THE BODLEY HEAD
Bernard Shaw
VOLUME
VI

THE BODLEY HEAD

Bernard Shaw

COLLECTED PLAYS WITH

THEIR PREFACES

⸢VOLUME VI⸣

Saint Joan, The Apple Cart
Too True to be Good
Village Wooing, On the Rocks
The Simpleton of the Unexpected Isles
The Millionairess, The Six of Calais

MAX REINHARDT
THE BODLEY HEAD
LONDON SYDNEY
TORONTO

EDITORIAL SUPERVISOR

Dan H. Laurence

ISBN 0 370 10225 8
Printed and bound in Great Britain for
Max Reinhardt, The Bodley Head Ltd
9 Bow Street, London, WC2E 7AL
by William Clowes & Sons Ltd, Beccles
Set in Monotype Plantin Light
First published 1924, 1929, 1932, 1933,
1934, 1935, 1936
This edition first published 1973

Publisher's Note

Bernard Shaw was, throughout his publishing career, an inveterate reviser. His most extensive revision of his plays was undertaken in 1930–32 for the Collected Edition. This text was subsequently reset and issued in 1931–32 as the Standard Edition: it contained corrections but no further textual revision. Shaw, however, did make further alterations in some of the plays and prefaces in the Standard Edition in later years. Accordingly, to ensure a definitive text, we have set type for the Bodley Head edition from the last printing of each volume of plays in the Standard Edition which was authorized for press by Shaw in his lifetime.

Shaw had strong personal opinions about style in printing, many of them highly idiosyncratic, and as he was his own publisher he had no difficulty implementing them. His spellings and contractions were often bizarre (*enterprize* and *wernt*), and sometimes archaic (*shew* for *show*, as in the title of his play *The Shewing-up of Blanco Posnet*). He had equally strong convictions about the superfluous use of punctuation, noting in *The Author* in April 1902:

"The apostrophes in ain't, don't, haven't, etc., look so ugly that the most careful printing cannot make a page of colloquial dialogue as handsome as a page of classical dialogue. Besides, shan't should be sha"n't, if the wretched pedantry of indicating the elision is to be carried out. I have written aint, dont, havnt, shant, shouldnt and wont for twenty years with perfect impunity, using the apostrophe only where its omission would suggest another word: for example, hell for he'll. There is not the faintest reason for persisting in the ugly and silly trick of peppering pages with these uncouth bacilli. I also write thats, whats, lets, for the colloquial forms of that is, what is, let us; and I have not yet been prosecuted."

Throughout this definitive edition we have undertaken to follow Shaw's dictates in all matters of spelling and punctuation. Except for a small number of corrections of obvious misprints, the texts are faithfully reproduced.

One additional technical matter must be noted here. Shaw's aesthetics of typography required that italics be reserved for stage directions. In all editions of Shaw's plays up to and including the Collected Edition emphasis within dialogue passages was obtained by letter-spacing. For technical reasons, however, Shaw's printer (William Maxwell, director of R. & R. Clark, Edinburgh) prevailed upon him to permit the setting of emphasised words in the Standard Edition in a slightly larger type. Shaw virtually eliminated accentuation of words in the plays published after 1934: an occasional stress in the later plays was obtained by use of bold face or uniform capitals. In the present edition the original spaced lettering has been restored. This move, we like to think, would have pleased Shaw.

CONTENTS

Saint Joan:
A Chronicle Play in Six Scenes and an Epilogue

The Apple Cart:
A Political Extravaganza

Too True to be Good:
A Political Extravaganza

Saint Joan:
A Chronicle Play in Six Scenes and an Epilogue

WITH

Preface

Statement to New York Theatre Audiences

Note by the Author

The Epilogue to "Saint Joan"

Saint Joan: A Radio Talk

Shaw Unperturbed by Immortality

Saint Joan Banned: Film Censorship in the United States

Where was "Saint Joan" Written?

Shaw's Saint Joan

Composition begun 29 April 1923; completed 24 August 1923. First published in German translation, as *Die heilige Johanna*, in the *Neue Rundschau* (Berlin), June–September 1924. Published in English, 1924. First presented by the Theatre Guild at the Garrick Theatre, New York, on 28 December 1923.

Robert de Baudricourt *Ernest Cossart*
Steward *William M. Griffith*
Joan ("The Maid") *Winifred Lenihan*
Bertrand de Poulengey *Frank Tweed*
La Trémouille, Constable of France *Herbert Ashton*
The Archbishop of Rheims *Albert Bruning*
Court Page *Jo Mielziner*
Gilles de Rais ("Bluebeard") *Walton Butterfield*
Captain La Hire *Morris Carnovsky*
The Dauphin (later Charles VII) *Philip Leigh*
The Duchesse de la Trémouille *Elizabeth Pearré*
Dunois, Bastard of Orleans *Maurice Colbourne*
Dunois' Page *James Norris*
Richard de Beauchamp, Earl of Warwick *A. H. Van Buren*
John Bowyer Spenser Neville de Stogumber (Warwick's Chaplain) *Henry Travers*
Warwick's Page *Seth Baldwin*
Peter Cauchon, Bishop of Beauvais *Ian Maclaren*

Brother John Lemaître (The Inquisitor)
   Joseph Macaulay
John d'Estivet, Canon of Bayeux   *Albert Perry*
De Courcelles, Canon of Paris   *Walton Butterfield*
Brother Martin Ladvenu   *Morris Carnovsky*
The Executioner   *Herbert Ashton*
An English Soldier   *Frank Tweed*
A Clerical Gentleman   *Ernest Cossart*
Also Courtiers, Monks, Soldiers, etc.

Period—The Fifteenth Century, during the Hundred Years War. In France

Scene 1: *The Castle of Vaucouleurs. 23 February 1429*

Scene 2: *Antechamber and Throne Room at Chinon. 8 March 1429*

Scene 3: *The Bank of the River Loire near Orléans. 29 May 1429*

Scene 4: *The Earl of Warwick's Tent in the English Camp*

Scene 5: *The Ambulatory of Rheims Cathedral. 17 July 1429*

Scene 6: *A Hall in the Castle at Rouen. The Trial of Joan. 30 May 1431*

Epilogue: *Bedroom in the Château of Charles VII. June 1456*

Preface

Contents

JOAN THE ORIGINAL AND PRESUMPTUOUS

Joan of Arc, a village girl from the Vosges, was born about 1412; burnt for heresy, witchcraft, and sorcery in 1431; rehabilitated after a fashion in 1456; designated Venerable in 1904; declared Blessed in 1908; and finally canonized in 1920. She is the most notable Warrior Saint in the Christian calendar, and the queerest fish among the eccentric worthies of the Middle Ages. Though a professed and most pious Catholic, and the projector of a Crusade against the Husites, she was in fact one of the first Protestant martyrs. She was also one of the first apostles of Nationalism, and the first French practitioner of Napoleonic realism in warfare as distinguished from the sporting ransom-gambling chivalry of her time. She was the pioneer of rational dressing for women, and, like Queen Christina of Sweden two centuries later, to say nothing of Catalina de Erauso and innumerable obscure heroines who have disguised themselves as men to serve as soldiers and sailors, she refused to accept the specific woman's lot, and dressed and fought and lived as men did.

As she contrived to assert herself in all these ways with such force that she was famous throughout western Europe before she was out of her teens (indeed she never got out of them), it is hardly surprising that she was judicially burnt, ostensibly for a number of capital crimes which we no longer punish as such, but essentially for what we call unwomanly and insufferable presumption. At eighteen Joan's pretensions were beyond those of the proudest Pope or the haughtiest emperor. She claimed to be the ambassador and plenipotentiary of God, and to be, in effect, a member of the Church Triumphant whilst still in the flesh on earth. She patronized her own king, and summoned the English king to repentance and obedience to her commands. She lectured, talked down, and overruled statesmen and prelates. She poohpoohed the plans of generals, leading their troops to victory on plans of her own. She had an unbounded and quite unconcealed contempt for official opinion, judgment, and authority, and for War Office tactics and strategy. Had she been a sage and monarch in whom the most venerable hierarchy and the most illustrious dynasty converged, her pretensions and proceedings would have been as trying to the official mind as the pretensions of Caesar were to Cassius. As her actual condition was pure upstart, there were only two opinions about her. One was that she was miraculous: the other that she was unbearable.

JOAN AND SOCRATES

If Joan had been malicious, selfish, cowardly or stupid, she would have been one of the most odious persons known to history instead of one of the most attractive.

If she had been old enough to know the effect she was producing on the men whom she humiliated by being right when they were wrong, and had learned to flatter and manage them, she might have lived as long as Queen Elizabeth. But she was too young and rustical and inexperienced to have any such arts. When she was thwarted by men whom she thought fools, she made no secret of her opinion of them or her impatience with their folly; and she was naïve enough to expect them to be obliged to her for setting them right and keeping them out of mischief. Now it is always hard for superior wits to understand the fury roused by their exposures of the stupidities of comparative dullards. Even Socrates, for all his age and experience, did not defend himself at his trial like a man who understood the long accumulated fury that had burst on him, and was clamoring for his death. His accuser, if born 2300 years later, might have been picked out of any first class carriage on a suburban railway during the evening or morning rush from or to the City; for he had really nothing to say except that he and his like could not endure being shewn up as idiots every time Socrates opened his mouth. Socrates, unconscious of this, was paralyzed by his sense that somehow he was missing the point of the attack. He petered out after he had established the fact that he was an old soldier and a man of honorable life, and that his accuser was a silly snob. He had no suspicion of the extent to which his mental superiority had roused fear and hatred against him in the hearts of men towards whom he was conscious of nothing but good will and good service.

CONTRAST WITH NAPOLEON

If Socrates was as innocent as this at the age of

seventy, it may be imagined how innocent Joan was at the age of seventeen. Now Socrates was a man of argument, operating slowly and peacefully on men's minds, whereas Joan was a woman of action, operating with impetuous violence on their bodies. That, no doubt, is why the contemporaries of Socrates endured him so long, and why Joan was destroyed before she was fully grown. But both of them combined terrifying ability with a frankness, personal modesty, and benevolence which made the furious dislike to which they fell victims absolutely unreasonable, and therefore inapprehensible by themselves. Napoleon, also possessed of terrifying ability, but neither frank nor disinterested, had no illusions as to the nature of his popularity. When he was asked how the world would take his death, he said it would give a gasp of relief. But it is not so easy for mental giants who neither hate nor intend to injure their fellows to realize that nevertheless their fellows hate mental giants and would like to destroy them, not only enviously because the juxtaposition of a superior wounds their vanity, but quite humbly and honestly because it frightens them. Fear will drive men to any extreme; and the fear inspired by a superior being is a mystery which cannot be reasoned away. Being immeasurable it is unbearable when there is no presumption or guarantee of its benevolence and moral responsibility: in other words, when it has no official status. The legal and conventional superiority of Herod and Pilate, and of Annas and Caiaphas, inspires fear; but the fear, being a reasonable fear of measurable and avoidable consequences which seem salutary and protective, is bearable; whilst the strange superiority of Christ and the fear it inspires elicit a shriek of Crucify Him from all who cannot divine its benevolence. Socrates has to drink the hemlock, Christ to hang on the cross, and Joan to burn at the stake, whilst Napoleon, though he ends in St Helena, at least dies in his bed there; and many terrifying but quite comprehensible official scoundrels die natural deaths in all the glory of the kingdoms of this world, proving that it is far more dangerous to be a saint than to be a conqueror. Those who have been both, like Mahomet and Joan, have found that it is the conqueror who must save the saint, and that defeat and capture mean martyrdom. Joan was burnt without a hand lifted on her own side to save her. The comrades she had led to victory and the enemies she had disgraced and defeated, the French king she had crowned and the English king whose crown she had kicked into the Loire, were equally glad to be rid of her.

WAS JOAN INNOCENT OR GUILTY?

As this result could have been produced by a crapulous inferiority as well as by a sublime superiority, the question which of the two was operative in Joan's case has to be faced. It was decided against her by her contemporaries after a very careful and conscientious trial; and the reversal of the verdict twentyfive years later, in form a rehabilitation of Joan, was really only a confirmation of the validity of the coronation of Charles VII. It is the more impressive reversal by a unanimous Posterity, culminating in her canonization, that has quashed the original proceedings, and put her judges on their trial, which, so far, has been much more unfair than their trial of her. Nevertheless the rehabilitation of 1456, corrupt job as it was, really did produce evidence enough to satisfy all reasonable critics that Joan was not a common termagant, not a harlot, not a witch, not a blasphemer, no more an idolater than the Pope himself, and not ill conducted in any sense apart from her soldiering, her wearing of men's clothes, and her audacity, but on the contrary good-humoured, an intact virgin, very pious, very temperate (we should call her meal of bread soaked in the common wine which is the drinking water of France ascetic), very kindly, and, though a brave and hardy soldier, unable to endure loose language or licentious conduct. She went to the stake without a stain on her character except the over-weening presumption, the superbity as they called it, that led her thither. It would therefore be waste of time now to prove that the Joan of the first part of the Elizabethan chronicle play of Henry VI (supposed to have been tinkered by Shakespear) grossly libels her in its concluding scenes in deference to Jingo patriotism. The mud that was thrown at her has dropped off by this time so completely that there is no need for any modern writer to wash up after it. What is far more difficult to get rid of is the mud that is being thrown at her judges, and the whitewash which disfigures her beyond recognition. When Jingo scurrility had done its worst to her, sectarian scurrility (in this case Protestant scurrility) used her stake to beat the Roman Catholic Church and the Inquisition. The easiest way to make these institutions the villains of a melodrama was to make The Maid its heroine. That melodrama may be dismissed as rubbish. Joan got a far fairer trial from the Church and the Inquisition than any prisoner of her type and in her situation gets nowadays in any official secular court; and the decision was strictly according to law. And she was not a melodramatic heroine: that is, a physically beautiful lovelorn parasite on an equally beautiful hero, but a genius and a saint, about as completely the opposite of a melodramatic heroine as it is possible for a human being to be.

Let us be clear about the meaning of the terms. A genius is a person who, seeing farther and probing deeper than other people, has a different set of ethical valuations from theirs, and has energy enough to give effect to this extra vision and its valuations in whatever manner best suits his or her specific talents. A saint is one who having practised heroic virtues, and enjoyed revelations or powers of the order which The Church classes technically as supernatural, is eligible for canonization. If a historian is an Anti-Feminist, and does not believe women to be capable of genius in the traditional masculine departments, he will never make anything of Joan, whose genius was turned to practical account mainly in soldiering and politics. If he is Rationalist enough to deny that saints exist, and to hold that new ideas cannot come otherwise than by conscious ratiocination, he will never catch Joan's likeness. Her ideal biographer must be free from nineteenth century prejudices and biases; must understand the Middle Ages, the Roman Catholic Church, and the Holy Roman Empire much more intimately than our Whig historians have ever understood them; and must be capable of throwing off sex partialities and their romance, and regarding woman as the female of the human species, and not as a different kind of animal with specific charms and specific imbecilities.

JOAN'S GOOD LOOKS

To put the last point roughly, any book about Joan which begins by describing her as a beauty may be at once classed as a romance. Not one of Joan's comrades, in village, court, or camp, even when they were straining themselves to please the king by praising her, ever claimed that she was pretty. All the men who alluded to the matter declared most emphatically that she was unattractive sexually to a degree that seemed to them miraculous, considering that she was in the bloom of youth, and neither ugly, awkward, deformed, nor unpleasant in her person. The evident truth is that like most women of her hardy managing type she seemed neutral in the conflict of sex because men were too much afraid of her to fall in love with her. She herself was not sexless: in spite of the virginity she had vowed up to a point, and preserved to her death, she never excluded the possibility of marriage for herself. But marriage, with its preliminary of the attraction, pursuit, and capture of a husband, was not her business: she had something else to do. Byron's formula, "Man's love is of man's life a thing apart: 'tis woman's whole existence," did not apply to her any more than to George Washington or any other masculine worker on the heroic scale. Had she lived in our time, picture postcards might have been sold of her as a general: they would not have been sold of her as a sultana. Nevertheless there is one reason for crediting her with a very remarkable face. A sculptor of her time in Orleans made a statue of a helmeted young woman with a face that is unique in art in point of being evidently not an ideal face but a portrait, and yet so uncommon as to be unlike any real woman one has ever seen. It is surmised that Joan served unconsciously as the sculptor's model. There is no proof of this; but those extraordinarily spaced eyes raise so powerfully the question "If this woman be not Joan, who is she?" that I dispense with further evidence, and challenge those who disagree with me to prove a negative. It is a wonderful face, but quite neutral from the point of view of the operatic beauty fancier.

Such a fancier may perhaps be finally chilled by the prosaic fact that Joan was the defendant in a suit for breach of promise of marriage, and that she conducted her own case and won it.

JOAN'S SOCIAL POSITION

By class Joan was the daughter of a working farmer who was one of the headmen of his village, and transacted its feudal business for it with the neighbouring squires and their lawyers. When the castle in which the villagers were entitled to take refuge from raids became derelict, he organized a combination of half a dozen farmers to obtain possession of it so as to occupy it when there was any danger of invasion. As a child, Joan could please herself at times with being the young lady of this castle. Her mother and brothers were able to follow and share her fortune at court without making themselves notably ridiculous. These facts leave us no excuse for the popular romance that turns every heroine into either a princess or a beggar maid. In the somewhat similar case of Shakespear a whole inverted pyramid of wasted research has been based on the assumption that he was an illiterate laborer, in the face of the plainest evidence that his father was a man of business, and at one time a very prosperous one, married to a woman of some social pretensions. There is the same tendency to drive Joan into the position of a hired shepherd girl, though a hired shepherd girl in Domrémy would have deferred to her as the young lady of the farm.

The difference between Joan's case and Shakespear's is that Shakespear was not illiterate. He had been to school, and knew as much Latin and Greek as most university passmen retain: that is, for practical purposes, none at all. Joan was absolutely illiterate. "I do not know A from B" she said. But many princesses at that time and for long after might have said the same. Marie Antoinette, for instance, at Joan's age could not spell her own name correctly. But this does not mean that Joan was an ignorant person, or that she suffered from the diffidence and sense of social disadvantage now felt by people who cannot read or write. If she could not write letters, she could and did dictate them and attach full and indeed excessive importance to them. When she was called a shepherd lass to her face she very warmly resented it, and challenged any woman to compete with her in the household arts of the mistress of well furnished houses. She understood the political and military situation in France much better than most of our newspaper fed university women-graduates understand the corresponding situation of their own country today. Her first convert was the neighbouring commandant at Vaucouleurs; and she converted him by telling him about the defeat of the Dauphin's troops at the Battle of Herrings so long before he had official news of it that he concluded she must have had a divine revelation. This knowledge of and interest in public affairs was nothing extraordinary among farmers in a war-swept countryside. Politicians came to the door too often sword in hand to be disregarded: Joan's people could not afford to be ignorant of what was going on in the feudal world. They were not rich; and Joan worked on the farm as her father did, driving the sheep to pasture and so forth; but there is no evidence or suggestion

[23]

of sordid poverty, and no reason to believe that Joan had to work as a hired servant works, or indeed to work at all when she preferred to go to confession, or dawdle about waiting for visions and listening to the church bells to hear voices in them. In short, much more of a young lady, and even of an intellectual, than most of the daughters of our petty bourgeoisie.

JOAN'S VOICES AND VISIONS

Joan's voices and visions have played many tricks with her reputation. They have been held to prove that she was mad, that she was a liar and impostor, that she was a sorceress (she was burned for this), and finally that she was a saint. They do not prove any of these things; but the variety of the conclusions reached shew how little our matter-of-fact historians know about other people's minds, or even about their own. There are people in the world whose imagination is so vivid that when they have an idea it comes to them as an audible voice, sometimes uttered by a visible figure. Criminal lunatic asylums are occupied largely by murderers who have obeyed voices. Thus a woman may hear voices telling her that she must cut her husband's throat and strangle her child as they lie asleep; and she may feel obliged to do what she is told. By a medico-legal superstition it is held in our courts that criminals whose temptations present themselves under these illusions are not responsible for their actions, and must be treated as insane. But the seers of visions and the hearers of revelations are not always criminals. The inspirations and intuitions and unconsciously reasoned conclusions of genius sometimes assume similar illusions. Socrates, Luther, Swedenborg, Blake saw visions and heard voices just as Saint Francis and Saint Joan did. If Newton's imagination had been of the same vividly dramatic kind he might have seen the ghost of Pythagoras walk into the orchard and explain why the apples were falling. Such an illusion would have invalidated neither the theory of gravitation nor Newton's general sanity. What is more, the visionary method of making the discovery would not be a whit more miraculous than the normal method. The test of sanity is not the normality of the method but the reasonableness of the discovery. If Newton had been informed by Pythagoras that the moon was made of green cheese, then Newton would have been locked up. Gravitation being a reasoned hypothesis which fitted remarkably well into the Copernican version of the observed physical facts of the universe, established Newton's reputation for extraordinary intelligence, and would have done so no matter how fantastically he had arrived at it. Yet his theory of gravitation is not so impressive a mental feat as his astounding chronology, which establishes him as the king of mental conjurors, but a Bedlamite king whose authority no one now accepts. On the subject of the eleventh horn of the beast seen by the prophet Daniel he was more fantastic than Joan, because his imagination was not dramatic but mathematical and therefore extraordinarily susceptible to numbers: indeed if all his works were lost except his chronology we should say that he was as mad as a hatter. As it is, who dares diagnose Newton as a madman?

In the same way Joan must be judged a sane woman in spite of her voices because they never gave her any advice that might not have come to her from her mother wit exactly as gravitation came to Newton. We can all see now, especially since the late war threw so many of our women into military life, that Joan's campaigning could not have been carried on in petticoats. This was not only because she did a man's work, but because it was morally necessary that sex should be left out of the question as between her and her comrades-in-arms. She gave this reason herself when she was pressed on the subject; and the fact that this entirely reasonable necessity came to her imagination first as an order from God delivered through the mouth of Saint Catherine does not prove that she was mad. The soundness of the order proves that she was unusually sane; but its form proves that her dramatic imagination played tricks with her senses. Her policy was also quite sound: nobody disputes that the relief of Orleans, followed up by the coronation at Rheims of the Dauphin as a counterblow to the suspicions then current of his legitimacy and consequently of his title, were military and political masterstrokes that saved France. They might have been planned by Napoleon or any other illusionproof genius. They came to Joan as an instruction from her Counsel, as she called her visionary saints; but she was none the less an able leader of men for imagining her ideas in this way.

THE EVOLUTIONARY APPETITE

What then is the modern view of Joan's voices and visions and messages from God? The nineteenth century said that they were delusions, but that as she was a pretty girl, and had been abominably ill-treated and finally done to death by a superstitious rabble of medieval priests hounded on by a corrupt political bishop, it must be assumed that she was the innocent dupe of these delusions. The twentieth century finds this explanation too vapidly commonplace, and demands something more mystic. I think the twentieth century is right, because an explanation which amounts to Joan being mentally defective instead of, as she obviously was, mentally excessive, will not wash. I cannot believe, nor, if I could, could I expect all my readers to believe, as Joan did, that three ocularly visible well dressed persons, named respectively Saint Catherine, Saint Margaret, and Saint Michael, came down from heaven and gave her certain instructions with which they were charged by God for her. Not that such a belief would be more improbable or fantastic than some modern beliefs which we all swallow; but there are fashions and family habits in belief, and it happens that, my fashion being Victorian and my family habit Protestant, I find myself unable to attach any such objective validity to the form of Joan's visions.

But that there are forces at work which use individuals for purposes far transcending the purpose of keeping these individuals alive and prosperous and respectable and safe and happy in the middle station in life, which is all any good bourgeois can reasonably require, is established by the fact that men will, in the pursuit of knowledge and of social readjustments for which they will not be a penny the better, and are indeed often many pence the worse, face poverty, infamy, exile, imprisonment, dreadful hardship, and death. Even the selfish pursuit of personal power does not nerve men to the efforts and sacrifices which are eagerly made in pursuit of extensions of our power over nature, though these extensions may not touch the personal life of the seeker at any point. There is no more mystery about this appetite for knowledge and power than about the appetite for food: both are known as facts and as facts only, the difference between them being that the appetite for food is necessary to the life of the hungry man and is therefore a personal appetite, whereas the other is an appetite for evolution, and therefore a superpersonal need.

The diverse manners in which our imaginations dramatize the approach of the superpersonal forces is a problem for the psychologist, not for the historian. Only, the historian must understand that visionaries are neither impostors nor lunatics. It is one thing to say that the figure Joan recognized as St Catherine was not really St Catherine, but the dramatization by Joan's imagination of that pressure upon her of the driving force that is behind evolution which I have just called the evolutionary appetite. It is quite another to class her visions with the vision of two moons seen by a drunken person, or with Brocken spectres, echoes and the like. Saint Catherine's instructions were far too cogent for that; and the simplest French peasant who believes in apparitions of celestial personages to favoured mortals is nearer to the scientific truth about Joan than the Rationalist and Materialist historians and essaysists who feel obliged to set down a girl who saw saints and heard them talking to her as either crazy or mendacious. If Joan was mad, all Christendom was mad too; for people who believe devoutly in the existence of celestial personages are every whit as mad in that sense as the people who think they see them. Luther, when he threw his inkhorn at the devil, was no more mad than any other Augustinian monk: he had a more vivid imagination, and had perhaps eaten and slept less: that was all.

THE MERE ICONOGRAPHY DOES NOT MATTER

All the popular religions in the world are made apprehensible by an array of legendary personages, with an Almighty Father, and sometimes a mother and divine child, as the central figures. These are presented to the mind's eye in childhood; and the result is a hallucination which persists strongly throughout life when it has been well impressed. Thus all the thinking of the hallucinated adult about the fountain of inspiration which is continually flowing in the universe, or about the promptings of virtue and the revulsions of shame: in short, about aspiration and conscience, both of which forces are matters of fact more obvious than electro-magnetism, is thinking in terms of the celestial vision. And when in the case of exceptionally imaginative persons, especially those practising certain appropriate austerities, the hallucination extends from the mind's eye to the body's, the visionary sees Krishna or the Buddha or the Blessed Virgin or St Catherine as the case may be.

THE MODERN EDUCATION WHICH JOAN ESCAPED

It is important to everyone nowadays to understand this, because modern science is making short work of the hallucinations without regard to the vital importance of the things they symbolize. If Joan were reborn today she would be sent, first to a convent school, in which she would be mildly taught to connect inspiration and conscience with St Catherine and St Michael exactly as she was in the fifteenth century, and then finished up with a very energetic training in the gospel of Saints Louis Pasteur and Paul Bert, who would tell her (possibly in visions but more probably

in pamphlets) not to be a superstitious little fool, and
to empty out St Catherine and the rest of the Catholic
hagiology as an obsolete iconography of exploded
myths. It would be rubbed into her that Galileo was
a martyr, and his persecutors incorrigible ignoramuses,
and that St Teresa's hormones had gone astray and
left her incurably hyperpituitary or hyperadrenal or
hysteroid or epileptoid or anything but asteroid. She
would have been convinced by precept and experiment that baptism and receiving the body of her Lord
were contemptible superstitions, and that vaccination
and vivisection were enlightened practices. Behind
her new Saints Louis and Paul there would be not
only Science purifying Religion and being purified by
it, but hypochondria, melancholia, cowardice, stupidity, cruelty, muckraking curiosity, knowledge without
wisdom, and everything that the eternal soul in
Nature loathes, instead of the virtues of which St
Catherine was the figure head. As to the new rites,
which would be the saner Joan ? the one who carried
little children to be baptized of water and the spirit,
or the one who sent the police to force their parents
to have the most villainous racial poison we know
thrust into their veins ? the one who told them the
story of the angel and Mary, or the one who questioned them as to their experiences of the Edipus
complex ? the one to whom the consecrated wafer was
the very body of the virtue that was her salvation, or
the one who looked forward to a precise and convenient regulation of her health and her desires by a
nicely calculated diet of thyroid extract, adrenalin,
thymin, pituitrin, and insulin, with pick-me-ups of
hormone stimulants, the blood being first carefully
fortified with antibodies against all possible infections
by inoculations of infected bacteria and serum from

infected animals, and against old age by surgical extirpation of the reproductive ducts or weekly doses of
monkey gland?

It is true that behind all these quackeries there is a
certain body of genuine scientific physiology. But
was there any the less a certain body of genuine
psychology behind St Catherine and the Holy Ghost?
And which is the healthier mind? the saintly mind or
the monkey gland mind? Does not the present cry of
Back to the Middle Ages, which has been incubating
ever since the pre-Raphaelite movement began, mean
that it is no longer our Academy pictures that are
intolerable, but our credulities that have not the
excuse of being superstitions, our cruelties that have
not the excuse of barbarism, our persecutions that
have not the excuse of religious faith, our shameless
substitution of successful swindlers and scoundrels
and quacks for saints as objects of worship, and our
deafness and blindness to the calls and visions of the
inexorable power that made us, and will destroy us
if we disregard it? To Joan and her contemporaries
we should appear as a drove of Gadarene swine,
possessed by all the unclean spirits cast out by the
faith and civilization of the Middle Ages, running
violently down a steep place into a hell of high explosives. For us to set up our condition as a standard of
sanity, and declare Joan mad because she never con-
descended to it, is to prove that we are not only lost
but irredeemable. Let us then once for all drop all
nonsense about Joan being cracked, and accept her
as at least as sane as Florence Nightingale, who also
combined a very simple iconography of religious
belief with a mind so exceptionally powerful that it
kept her in continual trouble with the medical and
military panjandrums of her time.

FAILURES OF THE VOICES

That the voices and visions were illusory, and their wisdom all Joan's own, is shewn by the occasions on which they failed her, notably during her trial, when they assured her that she would be rescued. Here her hopes flattered her; but they were not unreasonable: her military colleague La Hire was in command of a considerable force not so very far off; and if the Armagnacs, as her party was called, had really wanted to rescue her, and had put anything like her own vigor into the enterprise, they could have attempted it with very fair chances of success. She did not understand that they were glad to be rid of her, nor that the rescue of a prisoner from the hands of the Church was a much more serious business for a medieval captain, or even a medieval king, than its mere physical difficulty as a military exploit suggested. According to her lights her expectation of a rescue was reasonable; therefore she heard Madame Saint Catherine assuring her it would happen, that being her way of finding out and making up her own mind. When it became evident that she had miscalculated: when she was led to the stake, and La Hire was not thundering at the gates of Rouen nor charging Warwick's men at arms, she threw over Saint Catherine at once, and recanted. Nothing could be more sane or practical. It was not until she discovered that she had gained nothing by her recantation but close imprisonment for life that she withdrew it, and deliberately and explicitly chose burning instead: a decision which shewed not only the extraordinary decision of her character, but also a Rationalism carried to its ultimate human test of suicide. Yet even in this the illusion persisted; and she announced her relapse as dictated to her by her voices.

JOAN A GALTONIC VISUALIZER

The most sceptical scientific reader may therefore accept as a flat fact, carrying no implication of unsoundness of mind, that Joan was what Francis Galton and other modern investigators of human faculty call a visualizer. She saw imaginary saints just as some other people see imaginary diagrams and landscapes with numbers dotted about them, and are thereby able to perform feats of memory and arithmetic impossible to non-visualizers. Visualizers will understand this at once. Non-visualizers who have never read Galton will be puzzled and incredulous. But a very little inquiry among their acquaintances will reveal to them that the mind's eye is more or less a magic lantern, and that the street is full of normally sane people who have hallucinations of all sorts which they believe to be part of the normal permanent equipment of all human beings.

JOAN'S MANLINESS AND MILITARISM

Joan's other abnormality, too common among uncommon things to be properly called a peculiarity, was her craze for soldiering and the masculine life. Her father tried to frighten her out of it by threatening to drown her if she ran away with the soldiers, and ordering her brothers to drown her if he were not on the spot. This extravagance was clearly not serious: it must have been addressed to a child young enough to imagine that he was in earnest. Joan must therefore as a child have wanted to run away and be a soldier. The awful prospect of being thrown into the Meuse and drowned by a terrible father and her big brothers kept her quiet until the father had lost his terrors and the brothers yielded to her natural leadership; and by that time she had sense enough to know that the masculine and military life was not a mere matter of running away from home. But the taste for it never left her, and was fundamental in determining her career.

If anyone doubts this, let him ask himself why a maid charged with a special mission from heaven to the Dauphin (this was how Joan saw her very able plan for retrieving the desperate situation of the un-crowned king) should not have simply gone to the court as a maid, in woman's dress, and urged her counsel upon him in a woman's way, as other women with similar missions had come to his mad father and his wise grandfather. Why did she insist on having a soldier's dress and arms and sword and horse and equipment, and on treating her escort of soldiers as comrades, sleeping side by side with them on the floor at night as if there were no difference of sex between them? It may be answered that this was the safest way of travelling through a country infested with hostile troops and bands of marauding deserters from both sides. Such an answer has no weight because it applies to all the women who travelled in France at that time, and who never dreamt of travelling other-wise than as women. But even if we accept it, how does it account for the fact that when the danger was over, and she could present herself at court in feminine attire with perfect safety and obviously with greater propriety, she presented herself in her man's dress, and instead of urging Charles, like Queen Victoria urging the War Office to send Roberts to the Trans-vaal, to send D'Alençon, De Rais, La Hire and the rest to the relief of Dunois at Orleans, insisted that she must go herself and lead the assault in person? Why did she give exhibitions of her dexterity in handling a lance, and of her seat as a rider? Why did she accept presents of armor and chargers and masculine surcoats, and in every action repudiate the conventional character of a woman? The simple answer to all these questions is that she was the sort of woman that wants to lead a man's life. They are to be found wherever there are armies on foot or navies on the seas, serving in male disguise, eluding detection for astonishingly long periods, and sometimes, no doubt, escaping it entirely. When they are in a position to defy public opinion they throw off all concealment. You have your Rosa Bonheur painting in male blouse and trousers, and George Sand living a man's life and almost compelling her Chopins and De Mussets to live women's lives to amuse her. Had Joan not been one of those "unwomanly women", she might have been canonized much sooner.

But it is not necessary to wear trousers and smoke big cigars to live a man's life any more than it is necessary to wear petticoats to live a woman's. There are plenty of gowned and bodiced women in ordinary civil life who manage their own affairs and other people's, including those of their menfolk, and are entirely masculine in their tastes and pursuits. There always were such women, even in the Victorian days when women had fewer legal rights than men, and our modern women magistrates, mayors, and members of Parliament were unknown. In reactionary Russia in our own century a woman soldier organized an effective regiment of amazons, which disappeared only because it was Aldershottian enough to be against the Revolution. The exemption of women from military service is founded, not on any natural inaptitude that men do not share, but on the fact that communities cannot reproduce themselves without plenty of women. Men are more largely dispensable, and are sacrificed accordingly.

WAS JOAN SUICIDAL ?

These two abnormalities were the only ones that were irresistibly prepotent in Joan; and they brought her to the stake. Neither of them was peculiar to her. There was nothing peculiar about her except the vigor and scope of her mind and character, and the intensity of her vital energy. She was accused of a suicidal tendency; and it is a fact that when she attempted to escape from Beaurevoir Castle by jumping from a tower said to be sixty feet high, she took a risk beyond reason, though she recovered from the crash after a few days fasting. Her death was deliberately chosen as an alternative to life without liberty. In battle she challenged death as Wellington did at Waterloo, and as Nelson habitually did when he walked his quarter deck during his battles with all his decorations in full blaze. As neither Nelson nor Wellington nor any of those who have performed desperate feats, and preferred death to captivity, has been accused of suicidal mania, Joan need not be suspected of it. In the Beaurevoir affair there was more at stake than her freedom. She was distracted by the news that Compiègne was about to fall; and she was convinced that she could save it if only she could get free. Still, the leap was so perilous that her conscience was not quite easy about it; and she expressed this, as usual, by saying that Saint Catherine had forbidden her to do it, but forgave her afterwards for her disobedience.

JOAN SUMMED UP

We may accept and admire Joan, then, as a sane and

shrewd country girl of extraordinary strength of mind
and hardihood of body. Everything she did was
thoroughly calculated; and though the process was so
rapid that she was hardly conscious of it, and ascribed
it all to her voices, she was a woman of policy and not
of blind impulse. In war she was as much a realist as
Napoleon: she had his eye for artillery and his knowledge of what it could do. She did not expect besieged
cities to fall Jerichowise at the sound of her trumpet,
but, like Wellington, adapted her methods of attack
to the peculiarities of the defence; and she anticipated
the Napoleonic calculation that if you only hold on
long enough the other fellow will give in: for example,
her final triumph at Orleans was achieved after her
commander Dunois had sounded the retreat at the
end of a day's fighting without a decision. She was
never for a moment what so many romancers and
playwrights have pretended: a romantic young lady.
She was a thorough daughter of the soil in her peasant-
like matter-of-factness and doggedness, and her
acceptance of great lords and kings and prelates as
such without idolatry or snobbery, seeing at a glance
how much they were individually good for. She had
the respectable countrywoman's sense of the value of
public decency, and would not tolerate foul language
and neglect of religious observances, nor allow dis-
reputable women to hang about her soldiers. She had
one pious ejaculation "En nom Dé!" and one meaningless oath "Par mon martin"; and this much
swearing she allowed to the incorrigibly blasphemous
La Hire equally with herself. The value of this prudery was so great in restoring the self-respect of the
badly demoralized army that, like most of her policy,
it justified itself as soundly calculated. She talked to
and dealt with people of all classes, from laborers to

kings, without embarrassment or affectation, and got them to do what she wanted when they were not afraid or corrupt. She could coax and she could hustle, her tongue having a soft side and a sharp edge. She was very capable: a born boss.

JOAN'S IMMATURITY AND IGNORANCE

All this, however, must be taken with one heavy qualification. She was only a girl in her teens. If we could think of her as a managing woman of fifty we should seize her type at once; for we have plenty of managing women among us of that age who illustrate perfectly the sort of person she would have become had she lived. But she, being only a lass when all is said, lacked their knowledge of men's vanities and of the weight and proportion of social forces. She knew nothing of iron hands in velvet gloves: she just used her fists. She thought political changes much easier than they are, and, like Mahomet in his innocence of any world but the tribal world, wrote letters to kings calling on them to make millennial rearrangements. Consequently it was only in the enterprises that were really simple and compassable by swift physical force, like the coronation and the Orleans campaign, that she was successful.

Her want of academic education disabled her when she had to deal with such elaborately artificial structures as the great ecclesiastical and social institutions of the Middle Ages. She had a horror of heretics without suspecting that she was herself a heresiarch, one of the precursors of a schism that rent Europe in two, and cost centuries of bloodshed that is not yet staunched. She objected to foreigners on the sensible ground that they were not in their proper place in

France; but she had no notion of how this brought her into conflict with Catholicism and Feudalism, both essentially international. She worked by common-sense; and where scholarship was the only clue to institutions she was in the dark, and broke her shins against them, all the more rudely because of her enormous self-confidence, which made her the least cautious of human beings in civil affairs.

This combination of inept youth and academic ignorance with great natural capacity, push, courage, devotion, originality and oddity, fully accounts for all the facts in Joan's career, and makes her a credible historical and human phenomenon; but it clashes most discordantly both with the idolatrous romance that has grown up round her, and the belittling scepticism that reacts against that romance.

THE MAID IN LITERATURE

English readers would probably like to know how these idolizations and reactions have affected the books they are most familiar with about Joan. There is the first part of the Shakespearean, or pseudo-Shakespearean trilogy of Henry VI, in which Joan is one of the leading characters. This portrait of Joan is not more authentic than the descriptions in the London papers of George Washington in 1780, of Napoleon in 1803, of the German Crown Prince in 1915, or of Lenin in 1917. It ends in mere scurrility. The impression left by it is that the playwright, having begun by an attempt to make Joan a beautiful and romantic figure, was told by his scandalized company that English patriotism would never stand a sympathetic representation of a French conqueror of English troops, and that unless he at once introduced all the old charges against Joan of being a sorceress and a harlot, and assumed her to be guilty of all of them, his play could not be produced. As likely as not, this was what actually happened: indeed there is only one other apparent way of accounting for the sympathetic representation of Joan as a heroine culminating in her eloquent appeal to the Duke of Burgundy, followed by the blackguardly scurrility of the concluding scenes. That other way is to assume that the original play was wholly scurrilous, and that Shakespear touched up the earlier scenes. As the work belongs to a period at which he was only beginning his practice as a tinker of old works, before his own style was fully formed and hardened, it is impossible to verify this guess. His finger is not unmistakeably evident in the play, which is poor and base in its moral tone; but he may have tried to redeem it from downright infamy by shedding a momentary glamor on the figure of The Maid.

When we jump over two centuries to Schiller, we find Die Jungfrau von Orleans drowned in a witch's caldron of raging romance. Schiller's Joan has not a single point of contact with the real Joan, nor indeed with any mortal woman that ever walked this earth. There is really nothing to be said of his play but that it is not about Joan at all, and can hardly be said to pretend to be; for he makes her die on the battlefield, finding her burning unbearable. Before Schiller came Voltaire, who burlesqued Homer in a mock epic called La Pucelle. It is the fashion to dismiss this with virtuous indignation as an obscene libel; and I certainly cannot defend it against the charge of extravagant indecorum. But its purpose was not to depict Joan, but to kill with ridicule everything that Voltaire righteously hated in the institutions and fashions of his own day. He made Joan ridiculous, but not contemptible nor (comparatively) unchaste; and as he also made Homer and St Peter and St Denis and the brave Dunois ridiculous, and the other heroines of the poem very unchaste indeed, he may be said to have let Joan off very easily. But indeed the personal adventures of the characters are so outrageous, and so Homerically free from any pretence at or even possibility of historical veracity, that those who affect to take them seriously only make themselves Pecksniffian. Samuel Butler believed The Iliad to be a burlesque of Greek Jingoism and Greek religion, written by a hostage or a slave; and La Pucelle makes Butler's theory almost convincing. Voltaire represents Agnes Sorel, the Dauphin's mistress, whom Joan never met, as a woman with a consuming passion for the chastest concubinal fidelity, whose fate it was to be continually falling into the hands of licentious foes and suffering the worst extremities of rapine. The combats in which Joan rides a flying donkey, or in which, taken unaware with no clothes on, she defends Agnes with her sword, and inflicts appropriate mutilations on her assailants, can be laughed at as they are intended to be without scruple; for no sane person could mistake them for sober history; and it may be that their ribald irreverence is more wholesome than the beglamored sentimentality of Schiller. Certainly Voltaire should not have asserted that Joan's father was a priest; but when he was out to *écraser l'infâme* (the French Church) he stuck at nothing.

So far, the literary representations of The Maid were legendary. But the publication by Quicherat in 1841 of the reports of her trial and rehabilitation placed the subject on a new footing. These entirely realistic documents created a living interest in Joan which Voltaire's mock Homerics and Schiller's romantic nonsense missed. Typical products of that interest in America and England are the histories of Joan by Mark Twain and Andrew Lang. Mark Twain was converted to downright worship of Joan directly by Quicherat. Later on, another man of genius, Anatole France, reacted against the Quicheratic wave of enthusiasm, and wrote a Life of Joan in which he attributed Joan's ideas to clerical prompting and her military success to an adroit use of her by Dunois as a *mascotte*: in short, he denied that she had any serious military or political ability. At this Andrew saw red, and went for Anatole's scalp in a rival Life of her which should be read as a corrective to the other. Lang had no difficulty in shewing that Joan's ability was not unnatural fiction to be explained away as an illusion manufactured by priests and soldiers, but a straightforward fact.

It has been lightly pleaded in explanation that Anatole France is a Parisian of the art world, into whose scheme of things the able, hardheaded, hard-handed female, though she dominates provincial France and business Paris, does not enter; whereas Lang was a Scot, and every Scot knows that the grey mare is as likely as not to be the better horse. But this explanation does not convince me. I cannot believe that Anatole France does not know what everybody knows. I wish everybody knew all that he knows. One feels antipathies at work in his book. He is not anti-Joan; but he is anti-clerical, anti-mystic, and fundamentally unable to believe that there ever was any such person as the real Joan.

Mark Twain's Joan, skirted to the ground, and with as many petticoats as Noah's wife in a toy ark, is an attempt to combine Bayard with Esther Summerson from Bleak House into an unimpeachable

American school teacher in armor. Like Esther Summerson she makes her creator ridiculous, and yet, being the work of a man of genius, remains a credible human goodygoody in spite of her creator's infatuation. It is the description rather than the valuation that is wrong. Andrew Lang and Mark Twain are equally determined to make Joan a beautiful and most ladylike Victorian; but both of them recognize and insist on her capacity for leadership, though the Scots scholar is less romantic about it than the Mississippi pilot. But then Lang was, by lifelong professional habit, a critic of biographies rather than a biographer, whereas Mark Twain writes his biography frankly in the form of a romance.

PROTESTANT MISUNDERSTANDINGS OF THE MIDDLE AGES

They had, however, one disability in common. To understand Joan's history it is not enough to understand her character: you must understand her environment as well. Joan in a nineteenth-twentieth century environment is as incongruous a figure as she would appear were she to walk down Piccadilly today in her fifteenth century armor. To see her in her proper perspective you must understand Christendom and the Catholic Church, the Holy Roman Empire and the Feudal System, as they existed and were understood in the Middle Ages. If you confuse the Middle Ages with the Dark Ages, and are in the habit of ridiculing your aunt for wearing "medieval clothes," meaning those in vogue in the eighteen-nineties, and are quite convinced that the world has

progressed enormously, both morally and mechanically, since Joan's time, then you will never understand
why Joan was burnt, much less feel that you might
have voted for burning her yourself if you had been a
member of the court that tried her; and until you feel
that you know nothing essential about her.

That the Mississippi pilot should have broken
down on this misunderstanding is natural enough.
Mark Twain, the Innocent Abroad, who saw the
lovely churches of the Middle Ages without a throb
of emotion, author of A Yankee at the Court of King
Arthur, in which the heroes and heroines of medieval
chivalry are guys seen through the eyes of a street
arab, was clearly out of court from the beginning.
Andrew Lang was better read; but, like Walter Scott,
he enjoyed medieval history as a string of Border
romances rather than as the record of a high European
civilization based on a catholic faith. Both of them
were baptized as Protestants, and impressed by all
their schooling and most of their reading with the
belief that Catholic bishops who burnt heretics were
persecutors capable of any villainy; that all heretics
were Albigensians or Husites or Jews or Protestants of
the highest character; and that the Inquisition was a
Chamber of Horrors invented expressly and exclusively for such burnings. Accordingly we find them
representing Peter Cauchon, Bishop of Beauvais, the
judge who sent Joan to the stake, as an unconscionable scoundrel, and all the questions put to her as
"traps" to ensnare and destroy her. And they assume
unhesitatingly that the two or three score of canons
and doctors of law and divinity who sat with Cauchon
as assessors, were exact reproductions of him on
slightly less elevated chairs and with a different
headdress.

COMPARATIVE FAIRNESS OF JOAN'S TRIAL

The truth is that Cauchon was threatened and insulted by the English for being too considerate to Joan. A recent French writer denies that Joan was burnt, and holds that Cauchon spirited her away and burnt somebody or something else in her place, and that the pretender who subsequently personated her at Orleans and elsewhere was not a pretender but the real authentic Joan. He is able to cite Cauchon's pro-Joan partiality in support of his view. As to the assessors, the objection to them is not that they were a row of uniform rascals, but that they were political partisans of Joan's enemies. This is a valid objection to all such trials; but in the absence of neutral tribunals they are unavoidable. A trial by Joan's French partisans would have been as unfair as the trial by her French opponents; and an equally mixed tribunal would have produced a deadlock. Such recent trials as those of Edith Cavell by a German tribunal and Roger Casement by an English one were open to the same objection; but they went forward to the death nevertheless, because neutral tribunals were not available. Edith, like Joan, was an arch heretic: in the middle of the war she declared before the world that "Patriotism is not enough." She nursed enemies back to health, and assisted their prisoners to escape, making it abundantly clear that she would help any fugitive or distressed person without asking whose side he was on, and acknowledging no distinction before Christ between Tommy and Jerry and Pitou the *poilu*. Well might Edith have wished that she could bring the Middle Ages back, and have fifty civilians, learned in the law or vowed to the service of God, to support two skilled judges in trying her case according to the

Catholic law of Christendom, and to argue it out with her at sitting after sitting for many weeks. The modern military Inquisition was not so squeamish. It shot her out of hand; and her countrymen, seeing in this a good opportunity for lecturing the enemy on his intolerance, put up a statue to her, but took particular care not to inscribe on the pedestal "Patriotism is not enough," for which omission, and the lie it implies, they will need Edith's intercession when they are themselves brought to judgment, if any heavenly power thinks such moral cowards capable of pleading to an intelligible indictment.

The point need be no further labored. Joan was persecuted essentially as she would be persecuted today. The change from burning to hanging or shooting may strike us as a change for the better. The change from careful trial under ordinary law to recklessly summary military terrorism may strike us a change for the worse. But as far as toleration is concerned the trial and execution in Rouen in 1431 might have been an event of today; and we may charge our consciences accordingly. If Joan had to be dealt with by us in London she would be treated with no more toleration than Miss Sylvia Pankhurst, or the Peculiar People, or the parents who keep their children from the elementary school, or any of the others who cross the line we have to draw, rightly or wrongly, between the tolerable and the intolerable.

JOAN NOT TRIED AS A POLITICAL OFFENDER

Besides, Joan's trial was not, like Casement's, a national political trial. Ecclesiastical courts and the courts of the Inquisition (Joan was tried by a combination of the two) were Courts Christian: that is, international courts; and she was tried, not as a traitress, but as a heretic, blasphemer, sorceress and idolater. Her alleged offences were not political offences against England, nor against the Burgundian faction in France, but against God and against the common morality of Christendom. And although the idea we call Nationalism was so foreign to the medieval conception of Christian society that it might almost have been directly charged against Joan as an additional heresy, yet it was not so charged; and it is unreasonable to suppose that the political bias of a body of Frenchmen like the assessors would on this point have run strongly in favour of the English foreigners (even if they had been making themselves particularly agreeable in France instead of just the contrary) against a Frenchwoman who had vanquished them.

The tragic part of the trial was that Joan, like most prisoners tried for anything but the simplest breaches of the ten commandments, did not understand what they were accusing her of. She was much more like Mark Twain than like Peter Cauchon. Her attachment to the Church was very different from the Bishop's, and does not, in fact, bear close examination from his point of view. She delighted in the solaces the Church offers to sensitive souls: to her, confession and communion were luxuries beside which the vulgar pleasures of the senses were trash. Her prayers were wonderful conversations with her three saints. Her piety seemed superhuman to the formally dutiful people whose religion was only a task to them. But when the Church was not offering her her favorite luxuries, but calling on her to accept its interpretation of God's will, and to sacrifice her own, she flatly refused, and made it clear that her notion of a Catholic Church was one in which the Pope was Pope Joan. How could the Church tolerate that, when it had just

destroyed Hus, and had watched the career of
Wycliffe with a growing anger that would have brought
him, too, to the stake, had he not died a natural death
before the wrath fell on him in his grave? Neither
Hus nor Wycliffe was as bluntly defiant as Joan: both
were reformers of the Church like Luther; whilst
Joan, like Mrs Eddy, was quite prepared to supersede
St Peter as the rock on which the Church was built,
and, like Mahomet, was always ready with a private
revelation from God to settle every question and fit
every occasion.

The enormity of Joan's pretension was proved by
her own unconsciousness of it, which we call her
innocence, and her friends called her simplicity. Her
solutions of the problems presented to her seemed,
and indeed mostly were, the plainest commonsense,
and their revelation to her by her Voices was to her a
simple matter of fact. How could plain commonsense
and simple fact seem to her to be that hideous thing,
heresy? When rival prophetesses came into the field,
she was down on them at once for liars and humbugs;
but she never thought of them as heretics. She was in
a state of invincible ignorance as to the Church's view;
and the Church could not tolerate her pretensions
without either waiving its authority or giving her a
place beside the Trinity during her lifetime and in
her teens, which was unthinkable. Thus an irresistible
force met an immovable obstacle, and developed the
heat that consumed poor Joan.

Mark and Andrew would have shared her innocence and her fate had they been dealt with by the
Inquisition: that is why their accounts of the trial are
as absurd as hers might have been could she have
written one. All that can be said for their assumption
that Cauchon was a vulgar villain, and that the

questions put to Joan were traps, is that it has the
support of the inquiry which rehabilitated her twenty-
five years later. But this rehabilitation was as corrupt
as the contrary proceeding applied to Cromwell by
our Restoration reactionaries. Cauchon had been dug
up, and his body thrown into the common sewer.
Nothing was easier than to accuse him of cozenage,
and declare the whole trial void on that account. That
was what everybody wanted, from Charles the
Victorious, whose credit was bound up with The
Maid's, to the patriotic Nationalist populace, who
idolized Joan's memory. The English were gone; and
a verdict in their favour would have been an outrage
on the throne and on the patriotism which Joan had
set on foot.

We have none of these overwhelming motives of
political convenience and popularity to bias us. For us
the first trial stands valid; and the rehabilitation would
be negligible but for the mass of sincere testimony it
produced as to Joan's engaging personal character.
The question then arises: how did The Church get
over the verdict at the first trial when it canonized
Joan five hundred years later?

THE CHURCH UNCOMPROMISED BY ITS
AMENDS

Easily enough. In the Catholic Church, far more than
in law, there is no wrong without a remedy. It does not
defer to Joanesque private judgment as such, the
supremacy of private judgment for the individual
being the quintessence of Protestantism; nevertheless
it finds a place for private judgment *in excelsis* by
admitting that the highest wisdom may come as a
divine revelation to an individual. On sufficient evidence it will declare that individual a saint. Thus, as

revelation may come by way of an enlightenment of the private judgment no less than by the words of a celestial personage appearing in a vision, a saint may be defined as a person of heroic virtue whose private judgment is privileged. Many innovating saints, notably Francis and Clare, have been in conflict with the Church during their lives, and have thus raised the question whether they were heretics or saints. Francis might have gone to the stake had he lived longer. It is therefore by no means impossible for a person to be excommunicated as a heretic, and on further consideration canonized as a saint. Excommunication by a provincial ecclesiastical court is not one of the acts for which the Church claims infallibility. Perhaps I had better inform my Protestant readers that the famous Dogma of Papal Infallibility is by far the most modest pretension of the kind in existence. Compared with our infallible democracies, our infallible medical councils, our infallible astronomers, our infallible judges, and our infallible parliaments, the Pope is on his knees in the dust confessing his ignorance before the throne of God, asking only that as to certain historical matters on which he has clearly more sources of information open to him than anyone else his decision shall be taken as final. The Church may, and perhaps some day will, canonize Galileo without compromising such infallibility as it claims for the Pope, if not without compromising the infallibility claimed for the Book of Joshua by simple souls whose rational faith in more important things has become bound up with a quite irrational faith in the chronicle of Joshua's campaigns as a treatise on physics. Therefore the Church will probably not canonize Galileo yet awhile, though it might do worse. But it has been able to canonize Joan without any compromise at all. She never doubted that the sun went round the earth: she had seen it do so too often.

Still, there was a great wrong done to Joan and to the conscience of the world by her burning. *Tout comprendre, c'est tout pardonner*, which is the Devil's sentimentality, cannot excuse it. When we have admitted that the tribunal was not only honest and legal, but exceptionally merciful in respect of sparing Joan the torture which was customary when she was obdurate as to taking the oath, and that Cauchon was far more self-disciplined and conscientious both as priest and lawyer than any English judge ever dreams of being in a political case in which his party and class prejudices are involved, the human fact remains that the burning of Joan of Arc was a horror, and that a historian who would defend it would defend anything. The final criticism of its physical side is implied in the refusal of the Marquesas islanders to be persuaded that the English did not eat Joan. Why, they ask, should anyone take the trouble to roast a human being except with that object? They cannot conceive its being a pleasure. As we have no answer for them that is not shameful to us, let us blush for our more complicated and pretentious savagery before we proceed to unravel the business further, and see what other lessons it contains for us.

CRUELTY, MODERN AND MEDIEVAL

First, let us get rid of the notion that the mere physical cruelty of the burning has any special significance. Joan was burnt just as dozens of less interesting heretics were burnt in her time. Christ, in being crucified, only shared the fate of thousands of forgotten malefactors. They have no pre-eminence in mere physical pain: much more horrible executions than theirs are on record, to say nothing of the agonies of so-called natural death at its worst.

Joan was burnt more than five hundred years ago. More than three hundred years later: that is, only about a hundred years before I was born, a woman was burnt on Stephen's Green in my native city of Dublin for coining, which was held to be treason. In my preface to the recent volume on English Prisons under Local Government, by Sidney and Beatrice Webb, I have mentioned that when I was already a grown man I saw Richard Wagner conduct two concerts, and that when Richard Wagner was a young man he saw and avoided a crowd of people hastening to see a soldier broken on the wheel by the more cruel of the two ways of carrying out that hideous method of execution. Also that the penalty of hanging, drawing, and quartering, unmentionable in its details, was abolished so recently that there are men living who have been sentenced to it. We are still flogging criminals, and clamoring for more flogging. Not even the most sensationally frightful of these atrocities inflicted on its victim the misery, degradation, and conscious waste and loss of life suffered in our modern prisons, especially the model ones, without, as far as I can see, rousing any more compunction than the burning of heretics did in the Middle Ages. We have not even the excuse of getting some fun out of our prisons as the Middle Ages did out of their stakes and wheels and gibbets. Joan herself judged this matter when she had to choose between imprisonment and the stake, and chose the stake. And thereby she deprived The Church of the plea that it was guiltless of her death, which was the work of the secular arm. The Church should have confined itself to excommunicating her. There it was within its rights: she had refused to accept its authority or comply with its conditions; and it could say with truth "You are not one of us: go forth and find the religion that suits you, or found one for yourself." It had no right to say "You may return to us now that you have recanted; but you shall stay in a dungeon all the rest of your life." Unfortunately, The Church did not believe that there was any genuine soul saving religion outside itself; and it was deeply corrupted, as all the Churches were and still are, by primitive Calibanism (in Browning's sense), or the propitiation of a dreaded deity by suffering and sacrifice. Its method was not cruelty for cruelty's sake, but cruelty for the salvation of Joan's soul. Joan, however, believed that the saving of her soul was her own business, and not that of *les gens d'église*. By using that term as she did, mistrustfully and contemptuously, she announced herself as, in germ, an anti-Clerical as thoroughgoing as Voltaire or Anatole France. Had she said in so many words "To the dustbin with the Church Militant and its black-coated officials: I recognize only the Church Triumphant in heaven," she would hardly have put her view more plainly.

CATHOLIC ANTI-CLERICALISM

I must not leave it to be inferred here that one cannot be an anti-Clerical and a good Catholic too. All the reforming Popes have been vehement anti-Clericals, veritable scourges of the clergy. All the great Orders arose from dissatisfaction with the priests: that of the Franciscans with priestly snobbery, that of the Dominicans with priestly laziness and Laodiceanism, that of the Jesuits with priestly apathy and ignorance and indiscipline. The most bigoted Ulster Orangeman or Leicester Low Church bourgeois (as described by Mr Henry Nevinson) is a mere Gallio compared to Machiavelli, who, though no Protestant, was a fierce anti-Clerical. Any Catholic may, and many Catholics do, denounce any priest or body of priests, as lazy, drunken, idle, dissolute, and unworthy of their great Church and their functions as the pastors of their flocks of human souls. But to say that the souls of the people are no business of the Churchmen is to go a step further, a step across the Rubicon. Joan virtually took that step.

CATHOLICISM NOT YET CATHOLIC ENOUGH

And so, if we admit, as we must, that the burning of Joan was a mistake, we must broaden Catholicism sufficiently to include her in its charter. Our Churches must admit that no official organization of mortal men whose vocation does not carry with it extraordinary mental powers (and this is all that any Church Militant can in the face of fact and history pretend to be), can keep pace with the private judgment of persons of genius except when, by a very rare accident, the genius happens to be Pope, and not even then unless he is an exceedingly overbearing Pope. The Churches must learn humility as well as teach it. The Apostolic Succession cannot be secured or confined by the laying on of hands: the tongues of fire have descended on heathens and outcasts too often for that, leaving anointed Churchmen to scandalize History as worldly rascals. When the Church Militant behaves as if it were already the Church Triumphant, it makes these appalling blunders about Joan and Bruno and Galileo and the rest which make it so difficult for a Freethinker to join it; and a Church which has no place for Free-thinkers: nay, which does not inculcate and encourage freethinking with a complete belief that thought, when really free, must by its own law take the path that leads to The Church's bosom, not only has no future in modern culture, but obviously has no faith in the valid science of its own tenets, and is guilty of the heresy that theology and science are two different and opposite impulses, rivals for human allegiance.

I have before me the letter of a Catholic priest. "In your play," he writes, "I see the dramatic presentation of the conflict of the Regal, sacerdotal, and Prophetical powers, in which Joan was crushed. To me it is not the victory of any one of them over the others that will bring peace and the Reign of the Saints in the Kingdom of God, but their fruitful interaction in a costly but noble state of tension." The Pope himself could not put it better; nor can I. We must accept the tension, and maintain it nobly without letting ourselves be tempted to relieve it by burning the thread. This is Joan's lesson to The Church; and its formulation by the hand of a priest emboldens me to claim that her canonization was a magnificently Catholic gesture as the canonization of a Protestant saint by the Church of Rome. But its special value and virtue cannot be apparent until it is known and understood as such. If any simple priest for whom this is too hard a saying tells me that it was not so intended, I shall remind him that the Church is in the hands of God, and not, as simple priests imagine, God in the hands of the Church; so if he answers too confidently for God's intentions he may be asked "Hast thou entered into the springs of the sea? or hast thou walked in the recesses of the deep?" And Joan's own answer is also the answer of old: "Though He slay me, yet will I trust Him; *but I will maintain my own ways before Him.*"

THE LAW OF CHANGE IS THE LAW OF GOD

When Joan maintained her own ways she claimed, like Job, that there was not only God and the Church to be considered, but the Word made Flesh: that is, the unaveraged individual, representing life possibly at its highest actual human evolution and possibly at its lowest, but never at its merely mathematical average. Now there is no deification of the democratic average in the theory of the Church: it is an avowed hierarchy in which the members are sifted until at the end of the process an individual stands supreme as the Vicar of Christ. But when the process is examined it appears that its successive steps of selection and election are of the superior by the inferior (the cardinal vice of democracy), with the result that great popes are as rare and accidental as great kings, and that it has sometimes been safer for an aspirant to the Chair and the Keys to pass as a moribund dotard than as an energetic saint. At best very few popes have been canonized, or could be without letting down the standard of sanctity set by the self-elected saints.

No other result could have been reasonably expected; for it is not possible that an official organization of the spiritual needs of millions of men and women, mostly poor and ignorant, should compete successfully in the selection of its principals with the direct choice of the Holy Ghost as it flashes with unerring aim upon the individual. Nor can any College of Cardinals pray effectively that its choice may be inspired. The conscious prayer of the inferior may be that his choice may light on a greater than himself;

but the sub-conscious intention of his self-preserving individuality must be to find a trustworthy servant for his own purposes. The saints and prophets, though they may be accidentally in this or that official position or rank, are always really self-selected, like Joan. And since neither Church nor State, by the secular necessities of its constitution, can guarantee even the recognition of such self-chosen missions, there is nothing for us but to make it a point of honor to privilege heresy to the last bearable degree on the simple ground that all evolution in thought and conduct must at first appear as heresy and misconduct. In short, though all society is founded on intolerance, all improvement is founded on tolerance, or the recognition of the fact that the law of evolution is Ibsen's law of change. And as the law of God in any sense of the word which can now command a faith proof against science is a law of evolution, it follows that the law of God is a law of change, and that when the Churches set themselves against change as such, they are setting themselves against the law of God.

CREDULITY, MODERN AND MEDIEVAL

When Abernethy, the famous doctor, was asked why he indulged himself with all the habits he warned his patients against as unhealthy, he replied that his business was that of a direction post, which points out the way to a place, but does not go thither itself. He might have added that neither does it compel the traveller to go thither, nor prevent him from seeking some other way. Unfortunately our clerical direction posts always do coerce the traveller when they have the political power to do so. When the Church was a temporal as well as a spiritual power, and for long after to the full extent to which it could control or influence the temporal power, it enforced conformity by persecutions that were all the more ruthless because their intention was so excellent. Today, when the doctor has succeeded to the priest, and can do practically what he likes with parliament and the press through the blind faith in him which has succeeded to the far more critical faith in the parson, legal compulsion to take the doctor's prescription, however poisonous, is carried to an extent that would have horrified the Inquisition and staggered Archbishop Laud. Our credulity is grosser than that of the Middle Ages, because the priest had no such direct pecuniary interest in our sins as the doctor has in our diseases: he did not starve when all was well with his flock, nor prosper when they were perishing, as our private commercial doctors must. Also the medieval cleric believed that something extremely unpleasant would happen to him after death if he was unscrupulous, a belief now practically extinct among persons receiving a dogmatically materialist education. Our professional corporations are Trade Unions without souls to be damned; and they will soon drive us to remind them that they have bodies to be kicked. The Vatican was never soulless: at worst it was a political conspiracy to make the Church supreme temporally as well as spiritually. Therefore the question raised by Joan's burning is a burning question still, though the penalties involved are not so sensational. That is why I am probing it. If it were only an historical curiosity I would not waste my readers' time and my own on it for five minutes.

TOLERATION, MODERN AND MEDIEVAL

The more closely we grapple with it the more difficult

it becomes. At first sight we are disposed to repeat that Joan should have been excommunicated and then left to go her own way, though she would have protested vehemently against so cruel a deprivation of her spiritual food; for confession, absolution, and the body of her Lord were first necessaries of life to her. Such a spirit as Joan's might have got over that difficulty as the Church of England got over the Bulls of Pope Leo, by making a Church of her own, and affirming it to be the temple of the true and original faith from which her persecutors had strayed. But as such a proceeding was, in the eyes of both Church and State at that time, a spreading of damnation and anarchy, its toleration involved a greater strain on faith in freedom than political and ecclesiastical human nature could bear. It is easy to say that the Church should have waited for the alleged evil results instead of assuming that they would occur, and what they would be. That sounds simple enough; but if a modern Public Health Authority were to leave people entirely to their own devices in the matter of sanitation, saying, "We have nothing to do with drainage or your views about drainage; but if you catch smallpox or typhus we will prosecute you and have you punished very severely like the authorities in Butler's Erewhon," it would either be removed to the County Asylum or reminded that A's neglect of sanitation may kill the child of B two miles off, or start an epidemic in which the most conscientious sanitarians may perish.

We must face the fact that society is founded on intolerance. There are glaring cases of the abuse of intolerance; but they are quite as characteristic of our own age as of the Middle Ages. The typical modern example and contrast is compulsory inoculation replacing what was virtually compulsory baptism. But compulsion to inoculate is objected to as a crudely unscientific and mischievous anti-sanitary quackery, not in the least because we think it wrong to compel people to protect their children from disease. Its opponents would make it a crime, and will probably succeed in doing so; and that will be just as intolerant as making it compulsory. Neither the Pasteurians nor their opponents the Sanitarians would leave parents free to bring up their children naked, though that course also has some plausible advocates. We may prate of toleration as we will; but society must always draw a line somewhere between allowable conduct and insanity or crime, in spite of the risk of mistaking sages for lunatics and saviors for blasphemers. We must persecute, even to the death; and all we can do to mitigate the danger of persecution is, first, to be very careful what we persecute, and second, to bear in mind that unless there is a large liberty to shock conventional people, and a well informed sense of the value of originality, individuality, and eccentricity, the result will be apparent stagnation covering a repression of evolutionary forces which will eventually explode with extravagant and probably destructive violence.

VARIABILITY OF TOLERATION

The degree of tolerance attainable at any moment depends on the strain under which society is maintaining its cohesion. In war, for instance, we suppress the gospels and put Quakers in prison, muzzle the newspapers, and make it a serious offence to shew a light at night. Under the strain of invasion the French Government in 1792 struck off 4000 heads, mostly on grounds that would not in time of settled peace have provoked any Government to chloroform a dog; and in 1920 the British Government slaughtered and burnt in Ireland to persecute the advocates of a constitutional change which it had presently to effect itself. Later on the Fascisti in Italy did everything that the Black and Tans did in Ireland, with some grotesquely ferocious variations, under the strain of an unskilled attempt at industrial revolution by Socialists who understood Socialism even less than Capitalists understand Capitalism. In the United States an incredibly savage persecution of Russians took place during the scare spread by the Russian Bolshevik revolution after 1917. These instances could easily be multiplied; but they are enough to shew that between a maximum of indulgent toleration and a ruthlessly intolerant Terrorism there is a scale through which toleration is continually rising or falling, and that there was not the smallest ground for the self-complacent conviction of the nineteenth century that it was more tolerant than the fifteenth, or that such an event as the execution of Joan could not possibly occur in what we call our own more enlightened times. Thousands of women, each of them a thousand times less dangerous and terrifying to our Governments than Joan was to the Government of her day, have within the last ten years been slaughtered, starved to death, burnt out of house and home, and what not that Persecution and Terror could do to them, in the course of Crusades far more tyranically pretentious than the medieval Crusades which proposed nothing more hyperbolical than the rescue of the Holy Sepulchre from the Saracens. The Inquisition, with its English equivalent the Star Chamber, are gone in the sense that their names are now disused; but can any of the modern substitutes for the Inquisition, the

Special Tribunals and Commissions, the punitive expeditions, the suspensions of the Habeas Corpus Act, the proclamations of martial law and of minor states of siege, and the rest of them, claim that their victims have as fair a trial, as well considered a body of law to govern their cases, or as conscientious a judge to insist on strict legality of procedure as Joan had from the Inquisition and from the spirit of the Middle Ages even when her country was under the heaviest strain of civil and foreign war? From us she would have had no trial and no law except a Defence of The Realm Act suspending all law; and for judge she would have had, at best, a bothered major, and at worst a promoted advocate in ermine and scarlet to whom the scruples of a trained ecclesiastic like Cauchon would seem ridiculous and ungentlemanly.

THE CONFLICT BETWEEN GENIUS AND DISCIPLINE

Having thus brought the matter home to ourselves, we may now consider the special feature of Joan's mental constitution which made her so unmanageable. What is to be done on the one hand with rulers who will not give any reason for their orders, and on the other with people who cannot understand the reasons when they are given? The government of the world, political, industrial, and domestic, has to be carried on mostly by the giving and obeying of orders under just these conditions. "Dont argue: do as you are told" has to be said not only to children and soldiers, but practically to every body. Fortunately most people do not want to argue: they are only too glad to be saved the trouble of thinking for themselves. And the ablest and most independent thinkers are content to understand their own special department. In other departments they will unhesitatingly ask for and accept the instructions of a policeman or the advice of a tailor without demanding or desiring explanations.

Nevertheless, there must be some ground for attaching authority to an order. A child will obey its parents, a soldier his officer, a philosopher a railway porter, and a workman a foreman, all without question, because it is generally accepted that those who give the orders understand what they are about, and are duly authorized and even obliged to give them, and because, in the practical emergencies of daily life, there is no time for lessons and explanations, or for arguments as to their validity. Such obediences are as necessary to the continuous operation of our social system as the revolutions of the earth are to the succession of night and day. But they are not so spontaneous as they seem: they have to be very carefully arranged and maintained. A bishop will defer to and obey a king; but let a curate venture to give him an order, however necessary and sensible, and the bishop will forget his cloth and damn the curate's impudence. The more obedient a man is to accredited authority the more jealous he is of allowing any unauthorized person to order him about.

With all this in mind, consider the career of Joan. She was a village girl, in authority over sheep and pigs, dogs and chickens, and to some extent over her father's hired laborers when he hired any, but over no one else on earth. Outside the farm she had no authority, no prestige, no claim to the smallest deference. Yet she ordered everybody about, from her uncle to the king, the archbishop, and the military General Staff. Her uncle obeyed her like a sheep, and took her to the castle of the local commander, who, on being ordered about, tried to assert himself, but soon collapsed and obeyed. And so on up to the king, as we have seen. This would have been unbearably irritating even if her orders had been offered as rational solutions of the desperate difficulties in which her social superiors found themselves just then. But they were not so offered. Nor were they offered as the expression of Joan's arbitrary will. It was never "I say so," but always "God says so."

JOAN AS THEOCRAT

Leaders who take that line have no trouble with some people, and no end of trouble with others. They need never fear a lukewarm reception. Either they are messengers of God, or they are blasphemous impostors. In the Middle Ages the general belief in witchcraft greatly intensified this contrast, because when an apparent miracle happened (as in the case of the wind changing at Orleans) it proved the divine mission to the credulous, and proved a contract with the devil to the sceptical. All through, Joan had to depend on those who accepted her as an incarnate angel against those who added to an intense resentment of her presumption a bigoted abhorrence of her as a witch. To this abhorrence we must add the extreme irritation of those who did not believe in the voices, and regarded her as a liar and impostor. It is hard to conceive anything more infuriating to a statesman or a military commander, or to a court favourite, than to be overruled at every turn, or to be robbed of the ear of the reigning sovereign, by an impudent young upstart practising on the credulity of the populace and the vanity and silliness of an immature prince by exploiting a few of those lucky coincidences which pass as miracles with uncritical people. Not only were the envy, snobbery, and competitive ambition of the baser natures exacerbated by Joan's success, but among the friendly ones that were clever enough to be critical a quite reasonable scepticism and mistrust of her ability, founded on a fair observation of her obvious ignorance and temerity, were at work against her. And as she met all remonstrances and all criticisms, not with arguments or persuasion, but with a flat appeal to the authority of God and a claim to be in God's special confidence, she must have seemed, to all who were not infatuated by her, so insufferable that nothing but an unbroken chain of overwhelming successes in the military and political field could have saved her from the wrath that finally destroyed her.

UNBROKEN SUCCESS ESSENTIAL IN THEOCRACY

To forge such a chain she needed to be the King, the Archbishop of Rheims, the Bastard of Orleans, and herself into the bargain; and that was impossible. From the moment when she failed to stimulate Charles to follow up his coronation with a swoop on Paris she was lost. The fact that she insisted on this whilst the king and the rest timidly and foolishly thought they could square the Duke of Burgundy, and effect a combination with him against the English, made her a terrifying nuisance to them; and from that time onward she could do nothing but prowl about the battlefields waiting for some lucky chance to sweep the captains into a big move. But it was to the enemy that the chance came: she was taken prisoner by the Burgundians fighting before Compiègne, and at once discovered that she had not a friend in the political world. Had she escaped she would probably have fought on until the English were gone, and then had to shake the dust of the court off her feet, and retire to Domrémy as Garibaldi had to retire to Caprera.

MODERN DISTORTIONS OF JOAN'S HISTORY

This, I think, is all that we can now pretend to say about the prose of Joan's career. The romance of her rise, the tragedy of her execution, and the comedy of the attempts of posterity to make amends for that execution, belong to my play and not to my preface, which must be confined to a sober essay on the facts. That such an essay is badly needed can be ascertained by examining any of our standard works of reference. They give accurately enough the facts about the visit to Vaucouleurs, the annunciation to Charles at Chinon, the raising of the siege of Orleans and the subsequent battles, the coronation at Rheims, the capture at Compiègne, and the trial and execution at Rouen, with their dates and the names of the people concerned; but they all break down on the melodramatic legend of the wicked bishop and the entrapped maiden and the rest of it. It would be far less misleading if they were wrong as to the facts, and right in their view of the facts. As it is, they illustrate the too little considered truth that the fashion in which we think changes like the fashion of our clothes, and that it is difficult, if not impossible, for most people to think otherwise than in the fashion of their own period.

HISTORY ALWAYS OUT OF DATE

This, by the way, is why children are never taught contemporary history. Their history books deal with periods of which the thinking has passed out of fashion, and the circumstances no longer apply to active life. For example, they are taught history about Washington, and told lies about Lenin. In Washington's time they were told lies (the same lies) about Washington, and taught history about Cromwell. In the fifteenth and sixteenth centuries they were told lies about Joan, and by this time might very well be told the truth about her. Unfortunately the lies did not cease when the political circumstances became obsolete. The Reformation, which Joan had unconsciously anticipated, kept the questions which arose in her case burning up to our own day (you can see plenty of the burnt houses still in Ireland), with the result that Joan has remained the subject of anti-Clerical lies, of specifically Protestant lies, and of Roman Catholic evasions of her unconscious Protestantism. The truth sticks in our throats with all the sauces it is served with: it will never go down until we take it without any sauce at all.

THE REAL JOAN NOT MARVELLOUS ENOUGH FOR US

But even in its simplicity, the faith demanded by Joan is one which the anti-metaphysical temper of nineteenth century civilization, which remains powerful in England and America, and is tyrannical in France, contemptuously refuses her. We do not, like her contemporaries, rush to the opposite extreme in a recoil from her as from a witch self-sold to the devil, because we do not believe in the devil nor in the possibility of commercial contracts with him. Our credulity, though enormous, is not boundless; and our stock of it is quite used up by our mediums, clairvoyants, hand readers, slate writers, Christian Scientists, psycho-analysts, electronic vibration diviners, therapeutists of all schools registered and unregistered, astrologers, astronomers who tell us that the sun is nearly a hundred million miles away and that Betelgeuse is ten times as big as the whole universe, physicists who balance Betelgeuse by describing the incredible smallness of the atom, and a host of other marvel mongers whose credulity would have dissolved the Middle Ages in a roar of sceptical merriment. In the Middle Ages people believed that the earth was flat, for which they had at least the evidence of their senses: we believe it to be round, not because as many as one per cent of us could give the physical reasons for so quaint a belief, but because modern science has convinced us that nothing that is obvious is true, and that everything that is magical, improbable, extraordinary, gigantic, microscopic, heartless, or outrageous is scientific.

I must not, by the way, be taken as implying that the earth is flat, or that all or any of our amazing credulities are delusions or impostures. I am only defending my own age against the charge of being less imaginative than the Middle Ages. I affirm that the nineteenth century, and still more the twentieth, can knock the fifteenth into a cocked hat in point of susceptibility to marvels and miracles and saints and prophets and magicians and monsters and fairy tales of all kinds. The proportion of marvel to immediately credible statement in the latest edition of the Encyclopædia Britannica is enormously greater than in the Bible. The medieval doctors of divinity who did not pretend to settle how many angels could dance on the point of a needle cut a very poor figure as far as romantic credulity is concerned beside the modern

physicists who have settled to the billionth of a milli-
metre every movement and position in the dance of
the electrons. Not for worlds would I question the
precise accuracy of these calculations or the existence
of electrons (whatever they may be). The fate of Joan
is a warning to me against such heresy. But why the
men who believe in electrons should regard themselves as less credulous than the men who believed
in angels is not apparent to me. If they refuse to
believe, with the Rouen assessors of 1431, that Joan
was a witch, it is not because that explanation is
too marvellous, but because it is not marvellous
enough.

THE STAGE LIMITS OF HISTORICAL
REPRESENTATION

For the story of Joan I refer the reader to the play
which follows. It contains all that need be known about
her; but as it is for stage use I have had to condense
into three and a half hours a series of events which in
their historical happening were spread over four times
as many months; for the theatre imposes unities of
time and place from which Nature in her boundless
wastefulness is free. Therefore the reader must not
suppose that Joan really put Robert de Baudricourt in
her pocket in fifteen minutes, nor that her excommunication, recantation, relapse, and death at the
stake were a matter of half an hour or so. Neither do I
claim more for my dramatizations of Joan's contemporaries than that some of them are probably slightly
more like the originals than those imaginary portraits
of all the Popes from Saint Peter onward through the
Dark Ages which are still gravely exhibited in the
Uffizi in Florence (or were when I was there last).

My Dunois would do equally well for the Duc d'Alençon. Both left descriptions of Joan so similar that, as a man always describes himself unconsciously whenever he describes anyone else, I have inferred that these goodnatured young men were very like one another in mind; so I have lumped the twain into a single figure, thereby saving the theatre manager a salary and a suit of armor. Dunois' face, still on record at Châteaudun, is a suggestive help. But I really know no more about these men and their circle than Shakespear knew about Falconbridge and the Duke of Austria, or about Macbeth and Macduff. In view of the things they did in history, and have to do again in the play, I can only invent appropriate characters for them in Shakespear's manner.

A VOID IN THE ELIZABETHAN DRAMA

I have, however, one advantage over the Elizabethans. I write in full view of the Middle Ages, which may be said to have been rediscovered in the middle of the nineteenth century after an eclipse of about four hundred and fifty years. The Renascence of antique literature and art in the sixteenth century, and the lusty growth of Capitalism, between them buried the Middle Ages; and their resurrection is a second Renascence. Now there is not a breath of medieval atmosphere in Shakespear's histories. His John of Gaunt is like a study of the old age of Drake. Although he was a Catholic by family tradition, his figures are all intensely Protestant, individualist, sceptical, self-centred in everything but their love affairs, and completely personal and selfish even in them. His kings are not statesmen: his cardinals have no religion: a novice can read his plays from one end to the other without learning that the world is finally governed by forces expressing themselves in religions and laws which make epochs rather than by vulgarly ambitious individuals who make rows. The divinity which shapes our ends, rough hew them how we will, is mentioned fatalistically only to be forgotten immediately like a passing vague apprehension. To Shakesspear as to Mark Twain, Cauchon would have been a tyrant and a bully instead of a Catholic, and the inquisitor Lemaître would have been a Sadist instead of a lawyer. Warwick would have had no more feudal quality than his successor the King Maker has in the play of Henry VI. We should have seen them all completely satisfied that if they would only to their own selves be true they could not then be false to any man (a precept which represents the reaction against medievalism at its intensest) as if they were beings in the air, without public responsibilities of any kind. All Shakespear's characters are so: that is why they seem natural to our middle classes, who are comfortable and irresponsible at other people's expense, and are neither ashamed of that condition nor even conscious of it. Nature abhors this vacuum in Shakespear; and I have taken care to let the medieval atmosphere blow through my play freely. Those who see it performed will not mistake the startling event it records for a mere personal accident. They will have before them not only the visible and human puppets, but the Church, the Inquisition, the Feudal System, with divine inspiration always beating against their too inelastic limits: all more terrible in their dramatic force than any of the little mortal figures clanking about in plate armor or moving silently in the frocks and hoods of the order of St Dominic.

TRAGEDY, NOT MELODRAMA

There are no villains in the piece. Crime, like disease, is not interesting: it is something to be done away with by general consent, and that is all about it. It is what men do at their best, with good intentions, and what normal men and women find that they must and will do in spite of their intentions, that really concern us. The rascally bishop and the cruel inquisitor of Mark Twain and Andrew Lang are as dull as pickpockets; and they reduce Joan to the level of the even less interesting person whose pocket is picked. I have represented both of them as capable and eloquent exponents of The Church Militant and The Church Litigant, because only by doing so can I maintain my drama on the level of high tragedy and save it from becoming a mere police court sensation. A villain in a play can never be anything more than a *diabolus ex machina*, possibly a more exciting expedient than a *deus ex machina*, but both equally mechanical, and therefore interesting only as mechanism. It is, I repeat, what normally innocent people do that concerns us; and if Joan had not been burnt by normally innocent people in the energy of their righteousness her death at their hands would have no more significance than the Tokyo earthquake, which burnt a great many maidens. The tragedy of such murders is that they are not committed by murderers. They are judical murders, pious murders; and this contradiction at once brings an element of comedy into the tragedy: the angels may weep at the murder, but the gods laugh at the murderers.

THE INEVITABLE FLATTERIES OF TRAGEDY

Here then we have a reason why my drama of Saint

Joan's career, though it may give the essential truth of it, gives an inexact picture of some accidental facts. It goes almost without saying that the old Jeanne d'Arc melodramas, reducing everything to a conflict of villain and hero, or in Joan's case villain and heroine, not only miss the point entirely, but falsify the characters, making Cauchon a scoundrel, Joan a prima donna, and Dunois a lover. But the writer of high tragedy and comedy, aiming at the innermost attainable truth, must needs flatter Cauchon nearly as much as the melodramatist vilifies him. Although there is, as far as I have been able to discover, nothing against Cauchon that convicts him of bad faith or exceptional severity in his judicial relations with Joan, or of as much anti-prisoner, pro-police, class and sectarian bias as we now take for granted in our own courts, yet there is hardly more warrant for classing him as a great Catholic churchman, completely proof against the passions roused by the temporal situation. Neither does the inquisitor Lemaître, in such scanty accounts of him as are now recoverable, appear quite so able a master of his duties and of the case before him as I have given him credit for being. But it is the business of the stage to make its figures more intelligible to themselves than they would be in real life; for by no other means can they be made intelligible to the audience. And in this case Cauchon and Lemaître have to make intelligible not only themselves but the Church and the Inquisition, just as Warwick has to make the feudal system intelligible, the three between them having thus to make a twentieth-century audience conscious of an epoch fundamentally different from its own. Obviously the real Cauchon, Lemaître, and Warwick could not have done this: they were part of the Middle Ages themselves, and therefore as unconscious of its peculiarities as of the atomic formula of the air they breathed. But the play would be unintelligible if I had not endowed them with enough of this consciousness to enable them to explain their attitude to the twentieth century. All I claim is that by this inevitable sacrifice of verisimilitude I have secured in the only possible way sufficient veracity to justify me in claiming that as far as I can gather from the available documentation, and from such powers of divination as I possess, the things I represent these three exponents of the drama as saying are the things they actually would have said if they had known what they were really doing. And beyond this neither drama nor history can go in my hands.

SOME WELL-MEANT PROPOSALS FOR THE IMPROVEMENT OF THE PLAY

I have to thank several critics on both sides of the Atlantic, including some whose admiration for my play is most generously enthusiastic, for their heartfelt instructions as to how it can be improved. They point out that by the excision of the epilogue and all the references to such undramatic and tedious matters as the Church, the feudal system, the Inquisition, the theory of heresy and so forth, all of which, they point out, would be ruthlessly blue pencilled by any experienced manager, the play could be considerably shortened. I think they are mistaken. The experienced knights of the blue pencil, having saved an hour and a half by disembowelling the play, would at once proceed to waste two hours in building elaborate scenery, having real water in the river Loire and a real bridge across it, and staging an obviously sham fight for

possession of it, with the victorious French led by
Joan on a real horse. The coronation would eclipse
all previous theatrical displays, shewing, first, the
procession through the streets of Rheims, and then
the service in the cathedral, with special music written
for both. Joan would be burnt on the stage, as Mr
Matheson Lang always is in The Wandering Jew, on
the principle that it does not matter in the least why a
woman is burnt provided she is burnt, and people can
pay to see it done. The intervals between the acts
whilst these splendors were being built up and then
demolished by the stage carpenters would seem eternal,
to the great profit of the refreshment bars. And the
weary and demoralized audience would lose their
last trains and curse me for writing such inordinately
long and intolerably dreary and meaningless plays.
But the applause of the press would be unanimous.
Nobody who knows the stage history of Shakespear
will doubt that this is what would happen if I knew
my business so little as to listen to these well intentioned but disastrous counsellors: indeed it probably
will happen when I am no longer in control of the
performing rights. So perhaps it will be as well for
the public to see the play while I am still alive.

THE EPILOGUE

As to the epilogue, I could hardly be expected to
stultify myself by implying that Joan's history in the
world ended unhappily with her execution, instead of
beginning there. It was necessary by hook or crook to
shew the canonized Joan as well as the incinerated
one; for many a woman has got herself burnt by
carelessly whisking a muslin skirt into the drawing

room fireplace, but getting canonized is a different matter, and a more important one. So I am afraid the epilogue must stand.

TO THE CRITICS, LEST THEY SHOULD FEEL IGNORED

To a professional critic (I have been one myself) theatre-going is the curse of Adam. The play is the evil he is paid to endure in the sweat of his brow; and the sooner it is over, the better. This would seem to place him in irreconcilable opposition to the paying playgoer, from whose point of view the longer the play, the more entertainment he gets for his money. It does in fact so place him, especially in the provinces, where the playgoer goes to the theatre for the sake of the play solely, and insists so effectively on a certain number of hours' entertainment that touring managers are sometimes seriously embarrassed by the brevity of the London plays they have to deal in.

For in London the critics are reinforced by a considerable body of persons who go to the theatre as many others go to church, to display their best clothes and compare them with other people's; to be in the fashion, and have something to talk about at dinner parties; to adore a pet performer; to pass the evening anywhere rather than at home: in short, for any or every reason except interest in dramatic art as such. In fashionable centres the number of irreligious people who go to church, of unmusical people who go to concerts and operas, and of undramatic people who go to the theatre, is so prodigious that sermons have been cut down to ten minutes and plays to two hours; and, even at that, congregations sit longing for the

benediction and audiences for the final curtain, so
that they may get away to the lunch or supper they
really crave for, after arriving as late as (or later
than) the hour of beginning can possibly be made for
them.

Thus from the stalls and in the Press an atmosphere of hypocrisy spreads. Nobody says straight out
that genuine drama is a tedious nuisance, and that to
ask people to endure more than two hours of it (with
two long intervals of relief) is an intolerable imposi-
tion. Nobody says "I hate classical tragedy and
comedy as I hate sermons and symphonies; but I like
police news and divorce news and any kind of dancing
or decoration that has an aphrodisiac effect on me or
on my wife or husband. And whatever superior people
may pretend, I cannot associate pleasure with any
sort of intellectual activity; and I dont believe anyone
else can either." Such things are not said; yet nine-
tenths of what is offered as criticism of the drama in the
metropolitan Press of Europe and America is nothing
but a muddled paraphrase of it. If it does not mean
that, it means nothing.

I do not complain of this, though it complains very
unreasonably of me. But I can take no more notice of
it than Einstein of the people who are incapable of
mathematics. I write in the classical manner for those
who pay for admission to a theatre because they like
classical comedy or tragedy for its own sake, and like
it so much when it is good of its kind and well done
that they tear themselves away from it with reluctance
to catch the very latest train or omnibus that will take
them home. Far from arriving late from an eight or
half-past eight o'clock dinner so as to escape at least
the first half-hour of the performance, they stand in
queues outside the theatre doors for hours beforehand

in bitingly cold weather to secure a seat. In countries where a play lasts a week, they bring baskets of provisions and sit it out. These are the patrons on whom I depend for my bread. I do not give them performances twelve hours long, because circumstances do not at present make such entertainments feasible; though a performance beginning after breakfast and ending at sunset is as possible physically and artistically in Surrey or Middlesex as in Ober-Ammergau; and an all-night sitting in a theatre would be at least as enjoyable as an all-night sitting in the House of Commons, and much more useful. But in St Joan I have done my best by going to the well-established classical limit of three and a half hours practically continuous playing, barring the one interval imposed by considerations which have nothing to do with art. I know that this is hard on the pseudo-critics and on the fashionable people whose playgoing is a hypocrisy. I cannot help feeling some compassion for them when they assure me that my play, though a great play, must fail hopelessly, because it does not begin at a quarter to nine and end at eleven. The facts are overwhelmingly against them. They forget that all men are not as they are. Still, I am sorry for them; and though I cannot for their sakes undo my work and help the people who hate the theatre to drive out the people who love it, yet I may point out to them that they have several remedies in their own hands. They can escape the first part of the play by their usual practice of arriving late. They can escape the epilogue by not waiting for it. And if the irreducible minimum thus attained is still too painful, they can stay away altogether. But I deprecate this extreme course, because it is good neither for my pocket nor for their own souls. Already a few of them, noticing that what matters is not the absolute length of time occupied by a play, but the speed with which that time passes, are discovering that the theatre, though purgatorial in its Aristotelian moments, is not necessarily always the dull place they have so often found it. What do its discomforts matter when the play makes us forget them?

AYOT ST LAWRENCE, *May 1924*

SCENE I

A fine spring morning on the river Meuse, between Lorraine and Champagne, in the year 1429 A.D., in the castle of Vaucouleurs.

Captain Robert de Baudricourt, a military squire, handsome and physically energetic, but with no will of his own, is disguising that defect in his usual fashion by storming terribly at his steward, a trodden worm, scanty of flesh, scanty of hair, who might be any age from 18 to 55, being the sort of man whom age cannot wither because he has never bloomed.

The two are in a sunny stone chamber on the first floor of the castle. At a plain strong oak table, seated in chair to match, the captain presents his left profile. The steward stands facing him at the other side of the table, if so deprecatory a stance as his can be called standing. The mullioned thirteenth-century window is open behind him. Near it in the corner is a turret with a narrow arched doorway leading to a winding stair which descends to the courtyard. There is a stout fourlegged stool under the table, and a wooden chest under the window.

ROBERT. No eggs! No eggs!! Thousand thunders, man, what do you mean by no eggs?
STEWARD. Sir: it is not my fault. It is the act of God.
ROBERT. Blasphemy. You tell me there are no eggs; and you blame your Maker for it.
STEWARD. Sir: what can I do? I cannot lay eggs.
ROBERT [*sarcastic*] Ha! You jest about it.
STEWARD. No, sir, God knows. We all have to go without eggs just as you have, sir. The hens will not lay.

ROBERT. Indeed! [*Rising*] Now listen to me, you.

STEWARD [*humbly*] Yes, sir.

ROBERT. What am I?

STEWARD. What are you, sir?

ROBERT [*coming at him*] Yes: what am I? Am I Robert, squire of Baudricourt and captain of this castle of Vaucouleurs; or am I a cowboy?

STEWARD. Oh, sir, you know you are a greater man here than the king himself.

ROBERT. Precisely. And now, do you know what you are?

STEWARD. I am nobody, sir, except that I have the honor to be your steward.

ROBERT [*driving him to the wall, adjective by adjective*] You have not only the honor of being my steward, but the privilege of being the worst, most incompetent, drivelling snivelling jibbering jabbering idiot of a steward in France. [*He strides back to the table*].

STEWARD [*cowering on the chest*] Yes, sir: to a great man like you I must seem like that.

ROBERT [*turning*] My fault, I suppose. Eh?

STEWARD [*coming to him deprecatingly*] Oh, sir: you always give my most innocent words such a turn!

ROBERT. I will give your neck a turn if you dare tell me, when I ask you how many eggs there are, that you cannot lay any.

STEWARD [*protesting*] Oh sir, oh sir—

ROBERT. No: not oh sir, oh sir, but no sir, no sir. My three Barbary hens and the black are the best layers in Champagne. And you come and tell me that there are no eggs! Who stole them? Tell me that, before I kick you out through the castle gate for a liar and a seller of my goods to thieves. The milk was short yesterday, too: do not forget that.

STEWARD [*desperate*] I know, sir. I know only too

well. There is no milk: there are no eggs: tomorrow there will be nothing.

ROBERT. Nothing! You will steal the lot: eh?

STEWARD. No, sir: nobody will steal anything. But there is a spell on us: we are bewitched.

ROBERT. That story is not good enough for me. Robert de Baudricourt burns witches and hangs thieves. Go. Bring me four dozen eggs and two gallons of milk here in this room before noon, or Heaven have mercy on your bones! I will teach you to make a fool of me. [*He resumes his seat with an air of finality*].

STEWARD. Sir: I tell you there are no eggs. There will be none—not if you were to kill me for it—as long as The Maid is at the door.

ROBERT. The Maid! What maid? What are you talking about?

STEWARD. The girl from Lorraine, sir. From Domrémy.

ROBERT [*rising in fearful wrath*] Thirty thousand thunders! Fifty thousand devils! Do you mean to say that that girl, who had the impudence to ask to see me two days ago, and whom I told you to send back to her father with my orders that he was to give her a good hiding, is here still?

STEWARD. I have told her to go, sir, She wont.

ROBERT. I did not tell you to tell her to go: I told you to throw her out. You have fifty men-at-arms and a dozen lumps of able-bodied servants to carry out my orders. Are they afraid of her?

STEWARD. She is so positive, sir.

ROBERT [*seizing him by the scruff of the neck*] Positive! Now see here. I am going to throw you downstairs.

STEWARD. No, sir. Please.

ROBERT. Well, stop me by being positive. It's quite easy: any slut of a girl can do it.

STEWARD [*hanging limp in his hands*] Sir, sir: you cannot get rid of her by throwing me out. [*Robert has to let him drop. He squats on his knees on the floor, contemplating his master resignedly*]. You see, sir, you are much more positive than I am. But so is she.

ROBERT. I am stronger than you are, you fool.

STEWARD. No, sir: it isnt that: it's your strong character, sir. She is weaker than we are: she is only a slip of a girl; but we cannot make her go.

ROBERT. You parcel of curs: you are afraid of her.

STEWARD [*rising cautiously*] No, sir: we are afraid of you; but she puts courage into us. She really doesnt seem to be afraid of anything. Perhaps you could frighten her, sir.

ROBERT [*grimly*] Perhaps. Where is she now?

STEWARD. Down in the courtyard, sir, talking to the soldiers as usual. She is always talking to the soldiers except when she is praying.

ROBERT. Praying! Ha! You believe she prays, you idiot. I know the sort of girl that is always talking to soldiers. She shall talk to me a bit. [*He goes to the window and shouts fiercely through it*] Hallo, you there!

A GIRL'S VOICE [*bright, strong and rough*] Is it me, sir?

ROBERT. Yes, you.

THE VOICE. Be you captain?

ROBERT. Yes, damn your impudence, I be captain. Come up here. [*To the soldiers in the yard*] Shew her the way, you. And shove her along quick. [*He leaves the window, and returns to his place at the table, where he sits magisterially*].

STEWARD [*whispering*] She wants to go and be a soldier herself. She wants you to give her soldier's clothes. Armor, sir! And a sword! Actually! [*He steals behind Robert*].

Joan appears in the turret doorway. She is an able-bodied country girl of 17 *or* 18, *respectably dressed in red, with an uncommon face: eyes very wide apart and bulging as they often do in very imaginative people, a long well-shaped nose with wide nostrils, a short upper lip, resolute but full-lipped mouth, and handsome fighting chin. She comes eagerly to the table, delighted at having penetrated to Baudricourt's presence at last, and full of hope as to the result. His scowl does not check or frighten her in the least. Her voice is normally a hearty coaxing voice, very confident, very appealing, very hard to resist.*

JOAN [*bobbing a curtsey*] Good morning, captain squire. Captain: you are to give me a horse and armor and some soldiers, and send me to the Dauphin. Those are your orders from my Lord.

ROBERT [*outraged*] Orders from your lord! And who the devil may your lord be? Go back to him, and tell him that I am neither duke nor peer at his orders: I am squire of Baudricourt; and I take no orders except from the king.

JOAN [*reassuringly*] Yes, squire: that is all right. My Lord is the King of Heaven.

ROBERT. Why, the girl's mad. [*To the steward*] Why didnt you tell me so, you blockhead?

STEWARD. Sir: do not anger her: give her what she wants.

JOAN [*impatient, but friendly*] They all say I am mad until I talk to them, squire. But you see that it is the will of God that you are to do what He has put into my mind.

ROBERT. It is the will of God that I shall send you back to your father with orders to put you under lock and key and thrash the madness out of you. What have you to say to that?

JOAN. You think you will, squire; but you will find it all coming quite different. You said you would not see me; but here I am.

STEWARD [*appealing*] Yes, sir. You see, sir.

ROBERT. Hold your tongue, you.

STEWARD [*abjectly*] Yes, sir.

ROBERT [*to Joan, with a sour loss of confidence*] So you are presuming on my seeing you, are you?

JOAN [*sweetly*] Yes, squire.

ROBERT [*feeling that he has lost ground, brings down his two fists squarely on the table, and inflates his chest imposingly to cure the unwelcome and only too familiar sensation*] Now listen to me. I am going to assert myself.

JOAN [*busily*] Please do, squire. The horse will cost sixteen francs. It is a good deal of money; but I can save it on the armor. I can find a soldier's armor that will fit me well enough: I am very hardy; and I do not need beautiful armor made to my measure like you wear. I shall not want many soldiers: the Dauphin will give me all I need to raise the siege of Orleans.

ROBERT [*flabbergasted*] To raise the siege of Orleans!

JOAN [*simply*] Yes, squire: that is what God is sending me to do. Three men will be enough for you to send with me if they are good men and gentle to me. They have promised to come with me. Polly and Jack and—

ROBERT. Polly!! You impudent baggage, do you dare call squire Bertrand de Poulengey Polly to my face?

JOAN. His friends call him so, squire: I did not know he had any other name. Jack—

ROBERT. That is Monsieur John of Metz, I suppose?

JOAN. Yes, squire. Jack will come willingly: he is a

very kind gentleman, and gives me money to give to the poor. I think John Godsave will come, and Dick the Archer, and their servants John of Honecourt and Julian. There will be no trouble for you, squire: I have arranged it all: you have only to give the order.

ROBERT [*contemplating her in a stupor of amazement*] Well, I am damned!

JOAN [*with unruffled sweetness*] No, squire: God is very merciful; and the blessed saints Catherine and Margaret, who speak to me every day [*he gapes*], will intercede for you. You will go to paradise; and your name will be remembered for ever as my first helper.

ROBERT [*to the steward, still much bothered, but changing his tone as he pursues a new clue*] Is this true about Monsieur de Poulengey?

STEWARD [*eagerly*] Yes, sir, and about Monsieur de Metz too. They both want to go with her.

ROBERT [*thoughtful*] Mf! [*He goes to the window, and shouts into the courtyard*] Hallo! You there: send Monsieur de Poulengey to me, will you? [*He turns to Joan*] Get out; and wait in the yard.

JOAN [*smiling brightly at him*] Right, squire. [*She goes out*].

ROBERT [*to the steward*] Go with her, you, you dithering imbecile. Stay within call; and keep your eye on her. I shall have her up here again.

STEWARD. Do so in God's name, sir. Think of those hens, the best layers in Champagne: and—

ROBERT. Think of my boot; and take your backside out of reach of it.

The steward retreats hastily and finds himself confronted in the doorway by Bertrand de Poulengey, a lymphatic French gentleman-at-arms, aged 36 or thereabout, employed in the department of the provost-marshal, dreamily absent-minded, seldom speaking unless spoken to, and then slow and obstinate in reply: alto-gether in contrast to the self-assertive, loud-mouthed, superficially energetic, fundamentally will-less Robert. The steward makes way for him and vanishes.

Poulengey salutes, and stands awaiting orders.

ROBERT [*genially*] It isnt service, Polly. A friendly talk. Sit down. [*He hooks the stool from under the table with his instep*].

Poulengey, relaxing, comes into the room; places the stool between the table and the window; and sits down ruminatively. Robert, half sitting on the end of the table, begins the friendly talk.

ROBERT. Now listen to me, Polly. I must talk to you like a father.

Poulengey looks up at him gravely for a moment, but says nothing.

ROBERT. It's about this girl you are interested in. Now, I have seen her. I have talked to her. First, she's mad. That doesnt matter. Second, she's not a farm wench. She's bourgeoise. That matters a good deal. I know her class exactly. Her father came here last year to represent his village in a lawsuit: he is one of their notables. A farmer. Not a gentleman farmer: he makes money by it, and lives by it. Still, not a laborer. Not a mechanic. He might have a cousin a lawyer, or in the Church. People of this sort may be of no account socially; but they can give a lot of bother to the authorities. That is to say, to me. Now no doubt it seems to you a very simple thing to take this girl away, humbugging her into the belief that you are taking her to the Dauphin. But if you get her into trouble, you may get me into no end of a mess, as I am her father's lord, and responsible for her protection. So friends or no friends, Polly, hands off her.

POULENGEY [*with deliberate impressiveness*] I should

as soon think of the Blessed Virgin herself in that way, as of this girl.

ROBERT [*coming off the table*] But she says you and Jack and Dick have offered to go with her. What for? You are not going to tell me that you take her crazy notion of going to the Dauphin seriously, are you?

POULENGEY [*slowly*] There is something about her. They are pretty foulmouthed and foulminded down there in the guardroom, some of them. But there hasnt been a word that has anything to do with her being a woman. They have stopped swearing before her. There is something. Something. It may be worth trying.

ROBERT. Oh, come, Polly! pull yourself together. Commonsense was never your strong point; but this is a little too much. [*He retreats disgustedly*].

POULENGEY [*unmoved*] What is the good of commonsense? If we had any commonsense we should join the Duke of Burgundy and the English king. They hold half the country, right down to the Loire. They have Paris. They have this castle: you know very well that we had to surrender it to the Duke of Bedford, and that you are only holding it on parole. The Dauphin is in Chinon, like a rat in a corner, except that he wont fight. We dont even know that he is the Dauphin: his mother says he isnt; and she ought to know. Think of that! the queen denying the legitimacy of her own son!

ROBERT. Well, she married her daughter to the English king. Can you blame the woman?

POULENGEY. I blame nobody. But thanks to her, the Dauphin is down and out; and we may as well face it. The English will take Orleans: the Bastard will not be able to stop them.

ROBERT. He beat the English the year before last at Montargis. I was with him.

POULENGEY. No matter: his men are cowed now; and he cant work miracles. And I tell you that nothing can save our side now but a miracle.

ROBERT. Miracles are all right, Polly. The only difficulty about them is that they dont happen nowadays.

POULENGEY. I used to think so. I am not so sure now. [*Rising and moving ruminatively towards the window*] At all events this is not a time to leave any stone unturned. There is something about the girl.

ROBERT. Oh! You think the girl can work miracles, do you?

POULENGEY. I think the girl herself is a bit of a miracle. Anyhow, she is the last card left in our hand. Better play her than throw up the game. [*He wanders to the turret*].

ROBERT [*wavering*] You really think that?

POULENGEY [*turning*] Is there anything else left for us to think?

ROBERT [*going to him*] Look here, Polly. If you were in my place would you let a girl like that do you out of sixteen francs for a horse?

POULENGEY. I will pay for the horse.

ROBERT. You will!

POULENGEY. Yes: I will back my opinion.

ROBERT. You will really gamble on a forlorn hope to the tune of sixteen francs?

POULENGEY. It is not a gamble.

ROBERT. What else is it?

POULENGEY. It is a certainty. Her words and her ardent faith in God have put fire into me.

ROBERT [*giving him up*] Whew! You are as mad as she is.

POULENGEY [*obstinately*] We want a few mad people now. See where the sane ones have landed us!

ROBERT [*his irresoluteness now openly swamping his affected decisiveness*] I shall feel like a precious fool. Still, if you feel sure—?

POULENGEY. I feel sure enough to take her to Chinon—unless you stop me.

ROBERT. This is not fair. You are putting the responsibility on me.

POULENGEY. It is on you whichever way you decide.

ROBERT. Yes: thats just it. Which way am I to decide? You dont see how awkward this is for me. [*Snatching at a dilatory step with an unconscious hope that Joan will make up his mind for him*] Do you think I ought to have another talk to her?

POULENGEY [*rising*] Yes. [*He goes to the window and calls*] Joan!

JOAN'S VOICE. Will he let us go, Polly?

POULENGEY. Come up. Come in. [*Turning to Robert*] Shall I leave you with her?

ROBERT. No: stay here; and back me up.

Poulengey sits down on the chest. Robert goes back to his magisterial chair, but remains standing to inflate himself more imposingly. Joan comes in, full of good news.

JOAN. Jack will go halves for the horse.

ROBERT. Well!! [*He sits, deflated*].

POULENGEY [*gravely*] Sit down, Joan.

JOAN [*checked a little, and looking to Robert*] May I?

ROBERT. Do what you are told.

Joan curtsies and sits down on the stool between them. Robert outfaces his perplexity with his most peremptory air.

ROBERT. What is your name?

JOAN [*chattily*] They always call me Jenny in Lorraine. Here in France I am Joan. The soldiers call me The Maid.

ROBERT. What is your surname?

JOAN. Surname? What is that? My father sometimes calls himself d'Arc; but I know nothing about it. You met my father. He—

ROBERT. Yes, yes: I remember. You come from Domrémy in Lorraine, I think.

JOAN. Yes; but what does it matter? we all speak French.

ROBERT. Dont ask questions: answer them. How old are you?

JOAN. Seventeen: so they tell me. It might be nineteen. I dont remember.

ROBERT. What did you mean when you said that St Catherine and St Margaret talked to you every day?

JOAN. They do.

ROBERT. What are they like?

JOAN [*suddenly obstinate*] I will tell you nothing about that: they have not given me leave.

ROBERT. But you actually see them; and they talk to you just as I am talking to you?

JOAN. No: it is quite different. I cannot tell you: you must not talk to me about my voices.

ROBERT. How do you mean? voices?

JOAN. I hear voices telling me what to do. They come from God.

ROBERT. They come from your imagination.

JOAN. Of course. That is how the messages of God come to us.

POULENGEY. Checkmate.

ROBERT. No fear! [*To Joan*] So God says you are to raise the siege of Orleans?

JOAN. And to crown the Dauphin in Rheims Cathedral.

ROBERT [*gasping*] Crown the D——! Gosh!

JOAN. And to make the English leave France.

ROBERT [*sarcastic*] Anything else?

JOAN [*charming*] Not just at present, thank you, squire.

ROBERT. I suppose you think raising a siege is as easy as chasing a cow out of a meadow. You think soldiering is anybody's job?

JOAN. I do not think it can be very difficult if God is on your side, and you are willing to put your life in His hand. But many soldiers are very simple.

ROBERT [*grimly*] Simple! Did you ever see English soldiers fighting?

JOAN. They are only men. God made them just like us; but He gave them their own country and their own language; and it is not His will that they should come into our country and try to speak our language.

ROBERT. Who has been putting such nonsense into your head? Dont you know that soldiers are subject to their feudal lord, and that it is nothing to them or to you whether he is the duke of Burgundy or the king of England or the king of France? What has their language to do with it?

JOAN. I do not understand that a bit. We are all subject to the King of Heaven; and He gave us our countries and our languages, and meant us to keep to them. If it were not so it would be murder to kill an Englishman in battle; and you, squire, would be in great danger of hell fire. You must not think about your duty to your feudal lord, but about your duty to God.

POULENGEY. It's no use, Robert: she can choke you like that every time.

ROBERT. Can she, by Saint Dennis! We shall see. [*To Joan*] We are not talking about God: we are talking about practical affairs. I ask you again, girl, have you ever seen English soldiers fighting? Have you ever seen them plundering, burning, turning the countryside into a desert? Have you heard no tales of their

Black Prince who was blacker than the devil himself,
or of the English king's father?

JOAN. You must not be afraid, Robert—

ROBERT. Damn you, I am not afraid. And who gave
you leave to call me Robert?

JOAN. You were called so in church in the name of
our Lord. All the other names are your father's or
your brother's or anybody's.

ROBERT. Tcha!

JOAN. Listen to me, squire. At Domrémy we had to
fly to the next village to escape from the English
soldiers. Three of them were left behind, wounded.
I came to know these three poor goddams quite well.
They had not half my strength.

ROBERT. Do you know why they are called goddams?

JOAN. No. Everyone calls them goddams.

ROBERT. It is because they are always calling on their
God to condemn their souls to perdition. That is what
goddam means in their language. How do you like it?

JOAN. God will be merciful to them; and they will
act like His good children when they go back to the
country He made for them, and made them for. I have
heard the tales of the Black Prince. The moment he
touched the soil of our country the devil entered into
him and made him a black fiend. But at home, in the
place made for him by God, he was good. It is always
so. If I went into England against the will of God to
conquer England, and tried to live there and speak its
language, the devil would enter into me; and when I
was old I should shudder to remember the wicked-
nesses I did.

ROBERT. Perhaps. But the more devil you were the
better you might fight. That is why the goddams will
take Orleans. And you cannot stop them, nor ten
thousand like you.

JOAN. One thousand like me can stop them. Ten like me can stop them with God on our side. [*She rises impetuously, and goes at him, unable to sit quiet any longer*]. You do not understand, squire. Our soldiers are always beaten because they are fighting only to save their skins; and the shortest way to save your skin is to run away. Our knights are thinking only of the money they will make in ransoms: it is not kill or be killed with them, but pay or be paid. But I will teach them all to fight that the will of God may be done in France; and then they will drive the poor goddams before them like sheep. You and Polly will live to see the day when there will not be an English soldier on the soil of France; and there will be but one king there: not the feudal English king, but God's French one.

ROBERT [*to Poulengey*] This may be all rot, Polly; but the troops might swallow it, though nothing that we can say seems able to put any fight into them. Even the Dauphin might swallow it. And if she can put fight into him, she can put it into anybody.

POULENGEY. I can see no harm in trying. Can you? And there is something about the girl—

ROBERT [*turning to Joan*] Now listen you to me; and [*desperately*] dont cut in before I have time to think.

JOAN [*plumping down on the stool again, like an obedient schoolgirl*] Yes, squire.

ROBERT. Your orders are, that you are to go to Chinon under the escort of this gentleman and three of his friends.

JOAN [*radiant, clasping her hands*] Oh, squire! Your head is all circled with light, like a saint's.

POULENGEY. How is she to get into the royal presence?

ROBERT [*who has looked up for his halo rather*

apprehensively] I dont know: how did she get into my presence? If the Dauphin can keep her out he is a better man than I take him for. [*Rising*] I will send her to Chinon; and she can say I sent her. Then let come what may: I can do no more.

JOAN. And the dress? I may have a soldier's dress, maynt I, squire?

ROBERT. Have what you please. I wash my hands of it.

JOAN [*wildly excited by her success*] Come, Polly. [*She dashes out*].

ROBERT [*shaking Poulengey's hand*] Goodbye, old man, I am taking a big chance. Few other men would have done it. But as you say, there is something about her.

POULENGEY. Yes: there is something about her. Goodbye. [*He goes out*].

Robert, still very doubtful whether he has not been made a fool of by a crazy female, and a social inferior to boot, scratches his head and slowly comes back from the door.

The steward runs in with a basket.

STEWARD. Sir, sir—

ROBERT. What now?

STEWARD. The hens are laying like mad, sir. Five dozen eggs!

ROBERT [*stiffens convulsively; crosses himself; and forms with his pale lips the words*] Christ in heaven! [*Aloud but breathless*] She did come from God.

Chinon, in Touraine. An end of the throne room in the castle, curtained off to make an antechamber. The Archbishop of Rheims, close on 50, a full-fed political prelate with nothing of the ecclesiastic about him except his imposing bearing, and the Lord Chamberlain, Monseigneur de la Trémouille, a monstrous arrogant wineskin of a man, are waiting for the Dauphin. There is a door in the wall to the right of the two men. It is late in the afternoon on the 8th of March, 1429. The Archbishop stands with dignity whilst the Chamberlain, on his left, fumes about in the worst of tempers.

LA TRÉMOUILLE. What the devil does the Dauphin mean by keeping us waiting like this? I dont know how you have the patience to stand there like a stone idol.

THE ARCHBISHOP. You see, I am an archbishop; and an archbishop is a sort of idol. At any rate he has to learn to keep still and suffer fools patiently. Besides, my dear Lord Chamberlain, it is the Dauphin's royal privilege to keep you waiting, is it not?

LA TRÉMOUILLE. Dauphin be damned! saving your reverence. Do you know how much money he owes me?

THE ARCHBISHOP. Much more than he owes me, I have no doubt, because you are a much richer man. But I take it he owes you all you could afford to lend him. That is what he owes me.

LA TRÉMOUILLE. Twenty-seven thousand: that was his last haul. A cool twenty-seven thousand!

THE ARCHBISHOP. What becomes of it all? He never has a suit of clothes that I would throw to a curate.

LA TRÉMOUILLE. He dines on a chicken or a scrap of mutton. He borrows my last penny; and there is nothing to shew for it [*A page appears in the doorway*]. At last!

THE PAGE. No, my lord: it is not His Majesty. Monsieur de Rais is approaching.

LA TRÉMOUILLE. Young Bluebeard! Why announce him?

THE PAGE. Captain La Hire is with him. Something has happened, I think.

Gilles de Rais, a young man of 25, very smart and self-possessed, and sporting the extravagance of a little curled beard dyed blue at a clean-shaven court, comes in. He is determined to make himself agreeable, but lacks natural joyousness, and is not really pleasant. In fact when he defies the Church some eleven years later he is accused of trying to extract pleasure from horrible cruelties, and hanged. So far, however, there is no shadow of the gallows on him. He advances gaily to the Archbishop. The page withdraws.

BLUEBEARD. Your faithful lamb, Archbishop. Good day, my lord. Do you know what has happened to La Hire?

LA TRÉMOUILLE. He has sworn himself into a fit, perhaps.

BLUEBEARD. No: just the opposite. Foul Mouthed Frank, the only man in Touraine who could beat him at swearing, was told by a soldier that he shouldnt use such language when he was at the point of death.

THE ARCHBISHOP. Nor at any other point. But was Foul Mouthed Frank on the point of death?

BLUEBEARD. Yes: he has just fallen into a well and been drowned. La Hire is frightened out of his wits.

Captain La Hire comes in: a war dog with no court manners and pronounced camp ones.

BLUEBEARD. I have just been telling the Chamberlain and the Archbishop. The Archbishop says you are a lost man.

LA HIRE [*striding past Bluebeard, and planting himself between the Archbishop and La Trémouille*] This is nothing to joke about. It is worse than we thought. It was not a soldier, but an angel dressed as a soldier.

THE ARCHBISHOP
THE CHAMBERLAIN } [*exclaiming all together*] An angel!
BLUEBEARD

LA HIRE. Yes, an angel. She has made her way from Champagne with half a dozen men through the thick of everything: Burgundians, Goddams, deserters, robbers, and Lord knows who; and they never met a soul except the country folk. I know one of them: de Poulengey. He says she's an angel. If ever I utter an oath again may my soul be blasted to eternal damnation!

THE ARCHBISHOP. A very pious beginning, Captain.

Bluebeard and La Trémouille laugh at him. The page returns.

THE PAGE. His Majesty.

They stand perfunctorily at court attention. The Dauphin, aged 26, really King Charles the Seventh since the death of his father, but as yet uncrowned, comes in through the curtains with a paper in his hands. He is a poor creature physically; and the current fashion of shaving closely, and hiding every scrap of hair under the headcovering or headdress, both by women and men, makes the worst of his appearance. He has little narrow eyes, near together, a long pendulous nose that droops over his thick short upper lip, and the expression of a young dog accustomed to be kicked, yet incorrigible and irrepressible. But he is neither vulgar nor stupid; and he has a cheeky humor which enables him to hold his own in conversation. Just at present he is excited, like a child with a new toy. He comes to the Archbishop's left hand. Bluebeard and La Hire retire towards the curtains.

CHARLES. Oh, Archbishop, do you know what Robert de Baudricourt is sending me from Vaucouleurs?

THE ARCHBISHOP [*contemptuously*] I am not interested in the newest toys.

CHARLES [*indignantly*] It isnt a toy. [*Sulkily*] However, I can get on very well without your interest.

THE ARCHBISHOP. Your Highness is taking offence very unnecessarily.

CHARLES. Thank you. You are always ready with a lecture, arnt you?

LA TRÉMOUILLE [*roughly*] Enough grumbling. What have you got there?

CHARLES. What is that to you?

LA TRÉMOUILLE. It is my business to know what is passing between you and the garrison at Vaucouleurs. [*He snatches the paper from the Dauphin's hand, and begins reading it with some difficulty, following the words with his finger and spelling them out syllable by syllable.*]

CHARLES [*mortified*] You all think you can treat me as you please because I owe you money, and because I am no good at fighting. But I have the blood royal in my veins.

THE ARCHBISHOP. Even that has been questioned, your Highness. One hardly recognizes in you the grandson of Charles the Wise.

CHARLES. I want to hear no more of my grandfather. He was so wise that he used up the whole family stock

of wisdom for five generations, and left me the poor
fool I am, bullied and insulted by all of you.

THE ARCHBISHOP. Control yourself, sir. These outbursts of petulance are not seemly.

CHARLES. Another lecture! Thank you. What a pity
it is that though you are an archbishop saints and
angels dont come to see you!

THE ARCHBISHOP. What do you mean?

CHARLES. Aha! Ask that bully there [*pointing to La
Trémouille*].

LA TRÉMOUILLE [*furious*] Hold your tongue. Do you
hear?

CHARLES. Oh, I hear. You neednt shout. The whole
castle can hear. Why dont you go and shout at the
English, and beat them for me?

LA TRÉMOUILLE [*raising his fist*] You young—

CHARLES [*running behind the Archbishop*] Dont you
raise your hand to me. It's high treason.

LA HIRE. Steady, Duke! Steady!

THE ARCHBISHOP [*resolutely*] Come, come! this will
not do. My Lord Chamberlain: please! please! we
must keep some sort of order. [*To the Dauphin*] And
you, sir: if you cannot rule your kingdom, at least try
to rule yourself.

CHARLES. Another lecture! Thank you.

LA TRÉMOUILLE [*handing the paper to the Archbishop*] Here: read the accursed thing for me. He has
sent the blood boiling into my head: I cant distinguish
the letters.

CHARLES [*coming back and peering round La Trémouille's left shoulder*] I will read it for you if you like.
I can read, you know.

LA TRÉMOUILLE [*with intense contempt, not at all
stung by the taunt*] Yes: reading is about all you are fit
for. Can you make it out, Archbishop?

THE ARCHBISHOP. I should have expected more commonsense from De Baudricourt. He is sending some cracked country lass here—

CHARLES [*interrupting*] No: he is sending a saint: an angel. And she is coming to me: to me, the king, and not to you, Archbishop, holy as you are. She knows the blood royal if you dont. [*He struts up to the curtains between Bluebeard and La Hire*].

THE ARCHBISHOP. You cannot be allowed to see this crazy wench.

CHARLES [*turning*] But I am the king; and I will.

LA TRÉMOUILLE [*brutally*] Then she cannot be allowed to see you. Now!

CHARLES. I tell you I will. I am going to put my foot down—

BLUEBEARD [*laughing at him*] Naughty! What would your wise grandfather say?

CHARLES. That just shews your ignorance, Bluebeard. My grandfather had a saint who used to float in the air when she was praying, and told him everything he wanted to know. My poor father had two saints, Marie de Maillé and the Gasque of Avignon. It is in our family; and I dont care what you say: I will have my saint too.

THE ARCHBISHOP. This creature is not a saint. She is not even a respectable woman. She does not wear women's clothes. She is dressed like a soldier, and rides round the country with soldiers. Do you suppose such a person can be admitted to your Highness's court?

LA HIRE. Stop. [*Going to the Archbishop*] Did you say a girl in armor, like a soldier?

THE ARCHBISHOP. So De Baudricourt describes her.

LA HIRE. But by all the devils in hell—Oh, God forgive me, what am I saying?—by Our Lady and all

the saints, this must be the angel that struck Foul
Mouthed Frank dead for swearing.

CHARLES [*triumphant*] You see! A miracle!

LA HIRE. She may strike the lot of us dead if we cross
her. For Heaven's sake, Archbishop, be careful what
you are doing.

THE ARCHBISHOP [*severely*] Rubbish! Nobody has
been struck dead. A drunken blackguard who has been
rebuked a hundred times for swearing has fallen into
a well, and been drowned. A mere coincidence.

LA HIRE. I do not know what a coincidence is. I do
know that the man is dead, and that she told him he
was going to die.

THE ARCHBISHOP. We are all going to die, Captain.

LA HIRE [*crossing himself*] I hope not. [*He backs out of
the conversation*].

BLUEBEARD. We can easily find out whether she is an
angel or not. Let us arrange when she comes that I
shall be the Dauphin, and see whether she will find
me out.

CHARLES. Yes: I agree to that. If she cannot find the
blood royal I will have nothing to do with her.

THE ARCHBISHOP. It is for the Church to make saints:
let De Baudricourt mind his own business, and not
dare usurp the function of his priest. I say the girl
shall not be admitted.

BLUEBEARD. But, Archbishop—

THE ARCHBISHOP [*sternly*] I speak in the Church's
name. [*To the Dauphin*] Do you dare say she shall?

CHARLES [*intimidated but sulkily*] Oh, if you make it
an excommunication matter, I have nothing more to
say, of course. But you havnt read the end of the
letter. De Baudricourt says she will raise the siege of
Orleans, and beat the English for us.

LA TRÉMOUILLE. Rot!

CHARLES. Well, will you save Orleans for us, with all your bullying?

LA TRÉMOUILLE [*savagely*] Do not throw that in my face again: do you hear? I have done more fighting than you ever did or ever will. But I cannot be everywhere.

THE DAUPHIN. Well, thats something.

BLUEBEARD [*coming between the Archbishop and Charles*] You have Jack Dunois at the head of your troops in Orleans: the brave Dunois, the handsome Dunois, the wonderful invincible Dunois, the darling of all the ladies, the beautiful bastard. Is it likely that the country lass can do what he cannot do?

CHARLES. Why doesnt he raise the siege, then?

LA HIRE. The wind is against him.

BLUEBEARD. How can the wind hurt him at Orleans? It is not on the Channel.

LA HIRE. It is on the river Loire; and the English hold the bridgehead. He must ship his men across the river and upstream, if he is to take them in the rear. Well, he cannot, because there is a devil of a wind blowing the other way. He is tired of paying the priests to pray for a west wind. What he needs is a miracle. You tell me that what the girl did to Foul Mouthed Frank was no miracle. No matter: it finished Frank. If she changes the wind for Dunois, that may not be a miracle either; but it may finish the English. What harm is there in trying?

THE ARCHBISHOP [*who has read the end of the letter and become more thoughtful*] It is true that De Baudricourt seems extraordinarily impressed.

LA HIRE. De Baudricourt is a blazing ass; but he is a soldier; and if he thinks she can beat the English, all the rest of the army will think so too.

LA TRÉMOUILLE [*to the Archbishop, who is hesitating*]

Oh, let them have their way. Dunois' men will give up the town in spite of him if somebody does not put some fresh spunk into them.

THE ARCHBISHOP. The Church must examine the girl before anything decisive is done about her. However, since his Highness desires it, let her attend the Court.

LA HIRE. I will find her and tell her. [*He goes out*].

CHARLES. Come with me, Bluebeard; and let us arrange so that she will not know who I am. You will pretend to be me. [*He goes out through the curtains*].

BLUEBEARD. Pretend to be that thing! Holy Michael! [*He follows the Dauphin*].

LA TRÉMOUILLE. I wonder will she pick him out!

THE ARCHBISHOP. Of course she will.

LA TRÉMOUILLE. Why? How is she to know?

THE ARCHBISHOP. She will know what everybody in Chinon knows: that the Dauphin is the meanest-looking and worst-dressed figure in the Court, and that the man with the blue beard is Gilles de Rais.

LA TRÉMOUILLE. I never thought of that.

THE ARCHBISHOP. You are not so accustomed to miracles as I am. It is part of my profession.

LA TRÉMOUILLE [*puzzled and a little scandalized*] But that would not be a miracle at all.

THE ARCHBISHOP [*calmly*] Why not?

LA TRÉMOUILLE. Well, come! what is a miracle?

THE ARCHBISHOP. A miracle, my friend, is an event which creates faith. That is the purpose and nature of miracles. They may seem very wonderful to the people who witness them, and very simple to those who perform them. That does not matter: if they confirm or create faith they are true miracles.

LA TRÉMOUILLE. Even when they are frauds, do you mean?

THE ARCHBISHOP. Frauds deceive. An event which creates faith does not deceive: therefore it is not a fraud, but a miracle.

LA TRÉMOUILLE [*scratching his neck in his perplexity*] Well, I suppose as you are an archbishop you must be right. It seems a bit fishy to me. But I am no churchman, and dont understand these matters.

THE ARCHBISHOP. You are not a churchman; but you are a diplomatist and a soldier. Could you make our citizens pay war taxes, or our soldiers sacrifice their lives, if they knew what is really happening instead of what seems to them to be happening?

LA TRÉMOUILLE. No, by Saint Dennis: the fat would be in the fire before sundown.

THE ARCHBISHOP. Would it not be quite easy to tell them the truth?

LA TRÉMOUILLE. Man alive, they wouldnt believe it.

THE ARCHBISHOP. Just so. Well, the Church has to rule men for the good of their souls as you have to rule them for the good of their bodies. To do that, the Church must do as you do: nourish their faith by poetry.

LA TRÉMOUILLE. Poetry! I should call it humbug.

THE ARCHBISHOP. You would be wrong, my friend. Parables are not lies because they describe events that have never happened. Miracles are not frauds because they are often—I do not say always—very simple and innocent contrivances by which the priest fortifies the faith of his flock. When this girl picks out the Dauphin among his courtiers, it will not be a miracle for me, because I shall know how it has been done, and my faith will not be increased. But as for the others, if they feel the thrill of the supernatural, and forget their sinful clay in a sudden sense of the glory of God, it will be a miracle and a blessed one. And you will find that the girl herself will be more affected than anyone else. She will forget how she really picked him out. So, perhaps, will you.

LA TRÉMOUILLE. Well, I wish I were clever enough to know how much of you is God's archbishop and how much the most artful fox in Touraine. Come on, or we shall be late for the fun; and I want to see it, miracle or no miracle.

THE ARCHBISHOP [*detaining him a moment*] Do not think that I am a lover of crooked ways. There is a new spirit rising in men: we are at the dawning of a wider epoch. If I were a simple monk, and had not to rule men, I should seek peace for my spirit with Aristotle and Pythagoras rather than with the saints and their miracles.

LA TRÉMOUILLE. And who the deuce was Pythagoras?

THE ARCHBISHOP. A sage who held that the earth is round, and that it moves round the sun.

LA TRÉMOUILLE. What an utter fool! Couldnt he use his eyes?

They go out together through the curtains, which are presently withdrawn, revealing the full depth of the throne room with the Court assembled. On the right are two Chairs of State on a dais. Bluebeard is standing theatrically on the dais, playing the king, and, like the courtiers, enjoying the joke rather obviously. There is a curtained arch in the wall behind the dais; but the main door, guarded by men-at-arms, is at the other side of the room; and a clear path across is kept and lined by the courtiers. Charles is in this path in the middle of the room. La Hire is on his right. The Archbishop, on his left, has taken his place by the dais: La Trémouille at the other side of it. The Duchess de la Trémouille, pretending to be the Queen, sits in the Consort's chair, with a group of ladies in waiting close by, behind the Archbishop.

The chatter of the courtiers makes such a noise that nobody notices the appearance of the page at the door.

THE PAGE. The Duke of— [*Nobody listens*]. The Duke of— [*The chatter continues. Indignant at his failure to command a hearing, he snatches the halberd of the nearest man-at-arms, and thumps the floor with it. The chatter ceases; and everybody looks at him in silence*]. Attention! [*He restores the halberd to the man-at-arms*]. The Duke of Vendôme presents Joan the Maid to his Majesty.

CHARLES [*putting his finger on his lip*] Ssh! [*He hides behind the nearest courtier, peering out to see what happens*].

BLUEBEARD [*majestically*] Let her approach the throne.

Joan, dressed as a soldier, with her hair bobbed and hanging thickly round her face, is led in by a bashful and speechless nobleman, from whom she detaches herself to stop and look round eagerly for the Dauphin.

THE DUCHESS [*to the nearest lady in waiting*] My dear! Her hair! *All the ladies explode in uncontrollable laughter.*

BLUEBEARD [*trying not to laugh, and waving his hand in deprecation of their merriment*] Ssh—ssh! Ladies! Ladies!!

JOAN [*not at all embarrassed*] I wear it like this because I am a soldier. Where be Dauphin?

A titter runs through the Court as she walks to the dais.

BLUEBEARD [*condescendingly*] You are in the presence of the Dauphin.

Joan looks at him sceptically for a moment, scanning him hard up and down to make sure. Dead silence, all watching her. Fun dawns in her face.

JOAN. Coom, Bluebeard! Thou canst not fool me.
Where be Dauphin?

*A roar of laughter breaks out as Gilles, with a gesture
of surrender, joins in the laugh, and jumps down from
the dais beside La Trémouille. Joan, also on the broad
grin, turns back, searching along the row of courtiers,
and presently makes a dive, and drags out Charles by
the arm.*

JOAN [*releasing him and bobbing him a little curtsey*]
Gentle little Dauphin. I am sent to you to drive the
English away from Orleans and from France, and to
crown you king in the cathedral at Rheims, where all
true kings of France are crowned.

CHARLES [*triumphant, to the Court*] You see, all of
you: she knew the blood royal. Who dare say now
that I am not my father's son [*To Joan*] But if you
want me to be crowned at Rheims you must talk to
the Archbishop, not to me. There he is [*he is standing
behind her*]!

JOAN [*turning quickly, overwhelmed with emotion*] Oh,
my lord! [*She falls on both knees before him, with
bowed head, not daring to look up*] My lord: I am only
a poor country girl; and you are filled with the blessedness and glory of God Himself; but you will touch
me with your hands, and give me your blessing, wont
you?

BLUEBEARD [*whispering to La Trémouille*] The old fox
blushes.

LA TRÉMOUILLE. Another miracle!

THE ARCHBISHOP [*touched, putting his hand on her
head*] Child: you are in love with religion.

JOAN [*startled: looking up at him*] Am I? I never
thought of that. Is there any harm in it?

THE ARCHBISHOP. There is no harm in it, my child.
But there is danger.

JOAN [*rising, with a sunflush of reckless happiness irradiating her face*] There is always danger, except in heaven. Oh, my lord, you have given me such strength, such courage. It must be a most wonderful thing to be Archbishop.

The Court smiles broadly: even titters a little.

THE ARCHBISHOP [*drawing himself up sensitively*] Gentlemen: your levity is rebuked by this maid's faith. I am, God help me, all unworthy; but your mirth is a deadly sin.

Their faces fall. Dead silence.

BLUEBEARD. My lord: we were laughing at her, not at you.

THE ARCHBISHOP. What? Not at my unworthiness but at her faith! Gilles de Rais: this maid prophesied that the blasphemer should be drowned in his sin—

JOAN [*distressed*] No!

THE ARCHBISHOP [*silencing her by a gesture*] I prophesy now that you will be hanged in yours if you do not learn when to laugh and when to pray.

BLUEBEARD. My lord: I stand rebuked. I am sorry: I can say no more. But if you prophesy that I shall be hanged, I shall never be able to resist temptation, because I shall always be telling myself that I may as well be hanged for a sheep as a lamb.

The courtiers take heart at this. There is more tittering.

JOAN [*scandalized*] You are an idle fellow, Bluebeard; and you have great impudence to answer the Archbishop.

LA HIRE [*with a huge chuckle*] Well said, lass! Well said!

JOAN [*impatiently to the Archbishop*] Oh, my lord, will you send all these silly folks away so that I may speak to the Dauphin alone?

LA HIRE [*goodhumoredly*] I can take a hint. [*He salutes; turns on his heel; and goes out*].

THE ARCHBISHOP. Come, gentlemen. The Maid comes with God's blessing, and must be obeyed.

The courtiers withdraw, some through the arch, others at the opposite side. The Archbishop marches across to the door, followed by the Duchess and La Trémouille. As the Archbishop passes Joan, she falls on her knees, and kisses the hem of his robe fervently. He shakes his head in instinctive remonstrance; gathers the robe from her; and goes out. She is left kneeling directly in the Duchess's way.

THE DUCHESS [*coldly*] Will you allow me to pass, please?

JOAN [*hastily rising, and standing back*] Beg pardon, maam, I am sure.

The Duchess passes on. Joan stares after her; then whispers to the Dauphin.

JOAN. Be that Queen?

CHARLES. No. She thinks she is.

JOAN [*again staring after the Duchess*] Oo-oo-ooh! [*Her awestruck amazement at the figure cut by the magnificently dressed lady is not wholly complimentary*].

LA TRÉMOUILLE [*very surly*] I'll trouble your Highness not to gibe at my wife. [*He goes out. The others have already gone*].

JOAN [*to the Dauphin*] Who be old Gruff-and-Grum?

CHARLES. He is the Duke de la Trémouille.

JOAN. What be his job?

CHARLES. He pretends to command the army. And whenever I find a friend I can care for, he kills him.

JOAN. Why dost let him?

CHARLES [*petulantly moving to the throne side of the room to escape from her magnetic field*] How can I prevent him? He bullies me. They all bully me.

JOAN. Art afraid?

CHARLES. Yes: I am afraid. It's no use preaching to me about it. It's all very well for these big men with their armor that is too heavy for me, and their swords that I can hardly lift, and their muscle and their shouting and their bad tempers. They like fighting: most of them are making fools of themselves all the time they are not fighting; but I am quiet and sensible; and I dont want to kill people: I only want to be left alone to enjoy myself in my own way. I never asked to be a king: it was pushed on me. So if you are going to say "Son of St Louis: gird on the sword of your ancestors, and lead us to victory" you may spare your breath to cool your porridge; for I cannot do it. I am not built that way; and there is an end of it.

JOAN [*trenchant and masterful*] Blethers! We are all like that to begin with. I shall put courage into thee.

CHARLES. But I dont want to have courage put into me. I want to sleep in a comfortable bed, and not live in continual terror of being killed or wounded. Put courage into the others, and let them have their bellyful of fighting; but let me alone.

JOAN. It's no use, Charlie: thou must face what God puts on thee. If thou fail to make thyself king, thoult be a beggar: what else art fit for? Come! Let me see thee sitting on the throne. I have looked forward to that.

CHARLES. What is the good of sitting on the throne when the other fellows give all the orders? However! [*he sits enthroned, a piteous figure*] here is the king for you! Look your fill at the poor devil.

JOAN. Thourt not king yet, lad: thourt but Dauphin. Be not led away by them around thee. Dressing up dont fill empty noddle. I know the people: the real people that make thy bread for thee; and I tell thee

they count no man king of France until the holy oil
has been poured on his hair, and himself consecrated
and crowned in Rheims Cathedral. And thou needs
new clothes, Charlie. Why does not Queen look after
thee properly?

CHARLES. We're too poor. She wants all the money
we can spare to put on her own back. Besides, I like
to see her beautifully dressed; and I dont care what I
wear myself: I should look ugly anyhow.

JOAN. There is some good in thee, Charlie; but it is
not yet a king's good.

CHARLES. We shall see. I am not such a fool as I look.
I have my eyes open; and I can tell you that one good
treaty is worth ten good fights. These fighting fellows
lose all on the treaties that they gain on the fights. If
we can only have a treaty, the English are sure to have
the worst of it, because they are better at fighting than
at thinking.

JOAN. If the English win, it is they that will make the
treaty; and then God help poor France! Thou must
fight, Charlie, whether thou will or no. I will go first
to hearten thee. We must take our courage in
both hands: aye, and pray for it with both hands
too.

CHARLES [descending from his throne and again crossing
the room to escape from her dominating urgency] Oh do
stop talking about God and praying. I cant bear
people who are always praying. Isnt it bad enough to
have to do it at the proper times?

JOAN [pitying him] Thou poor child, thou hast never
prayed in thy life. I must teach thee from the beginning.

CHARLES. I am not a child: I am a grown man and a
father; and I will not be taught any more.

JOAN. Aye, you have a little son. He that will be Louis

the Eleventh when you die. Would you not fight for him?

CHARLES. No: a horrid boy. He hates me. He hates everybody, selfish little beast! I dont want to be bothered with children. I dont want to be a father; and I dont want to be a son: especially a son of St Louis. I dont want to be any of these fine things you all have your heads full of: I want to be just what I am. Why cant you mind your own business, and let me mind mine?

JOAN [*again contemptuous*] Minding your own business is like minding your own body: it's the shortest way to make yourself sick. What is my business? Helping mother at home. What is thine? Petting lapdogs and sucking sugar-sticks. I call that muck. I tell thee it is God's business we are here to do: not our own. I have a message to thee from God; and thou must listen to it, though thy heart break with the terror of it.

CHARLES. I dont want a message; but can you tell me any secrets? Can you do any cures? Can you turn lead into gold, or anything of that sort?

JOAN. I can turn thee into a king, in Rheims Cathedral; and that is a miracle that will take some doing, it seems.

CHARLES. If we go to Rheims, and have a coronation, Anne will want new dresses. We cant afford them. I am all right as I am.

JOAN. As you are! And what is that? Less than my father's poorest shepherd. Thourt not lawful owner of thy own land of France till thou be consecrated.

CHARLES. But I shall not be lawful owner of my own land anyhow. Will the consecration pay off my mortgages? I have pledged my last acre to the Archbishop and that fat bully. I owe money even to Bluebeard.

JOAN [*earnestly*] Charlie: I come from the land, and

have gotten my strength working on the land; and I tell thee that the land is thine to rule righteously and keep God's peace in, and not to pledge at the pawn-shop as a drunken woman pledges her children's clothes. And I come from God to tell thee to kneel in the cathedral and solemnly give thy kingdom to Him for ever and ever, and become the greatest king in the world as His steward and His bailiff, His soldier and His servant. The very clay of France will become holy: her soldiers will be the soldiers of God: the rebel dukes will be rebels against God: the English will fall on their knees and beg thee let them return to their lawful homes in peace. Wilt be a poor little Judas, and betray me and Him that sent me?

CHARLES [*tempted at last*] Oh, if I only dare!

JOAN. I shall dare, dare, and dare again, in God's name! Art for or against me?

CHARLES [*excited*] I'll risk it, I warn you I shant be able to keep it up; but I'll risk it. You shall see. [*Running to the main door and shouting*] Hallo! Come back, everybody. [*To Joan, as he runs back to the arch opposite*] Mind you stand by and dont let me be bullied. [*Through the arch*] Come along, will you: the whole Court. [*He sits down in the royal chair as they all hurry in to their former places, chattering and wondering*]. Now I'm in for it; but no matter: here goes! [*To the page*] Call for silence, you little beast, will you?

THE PAGE [*snatching a halberd as before and thumping with it repeatedly*] Silence for His Majesty the King. The King speaks. [*Peremptorily*] Will you be silent there? [*Silence*].

CHARLES [*rising*] I have given the command of the army to The Maid. The Maid is to do as she likes with it. [*He descends from the dais*].

General amazement. La Hire, delighted, slaps his steel thighpiece with his gauntlet.

LA TRÉMOUILLE [*turning threateningly towards Charles*] What is this? *I* command the army.

Joan quickly puts her hand on Charles's shoulder as he instinctively recoils. Charles, with a grotesque effort culminating in an extravagant gesture, snaps his fingers in the Chamberlain's face.

JOAN. Thou'rt answered, old Gruff-and-Grum. [*Suddenly flashing out her sword as she divines that her moment has come*] Who is for God and His Maid? Who is for Orleans with me?

LA HIRE [*carried away, drawing also*] For God and His Maid! To Orleans!

ALL THE KNIGHTS [*following his lead with enthusiasm*] To Orleans!

Joan, radiant, falls on her knees in thanksgiving to God. They all kneel, except the Archbishop, who gives his benediction with a sign, and La Trémouille, who collapses, cursing.

SCENE III

Orleans, April 29th, 1429. Dunois, aged 26, is pacing up and down a patch of ground on the south bank of the silver Loire, commanding a long view of the river in both directions. He has had his lance stuck up with a pennon, which streams in a strong east wind. His shield with its bend sinister lies beside it. He has his commander's baton in his hand. He is well built, carrying his armor easily. His broad brow and pointed chin give him an equilaterally triangular face, already marked by active service and responsibility, with the expression of a goodnatured and capable man who has no affectations and no foolish illusions. His page is sitting on the ground, elbows on knees, cheeks on fists, idly watching the water. It is evening; and both man and boy are affected by the loveliness of the Loire.

DUNOIS [*halting for a moment to glance up at the streaming pennon and shake his head wearily before he resumes his pacing*] West wind, west wind, west wind. Strumpet: steadfast when you should be wanton, wanton when you should be steadfast. West wind on the silver Loire: what rhymes to Loire? [*He looks again at the pennon, and shakes his fist at it*] Change, curse you, change, English harlot of a wind, change. West, west, I tell you. [*With a growl he resumes his march in silence, but soon begins again*] West wind, wanton wind, wilful wind, womanish wind, false wind from over the water, will you never blow again?

THE PAGE [*bounding to his feet*] See! There! There she goes!

DUNOIS [*startled from his reverie: eagerly*] Where? Who? The Maid?

THE PAGE. No: the kingfisher. Like blue lightning. She went into that bush.

DUNOIS [*furiously disappointed*] Is that all? You infernal young idiot: I have a mind to pitch you into the river.

THE PAGE [*not afraid, knowing his man*] It looked frightfully jolly, that flash of blue. Look! There goes the other!

DUNOIS [*running eagerly to the river brim*] Where? Where?

THE PAGE [*pointing*] Passing the reeds.

DUNOIS [*delighted*] I see.

They follow the flight till the bird takes cover.

THE PAGE. You blew me up because you were not in time to see them yesterday.

DUNOIS. You knew I was expecting The Maid when you set up your yelping. I will give you something to yelp for next time.

THE PAGE. Arnt they lovely? I wish I could catch them.

DUNOIS. Let me catch you trying to trap them, and I will put you in the iron cage for a month to teach you what a cage feels like. You are an abominable boy.

THE PAGE [*laughs, and squats down as before*]!

DUNOIS [*pacing*] Blue bird, blue bird, since I am friend to thee, change thou the wind for me. No: it does not rhyme. He who has sinned for thee: thats better. No sense in it, though. [*He finds himself close to the page*] You abominable boy! [*He turns away from him*] Mary in the blue snood, kingfisher color: will you grudge me a west wind?

A SENTRY'S VOICE WESTWARD. Halt! Who goes there?

JOAN'S VOICE. The Maid.

DUNOIS. Let her pass. Hither, Maid! To me!

Joan, in splendid armor, rushes in in a blazing rage. The wind drops; and the pennon flaps idly down the lance; but Dunois is too much occupied with Joan to notice it.

JOAN [*bluntly*] Be you Bastard of Orleans?

DUNOIS [*cool and stern, pointing to his shield*] You see the bend sinister. Are you Joan the Maid?

JOAN. Sure.

DUNOIS. Where are your troops?

JOAN. Miles behind. They have cheated me. They have brought me to the wrong side of the river.

DUNOIS. I told them to.

JOAN. Why did you? The English are on the other side!

DUNOIS. The English are on both sides.

JOAN. But Orleans is on the other side. We must fight the English there. How can we cross the river?

DUNOIS [*grimly*] There is a bridge.

JOAN. In God's name, then, let us cross the bridge, and fall on them.

DUNOIS. It seems simple; but it cannot be done.

JOAN. Who says so?

DUNOIS. I say so; and older and wiser heads than mine are of the same opinion.

JOAN [*roundly*] Then your older and wiser heads are fat-heads: they have made a fool of you; and now they want to make a fool of me too, bringing me to the wrong side of the river. Do you not know that I bring you better help than ever came to any general or any town?

DUNOIS [*smiling patiently*] Your own?

JOAN. No: the help and the counsel of the King of Heaven. Which is the way to the bridge?

DUNOIS. You are impatient, Maid.

JOAN. Is this a time for patience? Our enemy is at our gates; and here we stand doing nothing. Oh, why are you not fighting? Listen to me: I will deliver you from fear. I—

DUNOIS [*laughing heartily, and waving her off*] No, no, my girl: if you delivered me from fear I should be a good knight for a story book, but a very bad commander of the army. Come! let me begin to make a soldier of you. [*He takes her to the water's edge*]. Do you see these two forts at this end of the bridge? the big ones?

JOAN. Yes. Are they ours or the goddams'?

DUNOIS. Be quiet, and listen to me. If I were in either of those forts with only ten men I could hold it against an army. The English have more than ten times ten goddams in those forts to hold them against us.

JOAN. They cannot hold them against God. God did not give them the land under those forts: they stole it from Him. He gave it to us. I will take those forts.

DUNOIS. Single-handed?

JOAN. Our men will take them. I will lead them.

DUNOIS. Not a man will follow you.

JOAN. I will not look back to see whether anyone is following me.

DUNOIS [*recognizing her mettle, and clapping her heartily on the shoulder*] Good. You have the makings of a soldier in you. You are in love with war.

JOAN [*startled*] Oh! And the Archbishop said I was in love with religion.

DUNOIS. I, God forgive me, am a little in love with war myself, the ugly devil! I am like a man with two wives. Do you want to be like a woman with two husbands?

JOAN [*matter-of-fact*] I will never take a husband. A man in Toul took an action against me for breach of promise; but I never promised him. I am a soldier: I do not want to be thought of as a woman. I will not dress as a woman. I do not care for the things women care for. They dream of lovers, and of money. I dream of leading a charge, and of placing the big guns. You soldiers do not know how to use the big guns: you think you can win battles with a great noise and smoke.

DUNOIS [*with a shrug*] True. Half the time the artillery is more trouble than it is worth.

JOAN. Aye, lad; but you cannot fight stone walls with horses: you must have guns, and much bigger guns too.

DUNOIS [*grinning at her familiarity, and echoing it*] Aye, lass; but a good heart and a stout ladder will get over the stoniest wall.

JOAN. I will be first up the ladder when we reach the fort, Bastard. I dare you to follow me.

DUNOIS. You must not dare a staff officer, Joan: only company officers are allowed to indulge in displays of personal courage. Besides, you must know that I welcome you as a saint, not as a soldier. I have daredevils enough at my call, if they could help me.

JOAN. I am not a daredevil: I am a servant of God. My sword is sacred: I found it behind the altar in the church of St Catherine, where God hid it for me; and I may not strike a blow with it. My heart is full of courage, not of anger. I will lead; and your men will follow: that is all I can do. But I must do it: you shall not stop me.

DUNOIS. All in good time. Our men cannot take those forts by a sally across the bridge. They must come by water, and take the English in the rear on this side.

JOAN [*her military sense asserting itself*] Then make

rafts and put big guns on them; and let your men cross to us.

DUNOIS. The rafts are ready; and the men are embarked. But they must wait for God.

JOAN. What do you mean? God is waiting for them.

DUNOIS. Let Him send us a wind then. My boats are downstream: they cannot come up against both wind and current. We must wait until God changes the wind. Come: let me take you to the church.

JOAN. No. I love church; but the English will not yield to prayers: they understand nothing but hard knocks and slashes. I will not go to church until we have beaten them.

DUNOIS. You must: I have business for you there.

JOAN. What business?

DUNOIS. To pray for a west wind. I have prayed; and I have given two silver candlesticks; but my prayers are not answered. Yours may be: you are young and innocent.

JOAN. Oh yes: you are right. I will pray: I will tell St Catherine: she will make God give me a west wind. Quick: shew me the way to the church.

THE PAGE [*sneezes violently*] At-cha!!!

JOAN. God bless you, child! Coom, Bastard.

They go out. The page rises to follow. He picks up the shield, and is taking the spear as well when he notices the pennon, which is now streaming eastward.

THE PAGE [*dropping the shield and calling excitedly after them*] Seigneur! Seigneur! Mademoiselle!

DUNOIS [*running back*] What is it? The kingfisher? [*He looks eagerly for it up the river*].

JOAN [*joining them*] Oh, a kingfisher! Where?

THE PAGE. No: the wind, the wind, the wind [*pointing to the pennon*]: that is what made me sneeze.

DUNOIS [*looking at the pennon*] The wind has changed.

[*He crosses himself*] God has spoken. [*Kneeling and handing his baton to Joan*] You command the king's army. I am your soldier.

THE PAGE [*looking down the river*] The boats have put off. They are ripping upstream like anything.

DUNOIS [*rising*] Now for the forts. You dared me to follow. Dare you lead?

JOAN [*bursting into tears and flinging her arms round Dunois, kissing him on both cheeks*] Dunois, dear comrade in arms, help me. My eyes are blinded with tears. Set my foot on the ladder, and say "Up, Joan."

DUNOIS [*dragging her out*] Never mind the tears: make for the flash of the guns.

JOAN [*in a blaze of courage*] Ah!

DUNOIS [*dragging her along with him*] For God and Saint Dennis!

THE PAGE [*shrilly*] The Maid! The Maid! God and The Maid! Hurray-ay-ay! [*He snatches up the shield and lance, and capers out after them, mad with excitement*].

SCENE IV

A tent in the English camp. A bullnecked English chaplain of 50 is sitting on a stool at a table, hard at work writing. At the other side of the table an imposing nobleman, aged 46, is seated in a handsome chair turning over the leaves of an illuminated Book of Hours. The nobleman is enjoying himself: the chaplain is struggling with suppressed wrath. There is an unoccupied leather stool on the nobleman's left. The table is on his right.

THE NOBLEMAN. Now this is what I call workmanship. There is nothing on earth more exquisite than a bonny book, with well-placed columns of rich black writing in beautiful borders, and illuminated pictures cunningly inset. But nowadays, instead of looking at books, people read them. A book might as well be one of those orders for bacon and bran that you are scribbling.

THE CHAPLAIN. I must say, my lord, you take our situation very coolly. Very coolly indeed.

THE NOBLEMAN [*supercilious*] What is the matter?

THE CHAPLAIN. The matter, my lord, is that we English have been defeated.

THE NOBLEMAN. That happens, you know. It is only in history books and ballads that the enemy is always defeated.

THE CHAPLAIN. But we are being defeated over and over again. First, Orleans—

THE NOBLEMAN [*poohpoohing*] Oh, Orleans!

THE CHAPLAIN. I know what you are going to say, my lord: that was a clear case of witchcraft and sorcery. But we are still being defeated. Jargeau,

Meung, Beaugency, just like Orleans. And now we have been butchered at Patay, and Sir John Talbot taken prisoner. [*He throws down his pen, almost in tears*] I feel it, my lord: I feel it very deeply. I cannot bear to see my countrymen defeated by a parcel of foreigners.

THE NOBLEMAN. Oh! you are an Englishman, are you?

THE CHAPLAIN. Certainly not, my lord: I am a gentleman. Still, like your lordship, I was born in England; and it makes a difference.

THE NOBLEMAN. You are attached to the soil, eh?

THE CHAPLAIN. It pleases your lordship to be satirical at my expense: your greatness privileges you to be so with impunity. But your lordship knows very well that I am not attached to the soil in a vulgar manner, like a serf. Still, I have a feeling about it; [*with growing agitation*] and I am not ashamed of it; and [*rising wildly*] by God, if this goes on any longer I will fling my cassock to the devil, and take arms myself, and strangle the accursed witch with my own hands.

THE NOBLEMAN [*laughing at him goodnaturedly*] So you shall, chaplain: so you shall, if we can do nothing better. But not yet, not quite yet.

The Chaplain resumes his seat very sulkily.

THE NOBLEMAN [*airily*] I should not care very much about the witch—you see, I have made my pilgrimage to the Holy Land; and the Heavenly Powers, for their own credit, can hardly allow me to be worsted by a village sorceress—but the Bastard of Orleans is a harder nut to crack; and as he has been to the Holy Land too, honors are easy between us as far as that goes.

THE CHAPLAIN. He is only a Frenchman, my lord.

[125]

THE NOBLEMAN. A Frenchman! Where did you pick up that expression? Are these Burgundians and Bretons and Picards and Gascons beginning to call themselves Frenchmen, just as our fellows are beginning to call themselves Englishmen? They actually talk of France and England as their countries. Theirs, if you please! What is to become of me and you if that way of thinking comes into fashion?

THE CHAPLAIN. Why, my lord? Can it hurt us?

THE NOBLEMAN. Men cannot serve two masters. If this cant of serving their country once takes hold of them, goodbye to the authority of their feudal lords, and goodbye to the authority of the Church. That is, goodbye to you and me.

THE CHAPLAIN. I hope I am a faithful servant of the Church; and there are only six cousins between me and the barony of Stogumber, which was created by the Conqueror. But is that any reason why I should stand by and see Englishmen beaten by a French bastard and a witch from Lousy Champagne?

THE NOBLEMAN. Easy man, easy: we shall burn the witch and beat the bastard all in good time. Indeed I am waiting at present for the Bishop of Beauvais, to arrange the burning with him. He has been turned out of his diocese by her faction.

THE CHAPLAIN. You have first to catch her, my lord.

THE NOBLEMAN. Or buy her. I will offer a king's ransom.

THE CHAPLAIN. A king's ransom! For that slut!

THE NOBLEMAN. One has to leave a margin. Some of Charles's people will sell her to the Burgundians; the Burgundians will sell her to us; and there will probably be three or four middlemen who will expect their little commissions.

THE CHAPLAIN. Monstrous. It is all those scoundrels

of Jews: they get in every time money changes hands. I would not leave a Jew alive in Christendom if I had my way.

THE NOBLEMAN. Why not? The Jews generally give value. They make you pay; but they deliver the goods. In my experience the men who want something for nothing are invariably Christians.

A page appears.

THE PAGE. The Right Reverend the Bishop of Beauvais: Monseigneur Cauchon.

Cauchon, aged about 60, comes in. The page withdraws. The two Englishmen rise.

THE NOBLEMAN [*with effusive courtesy*] My dear Bishop, how good of you to come! Allow me to introduce myself: Richard de Beauchamp, Earl of Warwick, at your service.

CAUCHON. Your lordship's fame is well known to me.

WARWICK. This reverend cleric is Master John de Stogumber.

THE CHAPLAIN [*glibly*] John Bowyer Spenser Neville de Stogumber, at your service, my lord: Bachelor of Theology, and Keeper of the Private Seal to His Eminence the Cardinal of Winchester.

WARWICK [*to Cauchon*] You call him the Cardinal of England, I believe. Our king's uncle.

CAUCHON. Messire John de Stogumber: I am always the very good friend of His Eminence. [*He extends his hand to the chaplain, who kisses his ring*].

WARWICK. Do me the honor to be seated. [*He gives Cauchon his chair, placing it at the head of the table*].

Cauchon accepts the place of honor with a grave inclination. Warwick fetches the leather stool carelessly, and sits in his former place. The chaplain goes back to his chair.

Though Warwick has taken second place in calculated

*deference to the Bishop, he assumes the lead in opening
the proceedings as a matter of course. He is still cordial
and expansive; but there is a new note in his voice which
means that he is coming to business.*

WARWICK. Well, my Lord Bishop, you find us in one
of our unlucky moments. Charles is to be crowned at
Rheims, practically by the young woman from
Lorraine; and—I must not deceive you, nor flatter
your hopes—we cannot prevent it. I suppose it will
make a great difference to Charles's position.

CAUCHON. Undoubtedly. It is a masterstroke of The
Maid's.

THE CHAPLAIN [*again agitated*] We were not fairly
beaten, my lord. No Englishman is ever fairly beaten.

*Cauchon raises his eyebrow slightly, then quickly
composes his face.*

WARWICK. Our friend here takes the view that the
young woman is a sorceress. It would, I presume, be
the duty of your reverend lordship to denounce her
to the Inquisition, and have her burnt for that offence.

CAUCHON. If she were captured in my diocese: yes.

WARWICK [*feeling that they are getting on capitally*]
Just so. Now I suppose there can be no reasonable
doubt that she is a sorceress.

THE CHAPLAIN. Not the least. An arrant witch.

WARWICK [*gently reproving the interruption*] We are
asking for the Bishop's opinion, Messire John.

CAUCHON. We shall have to consider not merely our
own opinions here, but the opinions—the prejudices,
if you like—of a French court.

WARWICK [*correcting*] A Catholic court, my lord.

CAUCHON. Catholic courts are composed of mortal
men, like other courts, however sacred their function
and inspiration may be. And if the men are Frenchmen, as the modern fashion calls them, I am afraid

the bare fact that an English army has been defeated by a French one will not convince them that there is any sorcery in the matter.

THE CHAPLAIN. What! Not when the famous Sir John Talbot himself has been defeated and actually taken prisoner by a drab from the ditches of Lorraine!

CAUCHON. Sir John Talbot, we all know, is a fierce and formidable soldier, Messire; but I have yet to learn that he is an able general. And though it pleases you to say that he has been defeated by this girl, some of us may be disposed to give a little of the credit to Dunois.

THE CHAPLAIN [*contemptuously*] The Bastard of Orleans!

CAUCHON. Let me remind—

WARWICK [*interposing*] I know what you are going to say, my lord. Dunois defeated me at Montargis.

CAUCHON [*bowing*] I take that as evidence that the Seigneur Dunois is a very able commander indeed.

WARWICK. Your lordship is the flower of courtesy. I admit, on our side, that Talbot is a mere fighting animal, and that it probably served him right to be taken at Patay.

THE CHAPLAIN [*chafing*] My lord: at Orleans this woman had her throat pierced by an English arrow, and was seen to cry like a child from the pain of it. It was a death wound; yet she fought all day; and when our men had repulsed all her attacks like true Englishmen, she walked alone to the wall of our fort with a white banner in her hand; and our men were paralyzed, and could neither shoot nor strike whilst the French fell on them and drove them on to the bridge, which immediately burst into flames and crumbled under them, letting them down into the river, where they were drowned in heaps. Was this your bastard's generalship? or were those flames the flames of hell, conjured up by witchcraft?

WARWICK. You will forgive Messire John's vehemence, my lord; but he has put our case. Dunois is a great captain, we admit; but why could he do nothing until the witch came?

CAUCHON. I do not say that there were no supernatural powers on her side. But the names on that white banner were not the names of Satan and Beelzebub, but the blessed names of our Lord and His holy mother. And your commander who was drowned—Clahz-da I think you call him—

WARWICK. Glasdale. Sir William Glasdale.

CAUCHON. Glass-dell, thank you. He was no saint; and many of our people think that he was drowned for his blasphemies against The Maid.

WARWICK [*beginning to look very dubious*] Well, what are we to infer from all this, my lord? Has The Maid converted you?

CAUCHON. If she had, my lord, I should have known better than to have trusted myself here within your grasp.

WARWICK [*blandly deprecating*] Oh! oh! My lord!

CAUCHON. If the devil is making use of this girl—and I believe he is—

WARWICK [*reassured*] Ah! You hear, Messire John? I knew your lordship would not fail us. Pardon my interruption. Proceed.

CAUCHON. If it be so, the devil has longer views than you give him credit for.

WARWICK. Indeed? In what way? Listen to this, Messire John.

CAUCHON. If the devil wanted to damn a country girl, do you think so easy a task would cost him the winning of half a dozen battles? No, my lord: any trumpery imp could do that much if the girl could be damned at all. The Prince of Darkness does not condescend to such cheap drudgery. When he strikes, he strikes at the Catholic Church, whose realm is the whole spiritual world. When he damns, he damns the souls of the entire human race. Against that dreadful design The Church stands ever on guard. And it is as one of the instruments of that design that I see this girl. She is inspired, but diabolically inspired.

THE CHAPLAIN. I told you she was a witch.

CAUCHON [*fiercely*] She is not a witch. She is a heretic.

THE CHAPLAIN. What difference does that make?

CAUCHON. You, a priest, ask me that! You English are strangely blunt in the mind. All these things that you call witchcraft are capable of a natural explanation. The woman's miracles would not impose on a rabbit: she does not claim them as miracles herself. What do her victories prove but that she has a better head on her shoulders than your swearing Glass-dells and mad bull Talbots, and that the courage of faith, even though it be a false faith, will always outstay the courage of wrath?

THE CHAPLAIN [*hardly able to believe his ears*] Does your lordship compare Sir John Talbot, three times Governor of Ireland, to a mad bull?!!!

WARWICK. It would not be seemly for you to do so, Messire John, as you are still six removes from a barony. But as I am an earl, and Talbot is only a knight, I may make bold to accept the comparison. [*To the Bishop*] My lord: I wipe the slate as far as the witchcraft goes. None the less, we must burn the woman.

CAUCHON. I cannot burn her. The Church cannot take life. And my first duty is to seek this girl's salvation.

WARWICK. No doubt. But you do burn people occasionally.

CAUCHON. No. When The Church cuts off an obstinate heretic as a dead branch from the tree of life, the heretic is handed over to the secular arm. The Church has no part in what the secular arm may see fit to do.

WARWICK. Precisely. And I shall be the secular arm in this case. Well, my lord, hand over your dead branch; and I will see that the fire is ready for it. If you will answer for The Church's part, I will answer for the secular part.

CAUCHON [*with smouldering anger*] I can answer for nothing. You great lords are too prone to treat The Church as a mere political convenience.

WARWICK [*smiling and propitiatory*] Not in England, I assure you.

CAUCHON. In England more than anywhere else. No, my lord: the soul of this village girl is of equal value with yours or your king's before the throne of God; and my first duty is to save it. I will not suffer your lordship to smile at me as if I were repeating a meaningless form of words, and it were well understood between us that I should betray the girl to you. I am no mere political bishop: my faith is to me what your honor is to you; and if there be a loophole through which this baptized child of God can creep to her salvation, I shall guide her to it.

THE CHAPLAIN [*rising in a fury*] You are a traitor.

CAUCHON [*springing up*] You lie, priest. [*Trembling with rage*] If you dare do what this woman has done—set your country above the holy Catholic Church—you shall go to the fire with her.

THE CHAPLAIN. My lord: I—I went too far. I—[*he sits down with a submissive gesture*].

WARWICK [*who has risen apprehensively*] My Lord: I

apologize to you for the word used by Messire John de Stogumber. It does not mean in England what it does in France. In your language traitor means betrayer: one who is perfidious, treacherous, unfaithful, disloyal. In our country it means simply one who is not wholly devoted to our English interests.

CAUCHON. I am sorry: I did not understand. [*He subsides into his chair with dignity*].

WARWICK [*resuming his seat, much relieved*] I must apologize on my own account if I have seemed to take the burning of this poor girl too lightly. When one has seen whole countrysides burnt over and over again as mere items in military routine, one has to grow a very thick skin. Otherwise one might go mad: at all events, I should. May I venture to assume that your lordship also, having to see so many heretics burned from time to time, is compelled to take—shall I say a professional view of what would otherwise be a very horrible incident?

CAUCHON. Yes: it is a very painful duty: even, as you say, a horrible one. But in comparison with the horror of heresy it is less than nothing. I am not thinking of this girl's body, which will suffer for a few moments only, and which must in any event die in some more or less painful manner, but of her soul, which may suffer to all eternity.

WARWICK. Just so; and God grant that her soul may be saved! But the practical problem would seem to be how to save her soul without saving her body. For we must face it, my lord: if this cult of The Maid goes on, our cause is lost.

THE CHAPLAIN [*his voice broken like that of a man who has been crying*] May I speak, my lord?

WARWICK. Really, Messire John, I had rather you did not, unless you can keep your temper.

THE CHAPLAIN. It is only this. I speak under correction; but The Maid is full of deceit: she pretends to be devout. Her prayers and confessions are endless. How can she be accused of heresy when she neglects no observance of a faithful daughter of The Church?

CAUCHON [*flaming up*] A faithful daughter of The Church! The Pope himself at his proudest dare not presume as this woman presumes. She acts as if she herself were The Church. She brings the message of God to Charles; and The Church must stand aside. She will crown him in the cathedral of Rheims: she not The Church! She sends letters to the king of England giving him God's command through her to return to his island on pain of God's vengeance, which she will execute. Let me tell you that the writing of such letters was the practice of the accursed Mahomet, the anti-Christ. Has she ever in all her utterances said one word of The Church? Never. It is always God and herself.

WARWICK. What can you expect? A beggar on horseback! Her head is turned.

CAUCHON. Who has turned it? The devil. And for a mighty purpose. He is spreading this heresy everywhere. The man Hus, burnt only thirteen years ago at Constance, infected all Bohemia with it. A man named WcLeef, himself an anointed priest, spread the pestilence in England; and to your shame you let him die in his bed. We have such people here in France too: I know the breed. It is cancerous: if it be not cut out, stamped out, burnt out, it will not stop until it has brought the whole body of human society into sin and corruption, into waste and ruin. By it an Arab camel driver drove Christ and His Church out of Jerusalem, and ravaged his way west like a wild beast until at last there stood only the Pyrenees and God's mercy between France and damnation. Yet what did the camel driver do at the beginning more than this shepherd girl is doing? He had his voices from the angel Gabriel: she has her voices from St Catherine and St Margaret and the Blessed Michael. He declared himself the messenger of God, and wrote in God's name to the kings of the earth. Her letters to them are going forth daily. It is not the Mother of God now to whom we must look for intercession, but to Joan the Maid. What will the world be like when The Church's accumulated wisdom and knowledge and experience, its councils of learned, venerable pious men, are thrust into the kennel by every ignorant laborer or dairymaid whom the devil can puff up with the monstrous self-conceit of being directly inspired from heaven? It will be a world of blood, of fury, of devastation, of each man striving for his own hand: in the end a world wrecked back into barbarism. For now you have only Mahomet and his dupes, and the Maid and her dupes; but what will it be when every girl thinks herself a Joan and every man a Mahomet? I shudder to the very marrow of my bones when I think of it. I have fought it all my life; and I will fight it to the end. Let all this woman's sins be forgiven her except only this sin; for it is the sin against the Holy Ghost; and if she does not recant in the dust before the world, and submit herself to the last inch of her soul to her Church, to the fire she shall go if she once falls into my hand.

WARWICK [*unimpressed*] You feel strongly about it, naturally.

CAUCHON. Do not you?

WARWICK. I am a soldier, not a churchman. As a pilgrim I saw something of the Mahometans. They were not so ill-bred as I had been led to believe. In some respects their conduct compared favourably with ours.

CAUCHON [*displeased*] I have noticed this before. Men go to the East to convert the infidels. And the infidels pervert them. The Crusader comes back more than half a Saracen. Not to mention that all Englishmen are born heretics.

THE CHAPLAIN. Englishmen heretics!!! [*Appealing to Warwick*] My lord: must we endure this? His lordship is beside himself. How can what an Englishman believes be heresy? It is a contradiction in terms.

CAUCHON. I absolve you, Messire de Stogumber, on the ground of invincible ignorance. The thick air of your country does not breed theologians.

WARWICK. You would not say so if you heard us quarrelling about religion, my lord! I am sorry you think I must be either a heretic or a blockhead because, as a travelled man, I know that the followers of Mahomet profess great respect for our Lord, and are more ready to forgive St Peter for being a fisherman than your lordship is to forgive Mahomet for being a camel driver. But at least we can proceed in this matter without bigotry.

CAUCHON. When men call the zeal of the Christian Church bigotry I know what to think.

WARWICK. They are only east and west views of the same thing.

CAUCHON [*bitterly ironical*] Only east and west! Only!!

WARWICK. Oh, my Lord Bishop, I am not gainsaying you. You will carry The Church with you; but you have to carry the nobles also. To my mind there is a stronger case against The Maid than the one you have so forcibly put. Frankly, I am not afraid of this girl becoming another Mahomet, and superseding

The Church by a great heresy. I think you exaggerate that risk. But have you noticed that in these letters of hers, she proposes to all the kings of Europe, as she has already pressed on Charles, a transaction which would wreck the whole social structure of Christendom?

CAUCHON. Wreck The Church. I tell you so.

WARWICK [*whose patience is wearing out*] My lord: pray get The Church out of your head for a moment; and remember that there are temporal institutions in the world as well as spiritual ones. I and my peers represent the feudal aristocracy as you represent The Church. We are the temporal power. Well, do you not see how this girl's idea strikes at us?

CAUCHON. How does her idea strike at you, except as it strikes at all of us, through The Church?

WARWICK. Her idea is that the kings should give their realms to God, and then reign as God's bailiffs.

CAUCHON [*not interested*] Quite sound theologically, my lord. But the king will hardly care, provided he reign. It is an abstract idea: a mere form of words.

WARWICK. By no means. It is a cunning device to supersede the aristocracy, and make the king sole and absolute autocrat. Instead of the king being merely the first among his peers, he becomes their master. That we cannot suffer: we call no man master. Nominally we hold our lands and dignities from the king, because there must be a keystone to the arch of human society; but we hold our lands in our own hands, and defend them with our own swords and those of our own tenants. Now by The Maid's doctrine the king will take our lands—our lands!—and make them a present to God; and God will then vest them wholly in the king.

CAUCHON. Need you fear that? You are the makers

of kings after all. York or Lancaster in England, Lancaster or Valois in France: they reign according to your pleasure.

WARWICK. Yes; but only as long as the people follow their feudal lords, and know the king only as a travelling show, owning nothing but the highway that belongs to everybody. If the people's thoughts and hearts were turned to the king, and their lords became only the king's servants in their eyes, the king could break us across his knee one by one; and then what should we be but liveried courtiers in his halls?

CAUCHON. Still you need not fear, my lord. Some men are born kings; and some are born statesmen. The two are seldom the same. Where would the king find counsellors to plan and carry out such a policy for him?

WARWICK [*with a not too friendly smile*] Perhaps in the Church, my lord.

Cauchon, with an equally sour smile, shrugs his shoulders, and does not contradict him.

WARWICK. Strike down the barons; and the cardinals will have it all their own way.

CAUCHON [*conciliatory, dropping his polemical tone*] My lord: we shall not defeat The Maid if we strive against one another. I know well that there is a Will to Power in the world. I know that while it lasts there will be a struggle between the Emperor and the Pope, between the dukes and the political cardinals, between the barons and the kings. The devil divides us and governs. I see you are no friend to The Church: you are an earl first and last, as I am a churchman first and last. But can we not sink our differences in the face of a common enemy? I see now that what is in your mind is not that this girl has never once mentioned The Church, and thinks only of God and herself, but that she has never once mentioned the peerage, and thinks only of the king and herself.

WARWICK. Quite so. These two ideas of hers are the same idea at bottom. It goes deep, my lord. It is the protest of the individual soul against the interference of priest or peer between the private man and his God. I should call it Protestantism if I had to find a name for it.

CAUCHON [*looking hard at him*] You understand it wonderfully well, my lord. Scratch an Englishman, and find a Protestant.

WARWICK [*playing the pink of courtesy*] I think you are not entirely void of sympathy with The Maid's secular heresy, my lord. I leave you to find a name for it.

CAUCHON. You mistake me, my lord. I have no sympathy with her political presumptions. But as a priest I have gained a knowledge of the minds of the common people; and there you will find yet another most dangerous idea. I can express it only by such phrases as France for the French, England for the English, Italy for the Italians, Spain for the Spanish, and so forth. It is sometimes so narrow and bitter in country folk that it surprises me that this country girl can rise above the idea of her village for its villagers. But she can. She does. When she threatens to drive the English from the soil of France she is undoubtedly thinking of the whole extent of country in which French is spoken. To her the French-speaking people are what the Holy Scriptures describe as a nation. Call this side of her heresy Nationalism if you will: I can find you no better name for it. I can only tell you that it is essentially anti-Catholic and anti-Christian; for the Catholic Church knows only one realm, and that is the realm of Christ's kingdom. Divide that kingdom into nations, and you dethrone Christ.

Dethrone Christ, and who will stand between our throats and the sword? The world will perish in a welter of war.

WARWICK. Well, if you will burn the Protestant, I will burn the Nationalist, though perhaps I shall not carry Messire John with me there. England for the English will appeal to him.

THE CHAPLAIN. Certainly England for the English goes without saying: it is the simple law of nature. But this woman denies to England her legitimate conquests, given her by God because of her peculiar fitness to rule over less civilized races for their own good. I do not understand what your lordships mean by Protestant and Nationalist: you are too learned and subtle for a poor clerk like myself. But I know as a matter of plain commonsense that the woman is a rebel; and that is enough for me. She rebels against Nature by wearing man's clothes, and fighting. She rebels against The Church by usurping the divine authority of the Pope. She rebels against God by her damnable league with Satan and his evil spirits against our Army. And all these rebellions are only excuses for her great rebellion against England. That is not to be endured. Let her perish. Let her burn. Let her not infect the whole flock. It is expedient that one woman die for the people.

WARWICK [*rising*] My lord: we seem to be agreed.

CAUCHON [*rising also, but in protest*] I will not imperil my soul. I will uphold the justice of the Church. I will strive to the utmost for this woman's salvation.

WARWICK. I am sorry for the poor girl. I hate these severities. I will spare her if I can.

THE CHAPLAIN [*implacably*] I would burn her with with my own hands.

CAUCHON [*blessing him*] Sancta simplicitas!

The ambulatory in the cathedral of Rheims, near the door of the vestry. A pillar bears one of the stations of the cross. The organ is playing the people out of the nave after the coronation. Joan is kneeling in prayer before the station. She is beautifully dressed, but still in male attire. The organ ceases as Dunois, also splendidly arrayed, comes into the ambulatory from the vestry.

DUNOIS. Come, Joan! you have had enough praying. After that fit of crying you will catch a chill if you stay here any longer. It is all over: the cathedral is empty; and the streets are full. They are calling for The Maid. We have told them you are staying here alone to pray; but they want to see you again.

JOAN. No: let the king have all the glory.

DUNOIS. He only spoils the show, poor devil. No, Joan: you have crowned him; and you must go through with it.

JOAN [*shakes her head reluctantly*].

DUNOIS [*raising her*] Come come! it will be over in a couple of hours. It's better than the bridge at Orleans: eh?

JOAN. Oh, dear Dunois, how I wish it were the bridge at Orleans again! We lived at that bridge.

DUNOIS. Yes, faith, and died too: some of us.

JOAN. Isnt it strange, Jack? I am such a coward: I am frightened beyond words before a battle; but it is so dull afterwards when there is no danger: oh, so dull! dull! dull!

DUNOIS. You must learn to be abstemious in war, just as you are in your food and drink, my little saint.

JOAN. Dear Jack: I think you like me as a soldier likes his comrade.

DUNOIS. You need it, poor innocent child of God. You have not many friends at court.

JOAN. Why do all these courtiers and knights and churchmen hate me? What have I done to them? I have asked nothing for myself except that my village shall not be taxed; for we cannot afford war taxes. I have brought them luck and victory: I have set them right when they were doing all sorts of stupid things: I have crowned Charles and made him a real king; and all the honors he is handing out have gone to them. Then why do they not love me?

DUNOIS [*rallying her*] Sim-ple-ton! Do you expect stupid people to love you for shewing them up? Do blundering old military dug-outs love the successful young captains who supersede them? Do ambitious politicians love the climbers who take the front seats from them? Do archbishops enjoy being played off their own altars, even by saints? Why, I should be jealous of you myself if I were ambitious enough.

JOAN. You are the pick of the basket here, Jack: the only friend I have among all these nobles. I'll wager your mother was from the country. I will go back to the farm when I have taken Paris.

DUNOIS. I am not so sure that they will let you take Paris.

JOAN [*startled*] What!

DUNOIS. I should have taken it myself before this if they had all been sound about it. Some of them would rather Paris took you, I think. So take care.

JOAN. Jack: the world is too wicked for me. If the goddams and the Burgundians do not make an end of me, the French will. Only for my voices I should lose all heart. That is why I had to steal away to pray here alone after the coronation. I'll tell you something, Jack. It is in the bells I hear my voices. Not to-day, when they all rang: that was nothing but jangling. But here in this corner, where the bells come down from heaven, and the echoes linger, or in the fields, where they come from a distance through the quiet of the countryside, my voices are in them. [*The cathedral clock chimes the quarter*] Hark! [*She becomes rapt*] Do you hear? "Dear-child-of-God": just what you said. At the half-hour they will say "Be-brave-go-on." At the three-quarters they will say "I-am-thy-Help." But it is at the hour, when the great bell goes after "God-will-save-France": it is then that St Margaret and St Catherine and sometimes even the blessed Michael will say things that I cannot tell beforehand. Then, oh then—

DUNOIS [*interrupting her kindly but not sympathetically*] Then, Joan, we shall hear whatever we fancy in the booming of the bell. You make me uneasy when you talk about your voices: I should think you were a bit cracked if I hadnt noticed that you give me very sensible reasons for what you do, though I hear you telling others you are only obeying Madame Saint Catherine.

JOAN [*crossly*] Well, I have to find reasons for you, because you do not believe in my voices. But the voices come first; and I find the reasons after: whatever you may choose to believe.

DUNOIS. Are you angry, Joan?

JOAN. Yes. [*Smiling*] No: not with you. I wish you were one of the village babies.

DUNOIS. Why?

JOAN. I could nurse you for awhile.

DUNOIS. You are a bit of a woman after all.

[143]

JOAN. No: not a bit. I am a soldier and nothing else.
Soldiers always nurse children when they get a chance.
DUNOIS. That is true. [*He laughs*].

King Charles, with Bluebeard on his left and La Hire
on his right, comes from the vestry, where he has been
disrobing. Joan shrinks away behind the pillar. Dunois
is left between Charles and La Hire.

DUNOIS. Well, your Majesty is an anointed king at
last. How do you like it?

CHARLES. I would not go through it again to be
emperor of the sun and moon. The weight of those
robes! I thought I should have dropped when they
loaded that crown on to me. And the famous holy oil
they talked so much about was rancid: phew! The
Archbishop must be nearly dead: his robes must have
weighed a ton: they are stripping him still in the
vestry.

DUNOIS [*drily*] Your majesty should wear armor
oftener. That would accustom you to heavy dressing.

CHARLES. Yes: the old jibe! Well, I am not going to
wear armor: fighting is not my job. Where is The
Maid?

JOAN [*coming forward between Charles and Bluebeard,
and falling on her knee*] Sire: I have made you king:
my work is done. I am going back to my father's
farm.

CHARLES [*surprised, but relieved*] Oh, are you? Well,
that will be very nice.

Joan rises, deeply discouraged.

CHARLES [*continuing heedlessly*] A healthy life, you
know.

DUNOIS. But a dull one.

BLUEBEARD. You will find the petticoats tripping
you up after leaving them off for so long.

LA HIRE. You will miss the fighting. It's a bad habit,

but a grand one, and the hardest of all to break your-self of.

CHARLES [*anxiously*] Still, we dont want you to stay if you would really rather go home.

JOAN [*bitterly*] I know well that none of you will be sorry to see me go. [*She turns her shoulder to Charles and walks past him to the more congenial neighbourhood of Dunois and La Hire*].

LA HIRE. Well, I shall be able to swear when I want to. But I shall miss you at times.

JOAN. La Hire: in spite of all your sins and swears we shall meet in heaven; for I love you as I love Pitou, my old sheep dog. Pitou could kill a wolf. You will kill the English wolves until they go back to their country and become good dogs of God, will you not?

LA HIRE. You and I together: yes.

JOAN. No: I shall last only a year from the beginning.

ALL THE OTHERS. What!

JOAN. I know it somehow.

DUNOIS. Nonsense!

JOAN. Jack: do you think you will be able to drive them out?

DUNOIS [*with quiet conviction*] Yes: I shall drive them out. They beat us because we thought battles were tournaments and ransom markets. We played the fool while the goddams took war seriously. But I have learnt my lesson, and taken their measure. They have no roots here. I have beaten them before; and I shall beat them again.

JOAN. You will not be cruel to them, Jack?

DUNOIS. The goddams will not yield to tender hand-ling. We did not begin it.

JOAN [*suddenly*] Jack: before I go home, let us take Paris.

CHARLES [*terrified*] Oh no no. We shall lose everything

[145]

we have gained. Oh dont let us have any more fighting. We can make a very good treaty with the Duke of Burgundy.

JOAN. Treaty! [*She stamps with impatience*].

CHARLES. Well, why not, now that I am crowned and anointed? Oh, that oil!

The Archbishop comes from the vestry, and joins the group between Charles and Bluebeard.

CHARLES. Archbishop: The Maid wants to start fighting again.

THE ARCHBISHOP. Have we ceased fighting, then? Are we at peace?

CHARLES. No: I suppose not; but let us be content with what we have done. Let us make a treaty. Our luck is too good to last; and now is our chance to stop before it turns.

JOAN. Luck! God has fought for us; and you call it luck! And you would stop while there are still Englishmen on this holy earth of dear France!

THE ARCHBISHOP [*sternly*] Maid: the king addressed himself to me, not to you. You forget yourself. You very often forget yourself.

JOAN [*unabashed, and rather roughly*] Then speak, you; and tell him that it is not God's will that he should take his hand from the plough.

THE ARCHBISHOP. If I am not so glib with the name of God as you are, it is because I interpret His will with the authority of the Church and of my sacred office. When you first came you respected it, and would not have dared to speak as you are now speaking. You came clothed with the virtue of humility; and because God blessed your enterprises accordingly, you have stained yourself with the sin of pride. The old Greek tragedy is rising among us. It is the chastisement of hubris.

CHARLES. Yes: she thinks she knows better than everyone else.

JOAN [*distressed but naïvely incapable of seeing the effect she is producing*] But I do know better than any of you seem to. And I am not proud: I never speak unless I know I am right.

BLUEBEARD} [*exclaiming* {Ha ha!
CHARLES } *together*] {Just so.

THE ARCHBISHOP. How do you know you are right?

JOAN. I always know. My voices—

CHARLES. Oh, your voices, your voices. Why dont the voices come to me? I am king, not you.

JOAN. They do come to you; but you do not hear them. You have not sat in the field in the evening listening for them. When the angelus rings you cross yourself and have done with it; but if you prayed from your heart, and listened to the thrilling of the bells in the air after they stop ringing, you would hear the voices as well as I do. [*Turning brusquely from him*] But what voices do you need to tell you what the blacksmith can tell you: that you must strike while the iron is hot? I tell you we must make a dash at Compiégne and relieve it as we relieved Orleans. Then Paris will open its gates; or if not, we will break through them. What is your crown worth without your capital?

LA HIRE. That is what I say too. We shall go through them like a red hot shot through a pound of butter. What do you say, Bastard?

DUNOIS. If our cannon balls were all as hot as your head, and we had enough of them, we should conquer the earth, no doubt. Pluck and impetuosity are good servants in war, but bad masters: they have delivered us into the hands of the English every time we have trusted to them. We never know when we are beaten: that is our great fault.

JOAN. You never know when you are victorious: that is a worse fault. I shall have to make you carry looking-glasses in battle to convince you that the English have not cut off all your noses. You would have been besieged in Orleans still, you and your councils of war, if I had not made you attack. You should always attack; and if you only hold on long enough the enemy will stop first. You dont know how to begin a battle; and you dont know how to use your cannons. And I do.

She squats down on the flags with crossed ankles, pouting.

DUNOIS. I know what you think of us, General Joan.

JOAN. Never mind that, Jack. Tell them what you think of me.

DUNOIS. I think that God was on your side; for I have not forgotten how the wind changed, and how our hearts changed when you came; and by my faith I shall never deny that it was in your sign that we conquered. But I tell you as a soldier that God is no man's daily drudge, and no maid's either. If you are worthy of it He will sometimes snatch you out of the jaws of death and set you on your feet again; but that is all: once on your feet you must fight with all your might and all your craft. For He has to be fair to your enemy too: dont forget that. Well, He set us on our feet through you at Orleans; and the glory of it has carried us through a few good battles here to the coronation. But if we presume on it further, and trust to God to do the work we should do ourselves, we shall be defeated; and serve us right!

JOAN. But—

DUNOIS. Sh! I have not finished. Do not think, any

of you, that these victories of ours were won without generalship. King Charles: you have said no word in your proclamations of my part in this campaign; and I make no complaint of that; for the people will run after The Maid and her miracles and not after the Bastard's hard work finding troops for her and feeding them. But I know exactly how much God did for us through The Maid and how much He left me to do by my own wits; and I tell you that your little hour of miracles is over, and that from this time on he who plays the war game best will win—if the luck is on his side.

JOAN. Ah! if, if, if, if! If ifs and ans were pots and pans there'd be no need of tinkers. [*Rising impetuously*] I tell you, Bastard, your art of war is no use, because your knights are no good for real fighting. War is only a game to them, like tennis and all their other games: they make rules as to what is fair and what is not fair, and heap armor on themselves and on their poor horses to keep out the arrows; and when they fall they cant get up, and have to wait for their squires to come and lift them to arrange about the ransom with the man that has poked them off their horse. Cant you see that all the like of that is gone by and done with? What use is armor against gunpowder? And if it was, do you think men that are fighting for France and for God will stop to bargain about ransoms, as half your knights live by doing? No: they will fight to win; and they will give up their lives out of their own hand into the hand of God when they go into battle, as I do. Common folks understand this. They cannot afford armor and cannot pay ransoms; but they followed me half naked into the moat and up the ladder and over the wall. With them it is my life or thine, and God defend the right!

You may shake your head, Jack; and Bluebeard may twirl his billygoat's beard and cock his nose at me; but remember the day your knights and captains refused to follow me to attack the English at Orleans! You locked the gates to keep me in; and it was the townsfolk and the common people that followed me, and forced the gate, and shewed you the way to fight in earnest.

BLUEBEARD [*offended*] Not content with being Pope Joan, you must be Caesar and Alexander as well.

THE ARCHBISHOP. Pride will have a fall, Joan.

JOAN. Oh, never mind whether it is pride or not: is it true? is it commonsense?

LA HIRE. It is true. Half of us are afraid of having our handsome noses broken; and the other half are out for paying off their mortgages. Let her have her way, Dunois: she does not know everything; but she has got hold of the right end of the stick. Fighting is not what it was; and those who know the least about it often make the best job of it.

DUNOIS. I know all that. I do not fight in the old way: I have learnt the lesson of Agincourt, of Poitiers and Crecy. I know how many lives any move of mine will cost; and if the move is worth the cost I make it and pay the cost. But Joan never counts the cost at all: she goes ahead and trusts to God: she thinks she has God in her pocket. Up to now she has had the numbers on her side; and she has won. But I know Joan; and I see that some day she will go ahead when she has only ten men to do the work of a hundred. And then she will find that God is on the side of the big battalions. She will be taken by the enemy. And the lucky man that makes the capture will receive sixteen thousand pounds from the Earl of Ouareek.

JOAN [*flattered*] Sixteen thousand pounds! Eh, laddie,

have they offered that for me? There cannot be so
much money in the world.

DUNOIS. There is, in England. And now tell me, all
of you, which of you will lift a finger to save Joan once
the English have got her? I speak first, for the army.
The day after she has been dragged from her horse by
a goddam or a Burgundian, and he is not struck dead:
the day after she is locked in a dungeon, and the bars
and bolts do not fly open at the touch of St Peter's
angel: the day when the enemy finds out that she is as
vulnerable as I am and not a bit more invincible, she
will not be worth the life of a single soldier to us; and
I will not risk that life, much as I cherish her as a
companion-in-arms.

JOAN. I dont blame you, Jack: you are right. I am
not worth one soldier's life if God lets me be beaten;
but France may think me worth my ransom after
what God has done for her through me.

CHARLES. I tell you I have no money; and this
coronation, which is all your fault, has cost me the last
farthing I can borrow.

JOAN. The Church is richer than you. I put my trust
in the Church.

THE ARCHBISHOP. Woman: they will drag you
through the streets, and burn you as a witch.

JOAN [*running to him*] Oh, my lord, do not say that.
It is impossible. I a witch!

THE ARCHBISHOP. Peter Cauchon knows his business. The University of Paris has burnt a woman for
saying that what you have done was well done, and
according to God.

JOAN [*bewildered*] But why? What sense is there in it?
What I have done is according to God. They could
not burn a woman for speaking the truth.

THE ARCHBISHOP. They did.

JOAN. But you know that she was speaking the truth. You would not let them burn me.

THE ARCHBISHOP. How could I prevent them?

JOAN. You would speak in the name of the Church. You are a great prince of the Church. I would go anywhere with your blessing to protect me.

THE ARCHBISHOP. I have no blessing for you while you are proud and disobedient.

JOAN. Oh, why will you go on saying things like that? I am not proud and disobedient. I am a poor girl, and so ignorant that I do not know A from B. How could I be proud? And how can you say that I am disobedient when I always obey my voices, because they come from God.

THE ARCHBISHOP. The voice of God on earth is the voice of the Church Militant; and all the voices that come to you are the echoes of your own wilfulness.

JOAN. It is not true.

THE ARCHBISHOP [*flushing angrily*] You tell the Archbishop in his cathedral that he lies; and yet you say you are not proud and disobedient.

JOAN. I never said you lied. It was you that as good as said my voices lied. When have they ever lied? If you will not believe in them: even if they are only the echoes of my own commonsense, are they not always right? and are not your earthly counsels always wrong?

THE ARCHBISHOP [*indignantly*] It is waste of time admonishing you.

CHARLES. It always comes back to the same thing. She is right; and everyone else is wrong.

THE ARCHBISHOP. Take this as your last warning. If you perish through setting your private judgment above the instructions of your spiritual directors, the Church disowns you, and leaves you to whatever fate your presumption may bring upon you. The Bastard has told you that if you persist in setting up your military conceit above the counsels of your commanders—

DUNOIS [*interposing*] To put it quite exactly, if you attempt to relieve the garrison in Compiègne without the same superiority in numbers you had at Orleans—

THE ARCHBISHOP. The army will disown you, and will not rescue you. And His Majesty the King has told you that the throne has not the means of ransoming you.

CHARLES. Not a penny.

THE ARCHBISHOP. You stand alone: absolutely alone, trusting to your own conceit, your own ignorance, your own headstrong presumption, your own impiety in hiding all these sins under the cloak of a trust in God. When you pass through these doors into the sunlight, the crowd will cheer you. They will bring you their little children and their invalids to heal: they will kiss your hands and feet, and do what they can, poor simple souls, to turn your head, and madden you with the self-confidence that is leading you to your destruction. But you will be none the less alone: they cannot save you. We and we only can stand between you and the stake at which our enemies have burnt that wretched woman in Paris.

JOAN [*her eyes skyward*] I have better friends and better counsel than yours.

THE ARCHBISHOP. I see that I am speaking in vain to a hardened heart. You reject our protection, and are determined to turn us all against you. In future, then, fend for yourself; and if you fail, God have mercy on your soul.

DUNOIS. That is the truth, Joan. Heed it.

JOAN. Where would you all have been now if I had heeded that sort of truth? There is no help, no counsel, in any of you. Yes: I am alone on earth: I have always been alone. My father told my brothers to drown me if I would not stay to mind his sheep while France was bleeding to death: France might perish if only our lambs were safe. I thought France would have friends at the court of the king of France; and I find only wolves fighting for pieces of her poor torn body. I thought God would have friends everywhere, because He is the friend of everyone; and in my innocence I believed that you who now cast me out would be like strong towers to keep harm from me. But I am wiser now; and nobody is any the worse for being wiser. Do not think you can frighten me by telling me that I am alone. France is alone; and God is alone; and what is my loneliness before the loneliness of my country and my God? I see now that the loneliness of God is His strength: what would He be if He listened to your jealous little counsels? Well, my loneliness shall be my strength too; it is better to be alone with God: His friendship will not fail me, nor His counsel, nor His love. In His strength I will dare, and dare, and dare, until I die. I will go out now to the common people, and let the love in their eyes comfort me for the hate in yours. You will all be glad to see me burnt; but if I go through the fire I shall go through it to their hearts for ever and ever. And so, God be with me!

She goes from them. They stare after her in glum silence for a moment. Then Gilles de Rais twirls his beard.

BLUEBEARD. You know, the woman is quite impossible. I dont dislike her, really; but what are you to do with such a character?

DUNOIS. As God is my judge, if she fell into the Loire I would jump in in full armor to fish her out. But if she plays the fool at Compiègne, and gets caught, I must leave her to her doom.

LA HIRE. Then you had better chain me up; for I could follow her to hell when the spirit rises in her like that.

THE ARCHBISHOP. She disturbs my judgment too: there is a dangerous power in her outbursts. But the pit is open at her feet; and for good or evil we cannot turn her from it.

CHARLES. If only she would keep quiet, or go home!

They follow her dispiritedly.

Rouen, 30th May 1431. A great stone hall in the castle, arranged for a trial-at-law, but not a trial-by-jury, the court being the Bishop's court with the Inquisition participating: hence there are two raised chairs side by side for the Bishop and the Inquisitor as judges. Rows of chairs radiating from them at an obtuse angle are for the canons, the doctors of law and theology, and the Dominican monks, who act as assessors. In the angle is a table for the scribes, with stools. There is also a heavy rough wooden stool for the prisoner. All these are at the inner end of the hall. The further end is open to the courtyard through a row of arches. The court is shielded from the weather by screens and curtains.

Looking down the great hall from the middle of the inner end, the judicial chairs and scribes' table are to the right. The prisoner's stool is to the left. There are arched doors right and left. It is a fine sunshiny May morning.

Warwick comes in through the arched doorway on the judges' side, followed by his page.

THE PAGE [*pertly*] I suppose your lordship is aware that we have no business here. This is an ecclesiastical court; and we are only the secular arm.

WARWICK. I am aware of that fact. Will it please your impudence to find the Bishop of Beauvais for me, and give him a hint that he can have a word with me here before the trial, if he wishes?

THE PAGE [*going*] Yes, my lord.

WARWICK. And mind you behave yourself. Do not address him as Pious Peter.

THE PAGE. No, my lord. I shall be kind to him, because, when The Maid is brought in, Pious Peter will have to pick a peck of pickled pepper.

Cauchon enters through the same door with a Dominican monk and a canon, the latter carrying a brief.

THE PAGE. The Right Reverend his lordship the Bishop of Beauvais. And two other reverend gentlemen.

WARWICK. Get out; and see that we are not interrupted.

THE PAGE. Right, my lord [*he vanishes airily*].

CAUCHON. I wish your lordship good-morrow.

WARWICK. Good-morrow to your lordship. Have I had the pleasure of meeting your friends before? I think not.

CAUCHON [*introducing the monk, who is on his right*] This, my lord, is Brother John Lemaître, of the order of St Dominic. He is acting as deputy for the Chief Inquisitor into the evil of heresy in France. Brother John: the Earl of Warwick.

WARWICK. Your Reverence is most welcome. We have no Inquisitor in England, unfortunately; though we miss him greatly, especially on occasions like the present.

The Inquisitor smiles patiently, and bows. He is a mild elderly gentleman, but he has evident reserves of authority and firmness.

CAUCHON [*introducing the Canon, who is on his left*] This gentleman is Canon John D'Estivet, of the Chapter of Bayeux. He is acting as Promoter.

WARWICK. Promoter?

CAUCHON. Prosecutor, you would call him in civil law.

WARWICK. Ah! prosecutor. Quite, quite. I am very glad to make your acquaintance, Canon D'Estivet.

D'Estivet bows. [He is on the young side of middle age, well mannered, but vulpine beneath his veneer].

WARWICK. May I ask what stage the proceedings have reached? It is now more than nine months since The Maid was captured at Compiègne by the Burgundians. It is fully four months since I bought her from the Burgundians for a very handsome sum, solely that she might be brought to justice. It is very nearly three months since I delivered her up to you, my Lord Bishop, as a person suspected of heresy. May I suggest that you are taking a rather unconscionable time to make up your minds about a very plain case? Is this trial never going to end?

THE INQUISITOR [*smiling*] It has not yet begun, my lord.

WARWICK. Not yet begun! Why, you have been at it eleven weeks!

CAUCHON. We have not been idle, my lord. We have held fifteen examinations of The Maid: six public and nine private.

THE INQUISITOR [*always patiently smiling*] You see, my lord, I have been present at only two of these examinations. They were proceedings of the Bishop's court solely, and not of the Holy Office. I have only just decided to associate myself—that is, to associate the Holy Inquisition—with the Bishop's court. I did not at first think that this was a case of heresy at all. I regarded it as a political case, and The Maid as a prisoner of war. But having now been present at two of the examinations, I must admit that this seems to be one of the gravest cases of heresy within my experience. Therefore everything is now in order, and we proceed to trial this morning. [*He moves towards the judicial chairs*].

CAUCHON. This moment, if your lordship's convenience allows.

WARWICK [*graciously*] Well, that is good news, gentlemen. I will not attempt to conceal from you that our patience was becoming strained.

CAUCHON. So I gathered from the threats of your soldiers to drown those of our people who favour The Maid.

WARWICK. Dear me! At all events their intentions were friendly to you, my lord.

CAUCHON [*sternly*] I hope not. I am determined that the woman shall have a fair hearing. The justice of the Church is not a mockery, my lord.

THE INQUISITOR [*returning*] Never has there been a fairer examination within my experience, my lord. The Maid needs no lawyers to take her part: she will be tried by her most faithful friends, all ardently desirous to save her soul from perdition.

D'ESTIVET. Sir: I am the Promoter; and it has been my painful duty to present the case against the girl; but believe me, I would throw up my case today and hasten to her defence if I did not know that men far my superiors in learning and piety, in eloquence and persuasiveness, have been sent to reason with her, to explain to her the danger she is running, and the ease with which she may avoid it. [*Suddenly bursting into forensic eloquence, to the disgust of Cauchon and the Inquisitor, who have listened to him so far with patronizing approval*] Men have dared to say that we are acting from hate; but God is our witness that they lie. Have we tortured her? No. Have we ceased to exhort her; to implore her to have pity on herself; to come to the bosom of her Church as an erring but beloved child? Have we—

CAUCHON [*interrupting drily*] Take care, Canon. All that you say is true; but if you make his lordship believe it I will not answer for your life, and hardly for my own.

WARWICK [*deprecating, but by no means denying*] Oh, my lord, you are very hard on us poor English. But we certainly do not share your pious desire to save The Maid: in fact I tell you now plainly that her death is a political necessity which I regret but cannot help. If the Church lets her go—

CAUCHON [*with fierce and menacing pride*] If the Church lets her go, woe to the man, were he the Emperor himself, who dares lay a finger on her! The Church is not subject to political necessity, my lord.

THE INQUISITOR [*interposing smoothly*] You need have no anxiety about the result, my lord. You have an invincible ally in the matter: one who is far more determined than you that she shall burn.

WARWICK. And who is this very convenient partisan, may I ask?

THE INQUISITOR. The Maid herself. Unless you put a gag in her mouth you cannot prevent her from convicting herself ten times over every time she opens it.

D'ESTIVET. That is perfectly true, my lord. My hair bristles on my head when I hear so young a creature utter such blasphemies.

WARWICK. Well, by all means do your best for her if you are quite sure it will be of no avail. [*Looking hard at Cauchon*] I should be sorry to have to act without the blessing of the Church.

CAUCHON [*with a mixture of cynical admiration and contempt*] And yet they say Englishmen are hypocrites! You play for your side, my lord, even at the peril of your soul. I cannot but admire such devotion; but I dare not go so far myself. I fear damnation.

WARWICK. If we feared anything we could never govern England, my lord. Shall I send your people in to you?

CAUCHON. Yes: it will be very good of your lordship
to withdraw and allow the court to assemble.

*Warwick turns on his heel, and goes out through the
courtyard. Cauchon takes one of the judicial seats; and
D'Estivet sits at the scribes' table, studying his brief.*

CAUCHON [*casually, as he makes himself comfortable*]
What scoundrels these English nobles are!

THE INQUISITOR [*taking the other judicial chair on
Cauchon's left*] All secular power makes men scoundrels. They are not trained for the work; and they have
not the Apostolic Succession. Our own nobles are just
as bad.

*The Bishop's assessors hurry into the hall, headed by
Chaplain de Stogumber and Canon de Courcelles, a
young priest of 30. The scribes sit at the table, leaving a
chair vacant opposite D'Estivet. Some of the assessors
take their seats: others stand chatting, waiting for the
proceedings to begin formally. De Stogumber, aggrieved
and obstinate, will not take his seat: neither will the
Canon, who stands on his right.*

CAUCHON. Good morning, Master de Stogumber.
[*To the Inquisitor*] Chaplain to the Cardinal of England.

THE CHAPLAIN [*correcting him*] Of Winchester, my
lord. I have to make a protest, my lord.

CAUCHON. You make a great many.

THE CHAPLAIN. I am not without support, my lord.
Here is Master de Courcelles, Canon of Paris, who
associates himself with me in my protest.

CAUCHON. Well, what is the matter?

THE CHAPLAIN [*sulkily*] Speak you, Master de
Courcelles, since I do not seem to enjoy his lordship's
confidence. [*He sits down in dudgeon next to Cauchon,
on his right*].

COURCELLES. My lord: we have been at great pains
to draw up an indictment of The Maid on sixty-four

counts. We are now told that they have been reduced, without consulting us.

THE INQUISITOR. Master de Courcelles: I am the culprit. I am overwhelmed with admiration for the zeal displayed in your sixty-four counts; but in accusing a heretic, as in other things, enough is enough. Also you must remember that all the members of the court are not so subtle and profound as you, and that some of your very great learning might appear to them to be very great nonsense. Therefore I have thought it well to have your sixty-four articles cut down to twelve—

COURCELLES [*thunderstruck*] Twelve!!!

THE INQUISITOR. Twelve will, believe me, be quite enough for your purpose.

THE CHAPLAIN. But some of the most important points have been reduced almost to nothing. For instance, The Maid has actually declared that the blessed saints Margaret and Catherine, and the holy Archangel Michael, spoke to her in French. That is a vital point.

THE INQUISITOR. You think, doubtless, that they should have spoken in Latin?

CAUCHON. No: he thinks they should have spoken in English.

THE CHAPLAIN. Naturally, my lord.

THE INQUISITOR. Well, as we are all here agreed, I think, that these voices of The Maid are the voices of evil spirits tempting her to her damnation, it would not be very courteous to you, Master de Stogumber, or to the King of England, to assume that English is the devil's native language. So let it pass. The matter is not wholly omitted from the twelve articles. Pray take your places, gentlemen; and let us proceed to business.

All who have not taken their seats, do so.

THE CHAPLAIN. Well, I protest. That is all.

COURCELLES. I think it hard that all our work should go for nothing. It is only another example of the diabolical influence which this woman exercises over the court. [*He takes his chair, which is on the Chaplain's right*].

CAUCHON. Do you suggest that I am under diabolical influence?

COURCELLES. I suggest nothing, my lord. But it seems to me that there is a conspiracy here to hush up the fact that The Maid stole the Bishop of Senlis's horse.

CAUCHON [*keeping his temper with difficulty*] This is not a police court. Are we to waste our time on such rubbish?

COURCELLES [*rising, shocked*] My lord: do you call the Bishop's horse rubbish?

THE INQUISITOR [*blandly*] Master de Courcelles: The Maid alleges that she paid handsomely for the Bishop's horse, and that if he did not get the money the fault was not hers. As that may be true, the point is one on which The Maid may well be acquitted.

COURCELLES. Yes, if it were an ordinary horse. But the Bishop's horse! how can she be acquitted for that? [*He sits down again, bewildered and discouraged*].

THE INQUISITOR. I submit to you, with great respect, that if we persist in trying The Maid on trumpery issues on which we may have to declare her innocent, she may escape us on the great main issue of heresy, on which she seems so far to insist on her own guilt. I will ask you, therefore, to say nothing, when The Maid is brought before us, of these stealings of horses, and dancings round fairy trees with the village children, and prayings at haunted wells, and a dozen other things which you were diligently inquiring into until my arrival. There is not a village girl in France against whom you could not prove such things: they all dance round haunted trees, and pray at magic wells. Some of them would steal the Pope's horse if they got the chance. Heresy, gentlemen, heresy is the charge we have to try. The detection and suppression of heresy is my peculiar business: I am here as an inquisitor, not as an ordinary magistrate. Stick to the heresy, gentlemen; and leave the other matters alone.

CAUCHON. I may say that we have sent to the girl's village to make inquiries about her? and there is practically nothing serious against her.

THE CHAPLAIN *[rising and clamoring together]* Nothing serious, my lord—

COURCELLES *[rising and clamoring together]* What! The fairy tree not—

CAUCHON *[out of patience]* Be silent, gentlemen; or speak one at a time.

Courcelles collapses into his chair, intimidated.

THE CHAPLAIN *[sulkily resuming his seat]* That is what The Maid said to us last Friday.

CAUCHON. I wish you had followed her counsel, sir. When I say nothing serious, I mean nothing that men of sufficiently large mind to conduct an inquiry like this would consider serious. I agree with my colleague the Inquisitor that it is on the count of heresy that we must proceed.

LADVENU *[a young but ascetically fine-drawn Dominican who is sitting next Courcelles, on his right]* But is there any great harm in the girl's heresy? Is it not merely her simplicity? Many saints have said as much as Joan.

THE INQUISITOR *[dropping his blandness and speak-*

ing very gravely] Brother Martin: if you had seen what I have seen of heresy, you would not think it a light thing even in its most apparently harmless and even lovable and pious origins. Heresy begins with people who are to all appearance better than their neighbors. A gentle and pious girl, or a young man who has obeyed the command of our Lord by giving all his riches to the poor, and putting on the garb of poverty, the life of austerity, and the rule of humility and charity, may be the founder of a heresy that will wreck both Church and Empire if not ruthlessly stamped out in time. The records of the holy Inquisition are full of histories we dare not give to the world, because they are beyond the belief of honest men and innocent women; yet they all began with saintly simpletons. I have seen this again and again. Mark what I say: the woman who quarrels with her clothes, and puts on the dress of a man, is like the man who throws off his fur gown and dresses like John the Baptist: they are followed, as surely as the night follows the day, by bands of wild women and men who refuse to wear any clothes at all. When maids will neither marry nor take regular vows, and men reject marriage and exalt their lusts into divine inspirations, then, as surely as the summer follows the spring, they begin with polygamy, and end by incest. Heresy at first seems innocent and even laudable; but it ends in such a monstrous horror of unnatural wickedness that the most tender-hearted among you, if you saw it at work as I have seen it, would clamor against the mercy of the Church in dealing with it. For two hundred years the Holy Office has striven with these diabolical madnesses; and it knows that they begin always by vain and ignorant persons setting up their own judgment against the Church, and taking it upon themselves to be the interpreters of God's will. You must not fall into the common error of mistaking these simpletons for liars and hypocrites. They believe honestly and sincerely that their diabolical inspiration is divine. Therefore you must be on your guard against your natural compassion. You are all, I hope, merciful men: how else could you have devoted your lives to the service of our gentle Saviour? You are going to see before you a young girl, pious and chaste; for I must tell you, gentlemen, that the things said of her by our English friends are supported by no evidence, whilst there is abundant testimony that her excesses have been excesses of religion and charity and not of worldliness and wantonness. This girl is not one of those whose hard features are the sign of hard hearts, and whose brazen looks and lewd demeanor condemn them before they are accused. The devilish pride that has led her into her present peril has left no mark on her countenance. Strange as it may seem to you, it has even left no mark on her character outside those special matters in which she is proud; so that you will see a diabolical pride and a natural humility seated side by side in the selfsame soul. Therefore be on your guard. God forbid that I should tell you to harden your hearts; for her punishment if we condemn her will be so cruel that we should forfeit our own hope of divine mercy were there one grain of malice against her in our hearts. But if you hate cruelty—and if any man here does not hate it I command him on his soul's salvation to quit this holy court—I say, if you hate cruelty, remember that nothing is so cruel in its consequences as the toleration of heresy. Remember also that no court of law can be so cruel as the common people are to those whom they suspect of heresy. The heretic in the hands of the Holy Office is safe from violence, is assured of a fair trial, and cannot suffer death, even when guilty, if repentance follows sin. Innumerable lives of heretics have been saved because the Holy Office has taken them out of the hands of the people, and because the people have yielded them up, knowing that the Holy Office would deal with them. Before the Holy Inquisition existed, and even now when its officers are not within reach, the unfortunate wretch suspected of heresy, perhaps quite ignorantly and unjustly, is stoned, torn in pieces, drowned, burned in his house with all his innocent children, without a trial, unshriven, unburied save as a dog is buried: all of them deeds hateful to God and most cruel to man. Gentlemen: I am compassionate by nature as well as by my profession; and though the work I have to do may seem cruel to those who do not know how much more cruel it would be to leave it undone, I would go to the stake myself sooner than do it if I did not know its righteousness, its necessity, its essential mercy. I ask you to address yourself to this trial in that conviction. Anger is a bad counsellor: cast out anger. Pity is sometimes worse: cast out pity. But do not cast out mercy. Remember only that justice comes first. Have you anything to say, my lord, before we proceed to trial?

CAUCHON. You have spoken for me, and spoken better than I could. I do not see how any sane man could disagree with a word that has fallen from you. But this I will add. The crude heresies of which you have told us are horrible; but their horror is like that of the black death: they rage for a while and then die out, because sound and sensible men will not under any incitement be reconciled to nakedness and incest and polygamy and the like. But we are confronted today throughout Europe with a heresy that is spreading among men not weak in mind nor diseased in brain: nay, the stronger the mind, the more obstinate the heretic. It is neither discredited by fantastic extremes nor corrupted by the common lusts of the flesh; but it, too, sets up the private judgment of the single erring mortal against the considered wisdom and experience of the Church. The mighty structure of Catholic Christendom will never be shaken by naked madmen or by the sins of Moab and Ammon. But it may be betrayed from within, and brought to barbarous ruin and desolation, by this arch heresy which the English Commander calls Protestantism.

THE ASSESSORS [*whispering*] Protestantism! What was that? What does the Bishop mean? Is it a new heresy? The English Commander, he said. Did you ever hear of Protestantism? etc., etc.

CAUCHON [*continuing*] And that reminds me. What provision has the Earl of Warwick made for the defence of the secular arm should The Maid prove obdurate, and the people be moved to pity her?

THE CHAPLAIN. Have no fear on that score, my lord. The noble earl has eight hundred men-at-arms at the gates. She will not slip through our English fingers even if the whole city be on her side.

CAUCHON [*revolted*] Will you not add, God grant that she repent and purge her sin?

THE CHAPLAIN. That does not seem to me to be consistent; but of course I agree with your lordship.

CAUCHON [*giving him up with a shrug of contempt*] The court sits.

THE INQUISITOR. Let the accused be brought in.

LADVENU [*calling*] The accused. Let her be brought in.

Joan, chained by the ankles, is brought in through the

[168]

arched door behind the prisoner's stool by a guard of English soldiers. With them is the Executioner and his assistants. They lead her to the prisoner's stool, and place themselves behind it after taking off her chain. She wears a page's black suit. Her long imprisonment and the strain of the examinations which have preceded the trial have left their mark on her; but her vitality still holds: she confronts the court unabashed, without a trace of the awe which their formal solemnity seems to require for the complete success of its impressiveness.

THE INQUISITOR [*kindly*] Sit down, Joan. [*She sits on the prisoner's stool*]. You look very pale today. Are you not well?

JOAN. Thank you kindly: I am well enough. But the Bishop sent me some carp; and it made me ill.

CAUCHON. I am sorry. I told them to see that it was fresh.

JOAN. You meant to be good to me, I know; but it is a fish that does not agree with me. The English thought you were trying to poison me—

CAUCHON } [*together*] { What!
THE CHAPLAIN } { No, my lord.

JOAN [*continuing*] They are determined that I shall be burnt as a witch; and they sent their doctor to cure me; but he was forbidden to bleed me because the silly people believe that a witch's witchery leaves her if she is bled; so he only called me filthy names. Why do you leave me in the hands of the English? I should be in the hands of the Church. And why must I be chained by the feet to a log of wood? Are you afraid I will fly away?

D'ESTIVET [*harshly*] Woman: it is not for you to question the court: it is for us to question you.

COURCELLES. When you were left unchained, did you not try to escape by jumping from a tower sixty feet high? If you cannot fly like a witch, how is it that you are still alive?

JOAN. I suppose because the tower was not so high then. It has grown higher every day since you began asking me questions about it.

D'ESTIVET. Why did you jump from the tower?

JOAN. How do you know that I jumped?

D'ESTIVET. You were found lying in the moat. Why did you leave the tower?

JOAN. Why would anybody leave a prison if they could get out?

D'ESTIVET. You tried to escape?

JOAN. Of course I did; and not for the first time either. If you leave the door of the cage open the bird will fly out.

D'ESTIVET [*rising*] That is a confession of heresy. I call the attention of the court to it.

JOAN. Heresy, he calls it! Am I a heretic because I try to escape from prison?

D'ESTIVET. Assuredly, if you are in the hands of the Church, and you wilfully take yourself out of its hands, you are deserting the Church; and that is heresy.

JOAN. It is great nonsense. Nobody could be such a fool as to think that.

D'ESTIVET. You hear, my lord, how I am reviled in the execution of my duty by this woman. [*He sits down indignantly*].

CAUCHON. I have warned you before, Joan, that you are doing yourself no good by these pert answers.

JOAN. But you will not talk sense to me. I am reasonable if you will be reasonable.

THE INQUISITOR [*interposing*] This is not yet in order. You forget, Master Promoter, that the proceedings have not been formally opened. The time for questions is after she has sworn on the Gospels to tell us the whole truth.

JOAN. You say this to me every time. I have said again and again that I will tell you all that concerns this trial. But I cannot tell you the whole truth: God does not allow the whole truth to be told. You do not understand it when I tell it. It is an old saying that he who tells too much truth is sure to be hanged. I am weary of this argument: we have been over it nine times already. I have sworn as much as I will swear; and I will swear no more.

COURCELLES. My lord: she should be put to the torture.

THE INQUISITOR. You hear, Joan? That is what happens to the obdurate. Think before you answer. Has she been shewn the instruments?

THE EXECUTIONER. They are ready, my lord. She has seen them.

JOAN. If you tear me limb from limb until you separate my soul from my body you will get nothing out of me beyond what I have told you. What more is there to tell that you could understand? Besides, I cannot bear to be hurt; and if you hurt me I will say anything you like to stop the pain. But I will take it all back afterwards; so what is the use of it?

LADVENU. There is much in that. We should proceed mercifully.

COURCELLES. But the torture is customary.

THE INQUISITOR. It must not be applied wantonly. If the accused will confess voluntarily, then its use cannot be justified.

COURCELLES. But this is unusual and irregular. She refuses to take the oath.

LADVENU [*disgusted*] Do you want to torture the girl for the mere pleasure of it?

COURCELLES [*bewildered*] But it is not a pleasure. It is the law. It is customary. It is always done.

THE INQUISITOR. That is not so, Master, except when the inquiries are carried on by people who do not know their legal business.

COURCELLES. But the woman is a heretic. I assure you it is always done.

CAUCHON [*decisively*] It will not be done today if it is not necessary. Let there be an end of this. I will not have it said that we proceeded on forced confessions. We have sent our best preachers and doctors to this woman to exhort and implore her to save her soul and body from the fire: we shall not now send the executioner to thrust her into it.

COURCELLES. Your lordship is merciful, of course. But it is a great responsibility to depart from the usual practice.

JOAN. Thou art a rare noodle, Master. Do what was done last time is thy rule, eh?

COURCELLES [*rising*] Thou wanton: dost thou dare call me noodle?

THE INQUISITOR. Patience, Master, patience: I fear you will soon be only too terribly avenged.

COURCELLES [*mutters*] Noodle indeed! [*He sits down, much discontented*].

THE INQUISITOR. Meanwhile, let us not be moved by the rough side of a shepherd lass's tongue.

JOAN. Nay: I am no shepherd lass, though I have helped with the sheep like anyone else. I will do a lady's work in the house—spin or weave—against any woman in Rouen.

THE INQUISITOR. This is not a time for vanity, Joan. You stand in great peril.

JOAN. I know it: have I not been punished for my vanity? If I had not worn my cloth of gold surcoat in battle like a fool, that Burgundian soldier would never have pulled me backwards off my horse; and I should not have been here.

THE CHAPLAIN. If you are so clever at woman's work why do you not stay at home and do it?

JOAN. There are plenty of other women to do it; but there is nobody to do my work.

CAUCHON. Come! we are wasting time on trifles. Joan: I am going to put a most solemn question to you. Take care how you answer; for your life and salvation are at stake on it. Will you for all you have said and done, be it good or bad, accept the judgment of God's Church on earth? More especially as to the acts and words that are imputed to you in this trial by the Promoter here, will you submit your case to the inspired interpretation of the Church Militant?

JOAN. I am a faithful child of the Church. I will obey the Church—

CAUCHON [hopefully leaning forward] You will?

JOAN. —provided it does not command anything impossible.

Cauchon sinks back in his chair with a heavy sigh. The Inquisitor purses his lips and frowns. Ladvenu shakes his head pitifully.

D'ESTIVET. She imputes to the Church the error and folly of commanding the impossible.

JOAN. If you command me to declare that all that I have done and said, and all the visions and revelations I have had, were not from God, then that is impossible: I will not declare it for anything in the world. What God made me do I will never go back on; and what He has commanded or shall command I will not fail to do in spite of any man alive. That is what I mean by impossible. And in case the Church should bid me do anything contrary to the command I have from

God, I will not consent to it, no matter what it may be.

THE ASSESSORS [*shocked and indignant*] Oh! The Church contrary to God! What do you say now? Flat heresy. This is beyond everything, etc., etc.

D'ESTIVET [*throwing down his brief*] My lord: do you need anything more than this?

CAUCHON. Woman: you have said enough to burn ten heretics. Will you not be warned? Will you not understand?

THE INQUISITOR. If the Church Militant tells you that your revelations and visions are sent by the devil to tempt you to your damnation, will you not believe that the Church is wiser than you?

JOAN. I believe that God is wiser than I; and it is His commands that I will do. All the things that you call my crimes have come to me by the command of God. I say that I have done them by the order of God: it is impossible for me to say anything else. If any Churchman says the contrary I shall not mind him: I shall mind God alone, whose command I always follow.

LADVENU [*pleading with her urgently*] You do not know what you are saying, child. Do you want to kill yourself? Listen. Do you not believe that you are subject to the Church of God on earth?

JOAN. Yes. When have I ever denied it?

LADVENU. Good. That means, does it not, that you are subject to our Lord the Pope, to the cardinals, the archbishops, and the bishops for whom his lordship stands here today?

JOAN. God must be served first.

D'ESTIVET. Then your voices command you not to submit yourself to the Church Militant?

JOAN. My voices do not tell me to disobey the Church; but God must be served first.

CAUCHON. And you, and not the Church, are to be the judge?

JOAN. What other judgment can I judge by but my own?

THE ASSESSORS [*scandalized*] Oh! [*They cannot find words*].

CAUCHON. Out of your own mouth you have condemned yourself. We have striven for your salvation to the verge of sinning ourselves: we have opened the door to you again and again; and you have shut it in our faces and in the face of God. Dare you pretend, after what you have said, that you are in a state of grace?

JOAN. If I am not, may God bring me to it: if I am, may God keep me in it!

LADVENU. That is a very good reply, my lord.

COURCELLES. Were you in a state of grace when you stole the Bishop's horse?

CAUCHON [*rising in a fury*] Oh, devil take the Bishop's horse and you too! We are here to try a case of heresy; and no sooner do we come to the root of the matter than we are thrown back by idiots who understand nothing but horses. [*Trembling with rage, he forces himself to sit down*].

THE INQUISITOR. Gentlemen, gentlemen: in clinging to these small issues you are The Maid's best advocates. I am not surprised that his lordship has lost patience with you. What does the Promotor say? Does he press these trumpery matters?

D'ESTIVET. I am bound by my office to press everything; but when the woman confesses a heresy that must bring upon her the doom of excommunication, of what consequence is it that she has been guilty also of offences which expose her to minor penances? I share the impatience of his lordship as to these minor charges. Only, with great respect, I must emphasize the gravity of two very horrible and blasphemous crimes which she does not deny. First, she has intercourse with evil spirits, and is therefore a sorceress. Second, she wears men's clothes, which is indecent, unnatural, and abominable; and in spite of our most earnest remonstrances and entreaties, she will not change them even to receive the sacrament.

JOAN. Is the blessed St Catherine an evil spirit? Is St Margaret? Is Michael the Archangel?

COURCELLES. How do you know that the spirit which appears to you is an archangel? Does he not appear to you as a naked man?

JOAN. Do you think God cannot afford clothes for him?

The assessors cannot help smiling, especially as the joke is against Courcelles.

LADVENU. Well answered, Joan.

THE INQUISITOR. It is, in effect, well answered. But no evil spirit would be so simple as to appear to a young girl in a guise that would scandalize her when he meant her to take him for a messenger from the Most High? Joan: the Church instructs you that these apparitions are demons seeking your soul's perdition. Do you accept the instruction of the Church?

JOAN. I accept the messenger of God. How could any faithful believer in the Church refuse him?

CAUCHON. Wretched woman: again I ask you, do you know what you are saying?

THE INQUISITOR. You wrestle in vain with the devil for her soul, my lord: she will not be saved. Now as to this matter of the man's dress. For the last time, will you put off that impudent attire, and dress as becomes your sex?

JOAN. I will not.

D'ESTIVET [*pouncing*] The sin of disobedience, my lord.

JOAN [*distressed*] But my voices tell me I must dress as a soldier.

LADVENU. Joan, Joan: does not that prove to you that the voices are the voices of evil spirits? Can you suggest to us one good reason why an angel of God should give you such shameless advice?

JOAN. Why, yes: what can be plainer commonsense? I was a soldier living among soldiers. I am a prisoner guarded by soldiers. If I were to dress as a woman they would think of me as a woman; and then what would become of me? If I dress as a soldier they think of me as a soldier, and I can live with them as I do at home with my brothers. That is why St Catherine tells me I must not dress as a woman until she gives me leave.

COURCELLES. When will she give you leave?

JOAN. When you take me out of the hands of the English soldiers. I have told you that I should be in the hands of the Church, and not left night and day with four soldiers of the Earl of Warwick. Do you want me to live with them in petticoats?

LADVENU. My lord: what she says is, God knows, very wrong and shocking; but there is a grain of worldly sense in it such as might impose on a simple village maiden.

JOAN. If we were as simple in the village as you are in your courts and palaces, there would soon be no wheat to make bread for you.

CAUCHON. That is the thanks you get for trying to save her, Brother Martin.

LADVENU. Joan: we are all trying to save you. His lordship is trying to save you. The Inquisitor could not be more just to you if you were his own daughter. But you are blinded by a terrible pride of self-sufficiency.

JOAN. Why do you say that? I have said nothing wrong. I cannot understand.

THE INQUISITOR. The blessed St Athanasius has laid it down in his creed that those who cannot understand are damned. It is not enough to be simple. It is not enough even to be what simple people call good. The simplicity of a darkened mind is no better than the simplicity of a beast.

JOAN. There is great wisdom in the simplicity of a beast, let me tell you; and sometimes great foolishness in the wisdom of scholars.

LADVENU. We know that, Joan: we are not so foolish as you think us. Try to resist the temptation to make pert replies to us. Do you see that man who stands behind you [*he indicates the Executioner*]?

JOAN [*turning and looking at the man*] Your torturer? But the Bishop said I was not to be tortured.

LADVENU. You are not to be tortured because you have confessed everything that is necessary to your condemnation. That man is not only the torturer: he is also the Executioner. Executioner: let The Maid hear your answers to my questions. Are you prepared for the burning of a heretic this day?

THE EXECUTIONER. Yes, Master.

LADVENU. Is the stake ready?

THE EXECUTIONER. It is. In the market-place. The English have built it too high for me to get near her and make the death easier. It will be a cruel death.

JOAN [*horrified*] But you are not going to burn me now?

THE INQUISITOR. You realize it at last.

LADVENU. There are eight hundred English soldiers

waiting to take you to the market-place the moment the sentence of excommunication has passed the lips of your judges. You are within a few short moments of that doom.

JOAN [*looking round desperately for rescue*] Oh God!

LADVENU. Do not despair, Joan. The Church is merciful. You can save yourself.

JOAN [*hopefully*] Yes: my voices promised me I should not be burnt. St Catherine bade me be bold.

CAUCHON. Woman: are you quite mad? Do you not yet see that your voices have deceived you?

JOAN. Oh no: that is impossible.

CAUCHON. Impossible! They have led you straight to your excommunication, and to the stake which is there waiting for you.

LADVENU. [*pressing the point hard*] Have they kept a single promise to you since you were taken at Compiègne? The devil has betrayed you. The Church holds out its arms to you.

JOAN [*despairing*] Oh, it is true: it is true: my voices have deceived me. I have been mocked by devils: my faith is broken. I have dared and dared; but only a fool will walk into a fire: God, who gave me my common-sense, cannot will me to do that.

LADVENU. Now God be praised that He has saved you at the eleventh hour! [*He hurries to the vacant seat at the scribes' table, and snatches a sheet of paper, on which he sets to work writing eagerly*].

CAUCHON. Amen!

JOAN. What must I do?

CAUCHON. You must sign a solemn recantation of your heresy.

JOAN. Sign? That means to write my name. I cannot write.

CAUCHON. You have signed many letters before.

JOAN. Yes; but someone held my hand and guided the pen. I can make my mark.

THE CHAPLAIN [*who has been listening with growing alarm and indignation*] My lord: do you mean that you are going to allow this woman to escape us?

THE INQUISITOR. The law must take its course, Master de Stogumber. And you know the law.

THE CHAPLAIN [*rising, purple with fury*] I know that there is no faith in a Frenchman [*Tumult, which he shouts down*]. I know what my lord the Cardinal of Winchester will say when he hears of this. I know what the Earl of Warwick will do when he learns that you intend to betray him. There are eight hundred men at the gate who will see that this abominable witch is burnt in spite of your teeth.

THE ASSESSORS [*meanwhile*] What is this? What did he say? He accuses us of treachery! This is past bearing. No faith in a Frenchman! Did you hear that? This is an intolerable fellow. Who is he? Is this what English Churchmen are like? He must be mad or drunk, etc., etc.

THE INQUISITOR [*rising*] Silence, pray! Gentlemen: pray silence! Master Chaplain: bethink you a moment of your holy office: of what you are, and where you are. I direct you to sit down.

THE CHAPLAIN [*folding his arms doggedly, his face working convulsively*] I will NOT sit down.

CAUCHON. Master Inquisitor: this man has called me a traitor to my face before now.

THE CHAPLAIN. So you are a traitor. You are all traitors. You have been doing nothing but begging this damnable witch on your knees to recant all through this trial.

THE INQUISITOR [*placidly resuming his seat*] If you will not sit, you must stand: that is all.

THE CHAPLAIN. I will NOT stand [*he flings himself back into his chair*].

LADVENU [*rising with the paper in his hand*] My lord: here is the form of recantation for The Maid to sign.

CAUCHON. Read it to her.

JOAN. Do not trouble. I will sign it.

THE INQUISITOR. Woman: you must know what you are putting your hand to. Read it to her, Brother Martin. And let all be silent.

LADVENU [*reading quietly*] "I, Joan, commonly called The Maid, a miserable sinner, do confess that I have most grievously sinned in the following articles. I have pretended to have revelations from God and the angels and the blessed saints, and perversely rejected the Church's warnings that these were temptations by demons. I have blasphemed abominably by wearing an immodest dress, contrary to the Holy Scripture and the canons of the Church. Also I have clipped my hair in the style of a man, and, against all the duties which have made my sex specially acceptable in heaven, have taken up the sword, even to the shedding of human blood, inciting men to slay each other, invoking evil spirits to delude them, and stubbornly and most blasphemously imputing these sins to Almighty God. I confess to the sin of sedition, to the sin of idolatry, to the sin of disobedience, to the sin of pride, and to the sin of heresy. All of which sins I now renounce and abjure and depart from, humbly thanking you Doctors and Masters who have brought me back to the truth and into the grace of our Lord. And I will never return to my errors, but will remain in communion with our Holy Church and in obedience to our Holy Father the Pope of Rome. All this I swear by God Almighty and the Holy Gospels, in witness whereto I sign my name to this recantation."

THE INQUISITOR. You understand this, Joan?

JOAN [*listless*] It is plain enough, sir.

THE INQUISITOR. And it is true?

JOAN. It may be true. If it were not true, the fire would not be ready for me in the market-place.

LADVENU [*taking up his pen and a book, and going to her quickly lest she should compromise herself again*] Come, child: let me guide your hand. Take the pen. [*She does so; and they begin to write, using the book as a desk*] J. E. H. A. N. E. So. Now make your mark by yourself.

JOAN [*makes her mark, and gives him back the pen, tormented by the rebellion of her soul against her mind and body*] There!

LADVENU [*replacing the pen on the table, and handing the recantation to Cauchon with a reverence*] Praise be to God, my brothers, the lamb has returned to the flock; and the shepherd rejoices in her more than in ninety and nine just persons. [*He returns to his seat*].

THE INQUISITOR [*taking the paper from Cauchon*] We declare thee by this act set free from the danger of excommunication in which thou stoodest. [*He throws the paper down to the table*].

JOAN. I thank you.

THE INQUISITOR. But because thou hast sinned most presumptuously against God and the Holy Church, and that thou mayst repent thy errors in solitary contemplation, and be shielded from all temptation to return to them, we, for the good of thy soul, and for a penance that may wipe out thy sins and bring thee finally unspotted to the throne of grace, do condemn thee to eat the bread of sorrow and drink the water of affliction to the end of thy earthly days in perpetual imprisonment.

JOAN [*rising in consternation and terrible anger*]

Perpetual imprisonment! Am I not then to be set free?

LADVENU [*mildly shocked*] Set free, child, after such wickedness as yours! What are you dreaming of?

JOAN. Give me that writing. [*She rushes to the table; snatches up the paper; and tears it into fragments*] Light your fire: do you think I dread it as much as the life of a rat in a hole? My voices were right.

LADVENU. Joan! Joan!

JOAN. Yes: they told me you were fools [*the word gives great offence*], and that I was not to listen to your fine words nor trust to your charity. You promised me my life; but you lied [*indignant exclamations*]. You think that life is nothing but not being stone dead. It is not the bread and water I fear: I can live on bread: when have I asked for more? It is no hardship to drink water if the water be clean. Bread has no sorrow for me, and water no affliction. But to shut me from the light of the sky and the sight of the fields and flowers; to chain my feet so that I can never again ride with the soldiers nor climb the hills; to make me breathe foul damp darkness, and keep from me everything that brings me back to the love of God when your wickedness and foolishness tempt me to hate Him: all this is worse than the furnace in the Bible that was heated seven times. I could do without my warhorse; I could drag about in a skirt; I could let the banners and the trumpets and the knights and soldiers pass me and leave me behind as they leave the other women, if only I could still hear the wind in the trees, the larks in the sunshine, the young lambs crying through the healthy frost, and the blessed blessed church bells that send my angel voices floating to me on the wind. But without these things I cannot live; and by your wanting to take them away from me, or from any human creature, I know that your counsel is of the devil, and that mine is of God.

THE ASSESSORS [*in great commotion*] Blasphemy! blasphemy! She is possessed. She said our counsel was of the devil. And hers of God. Monstrous! The devil is in our midst, etc., etc.

D'ESTIVET [*shouting above the din*] She is a relapsed heretic, obstinate, incorrigible, and altogether unworthy of the mercy we have shewn her. I call for her excommunication.

THE CHAPLAIN [*to the Executioner*] Light your fire, man. To the stake with her.

The Executioner and his assistants hurry out through the courtyard.

LADVENU. You wicked girl: if your counsel were of God would He not deliver you?

JOAN. His ways are not your ways. He wills that I go through the fire to His bosom; for I am His child, and you are not fit that I should live among you. That is my last word to you.

The soldiers seize her.

CAUCHON [*rising*] Not yet.

They wait. There is a dead silence. Cauchon turns to the Inquisitor with an inquiring look. The Inquisitor nods affirmatively. They rise solemnly, and intone the sentence antiphonally.

CAUCHON. We decree that thou art a relapsed heretic.

THE INQUISITOR. Cast out from the unity of the Church.

CAUCHON. Sundered from her body.

THE INQUISITOR. Infected with the leprosy of heresy.

CAUCHON. A member of Satan.

THE INQUISITOR. We declare that thou must be excommunicate.

CAUCHON. And now we do cast thee out, segregate thee, and abandon thee to the secular power.

THE INQUISITOR. Admonishing the same secular power that it moderate its judgment of thee in respect of death and division of the limbs. [*He resumes his seat*].

CAUCHON. And if any true sign of penitence appear in thee, to permit our Brother Martin to administer to thee the sacrament of penance.

THE CHAPLAIN. Into the fire with the witch [*he rushes at her, and helps the soldiers to push her out*].

Joan is taken away through the courtyard. The assessors rise in disorder, and follow the soldiers, except Ladvenu, who has hidden his face in his hands.

CAUCHON [*rising again in the act of sitting down*] No, no: this is irregular. The representative of the secular arm should be here to receive her from us.

THE INQUISITOR [*also on his feet again*] That man is an incorrigible fool.

CAUCHON. Brother Martin: see that everything is done in order.

LADVENU. My place is at her side, my lord. You must exercise your own authority. [*He hurries out*].

CAUCHON. These English are impossible: they will thrust her straight into the fire. Look!

He points to the courtyard, in which the glow and flicker of fire can now be seen reddening the May daylight. Only the Bishop and Inquisitor are left in the court.

CAUCHON [*turning to go*] We must stop that.

THE INQUISITOR [*calmly*] Yes; but not too fast, my lord.

CAUCHON [*halting*] But there is not a moment to lose.

THE INQUISITOR. We have proceeded in perfect order. If the English choose to put themselves in the wrong, it is not our business to put them in the right. A flaw in the procedure may be useful later on: one never knows. And the sooner it is over, the better for that poor girl.

CAUCHON [*relaxing*] That is true. But I suppose we must see this dreadful thing through.

THE INQUISITOR. One gets used to it. Habit is everything. I am accustomed to the fire: it is soon over. But it is a terrible thing to see a young and innocent creature crushed between these mighty forces, the Church and the Law.

CAUCHON. You call her innocent!

THE INQUISITOR. Oh, quite innocent. What does she know of the Church and the Law? She did not understand a word we were saying. It is the ignorant who suffer. Come, or we shall be late for the end.

CAUCHON [*going with him*] I shall not be sorry if we are: I am not so accustomed as you.

They are going out when Warwick comes in, meeting them.

WARWICK. Oh, I am intruding. I thought it was all over. [*He makes a feint of retiring*].

CAUCHON. Do not go, my lord. It is all over.

THE INQUISITOR. The execution is not in our hands, my lord; but it is desirable that we should witness the end. So by your leave— [*He bows, and goes out through the courtyard*].

CAUCHON. There is some doubt whether your people have observed the forms of law, my lord.

WARWICK. I am told that there is some doubt whether your authority runs in this city, my lord. It is not in your diocese. However, if you will answer for that I will answer for the rest.

CAUCHON. It is to God that we both must answer. Good morning, my lord.

WARWICK. My lord: good morning.

They look at one another for a moment with uncon-
cealed hostility. Then Cauchon follows the Inquisitor out.
Warwick looks round. Finding himself alone, he calls for
attendance.

WARWICK. Hallo: some attendance here! [*Silence*].
Hallo, there! [*Silence*]. Hallo! Brian, you young black-
guard, where are you? [*Silence*]. Guard! [*Silence*].
They have all gone to see the burning: even that child.

The silence is broken by someone frantically howling
and sobbing.

WARWICK. What in the devil's name—?

The Chaplain staggers in from the courtyard like a
demented creature, his face streaming with tears, making
the piteous sounds that Warwick has heard. He stumbles
to the prisoner's stool, and throws himself upon it with
heartrending sobs.

WARWICK [*going to him and patting him on the shoulder*]
What is it, Master John? What is the matter?

THE CHAPLAIN [*clutching at his hands*] My lord, my
lord: for Christ's sake pray for my wretched guilty
soul.

WARWICK [*soothing him*] Yes, yes: of course I will.
Calmly, gently—

THE CHAPLAIN [*blubbering miserably*] I am not a
bad man, my lord.

WARWICK. No, no: not at all.

THE CHAPLAIN. I meant no harm. I did not know
what it would be like.

WARWICK [*hardening*] Oh! You saw it, then?

THE CHAPLAIN. I did not know what I was doing.
I am a hot-headed fool; and I shall be damned to all
eternity for it.

WARWICK. Nonsense! Very distressing, no doubt;
but it was not your doing.

THE CHAPLAIN [*lamentably*] I let them do it. If I had known, I would have torn her from their hands. You dont know: you havnt seen: it is so easy to talk when you dont know. You madden yourself with words: you damn yourself because it feels grand to throw oil on the flaming hell of your own temper. But when it is brought home to you; when you see the thing you have done; when it is blinding your eyes, stifling your nostrils, tearing your heart, then—then— [*Falling on his knees*] O God, take away this sight from me! O Christ, deliver me from this fire that is consuming me! She cried to Thee in the midst of it: Jesus! Jesus! Jesus! She is in Thy bosom; and I am in hell for evermore.

WARWICK [*summarily hauling him to his feet*] Come come, man! you must pull yourself together. We shall have the whole town talking of this. [*He throws him not too gently into a chair at the table*] If you have not the nerve to see these things, why do you not do as I do, and stay away?

THE CHAPLAIN [*bewildered and submissive*] She asked for a cross. A soldier gave her two sticks tied together. Thank God he was an Englishman! I might have done it; but I did not: I am a coward, a mad dog, a fool. But he was an Englishman too.

WARWICK. The fool! they will burn him too if the priests get hold of him.

THE CHAPLAIN [*shaken with a convulsion*] Some of the people laughed at her. They would have laughed at Christ. They were French people, my lord: I know they were French.

WARWICK. Hush? someone is coming. Control yourself.

Ladvenu comes back through the courtyard to War-wick's right hand, carrying a bishop's cross which he has taken from a church. He is very grave and composed.

WARWICK. I am informed that it is all over, Brother Martin.

LADVENU [*enigmatically*] We do not know, my lord. It may have only just begun.

WARWICK. What does that mean, exactly?

LADVENU. I took this cross from the church for her that she might see it to the last: she had only two sticks that she put into her bosom. When the fire crept round us, and she saw that if I held the cross before her I should be burnt myself, she warned me to get down and save myself. My lord: a girl who could think of another's danger in such a moment was not inspired by the devil. When I had to snatch the cross from her sight, she looked up to heaven. And I do not believe that the heavens were empty. I firmly believe that her Savior appeared to her then in His tenderest glory. She called to Him and died. This is not the end for her, but the beginning.

WARWICK. I am afraid it will have a bad effect on the people.

LADVENU. It had, my lord, on some of them. I heard laughter. Forgive me for saying that I hope and believe it was English laughter.

THE CHAPLAIN [*rising frantically*] No: it was not. There was only one Englishman there that disgraced his country; and that was the mad dog, de Stogumber. [*He rushes wildly out, shrieking*] Let them torture him. Let them burn him. I will go pray among her ashes. I am no better than Judas: I will hang myself.

WARWICK. Quick, Brother Martin: follow him: he will do himself some mischief. After him, quick.

Ladvenu hurries out, Warwick urging him. The Executioner comes in by the door behind the judges' chairs; and Warwick, returning, finds himself face to face with him.

WARWICK. Well, fellow: who are you?

THE EXECUTIONER [*with dignity*] I am not addressed as fellow, my lord. I am the Master Executioner of Rouen: it is a highly skilled mystery. I am come to tell your lordship that your orders have been obeyed.

WARWICK. I crave your pardon, Master Executioner; and I will see that you lose nothing by having no relics to sell. I have your word, have I, that nothing remains, not a bone, not a nail, not a hair?

THE EXECUTIONER. Her heart would not burn, my lord; but everything that was left is at the bottom of the river. You have heard the last of her.

WARWICK [*with a wry smile, thinking of what Ladvenu said*] The last of her? Hm! I wonder!

EPILOGUE

A restless fitfully windy night in June 1456, full of summer lightning after many days of heat. King Charles the Seventh of France, formerly Joan's Dauphin, now Charles the Victorious, aged 51, is in bed in one of his royal chateaux. The bed, raised on a dais of two steps, is towards the side of the room so as to avoid blocking a tall lancet window in the middle. Its canopy bears the royal arms in embroidery. Except for the canopy and the huge down pillows there is nothing to distinguish it from a broad settee with bed-clothes and a valance. Thus its occupant is in full view from the foot.

Charles is not asleep: he is reading in bed, or rather looking at the pictures in Fouquet's Boccaccio with his knees doubled up to make a reading desk. Beside the bed on his left is a little table with a picture of the Virgin,

*lighted by candles of painted wax. The walls are hung
from ceiling to floor with painted curtains which stir at
times in the draughts. At first glance the prevailing
yellow and red in these hanging pictures is somewhat
flamelike when the folds breathe in the wind.*

*The door is on Charles's left, but in front of him close
to the corner farthest from him. A large watchman's
rattle, handsomely designed and gaily painted, is in the
bed under his hand.*

*Charles turns a leaf. A distant clock strikes the half-
hour softly. Charles shuts the book with a clap; throws
it aside; snatches up the rattle; and whirls it energetically,
making a deafening clatter. Ladvenu enters, 25 years
older, strange and stark in bearing, and still carrying
the cross from Rouen. Charles evidently does not expect
him; for he springs out of bed on the farther side from
the door.*

CHARLES. Who are you? Where is my gentleman of
the bedchamber? What do you want?

LADVENU [*solemnly*] I bring you glad tidings of great
joy. Rejoice, O king; for the taint is removed from
your blood, and the stain from your crown. Justice,
long delayed, is at last triumphant.

CHARLES. What are you talking about? Who are you?

LADVENU. I am Brother Martin.

CHARLES. And who, saving your reverence, may
Brother Martin be?

LADVENU. I held this cross when The Maid perished
in the fire. Twenty-five years have passed since then:
nearly ten thousand days. And on every one of those
days I have prayed God to justify His daughter on
earth as she is justified in heaven.

CHARLES [*reassured, sitting down on the foot of the bed*]

Oh, I remember now. I have heard of you. You have a bee in your bonnet about The Maid. Have you been at the inquiry?

LADVENU. I have given my testimony.

CHARLES. Is it over?

LADVENU. It is over.

CHARLES. Satisfactorily?

LADVENU. The ways of God are very strange.

CHARLES. How so?

LADVENU. At the trial which sent a saint to the stake as a heretic and a sorceress, the truth was told; the law was upheld; mercy was shewn beyond all custom; no wrong was done but the final and dreadful wrong of the lying sentence and the pitiless fire. At this inquiry from which I have just come, there was shameless perjury, courtly corruption, calumny of the dead who did their duty according to their lights, cowardly evasion of the issue, testimony made of idle tales that could not impose on a ploughboy. Yet out of this insult to justice, this defamation of the Church, this orgy of lying and foolishness, the truth is set in the noonday sun on the hilltop; the white robe of innocence is cleansed from the smirch of the burning faggots; the holy life is sanctified; the true heart that lived through the flame is consecrated; a great lie is silenced for ever; and a great wrong is set right before all men.

CHARLES. My friend: provided they can no longer say that I was crowned by a witch and a heretic, I shall not fuss about how the trick has been done. Joan would not have fussed about it if it came all right in the end: she was not that sort: I knew her. Is her rehabilitation complete? I made it pretty clear that there was to be no nonsense about it.

LADVENU. It is solemnly declared that her judges

were full of corruption, cozenage, fraud, and malice. Four falsehoods.

CHARLES. Never mind the falsehoods: her judges are dead.

LADVENU. The sentence on her is broken, annulled, annihilated, set aside as non-existent, without value or effect.

CHARLES. Good. Nobody can challenge my consecration now, can they?

LADVENU. Not Charlemagne nor King David himself was more sacredly crowned.

CHARLES [*rising*] Excellent. Think of what that means to me!

LADVENU. I think of what it means to her!

CHARLES. You cannot. None of us ever knew what anything meant to her. She was like nobody else; and she must take care of herself wherever she is; for *I* cannot take care of her; and neither can you, whatever you may think: you are not big enough. But I will tell you this about her. If you could bring her back to life, they would burn her again within six months, for all their present adoration of her. And you would hold up the cross, too, just the same. So [*crossing himself*] let her rest; and let you and I mind our own business, and not meddle with hers.

LADVENU. God forbid that I should have no share in her, nor she in me! [*He turns and strides out as he came, saying*] Henceforth my path will not lie through palaces, nor my conversation be with kings.

CHARLES [*following him towards the door, and shouting after him*] Much good may it do you, holy man! [*He returns to the middle of the chamber, where he halts, and says quizzically to himself*] That was a funny chap. How did he get in? Where are my people? [*He goes impatiently to the bed, and swings the rattle. A rush of*

wind through the open door sets the walls swaying agita-
tedly. The candles go out. He calls in the darkness]
Hallo! Someone come and shut the windows: everything is being blown all over the place. [*A flash of*
summer lightning shews up the lancet window. A figure is
seen in silhouette against it] Who is there? Who is
that? Help! Murder! [*Thunder. He jumps into bed,*
and hides under the clothes].

JOAN'S VOICE. Easy, Charlie, easy. What art making
all that noise for? No one can hear thee. Thourt
asleep. [*She is dimly seen in a pallid greenish light by*
the bedside].

CHARLES [*peeping out*] Joan! Are you a ghost, Joan?

JOAN. Hardly even that, lad. Can a poor burnt-up
lass have a ghost? I am but a dream that thourt
dreaming. [*The light increases: they become plainly*
visible as he sits up] Thou looks older, lad.

CHARLES. I am older. Am I really asleep?

JOAN. Fallen asleep over thy silly book.

CHARLES. That's funny.

JOAN. Not so funny as that I am dead, is it?

CHARLES. Are you really dead?

JOAN. As dead as anybody ever is, laddie. I am out of
the body.

CHARLES. Just fancy! Did it hurt much?

JOAN. Did what hurt much?

CHARLES. Being burnt.

JOAN. Oh, that! I cannot remember very well. I
think it did at first; but then it all got mixed up; and
I was not in my right mind until I was free of the body.
But do not thou go handling fire and thinking it will
not hurt thee. How hast been ever since?

CHARLES. Oh, not so bad. Do you know, I actually
lead my army out and win battles? Down into the
moat up to my waist in mud and blood. Up the ladders

with the stones and hot pitch raining down. Like you.

JOAN. No! Did I make a man of thee after all, Charlie?

CHARLES. I am Charles the Victorious now. I had to be brave because you were. Agnes put a little pluck into me too.

JOAN. Agnes! Who was Agnes?

CHARLES. Agnes Sorel. A woman I fell in love with. I dream of her often. I never dreamed of you before.

JOAN. Is she dead, like me?

CHARLES. Yes. But she was not like you. She was very beautiful.

JOAN [*laughing heartily*] Ha ha! I was no beauty: I was always a rough one: a regular soldier. I might almost as well have been a man. Pity I wasnt: I should not have bothered you all so much then. But my head was in the skies; and the glory of God was upon me; and, man or woman, I should have bothered you as long as your noses were in the mud. Now tell me what has happened since you wise men knew no better than to make a heap of cinders of me?

CHARLES. Your mother and brothers have sued the courts to have your case tried over again. And the courts have declared that your judges were full of corruption and cozenage, fraud and malice.

JOAN. Not they. They were as honest a lot of poor fools as ever burned their betters.

CHARLES. The sentence on you is broken, annihilated, annulled: null, non-existent, without value or effect.

JOAN. I was burned, all the same. Can they unburn me?

CHARLES. If they could, they would think twice before they did it. But they have decreed that a beautiful cross be placed where the stake stood, for your perpetual memory and for your salvation.

JOAN. It is the memory and the salvation that sanctify

the cross, not the cross that sanctifies the memory and the salvation. [*She turns away, forgetting him*] I shall outlast that cross. I shall be remembered when men will have forgotten where Rouen stood.

CHARLES. There you go with your self-conceit, the same as ever! I think you might say a word of thanks to me for having had justice done at last.

CAUCHON [*appearing at the window between them*] Liar!

CHARLES. Thank you.

JOAN. Why, if it isnt Peter Cauchon! How are you, Peter? What luck have you had since you burned me?

CAUCHON. None. I arraign the justice of Man. It is not the justice of God.

JOAN. Still dreaming of justice, Peter? See what justice came to with me! But what has happened to thee? Art dead or alive?

CAUCHON. Dead, Dishonored. They pursued me beyond the grave. They excommunicated my dead body: they dug it up and flung it into the common sewer.

JOAN. Your dead body did not feel the spade and the sewer as my live body felt the fire.

CAUCHON. But this thing that they have done against me hurts justice; destroys faith; saps the foundation of the Church. The solid earth sways like the treacherous sea beneath the feet of men and spirits alike when the innocent are slain in the name of law, and their wrongs are undone by slandering the pure of heart.

JOAN. Well, well, Peter, I hope men will be the better for remembering me; and they would not remember me so well if you had not burned me.

CAUCHON. They will be the worse for remembering me: they will see in me evil triumphing over good, falsehood over truth, cruelty over mercy, hell over heaven. Their courage will rise as they think of you, only to faint as they think of me. Yet God is my witness I was just: I was merciful: I was faithful to my light: I could do no other than I did.

CHARLES [*scrambling out of the sheets and enthroning himself on the side of the bed*] Yes: it is always you good men that do the big mischiefs. Look at me! I am not Charles the Good, nor Charles the Wise, not Charles the Bold. Joan's worshippers may even call me Charles the Coward because I did not pull her out of the fire. But I have done less harm than any of you. You people with your heads in the sky spend all your time trying to turn the world upside down; but I take the world as it is, and say that top-side-up is right-side-up; and I keep my nose pretty close to the ground. And I ask you, what king of France has done better, or been a better fellow in his little way?

JOAN. Art really king of France, Charlie? Be the English gone?

DUNOIS [*coming through the tapestry on Joan's left, the candles relighting themselves at the same moment, and illuminating his armor and surcoat cheerfully*] I have kept my word: the English are gone.

JOAN. Praised be God! now is fair France a province in heaven. Tell me all about the fighting, Jack. Was it thou that led them? Wert thou God's captain to thy death?

DUNOIS. I am not dead. My body is very comfortably asleep in my bed at Chateaudun; but my spirit is called here by yours.

JOAN. And you fought them my way, Jack: eh? Not the old way, chaffering for ransoms; but The Maid's way: staking life against death, with the heart high and humble and void of malice, and nothing counting under God but France free and French. Was it my way, Jack?

DUNOIS. Faith, it was any way that would win. But the way that won was always your way. I give you best, lassie. I wrote a fine letter to set you right at the new trial. Perhaps I should never have let the priests burn you; but I was busy fighting; and it was the Church's business, not mine. There was no use in both of us being burned, was there?

CAUCHON. Ay! put the blame on the priests. But I, who am beyond praise and blame, tell you that the world is saved neither by its priests nor its soldiers, but by God and His Saints. The Church Militant sent this woman to the fire; but even as she burned, the flames whitened into the radiance of the Church Triumphant.

The clock strikes the third quarter. A rough male voice is heard trolling an improvised tune.

Rum tum trumpledum,
Bacon fat and rumpledum,
Old Saint mumpledum,
Pull his tail and stumpledum
O my Ma—ry Ann!

A ruffianly English soldier comes through the curtains and marches between Dunois and Joan.

DUNOIS. What villainous troubadour taught you that doggrel?

THE SOLDIER. No troubadour. We made it up our-selves as we marched. We were not gentlefolks and troubadours. Music straight out of the heart of the people, as you might say. Rum tum trumpledum, Bacon fat and rumpledum, Old Saint mumpledum, Pull his tail and stumpledum: that dont mean anything, you know; but it keeps you marching. Your servant, ladies and gentlemen. Who asked for a saint?

JOAN. Be you a saint?

THE SOLDIER. Yes, lady, straight from hell.

DUNOIS. A saint, and from hell!

THE SOLDIER. Yes, noble captain: I have a day off. Every year, you know. Thats my allowance for my one good action.

CAUCHON. Wretch! In all the years of your life did you do only one good action?

THE SOLDIER. I never thought about it: it came natural like. But they scored it up for me.

CHARLES. What was it?

THE SOLDIER. Why, the silliest thing you ever heard of. I—

JOAN [*interrupting him by strolling across to the bed, where she sits beside Charles*] He tied two sticks together, and gave them to a poor lass that was going to be burned.

THE SOLDIER. Right. Who told you that?

JOAN. Never mind. Would you know her if you saw her again?

THE SOLDIER. Not I. There are so many girls! and they all expect you to remember them as if there was only one in the world. This one must have been a prime sort; for I have a day off every year for her; and so, until twelve o'clock punctually, I am a saint, at your service, noble lords and lovely ladies.

CHARLES. And after twelve?

THE SOLDIER. After twelve, back to the only place fit for the likes of me.

JOAN [*rising*] Back there! You! that gave the lass the cross!

THE SOLDIER [*excusing his unsoldierly conduct*] Well, she asked for it; and they were going to burn her. She had as good a right to a cross as they had; and they had dozens of them. It was her funeral, not theirs. Where was the harm in it?

JOAN. Man: I am not reproaching you. But I cannot bear to think of you in torment.

THE SOLDIER [*cheerfully*] No great torment, lady. You see I was used to worse.

CHARLES. What! worse than hell?

THE SOLDIER. Fifteen years' service in the French wars. Hell was a treat after that.

Joan throws up her arms, and takes refuge from despair of humanity before the picture of the Virgin.

THE SOLDIER [*continuing*]—Suits me somehow. The day off was dull at first, like a wet Sunday. I dont mind it so much now. They tell me I can have as many as I like as soon as I want them.

CHARLES. What is hell like?

THE SOLDIER. You wont find it so bad, sir. Jolly. Like as if you were always drunk without the trouble and expense of drinking. Tip top company too: emperors and popes and kings and all sorts. They chip me about giving that young judy the cross; but I dont care: I stand up to them proper, and tell them that if she hadnt a better right to it than they, she'd be where they are. That dumbfounds them, that does. All they can do is gnash their teeth, hell fashion; and I just laugh, and go off singing the old chanty: Rum tum trumple— Hullo! Who's that knocking at the door?

They listen. A long gentle knocking is heard.

CHARLES. Come in.

The door opens; and an old priest, white-haired, bent, with a silly but benevolent smile, comes in and trots over to Joan.

THE NEWCOMER. Excuse me, gentle lords and ladies. Do not let me disturb you. Only a poor old harmless English rector. Formerly chaplain to the cardinal: to my lord of Winchester. John de Stogumber, at your service. [*He looks at them inquiringly*] Did you say anything? I am a little deaf, unfortunately. Also a little—well, not always in my right mind, perhaps; but still, it is a small village with a few simple people. I suffice: I suffice: they love me there; and I am able to do a little good. I am well connected, you see; and they indulge me.

JOAN. Poor old John! What brought thee to this state?

DE STOGUMBER. I tell my folks they must be very careful. I say to them, "If you only saw what you think about you would think quite differently about it. It would give you a great shock. Oh, a great shock." And they all say "Yes, parson: we all know you are a kind man, and would not harm a fly." That is a great comfort to me. For I am not cruel by nature, you know.

THE SOLDIER. Who said you were?

DE STOGUMBER. Well, you see, I did a very cruel thing once because I did not know what cruelty was like. I had not seen it, you know. That is the great thing: you must see it. And then you are redeemed and saved.

CAUCHON. Were not the sufferings of our Lord Christ enough for you?

DE STOGUMBER. No. Oh no: not at all. I had seen them in pictures, and read of them in books, and been greatly moved by them, as I thought. But it was no use: it was not our Lord that redeemed me, but a young woman whom I saw actually burned to death. It was dreadful: oh, most dreadful. But it saved me. I have been a different man ever since, though a little astray in my wits sometimes.

CAUCHON. Must then a Christ perish in torment in every age to save those that have no imagination?

JOAN. Well, if I saved all those he would have been cruel to if he had not been cruel to me, I was not burnt for nothing, was I?

DE STOGUMBER. Oh no; it was not you. My sight is bad: I cannot distinguish your features: but you are not she: oh no: she was burned to a cinder: dead and gone, dead and gone.

THE EXECUTIONER [*stepping from behind the bed curtains on Charles's right, the bed being between them*] She is more alive than you, old man. Her heart would not burn; and it would not drown. I was a master at my craft: better than the master of Paris, better than the master of Toulouse; but I could not kill The Maid. She is up and alive everywhere.

THE EARL OF WARWICK [*sallying from the bed curtains on the other side, and coming to Joan's left hand*] Madam: my congratulations on your rehabilitation. I feel that I owe you an apology.

JOAN. Oh, please dont mention it.

WARWICK [*pleasantly*] The burning was purely political. There was no personal feeling against you, I assure you.

JOAN. I bear no malice, my lord.

WARWICK. Just so. Very kind of you to meet me in that way: a touch of true breeding. But I must insist on apologizing very amply. The truth is, these political necessities sometimes turn out to be political mistakes; and this one was a veritable howler; for your spirit conquered us, madam, in spite of our faggots. History will remember me for your sake, though the incidents of the connection were perhaps a little unfortunate.

JOAN. Ay, perhaps just a little, you funny man.

WARWICK. Still, when they make you a saint, you will owe your halo to me, just as this lucky monarch owes his crown to you.

JOAN [*turning from him*] I shall owe nothing to any man: I owe everything to the spirit of God that was within me. But fancy me a saint! What would St Catherine and St Margaret say if the farm girl was cocked up beside them!

A clerical-looking gentleman in black frockcoat and trousers, and tall hat, in the fashion of the year 1920, suddenly appears before them in the corner on their right. They all stare at him. Then they burst into uncontrollable laughter.

THE GENTLEMAN. Why this mirth, gentlemen?

WARWICK. I congratulate you on having invented a most extraordinarily comic dress.

THE GENTLEMAN. I do not understand. You are all in fancy dress: I am properly dressed.

DUNOIS. All dress is fancy dress, is it not, except our natural skins?

THE GENTLEMAN. Pardon me: I am here on serious business, and cannot engage in frivolous discussions. [*He takes out a paper, and assumes a dry official manner*]. I am sent to announce to you that Joan of Arc, formerly known as The Maid, having been the subject of an inquiry instituted by the Bishop of Orleans—

JOAN [*interrupting*] Ah! They remember me still in Orleans.

THE GENTLEMAN [*emphatically, to mark his indignation at the interruption*]—by the Bishop of Orleans into the claim of the said Joan of Arc to be canonized as a saint—

JOAN [*again interrupting*] But I never made any such claim.

THE GENTLEMAN [*as before*]—the Church has examined the claim exhaustively in the usual course, and, having admitted the said Joan successively to the ranks of Venerable and Blessed,—

JOAN [*chuckling*] Me venerable!

THE GENTLEMAN.—has finally declared her to have been endowed with heroic virtues and favoured with private revelations, and calls the said Venerable and Blessed Joan to the communion of the Church Triumphant as Saint Joan.

JOAN [*rapt*] Saint Joan!

THE GENTLEMAN. On every thirtieth day of May, being the anniversary of the death of the said most blessed daughter of God, there shall in every Catholic church to the end of time be celebrated a special office in commemoration of her; and it shall be lawful to dedicate a special chapel to her, and to place her image on its altar in every such church. And it shall be lawful and laudable for the faithful to kneel and address their prayers through her to the Mercy Seat.

JOAN. Oh no. It is for the saint to kneel. [*She falls on her knees, still rapt*].

THE GENTLEMAN [*putting up his paper, and retiring beside the Executioner*] In Basilica Vaticana, the sixteenth day of May, nineteen hundred and twenty.

DUNOIS [*raising Joan*] Half an hour to burn you, dear Saint: and four centuries to find out the truth about you!

DE STOGUMBER. Sir: I was chaplain to the Cardinal of Winchester once. They always would call him the Cardinal of England. It would be a great comfort to me and to my master to see a fair statue to The Maid in Winchester Cathedral. Will they put one there, do you think?

THE GENTLEMAN. As the building is temporarily in the hands of the Anglican heresy, I cannot answer for that.

A vision of the statue in Winchester Cathedral is seen through the window.

DE STOGUMBER. Oh look! look! that is Winchester.

JOAN. Is that meant to be me? I was stiffer on my feet.

The vision fades.

THE GENTLEMAN. I have been requested by the temporal authorities of France to mention that the multiplication of public statues to The Maid threatens to become an obstruction to traffic. I do so as a matter of courtesy to the said authorities, but must point out on behalf of the Church that The Maid's horse is no greater obstruction to traffic than any other horse.

JOAN. Eh! I am glad they have not forgotten my horse.

A vision of the statue before Rheims Cathedral appears.

JOAN. Is that funny little thing me too?

CHARLES. That is Rheims Cathedral where you had me crowned. It must be you.

JOAN. Who has broken my sword? My sword was never broken. It is the sword of France.

DUNOIS. Never mind. Swords can be mended. Your soul is unbroken; and you are the soul of France.

The vision fades. The Archbishop and the Inquisitor are now seen on the right and left of Cauchon.

JOAN. My sword shall conquer yet: the sword that never struck a blow. Though men destroyed my body, yet in my soul I have seen God.

CAUCHON [*kneeling to her*] The girls in the field praise thee; for thou hast raised their eyes; and they see that there is nothing between them and heaven.

DUNOIS [*kneeling to her*] The dying soldiers praise thee, because thou art a shield of glory between them and the judgment.

THE ARCHBISHOP [*kneeling to her*] The princes of the Church praise thee, because thou hast redeemed the faith their worldlinesses have dragged through the mire.

WARWICK [*kneeling to her*] The cunning counsellors praise thee, because thou hast cut the knots in which they have tied their own souls.

DE STOGUMBER [*kneeling to her*] The foolish old men on their deathbeds praise thee, because their sins against thee are turned into blessings.

THE INQUISITOR [*kneeling to her*] The judges in the blindness and bondage of the law praise thee, because thou hast vindicated the vision and the freedom of the living soul.

THE SOLDIER [*kneeling to her*] The wicked out of hell praise thee, because thou hast shewn them that the fire that is not quenched is a holy fire.

THE EXECUTIONER [*kneeling to her*] The tormentors and executioners praise thee, because thou hast shewn that their hands are guiltless of the death of the soul.

CHARLES [*kneeling to her*] The unpretending praise thee, because thou hast taken upon thyself the heroic burdens that are too heavy for them.

JOAN. Woe unto me when all men praise me! I bid you remember that I am a saint, and that saints can work miracles. And now tell me: shall I rise from the dead, and come back to you a living woman?

A sudden darkness blots out the walls of the room as they all spring to their feet in consternation. Only the figures and the bed remain visible.

JOAN. What! Must I burn again? Are none of you ready to receive me?

CAUCHON. The heretic is always better dead. And mortal eyes cannot distinguish the saint from the heretic. Spare them. [*He goes out as he came*].

DUNOIS. Forgive us, Joan: we are not yet good enough for you. I shall go back to my bed. [*He also goes*].

WARWICK. We sincerely regret our little mistake; but political necessities, though occasionally erroneous, are still imperative; so if you will be good enough to excuse me— [*He steals discreetly away*].

THE ARCHBISHOP. Your return would not make me the man you once thought me. The utmost I can say is that though I dare not bless you, I hope I may one day enter into your blessedness. Meanwhile, however— [*He goes*].

THE INQUISITOR. I who am of the dead, testified that day that you were innocent. But I do not see how The Inquisition could possibly be dispensed with under existing circumstances. Therefore— [*He goes*].

DE STOGUMBER. Oh, do not come back: you must not come back. I must die in peace. Give us peace in our time, O Lord! [*He goes*].

THE GENTLEMAN. The possibility of your resurrection was not contemplated in the recent proceedings for your canonization. I must return to Rome for fresh instructions. [*He bows formally, and withdraws*].

THE EXECUTIONER. As a master in my profession I have to consider its interests. And, after all, my first duty is to my wife and children. I must have time to think over this. [*He goes*].

CHARLES. Poor old Joan! They have all run away from you except this blackguard who has to go back to hell at twelve o'clock. And what can I do but follow Jack Dunois' example, and go back to bed too ? [*He does so*].

JOAN [*sadly*] Goodnight, Charlie.

CHARLES [*mumbling in his pillows*] Goo ni. [*He sleeps. The darkness envelops the bed*].

JOAN [*to the soldier*] And you, my one faithful ? What comfort have you for Saint Joan ?

THE SOLDIER. Well, what do they all amount to, these kings and captains and bishops and lawyers and such like ? They just leave you in the ditch to bleed to death; and the next thing is, you meet them down there, for all the airs they give themselves. What I say is, you have as good a right to your notions as they have to theirs, and perhaps better. [*Settling himself for a lecture on the subject*] You see, it's like this. If— [*the first stroke of midnight is heard softly from a distant bell*]. Excuse me: a pressing appointment— [*He goes on tiptoe*].

The last remaining rays of light gather into a white radiance descending on Joan. The hour continues to strike.

JOAN. O God that madest this beautiful earth, when will it be ready to receive Thy saints ? How long, O Lord, how long ?

Statement to
New York Theatre Audiences

(Written 3 January 1924 for the Theatre Guild, but
not released to the Press. First published in *Life
Magazine*, New York, 22 October 1951)

As there seems to be some misunderstanding in the
New York press of my intention in writing Saint Joan,
I had better make myself quite clear. I am supposed
to have set myself the task of providing the playgoing
public with a pleasant theatrical entertainment whilst
keeping the working hours of the professional critics
within their customary limits; and it is accordingly
suggested that I can improve the play vastly by cutting off a sufficient length from it to enable the curtain
to rise at half past eight and descend finally at ten
minutes to eleven. Certainly nothing could be easier.
In the popular entertainment business, if your cradle
is too short for your baby, you can always cut down
your baby to fit the cradle.

But I am not in the popular entertainment business.
The sort of entertainment provided by the fate of
Joan of Arc seems to be quite sufficiently looked after
in the United States by the Ku-Klux Klan, and is all
the more entertaining for being the real thing instead
of a stage show.

As to the grievance of the professional critics, I,
as an ex-critic, understand it only too well. It is a
hideous experience for a critic, when at half past ten
he has all the material for a good long notice, and is
longing to get back to his newspaper office and write it
at comparative leisure, to be forced to sit for another
hour by that rival artist the author, until all the leisure
is gone and nothing but a hurried scramble to feed the

clamoring compositors is possible. But the remedy for that is, not to demand that the play shall be mutilated for the convenience of a score or two of gentlemen who see it as their breadwinning job on the first night only but to combine as other professional men do, and establish the custom of beginning plays of full classical length an hour earlier on the first night.

So much for the negative side of the situation. As to the positive side, I am, like all educated persons, intensely interested, and to some extent conscience stricken, by the great historical case of Joan of Arc. I know that many others share that interest and that compunction, and that they would eagerly take some trouble to have it made clear to them how it all happened. I conceive such a demonstration to be an act of justice for which the spirit of Joan, yet incarnate among us, is still calling. Every step in such a demonstration is intensely interesting to me; and the real protagonists of the drama, the Catholic Church, the Holy Roman Empire, and the nascent Reformation, appeal to my imagination and my intellect with a grip and fascination far beyond those of Dick Dudgeon and General Burgoyne. When in the face of that claim of a great spirit for justice, and of a world situation in which we see whole peoples perishing and dragging us towards the abyss which has swallowed them all for want of any grasp of the political forces that move civilizations, I am met with peevish complaints that three hours or so is too long, and with petitions to cut the cackle and come to the burning, and promises that if I adapt the play to the outlook and tastes and capacities of the purblind people who have made the word suburban a derisive epithet, it will run for eighteen months and make a fortune for me and the Theatre Guild, the effect is to make me seem ten feet high and these poor people ten inches, which is bad for my soul, and not particularly healthy for theirs.

In theatres as elsewhere, people must learn to know their places. When a man goes to church and does not like the service nor understand the doctrine, he does not ask to have it changed to suit him: he goes elsewhere until he is suited. When he goes to a classical concert and is bored by Beethoven, he does not scream to the conductor for a fox trot, and suggest that Beethoven should introduce a saxophone solo into the Ninth Symphony: he goes to the nearest hall where a jazz band is at work. I plead for equally reasonable behaviour in the theatre. Saint Joan is not for connoisseurs of the police and divorce drama, or of the languors and lilies and roses and raptures of the cinema; and it is not going to be altered to suit them. It is right over their heads, and they must either grow up to it or let it alone. Fortunately for me, it interests and even enthralls serious people who would not enter an ordinary theatre if they were paid to, and draws novices who have never crossed the threshold of a theatre in their lives, and were taught by their parents that it is the threshold of hell. And the class of intelligent and cultivated playgoers whose neglected needs have brought the Theatre Guild into existence, naturally jump at it.

However, even at the risk of a comprehensive insult to the general public of New York, I must add that the limitation of the audience to serious, intelligent, and cultivated Americans means that Saint Joan must be regarded for the present as an Exceptional Play for Exceptional People. It has cost a good deal to produce it for them, and is costing a good deal to keep the opportunity open. This will not matter if they seize the opportunity promptly with a sense that if they do not, they will miss it, and discourage the Guild from future public spirited enterprises of this class. The solvency of a play depends not only on the number of persons who pay to witness it, but on the length of time over which their attendances are spread. Even a million enthusiasts will not help if they arrive at the rate of ten per week. A thousand can do a great deal if they do it in two days. Saint Joan's present prosperity cannot in the nature of things last many months. Those who come early and come often are the pillars of the sort of play that gives you something to take home with you.

G.B.S.

Note by the Author

(From the programme of the New Theatre, London, 26 March 1924)

For the convenience of professional critics, and the satisfaction of the general interest in Saint Joan, I had better point out how far the play this evening will depart from historical facts. It does not depart from ascertainable historical truth in any essential particular; but historical facts cannot be put on the stage exactly as they occurred, because they will not fit into its limits of time and space.

The visit of Joan to the castle of Vaucouleurs, and her conquest of its captain, occupy about twenty minutes on the stage. Actually she made three visits, before she carried her point with him. The apparent miracle which impressed him was the news of the Battle of Herrings. Joan learnt this from the mouth to mouth wireless of the peasantry. She was therefore able to tell him what had happened several days before the news reached him by the official routine of mounted messenger. This seemed to him miraculous. A much simpler form of miracle has been substituted in the play to save tedious and unnecessary explanations.

Joan's second adventure: the visit to Chinon and the conquest of the Dauphin, has been compressed in the same way. Actually, Joan was received after days of hesitation, and sent to Poitiers to be examined by a body of Churchmen there before she was sent with reinforcements to Orleans. The miracles of the drowned blasphemer and the change of wind on the Loire are historical.

Joan's unconscious confessions of heresy at her trial, her recantation, her relapse, and her execution, occupied several days. On the stage they occupy forty minutes; but nothing essential is misrepresented; and nothing is omitted except the adjournments and matters irrelevant to the final issue.

The Epilogue is obviously not a representation of an actual scene, or even of a recorded dream; but it is none the less historical. Without it the play would be only a sensational tale of a girl who was burnt, leaving the spectators plunged in horror, despairing of humanity. The true tale of Saint Joan is a tale with a glorious ending; and any play that did not make this clear would be an insult to her memory.

But this play is more likely to puzzle by its conflict with current fictions about Saint Joan than by its adaptation of facts to the stage. In any generally accessible work of reference, and in such well known books as those by Mark Twain and Andrew Lang, it is stated that Joan's trial was corrupt, her judges scoundrels, and the questions put to her devised to trap her into fatal admissions. For these slanders of the Church and the Inquisition there is not a shred of evidence in the records of the trial. Joan's judges were as straightforward as Joan herself: and the law took its regular course. She was burnt for heresy because she was guided by her inner light to the position taken two hundred years later by the Society of Friends, for which women were judicially flogged mercilessly at the instance of the Church of England, and would have been burnt had they been Joan's contemporaries. Her insistence on wearing male attire is still a punishable offence. The opinion of the court that her visions were temptations of the devil was quite sincere. Like all prisoners of war, Joan was tried by her political enemies instead of by an impartial international tribunal; but a medieval Catholic court was far more impartial than a modern national one. How violently the English were prejudiced against her may be seen in the scurrilous popular representation of her in the XVI century play of Henry VI (supposed to have been touched up by Shakespeare); but it was not an English court that excommunicated her; and she would have been burnt equally if the Hundred Years War in France had been a purely civil one. Not until the Church privileged her private judgment and classed her visions and her inner light as celestial by canonizing her in 1904–1920 was the verdict of 1431 really reversed. Thus it cannot be too clearly understood that there were no villains in the tragedy of Joan's death. She was entirely innocent; but her excommunication was a genuine act of faith and piety; and her execution followed inevitably.

All the characters in the play are historical to the extent that they bear the names of persons who actually existed in Joan's time and were concerned with her as represented. But the information we have about them varies from such comparatively documented lives as those of Charles, Dunois, and Warwick, to that of Chaplain de Stogumber, who is known only by his having lost his temper and called Cauchon a traitor for accepting Joan's recantation. His Devonshire name is borrowed for the occasion. The English soldier represents a cherished tradition if not an authentic fact.

Several of the speeches and sallies in the play, especially those of Joan, are historical; and some of them may possibly sound like modern jokes; for instance, her use of the word *godons* (God damns) to denote English soldiers. One or two speeches have been transposed for stage purposes; and it has been assumed that the military conversation of Dunois may safely be founded on that of his colleague the Duc d'Alençon, who does not appear in the play.

To the more romantic spectators I must break the news that though Joan inspired strong likes and dislikes, and was not at all badlooking, she had no love affairs. There is overwhelming testimony that her complete neutrality in this respect was accepted as evidence of her divine mission by her soldier comrades.

No portrait of Joan was made to her knowledge; but a St. Maurice sculptured at Orleans by an artist who presumably saw her is so extraordinary, being obviously a portrait and yet stranger in its impressiveness and the spacing of its features than any ideal head, that it can be accounted for only as an image of a very singular woman; and no other such woman than Joan is discoverable.

G. BERNARD SHAW

The Epilogue to " St Joan "
(A letter to the Editor of *The Spectator*,
London, 21 February 1925)

Sir,—I need not say anything about Mrs Kimball's
complaint in your issue of January 31st (which has
reached me a little late in Madeira), except that the
epilogue is incidentally useful as what impolite people
call a Foolometer, a term which I allow myself to use,
with apologies to Mrs. Kimball, only for the sake of
brevity.

The truth is, I am using her letter as an excuse for
calling attention to a point in the critical reception of
the epilogue which has surprised me. In the story of
St. Joan the tradition that a common English soldier
tied two sticks together and gave them to her, and
that she died with that cross in her bosom, has always
seemed to me so heroic, and so redemptive of the
otherwise unrelieved ferocity of our share in the
tragedy, that I innocently supposed my feeling about
it to be a general possession and consolation in no
way peculiar to myself. Mr. Chesterton, who hyper-
bolically made the soldier break his spear, seemed to
me to voice the national sentiment. It never occurred
to me that it would be possible to tell Joan's story on
the stage and leave that soldier out. Of course, he
understood the historical situation too well to believe
that any of Stafford's or Warwick's men-at-arms,
under the eye of their commanders and of the Church
dared have combined mutiny with heresy by such an
act; and I also know my business as a playwright too
well to suppose that it could be effectively and credibly
exhibited on the stage. Nevertheless it was clear that
the soldier must have his part as the hero of that
frightful scene.

This consideration alone, I should have thought, would have justified the epilogue, even if those which I thought it necessary to mention in my note in the playbill had not existed.

To my astonishment none of my critics attached the smallest importance to the soldier; and most of them, when they mentioned him at all, seemed to regard him as a silly invention of my own. I gasped, and demanded of my soul whether this was the ignorance of utter illiteracy or a hopeless degeneration of the English spirit. I do not find Mrs. Kimball very reassuring.

Perhaps if I were to rewrite the play, making Joan and the soldier playmates, and child lovers at the beginning, with a long separation, and then, on that fatal day, a thrilling recognition by the Maid of her old love in the Earl of Warwick, the Earl could fling her his cross-hilted sword, and the two together could sweep the wretched foreigners from the field (Cauchon and the Inquisitor incidentally perishing in the flames), and marry and live happily ever after. Joan as Countess of Warwick would please those who feel that in my present version she is hardly a lady; and the advantage of making the soldier an Earl instead of a common blackguard, with all the stains of that miserable war on his soul, is obvious.

Only, it might turn out that the inarticulate British playgoer, with all his faults, is more faithful to a heroic tradition than the professional playgoer who prints his opinions.—I am, Sir, &c.,

G. BERNARD SHAW

[Our readers may have forgotten that in our issue of January 31st Mrs. Kimball protested against the epilogue as a "perfectly appalling" ending to the play. She said that all the impressions of three enchanted hours were for her wantonly destroyed by Mr. Shaw himself. Mr. Shaw, however, need not defend his soldier against us. The soldier is not only one of the most moving persons in a great play but he is also true to kind. That must be clear to anyone who knows the rank and file of our Army. If the tale of the soldier's two sticks is only a legend, the inventor knew his subject.—Ed. *Spectator*.]

Saint Joan: A Radio Talk

(BBC broadcast talk, delivered on the five hundredth anniversary of the burning of Joan of Arc, 30 May 1931. First published in *The Listener*, London, 3 June 1931)

I have promised to give a chat here tonight about that very extraordinary young woman who was burnt 500 years ago. Now, when I say that I promised to give a chat, I really mean that. I am playing the game quite strictly with you. I have not got a manuscript, mostly copied out of the *Encyclopaedia Britannica*, to read solemnly to you giving all the historical details about Joan of Arc. I am sitting here in London quite comfortably, and I shall say anything about her that comes into my head, quite obviously.

You know, of course, that Joan of Arc was a young girl who was burnt. But I want you to get that out of your head; it is not really a matter of very great consequence to us now, the particular way in which she died, and the fact that she was burnt does not distinguish her at all, and does not explain why we are talking about her here tonight, although hundreds of thousands of women have been burnt, just as she was burnt, and yet they are quite forgotten and nobody talks about them.

It was not that she was young, because after the Bull of Pope Innocent VIII, which began the burning of witches (and Joan was burnt because she was a witch), young girls were burnt; but also young children were burnt; quite beautiful young children were thrown into the flames. All that you read. She is only one of a great many people.

There is a parallel case really to Joan's which is very well known throughout all Christendom, and that is the case of the Founder of Christianity Himself, and I sometimes have to remind people that a belief in Christianity does not mean getting very excited in a sensational way about the very horrible way in which the Founder of Christianity was executed. I think of all the hymns in the English Hymnal the one that I dislike the most is "When I survey the wondrous Cross". When people sing that I always feel inclined to say, "Will you please stop surveying the wondrous Cross, which is not an emblem of Christianity but an emblem of what the Romans called justice, a very cruel, unchristian and horrible thing, and I am sorry to say that we still call exactly the same sort of thing justice". Not very long before Jesus Christ was crucified 60,000 persons were crucified because they had revolted against their conditions as slaves and gladiators, and they all suffered in the same way that Jesus suffered. And, therefore, in talking of people like Joan and of Jesus Christ you must not think of Jesus Christ as the Crucified one, because there were a great many crucified ones, and the two who were crucified with Him were not persons of very respectable character.

What we have to consider then is, simply, what

manner of persons these executed people were that we should, 500 years and 1,900 years after their execution, be still talking about them. And I want particularly to insist on this in the case of Joan, because people think it is such a romantic thing to be burnt, and to be a young woman being burnt, that they begin to insist on the young woman being a beautiful young woman and they begin to imagine that she must have had some very touching and charming love-affairs in her life. Now, I am sorry to disappoint those of my hearers who have that particular romantic turn, but it is a perfectly well-established fact that Joan was not beautiful. It is not merely that people have not mentioned whether she was beautiful or not, but it has been placed on record by her military comrades, by the officers with whom she worked in battle and also by the men, who adored her and believed her to be something divine. These officers liked her very much, always remembered her with affection as a comrade, and the men, as I have said, worshipped her; but they all expressly—those of them whose testimony we have still got—explicitly said that the reason, or one of the reasons, why they believed her to be divine was that, although she was a woman, she had none of what our American friends in Hollywood and elsewhere call "sex appeal". She was outside that. They felt towards her as they felt towards the Saints and towards the Blessed Virgin; but all that romantic kind of thing was out of the way, was a thing almost blasphemous. And so you must make up your minds to Joan of Arc as being a person who was not beautiful, who was not romantic, but who, as I said, was a very extraordinary person.

Now, she was burned by a Christian Tribunal. You hear people occasionally discussing whether the

French burned her or whether the English burned
her and who was to blame in the matter. You need not
worry about that. The really significant thing for us
today is that she was burnt by a Tribunal which represented Christianity in the world. She was burnt by a
Catholic Tribunal, one which at that time really represented the whole Christian feeling of the world. And,
furthermore, they gave her a very long, a very careful,
and a very conscientious trial; they found her guilty on
all the counts of the indictment that was made against
her, and she was guilty on every one of those counts
according to the ideas of those people, and, I may say,
probably according to the ideas of a great many of
you ladies and gentlemen whom I am now addressing.
She was found guilty of heresy; she was found guilty
of witchcraft; she was found guilty of homicidal
soldiering, which was a horrible sin for a woman; and
she was found guilty of a blasphemous habit of wearing men's attire, which also was considered a very
grave and frightful thing for a woman to do. But I
may say that the reason it was called blasphemous
was, that she not only wore men's dress and insisted
on wearing it, but she said that she had been ordered
to do it by St. Margaret and by St. Catherine, and
that was an appalling blasphemy in those days, and I
think it may possibly shock one or two of those whom
I am now addressing.

You cannot deny that all these accusations were
true accusations. To begin with the heresy. At a time
when the whole world was Catholic and when the
Reformation had not yet taken place, she was a
Protestant; that is to say, she said that God came first
with her. He came before the Church; and when she
was asked, "Will you not accept the Church's interpretation of God for you?" she said, "No; God must

come first". That was heresy. That was about the most shocking thing that could be said to a true Catholic by a true Catholic. And she said this quite naturally. She was not a person who had studied the works of Wycliffe or any of the early Reformers or their precursors. She said that as a mere obvious matter of course. She was so ignorant of the fact that she was a Protestant—she had never heard the word— that she actually proposed to go and lead a Crusade against the Bohemian Protestants, against the follow- ers of John Huss—as we call them, Hussites; and she was quite ready to lead a Crusade to fight and suppress those people, not knowing that she herself was utter- ing precisely the thing for which the Church had quarrelled with them. They tried her quite mercifully, they did everything they possibly could when they were trying her to get her to take that back; they implored her to consider what she was saying, but she did not realise herself its gravity; it seemed to her to be the perfectly natural thing. She could not under- stand that the 'men of the Church', as she spoke of them, rather slightingly, although she was such a devout Catholic, as she believed—she could not under- stand how anybody could propose to come between her and God. In that way she was guilty of heresy, in a manner of speaking the most shocking heresy, the most terrible thing that you could be guilty of in those days, the crime for which people were burnt; and it was that mainly for which she was burnt.

Furthermore, she was guilty of witchcraft in the sense of the Tribunal before which she was standing, because she declared that her inspiration had been conveyed to her by voices and by visions. In particular, there were three saints—St. Catherine, St. Margaret, and St. Michael—and these, she said, visited her,

spoke to her, told her what to do, and she undoubtedly honestly believed that these voices that
came to her did come from these saints. Now, the
main sin of witchcraft in these days was having intercourse with spirits, and the Church told her that
those spirits were evil spirits come to tempt her to
damnation. As I have just told you, she said that one
of the things that they told her to do was to dress like
a man, and furthermore, to take a sword and go and
slay men, and to take part in war. In saying that, in
claiming it proudly as being her justification, she was
condemning herself to execution for the crime of
witchcraft. There was no question of trapping her
into these admissions. They did not try to trap her.
On the contrary, they really did their best, as you
will find, if you read the accounts of the trial; they
did all that could be expected of them to make her
withdraw them. But she was perfectly steadfast in
these statements.

As for the soldiering, that was considered a dreadful thing for a woman to undertake; and I think we
who are now speaking to one another may say that it
is a shocking thing to think of a woman going out to
kill, and risking being killed; I happen to think that
it is an equally shocking thing for a man to do, and
perhaps some of you will agree with me. But there
are certain people who have the misfortune to be
born with a talent for soldiering, and there is no doubt
that Joan was an inveterate soldier. Whenever there
was a battle within her reach Joan got into the thick
of it. She fought as a company officer; when her men
were flinching or faltering she threw herself into
battle, she led them into danger, right up to the
danger point. When they were storming a fort she
was the first officer at the fort wall and made them

come after her. Even when her battles had been successful, to such a point that many of the statesmen and soldiers of her time wanted to stop the fighting, she wanted to go on with it, and, as I told you, even when there was no more fighting to be done in France, she was looking forward to having some more fighting in Bohemia, by conducting a Crusade against the Hussites in that country.

I have already spoken to you about the male attire. So that you see on these counts—heresy, witchcraft, homicidal soldiering, male attire—Joan was guilty. If you consider that sort of conduct guilty, she was unquestionably and on her own confession guilty. She was accordingly sentenced to be burnt to death, that being the usual punishment, the allotted punishment, by the custom of the time, and practically by the rules of the Inquisition, because although the Catholic Church and the Inquisition would not kill anybody directly, they nevertheless handed the condemned person over to what they called the secular arm—that is to say, the military or the civil power—knowing perfectly well the result would be that the person would be burnt to death.

On that particular point of the burning, I want to remind you of one thing. Joan chose to be burnt. She could have escaped being burnt. She tried to escape being burnt by recanting. When they told her that she would be burnt if she persisted, she then said, very well, she did not want to be burnt; she was a very sensible kind of woman and she said, 'Since you say so, I do not want to be burnt; I will take it all back and I will sign a recantation'. She signed a recantation and then it became impossible to burn her. But when she learned that she was not going to be set free, but that she was to be condemned to perpetual imprisonment, she then deliberately withdrew her recantation; she put on her man's dress again, she reaffirmed that her voices, her saints, were saints and not devils, and that she was going to obey their instructions; she relapsed, as they called it, completely into her heresy, and by her own deliberate choice was burnt instead of being perpetually imprisoned. Now, I recommend that to all of you who are listening to me; because in almost all your criminal codes, here in England, in America, in Italy, in France, we are always condemning people for crimes to this very punishment of imprisonment, of long terms of imprisonment, sometimes of solitary imprisonment, and in that we are using a crueller punishment than burning, according to the judgment of this woman who had her open choice between the two. That is something for you to think about. I will not dwell any more on it.

Now let me say a word as to Joan's life and her abilities. She was, unquestionably, an exceptionally and extraordinarily able woman. She was a farmer's daughter, with no special advantages of education. She could not read and she could not write, although she could dictate letters and did. She had, unquestionably, military ability. In her campaign, the campaign by which she brought King Charles to the throne, she knew exactly what to do at the time when the military commanders of her time were muddling, were hesitating, were wasting their forces in all directions. She concentrated them, she knew how to make soldiers fight, which they did not; she made them fight, she made them conquer soldiers by whom they were accustomed to be conquered. She had great political ability. She saw exactly what was needed to strike the imagination of the French people in getting the Dauphin crowned in the cathedral at Rheims, and she fought her way and made him fight his way to that cathedral and that place, and saw that he was consecrated with the holy oil. She knew that that was the way in which you could swing the political feeling in France to his side as being the anointed King. She had tremendous parliamentary ability. Her trial was a very long business, in which she had to discuss, dispute, argue, and debate with very clever persons. And there she was in a very desperate situation, as she very well knew, and she held her own with all of them.

The trial is very curious. It is not so much the trial of judges who are speaking from the height of their position to a culprit. The whole thing became something like a parliamentary argument, of which she very often got the best, or the better. I cannot elaborate that because my time has drawn to an end. I want only to tell you this: that although the burning of Joan was an inexcusable thing, because it was a uselessly cruel thing, the question arises whether she was not a dangerous woman.

That question arises with almost every person of distinguished or extraordinary ability. Let us take an example from our own times. After the late war the late Marshal Foch was asked by somebody, 'How would Napoleon have fought this war?' Foch answered, 'Oh! he would have fought it magnificently, superbly. But', he said, 'what on earth should we have done with him afterwards?' Now, that question arose in Joan's case. I want to bring it close to the present day. It is arising today in the case of a very extraordinary man, a man whose name is Leon Trotsky. Leon Trotsky's military exploits will probably rank with those of the greatest commanders in future history. The history of Trotsky's train—the railway train in which for a couple of years he practically lived while he threw back the whole forces of Europe, at a time when the condition of his country seemed desperate—that was a military exploit which we are too close to appreciate, but there is no doubt whatever as to what history will say about him; it will rank him along with the greatest commanders. But he is just in the position of Napoleon: when the question arose what was to be done with him afterwards, his own country, Russia, banished him. They banished him to a place at first very much like St. Helena, which we put Napoleon into because we believed it would kill him, and it did kill him. Trotsky was put in a very unpleasant place. He is now in Turkey, under happier circumstances. But the question arises there. We are all very much afraid of him: we dare not allow him to come to England, not so much because we are afraid of him making war here, but because his own country is so afraid of him that we feel that any hospitality that we extended to him would be almost interpreted as an attack on the Russian Government. You may think of Trotsky as being a sort of male St. Joan, in his day, who has not been burnt. You may connect him, again, as I say, with Napoleon. You will have to think it all out for yourself because I have no time here tonight to go into it. I have already exceeded my time.

I will just give you one more thing to think about. If you want to have an example from your own time, if you want to find what women can feel when they suddenly find the whole power of society marshalled against them and they have to fight it, as it were, then read a very interesting book which has just appeared by Miss Sylvia Pankhurst describing what women did in the early part of this century in order to get the parliamentary vote. Miss Sylvia Pankhurst, like so many other women in that movement, was tortured. In fact, except for burning, she suffered actual physical torture which Joan was spared. Other women suffered in that way with her. She describes from her own experience what those women felt, and how they did it. They were none of them exactly like St. Joan, but I believe every one of them did regard herself as, in a measure, repeating the experiences of St. Joan. St. Joan inspired that movement, that curious movement, which I think is within the recollection of most of you. Think of it in that way. If you read Miss Pankhurst, you will understand a great deal more about the psychology of Joan, and her position at the trial, than you will by reading the historical accounts, which are very dry.

I say one thing finally. Joan was killed by the Inquisition. The Inquisition, you think, is dead. The Inquisition is not dead. Whenever you have a form of government which cannot deal with spiritual affairs, sooner or later you will have the Inquisition. In England it was said there was no Inquisition. That was not true. It was called by another name—it was called 'Star Chamber'; but you always will have a spiritual tribunal of some kind, and unless it is an organised and recognised thing, with a body of law behind it, it will become a secret thing, and a very terrible thing; it will have all the worst qualities of the Inquisition without that subjection to a body of law which the Inquisition finally had. And when in modern times you fall behindhand with your political institutions, as we are doing, and try to get on with a parliamentary institution which is entirely unfitted to modern needs, you get dictatorships, as you have got in Hungary, and in Italy, and—I need not go through the whole list—as you may have at any moment almost in any country, because, as Signor Mussolini has so well said, there is a vacant throne in almost every country in Europe; and when you get your dictatorship you may take it from me that you will with the greatest certainty get a secret tribunal, dealing with sedition, with political heresy, exactly like the Inquisition.

That is all I can say to you tonight. I have not, I am aware, said the conventional thing, or said the historical thing. Well, you can read that. You will find it told very often in a very dull way. I have only spoken here because the whole value of Joan to us is how you can bring her and her circumstances into contact with our life and our circumstances. Now, the British Broadcasting Corporation is in a state of great impatience because I have already stolen nearly ten minutes. I should have taken twenty minutes; I have taken half an hour. Just like me, isn't it? Good night.

Shaw Unperturbed by Immortality

(Replies to a questionnaire by Leslie Rees after *Saint Joan* had been singled out overwhelmingly in a symposium by representative theatre people on "what play of the last ten years will survive in 1984." *The Era*, London, 10 January 1934)

A large number of critics, actors, managers and producers chose "Saint Joan" as the play of 1923–33 that they consider worthy to be a classic in 1984. Which play would you have chosen? If one of your own, would it have been "Saint Joan"—or another?

G. B. S.—These speculations do not interest me: I know how futile they are. My hope is that in 1984 all our plays will be as ridiculously behind the times as "London Assurance" and "Money" are now. But historical plays are in a special category. They last a long time because great actors and actresses have very few one-part plays to choose from. It is quite likely that sixty years hence, every great English and American actress will have a shot at "St. Joan" just as every great actor will have a shot at "Hamlet" or Lytton's "Richelieu." Plays which project great personalities will survive when much more profound and important topical plays—Ibsen's "Doll's House," for example—become quite obsolete.

Will you now tell me whether, in your opinion, writers can or should "write for posterity," or should and must they write only for immediate consumption, leaving the question and hope of "immortality" entirely to chance?

G. B. S.—They must write the best they can and then let come what may. I wrote the third act of "Man and Superman" and the whole of "Back to Methuselah" without the least prospect of their being performed in my lifetime; but they have proved more popular than some of the plays I wrote for immediate consumption.

Reverting to "Saint Joan," do you privately believe that most people miss the point of the play, thinking you have sentimentalised the character, when actually you have done your best to unsentimentalise it? And do not most performances assist the public in that belief?

G. B. S.—The point was certainly not missed in England. Miss Thorndike, who established the English tradition of the part, hit it exactly. Ludmila Pitoeff missed it completely, and revived the snivelling womanly heroine of the old sentimental melodramas with appalling intensity. But the effect she made in Paris was not repeated in London, and will never, I hope, overcome that made by Miss Thorndike in London and Miss Dorothy Holmes Gore in the provinces.

I believe you wrote "Saint Joan," or some of it, at Stratford-on-Avon. Did you feel then that you were producing your most lasting work? Did some subtle influence from the Bard leap into your pen and permeate your words? If so (and I am not being facetious), would you advise all writers to go to Stratford when they feel they are about to give birth to their greatest masterpiece?

G. B. S.—I did not write a line of it in Stratford. Most of it was written in County Kerry, in Ireland. You forget that Shakespeare is still held responsible for the first part of "Henry VI.," with its infamous libel on Joan. She would have risen from the Seine and punched my head if I had penned her name in Stratford.

Finally, may I ask, does it matter to you whether your plays are to be remembered afterwards or not? Or would such caring be empty vanity?

G. B. S.—It matters to me and to my executors until the copyright and performing rights expire. Apart from that, I am not prepared to say in any large sense that it matters at all.

Anyhow, I am too busy to bother about it.

Saint Joan Banned: Film Censorship in the United States

(Appeared as a letter to the Editor of the *New York Times*, 14 September 1936, and as an article in the *London Mercury*, October 1936)

Some months ago statements appeared in the Press to the effect that my play, St. Joan, had been adapted to the cinema by myself, and a syndicate formed for the production of the film version with Miss Elisabeth Bergner in the title part. These statements were duly authorized by me and by Miss Bergner's Press representatives. The facts were as stated; and the way seemed clear before us. The play had held the stage for eleven years throughout the civilized world with such general approval, and especially with such religious encouragement, that the possibility of a conflict with the censorships which now control the film world never occurred to me. Its revival in America by Miss Katharine Cornell has almost taken on the character of a religious mission.

I am, of course, aware that there has been in the United States a genuine revolt against pornography and profanity in the picture theatres by good Catholics who want to enjoy a beautiful art without being disgusted and insulted by exhibitions of silly blackguardism financed by film speculators foolish enough to think that such trash pays. A body called the Hays Organization has taken the matter in hand so vigorously that it now has Hollywood completely terrorized. Without its sanction nothing can be done there in the film business. The section of the screen industry which is out for making money on the assumption that the public is half-witted and depraved, has had a thorough scare, which was badly needed.

As I thought that the Hays Organization represented unsectarian American decency I never dreamt that St. Joan had anything to fear from it. Conceive my amazement when I found that the censorship of the Hays Organization includes that of a body called the Catholic Action, professing, on what authority I know not, to be a Roman Catholic doctrinal censorship.

It may be asked how a Catholic censorship can possibly hurt me, as St. Joan was hailed by all instructed Catholics as a very unexpected first instalment of justice to the Church from Protestant quarters, and in effect, a vindication of the good faith of the famous trial at Rouen which had been held up to public execration for centuries as an abominable conspiracy by a corrupt and treacherous bishop and a villainous inquisitor to murder an innocent girl. The reply is that I have certainly nothing to fear from Catholics who understand the conditions imposed on history by stage representation and are experts in Catholic history and teaching; but as hardly one percent of Catholics can answer to this description I have everything to fear from any meddling by amateur busybodies who do not know that the work of censorship requires any qualification beyond Catholic baptism. And the Catholic Action turns out to be a body of just such conceited amateurs.

Accordingly, I find myself presented with certain specific requisitions from the Action to be complied with on pain of having all Roman Catholics forbidden to witness an exhibition of my St. Joan film. What will happen to them if they do, whether excommunication or a mild penance from the confessional, is not

specified. On my compliance and submission, and "if
the final film appears to be according to the truth of
the story, and does not contain anything against the
prestige of the Roman Catholic Church, the Catholic
Action (Azione Catholica) will declare that the shooting of such a picture has not met with any objections
from the Catholic authorities."

The censors of the Action object primarily that I
am "a mocking Irishman" (Ireland is now apparently
in partibus infidelium) and that my play is "a satire
against Church and State which are made to appear
stupid and inept." They follow this up with a heresy
which will make the Pope's hair lift the triple crown
from his head. In the play it is necessarily explained
that the Church must not take life. It could excommunicate Joan and hand her over to the secular arm,
but it could not under any circumstances kill her.
The Catholic Action is unaware of the existence of
any such scruple. It prescribes the following correction. The Bishop must not say "the Church cannot
take life." He must say "The Church does not wish
death."

At the Rouen trial Joan was spared the customary
torture, though she was threatened with it, and actually shewn the rack, where the tormentors were waiting for her. This incident, credited in my play to the
mercy of the Church, must, the Catholic Action
demands, be omitted from the film, not because it is
not true, but because it is "essentially damaging."
The common use of torture by all tribunals, secular
and clerical, in fifteenth-century France, must not be
revealed to the frequenters of picture palaces. No
objection, however, is made to the revelation of the
fact that Joan was deliberately burnt alive. The Action
would have me teach that the Holy Office was far too

humane to use the rack, but had no objection to the use of the stake by the secular arm.

But it is at the crux of the trial that the Action censor gets deepest out of his depth. There is no longer any obscurity on that crux: those who have not French enough to read Quicherat or Champion can read the excellent account by Mr. Milton Waldmann just published. When the Holy Office cleaned all the childish trifles out of the indictment, there was a perfectly clear issue left: the issue already raised by Wycliffe and Hus which subsequently developed into the issue between the Church and Luther. On this issue Joan convicted herself again and again in spite of the vain efforts of Cauchon and others of her judges to make her understand it. The question on which her fate turned was, would she accept the Church as the inspired interpreter of the will of God instead of setting up her own private judgment against it and claiming that her conduct was a matter between God and herself. In this heresy she was adamant: no threat of torture, no argument, no affectionate appeal to her feelings could move her from it: George Fox himself could not have taken the Quaker position with more heroic obstinacy. The legal consequence was inevitable: there was nothing for it but to excommunicate her and deliver her over to the secular arm to be burnt; for no appeal to the Pope could have saved her: such an appeal must have had the same result as Cauchon's appeal to the University of Paris, which could not understand why he was hesitating.

To the last, Joan, strong in her spiritual experiences and her voices, was sure she knew better than "*les gens de l'Église*," of whom apparently she had much the same opinion as I now have of the Catholic Action's film censors. But when she did at last understand that she would certainly be burnt unless she recanted, she said with her rough common sense she would sign anything rather than be burnt. And sign she did: her immediate object, apart from the fire, being to escape from the indecent custody of Warwick's soldiers into the custody of the Church under conditions proper to her sex. But as Warwick would not let her go, her judges perforce broke their promise to her. Her voices reproached her for having betrayed them. She recanted her recantation, and thus became a relapsed heretic. As such she was beyond redemption. She had to face the stake and go through with it.

Perhaps as Joan could not make head or tail of the ecclesiastical law, the Action's censors may be excused for being equally at a loss. In desperation they have demanded the excision of all that part of the trial and of the incident of the recantation. This trenchant stroke would convert my account of a perfectly legal trial, in which the accused was, as far as the Church and the Holy Office were concerned, treated with special consideration and meticulous regard for the law, into a judicial murder like nothing except the trial of Faithful in *The Pilgrim's Progress*. It would restore the Belfast Protestant view of the Church which prevailed in literature until my play exploded it. That is what comes of conferring a power over the drama which would tax the qualifications of a Gregory or a Hildebrand on a body pretending to represent the Vatican without as much knowledge of Catholicism as any village gravedigger.

Besides, the Church was not finally beaten in the matter of Joan. The Church has a place for all types of character, including the ultra-Protestant. It admits that there are certain extraordinary persons to whom direct celestial revelations are vouchsafed. St.

Catherine and St. Michael, revealing themselves to Joan in the fields at Domremy, and giving her divine instruction as to her work and destiny, are no more outside the belief of the Church than the Blessed Virgin in the cave at Lourdes revealing herself to Bernadette Soubirous. But just as persons of deep piety can attract to themselves heavenly patrons and counsellors, so equally can diabolically wicked persons, called witches and sorcerers, attract to themselves hellish tempters, personified in the fifteenth century as Satan, Belial, and Behemoth, in heavenly disguises. It was inconceivable to the Rouen tribunal that Joan could be a saint; and the alternative was to condemn her as a witch. That procedure was strictly legal, strictly reasonable, strictly pious. In 1920, however, the Church finally decided that Joan was a saint after all, and canonized her.

This has settled the whole question for the Church. Joan's voices came from heaven, not from hell. And the Rouen judges were not corrupt, unjust, lawless, nor any of the infamous things the Rehabilitation inquiry imputed: they simply mistook a very extraordinary saint for a witch. The Catholic Action must be aware of the fact of the canonization; but it has not yet readjusted its views to the 1920 situation. One of the consequences is that Miss Elisabeth Bergner is to be seen everywhere on the screen as Catherine of Russia, Empress of Freethinkers and Free Lovers, but may not make the world fall in love with a Catholic saint as she did when she created the part of Joan in Protestant Berlin when my play was new.

I cannot accept the pretension of the Catholic Action to represent the Vatican. It has neither the knowledge nor the manners to sustain such a part. It is as obnoxious to the United States Constitution as any of the features of the New Deal forbidden by the Supreme Court. It has no legal authority to enforce its vetoes. Yet it has brought all the Hollywood financiers and corporations to their knees by the threat that if they dare to produce a film banned by it not one of the twenty million Catholics in the United States will be allowed to cross the threshold of any picture house exhibiting it.

But what a paltry understatement of the Catholic position! The United States is not the whole realm of the Catholic Church, nor even as much as half that realm in America. What about South America and Quebec? What about the rest of the world? The Catholic population of the globe is estimated at 324 millions, of whom less than 50 millions are in the dominions of the United States and the British Empire. The Hollywood financiers believe that the Action can by a shake of its head keep twenty millions of Catholics out of the picture theatres. But if their belief is well founded it has but to hold up its finger to keep more than 324 millions of Catholics at home in the evenings.

I am not quite so credulous as the Hollywood financiers. I was impressed in my Irish Protestant infancy with the belief that every Catholic, including especially the Pope, must go to hell as a matter of divine routine. When I was seven years old, Pope Pius IX ruled that I, though a little Protestant, might go to heaven, in spite of my invincible ignorance regarding the Catholic religion, if I behaved myself properly. But I made no reciprocal concession at the time; and no Catholic alive can bluff me into believing that, even had he the Vatican behind him, he could keep Papists (as I used to call them) even out of the saloons and speakeasies, much less out of the much more enjoyable theatres and picture palaces. I will make the Action a present of all the Catholics who never dream of going to a theatre under any circumstances; but I defy it to add a baker's dozen to that number by any interdict it can utter. And I promise it, in the case of St. Joan, that wherever there is a cultivated Catholic priest who knows my play, he will do everything in his power to deepen the piety of his flock by making them go to see it, and urging them to make converts by inducing Protestants to do the same. Did not one of the princes of the Church in America publicly decorate the first American impersonatress of St. Joan? I hope this service of mine to the Church may be accepted as a small set-off against the abominable bigotry of my Irish Protestant childhood, which I renounced so vigorously when I grew up to some sort of discretion and decency that I emptied the baby out with the bath, and left myself for a while with no religion at all.

I make all this public because I believe very few inhabitants of the United States, Catholic or Protestant, lay or secular, have the least suspicion that an irresponsible Catholic Society has assumed public control of their artistic recreations. I do not consider public control a bad thing in itself. I greatly prefer it to the irresponsible and sometimes vicious private control which is the real alternative. But I have again to point out that censorship is the wrong method. Whatever its moral and religious pretences may be, it always comes in practice to postulating the desirability of an official with the attributes of a god, and then offering the salary of a minor railway stationmaster plus a fee per play to some erring mortal to deputize for Omniscience. He who is fool enough or needy enough to accept such a post soon finds that except in the plainest cases judgment is impossible. He therefore makes an office list of words that must not be used and subjects that must not be mentioned (usually religion and sex); and though this brings his job within the capacity of an office boy, it also reduces it to absurdity. I find in the copy of my scenario that fell into the hands of the Catholic Action that the word paradise, and an allusion to a halo, are struck out because they are classed as religious. The word damned is cut out apparently because it is profane. The word God is cut out, St Denis is cut out, sentences containing the words religion, archbishop, deadly sin, holy, infernal, sacred office, and the like are cut out quite senselessly because they are on the list. Even the word babes is forbidden, presumably as immodest. These absurdities represent, not the wisdom of the Catholic Church but the desperation of a minor official's attempts to reduce that wisdom to an office routine.

There is an epidemic of censorships at present raging through the United States as a protest against the very licentious anarchy which has hitherto prevailed. Through a crowd of amateur regulations and lists of words varying from State to State and even from city to city the anarchists, the pugilists, the pornographers can easily drive a coach and six, as it is useless to check up on the letter if the spirit still eludes. But the serious plays like St. Joan get stopped because they take the censorships completely out of their depth. Presently the epidemic will abate, and the picture trade pluck up enough courage and public spirit to insist on the control of film morality being made a federal matter, independent of prudes, of parochial busybodies, and doctrinaire enemies of the theatre as such. As to the method of that control there is only one which has proved sensible and practicable. Have your picture houses and theatres licensed from year to year by the local municipal corporation, with power to the corporation to discontinue the licence on evidence that the house is ill conducted or for other "judicial reasons." That will put an end to the irresponsibility of the exhibitor without destroying the liberty that is vital in those departments of social activity which are roughly classed as highbrow. And as such departments must be jealously guarded against the simplicity of the lowbrowed (else must we stick in the mud for ever) the initiative in prosecutions for sedition, blasphemy, and obscenity should be taken out of the hands of the common informer, and treated as a very delicate and difficult function of the most responsible constitutional department available.

For it must not be forgotten that the alternative to amateur censorships is not complete anarchy but police interference. The censorships are popular with theatrical managers and speculators because their licences act as insurance policies against police prosecution, and keep the agents of the criminal law quiet, without imposing any effective restrictions on the exploitation of vulgar pornography and criminal sensationalism. But as they do interfere very seriously with work of the class to which St. Joan belongs I must continue to insist on the evil they do, on the good that they fail to do, and on the better ways of achieving their purpose that are readily available.

Where was " Saint Joan " Written?

(A letter to the Editor of the *Irish Independent*, Dublin, 13 November 1943)

Sir—I see that a controversy has arisen as to whether

I wrote "St. Joan" at Glengarriff, in the County Cork, or at Parknasilla, in the County Kerry. It is assumed on both sides that it must have been written either in one place or the other. This assumption is evidently founded on the belief that a dramatic poet, when he writes a play, sits down on a particular spot on the earth's surface and does not rise until in a frenzy of inspiration, he has dashed off the play, the process taking, say, two hours or less.

That is not what happens. Writing a play of full Shakesperean length like "St. Joan," with the necessary intervals for feeding, sleeping, dressing and undressing, locomotion, business, and even a little rest and recreation, occupies at least several months, and sometimes several years. Goethe's "Faust" was the work of a lifetime.

Now for the facts as to "St. Joan." I wrote it in 1923. During that year I was at Glengarriff from the 18th July to the 15th August, and at Parknasilla from the 15th August to the 18th September working at the play all the time. Between these two places, therefore, honours are easy: and their respective champions need no longer regard each other as hardened liars.

But the play was neither begun nor finished in Eire. A good deal of it was written in rapidly moving trains between King's Cross and Hatfield on the London Midland and Scottish Railways: and to locate this part of it is a problem in Cartesian geometry which I leave to Mr. de Valera, as he is an expert in mathematics and I a hopeless duffer.

During the year 1923 I resided half the week in London and the other half at Ayot St. Lawrence in Hertfordshire. And I visited not only Glengarriff and Parknasilla, but made some stay at Bournemouth,

Minehead, Malvern, Stratford-upon-Avon, Birmingham, and Oxford: ten birthplaces in all.

I hope the question may now be regarded as settled to the satisfaction of all parties.

Faithfully,

G. Bernard Shaw

Shaw's Saint Joan

(A letter to the Editor of the *Catholic Herald*, London, 9 January 1948)

Sir,—What your correspondent Ruth is asking for is not a history of the trial of Jehanne la Pucelle, Maid of Orleans, but a set of character sketches of Cauchon, Lemaitre, and the rest of the entirely uninteresting and irrelevant personalities who happened to be in court officially.

That sort of dry-as-dust rubbish reduced the biographies by Mark Twain and Andrew Lang to worthless and mischievous outbursts of Protestant scurrility. Whoever reads them will be completely misled. My account is essentially correct and historical. I do not mean that Cauchon was in fact a great Catholic, Lemaitre a great lawyer, or Warwick a student of Bryce's Holy Roman Empire as they are in my play. For all I know or care the worst that Clemens and Lang wrote about them may have been deserved. The real parties in the case were the Catholic Church, the Holy Office, and militarist Whig Feudalism.

Anatole France's book (as far as it is really his) is as absurd as the lampoons of Voltaire and Shakespeare.

G. Bernard Shaw

The Apple Cart
A Political Extravaganza

Preface

Mr Shaw Replies to His Critics

A Walk and a Talk with Mr Shaw

Bernard Shaw's Denial

Mr Shaw and Democracy

The Apple Cart Again

Composition begun 5 November 1928; completed 29 December 1928. First published in German translation, as *Der Kaiser von Amerika*, 1929. Published in English, 1930. First presented in Polish at the Teatr Polski, Warsaw, on 14 June 1929. First presented in English at the Festival Theatre, Malvern, on 19 August 1929.

Pamphilius ⎱ Private Sec- ⎰ *Wallace Evennett*
Sempronius ⎰ retaries to ⎱
     the King   *Scott Sunderland*

Boanerges (President of the Board of Trade) *Matthew Boulton*

Magnus (King of England)   *Cedric Hardwicke*

Alice (The Princess Royal)   *Eve Turner*

Proteus (Prime Minister) *Charles Carson*

Balbus (Home Secretary)   *Frank Moore*

Nicobar (Foreign Secretary)   *Clifford Marquand*

Crassus (Colonial Secretary)   *Julian d'Albie*

Pliny (Chancellor of the Exchequer)   *Aubrey Mallalieu*

Lysistrata (Powermistress-General)   *Eileen Beldon*

Amanda (Postmistress-General)   *Dorothy Holmes-Gore*

Orinthia   *Edith Evans*

Queen Jemima   *Barbara Everest*

Mr Vanhattan (American Ambassador)   *James Carew*

Period—The Future

ACT I *An Office in the Royal Palace. A Summer Morning. 11 a.m.*

An Interlude: *Orinthia's Boudoir. The Same Day. 3.15 p.m.*
ACT II *A Terrace overlooking the Palace Gardens. Later in the Afternoon*

Preface

The first performances of this play at home and abroad provoked several confident anticipations that it would be published with an elaborate prefatory treatise on Democracy to explain why I, formerly a notorious democrat, have apparently veered round to the opposite quarter and become a devoted Royalist. In Dresden the performance was actually prohibited as a blasphemy against Democracy.

What was all this pother about? I had written a comedy in which a King defeats an attempt by his popularly elected Prime Minister to deprive him of the right to influence public opinion through the press and the platform: in short, to reduce him to a cipher. The King's reply is that rather than be a cipher he will abandon his throne and take his obviously very rosy chance of becoming a popularly elected Prime Minister himself. To those who believe that our system of votes for everybody produces parliaments which represent the people it should seem that this solution of the difficulty is completely democratic, and that the Prime Minister must at once accept it joyfully as such. He knows better. The change would rally the anti-democratic royalist vote against him, and impose on him a rival in the person of the only public man whose ability he has to fear. The comedic paradox of the situation is that the King wins, not by exercising his royal authority, but by threatening to resign it and go to the democratic poll.

That so many critics who believe themselves to be ardent democrats should take the entirely personal triumph of the hereditary king over the elected minister to be a triumph of autocracy over democracy, and its dramatization an act of political apostasy on the part of the author, convinces me that our professed devotion to political principles is only a mask for our idolatry of eminent persons. The Apple Cart exposes the unreality of both democracy and royalty as our idealists conceive them. Our Liberal democrats believe in a figment called a constitutional monarch, a sort of Punch puppet who cannot move until his Prime Minister's fingers are in his sleeves. They believe in another figment called a responsible minister, who moves only when similarly actuated by the million fingers of the electorate. But the most superficial inspection of any two such figures shews that they are not puppets but living men, and that the supposed control of one by the other and of both by the electorate amounts to no more than a not very deterrent fear of uncertain and under ordinary circumstances quite remote consequences. The nearest thing to a puppet in our political system is a Cabinet minister at the head of a great public office. Unless he possesses a very exceptional share of dominating ability and relevant knowledge he is helpless in the hands of his officials. He must sign whatever documents they present to him, and repeat whatever words they put into his mouth when answering questions in parliament, with a docility which cannot be imposed on a king who works at his job; for the king works continuously whilst his ministers are in office for spells only, the spells being few and brief, and often occurring for the first time to men of advanced age with little or no training for and experience of supreme responsibility. George the Third and Queen Victoria were not, like Queen Elizabeth, the natural superiors of their ministers in political genius and general capacity; but they were for many purposes of State necessarily superior to them in experience, in cunning, in exact knowledge of the limits of their responsibility and consequently of the limits of their irresponsibility: in short, in the authority and practical power that these superiorities produce. Very clever men who have come into contact with monarchs have been so impressed that they have attributed to them extraordinary natural qualifications which they, as now visible to us in historical perspective, clearly did not possess. In conflicts between monarchs and popularly elected ministers the monarchs win every time when personal ability and good sense are at all equally divided.

In The Apple Cart this equality is assumed. It is masked by a strong contrast of character and methods which has led my less considerate critics to complain that I have packed the cards by making the King a wise man and the minister a fool. But that is not at all the relation between the two. Both play with equal skill; and the King wins, not by greater astuteness, but because he has the ace of trumps in his hand and knows when to play it. As the prettier player of the two he has the sympathy of the audience. Not being as pampered and powerful as an operatic prima donna, and depending as he does not on some commercially valuable talent but on his conformity to the popular ideal of dignity and perfect breeding, he has to be trained, and to train himself, to accept good manners as an indispensable condition of his intercourse with his subjects, and to leave to the less highly placed such indulgences as tempers, tantrums, bullyings, sneerings, swearings, kickings: in short, the commoner violences and intemperances of authority.

His ministers have much laxer standards. It is open to them, if it will save their time, to get their own way by making scenes, flying into calculated rages, and substituting vulgar abuse for argument. A clever minister, not having had a royal training, will, if he finds himself involved in a duel with his king, be careful not to choose the weapons at which the king can beat him. Rather will he in cold blood oppose to the king's perfect behavior an intentional misbehavior and apparently childish petulance which he can always drop at the right moment for a demeanor as urbane as that of the king himself, thus employing two sets of weapons to the king's one. This gives him the advantages of his own training as a successful ambitious man who has pushed his way from obscurity to celebrity: a process involving a considerable use of the shorter and more selfish methods of dominating the feebly recalcitrant, the unreasonable, the timid, and the stupid, as well as a sharp sense of the danger of these methods when dealing with persons of strong character in strong positions.

In this light the style of fighting adopted by the antagonists in the scrap between King Magnus and Mr Joseph Proteus is seen to be a plain deduction from their relative positions and antecedents, and not a manufactured contrast between democracy and royalty to the disadvantage of the former. Those who so mistook it are out of date. They still regard democracy as the under dog in the conflict. But to me it is the king who is doomed to be tragically in that position in the future into which the play is projected: in fact, he is visibly at least half in it already; and the theory of constitutional monarchy assumes that he is wholly in it, and has been so since the end of the seventeenth century.

Besides, the conflict is not really between royalty and democracy. It is between both and plutocracy, which, having destroyed the royal power by frank force under democratic pretexts, has bought and swallowed democracy. Money talks: money prints: money broadcasts: money reigns; and kings and labor leaders alike have to register its decrees, and even, by a staggering paradox, to finance its enterprises and guarantee its profits. Democracy is no longer bought: it is bilked. Ministers who are Socialists to the backbone are as helpless in the grip of Breakages Limited as its acknowledged henchmen: from the moment when they attain to what is with unintentional irony called power (meaning the drudgery of carrying on for the plutocrats) they no longer dare even to talk of nationalizing any industry, however socially vital, that has a farthing of profit for plutocracy still left in it, or that can be made to yield a farthing for it by subsidies.

King Magnus's little tactical victory, which bulks so largely in the playhouse, leaves him in a worse plight than his defeated opponent, who can always plead that he is only the instrument of the people's will, whereas the unfortunate monarch, making a desperate bid for dictatorship on the perfectly true plea that democracy has destroyed all other responsibility (has not Mussolini said that there is a vacant throne in every country in Europe waiting for a capable man to fill it?), is compelled to assume full responsibility himself, and face all the reproaches that Mr Proteus can shirk. In his Cabinet there is only one friendly man who has courage, principle, and genuine good manners when he is courteously treated; and that man is an uncompromising republican, his rival for the dictatorship. The splendidly honest and devoted Die-hard lady is too scornfully tactless to help much; but with a little more experience in the art of handling effective men and women as distinguished from the art of handling mass meetings Mr Bill Boanerges might surprise those who, because he makes them laugh, see nothing in him but a caricature.

In short, those critics of mine who have taken The Apple Cart for a story of a struggle between a hero and a roomful of guys have been grossly taken in. It is never safe to take my plays at their suburban face value: it ends in your finding in them only what you bring to them, and so getting nothing for your money.

On the subject of Democracy generally I have nothing to say that can take the problem farther than I have already carried it in my Intelligent Woman's Guide to Socialism and Capitalism. We have to solve two inseparable main problems: the economic problem of how to produce and distribute our subsistence, and the political problem of how to select our rulers and prevent them from abusing their authority in their own interests or those of their class or religion. Our solution of the economic problem is the Capitalist system, which achieves miracles in production, but fails so ludicrously and disastrously to distribute its products rationally, or to produce in the order of social need, that it is always complaining of being paralysed by its "overproduction" of things of which millions of us stand in desperate want. Our solution of the political problem is Votes for Everybody and Every Authority Elected by Vote, an expedient originally devised to prevent rulers from tyrannizing by the very effectual method of preventing them from doing anything, and thus leaving everything to irresponsible private enterprise. But as private enterprise will do nothing that is not profitable to its little self, and the very existence of civilization now depends on the swift and unhampered public execution of enterprises that supersede private enterprise and are not merely profitable but vitally necessary to the whole community, this purely inhibitive check on tyranny has become a stranglehold on genuine democracy. Its painfully evolved machinery of parliament and Party System and Cabinet is so effective in obstruction that we take thirty years by constitutional methods to do thirty minutes work, and shall presently be forced to clear up thirty years arrears in thirty minutes by unconstitutional ones unless we pass a Reform Bill that will make a complete revolution in our political machinery and procedure. When we see parliaments like ours kicked into the gutter by dictators, both in kingdoms and republics, it is foolish to wait until the dictator dies or collapses, and then do nothing but pick the poor old things up and try to scrape the mud off them: the only sane course is to take the step by which the dictatorship could have been anticipated and averted, and construct a political system for rapid positive work instead of slow nugatory work, made to fit into the twentieth century instead of into the sixteenth.

Until we face this task and accomplish it we shall not be able to produce electorates capable of doing anything by their votes except pave the way to their own destruction. An election at present, considered as a means of selecting the best qualified rulers, is so absurd that if the last dozen parliaments had consisted of the candidates who were at the foot of the poll instead of those who were at the head of it there is no reason to suppose that we should have been a step more or less advanced than we are today. In neither case would the electorate have had any real choice of representatives. If it had, we might have had to struggle with parliaments of Titus Oateses and

Lord George Gordons dominating a few generals and artists, with Cabinets made up of the sort of orator who is said to carry away his hearers by his eloquence because, having first ascertained by a few cautious feelers what they are ready to applaud, he gives it to them a dozen times over in an overwhelming crescendo, and is in effect carried away by them. As it is, the voters have no real choice of candidates: they have to take what they can get and make the best of it according to their lights, which is often the worst of it by the light of heaven. By chance rather than by judgment they find themselves represented in parliament by a fortunate proportion of reasonably honest and public spirited persons who happen to be also successful public speakers. The rest are in parliament because they can afford it and have a fancy for it or an interest in it.

Last October (1929) I was asked to address the enormous audience created by the new invention of Wireless Broadcast on a range of political and cultural topics introduced by a previous speaker under the general heading of Points of View. Among the topics was Democracy, presented, as usual, in a completely abstract guise as an infinitely beneficent principle in which we must trust though it slay us. I was determined that this time Votes for Everybody and Every Authority Elected by Vote should not escape by wearing its imposing mask. I delivered myself as follows:

Your Majesties, your Royal Highnesses, your Excellencies, your Graces and Reverences, my Lords, Ladies and Gentlemen, fellow-citizens of all degrees: I am going to talk to you about Democracy objectively: that is, as it exists and as we must all reckon with it equally, no matter what our points of view may be. Suppose I were to talk to you not about Democracy, but about the sea, which is in some respects rather like Democracy! We all have our own views .of the sea. Some of us hate it and are never well when we are at it or on it. Others love it, and are never so happy as when they are in it or on it or looking at it. Some of us regard it as Britain's natural realm and surest bulwark: others want a Channel Tunnel. But certain facts about the sea are quite independent of our feelings towards it. If I take it for granted that the sea exists, none of you will contradict me. If I say that the sea is sometimes furiously violent and always uncertain, and that those who are most familiar with it trust it least, you will not immediately shriek out that I do not believe in the sea; that I am an enemy of the sea; that I want to abolish the sea; that I am going to make bathing illegal; that I am out to ruin our carrying trade and lay waste all our seaside resorts and scrap the British Navy. If I tell you that you cannot breathe in the sea, you will not take that as a personal insult and ask me indignantly if I consider you inferior to a fish. Well, you must please be equally sensible when I tell you some hard facts about Democracy. When I tell you that it is sometimes furiously violent and always dangerous and treacherous, and that those who are familiar with it as practical statesmen trust it least, you must not at once denounce me as a paid agent of Benito Mussolini, or declare that I have become a Tory Die-hard in my old age, and accuse me of wanting to take away your votes and make an end of parliament, and the franchise, and free speech, and public meeting, and trial by jury. Still less must you rise in your places and give me three rousing cheers as a champion of medieval monarchy and feudalism. I am quite innocent of any such extravagances. All I mean is that whether we are Democrats or Tories, Catholics or Protestants, Communists or Fascists, we are all face to face with a certain force in the world called Democracy; and we must understand the nature of that force whether we want to fight it or to forward it. Our business is not to deny the perils of Democracy, but to provide against them as far as we can, and then consider whether the risks we cannot provide against are worth taking.

Democracy, as you know it, is seldom more than a long word beginning with a capital letter, which we accept reverently or disparage contemptuously without asking any questions. Now we should never accept anything reverently until we have asked it a great many very searching questions, the first two being What are you? and Where do you live? When I put these questions to Democracy the answer I get is "My name is Demos; and I live in the British Empire, the United States of America, and wherever the love of liberty burns in the heart of man. You, my friend Shaw, are a unit of Democracy: your name is also Demos: you are a citizen of a great democratic community: you are a potential constituent of the Parliament of Man, The Federation of the World." At this I usually burst into loud cheers, which do credit to my enthusiastic nature. To-night, however, I shall do nothing of the sort: I shall say "Dont talk nonsense. My name is not Demos: it is Bernard Shaw. My address is not the British Empire, nor the United States of America, nor wherever the love of liberty burns in the heart of man: it is at such and such a number in such and such a street in London; and it will be time enough to discuss my seat in the Parliament of Man when that celebrated institution comes into existence. I dont believe your name is Demos: nobody's name is Demos; and all I can make of your address is that you have no address, and are just a tramp—if indeed you exist at all."

You will notice that I am too polite to call Demos a windbag or a hot air merchant; but I am going to ask you to begin our study of Democracy by considering it first as a big balloon, filled with gas or hot air, and sent up so that you shall be kept looking up at the sky whilst other people are picking your pockets. When the balloon comes down to earth every five years or so you are invited to get into the basket if you can throw out one of the people who are sitting tightly in it; but as you can afford neither the time nor the money, and there are forty millions of you and hardly room for six hundred in the basket, the balloon goes up again with much the same lot in it and leaves you where you were before. I think you will admit that the balloon as an image of Democracy corresponds to the parliamentary facts.

Now let us examine a more poetic conception of Democracy. Abraham Lincoln is represented as standing amid the carnage of the battlefield of Gettysburg, and declaring that all that slaughter of Americans by Americans occurred in order that Democracy, defined as government *of* the people *for* the people *by* the people, should not perish from the earth. Let us pick this famous peroration to pieces and see what there really is inside it. (By the way, Lincoln did not really declaim it on the field of Gettysburg; and the American Civil War was not fought in defence of any such principle, but, on the contrary, to enable one half of the United States to force the other half to be governed as they did not wish to be governed. But never mind that. I mentioned it only to remind you that it seems impossible for statesmen to make speeches about Democracy, or journalists to report them, without obscuring it in a cloud of humbug.)

Now for the three articles of the definition. Number One: Government *of* the people: that, evidently, is necessary: a human community can no more exist without a government than a human being can exist without a co-ordinated control of its breathing and blood circulation. Number Two: Government *for* the people, is most important. Dean Inge put it perfectly for us when he called Democracy a form of society which means equal consideration for all. He added that it is a Christian principle, and that, as a Christian, he believes in it. So do I. That is why I insist on equality of income. Equal consideration for a person with a hundred a year and one with a hundred thousand is impossible. But Number Three: Government *by* the people, is quite a different matter. All the monarchs, all the tyrants, all the dictators, all the Diehard Tories are agreed that we must be governed. Democrats like the Dean and myself are agreed that we must be governed with equal consideration for everybody. But we repudiate Number Three on the ground that the people cannot govern. The thing is a physical impossibility. Every citizen cannot be a ruler any more than every boy can be an engine driver or a pirate king. A nation of prime ministers or dictators is as absurd as an army of field marshals. Government by the people is not and never can be a reality: it is only a cry by which demagogues humbug us into voting for them. If you doubt this—if you ask me "Why should not the people make their own laws?" I need only ask you "Why should not the people write their own plays?" They cannot. It is much easier to write a good play than to make a good law. And there are not a hundred men in the world who can write a play good enough to stand daily wear and tear as long as a law must.

Now comes the question, If we cannot govern ourselves, what can we do to save ourselves from being at the mercy of those who *can* govern, and who may quite possibly be thoroughpaced grafters and scoundrels? The primitive answer is that as we are always in a huge majority we can, if rulers oppress us intolerably, burn their houses and tear them to pieces. This is not satisfactory. Decent people never do it until they have quite lost their heads; and when they have lost their heads they are as likely as not to burn the wrong house and tear the wrong man to pieces. When we have what is called a popular movement very few people who take part in it know what it is all about. I once saw a real popular movement in London. People were running excitedly through the streets. Everyone who saw them doing it immediately joined in the rush. They ran simply because everyone else was doing it. It was most impressive to see thousands of people sweeping along at full speed like that. There could be no doubt that it was literally a popular movement. I ascertained afterwards that it was started by a runaway cow. That cow had an important share in my education as a political philosopher; and I can assure you that if you will study crowds, and lost and terrified animals, and things like that, instead of reading books and newspaper articles, you will learn a great deal about politics from them. Most general elections, for instance, are nothing but stampedes. Our last but one was a conspicuous example of this. The cow was a Russian one.

I think we may take it that neither mob violence nor popular movements can be depended on as checks upon the abuse of power by governments. One might suppose that at least they would act as a last resort when an autocrat goes mad and commits outrageous excesses of tyranny and cruelty. But it is a curious fact that they never do. Take two famous cases: those of Nero and Tsar Paul the First of Russia. If Nero had been an ordinary professional fiddler he would probably have been no worse a man than any member of the wireless orchestra. If Paul had been a lieutenant in a line regiment we should never have heard of him. But when these two poor fellows were invested with absolute powers over their fellow-creatures they went mad, and did such appalling things that they had to be killed like mad dogs. Only, it was not the people that rose up and killed them. They were dispatched quite privately by a very select circle of their own bodyguards. For a genuinely democratic execution of unpopular statesmen we must turn to the brothers De Witt, who were torn to pieces by a Dutch mob in the seventeenth century. They were neither tyrants nor autocrats. On the contrary, one of them had been imprisoned and tortured for his resistance to the despotism of William of Orange; and the other had come to meet him as he came out of prison. The mob was on the side of the autocrat. We may take it that the shortest way for a tyrant to get rid of a troublesome champion of liberty is to raise a hue and cry against him as an unpatriotic person, and leave the mob to do the rest after supplying them with a well tipped ringleader. Nowadays this is called direct action by the revolutionary proletariat. Those who put their faith in it soon find that proletariats are never revolutionary, and that their direct action, when it is controlled at all, is usually controlled by police agents.

Democracy, then, cannot be government by the people: it can only be government by consent of the governed. Unfortunately, when democratic statesmen propose to govern us by our own consent, they find that we dont want to be governed at all, and that we regard rates and taxes and rents and death duties as intolerable burdens. What we want to know is how little government we can get along with without being murdered in our beds. That question cannot be answered until we have explained what we mean by getting along. Savages manage to get along. Unruly Arabs and Tartars get along. The only rule in the matter is that the civilized way of getting along is the way of corporate action, not individual action; and corporate action involves more government than individual action.

Thus government, which used to be a comparatively simple affair, today has to manage an enormous development of Socialism and Communism. Our industrial and social life is set in a huge communistic framework of public roadways, streets, bridges, water supplies, power supplies, lighting, tramways, schools, dockyards, and public aids and conveniences, employing a prodigious army of police, inspectors, teachers, and officials of all grades in hundreds of departments. We have found by bitter experience that it is impossible to trust factories, workshops, and mines to private management. Only by stern laws enforced by constant inspection have we stopped the monstrous waste of human life and welfare it cost when it was left uncontrolled by the Government. During the war our attempt to leave the munitioning of the army to private enterprise led us to the verge of defeat and caused an appalling slaughter of our soldiers. When the Government took the work out of private hands and had it done in national factories it was at once successful. The private firms were still allowed to do what little they could; but they had to be taught to do it economically, and to keep their accounts properly, by Government officials. Our big capitalist enterprises now run to the Government for help as a lamb runs to its mother. They cannot even make an extension of the Tube railway in London without Government aid. Unassisted private capitalism is breaking down or getting left behind in all directions. If all our Socialism and Communism and the drastic taxation of unearned incomes which finances it were to stop, our private enterprises would drop like shot stags, and we should all be dead in a month. When Mr Baldwin tried to win the last election by declaring that Socialism had been a failure whenever and wherever it had been tried, Socialism went over him like a steam roller and handed his office to a Socialist Prime Minister. Nothing could save us in the war but a great extension of Socialism; and now it is clear enough that only still greater extensions of it can repair the ravages of the war and keep pace with the growing requirements of civilization.

What we have to ask ourselves, then, is not whether we will have Socialism and Communism or not, but whether Democracy can keep pace with the developments of both that are being forced on us by the growth of national and international corporate action.

Now corporate action is impossible without a governing body. It may be the central Government: it may be a municipal corporation, a county council, a district council, or a parish council. It may be the board of directors of a joint stock company, or of a trust made by combining several joint stock companies. Such boards, elected by the votes of the shareholders, are little States within the State, and very powerful ones, too, some of them. If they have not laws and kings, they have by-laws and chairmen. And you and I, the consumers of their services, are more at the mercy of the boards that organize them than we are at the mercy of parliament. Several active politicians who began as Liberals and are now Socialists have said to me that they were converted by seeing that the nation had to choose, not between governmental control of industry and control by separate private individuals kept in order by their competition for our custom, but between governmental control and control by gigantic trusts wielding great power without responsibility, and having no object but to make as much money out of us as possible. Our Government is at this moment having much more trouble with the private corporations on whom we are dependent for our coals and cotton goods than with France or the United States of America. We are in the hands of our corporate bodies, public or private, for the satisfaction of our everyday needs. Their powers are life and death powers. I need not labor this point: we all know it.

But what we do not all realize is that we are equally dependent on corporate action for the satisfaction of our religious needs. Dean Inge tells us that our general elections have become public auctions at which the contending parties bid against one another for our votes by each promising us a larger share than the other of the plunder of the minority. Now that is perfectly true. The contending parties do not as yet venture to put it exactly in those words; but that is what it comes to. And the Dean's profession obliges him to urge his congregation, which is much wider than that of St. Paul's (it extends across the Atlantic), always to vote for the party which pledges itself to go farthest in enabling those of us who have great possessions to sell them and give the price to the poor. But we cannot do this as private persons. It must be done by the Government or not at all. Take my own case. I am not a young man with great possessions; but I am an old man paying enough income tax and surtax to provide doles for some hundreds of unemployed and old age pensioners. I have not the smallest objection to this: on the contrary, I advocated it strongly for years before I had any income worth taxing. But I could not do it if the Government did not arrange it for me. If the Government ceased taxing my superfluous money and redistributing it among people who have no incomes at all, I could do nothing by myself. What could I do? Can you suggest anything? I could send my war bonds to the Chancellor of the Exchequer and invite him to cancel the part of the National Debt that they represent; and he would undoubtedly thank me in the most courteous official terms for my patriotism. But the poor would not get any of it. The other payers of surtax and income tax and death duties would save the interest they now have to pay on it: that is all. I should only have made the rich richer and myself poorer. I could burn all my share certificates and inform the secretaries of the companies that they might write off that much of their capital indebtedness. The result would be a bigger dividend for the rest of the shareholders, with the poor out in the cold as before. I might sell my war bonds and share certificates for cash, and throw the money into the street to be scrambled for;

but it would be snatched up, not by the poorest, but
by the best fed and most able-bodied of the scram-
blers. Besides, if we all tried to sell our bonds and
shares—and this is what you have to consider; for
Christ's advice was not addressed to me alone but to
all who have great possessions—the result would be
that their value would fall to nothing, as the Stock
Exchange would immediately become a market in
which there were all sellers and no buyers. Accordingly, any spare money that the Government leaves
me is invested where I can get the highest interest and
the best security, as thereby I can make sure that it
goes where it is most wanted and gives immediate
employment. This is the best I can do without
Government interference: indeed any other way of
dealing with my spare money would be foolish and
demoralizing; but the result is that I become richer
and richer, and the poor become relatively poorer and
poorer. So you see I cannot even be a Christian
except through Government action; and neither can
the Dean.

Now let us get down to our problem. We cannot
govern ourselves; yet if we entrust the immense
powers and revenues which are necessary in an effective modern Government to an absolute monarch or
dictator, he goes more or less mad unless he is a quite
extraordinary and therefore very seldom obtainable
person. Besides, modern government is not a one-man
job: it is too big for that. If we resort to a committee or
parliament of superior persons, they will set up an
oligarchy and abuse their power for their own benefit. Our dilemma is that men in the lump cannot
govern themselves; and yet, as William Morris put
it, no man is good enough to be another man's master.
We need to be governed, and yet to control our

governors. But the best governors will not accept any control except that of their own consciences; and, as we who are governed are also apt to abuse any power of control we have, our ignorance, our passions, our private and immediate interests are constantly in conflict with the knowledge, the wisdom, and the public spirit and regard for the future of our best qualified governors.

Still, if we cannot control our governors, can we not at least choose them and change them if they do not suit?

Let me invent a primitive example of democratic choice. It is always best to take imaginary examples: they offend nobody. Imagine then that we are the inhabitants of a village. We have to elect somebody for the office of postman. There are several candidates; but one stands out conspicuously, because he has frequently treated us at the public-house, has subscribed a shilling to our little flower show, has a kind word for the children when he passes, and is a victim of oppression by the squire because his late father was one of our most successful poachers. We elect him triumphantly; and he is duly installed, uniformed, provided with a red bicycle, and given a batch of letters to deliver. As his motive in seeking the post has been pure ambition, he has not thought much beforehand about his duties; and it now occurs to him for the first time that he cannot read. So he hires a boy to come round with him and read the addresses. The boy conceals himself in the lane whilst the postman delivers the letters at the house, takes the Christmas boxes, and gets the whole credit of the transaction. In course of time he dies with a high reputation for efficiency in the discharge of his duties; and we elect another equally illiterate successor on similar grounds. But by this time the boy has grown up and become an institution. He presents himself to the new postman as an established and indispensable feature of the postal system, and finally becomes recognized and paid by the village as such.

Here you have the perfect image of a popularly elected Cabinet Minister and the Civil Service department over which he presides. It may work very well; for our postman, though illiterate, may be a very capable fellow; and the boy who reads the addresses for him may be quite incapable of doing anything more. But this does not always happen. Whether it happens or not, the system is not a democratic reality: it is a democratic illusion. The boy, when he has ability to take advantage of the situation, is the master of the man. The person elected to do the work is not really doing it: he is a popular humbug who is merely doing what a permanent official tells him to do. That is how it comes about that we are now governed by a Civil Service which has such enormous power that its regulations are taking the place of the laws of England, though some of them are made for the convenience of the officials without the slightest regard to the convenience or even the rights of the public. And how are our Civil Servants selected? Mostly by an educational test which nobody but an expensively schooled youth can pass, thus making the most powerful and effective part of our government an irresponsible class government.

Now, what control have you or I over the Services? We have votes. I have used mine a few times to see what it is like. Well, it is like this. When the election approaches, two or three persons of whom I know nothing write to me soliciting my vote and enclosing a list of meetings, an election address, and a polling

card. One of the addresses reads like an article in
The Morning Post, and has a Union Jack on it.
Another is like The Daily News or Manchester
Guardian. Both might have been compiled from the
editorial waste paper baskets of a hundred years ago.
A third address, more up-to-date and much better
phrased, convinces me that the sender has had it
written for him at the headquarters of the Labor
Party. A fourth, the most hopelessly out of date of
them all, contains scraps of the early English trans-
lations of the Communist Manifesto of 1848. I have
no guarantee that any of these documents were
written by the candidates. They convey nothing
whatever to me as to their character or political
capacity. The half-tone photographic portraits which
adorn the front pages do not even tell me their ages,
having been taken twenty years ago. If I go to one of
the meetings I find a schoolroom packed with people
who find an election meeting cheaper and funnier than
a theatre. On the platform sit one or two poor men
who have worked hard to keep party politics alive in
the constituency. They ought to be the candidates;
but they have no more chance of such eminence than
they have of possessing a Rolls-Royce car. They move
votes of confidence in the candidate, though as the
candidate is a stranger to them and to everybody else
present nobody can possibly feel any such confidence.
They lead the applause for him; they prompt him
when questions are asked; and when he is completely
floored they jump up and cry "Let me answer that,
Mr Chairman!" and then pretend that he has
answered it. The old shibboleths are droned over; and
nothing has any sense or reality in it except the
vituperation of the opposition party, which is received
with shouts of relief by the audience. Yet it is nothing

but an exhibition of bad manners. If I vote for one of these candidates, and he or she is elected, I am supposed to be enjoying a democratic control of the government—to be exercising government *of* myself, *for* myself, *by* myself. Do you wonder that the Dean cannot believe such nonsense? If I believed it I should not be fit to vote at all. If this is Democracy, who can blame Signor Mussolini for describing it as a putrefying corpse?

The candidates may ask me what more they can do for me but present themselves and answer any questions I may put to them. I quite admit that they can do nothing; but that does not mend matters. What I should like is a real test of their capacity. Shortly before the war a doctor in San Francisco discovered that if a drop of a candidate's blood can be obtained on a piece of blotting paper it is possible to discover within half an hour what is wrong with him physically. What I am waiting for is the discovery of a process by which on delivery of a drop of his blood or a lock of his hair we can ascertain what is right with him mentally. We could then have a graded series of panels of capable persons for all employments, public or private, and not allow any person, however popular, to undertake the employment of governing us unless he or she were on the appropriate panel. At the lower end of the scale there would be a panel of persons qualified to take part in a parish meeting; at the higher end a panel of persons qualified to act as Secretaries of State for Foreign Affairs or Finance Ministers. At present not more than two per thousand of the population would be available for the highest panel. I should then be in no danger of electing a postman and finding that he could neither read nor write. My choice of candidates would be perhaps more restricted than at present; but I do not desire liberty to choose windbags and nincompoops to represent me in parliament; and my power to choose between one qualified candidate and another would give me as much control as is either possible or desirable. The voting and counting would be done by machinery: I should connect my telephone with the proper office; touch a button; and the machinery would do the rest.

Pending such a completion of the American doctor's discovery, how are we to go on? Well, as best we can, with the sort of government that our present system produces. Several reforms are possible without any new discovery. Our present parliament is obsolete: it can no more do the work of a modern State than Julius Cæsar's galley could do the work of an Atlantic liner. We need in these islands two or three additional federal legislatures, working on our municipal committee system instead of our parliamentary party system. We need a central authority to co-ordinate the federal work. Our obsolete little internal frontiers must be obliterated, and our units of local government enlarged to dimensions compatible with the recent prodigious advances in facility of communication and co-operation. Commonwealth affairs and supernational activities through the League of Nations or otherwise will have to be provided for, and Cabinet function to be transformed. All the pseudo-democratic obstructive functions of our political machinery must be ruthlessly scrapped, and the general problem of government approached from a positive viewpoint at which mere anarchic national sovereignty as distinguished from self-government will have no meaning.

I must conclude by warning you that when everything has been done that can be done, civilization will still be dependent on the consciences of the governors and the governed. Our natural dispositions may be good; but we have been badly brought up, and are full of anti-social personal ambitions and prejudices and snobberies. Had we not better teach our children to be better citizens than ourselves? We are not doing that at present. The Russians *are*. That is my last word. Think over it.

So much for my broadcast on Democracy! And now a word about Breakages, Limited. Like all Socialists who know their business I have an exasperated sense of the mischief done by our system of private Capitalism in setting up huge vested interests in destruction, waste, and disease. The armament firms thrive on war; the glaziers gain by broken windows; the operating surgeons depend on cancer for their children's bread; the distillers and brewers build cathedrals to sanctify the profits of drunkenness; and the prosperity of Dives costs the privation of a hundred Lazaruses.

The title Breakages, Limited, was suggested to me by the fate of that remarkable genius, the late Alfred Warwick Gattie, with whom I was personally acquainted. I knew him first as the author of a play. He was a disturbing man, afflicted—or, as it turned out, gifted—with chronic hyperæsthesia, feeling everything violently and expressing his feelings vehemently and on occasion volcanically. I concluded that he was not sufficiently cold-blooded to do much as a playwright; so that when, having lost sight of him for some years, I was told that he had made an invention of first-rate importance, I was incredulous, and concluded that the invention was only a Utopian project. Our friend Henry Murray was so provoked by my attitude that to appease him I consented to investigate the alleged great invention in person on Gattie's promising to behave like a reasonable being during the process, a promise which he redeemed with the greatest dignity, remaining silent whilst an engineer explained his miracles to me, and contenting himself with the reading of a brief statement shewing that the adoption of his plan would release from industry enough men to utterly overwhelm the Central Empires with whom we were then at war.

I approached the investigation very sceptically. Our friend spoke of "the works." I could not believe that Gattie had any works, except in his fervid imagination. He mentioned "the company." That was more credible: anyone may form a company; but that it had any resources seemed to me doubtful. However, I suffered myself to be taken to Battersea; and there, sure enough, I found a workshop, duly labelled as the premises of The New Transport Company, Limited, and spacious enough to accommodate a double railway line with a platform. The affair was unquestionably real, so far. The platform was not provided with a station: its sole equipment was a table with a row of buttons on it for making electrical contacts. Each line of railway had on it a truck with a steel lid. The practical part of the proceedings began by placing an armchair on the lid of one of the trucks and seating me in it. A brimming glass of water was then set at my feet. I could not imagine what I was expected to do with the water or what was going to happen; and there was a suggestion of electrocution about the chair which made me nervous. Gattie then sat down majestically at the table on the platform with his hand hovering over the buttons. Intimating that the miracle would take place when my truck passed the other truck, he asked me to choose whether it should occur at the first passage or later, and to dictate the order in which it should be repeated. I was by that time incapable of choosing; so I said the sooner the better; and the two trucks started. When the other truck had passed mine I found myself magically sitting on it, chair and all, with the glass of water unspilled at my feet.

The rest of the story is a tragi-comedy. When I said to Gattie apologetically (I felt deeply guilty of having underrated him) that I had never known that he was an engineer, and had taken him to be the usual amateur inventor with no professional training, he told me that this was exactly what he was: just like Sir Christopher Wren. He had been concerned in an electric lighting business, and had been revolted by the prodigious number of breakages of glass bulbs involved by the handling of the crates in which they were packed for transport by rail and road. What was needed was a method of transferring the crates from truck to truck, and from truck to road lorry, and from road lorry to warehouse lift without shock, friction, or handling. Gattie, being, I suppose, by natural genius an inventor though by mistaken vocation a playwright, solved the mechanical problem without apparent difficulty, and offered his nation the means of effecting an enormous saving of labor and smash. But instead of being received with open arms as a social bene- factor he found himself up against Breakages, Limited. The glass blowers whose employment was threatened, the exploiters of the great industry of repairing our railway trucks (every time a goods train is stopped a series of 150 violent collisions is propagated from end to end of the train, as those who

live within earshot know to their cost), and the railway
porters who dump the crates from truck to platform
and then hurl them into other trucks, shattering
bulbs, battering cans, and too often rupturing themselves in the process, saw in Gattie an enemy of the
human race, a wrecker of homes and a starver of
innocent babes. He fought them undauntedly; but
they were too strong for him; and in due time his
patents expired and he died almost unrecognized,
whilst Unknown Soldiers were being canonized
throughout the world. So far, The Apple Cart is his
only shrine; and as it does not even bear his name, I
have written it here pending its tardy appearance in
the roll of fame.

I must not leave my readers to assume that Gattie
was an easy man to deal with, or that he handled the
opposition in a conciliatory manner with due allowance for the inertia of a somewhat unimaginative
officialdom which had not, like myself, sat on his
trucks, and probably set him down as a Utopian (a
species much dreaded in Government departments)
and thus missed the real point, which was that he was
an inventor. Like many men of genius he could not
understand why things obvious to him should not be
so at once to other people, and found it easier to
believe that they were corrupt than that they could be
so stupid. Once, after I had urged him to be more
diplomatic, he brought me, with some pride, a letter
to the Board of Trade which he considered a masterpiece of tact and good temper. It contained not a word
descriptive of his invention; and it began somewhat in
this fashion: "Sir: If you are an honest man you cannot deny that among the worst abuses of this corrupt
age is the acceptance of city directorships by retired
members of the Board of Trade." Clearly it was not

easy for the Board of Trade to deal with an inventor who wished to interest them, not in his new machines, but in the desirability of its abolishing itself as infamous.

The last time I saw him he called on me to unfold a new scheme of much greater importance, as he declared, than his trucks. He was very interesting on that occasion. He began by giving me a vivid account of the pirates who used to infest the Thames below London Bridge before the docks were built. He described how the docks had come into existence not as wharves for loading and unloading but as strongholds in which ships and their cargoes could be secure from piracy. They are now, he declared, a waste of fabulously valuable ground; and their work should be done in quite another way. He then produced plans of a pier to be built in the middle of the river, communicating directly by rail and road with the shore and the great main lines. The ships would come alongside the pier; and by a simple system of hoists the contents of their holds would be lifted out and transferred (like myself in the armchair) to railway trucks or motor lorries without being touched by a human hand and therefore without risk of breakage. It was all so masterly, so simple in its complexity, so convincing as to its practicability, and so prodigiously valuable socially, that I, taking it very seriously, proceeded to discuss what could be done to interest the proper people in it.

To my amazement Gattie began to shew unmistakeable signs of disappointment and indignation. "You do not seem to understand me," he said. "I have shewn you all this mechanical stuff merely by way of illustration. What I have come to consult you about is a great melodrama I am going to write, the scene of which will be the Pool of London in the seventeenth century among the pirates!"

What could I or anyone do with a man like that? He was naïvely surprised when I laughed; and he went away only half persuaded that his scheme for turning the docks into building land; expediting the Thames traffic; saving much dangerous and demoralizingly casual labor; and transfiguring the underpaid stevedore into a fullfed electrician, was stupendously more important than any ridiculous melodrama. He admitted that there was of course all that in it; but I could see that his heart was in the melodrama.

As it was evident that officialdom, writhing under his insults and shocked by his utter lack of veneration for bigwigs, besides being hampered as all our Government departments are by the vested interests of Breakages, Limited, would do nothing for him, I induced some less embarrassed public persons to take a ride in the trucks and be convinced that they really existed and worked. But here again the parallel between Gattie and his fellow-amateur Sir Christopher Wren came in. Wren was not content to redesign and rebuild St Paul's: he wanted to redesign London as well. He was quite right: what we have lost by not letting him do it is incalculable. Similarly, Gattie was not content to improve the luggage arrangements of our railways: he would not listen to you if your mind was not large enough to grasp the immediate necessity for a new central clearing house in Farringdon Market, connected with the existing railways by a system of new tubes. He was of course right; and we have already lost by sticking to our old ways more than the gigantic sum his scheme would have cost. But neither the money nor the enterprise was available just then, with the war on our hands.

The Clearing House, like the Thames pier, remains on paper; and Gattie is in his grave. But I still hold that there must have been something great in a man who, having not only imagined them but invented their machinery, could, far from being crushed by their rejection, exclaim "Perish all my mechanical trash if only it provides material for one bad play!"

This little history will explain how it actually did provide material for Breakages, Limited, and for the bitter cry of the Powermistress General. Not until Breakages is itself broken will it cease to have a message for us.

AYOT ST LAWRENCE, *March 1930*

$\begin{bmatrix} \text{ACT I} \end{bmatrix}$

*An office in the royal palace. Two writing-tables face
each other from opposite sides of the room, leaving
plenty of room between them. Each table has a chair by
it for visitors. The door is in the middle of the farthest
wall. The clock shews that it is a little past 11; and the
light is that of a fine summer morning.*

*Sempronius, smart and still presentably young, shews
his right profile as he sits at one of the tables opening the
King's letters. Pamphilius, middle aged, shews his left as
he leans back in his chair at the other table with a pile
of the morning papers at his elbow, reading one of them.
This goes on silently for some time. Then Pamphilius,
putting down his paper, looks at Sempronius for a
moment before speaking.*

PAMPHILIUS. What was your father?
SEMPRONIUS [*startled*] Eh?
PAMPHILIUS. What was your father?
SEMPRONIUS. My father?
PAMPHILIUS. Yes. What was he?
SEMPRONIUS. A Ritualist.
PAMPHILIUS. I dont mean his religion. I mean his
profession. And his politics.
SEMPRONIUS. He was a Ritualist by profession, a
Ritualist in politics, a Ritualist in religion: a raging
emotional Die Hard Ritualist right down to his boots.
PAMPHILIUS. Do you mean that he was a parson?
SEMPRONIUS. Not at all. He was a sort of spectacular
artist. He got up pageants and Lord Mayors' Shows

and military tattoos and big public ceremonies and things like that. He arranged the last two coronations. That was how I got my job here in the palace. All our royal people knew him quite well: he was behind the scenes with them.

PAMPHILIUS. Behind the scenes and yet believed they were all real!

SEMPRONIUS. Yes. Believed in them with all his soul.

PAMPHILIUS. Although he manufactured them himself?

SEMPRONIUS. Certainly. Do you suppose a baker cannot believe sincerely in the sacrifice of the Mass or in holy communion because he has baked the consecrated wafer himself?

PAMPHILIUS. I never thought of that.

SEMPRONIUS. My father might have made millions in the theatres and film studios. But he refused to touch them because the things they represented hadnt really happened. He didnt mind doing the christening of Queen Elizabeth in Shakespear's Henry the Eighth because that had really happened. It was a celebration of royalty. But not anything romantic: not though they offered him thousands.

PAMPHILIUS. Did you ever ask him what he really thought about it all? But of course you didnt: one cant ask one's father anything about himself.

SEMPRONIUS. My dear Pam: my father never thought. He didnt know what thought meant. Very few people do, you know. He had vision: actual bodily vision, I mean; and he had an oddly limited sort of imagination. What I mean is that he couldnt imagine anything he didnt see; but he could imagine that what he did see was divine and holy and omniscient and omnipotent and eternal and everything that is im-

possible if only it looked splendid enough, and the
organ was solemn enough, or the military bands
brassy enough.

PAMPHILIUS. You mean that he had to get everything from outside.

SEMPRONIUS. Exactly. He'd never have felt anything if he hadnt had parents to feel about in his
childhood, and a wife and babies to feel about when
he grew up. He'd never have known anything if he
hadnt been taught at school. He couldnt amuse
himself: he had to pay oceans of money to other
people to amuse him with all sorts of ghastly sports
and pleasures that would have driven me into a
monastery to escape from them. You see it was all
ritual: he went to the Riviera every winter just as he
went to church.

PAMPHILIUS. By the way, is he alive? I should like
to know him.

SEMPRONIUS. No. He died in 1962, of solitude.

PAMPHILIUS. What do you mean? of solitude?

SEMPRONIUS. He couldnt bear to be alone for a
moment: it was death to him. Somebody had to be
with him always.

PAMPHILIUS. Oh well, come! That was friendly and
kindly. It shews he had something inside him after all.

SEMPRONIUS. Not a bit. He never talked to his
friends. He played cards with them. They never
exchanged a thought.

PAMPHILIUS. He must have been a rum old bird.

SEMPRONIUS. Not rum enough to be noticed. There
are millions like him.

PAMPHILIUS. But what about his dying of solitude?
Was he imprisoned?

SEMPRONIUS. No. His yacht struck a reef and sank
somewhere off the north of Scotland; and he managed

to swim to an uninhabited island. All the rest were drowned; and he was not taken off for three weeks. When they found him he was melancholy mad, poor old boy; and he never got over it. Simply from having no one to play cards with, and no church to go to.

PAMPHILIUS. My dear Sem: one isnt alone on an uninhabited island. My mother used to stand me on the table and make me recite about it.

[*He declaims*]

> To sit on rocks; to muse o'er flood and fell;
> To slowly trace the forest's shady scene
> Where things that own not man's dominion
>   dwell
> And mortal foot hath ne'er or rarely been;
> To climb the trackless mountain all unseen
> With the wild flock that never needs a fold;
> Alone o'er steeps and foaming falls to lean:
> This is not solitude: 'tis but to hold
> Converse with Nature's charms, and view her
>   stores unrolled.

SEMPRONIUS. Now you have hit the really funny thing about my father. All that about the lonely woods and the rest of it—what you call Nature—didnt exist for him. It had to be something artificial to get at him. Nature to him meant nakedness; and nakedness only disgusted him. He wouldnt look at a horse grazing in a field; but put splendid trappings on it and stick it into a procession and he just loved it. The same with men and women: they were nothing to him until they were dressed up in fancy costumes and painted and wigged and titled. To him the sacredness of the priest was the beauty of his vestment, the loveliness of women the dazzle of their jewels and robes, the charm of the countryside not in its hills and trees, nor in the blue smoke from its cottages in the winter evenings, but of its temples, palaces, mansions, park gates, and porticoed country houses. Think of the horror of that island to him! A void! a place where he was deaf and dumb and blind and lonely! If only there had been a peacock with its tail in full bloom it might have saved his reason; but all the birds were gulls; and gulls are not decorative. Our King could have lived there for thirty years with nothing but his own thoughts. You would have been all right with a fishing rod and a golf ball with a bag of clubs. I should have been as happy as a man in a picture gallery looking at the dawns and sunsets, the changing seasons, the continual miracle of life ever renewing itself. Who could be dull with pools in the rocks to watch? Yet my father, with all that under his nose, was driven mad by its nothingness. They say that where there is nothing the king loses his rights. My father found that where there is nothing a man loses his reason and dies.

PAMPHILIUS. Let me add that in this palace, when the king's letters are not ready for him at 12 o'clock, a secretary loses his job.

SEMPRONIUS [*hastily resuming his work*] Yes, devil take you: why did you start me talking before I had finished my work? You have nothing to do but pretend to read the newspapers for him; and when you say "Nothing particular this morning, Sir," all he says is "Thank Heaven!" But if I missed a note from one of his aunts inviting herself to tea, or a little line from Orinthia the Beloved marked "Strictly private and confidential: to be opened by His Majesty alone," I should never hear the end of it. He had six love letters yesterday; and all he said when I told him was "Take them to the Queen." He thinks they amuse her. I believe they make her as sick as they make me.

PAMPHILIUS. Do Orinthia's letters go to the Queen?

SEMPRONIUS. No, by George! Even I dont read Orinthia's letters. My instructions are to read everything; but I take care to forget to open hers. And I notice that I am not rebuked for my negligence.

PAMPHILIUS [*thoughtfully*] I suppose—

SEMPRONIUS. Oh shut up, Pam. I shall never get through if you go on talking.

PAMPHILIUS. I was only going to say that I suppose—

SEMPRONIUS. Something about Orinthia. Dont. If you indulge in supposition on that subject, you will lose your job, old chap. So stow it.

PAMPHILIUS. Dont cry out before Orinthia is hurt, young chap. I was going to say that I suppose you know that that bull-roarer Boanerges has just been taken into the Cabinet as President of the Board of Trade, and that he is coming here today to give the King a piece of his mind, or what he calls his mind, about the crisis.

SEMPRONIUS. What does the King care about the crisis? There has been a crisis every two months since he came to the throne; but he has always been too clever for them. He'll turn Boanerges inside out after letting him roar the palace down.

Boanerges enters, dressed in a Russian blouse and peaked cap, which he keeps on. He is fifty, heavily built and aggressively self-assertive.

BOANERGES. Look here. The King has an appointment with me at a quarter to twelve. How long more am I to be kept waiting?

SEMPRONIUS [*with cheerful politeness*] Good morning. Mr Boanerges, I think.

[286]

BOANERGES [*shortly, but a little taken aback*] Oh, good morning to you. They say that politeness is the punctuality of kings—

SEMPRONIUS. The other way about, Mr Boanerges. Punctuality is the politeness of kings; and King Magnus is a model in that respect. Your arrival cannot have been announced to His Majesty. I will see about it. [*He hurries out*].

PAMPHILIUS. Be seated, Mr Boanerges.

BOANERGES [*seating himself by Pamphilius's writing-table*] A nice lot of young upstarts you have in this palace, Mr—?

PAMPHILIUS. Pamphilius is my name.

BOANERGES. Oh yes: Ive heard of you. Youre one of the king's private secretaries.

PAMPHILIUS. I am. And what have our young up-starts been doing to you, Mr Boanerges?

BOANERGES. Well, I told one of them to tell the king I was here, and to look sharp about it. He looked at me as if I was a performing elephant, and took himself off after whispering to another flunkey. Then this other chap comes over to me and pretends he doesnt know who I am! asks me can he have my name! "My lad" I said: "not to know me argues yourself unknown. You know who I am as well as I do myself. Go and tell the king I'm waiting for him, d'ye see?" So he took himself off with a flea in his ear. I waited until I was fed up with it, and then opened the nearest door and came in here.

PAMPHILIUS. Young rascals! However, my friend Mr Sempronius will make it all right for you.

BOANERGES. Oh: that was Sempronius, was it. Ive heard of him too.

PAMPHILIUS. You seem to have heard of all of us. You will be quite at home in the palace now that you

are a Cabinet Minister. By the way, may I congratulate you on your appointment—or rather
congratulate the Cabinet on your accession?

SEMPRONIUS [*returning*] The King. [*He goes to his
table and takes the visitor's chair in his hand, ready for
the king's instructions as to where to place it*].

*Pamphilius rises. Boanerges turns to the door in his
chair without rising. King Magnus, a tallish studious
looking gentleman of 45 or thereabouts, enters, and
comes quickly down the middle of the room to Boanerges,
proffering his hand cordially.*

MAGNUS. You are very welcome to my little palace,
Mr Boanerges. Wont you sit down?

BOANERGES. I am sitting down.

MAGNUS. True, Mr Boanerges. I had not noticed it.
Forgive me: force of habit.

*He indicates to Sempronius that he wishes to sit near
Boanerges, on his right. Sempronius places the chair
accordingly.*

MAGNUS. You will allow me to be seated?

BOANERGES. Oh, sit down, man, sit down. Youre in
your own house: ceremony cuts no ice with me.

MAGNUS [*gratefully*] Thank you.

*The King sits. Pamphilius sits. Sempronius returns to
his table and sits.*

MAGNUS. It is a great pleasure to meet you at last,
Mr Boanerges. I have followed your career with
interest ever since you contested Northampton
twenty-five years ago.

BOANERGES [*pleased and credulous*] I should just
think you have, King Magnus. I have made you sit
up once or twice, eh?

MAGNUS [*smiling*] Your voice has shaken the throne
oftener than that.

BOANERGES [*indicating the secretaries with a jerk of*

his head] What about these two? Are they to over-
hear everything that passes?

MAGNUS. My private secretaries. Do they incommode you?

BOANERGES. Oh, they dont incommode me. I am
ready to have our talk out in Trafalgar Square if you
like, or have it broadcast on the wireless.

MAGNUS. That would be a treat for my people, Mr
Boanerges. I am sorry we have not arranged for
it.

BOANERGES [*gathering himself together formidably*]
Yes; but do you realize that I am going to say things
to you that have never been said to a king before?

MAGNUS. I am very glad indeed to hear it, Mr Boanerges. I thought I had already heard everything that
could be said to a king. I shall be grateful for the
smallest novelty.

BOANERGES. I warn you it wont be agreeable. I am
a plain man, Magnus: a very plain man.

MAGNUS. Not at all, I assure you—

BOANERGES [*indignantly*] I was not alluding to my
personal appearance.

MAGNUS [*gravely*] Nor was I. Do not deceive yourself, Mr Boanerges. You are very far from being a
plain man. To me you have always been an Enigma.

BOANERGES [*surprised and enormously flattered: he
cannot help smiling with pleasure*] Well, perhaps I am
a bit of an enigma. Perhaps I am.

MAGNUS [*humbly*] I wish I could see through you, Mr
Boanerges. But I have not your sort of cleverness. I
can only ask you to be frank with me.

BOANERGES [*now convinced that he has the upper
hand*] You mean about the crisis. Well, frank is just
what I have come here to be. And the first thing I am
going to tell you frankly about it is that this country

has got to be governed, not by you, but by your ministers.

MAGNUS. I shall be only too grateful to them for taking a very difficult and thankless job off my hands.

BOANERGES. But it's not on your hands. It's on your ministers' hands. You are only a constitutional monarch. Do you know what they call that in Belgium?

MAGNUS. An indiarubber stamp, I think. Am I right?

BOANERGES. You are, King Magnus. An india-rubber stamp. Thats what you have got to be; and dont you forget it.

MAGNUS. Yes: thats what we are most of the time: both of us.

BOANERGES [*outraged*] What do you mean? both of us?

MAGNUS. They bring us papers. We sign. You have no time to read them, luckily for you. But I am expected to read everything. I do not always agree; but I must sign: there is nothing else to be done. For instance, death warrants. Not only have I to sign the death warrants of persons who in my opinion ought not to be killed; but I may not even issue death warrants for a great many people who in my opinion ought to be killed.

BOANERGES [*sarcastic*] Youd like to be able to say "Off with his head!" wouldnt you?

MAGNUS. Many men would hardly miss their heads, there is so little in them. Still, killing is a serious business: at least the person who is to be killed is usually conceited enough to think so. I think that if there were a question of killing me—

BOANERGES [*grimly*] There may be, someday. I have heard it discussed.

MAGNUS. Oh, quite. I have not forgotten King

Charles's head. Well, I hope it will be settled by a living person and not by an indiarubber stamp.

BOANERGES. It will be settled by the Home Secretary, your duly constituted democratic minister.

MAGNUS. Another indiarubber stamp, eh?

BOANERGES. At present, perhaps. But not when I am Home Secretary, by Jingo! Nobody will make an indiarubber stamp of Bill Boanerges: take that from me.

MAGNUS. Of course not. Is it not curious how people idealize their rulers? In the old days the king—poor man!—was a god, and was actually called God and worshipped as infallible and omniscient. That was monstrous—

BOANERGES. It was silly: just silly.

MAGNUS. But was it half so silly as our pretence that he is an indiarubber stamp? The ancient Roman emperor-god had not infinite wisdom, infinite knowledge, infinite power; but he had some: perhaps even as much as his ministers. He was alive, not dead. What man has ever approached either a king or a minister and been able to pick him up from the table and use him as one picks up and uses a piece of wood and brass and rubber? Permanent officials of your department will try to pick you up and use you like that. Nineteen times out of twenty you will have to let them do it, because you cannot know everything; and even if you could you cannot do everything and be everywhere. But what about the twentieth time?

BOANERGES. The twentieth time they will find they are up against Bill Boanerges, eh?

MAGNUS. Precisely. The indiarubber stamp theory will not work, Mr Boanerges. The old divine theory worked because there is a divine spark in us all; and the stupidest or worst monarch or minister, if not

wholly god, is a bit of a god—an attempt at a god—
however little the bit and unsuccessful the attempt.
But the indiarubber stamp theory breaks down in
every real emergency, because no king or minister is
the very least little bit like a stamp: he is a living soul.

BOANERGES. A soul, eh? You kings still believe in
that, I suppose.

MAGNUS. I find the word convenient: it is short and
familiar. But if you dislike being called a soul, let us
say that you are animate matter as distinguished
from inanimate.

BOANERGES [*not quite liking this*] I think I'd rather
you called me a soul, you know, if you must call me
anything at all. I know I have too much matter about
me: the doctor says I ought to knock off a stone or
two; but there's something more to me than beef.
Call it a soul if you like; only not in a superstitious
sense, if you understand me.

MAGNUS. Perfectly. So you see, Mr Boanerges, that
though we have been dealing with one another for
less than ten minutes, you have already led me into an
intellectual discussion which shews that we are something more than a pair of indiarubber stamps. You are
up against my brains, such as they are.

BOANERGES. And you are up against mine.

MAGNUS [*gallantly*] There can be no doubt of
that.

BOANERGES [*grinning*] Such as they are, eh?

MAGNUS. It is not for me to make that qualification,
except in my own case. Besides, you have given your
proofs. No common man could have risen as you have
done. As for me, I am a king because I was the nephew
of my uncle, and because my two elder brothers died.
If I had been the stupidest man in the country I
should still be its king. I have not won my position by

my merits. If I had been born as you were in the—in the—

BOANERGES. In the gutter. Out with it. Picked up by a policeman at the foot of Captain Coram's statue. Adopted by the policeman's grandmother, bless her!

MAGNUS. Where should *I* have been if the policeman had picked me up?

BOANERGES. Ah! Where? Not, mind you, that you mightnt have done pretty well for yourself. Youre no fool, Magnus: I will say that for you.

MAGNUS. You flatter me.

BOANERGES. Flatter a king! Never. Not Bill Boanerges.

MAGNUS. Yes, yes: everybody flatters the King. But everybody has not your tact, and, may I say? your good nature.

BOANERGES [*beaming with self-satisfaction*] Perhaps not. Still, I am a Republican, you know.

MAGNUS. That is what has always surprised me. Do you really think that any man should have as much personal power as the presidents of the republican States have? Ambitious kings envy them.

BOANERGES. What's that? I dont follow that.

MAGNUS [*smiling*] You cannot humbug me, Mr Boanerges. I see why you are a Republican. If the English people send me packing and establish a republic, no man has a better chance of being the first British president than you.

BOANERGES [*almost blushing*] Oh! I dont say that.

MAGNUS. Come come! You know it as well as I do. Well, if it happens you will have ten times more power than I have ever had.

BOANERGES [*not quite convinced*] How can that be? Youre King.

MAGNUS. And what is the King? An idol set up by a

group of plutocrats so that they can rule the country with the King as their scapegoat and puppet. Presidents, now, are chosen by the people, who always want a Strong Man to protect them against the rich.

BOANERGES. Well, speaking as a bit of a Strong Man myself, there may be something in that. But honestly, Magnus, as man to man, do you tell me youd rather be a president than what you are?

MAGNUS. By no means. You wouldnt believe me if I did; and you would be quite right. You see, my security is very comfortable.

BOANERGES. Security, eh? You admitted just now that even a modest individual like myself had given your throne a shake or two.

MAGNUS. True. You are quite right to remind me of it. I know that the monarchy may come to an end at any moment. But while the monarchy lasts—while it lasts, mark you—I am very secure. I escape the dreadful and demoralizing drudgery of electioneering. I have no voters to please. Ministers come and ministers go; but I go on for ever. The terrible precariousness of your position—

BOANERGES. What's that? How is my position precarious?

MAGNUS. The vote may go against you. Yours is a Trade Union seat, is it not? If the Hydro-Electric Workers Federation throw you over, where would you be?

BOANERGES [*confidently*] They wont throw me over. You dont know the workers, Magnus: you have never been a worker.

MAGNUS [*lifts his eyebrows*]!

BOANERGES [*continuing*] No king on earth is as safe in his job as a Trade Union Official. There is only one thing that can get him sacked; and that is drink. Not even that, as long as he doesnt actually fall down. I talk democracy to these men and women. I tell them that they have the vote, and that theirs is the kingdom and the power and the glory. I say to them "You are supreme: exercise your power." They say, "That's right: tell us what to do"; and I tell them. I say "Exercise your vote intelligently by voting for me." And they do. That's democracy; and a splendid thing it is too for putting the right men in the right place.

MAGNUS. Magnificent! I have never heard it better described. You certainly have a head on you, Mr Boanerges. You should write an essay on democracy. But—

BOANERGES. But what?

MAGNUS. Suppose a man with a bigger voice comes along! Some fool! Some windbag! Some upstart with a platform trick of gulling the multitude!

BOANERGES. Youre thinking of Iky Jacobus? He is only a talker. [*Snapping his fingers*] I dont give that for him.

MAGNUS. I never even heard of Mr Jacobus. But why do you say "only a talker." Talkers are very formidable rivals for popular favor. The multitude understands talk: it does not understand work. I mean brain work, like yours and mine.

BOANERGES. That's true. But I can talk Iky's head off.

MAGNUS. Lucky man: you have all the trumps in your hand. But I, who cannot pretend to your gifts, am very glad that Iky cannot upset me as long as I am the nephew of my uncle.

A young lady, dressed for walking, rushes in impetuously.

THE YOUNG LADY. Papa: I cannot find the address—
MAGNUS [*cutting her short*] No, no, no, dear: not now.

Go away. Dont you see that I am particularly engaged with the President of the Board of Trade? You must excuse my unruly daughter, Mr Boanerges. May I present her to you? Alice, my eldest girl. Mr Boanerges, dear.

ALICE. Oh! Are you the great Mr Boanerges?

BOANERGES [*rising in a glow of gratification*] Well, I dont call myself that, you know. But I believe the expression is in use, as you might say. I am very pleased indeed to make the aquaintance of the Princess Royal.

They shake hands.

ALICE. Why do you wear such awful clothes, Mr Boanerges?

MAGNUS [*remonstrating*] My dear—!

ALICE [*continuing*] I cant go out walking with you in that [*pointing to his blouse*].

BOANERGES. The uniform of Labor, your Royal Highness. I'm proud of it.

ALICE. Oh yes, I know all that, Mr Boanerges. But you dont look the part, you know. Anyone can see that you belong naturally to the governing class.

BOANERGES [*struck by this view*] In a way, perhaps. But I have earned my bread by my hands. Not as a laborer, though. I am a skilled mechanic, or was until my country called on me to lead it.

MAGNUS [*to Alice*] Well, my dear, you have broken up a most interesting conversation, and to me a most instructive one. It's no use our trying to go on, Mr Boanerges: I must go and find what my daughter wants, though I strongly suspect that what she really came in for was to see my wonderful new minister. We shall meet again presently: you know that the Prime Minister is calling on me today with some of his colleagues—including, I hope, yourself—to discuss the crisis. [*Taking Alice's arm and turning towards the door*] You will excuse us, wont you?

BOANERGES [*graciously*] Oh, thats all right. Thats quite all right.

The King and the Princess go out, apparently much pleased.

BOANERGES [*to Sempronius and Pamphilius comprehensively*] Well, say what you will, the King is no fool. Not when you know how to handle him.

PAMPHILIUS. Of course, that makes all the difference.

BOANERGES. And the girl hasnt been spoilt. I was glad to see that. She doesnt seem to know that she is the Princess Royal, eh?

SEMPRONIUS. Well, she wouldnt dream of giving herself any airs with you.

BOANERGES. What! Isnt she always like that?

SEMPRONIUS. Oh no. It's not everybody who is received as you have been. I hope you have enjoyed your visit.

BOANERGES. Well, I pulled Magnus through it pretty well: eh? Dont you think so?

SEMPRONIUS. He was pleased. You have a way with him, Mr President.

BOANERGES. Well, perhaps I have, perhaps I have.

A bevy of five Cabinet Ministers, resplendent in diplomatic uniforms, enters. Proteus the Prime Minister has on his left, Pliny, Chancellor of the Exchequer, good-humored and conciliatory, and Nicobar, Foreign Secretary, snaky and censorious. On his right Crassus, Colonial Secretary, elderly and anxious, and Balbus, Home Secretary, rude and thoughtless.

BALBUS. Holy snakes! look at Bill. [*To Boanerges*] Go home and dress yourself properly, man.

NICOBAR. Where do you think you are?

CRASSUS. Who do you think you are?

PLINY [*fingering the blouse*] Where did you buy it, Bill?

BOANERGES [*turning on them like a baited bear*] Well, if you come to that, who do you think you are, the lot of you?

PROTEUS [*conciliatory*] Never mind them, Bill: theyre jealous because they didnt think of it themselves. How did you get on with the King?

BOANERGES. Right as rain, Joe. You leave the King to me. I know how to handle him. If I'd been in the Cabinet these last three months there'd have been no crisis.

NICOBAR. He put you through it, did he?

BOANERGES. What do you mean? put me through it? Is this a police office?

PLINY. The third degree is not unknown in this palace, my boy. [*To Pamphilius*] Did the matron take a hand?

PAMPHILIUS. No. But the Princess Alice happened to drop in. She was greatly impressed by the President.

They all laugh uproariously at Boanerges.

BOANERGES. What in hell are you laughing at?

PROTEUS. Take no notice of them, Bill: they are only having their bit of fun with you as a new comer. Come, lads! enough of fooling: lets get to business. [*He takes the chair vacated by the King*].

Sempronius and Pamphilius at once rise and go out busily, taking some of their papers with them. Pliny takes Boanerges' chair, Balbus that of Sempronius, Boanerges that of Pamphilius, whilst Nicobar and Crassus take chairs from the wall and sit down at the ends of the writing tables, left and right of the Prime Minister respectively.

PROTEUS. Now to start with, do you chaps all fully realize that though we wiped out every other party at the last election, and have been in power for the last three years, this country has been governed during that time by the King?

NICOBAR. I dont see that. We—

PROTEUS [*impatiently*] Well, if you dont, then for Heaven's sake either resign and get out of the way of men who can see facts and look them in the face, or else take my job and lead the party yourself.

NICOBAR. The worst of you is that you wont face the fact that though youre Prime Minister youre not God Almighty. The king cant do anything except what we advise him to do. How can he govern the country if we have all the power and he has none?

BOANERGES. Dont talk silly, Nick. This indiarubber stamp theory doesnt work. What man has ever approached a king or a minister and been able to pick him up from the table and use him as youd use a bit of wood and brass and rubber? The King's a live man; and what more are you, with your blessed advice?

PLINY. Hullo, Bill! You have been having your mind improved by somebody.

BOANERGES. What do you mean? Isnt it what I have always said?

PROTEUS [*whose nerves are on edge*] Oh, will you stop squabbling. What are we going to say to the King when he comes in? If you will only hold together and say the same thing—or let me say it—he must give way. But he is as artful as the very devil. He'll have a pin to stick into the seat of every man of you. If you all start quarrelling and scolding and bawling, which is just what he wants you to do, it will end in his having his own way as usual, because one man that has a mind and knows it can always beat ten men who havnt and dont.

PLINY. Steady, Prime Minister. Youre overwrought.

PROTEUS. It's enough to drive a man mad. I am sorry.

PLINY [*changing the subject*] Where's Mandy?

NICOBAR. And Lizzie?

PROTEUS. Late as usual. Come! Business, business, business.

BOANERGES [*thunderously*] Order order!

PROTEUS. The King is working the Press against us. The King is making speeches. Things have come to a head. He said yesterday on the opening of the new Chamber of Commerce building that the king's veto is the only remaining defence of the people against corrupt legislation.

BOANERGES. So it is, by Jingo. What other defence is there? Democracy? Yah! We know what Democracy is worth. What we need is a Strong Man.

NICOBAR [*sneering*] Yourself for instance.

BOANERGES. I should stand a better chance than you, my lad, if we were a Republic, and the people could choose. And let me tell you that a republican president has more power than a king because the people know that they need a Strong Man to protect them against the rich.

PROTEUS [*flinging himself back in his chair in desperation*] This is a nice thing. Two Labor papers have leading articles this morning supporting the King; and the latest addition to the Cabinet here is a King's man. I resign.

General consternation except on the part of Nicobar, who displays cheerful unconcern, and of Boanerges, who squares himself with an iron face.

PLINY. } No: dont do that, Joe.
BALBUS. } What! Now! You cant. You mustnt.
CRASSUS. } Of course not. Out of the question.

PROTEUS. No use. [*Rising*] I resign, I tell you. You

can all go to the devil. I have lost my health, and almost lost my reason, trying to keep this Cabinet together in the face of the cunningest enemy popular government has ever had to face. I have had enough of it. [*Sitting down again*] I resign.

CRASSUS. But not at such a moment as this. Dont let us swop horses when crossing a stream.

NICOBAR. Why not, if the horse you have got is subject to hysterics?

BOANERGES. Not to mention that you may have more than one horse at your disposal.

PROTEUS. Right you are. Perfectly true. Take my job, Nick. It's vacant for you, Bill. I wish you joy of it.

PLINY. Now boys, boys, boys: be good. We cant make a new Cabinet before Magnus comes in. You have something in your pocket, Joe. Out with it. Read it to them.

PROTEUS [*taking a paper from his pocket*] What I was going to propose—and you can take it or leave it—is an ultimatum.

CRASSUS. Good!

PROTEUS. Either he signs this, or—[*he pauses significantly*]—!

NICOBAR. Or what?

PROTEUS [*disgusted*] Oh, you make me sick.

NICOBAR. Youre sick already, by your own account. I only ask, suppose he refuses to sign your ultimatum?

PROTEUS. You call yourself a Cabinet Minister, and you cant asnwer that!

NICOBAR. No I cant. I press my question. You said he must sign, OR. I ask, or what?

PROTEUS. Or we resign and tell the country that we cant carry on the King's Government under conditions which destroy our responsibility.

BALBUS. Thatll do it. He couldnt face that.

CRASSUS. Yes: thatll bunker him.

PROTEUS. Is that agreed?

PLINY.
CRASSUS. } Yes, yes, yes, 'greed 'greed 'greed.
BALBUS.

BOANERGES. I retain an open mind. Let us hear the ultimatum.

NICOBAR. Yes: lets hear it.

PROTEUS. Memorandum of understanding arrived at—

The King enters, with Amanda, Postmistress General, a merry lady in uniform like the men, on his left, and Lysistrata, Powermistress General, a grave lady in academic robes, on his right. All rise. The Prime Minister's face darkens.

MAGNUS. Welcome, gentlemen. I hope I am not too early. [*Noting the Prime Minister's scowl*] Am I intruding?

PROTEUS. I protest. It is intolerable. I call a conference of my Cabinet to consider our position in regard to the prerogative; and I find the two lady members, the Postmistress General and the Powermistress General, closeted with your Majesty instead of being in their places to confer with me.

LYSISTRATA. You mind your own business, Joe.

MAGNUS. Oh no: really, really, my dear Lysistrata, you must not take that line. Our business is to meddle in everybody's business. A Prime Minister is a busybody by profession. So is a monarch. So are we all.

LYSISTRATA. Well, they say everybody's business is nobody's business, which is just what Joe is fit for. [*She takes a chair from the wall with a powerful hand, and swings it forward to the inside corner of Sempronius's table, where she stands waiting for the King to sit down.*]

PROTEUS. This is what I have to put up with when I am on the verge of a nervous breakdown [*he sits down distractedly, and buries his face in his hands*].

AMANDA [*going to him and petting him*] Come, Joe! dont make a scene. You asked for it, you know.

NICOBAR. What do you go provoking Lizzie for like that? You know she has a temper.

LYSISTRATA. There is nothing whatever wrong with my temper. But I am not going to stand any of Joe's nonsense; and the sooner he makes up his mind to that the smoother our proceedings are likely to be.

BOANERGES. I protest. I say, let us be dignified. I say, let us respect ourselves and respect the throne. All this Joe and Bill and Nick and Lizzie: we might as well be hobnobbing in a fried fish shop. The Prime Minister is the prime minister: he isnt Joe. The Powermistress isnt Lizzie: she's Lysis Traitor.

LYSISTRATA [*who has evidently been a schoolmistress*] Certainly not, Bill. She is Ly Sistrata. You had better say Lizzie: it is easier to pronounce.

BOANERGES [*scornfully*] Ly Sistrata! A more foolish affectation I never heard: you might as well call me Bo Annerjeeze [*he flings himself into his chair*].

MAGNUS [*sweetly*] Shall we sit, ladies and gentlemen!

Boanerges hastily rises and sits down again. The King sits in Pliny's chair. Lysistrata and the rest of the men resume their seats, leaving Pliny and Amanda standing. Amanda takes an empty chair in each hand and plants them side by side between the King and the table of Pamphilius.

AMANDA. There you are, Plin. [*She sits next the table*].

PLINY. Ta ta, Mandy. Pardon me: I should have said Amanda. [*He sits next the King*].

AMANDA. Don't mention it, darling.

BOANERGES. Order, order!

AMANDA [*waves him a kiss*]!!

MAGNUS. Prime Minister: the word is with you. Why have you all simultaneously given me the great pleasure of exercising your constitutional right of access to the sovereign?

LYSISTRATA. Have I that right, sir; or havnt I?

MAGNUS. Most undoubtedly you have.

LYSISTRATA. You hear that, Joe?

PROTEUS. I—

BALBUS. Oh for Heaven's sake dont contradict her, Joe. We shall never get anywhere at this rate. Come to the crisis.

NICOBAR. ⎫   ⎧Yes yes: the crisis!
CRASSUS. ⎬[*together*]⎨Yes yes: come along!
PLINY.   ⎭   ⎩The crisis: out with it!

BALBUS. The ultimatum. Lets have the ultimatum.

MAGNUS. Oh, there is an ultimatum! I gathered from yesterday's evening papers that there is a crisis —another crisis. But the ultimatum is new to me. [*To Proteus*] Have you an ultimatum?

PROTEUS. Your Majesty's allusion to the royal veto in a speech yesterday has brought matters to a head.

MAGNUS. It was perhaps indelicate. But you all allude so freely to your own powers—to the supremacy of Parliament and the voice of the people and so forth—that I fear I have lost any little delicacy I ever possessed. If you may flourish your thunderbolts why may I not shoulder my little popgun of a veto and strut up and down with it for a moment?

NICOBAR. This is not a subject for jesting—

MAGNUS [*interrupting him quickly*] I am not jesting, Mr Nicobar. But I am certainly trying to discuss our differences in a good-humored manner. Do you wish me to lose my temper and make scenes?

[304]

AMANDA. Oh please no, your Majesty. We get enough of that from Joe.

PROTEUS. I pro—

MAGNUS [*his hand persuasively on the Prime Minister's arm*] Take care, Prime Minister: take care: do not let your wily Postmistress General provoke you to supply the evidence against yourself.

All the rest laugh.

PROTEUS [*coolly*] I thank your Majesty for the caution. The Postmistress General has never forgiven me for not making her First Lady of the Admiralty. She has three nephews in the navy.

AMANDA. Oh you— [*She swallows the epithet, and contents herself with shaking her fist at the Premier*].

MAGNUS. Tch-tch-tch! Gently, Amanda, gently. Three very promising lads: they do you credit.

AMANDA. I never wanted them to go to sea. I could have found them better jobs in the Post Office.

MAGNUS. Apart from Amanda's family relations, am I face to face with a united Cabinet.

PLINY. No, sir. You are face to face with a squabbling Cabinet; but, on the constitutional question, united we stand: divided we fall.

BALBUS. That is so.

NICOBAR. Hear hear!

MAGNUS. What is the constitutional question? Do you deny the royal veto? or do you object only to my reminding my subjects of its existence?

NICOBAR. What we say is that the king has no right to remind his subjects of anything constitutional except by the advice of the Prime Minister, and in words which he has read and approved.

MAGNUS. Which Prime Minister? There are so many of them in the Cabinet.

BOANERGES. There! Serves you all right! Arnt you

ashamed of yourselves? But I am not surprised, Joseph Proteus. I own I like a Prime Minister that knows how to be a Prime Minister. Why do you let them take the word out of your mouth every time?

PROTEUS. If His Majesty wants a Cabinet of dumb dogs he will not get it from my party.

BALBUS. Hear, hear, Joe!

MAGNUS. Heaven forbid! The variety of opinion in the Cabinet is always most instructive and interesting. Who is to be its spokesman today?

PROTEUS. I know your Majesty's opinion of me; but let—

MAGNUS [*before he can proceed*] Let me state it quite frankly. My opinion of you is that no man knows better than you when to speak and when to let others speak for you; when to make scenes and threaten resignation; and when to be as cool as a cucumber.

PROTEUS [*not altogether displeased*] Well, sir, I hope I am not such a fool as some fools think me. I may not always keep my temper. You would not be surprised at that if you knew how much temper I have to keep. [*He straightens up and becomes impressively eloquent*]. At this moment my cue is to shew you, not my own temper, but the temper of my Cabinet. What the Foreign Secretary and the Chancellor of the Exchequer and the Home Secretary have told you is true. If we are to carry on your government we cannot have you making speeches that express your own opinions and not ours. We cannot have you implying that everything that is of any value in our legislation is your doing and not ours. We cannot have you telling people that their only safeguard against the political encroachments of big business

[306]

whilst we are doing nothing but bungling and squabbling is your power of veto. It has got to stop, once for all.

BALBUS. } Hear hear!
NICOBAR. }

PROTEUS. Is that clear?

MAGNUS. Far clearer than I have ever dared to make it, Mr Proteus. Except, by the way, on one point. When you say that all this of which you complain must cease once for all, do you mean that henceforth I am to agree with you or you with me?

PROTEUS. I mean that when you disagree with us you are to keep your disagreement to yourself.

MAGNUS. That would be a very heavy responsibility for me. If I see you leading the nation over the edge of a precipice may I not warn it?

BALBUS. It is our business to warn it, not yours.

MAGNUS. Suppose you dont do your business! Suppose you dont see the danger! That has happened. It may happen again.

CRASSUS [*insinuating*] As democrats, I think we are bound to proceed on the assumption that such a thing cannot happen.

BOANERGES. Rot! It's happening all the time until somebody has the gumption to put his foot down and stop it.

CRASSUS. Yes: I know. But that is not democracy.

BOANERGES. Democracy be— [*he leaves the word unspoken*]! I have thirty years experience of democracy. So have most of you. I say no more.

BALBUS. Wages are too high, if you ask me. Anybody can earn from five to twenty pounds a week now, and a big dole when there is no job for him. And what Englishman will give his mind to politics as long as he can afford to keep a motor car?

NICOBAR. How many voted at the last election? Not seven per cent of the register.

BALBUS. Yes; and the seven per cent were only a parcel of sillies playing at ins and outs. To make democracy work in Crassus's way we need poverty and hardship.

PROTEUS [*emphatically*] And we have abolished poverty and hardship. That is why the people trust us. [*To the King*] And that is why you will have to give way to us. We have the people of England in comfort —solid middle class comfort—at our backs.

MAGNUS. No: we have not abolished poverty and hardship. Our big business men have abolished them. But how? By sending our capital abroad to places where poverty and hardship still exist: in other words, where labor is cheap. We live in comfort on the imported profits of that capital. We are all ladies and gentlemen now.

NICOBAR. Well, what more do you want?

PLINY. You surely dont grudge us our wonderful prosperity, sir.

MAGNUS. I want it to last.

NICOBAR. Why shouldnt it last? [*Rising*] Own the truth. You had rather have the people poor, and pose as their champion and savior, than have to admit that the people are better off under our government— under our squabbling and bungling, as you call it.

MAGNUS. No: it was the Prime Minister who used those expressions.

NICOBAR. Dont quibble: he was quoting them from your reptile press. What I say is that we stand for high wages, and you are always belittling and opposing the men that pay them. Well, the voters like high wages. They know when they are well off; and they dont know what you are grumbling about; and thats what will beat you every time you try to stir them against us [*he resumes his seat*].

PLINY. There is no need to rub it in like that, Nick. We're all good friends. Nobody objects to prosperity.

MAGNUS. You think this prosperity is safe?

NICOBAR. Safe!

PLINY. Oh come, sir! Really!

BALBUS. Safe! Look at my constituency: Northeast-by-north Birmingham, with its four square miles of confectionery works! Do you know that in the Christmas cracker trade Birmingham is the workshop of the world?

CRASSUS. Take Gateshead and Middlesbrough alone! Do you know that there has not been a day's unemployment there for five years past, and that their daily output of chocolate creams totals up to twenty thousand tons?

MAGNUS. It is certainly a consoling thought that if we were peacefully blockaded by the League of Nations we could live for at least three weeks on our chocolate creams.

NICOBAR. You neednt sneer at the sweets: we turn out plenty of solid stuff. Where will you find the equal of the English golf club?

BALBUS. Look at the potteries: the new crown Derby! the new Chelsea! Look at the tapestries! Why, Greenwich Goblin has chased the French stuff out of the market.

CRASSUS. Dont forget our racing motor boats and cars, sir: the finest on earth, and all individually designed. No cheap mass production stuff there.

PLINY. And our live stock! Can you beat the English polo pony?

AMANDA. Or the English parlormaid? She wins in all the international beauty shows.

PLINY. Now Mandy, Mandy! None of your triviality.

MAGNUS. I am not sure that the British parlormaid is not the only real asset in your balance sheet.

AMANDA [*triumphant*] Aha! [*To Pliny*] You go home to bed and reflect on that, old man.

PROTEUS. Well, sir? Are you satisfied that we have the best paid proletariat in the world on our side?

MAGNUS [*gravely*] I dread revolution.

All except the two women laugh uproariously at this.

BOANERGES. I must join them there, sir. I am as much against chocolate creams as you are: they never agree with me. But a revolution in England!!! Put that out of your head, sir. Not if you were to tear up Magna Carta in Trafalgar Square, and light the fires of Smithfield to burn every member of the House of Commons.

MAGNUS. I was not thinking of a revolution in England. I was thinking of the countries on whose tribute we are living. Suppose it occurs to them to stop paying it! That has happened before.

PLINY. Oh no, sir: no, no, no. What would become of their foreign trade with us?

MAGNUS. At a pinch, I think they could do without the Christmas crackers.

CRASSUS. Oh, thats childish.

MAGNUS. Children in their innocence are sometimes very practical, Mr Colonial Secretary. The more I see of the sort of prosperity that comes of your leaving our vital industries to big business men as long as they keep your constituents quiet with high wages, the more I feel as if I were sitting on a volcano.

LYSISTRATA [*who has been listening with implacable contempt to the discussion, suddenly breaks in in a sepulchral contralto*] Hear hear! My department was perfectly able and ready to deal with the supply of power from the tides in the north of Scotland, and you gave it away, like the boobs you are, to the Pentland Firth Syndicate: a gang of foreign capitalists who will make billions out of it at the people's expense while we are bungling and squabbling. Crassus worked that. His uncle is chairman.

CRASSUS. A lie. A flat lie. He is not related to me. He is only my stepson's father-in-law.

BALBUS. I demand an explanation of the words bungling and squabbling. We have had quite enough of them here today. Who are you getting at? It was not I who bungled the Factory Bill. I found it on my desk when I took office, with all His Majesty's suggestions in the margin; and you know it.

PROTEUS. Have you all done playing straight into His Majesty's hand, and making my situation here impossible?

Guilty silence.

PROTEUS [*proceeding deliberately and authoritatively*] The question before us is not one of our manners and our abilities. His Majesty will not press that question, because if he did he would oblige us to raise the question of his own morals.

MAGNUS [*starts*] What!

BALBUS. Good, Joe!

CRASSUS [*aside to Amanda*] Thats got him.

MAGNUS. Am I to take that threat seriously, Mr Proteus?

PROTEUS. If you try to prejudice what is a purely constitutional question by personal scandal, it will be easy enough for us to throw your mud back. In this conflict we are the challengers. You have the choice of weapons. If you choose scandal, we'll take you on at that. Personally I shall deplore it if you do. No good will come of washing our dirty linen in public. But dont make any mistake as to what will happen. I will be plain with you: I will dot the Is and cross the Ts. You will say that Crassus is a jobber.

CRASSUS [*springing up*] I—

PROTEUS [*fiercely crushing him*] Sit down. Leave this to me.

CRASSUS [*sits*] I a jobber! Well!

PROTEUS [*continuing*] You will say that I should never have given the Home Office to a bully like Balbus—

BALBUS [*intimidated by the fate of Crassus, but unable to forbear a protest*] Look here, Joe—

PROTEUS. You shut up, Bert. It's true.

BALBUS [*subsides with a shrug*]!

PROTEUS. Well, what will happen? There will be no denials, no excuses, no vindications. We shall not fall into that trap, clever as you are at setting it. Crassus will say just simply that you are a freethinker. And Balbus will say that you are a libertine.

THE MALE CABINET [*below their breaths*] Aha-a-a-a-h!!!

PROTEUS. Now, King Magnus! Our cards are on the table. What have you to say?

MAGNUS. Admirably put! People ask how it is that with all these strong characters around you hold your own as the only possible Prime Minister, in spite of your hysterics and tantrums, your secretiveness and your appalling laziness—

BALBUS [*delighted*] Hear hear! Youre getting it now, Joe.

MAGNUS [*continuing*] But when the decisive moment comes, they find out what a wonderful man you are.

PROTEUS. I am not a wonderful man. There is not a man or woman here whose job I could do as well as they do it. I am Prime Minister for the same reason

[312]

that all Prime Ministers have been Prime Ministers: because I am good for nothing else. But I can keep to the point—when it suits me. And I can keep you to the point, sir, whether it suits you or not.

MAGNUS. At all events you do not flatter kings. One of them, at least, is grateful to you for that.

PROTEUS. Kings, as you and I very well know, rule their ministers by flattering them; and now that you are the only king left in the civilized half of Europe Nature seems to have concentrated in you all the genius for flattery that she used to have to divide between half a dozen kings, three emperors, and a Sultan.

MAGNUS. But what interest has a king in flattering a subject?

AMANDA. Suppose she's a goodlooking woman, sir!

NICOBAR. Suppose he has a lot of money, and the king's hard up!

PROTEUS. Suppose he is a Prime Minister, and you can do nothing except by his advice.

MAGNUS [*smiling with his utmost charm*] Ah, there you have hit the nail on the head. Well, I suppose I must surrender. I am beaten. You are all too clever for me.

BOANERGES. Well, nothing can be fairer than that.

PLINY [*rubbing his hands*] You are a gentleman, sir. We shant rub it in, you know.

BALBUS. Ever the best of friends. I am the last to kick a man when he's down.

CRASSUS. I may be a jobber; but nobody shall say that I am an ungenerous opponent.

BOANERGES [*suddenly overwhelmed with emotion, rises and begins singing in stentorian tones*]

> Should auld acquaintance be forgot,
> And never brought to mind—

Amanda bursts into uncontrollable laughter. The King looks reproachfully at her, struggling hard to keep his countenance. The others are beginning to join in the chorus when Proteus rises in a fury.

PROTEUS. Are you all drunk?

Dead silence. Boanerges sits down hastily. The other singers pretend that they have disapproved of his minstrelsy.

PROTEUS. You are at present engaged in a tug of war with the King: the tug of your lives. You think you have won. You havnt. All that has happened is that the King has let go the rope. You are sprawling on your backs; and he is laughing at you. Look at him! [*He sits down contemptuously*].

MAGNUS [*making no further attempt to conceal his merriment*] Come to my rescue, Amanda. It was you who set me off.

AMANDA [*wreathed with smiles*] You got me so nicely, sir. [*To Boanerges*] Bill: you are a great boob.

BOANERGES. I dont understand this, I understood His Majesty to give way to us in, I must say, the handsomest manner. Cant we take our victory like gentlemen?

MAGNUS. Perhaps I had better explain. I quite appreciate the frank and magnanimous spirit—may I say the English spirit?—in which my little concession has been received, especially by you, Mr Boanerges. But in truth it leaves matters just where they were; for I should never have dreamt of entering on a campaign of recrimination such as the Prime Minister suggested. As he has reminded you, my own character is far too vulnerable. A king is not allowed the luxury of a good character. Our country has produced millions of blameless greengrocers, but not

one blameless monarch. I have to rule over more
religious sects than I can count. To rule them impartially I must not belong to any of them; and they all
regard people who do not belong to them as atheists.
My court includes several perfectly respectable wives
and mothers whose strange vanity it is to be talked
about as abandoned females. To gain the reputation
of being the king's mistress they would do almost
anything except give the unfortunate monarch the
pleasure of substantiating their claim. Side by side
with them are the ladies who are really unscrupulous.
They are so careful of their reputations that they lose
no opportunity of indignantly denying that they have
ever yielded to solicitations which have in fact never
been made to them. Thus every king is supposed to
be a libertine; and as, oddly enough, he owes a great
part of his popularity to this belief, he cannot deny it
without deeply disappointing his subjects.

*There is a rather grim silence, during which the King
looks round in vain for some encouraging response.*

LYSISTRATA [*severely*] Your Majesty's private affairs
do not concern us, in any case.

AMANDA [*splutters into an irrepressible laugh*]!!

MAGNUS [*looks reproachfully at Amanda*]!

AMANDA [*composing her features as best she can*]
Excuse me.

CRASSUS. I hope your Majesty recognizes that kings
are not the only people to whom certain sorts of mud
always stick, no matter what fool throws them. Call
a minister a jobber—

BALBUS. Or a bungler.

CRASSUS. Yes, or a bungler, and everybody believes
it. Jobbery and incompetence are the two sorts of mud
that stick to us, no matter how honest or capable we
are; and we havnt the royal advantage that you enjoy,

that the more the ladies take away your character the better the people like you.

BOANERGES [*suddenly*] Prime Minister: will you tell me what the Postmistress General is sniggering at?

AMANDA. This a free country, Bill. A sense of humor is not a crime. And when the King is not setting me off, you are.

BOANERGES. Where is the joke? I dont see it.

AMANDA. If you could see a joke, Bill, you wouldnt be the great popular orator you are.

BOANERGES. Thank Heaven, I am not a silly giggler like some I could mention.

AMANDA. Thanks, dearest Bill. Now, Joe: dont you think you have let us run loose long enough? What about that ultimatum?

MAGNUS [*shaking his head at her*] Traitor!

PROTEUS. I am in no hurry. His Majesty's speeches are very wise and interesting; and your back chat amuses both you and him. But the ultimatum is here all the time; and I shall not leave this room until I have His Majesty's signed pledge that its conditions will be observed.

All become gravely attentive.

MAGNUS. What are its terms?

PROTEUS. First, no more royal speeches.

MAGNUS. What! Not even if you dictate them?

PROTEUS. Not even if we dictate them. Your Majesty has a way of unrolling the manuscript and winking—

MAGNUS. Winking!

PROTEUS. You know what I mean. The best speech in the world can be read in such a way as to set the audience laughing at it. We have had enough of that. So, in future, no speeches.

MAGNUS. A dumb king?

PROTEUS. Of course we cannot object to such

speeches as "We declare this foundation stone well and truly laid" and so forth. But politically, yes: a dumb king.

PLINY [*to soften it*] A constitutional king.

PROTEUS [*implacably*] A dumb king.

MAGNUS. Hm! What next?

PROTEUS. The working of the Press from the palace back stairs must cease.

MAGNUS. You know that I have no control of the Press. The Press is in the hands of men much richer than I, who would not insert a single paragraph against their own interests even if it were signed by my own hand and sent to them with a royal command.

PROTEUS. We know that. But though these men are richer than you, they are not cleverer. They get amusing articles, spiced with exclusive backstairs information, that dont seem to them to have anything to do with politics. The next thing they know is that their pet shares have dropped fifteen points; that capital is frightened off their best prospectuses; and that some of the best measures in our party program are made to look like city jobs.

MAGNUS. Am I supposed to write these articles?

NICOBAR. Your man Sempronius does. I can spot his fist out of fifty columns.

CRASSUS. So can I. When he is getting at me he always begins the sentence with "Singularly enough."

PLINY [*chuckling*] Thats his trademark. "Singularly enough." Ha! ha!

MAGNUS. Is there to be any restriction on the other side? I have noticed, for instance, that in a certain newspaper which loses no opportunity of disparaging the throne, the last sentence of the leading article almost invariably begins with the words "Once for all." Whose trademark is that?

PROTEUS. Mine.

MAGNUS. Frank, Mr Proteus.

PROTEUS. I know when to be frank. I learnt the trick from Your Majesty.

AMANDA [*tries not to laugh*]!

MAGNUS [*gently reproachful*] Amanda: what is the joke now? I am surprised at you.

AMANDA. Joe frank! When I want to find out what he is up to I have to come and ask your Majesty.

LYSISTRATA. That is perfectly true. In this Cabinet there is no such thing as a policy. Every man plays for his own hand.

NICOBAR. It's like a game of cards.

BALBUS. Only there are no partners.

LYSISTRATA. Except Crassus and Nicobar.

PLINY. Good, Lizzie! He! he! he!

NICOBAR. What do you mean?

LYSISTRATA. You know quite well what I mean. When will you learn, Nicobar, that it is no use trying to browbeat me. I began life as a schoolmistress; and I can browbeat any man in this Cabinet or out of it if he is fool enough to try to compete with me in that department.

BOANERGES. Order! order! Cannot the Prime Minister check these unseemly personalities?

PROTEUS. They give me time to think, Bill. When you have had as much parliamentary experience as I have you will be very glad of an interruption occasionally. May I proceed?

Silence.

PROTEUS. His Majesty asks whether the restriction on press campaigning is to be entirely onesided. That, I take it, sir, is your question.

MAGNUS [*nods assent*]!

PROTEUS. The answer is in the affirmative.

BALBUS. Good!

MAGNUS. Anything more?

PROTEUS. Yes: one thing more. The veto must not be mentioned again. That can apply to both sides, if you like. The veto is dead.

MAGNUS. May we not make a historical reference to the corpse?

PROTEUS. No. I cannot carry on the King's government unless I can give pledges and carry them out. What is my pledge worth if our constituents are reminded every day that the King may veto anything that Parliament does? Do you expect me to say, when I am asked for a pledge. "You must ask the King"?

MAGNUS. I have to say "You must ask the Prime Minister."

PLINY [consoling him] Thats the constitution, you know.

MAGNUS. Quite. I only mention it to shew that the Prime Minister does not really wish to kill the veto. He only wishes to move it next door.

PROTEUS. The people live next door. The name on the brass plate is Public Opinion.

MAGNUS [gravely] Admirably turned, Mr Prime Minister; but unreal. I am far more subject to public opinion than you, because, thanks to the general belief in democracy, you can always pretend that what you do is done by the will of the people, who, God knows, never dreamt of it, and would not have understood it if they had; whereas, for what a king does, he, and he alone, is held responsible. A demagogue may steal a horse where a king dare not look over a hedge.

LYSISTRATA. I doubt if that is any longer true, sir. I know that I get blamed for everything that goes wrong in my department.

MAGNUS. Ah! But what a despot you are, Lysistrata!

Granted, however, that the people have found out long ago that democracy is humbug, and that instead of establishing responsible government it has abolished it, do you not see what this means?

BOANERGES [*scandalized*] Steady, steady! I cannot sit here and listen to such a word as humbug being applied to democracy. I am sorry, sir; but with all respect for you, I really must draw the line at that.

MAGNUS. You are right, Mr Boanerges, as you always are. Democracy is a very real thing, with much less humbug about it than many older institutions. But it means, not that the people govern, but that the responsibility and the veto now belong neither to kings nor demagogues as such, but to whoever is clever enough to get them.

LYSISTRATA. Yourself, sir, for example?

MAGNUS. I think I am in the running. That is why I do not feel bound to accept this ultimatum. By signing it I put myself out of the running. Why should I?

BALBUS. Because youre the king: thats why.

MAGNUS. Does it follow?

PROTEUS. If two men ride the same horse, one must ride behind.

LYSISTRATA. Which?

PROTEUS [*turning to her sharply*] What was that you said?

LYSISTRATA [*with placid but formidable obstinacy and ironical explicitness*] I said Which? You said that if two men rode the same horse one of them must ride behind. I said Which? [*Explanatorily*] Which man must ride behind?

AMANDA. Got it, Joe?

PROTEUS. That is exactly the question that has to be settled here and now.

AMANDA. "Once for all."

Everybody laughs except Proteus, who rises in a fury.

PROTEUS. I will not stand this perpetual tomfooling. I had rather be a dog than the Prime Minister of a country where the only things the inhabitants can be serious about are football and refreshments. Lick the King's boots: that is all you are fit for. [*He dashes out of the room*].

BALBUS. Youve done it now, Mandy. I hope youre proud of yourself.

MAGNUS. It is you, Amanda, who should go and coax him back. But I suppose I must do it myself, as usual. Excuse me, ladies and gentlemen.

He rises. The rest rise. He goes out.

BOANERGES. I told you. I told you what would come of conducting a conference with His Majesty as if it were a smoking concert. I am disgusted. [*He flings himself back into his chair*].

BALBUS. We'd just cornered the old fox; and then Amanda must have her silly laugh and lets him out of it [*he sits*].

NICOBAR. What are we to do now? thats what I want to know.

AMANDA [*incorrigible*] I suggest a little community singing [*she makes conductorlike gestures*].

NICOBAR. Yah!! [*he sits down very sulkily*].

AMANDA [*sits down with a little splutter of laughter*]!

CRASSUS [*thoughtful*] Take it easy, friends. Joe knows what he is about.

LYSISTRATA. Of course he does. I can excuse you, Bill, because it's your first day in the Cabinet. But if the rest of you havnt found out by this time that Joe's rages are invariably calculated, then nothing will ever teach you anything [*she sits down contemptuously*].

BOANERGES [*in his grandest manner*] Well, madam, I know I am a newcomer: everything must have a beginning. I am open to argument and conviction. The Prime Minister brought this conference, in what I admit was a very able and resolute manner, to the verge of a decision. Then, in a fit of childish temper he breaks up the conference, leaving us looking like fools with nothing done. And you tell me he did it on purpose! Where was the advantage to him in such a display? answer me that.

LYSISTRATA. He is settling the whole business with the King behind our backs. That is what Joe always contrives to do, by hook or crook.

PLINY. You didnt arrange it with him, Mandy: did you?

AMANDA. There wasnt any need to arrange it. Joe can always depend on one or other of us saying something that will give him an excuse for flying out.

CRASSUS. In my opinion, ladies and gentlemen, we have done our bit, and may leave the rest to Joe. Matters had reached a point at which it was yes or no between the Cabinet and the Crown. There is only one sort of committee that is better than a committee of two; and that is a committee of one. Like the family in Wordsworth's poem, we are seven—

LYSISTRATA. Eight.

CRASSUS. Well, seven or eight, we were too many for the final grapple. Two persons sticking to the point are worth eight all over the shop. So my advice is that we just sit here quietly until Joe comes back and tells us whats been settled. Perhaps Amanda will oblige with a song. [*He resumes his seat*].

The King returns with Proteus, who looks glum. All rise. The two resume their seats in silence. The rest sit down.

MAGNUS [*very grave*] The Prime Minister has been good enough to pursue the discussion with me in private to a point at which the issue is now clear. If I do not accept the ultimatum I shall receive your resignations and his; and the country will learn from his explanatory speech in the House of Commons that it is to choose between Cabinet government and monarchical government: an issue on which I frankly say that I should be very sorry to win, as I cannot carry on without the support of a body of ministers whose existence gives the English people a sensation of self-government.

AMANDA [*splutters*]!

CRASSUS [*whispers*] Shut up, will you?

MAGNUS [*continuing*] Naturally I want to avert a conflict in which success would damage me and failure disable me. But you tell me that I can do so only by signing pledges which would make me a mere Lord Chamberlain, without even the despotism which he exercises over the theatre. I should sink below the level of the meanest of my subjects, my sole privilege being that of being shot at when some victim of misgovernment resorts to assassination to avenge himself. How am I to defend myself? You are many: I oppose you single-handed. There was a time when the king could depend on the support of the aristocracy and the cultivated bourgeoisie. Today there is not a single aristocrat left in politics, not a single member of the professions, not a single leading personage in big business or finance. They are richer than ever, more powerful than ever, more able and better educated than ever. But not one of them will touch this drudgery of government, this public work that never ends because we cannot finish one job without creating ten fresh ones. We get no thanks for it because ninety-nine hundredths of it is unknown to the people, and the remaining hundredth is resented by them as an invasion of their liberty or an increase in their taxation. It wears out the strongest man, and even the strongest woman, in five or six years. It slows down to nothing when we are fresh from our holidays and best able to bear it, and rises in an overwhelming wave through some unforeseen catastrophe when we are on the verge of nervous breakdown from overwork and fit for rest and sleep only. And this drudgery, remember, is a sweated trade, the only one now left in this country. My civil list leaves me a poor man among multi-millionaires. Your salaries can be earned ten times over in the city by anyone with outstanding organizing or administrative ability. History tells us that the first Lord Chancellor who abandoned the woolsack for the city boardroom struck the nation with amazement: today the nation would be equally amazed if a man of his ability thought it worth his while to prefer the woolsack even to the stool of an office boy as a jumping-off place for his ambition. Our work is no longer even respected. It is looked down on by our men of genius as dirty work. What great actor would exchange his stage? what great barrister his court? what great preacher his pulpit? for the squalor of the political arena in which we have to struggle with foolish factions in parliament and with ignorant voters in the constituencies? The scientists will have nothing to do with us; for the atmosphere of politics is not the atmosphere of science. Even political science, the science by which civilization must live or die, is busy explaining the past whilst we have to grapple with the present: it leaves the ground before our feet in black darkness whilst it lights up every corner of the landscape behind us. All the talent and genius of the country is bought up by the flood of unearned money.

On that poisoned wealth talent and genius live far more luxuriously in the service of the rich than we in the service of our country. Politics, once the centre of attraction for ability, public spirit, and ambition, has now become the refuge of a few fanciers of public speaking and party intrigue who find all the other avenues to distinction closed to them either by their lack of practical ability, their comparative poverty and lack of education, or, let me hasten to add, their hatred of oppression and injustice, and their contempt for the chicaneries and false pretences of commercialized professionalism. History tells us of a gentleman-statesman who declared that such people were not fit to govern. Within a year it was discovered that they could govern at least as well as anyone else who could be persuaded to take on the job. Then began that abandonment of politics by the old governing class which has ended in all Cabinets, conservative no less than progressive, being what were called in the days of that rash statesman Labor Cabinets. Do not misunderstand me: I do not want the old governing class back. It governed so selfishly that the people would have perished if democracy had not swept it out of politics. But evil as it was in many ways, at least it stood above the tyranny of popular ignorance and popular poverty. Today only the king stands above that tyranny. You are dangerously subject to it. In spite of my urgings and remonstrances you have not yet dared to take command of our schools and put a stop to the inculcation upon your unfortunate children of superstitions and prejudices that stand like stone walls across every forward path. Are you well advised in trying to reduce me to your own slavery to them? If I do not stand above them there is no longer any reason for my existence at all. I stand for the future and the past, for the posterity that has no vote and the tradition that never had any. I stand for the great abstractions: for conscience and virtue; for the eternal against the expedient; for the evolutionary appetite against the day's gluttony; for intellectual integrity, for humanity, for the rescue of industry from commercialism and of science from professionalism, for everything that you desire as sincerely as I, but which in you is held in leash by the Press, which can organize against you the ignorance and superstition, the timidity and credulity, the gullibility and prudery, the hating and hunting instinct of the voting mob, and cast you down from power if you utter a word to alarm or displease the adventurers who have the Press in their pockets. Between you and that tyranny stands the throne. I have no elections to fear; and if any newspaper magnate dares offend me, that magnate's fashionable wife and marriageable daughters will soon make him understand that the King's displeasure is still a sentence of social death within range of St James's Palace. Think of the things you dare not do! the persons you dare not offend! Well, a king with a little courage may tackle them for you. Responsibilities which would break your backs may still be borne on a king's shoulders. But he must be a king, not a puppet. You would be responsible for a puppet: remember that. But whilst you continue to support me as a separate and independent estate of the realm, I am your scapegoat: you get the credit of all our popular legislation whilst you put the odium of all our resistance to ignorant popular clamor on me. I ask you, before you play your last card and destroy me, to consider where you will be without me. Think once: think twice: for your danger is, not that I may defeat you, but that your success is certain if you insist.

LYSISTRATA. Splendid!

AMANDA. You did speak that piece beautifully, sir.

BALBUS [*grumbling*] All very well; but what about my brother-in-law Mike?

LYSISTRATA [*maddened*] Oh, confound your brother-in-law Mike!

BOANERGES. Order! order!

LYSISTRATA [*to the King*] I beg your pardon, sir; but really—at a moment like this—[*words fail her*].

MAGNUS [*to Balbus*] If I had not put my foot down, Mr Balbus, the Prime Minister would have been unable to keep your brother-in-law out of the Cabinet.

BALBUS [*aggressively*] And why should he not be in the Cabinet?

AMANDA. Booze, my Balby: booze. Raising the elbow!

BALBUS [*bullying*] Who says so?

AMANDA. I do, darling.

BALBUS [*subsiding*] Well, perhaps it would surprise you all to know that Mike doesnt drink as much as I do.

AMANDA. You carry it better, Bert.

PLINY. Mike never knows when to stop.

CRASSUS. The time for Mike to stop is before he begins, if you ask me.

LYSISTRATA [*impetuously*] What sort of animals are you—you men? The King puts before us the most serious question of principle we shall ever have to deal with; and off you start discussing whether this drunken wretch takes honest whisky like Balbus or methylated spirit or petrol or whatever he can lay his hands on when the fit takes him.

BALBUS. I agree with that. What does it matter what Mike drinks? What does it matter whether he drinks or not? Mike would strengthen the Cabinet because he represents Breakages, Limited, the biggest industrial corporation in the country.

LYSISTRATA [*letting herself go*] Just so! Breakages, Limited! just so! Listen to me, sir; and judge whether I have not reason to feel everything you have just said to the very marrow of my bones. Here am I, the Powermistress Royal. I have to organize and administer all the motor power in the country for the good of the country. I have to harness the winds and the tides, the oils and the coal seams. I have to see that every little sewing machine in the Hebrides, every dentist's drill in Shetland, every carpet sweeper in Margate, has its stream of driving power on tap from a switch in the wall as punctually as the great thundering dynamos of our big industrial plants. I do it; but it costs twice as much as it should. Why? Because every new invention is bought up and suppressed by Breakages, Limited. Every breakdown, every accident, every smash and crash, is a job for them. But for them we should have unbreakable glass, unbreakable steel, imperishable materials of all sorts. But for them our goods trains could be started and stopped without battering and tearing the vitals out of every wagon and sending it to their repair shops once a week instead of once a year. Our national repair bill runs up to hundreds of millions. I could name you a dozen inventions within my own term of office which would have effected enormous economies in breakages and breakdowns; but these people can afford to pay an inventor more for his machine or his process or whatever it may be than he could hope to make by a legitimate use of it; and when they have bought it they smother it. When the inventor is poor and not good at defending himself they make bogus trials of his machine and report that it is no use. I have been shot at twice by inventors driven crazy by this sort of thing: they blamed me for it—as if I could stand up against this monster with its millions and its newspapers and its fingers in every pie. It is heartbreaking. I love my department: I dream of nothing but its efficiency: with me it comes before every personal tie, every happiness that common women run after. I would give my right hand to see these people in the bankruptcy court with half their business abolished and the other half done in public workshops where public losses are not private gains. You stand for that, sir; and I would be with you to the last drop of my blood if I dared. But what can I do? If I said one word of this in public, not a week would pass in the next two years without an article on the inefficiency and corruption of all Government departments, especially departments managed, like mine, by females. They would dig up the very machines they have buried, and make out that it is my fault that they have never been brought into use. They would set their private police to watch me day and night to get something against my private character. One of their directors told me to my face that by lifting up his finger he could get my windows broken by the mob; and that Breakages, Limited, would get the job of putting in new glass. And it is true. It is infamous; it is outrageous; but if I attempt to fight them I shall be hounded out of public life, and they will shove Mouldly Mike into the Cabinet to run my department in their interests: that is, to make such a failure of it that Joe will have to sell it to Breakages, Limited, at scrap iron prices. I—I—oh, it is beyond bearing [*she breaks down*].

There is a troubled silence for a moment. Then the

voice of the Prime Minister breaks it impressively as he addresses the King.

PROTEUS. You hear that, sir. Your one supporter in the Cabinet admits that the industrial situation is too strong for her. I do not pretend to be able to control the women in my Cabinet; but not one of them dare support you.

AMANDA [*springing up*] Whats that? Not dare! What do you bet that I dont go down to Mouldy Mike's constituency and say everything that Lizzie has said and a lot more too, if I choose? I tell you, Breakages, Limited, never interferes in my department. I'd like to catch them at it.

MAGNUS. I am afraid that that is only because the efficiency of the Post Office is as important to them as to the general public.

AMANDA. Stuff! They could get rid of me without shutting up the Post Office. Theyre afraid of me—of me, Amanda Postlethwaite.

MAGNUS. You coax them, I am afraid.

AMANDA. Coax! What do you think they care for coaxing? They can have all the coaxing they want from younger and prettier women than I by paying for it. No use trying to coax that lot. Intimidate them: thats the way to handle them.

LYSISTRATA [*her voice still broken*] I wish I could intimidate them.

MAGNUS. But what can Amanda do that you cannot do?

AMANDA. I'll tell you. She cant mimic people. And she cant sing funny songs. I can do both; and that—with all respect, sir—makes me the real queen of England.

BOANERGES. Oh, come! Disgraceful! Shame!

AMANDA. If you provoke me, Bill, I'll drive you out of your constituency inside of two months.

BOANERGES. Ho! You will, will you? How?

AMANDA. Just as I drove the Chairman of Breakages out of my own constituency when he came down there and tried to take my seat from me.

MAGNUS. I never quite understood why he turned tail. How did you do it?

AMANDA. I'll tell you. He opened his campaign with a great Saturday night speech against me in the Home Lovers' Hall to five thousand people. In that same hall a week later, I faced a meeting of the very same people. I didnt argue. I mimicked him. I took all the high-falutin passages in his speech, and repeated them in his best manner until I had the whole five thousand laughing at him. Then I asked them would they like me to sing; and their Yes nearly lifted the roof off. I had two songs. They both had choruses. One went "She lets me go out on Saturday night, on Saturday night, on Saturday night"—like that. The other went "Boo! Hoo! I want Amanda's Teddy bear to play with." They sang it under the windows of his hotel next time he came. He cancelled his meeting and left. And thats how England is governed by yours truly, sir. Lucky for England that Queen Amanda is a good sort, in spite of some surface faults. [*She resumes her seat with triumphant self-satisfaction*].

BALBUS. Lucky for England theres only one of you: thats what *I* say.

AMANDA [*wafts him a kiss*]!

MAGNUS. Should not the Queen support the King, your Majesty?

AMANDA. Sorry, sir; but there isnt room for two monarchs in my realm. I am against you on principle because the talent for mimicry isnt hereditary.

PROTEUS. Now, anybody else? We have heard why the two ladies cannot support the King. Is there anybody who can?

Silence.

MAGNUS. I see that my appeal has been in vain. I do not reproach you, ladies and gentlemen, because I perceive that your situation is a difficult one. The question is how to change it.

NICOBAR. Sign the ultimatum: that is how.

MAGNUS. I am not quite convinced of that. The Home Secretary's brother-in-law was quite willing to sign the pledge of total abstinence if I would admit him to the Cabinet. His offer was not accepted, because, though none of us doubted that he would sign the pledge, we were not equally certain that the infirmities of his nature would allow him to keep it. My nature is also subject to infirmity. Are you satisfied, Mr Proteus, that if I sign this ultimatum, I shall not inevitably relapse into the conduct that my nature dictates?

PROTEUS [*his patience strained*] What is the use of going on like this? You are a man on the scaffold, spinning out his prayers to put off the inevitable execution as long as possible. Nothing that you can say will make any difference. You know you must sign. Why not sign and have done with it?

NICOBAR. Now youre talking, Joe.

BALBUS. Thats the stuff to give him.

PLINY. Gulp it down, sir. It wont get any sweeter by keeping: what?

LYSISTRATA. Oh, for God's sake, sign, sir. This is torture to me.

MAGNUS. I perceive, gentlemen, that I have come to the end of your patience. I will tax it no further: you have been very forbearing; and I thank you for it. I will say no more by way of discussion; but I must have until five o'clock this evening to consider my decision. At that hour, if I can find no other way out, I will sign without another word. Meanwhile, ladies and gentlemen, au revoir!

He rises. All rise. He marches out.

PROTEUS. His last wriggle. Never mind: we have him safe enough. What about lunch? I am starving. Will you lunch with me, Lizzie.

LYSISTRATA. Dont speak to me. [*She rushes out distractedly*].

AMANDA. Poor darling Lizzie! She's a regular old true blue Diehard. If only I had her brains and education! or if she had my variety talent! what a queen she'd make! Like old Queen Elizabeth, eh? Dont grieve, Joe: I'll lunch with you since youre so pressing.

CRASSUS. Come and lunch with me—all of you.

AMANDA. What opulence! Can you afford it?

CRASSUS. Breakages will pay. They have a standing account at the Ritz. Over five thousand a year, it comes to.

PROTEUS. Right. Let us spoil the Egyptians.

BOANERGES [*with Roman dignity*] My lunch will cost me one and sixpence; and I shall pay for it myself [*he stalks out*].

AMANDA [*calling after him*] Dont make a beast of yourself, Bill. Ta ta!

PROTEUS. Come on, come on: it's ever so late.

They all hurry out. Sempronius and Pamphilius, entering, have to stand aside to let them pass before returning to their desks. Proteus, with Amanda on his arm, stops in the doorway on seeing them.

PROTEUS. Have you two been listening, may I ask?

PAMPHILIUS. Well, it would be rather inconvenient wouldnt it, if we had to be told everything that passed?

SEMPRONIUS. Once for all, Mr Proteus, the King's

[333]

private secretaries must hear everything, see everything, and know everything.

PROTEUS. Singularly enough, Mr Sempronius, I havnt the slightest objection [*he goes*].

AMANDA [*going with him*] Goodbye, Semmy. So long, Pam.

SEMPRONIUS.
PAMPHILIUS. } [*seating themselves at their writing tables and yawning prodigiously*] Ou-ou-ou-ou-ou-fff!!!

AN INTERLUDE

Orinthia's boudoir at half-past fifteen on the same day. She is at her writing-table scribbling notes. She is romantically beautiful, and beautifully dressed. As the table is against the wall near a corner, with the other wall on her left, her back alone is visible from the middle of the room. The door is near the corner diagonally opposite. There is a large settee in the middle of the room.

The King enters and waits on the threshold.

ORINTHIA [*crossly, without looking round*] Who is that?

MAGNUS. His Majesty the King.

ORINTHIA. I dont want to see him.

MAGNUS. How soon will you be disengaged?

ORINTHIA. I didnt say I was engaged. Tell the king I dont want to see him.

MAGNUS. He awaits your pleasure [*he comes in and seats himself on the settee*].

ORINTHIA. Go away. [*A pause*]. I wont speak to you. [*Another pause*]. If my private rooms are to be broken into at any moment because they are in the palace, and the king is not a gentleman, I must take a house outside. I am writing to the agents about one now.

MAGNUS. What is our quarrel today, belovéd?

ORINTHIA. Ask your conscience.

MAGNUS. I have none when you are concerned. You must tell me.

She takes a book from the table and rises; then sweeps superbly forward to the settee and flings the book into his hands.

ORINTHIA. There!

MAGNUS. What is this?

ORINTHIA. Page 16. Look at it.

MAGNUS [*looking at the title on the back of the book*] "Songs of our Great Great Grandparents." What page did you say?

ORINTHIA [*between her teeth*] Six-teen.

MAGNUS [*opening the book and finding the page, his eye lighting up with recognition as he looks at it*] Ah! The Pilgrim of Love!

ORINTHIA. Read the first three words—if you dare.

MAGNUS [*smiling as he caresses the phrase*] "Orinthia, my belovéd".

ORINTHIA. The name you pretended to invent specially for me, the only women in the world for you. Picked up out of the rubbish basket in a secondhand bookseller's! And I thought you were a poet!

MAGNUS. Well, one poet may consecrate a name for another. Orinthia is a name full of magic for me. It could not be that if I had invented it myself. I heard it at a concert of ancient music when I was a child; and I have treasured it ever since.

ORINTHIA. You always have a pretty excuse. You are the King of liars and humbugs. You cannot understand how a falsehood like that wounds me.

MAGNUS [*remorsefully, stretching out his arms towards her*] Belovéd: I am sorry.

ORINTHIA. Put your hands in your pockets: they shall not touch me ever again.

MAGNUS [*obeying*] Dont pretend to be hurt unless you really are, dearest. It wrings my heart.

ORINTHIA. Since when have you set up a heart? Did you buy that, too, secondhand?

MAGNUS. I have something in me that winces when you are hurt—or pretend to be.

[336]

ORINTHIA [*contemptuously*] Yes: I have only to squeal, and you will take me up and pet me as you would a puppy run over by a car. [*Sitting down beside him, but beyond arm's length*] That is what you give me when my heart demands love. I had rather you kicked me.

MAGNUS. I should like to kick you sometimes, when you are specially aggravating. But I shouldnt do it well. I should be afraid of hurting you all the time.

ORINTHIA. I believe you would sign my death warrant without turning a hair.

MAGNUS. That is true, in a way. It is wonderful how subtle your mind is, as far as it goes.

ORINTHIA. It does not go as far as yours, I suppose.

MAGNUS. I dont know. Our minds go together half way. Whether it is that your mind stops there or else that the road forks, and you take the high road and I take the low road, I cannot say; but somehow after a certain point we lose one another.

ORINTHIA. And then you go back to your Amandas and Lysistratas: creatures whose idea of romance is a minister in love with a department, and whose bedside books are blue books.

MAGNUS. They are not always thinking of some man or other. That is a rather desirable extension of their interests, in my opinion. If Lysistrata had a lover I should not be interested in him in the least; and she would bore me to distraction if she could talk of nothing else. But I am very much interested in her department. Her devotion to it gives us a topic of endless interest.

ORINTHIA. Well, go to her: I am not detaining you. But dont tell her that I have nothing to talk about but men; for that is a lie; and you know it.

MAGNUS. It is, as you say, a lie; and I know it. But I did not say it.

ORINTHIA. You implied it. You meant it. When those ridiculous political women are with us you talk to them all the time, and never say a word to me.

MAGNUS. Nor you to me. We cannot talk to one another in public: we have nothing to say that could be said before other people. Yet we find enough to say to one another when we are alone together. Would you change that if you could?

ORINTHIA. You are as slippery as an eel; but you shall not slip through my fingers. Why do you surround yourself with political bores and frumps and dowdy busybodies who cant talk: they can only debate about their dull departments and their fads and their election chances. [*Rising impatiently*] Who could talk to such people? If it were not for the nonentities of wives and husbands they drag about with them, there would be nobody to talk to at all. And even they can talk of nothing but the servants and the baby. [*Suddenly returning to her seat*] Listen to me, Magnus. Why can you not be a real king?

MAGNUS. In what way, belovédest?

ORINTHIA. Send all these stupid people packing. Make them do their drudgeries in their departments without bothering you about it, as you make your servants sweep the floors and dust the furniture. Live a really noble and beautiful life—a kingly life—with me. What you need to make you a real king is a real queen.

MAGNUS. But I have got one.

ORINTHIA. Oh, you are blind. You are worse than blind: you have low tastes. Heaven is offering you a rose; and you cling to a cabbage.

MAGNUS [*laughing*] That is a very apt metaphor, belovéd. But what wise man, if you force him to choose between doing without roses and doing with-

[338]

out cabbages, would not secure the cabbages? Besides, all these old married cabbages were once roses; and, though young things like you dont remember that, their husbands do. They dont notice the change. Besides, you should know better than anyone else that when a man gets tired of his wife and leaves her it is never because she has lost her good looks. The new love is often older and uglier than the old.

ORINTHIA. Why should I know it better than anyone else?

MAGNUS. Why, because you have been married twice; and both your husbands have run away from you to much plainer and stupider women. When I begged your present husband to come back to court for a while for the sake of appearances he said no man could call his soul his own in the same house with you. And yet that man was utterly infatuated with your beauty when he married you. Your first husband actually forced a good wife to divorce him so that he might marry you; but before two years were out he went back to her and died in her arms, poor chap.

ORINTHIA. Shall I tell you why these men could not live with me? It was because I am a thoroughbred, and they were only hacks. They had nothing against me: I was perfectly faithful to them. I kept their houses beautifully: I fed them better than they had ever been fed in their lives. But because I was higher than they were, and greater, they could not stand the strain of trying to live up to me. So I let them go their way, poor wretches, back to their cabbages. Look at the old creature Ignatius is living with now! She gives you his real measure.

MAGNUS. An excellent woman. Ignatius is quite happy with her. I never saw a man so changed.

ORINTHIA. Just what he is fit for. Commonplace. Bourgeoise. She trots through the streets shopping. [*Rising*] I tread the plains of Heaven. Common women cannot come where I am; and common men find themselves out and slink away.

MAGNUS. It must be magnificent to have the consciousness of a goddess without ever doing a thing to justify it.

ORINTHIA. Give me a goddess's work to do; and I will do it. I will even stoop to a queen's work if you will share the throne with me. But do not pretend that people become great by doing great things. They do great things because they are great, if the great things come along. But they are great just the same when the great things do not come along. If I never did anything but sit in this room and powder my face and tell you what a clever fool you are, I should still be heavens high above the millions of common women who do their domestic duty, and sacrifice themselves, and run Trade departments and all the rest of the vulgarities. Has all the tedious public work you have done made you any the better? I have seen you before and after your boasted strokes of policy; and you were the same man, and would have been the same man to me and to yourself if you had never done them. Thank God my self-consciousness is something nobler than vulgar conceit in having done something. It is what I am, not what I do, that you must worship in me. If you want deeds, go to your men and women of action, as you call them, who are all in a conspiracy to pretend that the mechanical things they do, the foolhardy way they risk their worthless lives, or their getting up in the morning at four and working sixteen hours a day for thirty years, like coral insects, make them great. What are they for? these dull slaves? To keep the streets swept for me. To enable me to reign over them in beauty like the stars without having anything to do with their slavery except to console it, to dazzle it, to enable them to forget it in adoring dreams of me. Am I not worth it? [*She sits, fascinating him*]. Look into my eyes and tell the truth. Am I worth it or not?

MAGNUS. To me, who love beauty, yes. But you should hear the speeches Balbus makes about your pension.

ORINTHIA. And my debts: do not forget my debts, my mortgages, the bill of sale on my furniture, the thousands I have had from the moneylenders to save me from being sold up because I will not borrow from my friends. Lecture me again about them; but do not dare pretend that the people grudge me my pension. They glory in it, and in my extravagance, as you call it.

MAGNUS [*more gravely*] By the way, Orinthia, when your dressmakers took up that last bill for you, they were speculating, were they not, in your chances of becoming my queen some day?

ORINTHIA. Well, what if they were?

MAGNUS. They would hardly have ventured on that without a hint from somebody. Was it from you?

ORINTHIA. You think me capable of that! You have a very low side to you, Magnus.

MAGNUS. No doubt: like other mortal fabrics I have a wrong side and a right side. But it is no use your giving yourself airs, belovédest. You are capable of anything. Do you deny that there was some suggestion of the kind?

ORINTHIA. How dare you challenge me to deny it? I never deny. Of course there was a suggestion of the kind.

MAGNUS. I thought so.

ORINTHIA. Oh, stupid! stupid! Go keep a grocer's shop: that is what you are fit for. Do you suppose that the suggestion came from me? Why, you great oaf, it is in the air: when my dressmaker hinted at it I told her that if she ever dared to repeat such a thing she should never get another order from me. But can I help people seeing what is as plain as the sun in the heavens? [*Rising again*] Everyone knows that I am the real queen. Everyone treats me as the real queen. They cheer me in the streets. When I open one of the art exhibitions or launch a new ship they crowd the place out. I am one of Nature's queens; and they know it. If you do not, you are not one of Nature's kings.

MAGNUS. Sublime! Nothing but genuine inspiration could give a woman such cheek.

ORINTHIA. Yes: inspiration, not cheek. [*Sitting as before*] Magnus: when are you going to face my destiny, and your own?

MAGNUS. But my wife? the queen? What is to become of my poor dear Jemima?

ORINTHIA. Oh, drown her: shoot her: tell your chauffeur to drive her into the Serpentine and leave her there. The woman makes you ridiculous.

MAGNUS. I dont think I should like that. And the public would think it illnatured.

ORINTHIA. Oh, you know what I mean. Divorce her. Make her divorce you. It is quite easy. That was how Ronny married me. Everybody does it when they need a change.

MAGNUS. But I cant imagine what I should do without Jemima.

ORINTHIA. Nobody else can imagine what you do with her. But you need not do without her. You can see as much of her as you like when we are married. I shall not be jealous and make scenes.

MAGNUS. That is very magnanimous of you. But I am afraid it does not settle the difficulty. Jemima would not think it right to keep up her present intimacy with me if I were married to you.

ORINTHIA. What a woman! Would she be in any worse position then than I am in now?

MAGNUS. No.

ORINTHIA. You mean, then, that you do not mind placing me in a position that you do not think good enough for her?

MAGNUS. Orinthia: I did not place you in your present position. You placed yourself in it. I could not resist you. You gathered me like a daisy.

ORINTHIA. Did you want to resist me?

MAGNUS. Oh no. I never resist temptation, because I have found that things that are bad for me do not tempt me.

ORINTHIA. Well, then, what are we talking about?

MAGNUS. I forget. I think I was explaining the impossibility of my wife changing places with you.

ORINTHIA. Why impossible, pray?

MAGNUS. I cannot make you understand: you see you have never been really married, though you have led two captives to the altar, and borne children to one of them. Being your husband is only a job for which one man will do as well as another, and which the last man holds subject to six months notice in the divorce court. Being my wife is something quite different. The smallest derogation to Jemima's dignity would hit me like the lash of a whip across the face. About yours, somehow, I do not care a rap.

ORINTHIA. Nothing can derogate from my dignity: it is divine. Hers is only a convention: that is why you tremble when it is challenged.

MAGNUS. Not a bit. It is because she is a part of my real workaday self. You belong to fairyland.

ORINTHIA. Suppose she dies! Will you die too?

MAGNUS. Not immediately. I shall have to carry on as best I can without her, though the prospect terrifies me.

ORINTHIA. Might not carrying on without her include marrying me?

MAGNUS. My dear Orinthia, I had rather marry the devil. Being a wife is not your job.

ORINTHIA. You think so because you have no imagination. And you dont know me because I have never let you really possess me. I should make you more happy than any man has ever yet been on earth.

MAGNUS. I defy you to make me more happy than our strangely innocent relations have already made me.

ORINTHIA [*rising restlessly*] You talk like a child or a saint. [*Turning on him*] I can give you a new life: one of which you have no conception. I can give you beautiful, wonderful children: have you ever seen a lovelier boy than my Basil?

MAGNUS. Your children are beautiful; but they are fairy children; and I have several very real ones already. A divorce would not sweep them out of the way of the fairies.

ORINTHIA. In short, when your golden moment comes—when the gates of heaven open before you, you are afraid to come out of your pigsty.

MAGNUS. If I am a pig, a pigsty is the proper place for me.

ORINTHIA. I cannot understand it. All men are fools and moral cowards when you come to know them. But you are less of a fool and less of a moral coward than any man I have ever known. You have almost the makings of a first rate woman in you. When I leave the earth and soar up to the regions which are my real eternal home, you can follow me: I can speak to you as I can speak to no one else; and you can say things to me that would just make your stupid wife cry. There is more of you in me than of any other man within my reach. There is more of me in you than of any other woman within your reach. We are meant for oneanother: it is written across the sky that you and I are queen and king. How can you hesitate? What attraction is there for you in your common healthy jolly lumps of children and your common housekeeper wife and the rabble of dowdies and upstarts and intriguers and clowns that think they are governing the country when they are only squabbling with you? Look again at me, man: again and again. Am I not worth a million such? Is not life with me as high above them as the sun is above the gutter?

MAGNUS. Yes yes yes yes, of course. You are lovely: you are divine [*she cannot restrain a gesture of triumph*]. And you are enormously amusing.

This anti-climax is too much for Orinthia's exaltation; but she is too clever not to appreciate it. With another gesture, this time of deflation, she sits down at his left hand with an air of suffering patience, and listens in silence to the harangue which follows.

MAGNUS. Some day perhaps Nature will graft the roses on the cabbages and make every woman as enchanting as you; and then what a glorious lark life will be! But at present, what I come here for is to enjoy talking to you like this when I need an hour's respite from royalty: when my stupid wife has been worrying me, or my jolly lumps of children bothering me, or my turbulent Cabinet obstructing me: when, as the doctors say, what I need is a change. You see, my dear, there is no wife on earth so precious, no children so jolly, no Cabinet so tactful that it is impossible ever to get tired of them. Jemima has her limitations, as you have observed. And I have mine. Now if our limitations exactly corresponded I should never want to talk to anyone else; and neither would she. But as that never happens, we are like all other married couples: that is, there are subjects which can never be discussed between us because they are sore subjects. There are people we avoid mentioning to oneanother because one of us likes them and the other doesnt. Not only individuals, but whole sorts of people. For instance, your sort. My wife doesnt like your sort, doesnt understand it, mistrusts and dreads it. Not without reason; for women like you are dangerous to wives. But I dont dislike your sort: I understand it, being a little in that line myself. At all events I am not afraid of it; though the least allusion to it brings a cloud over my wife's face. So when I want to talk freely about it I come and talk to you. And I take it she talks to friends of hers about people of whom she never talks to me. She has men friends from whom she can get some things that she cannot get from me. If she didnt do so she would be limited by my limitations, which would end in her hating me. So I always do my best to make her men friends feel at home with us.

ORINTHIA. A model husband in a model household! And when the model household becomes a bore, I am the diversion.

MAGNUS. Well, what more can you ask? Do not let us fall into the common mistake of expecting to become one flesh and one spirit. Every star has its own orbit; and between it and its nearest neighbor there is not only a powerful attraction but an infinite distance. When the attraction becomes stronger than the distance the two do not embrace: they crash together in ruin. We two also have our orbits, and must keep an infinite distance between us to avoid a disastrous collision. Keeping our distance is the whole secret of good manners; and without good manners human society is intolerable and impossible.

ORINTHIA. Would any other woman stand your sermons, and even like them?

MAGNUS. Orinthia: we are only two children at play; and you must be content to be my queen in fairyland. And [*rising*] I must go back to my work.

ORINTHIA. What work have you that is more important than being with me?

MAGNUS. None.

ORINTHIA. Then sit down.

MAGNUS. Unfortunately, this silly business of government must be carried on. And there is a crisis this evening, as usual.

ORINTHIA. But the crisis is not until five: I heard all about it from Sempronius. Why do you encourage that greedy schemer Proteus? He humbugs you. He humbugs everybody. He even humbugs himself; and of course he humbugs that Cabinet which is a disgrace to you: it is like an overcrowded third class carriage. Why do you allow such riffraff to waste your time? After all, what are you paid for? To be a king: that is, to wipe your boots on common people.

MAGNUS. Yes: but this king business, as the Americans call it, has got itself so mixed up with democracy that half the country expects me to wipe my perfectly polished boots on the Cabinet, and the other half expects me to let the Cabinet wipe its muddy boots on me. The Crisis at five o'clock is to decide which of us is to be the doormat.

ORINTHIA. And you will condescend to fight with Proteus for power?

MAGNUS. Oh no: I never fight. But I sometimes win.

ORINTHIA. If you let yourself be beaten by that trickster and poseur, never dare to approach me again.

MAGNUS. Proteus is a clever fellow: even on occasion a fine fellow. It would give me no satisfaction to beat him: I hate beating people. But there would be some innocent fun in outwitting him.

ORINTHIA. Magnus: you are a mollycoddle. If you were a real man you would just delight in beating him to a jelly.

MAGNUS. A real man would never do as a king. I am only an idol, my love; and all I can do is to draw the line at being a cruel idol. [*He looks at his watch*] Now I must really be off. Au revoir.

ORINTHIA [*looking at her wrist watch*] But it is only twenty-five minutes past four. You have heaps of time before five.

MAGNUS. Yes; but tea is at half-past four.

ORINTHIA [*catching him by the arm with a snakelike dart*] Never mind your tea. I will give you your tea.

MAGNUS. Impossible, belovéd. Jemima does not like to be kept waiting.

ORINTHIA. Oh, bother Jemima! You shall not leave me to go to Jemima [*she pulls him back so vigorously that he falls into the seat beside her*].

MAGNUS. My dear, I must.

ORINTHIA. No, not today. Listen, Magnus. I have something very particular to say to you.

MAGNUS. You have not. You are only trying to make me late to annoy my wife. [*He tries to rise, but is pulled back*]. Let me go, please.

ORINTHIA [*holding on*] Why are you so afraid of your

wife? You are the laughing stock of London, you poor henpecked darling.

MAGNUS. Henpecked! What do you call this? At least my wife does not restrain me by bodily violence.

ORINTHIA. I will not be deserted for your old Dutch.

MAGNUS. Listen, Orinthia. Dont be absurd. You know I must go. Do be good.

ORINTHIA. Only ten minutes more.

MAGNUS. It is half-past already.

He tries to rise; but she holds him back.

MAGNUS [*pausing for breath*] You are doing this out of sheer devilment. You are so abominably strong that I cannot break loose without hurting you. Must I call the guard?

ORINTHIA. Do, do. It will be in all the papers to-morrow.

MAGNUS. Fiend. [*Summoning all his dignity*] Orinthia: I command you.

ORINTHIA [*laughs wildly*]!!!

MAGNUS [*furious*] Very well, then, you she-devil: you shall let go.

He tackles her in earnest. She flings her arms round him and holds on with mischievous enjoyment. There is a tapping at the door; they do not hear it. As he is breaking loose she suddenly shifts her grip to his waist and drags him on to the floor, where they roll over one another. Sempronius enters. He stares at the scandalous scene for a moment; then hastily slips out; shuts the door; clears his throat and blows his nose noisily; and knocks loudly and repeatedly. The two combatants cease hostilities and scramble hastily to their feet.

MAGNUS. Come in.

SEMPRONIUS [*entering*] Her Majesty sent me to remind you that tea is waiting, sir.

MAGNUS. Thank you. [*He goes quickly out*].

[349]

ORINTHIA [*panting but greatly pleased with herself*]
The King forgets everything when he is here. So do
I, I am afraid. I am so sorry.

SEMPRONIUS [*stiffly*] No explanations are needed. I
saw what happened. [*He goes out*].

ORINTHIA. The beast! He must have looked through
the keyhole. [*She throws her hand up with a gesture of
laughing defiance, and dances back to her seat at the
writing-table*].

[ACT II]

Later in the afternoon. The Terrace of the Palace. A low balustrade separates it from the lawn. Terrace chairs in abundance, ranged along the balustrade. Some dining room chairs also, not ranged, but standing about as if they had just been occupied. The terrace is accessible from the lawn by a central flight of steps.

The King and Queen are sitting apart near the corners of the steps, the Queen to the King's right. He is reading the evening paper: she is knitting. She has a little work table on her right, with a small gong on it.

THE QUEEN. Why did you tell them to leave the chairs when they took away the tea?

MAGNUS. I shall receive the Cabinet here.

THE QUEEN. Here! Why?

MAGNUS. Well, I think the open air and the evening light will have a quieting effect on them. They cannot make speeches at me so easily as in a room.

THE QUEEN. Are you sure? When Robert asked Boanerges where he learnt to speak so beautifully, he said "In Hyde Park."

MAGNUS. Yes; but with a crowd to stimulate him.

THE QUEEN. Robert says you have tamed Boanerges.

MAGNUS. No: I have not tamed him. I have taught him how to behave. I have to valet all the beginners; but that does not tame them: it teaches them how to use their strength instead of wasting it in making fools of themselves. So much the worse for me when I have to fight them.

THE QUEEN. You get no thanks for it. They think you are only humbugging them.

MAGNUS. Well, so I am, in the elementary lessons. But when it comes to real business humbug is no use: they pick it up themselves too quickly.

Pamphilius enters along the terrace, from the Queen's side.

MAGNUS [*looking at his watch*] Good Heavens! They havnt come, have they? It's not five yet.

PAMPHILIUS. No, sir. It's the American ambassador.

THE QUEEN [*resenting this a little*] Has he an audience?

PAMPHILIUS. No, maam. He is rather excited about something, I think. I cant get anything out of him. He says he must see His Majesty at once.

THE QUEEN. Must!! An American must see the King at once, without an audience! Well!

MAGNUS [*rising*] Send him in, Pam.

Pamphilius goes out.

THE QUEEN. *I* should have told him to write for an audience, and then kept him waiting a week for it.

MAGNUS. What! When we still owe America that old war debt. And with a mad imperialist president like Bossfield! No you wouldnt, my dear: you would be crawlingly civil to him, as I am going to be, confound him!

PAMPHILIUS [*re-appearing*] His Excellency the American Ambassador. Mr Vanhattan.

He retires as Mr Vanhattan enters in an effusive condition, and, like a man assured of an enthusiastic welcome, hurries to the Queen, and salutes her with a handshake so prolonged that she stares in astonishment, first at him, and then appealingly at the King, with her hands being vigorously wrung and waved up and down all the time.

MAGNUS. What on earth is the matter, Mr Vanhattan? You are shaking Her Majesty's rings off.

VANHATTAN [*desisting*] Her Majesty will excuse me when she learns the nature of my errand here. This, King Magnus, is a great historic scene: one of the greatest, perhaps, that history has ever recorded or will ever again record.

MAGNUS. Have you had tea?

VANHATTAN. Tea! Who can think of tea at such a moment as this?

THE QUEEN [*rather coldly*] It is hard for us to share your enthusiasm in complete ignorance of its cause.

VANHATTAN. That is true, maam. I am just behaving like a crazy man. But you shall hear. You shall judge. and then you shall say whether I exaggerate the importance—the immensity—of an occasion that cannot be exaggerated.

MAGNUS. Goodness gracious! Wont you sit down?

VANHATTAN [*taking a chair and placing it between them*] I thank your Majesty. [*He sits*].

MAGNUS. You have some exciting news for us, apparently. Is it private or official?

VANHATTAN. Official, sir. No mistake about it. What I am going to tell you is authentic from the United States of America to the British Empire.

THE QUEEN. Perhaps I had better go.

VANHATTAN. No, maam: you shall not go. Whatever may be the limits of your privileges as the consort of your sovereign, it is your right as an Englishwoman to learn what I have come here to communicate.

MAGNUS. My dear Vanhattan, what the devil is the matter?

VANHATTAN. King Magnus: between your country and mine there is a debt.

MAGNUS. Does that matter, now that our capitalists

[353]

have invested so heavily in American concerns that after paying yourselves the interest on the debt you have to send us two thousand million dollars a year to balance the account.

VANHATTAN. King Magnus: for the moment, forget figures. Between your country and mine there is not only a debt but a frontier: the frontier that has on it not a single gun nor a single soldier, and across which the American citizen every day shakes the hand of the Canadian subject of your throne.

MAGNUS. There is also the frontier of the ocean, which is somewhat more expensively defended at our joint expense by the League of Nations.

VANHATTAN [*rising to give his words more impressiveness*] Sir: the debt is cancelled. The frontier no longer exists.

THE QUEEN. How can that be?

MAGNUS. Am I to understand, Mr Vanhattan, that by some convulsion of Nature the continent of North America has been submerged in the Atlantic?

VANHATTAN. Something even more wonderful than that has happened. One may say that the Atlantic Ocean has been submerged in the British Empire.

MAGNUS. I think you had better tell us as succinctly as possible what has happened. Pray sit down.

VANHATTAN [*resuming his seat*] You are aware, sir, that the United States of America at one time formed a part of your empire.

MAGNUS. There is a tradition to that effect.

VANHATTAN. No mere tradition, sir. An undoubted historical fact. In the eighteenth century—

MAGNUS. That is a long time ago.

VANHATTAN. Centuries count for but little in the lifetimes of great nations, sir. Let me recall the parable of the prodigal son.

MAGNUS. Oh really, Mr Vanhattan, that was a very very long time ago. I take it that something important has happened since yesterday.

VANHATTAN. It has. It has indeed, King Magnus.

MAGNUS. Then what is it? I have not time to attend to the eighteenth century and the prodigal son at this moment.

THE QUEEN. The King has a Cabinet meeting in ten minutes, Mr Vanhattan.

VANHATTAN. I should like to see the faces of your Cabinet ministers, King Magnus, when they hear what I have to tell you.

MAGNUS. So should I. But I am not in a position to tell it to them, because I dont know what it is.

VANHATTAN. The prodigal, sir, has returned to his father's house. Not poor, not hungry, not ragged, as of old. Oh no. This time he returns bringing with him the riches of the earth to the ancestral home.

MAGNUS [*starting from his chair*] You dont mean to say—

VANHATTAN [*rising also, blandly triumphant*] I do, sir. The Declaration of Independence is cancelled. The treaties which endorsed it are torn up. We have decided to rejoin the British Empire. We shall of course enjoy Dominion Home Rule under the Presidency of Mr Bossfield. I shall revisit you here shortly, not as the Ambassador of a foreign power, but as High Commissioner for the greatest of your dominions, and your very loyal and devoted subject, sir.

MAGNUS [*collapsing into his chair*] The devil you will! [*He stares haggardly into futurity, now for the first time utterly at a loss*].

THE QUEEN. What a splendid thing, Mr Vanhattan!

VANHATTAN. I thought your Majesty would say so.

The most splendid thing that has ever happened. [*He resumes his seat*].

THE QUEEN [*looking anxiously at the King*] Dont you think so, Magnus?

MAGNUS [*pulling himself together with a visible effort*] May I ask, Mr Vanhattan, with whom did this—this —this masterstroke of American policy originate? Frankly, I have been accustomed to regard your President as a statesman whose mouth was the most efficient part of his head. He cannot have thought of this himself. Who suggested it to him?

VANHATTAN. I must accept your criticism of Mr Bossfield with all doo reserve, but I may mention that we Americans will probably connect the good news with the recent visit to our shores of the President of the Irish Free State. I cannot pronounce his name in its official Gaelic form; and there is only one typist in our bureau who can spell it; but he is known to his friends as Mick O'Rafferty.

MAGNUS. The rascal! Jemima: we shall have to live in Dublin. This is the end of England.

VANHATTAN. In a sense that may be so. But England will not perish. She will merge—merge, sir—into a bigger and brighter concern. Perhaps I should have mentioned that one of our conditions will be that you shall be Emperor. King may be good enough for this little island; but if we come in we shall require something grander.

MAGNUS. This little island! "This little gem set in a silver sea!" Has it occurred to you, Mr Vanhattan, that rather than be reduced to a mere appendage of a big American concern, we might raise the old warcry of Sinn Fein, and fight for our independence to the last drop of our blood?

VANHATTAN. I should be right sorry to contemplate

such a reversion to a barbarous past. Fortunately, it's impossible—immpawsibl. The old warcry would not appeal to the cosmopolitan crews of the fleet of the League of Nations in the Atlantic. That fleet would blockade you, sir. And I fear we should be obliged to boycott you. The two thousand million dollars a year would stop.

MAGNUS. But the continental Powers! Do you suppose they would consent for a moment to such a change in the balance of power?

VANHATTAN. Why not? The change would be only nominal.

MAGNUS. Nominal! You call an amalgamation of the British Commonwealth with the United States a nominal change! What will France and Germany call it?

VANHATTAN [*shaking his head indulgently*] France and Germany? These queer old geographical expressions which you use here from old family habit do not trouble us. I suppose you mean by Germany the chain of more or less Soviet Republics between the Ural Mountains and the North Sea. Well, the clever people at Moscow and Berlin and Geneva are trying to federate them; and it is fully understood between us that if we dont object to their move they will not object to ours. France, by which I take it you mean the Government at New Timgad, is too busy in Africa to fuss about what is happening at the ends of your little Channel Tube. So long as Paris is full of Americans, and Americans are full of money, all's well in the west from the French point of view. One of the great attractions of Paris for Americans is the excursion to Old England. The French want us to feel at home here. And so we do. Why shouldnt we? After all, we are at home here.

[357]

MAGNUS. In what sense, may I ask?

VANHATTAN. Well, we find here everything we are accustomed to: our industrial products, our books, our plays, our sports, our Christian Science churches, our osteopaths, our movies and talkies. Put it in a small parcel and say our goods and our ideas. A political union with us will be just the official recognition of an already accomplished fact. A union of hearts, you might call it.

THE QUEEN. You forget, Mr Vanhattan. We have a great national tradition.

VANHATTAN. The United States, maam, have absorbed all the great national traditions, and blended them with their own glorious tradition of Freedom into something that is unique and universal.

THE QUEEN. We have a civilized culture which is peculiar to ourselves. It may not be better than yours; but it is different.

VANHATTAN. Well, is it? We found that culture enshrined in British material works of art: in the stately country homes of your nobility, in the cathedrals our common forefathers built as the country houses of God. What did you do with them? You sold them to us. I was brought up in the shade of Ely cathedral, the removal of which from the county of Cambridge to New Jersey was my dear old father's first big professional job. The building which stands on its former site is a very fine one: in my opinion the best example of reinforced concrete of its period; but it was designed by an American architect, and built by the Synthetic Building Materials Trust, an international affair. Believe me, the English people, the real English people who take things as they come instead of reading books about them, will be more at home with us than they are with the old English notions which our tourists try to keep alive. When you find some country gentleman keeping up the old English customs at Christmas and so forth, who is he? An American who has bought the place. Your people get up the show for him because he pays for it, not because it is natural to them.

THE QUEEN [*with a sigh*] Our own best families go so much to Ireland nowadays. People should not be allowed to go from England to Ireland. They never come back.

VANHATTAN. Well, can you blame them, maam? Look at the climate!

THE QUEEN. No: it is not the climate. It is the Horse Show.

The King rises very thoughtfully; and Vanhattan follows his example.

MAGNUS. I must think over this. I have known for years past that it was on the cards. When I was young, and under the influence of our family tradition, which of course never recognized the rebellion of the American colonies as valid, I actually dreamt of a reunited English speaking empire at the head of civilization.

VANHATTAN. Fine! Great! And now come true.

MAGNUS. Not yet. Now that I am older and wiser I find the reality less attractive than the dream.

VANHATTAN. And is that all I am to report to the President, sir? He will be disappointed. I am a little taken aback, myself.

MAGNUS. For the present, that is all. This may be a great idea—

VANHATTAN. Surely, surely.

MAGNUS. It may also be a trap in which England will perish.

VANHATTAN [*encouragingly*] Oh, I shouldnt look at

it that way. Besides, nothing—not even dear old England—can last for ever. Progress, you know, sir, progress, progress!

MAGNUS. Just so, just so. We may survive only as another star on your flag. Still, we cling to the little scrap of individuality you have left us. If we must merge, as you call it—or did you say submerge?— some of us will swim to the last. [*To the Queen*] My dear.

The Queen strikes her gong.

Pamphilius returns.

MAGNUS. You shall hear from me after the Cabinet meets. Not tonight: you must not sit up waiting for a message. Early tomorrow, I hope. Thank you for bringing me the news before the papers got it: that seldom happens now. Pamphilius: you will reconduct his Excellency. Good evening. [*He shakes hands*].

VANHATTAN. I thank your Majesty. [*To the Queen*] Good evening, maam. I look forward to presenting myself in court dress soon.

THE QUEEN. You will look very nice in it, Mr Vanhattan. Good evening.

The Ambassador goes out with Pamphilius.

MAGNUS [*striding grimly to and fro*] The scoundrels! That blackguard O'Rafferty! That booby bullroarer Bossfield! Breakages, Limited, have taken it into their heads to mend the British Commonwealth.

THE QUEEN [*quietly*] I think it is a very good thing. You will make a very good emperor. We shall civilize these Americans.

MAGNUS. How can we when we have not yet civilized ourselves? They have come to regard us as a mere tribe of redskins. England will be just a reservation.

THE QUEEN. Nonsense, dear! They know that we are their natural superiors. You can see it by the way their women behave at court. They really love and reverence royalty; while our English peeresses are hardly civil —when they condescend to come at all.

MAGNUS. Well, my dear, I do many things to please you that I should never do to please myself; and I suppose I shall end as American Emperor just to keep you amused.

THE QUEEN. I never desire anything that is not good for you, Magnus. You do not always know what is good for you.

MAGNUS. Well, well, well, well! Have it your own way, dearest. Where are these infernal ministers? Theyre late.

THE QUEEN [*looking out into the garden*] Coming across the lawn with Sempronius.

The Cabinet arrives. The men take off their hats as they come up the steps. Boanerges has taken advantage of the interval to procure a brilliant uniform and change into it. Proteus, with Sempronius, heads the procession, followed immediately by the two lady ministers. The Queen rises as Proteus turns to her. Sempronius moves the little table quickly back to the balustrade out of the way, and puts the Queen's chair in the centre for the King.

THE QUEEN [*shaking hands*] How do you do, Mr Proteus?

PROTEUS. May I present the President of the Board of Trade, Mr Boanerges?

THE QUEEN. I remember seeing you, Mr Boanerges, at the opening of the Transport Workers' Summer Palace. You wore a most becoming costume then. I hope you have not given it up.

BOANERGES. But the Princess told me I looked ridiculous in it!

THE QUEEN. That was very naughty of the Princess.

You looked particularly well in it. However, you look well in anything. And now I leave you all to your labors.

She goes out along the terrace. Sempronius follows with her knitting.

MAGNUS [*sitting down*] Be seated, ladies and gentlemen.

They take chairs of one sort or another where they can find them, first leaving their hats on the balustrade. When they are seated, their order from the King's right to his left is Nicobar, Crassus, Boanerges, Amanda, the King, Proteus, Lysistrata, Pliny, and Balbus.

A pause, Proteus waiting for the King to begin. He, deep in thought, says nothing. The silence becomes oppressive.

PLINY [*chattily*] Nice weather we're having, these evenings.

AMANDA [*splutters*]!!!

MAGNUS. There is rather a threatening cloud on the western horizon, Mr Pliny. [*To Proteus*] Have you heard the news from America?

PROTEUS. I have, sir.

MAGNUS. Am I to be favored with the advice of my ministers on that subject?

PROTEUS. By your Majesty's leave, we will take the question of the ultimatum first.

MAGNUS. Do you think the ultimatum will matter much when the capital of the British Commonwealth is shifted to Washington?

NICOBAR. We'll see it shifted to Melbourne or Montreal or Johannesburg first.

MAGNUS. It would not stay there. It will stay at a real centre of gravity only.

PROTEUS. We are agreed about that. If it shifts at all it will shift either west to Washington or east to Moscow.

BOANERGES. Moscow thinks a lot of itself. But what has Moscow to teach us that we cannot teach ourselves? Moscow is built on English history, written in London by Karl Marx.

PROTEUS. Yes; and the English king has sidetracked you again. [*To Magnus*] What about the ultimatum, sir? You promised us your decision at five o'clock. It is now a quarter past.

MAGNUS Are you inexorably determined to force this issue to its logical end? You know how unEnglish it is to do that?

PROTEUS. My people came from Scotland.

LYSISTRATA. I wish they had stayed there. I am English: every bone in my body.

BOANERGES [*vociferously*] Same here!

PROTEUS. God help England if she had no Scots to think for her!

MAGNUS. What does the Cabinet say to that?

AMANDA. All their people came from Scotland or Ireland or Wales or Jerusalem or somewhere, sir. It is no use appealing to English sentiment here.

CRASSUS. Politics are not suited to the English, if you ask me.

MAGNUS. Then I, the only Englishman left in politics, apparently, am to be reduced to complete nullity?

PROTEUS [*bluntly*] Yes. You cannot frighten us out of our position by painting it red. I could paint your position black if I liked. In plain terms we require from you an unconditional surrender. If you refuse it then I go to the country on the question whether England is to be an absolute monarchy or a constitutional one. We are all agreed on that: there will be no resignations. I have letters from the absent members of the Government: those present will speak for themselves.

ALL THE OTHER MEN. Agreed, agreed.

PROTEUS. Now, what is your answer?

MAGNUS. The day for absolute monarchies is past. You think you can do without me; and I know that I cannot do without you. I decide, of course, in favor of a constitutional monarchy.

THE MEN [*greatly relieved and delighted*] Hear! hear!

MAGNUS. Wait a moment.

Sudden silence and mistrust.

PROTEUS. So! There is a catch in it, is there?

MAGNUS. Not exactly a catch. But you have driven me to face the fact that I am unfitted to be a constitutional monarch. I am by nature incapable of the necessary self-effacement.

AMANDA. Well, thats true, at all events. You and I are a pair, sir.

MAGNUS. Thank you. Therefore, whilst accepting your constitutional principle without the slightest reserve, I cannot sign your ultimatum, because by doing so I should be making personal promises which I know I should break—which in fact I must break because I have forces within me which your constitutional limits cannot hold in check.

BALBUS. How can you accept our principle if you dont sign the ultimatum?

MAGNUS. Oh, there is no difficulty about that. When an honest man finds himself incapable of discharging the duties of a public post, he resigns.

PROTEUS [*alarmed*] Resigns! What are you driving at?

CRASSUS. A king cannot resign.

NICOBAR. You might as well talk of beheading yourself. You cant behead yourself.

BOANERGES. Other people can, though.

MAGNUS. Do not let us quarrel about words, gentlemen. I cannot resign. But I can abdicate.

ALL THE REST [*starting to their feet*] Abdicate! [*They stare at him in consternation*].

AMANDA [*whistling a descending minor scale very expressively*] !!!!!!!! [*She sits down*].

MAGNUS. Of course, abdicate. Lysistrata: you have been a teacher of history. You can assure your colleagues that there is nothing unprecedented in an abdication. The Emperor Charles the Fifth, for instance—

LYSISTRATA. Oh, Charles the Fifth be—be bothered! he's not good enough. Sir: I have stood by you as far as I dared. Dont throw me over. You must not abdicate. [*She sits down, distressed*].

PROTEUS. You cannot abdicate except by my advice.

MAGNUS. I am acting upon your advice.

PROTEUS. Nonsense! [*He sits down*].

BALBUS. Ridiculous! [*He sits down*].

PLINY. Youre not serious, you know. [*He sits down*].

NICOBAR. You cant upset the apple cart like this. [*He sits down*].

CRASSUS. I must say this is not playing the game. [*He sits down*].

BOANERGES [*powerfully*] Well, why not? Why not? Though as an old Republican I have no respect for His Majesty as a King, I have a great respect for him as a Strong Man. But he is not the only pebble on the beach. Why not have done with this superstition of monarchy, and bring the British Commonwealth into line with all the other great Powers today as a republic? [*He sits down*].

MAGNUS. My abdication does not involve that, Mr Boanerges. I am abdicating to save the monarchy, not to destroy it. I shall be succeeded by my son Robert, Prince of Wales. He will make an admirable constitutional monarch.

[365]

PLINY. Oh, come! Dont be hard on the lad, sir. He has plenty of brains.

MAGNUS. Oh yes, yes, yes: I did not mean that he is a nonentity: quite the contrary: he is much cleverer than I am. But I have never been able to induce him to take any interest in parliamentary politics. He prefers intellectual pursuits.

NICOBAR. Dont you believe it. He is up to his neck in business.

MAGNUS. Just so. He asks me why I waste my time with you here pretending to govern the country when it is really governed by Breakages, Limited. And really I hardly know how to answer him.

CRASSUS. Things are like that nowadays. My son says just the same.

LYSISTRATA. Personally I get on very well with the Prince; but somehow I do not feel that he is interested in what I am doing.

BALBUS. He isnt. He wont interfere with you as long as you dont interfere with him. Just the right king for us. Not pigheaded. Not meddlesome. Thinks that nothing we do matters a rap. What do you say, Joe?

PROTEUS. After all, why not? if your Majesty is in earnest.

MAGNUS. I assure you I am very much in earnest.

PROTEUS. Well, I confess I did not foresee this turn of events. But I ought to have foreseen it. What your Majesty proposes is the straightforward, logical, intellectually honest solution of our difficulty. Consequently it is the last solution I could have expected in politics. But I reckoned without your Majesty's character. The more I think of it the more clearly I see that you are right—that you are taking the only course open to you.

CRASSUS. I never said I was against it, Joe.

BALBUS. Neither did I.

NICOBAR. I think theres a great deal to be said for it. *I* have no objection.

PLINY. One king is no worse than another, is he?

BOANERGES. Is he any better? The way you fellows scuttle backward and forward from one mind to another whenever Joe holds up his finger is disgusting. This is a Cabinet of sheep.

PROTEUS. Well, give the flock a better lead if you can. Have you anything else to propose?

BOANERGES. I dont know that I have on the spur of the moment. We should have had notice of this. But I suppose the King must do as he thinks right.

PROTEUS. Then the goat goes with the sheep; so thats all right.

BOANERGES. Who are you calling a goat?

NICOBAR. If you come to that, who are you calling sheep?

AMANDA. Steady there, children! steady! steady! [*To the King*] You have brought us all round, sir, as usual.

PROTEUS. There is nothing more to be said.

AMANDA. That means another half hour at least.

BOANERGES. Woman: this is not the moment for your tomfooleries.

PROTEUS [*impressively*] Bill is right, Amanda. [*He rises and becomes the conventional House of Commons orator*].

Ministers compose themselves to listen with grave attention, as if in church; but Lysistrata is contemptuous and Amanda amused.

PROTEUS [*continuing*] It is a solemn moment. It is a moment in which an old tie is being broken. I am not ashamed to confess that it is a tie from which I have learned something.

MALE MINISTERS [*murmur*] Hear hear! Hear hear!

PROTEUS. For my own part—and I think I may speak for others here as well—it has been no mere political tie, but a tie of sincere friendship.

Renewed murmurs of sympathy. Increasing emotion.

PROTEUS. We have had our disagreements—as which of us has not?—but they have been family quarrels.

CRASSUS. Thats all. Nothing more.

PROTEUS. May I say lovers' quarrels?

PLINY [*wiping his eyes*] You may, Joe. You may.

PROTEUS. My friends, we came here to a meeting. We find, alas! that the meeting is to be a leavetaking. [*Crassus sniffs tearfully*]. It is a sad leavetaking on our part, but a cordial one. [Hear Hear *from Pliny*]. We are cast down, but not discouraged. Looking back to the past with regret, we can still look forward to the future with hope. That future has its dangers and its difficulties. It will bring us new problems; and it will bring us face to face with a new king. But the new problems and the new king will not make us forget our old counsellor, monarch, and—he will allow me to say—comrade. [Hear Hears *ad libitum*]. I know my words will find an echo in all your hearts when I conclude by saying that whatsoever king shall reign—

AMANDA. Youll be the Vicar of Bray, Joe.

Uproar. Proteus flings himself into his chair indignantly.

BALBUS. Shame!

NICOBAR. Shut up, you b—

PLINY. A joke's a joke; but really—

CRASSUS. Too bad, Amanda! Behave yourself.

LYSISTRATA. She has a perfect right to speak. You are a parcel of sentimental fools.

BOANERGES [*rising*] Silence. Order.

AMANDA. Sorry.

BOANERGES. So you ought to be. Where's your manners? Where's your education? King Magnus: we part; but we part as strong men part: as friends. The Prime Minister has correctly represented the sentiments of all the men present. I call on them to express those sentiments in the good old English fashion. [*Singing in stentorian tones*] Fo-o-o-o-r-r-r

MALE MINISTERS EXCEPT PROTEUS [*rising and singing*]

> — he's a jolly good fel-low
> For he's a jolly good fel-low
> For he's—

MAGNUS [*peremptorily*] Stop. Stop.

Sudden silence and misgiving. They sit down furtively.

MAGNUS. I thank you with all my heart; but there is a misapprehension. We are not taking leave of one another. I have no intention of withdrawing from an active part in politics.

PROTEUS. What!!

MAGNUS. You are looking on me, with an emotion which has deeply touched me, as a man with a political past. But I look on myself rather as a man with a political future. I have not yet told you my plans.

NICOBAR. What plans?

BALBUS. A retired king cant have plans and a future.

MAGNUS. Why not? I am looking forward to a most exciting and enjoyable time. As I shall of course dissolve parliament, the fun will begin with a general election.

BOANERGES [*dismayed*] But Ive only just been elected. Do you mean that I shall have to stand two elections in one month? Have you thought of the expenses?

MAGNUS. Surely your expenses will be paid by the State.

BOANERGES. Paid by the State! Is that all you know about electioneering in England?

PROTEUS. You will get your whack out of the party funds, Bill; and if you cant find the extras you must put up with straight votes. Go on, sir: we want to hear about those plans of yours.

MAGNUS. My last act of royal authority will be to divest myself of all titles and dignities; so that I may step down at once into the position of a commoner.

BOANERGES. Step up, you mean. The common man is the superior, not the inferior, of the titled man.

MAGNUS. That is why I am going to make myself a common man, Mr Boanerges.

PLINY. Well, it does you honor.

CRASSUS. Not all of us would be capable of a sacrifice like that.

BOANERGES. A fine gesture, sir. A fine gesture. I admit it.

PROTEUS [*suspicious*] And since when, pray, has your Majesty taken to making gestures? Whats the game this time?

BOANERGES. Shame!

PROTEUS. Shut up, you gaby. [*To the King*] I say, whats the game?

MAGNUS. There is no imposing on you, Prime Minister. The game is, of course, that when I come back into politics I shall be in a better position as a commoner than as a peer. I shall seek a parliamentary seat.

PROTEUS. You in the House of Commons!

MAGNUS [*blandly*] It is my intention to offer myself to the Royal Borough of Windsor as a candidate at the forthcoming General Election.

All the rest except Boanerges and the ladies rise in consternation.

PROTEUS. This is treachery.

BALBUS. A dirty trick.

NICOBAR. The meanest on record.

PLINY. He'll be at the top of the poll.

CRASSUS. There wont be any poll: it will be a walk-over.

BALBUS. This shews what all your fine manners and friendly ways are worth.

NICOBAR. Hypocrite!

CRASSUS. Humbug!

LYSISTRATA. I wish your Majesty every success.

AMANDA. Hear hear! Fair play, boys. Why shouldnt he go into parliament with us?

BOANERGES. Well said! well said! Why not?

THE OTHER MALE MINISTERS. Ya-a-a-ah! [*They sit down in utter disgust*].

PROTEUS [*very sullen*] And when you are in Parliament, what then?

MAGNUS. There are several possibilities. I shall naturally endeavor to form a party. My son King Robert will have to call on some Party leader who can depend on the support of the House of Commons to form a Government. He may call on you. He may even call on me.

AMANDA [*breaks the glum silence by whistling a bar or two of the National Anthem*]!!

MAGNUS. Whatever happens, it will be a great relief to us to be able to speak out quite frankly about one-another in public. You have never been able to tell the British people what you really think of me: no real criticism of the King is possible. I have never been able to speak my mind as to your various capacities and characters. All that reserve, that tedious affectation, that unwholesome concealment will end. I hope you look forward to our new footing as pleasurably as I do.

LYSISTRATA. I am delighted, sir. You will fight Breakages for me.

AMANDA. It will be awful fun.

BOANERGES. Now, Mr Prime Minister, we are waiting for you. What have you to say about it?

PROTEUS [*rising and speaking slowly, with his brows deeply knitted*] Has Your Majesty got that ultimatum on you?

MAGNUS [*produces it from his breast pocket and presents it to him*]!

PROTEUS [*with measured emphasis, after tearing the paper up into four pieces at two deliberate strokes, and throwing the pieces away*] There is not going to be any abdication. There is not going to be any general election. There is not going to be any ultimatum. We go on as before. The crisis is a washout. [*To the King, with deadly concentration*] I will never forgive you for this. You stole your ace of trumps from the hand I played this morning. [*He takes his hat from the balustrade and goes away through the park*].

BOANERGES [*rising*] That was a very deplorable exhibition of temper on the part of the Prime Minister, sir. It was not the gesture of a Strong Man. I will remonstrate with him. You may depend on me. [*He takes his hat and follows Proteus in a serious and dignified manner*].

NICOBAR [*rising*] Well, I shall not say what I think. [*He is taking his hat when the King addresses him*].

MAGNUS. So I have not upset the apple cart after all, Mr Nicobar.

NICOBAR. You can upset it as soon as you like for all I care. I am going out of politics. Politics is a mug's game. [*He goes*].

CRASSUS [*rising reluctantly and taking his hat*] If Nick goes, I shall have to go too.

MAGNUS. Can you really tear yourself away from politics?

CRASSUS. Only too glad to be well out of them, if Breakages will let me. They shoved me into it; and I daresay theyll find another job for me. [*He goes*].

PLINY [*cheerful to the last as he, too, goes for his hat*] Well, I am glad nothing's happened. You know, sir, nothing ever really does happen in the Cabinet. Never mind their bit of temper. Theyll feed out of your hand tomorrow. [*He goes*].

BALBUS [*after taking his hat*] Now that theyre all gone I dont mind saying that if anything should ever happen to the throne, and your Majesty should become a President with a Cabinet to pick, you might easily find a worse Home Secretary than me, with all my faults.

MAGNUS. I shall bear it in mind. By the way, if you should happen to overtake the Prime Minister, will you be so good as to remind him that we quite forgot to settle that little affair of the proposal of America to annex the British Commonwealth.

BALBUS. By the Lord, so we did! Well, thats a good one! Ha ha! Ha ha ha ha ha! [*He goes out laughing heartily*].

MAGNUS. They dont take it in, Lizzie: not one bit. It is as if another planet were crashing into us. The kingdom and the power and the glory will pass from us and leave us naked, face to face with our real selves at last.

LYSISTRATA. So much the better, if by our real selves you mean the old English stock that was unlike any other. Nowadays men all over the world are as much alike as hotel dinners. It's no use pretending that the America of George Washington is going to swallow up the England of Queen Anne. The America of George Washington is as dead as Queen Anne. What they call an American is only a wop pretending to be a Pilgrim Father. He is no more Uncle Jonathan than you are John Bull.

MAGNUS. Yes: we live in a world of wops, all melting into one another; and when all the frontiers are down London may be outvoted by Tennessee, and all the other places where we still madly teach our children the mentality of an eighteenth century village school.

LYSISTRATA. Never fear, sir. It is not the most ignorant national crowd that will come out on top, but the best power station; for you cant do without power stations, and you cant run them on patriotic songs and hatred of the foreigner, and guff and bugaboo, though you can run nationalism on nothing else. But I am heartbroken at your not coming into the House with us to keep old England in front and lead a new Party against Breakages [*tears come into her eyes*].

MAGNUS [*patting her consolingly on the back*] That would have been splendid, wouldnt it? But I am too old fashioned. This is a farce that younger men must finish.

AMANDA [*taking her arm*] Come home with me, dear. I will sing to you until you cant help laughing. Come.

Lysistrata pockets her handkerchief; shakes the King's hands impulsively; and goes with Amanda. The King plunges into deep thought. Presently the Queen comes back.

THE QUEEN. Now Magnus: it's time to dress for dinner.

MAGNUS [*much disturbed*] Oh, not now. I have something very big to think about. I dont want any dinner.

THE QUEEN [*peremptorily*] No dinner! Did anyone ever hear of such a thing! You know you will not sleep if you think after seven o'clock.

MAGNUS [*worried*] But really, Jemima—

THE QUEEN [*going to him and taking his arm*] Now, now, now! dont be naughty. I musnt be late for dinner. Come on, like a good little boy.

The King, with a grimace of hopeless tenderness, allows himself to be led away.

Mr Shaw Replies to His Critics

(Written statement, presented as interview,
Daily Mail, London, 21 August 1929)

*Mr Bernard Shaw laughingly declined to discuss the
Press notices of his new play, " The Apple Cart," when
I saw him this evening. " Surely you have formed some
opinion about it all?" I asked. He replied:*

Well, I am very pleased with the nice notices, but
what can I say on the subject? It is getting an
extremely serious matter nowadays.

In the old days one used to write a play and have it
produced and criticised and there was an end of it.
But now the Press has been clamouring throughout
the day for a statement of what I think about the
critics' reviews.

One can only say that the people had better read
the criticisms of the play and criticise the critics for
themselves.

I am an old dramatic critic so that I know all about
it.

Of course I read the criticisms, and if the critics say
anything helpful I should be prepared to make use of
it, but that does not usually happen.

Whatever they said, I should not rewrite the play.
When I had finished writing it I had said exactly what
I wanted to say.

Some of the criticisms might have been better
done. There are different sorts.

A Walk and a Talk with Mr Shaw

(Interview by G. W. Bishop, large portions of which were provided by Shaw in written statements, *The Observer*, London, 8 September 1929)

No play, not even any other one of Mr. Shaw's, has been talked about so much as "The Apple Cart"; it is all so like the epilogue to "Fanny's First Play"! "Shaw—what I've always told you about Shaw." . . . "Let's talk about Shaw"—for the last three weeks has been the favourite occupation of everybody who saw the play at Malvern, and of a good many who didn't.

I enjoyed the play so much that I made a special journey to Birmingham on Monday last to see it again. I travelled up with Cedric Hardwicke (who plays King Magnus), and Charles Carson (the Prime Minister), and on the journey we talked about Shaw; at supper after the performance we met again and, until the early hours, again talked about Shaw. At another table there were two other members of the cast—also, I am certain, talking about Shaw, and when I met Miss Edith Evans, who takes the part of Orinthia, we plunged at once into the subject of the moment and started discussing the controversial second act.

Nobody, of course, talks more illuminatingly, more amusingly, more provocatively or more interestingly about Shaw than G. B. S. himself. And it was Cedric Hardwicke's idea that we should continue the discussion the following day at Malvern, where the author of "The Apple Cart" was staying on for a few days of recuperating from the excitement of watching his own plays for a fortnight. There was something that Hardwicke wanted to ask him; I had a hundred things I wanted to talk to Mr Shaw about.

*   *   *   *   *

Shaw is, of course, the kindest, gentlest, and most courteous person living. He finds it difficult to refuse anybody anything—except newspaper men seeking an interview—and even then, if he is without the protection of his secretary. . . .

Perhaps it was because I came clinging to Hardwicke's mudguard, as it were: I like to think, however, that it was for my own sake—sublime vanity!—that he said when we arrived: "I feel stuffy; will you let me take you for a walk while Hardwicke entertains Mrs. Shaw!"

Away we strode. With some difficulty I managed to keep up with his pace; it was with considerably more difficulty that I could keep up with his talk. We happened to pass a cinema poster and I mentioned the "talkies." "Of course the 'talkies' have come to stay," he said; "a producer can spend £50,000 on a talking film, and is often guaranteed most of what he has spent before it is released, and it is bound to take the place of an ordinary stage production, upon which £50 has been spent."

*   *   *   *   *

"But surely theatre-goers will still demand the three-dimensional actor?" I suggested.

"Certainly," he replied, "but not the same person. The ordinary actor—as such—is unsuitable for talking film work. It is an entirely different technique. I tested that for myself. When I was shown the first picture I made I said to the producer, 'This is ludicrous; it is all wrong; it isn't me at all.' He replied:

[378]

'The camera cannot lie.' To which I retorted: 'The camera can lie and it has.' I then realised that in order to present a talking picture of Shaw I had to master a new method of moving and talking. If one acts naturally the result is simply—fussy.

"Look at the pictures taken of street scenes in the animated gazettes. The people who are walking give the impression of moving their legs quickly and running like this"—here Mr. Shaw illustrated what he meant—"whereas a movie actor has to walk in this way"—a few solemn steps were then "registered" in the middle of Malvern—"and the result on the screen is the ordinary natural walk. The screen magnifies and intensifies, and the technique is an entirely different one from the stage. 'Movie' actresses like Mary Pickford are clever enough not to appear on the stage without the glorious intensification of the camera. She knows that her public would consider that the real Mary Pickford is an insignificant person. She isn't, of course, but having always seen her magnified it would be like looking at her suddenly through the wrong end of the telescope.

*   *   *   *   *

"'Movie' acting is a different art," Mr. Shaw went on; "mainly it is the art of not moving at all! Then, along came the 'talkies,' and in rushed the ordinary 'movie' actor, and he has, on the whole, failed because he knows all about the reproduction of movement, but nothing about the voice. The stage actor, as such, is no good, and we shall have to breed a new race of 'talkie' actors and, what is more important, a race of intelligent producers."

"You will then allow your plays to be made into 'talkies'?"

"I know it is possible to reproduce dialogue, and it is now established that action can be reproduced on the screen. When it is as certain that the actual performers have mastered the technique and that there are some artistic producers who also understand the technique I shall consent."

"Don't you think that authors will have to write specifically for the screen?" I asked him as we finished our round and got back to the hotel.

"Possibly. I may write a 'talkie' myself, but I see no reason, given the conditions I have mentioned, that 'The Apple Cart' should not be reproduced exactly as it is written."

We had been out for nearly half an hour and I have only given the bare bones, a slight impression, of a talk which illuminated the whole subject as far as I was concerned. It gives little idea of the witty phrase, the apt illustration and Mr. Shaw's description of the banalities of the average moving picture.

     *   *   *   *   *

Inside, Mrs. Shaw was waiting for us with tea and we plunged into the subject of "The Apple Cart" at once. I mentioned the criticisms.

"Critics rely very much on labels," Mr. Shaw said. "I was not shown a proof of the programme and therefore the sub-title which will be printed when the play is seen in London, was omitted. The full title should have read: 'The Apple Cart—A Political Extravaganza in Two Acts and an Interlude.' The word 'extravaganza' would have helped them and they might then have been less worried by the short second act."

"Although it is an 'extravaganza' the play has a serious background?" I said.

"So serious that I intend to tell Mr. MacDonald when he returns from Geneva that he must refuse to take any young man into his Cabinet who hasn't seen 'The Apple Cart' at least six times. It is intended as a salutary lesson, as I feel it is a state of things into which we could drift.

★   ★   ★   ★   ★

"Few of the critics have realised that one of the points of the play is the recognition that there is no governing class. By which I mean the real governors are not a class, but are members of all classes. The King sees at once that Boanerges, who was picked out of the gutter by a policeman, is of the governing class. The great revelation that comes to Boanerges is that the King is also a member of the governing class. The 'plain-man' joke between the King and Boanerges has upset one or two people, but as a matter of fact it is a piece of tactful diplomacy on the part of the King. 'I'm a plain man,' boasts Boanerges. 'Not at all,' protests the King—the usual joke, it is asserted—but the King, after a pause, adds, 'you are anything but plain; in fact, to me, you have always been an enigma.' This flatters Boanerges, and puts him at his ease.

"Curiously, too, the Prime Minister has been called a dummy and a fool. But Proteus is really a very elaborate study of an able man. The King represents the classical example of the governing type; Proteus the womanly type—'I use the word woman,' Mr. Shaw added to his wife, 'in the stage sense'. He is hysterical and gets flustered, but he jumps at the true position of things at once, as I show at the end of the play, when he immediately grasps the fact that the King has beaten them. In the first act, too, Proteus and the King, in the two minutes they have alone together, arrive at a complete understanding. More is accomplished in that time than in the half an hour's previous talk."

★   ★   ★   ★   ★

"But the main oversight in the criticism of 'The Apple Cart,'" Mr. Shaw said, "is the failure to grasp the significance of the fact that the King wins, not *qua* King, but *qua* potential Commoner. The tearing up of the ultimatum is almost a defeat for him. It is certainly a defeat for Lysistrata (the Power Mistress), whose depression the King shares when the shouting is over.

"The critics have also missed the point of Boanerges' refusal to listen to a word against the Democracy which he himself ridiculed as an instrument of popular government. The Strong Man is a democrat because Democracy places power within his reach. As Magnus expressly says, Democracy has destroyed responsible government and gives the power to (as Bunyan put it) 'him that can get it.' 'Yourself, sir, for instance?' says Lysistrata. 'I think I am in the running,' replies the King.' But the great point is that he thinks he is in the running as Able Man, not as monarch. Only once in the whole play does Magnus assume royal authority, and that is in the interlude when he cries, 'Orinthia, I command you.' And then both Orinthia and the audience laugh him to scorn.

"No serious student of how monarchy and democracy actually work will demur to my handling of them," Mr. Shaw added.

"The protests that have actually been made sound as if George Odger had risen from his grave.

But you have probably never heard of George Odger*——"

     ★   ★   ★   ★   ★

"Now, about the second act—the interlude?"

"Composers are permitted a slow second movement in their symphony; why shouldn't I be allowed one in my composition?" Mr. Shaw protested. "Or, if you prefer it, the second act is a piece of relief, comic relief, if you like. What has the grave-diggers' scene to do with the character of Hamlet? But Shakespeare understood what I understand—if you put humour into a play it must be cheap humour!"

"The second act has, of course, a great dramatic significance, as great a significance as the porter's scene in 'Macbeth.' It completes the portrait of the King who in the middle of the crisis is seen, not merely as a statesman but as a human being with a domestic life."

Here Mr. Hardwicke suggested that the King held the Cabinet in the third act with some of Orinthia's powder still on his uniform. "Symbolically, yes," Mr. Shaw said, "nevertheless, Hardwicke, I hope that you will always brush your coat before the third act. The King knows that in married life the important thing is the recognition of the other's limitations. There are some subjects he cannot talk about to

---

* George Odger was born in 1820 and died in 1877. He was one of the early trade-unionists who exercised remarkable influence on the labour movement. He became a member of the National Reform League and helped to organise a popular welcome to Garibaldi in 1862, and the great meeting in St. James's Hall in support of the Northern States of America against slavery. He made five unsuccessful attempts to get into Parliament as an independent labour candidate. His funeral was the occasion of a great demonstration by the London working men, who regarded him as their leader. [Note by G. W. Bishop]

Jemima, his wife, and, on the other hand, the beautiful Orinthia certainly has *her* limitations. It is an important scene, and not there merely to amuse. I can only conclude that the critics who did not understand it are happily married to wives who combine in themselves Orinthia and Jemima. The average man is not so fortunate. There are hundreds of nice middle-class families who do not understand why they squabble. The scene between the King and Orinthia will serve as a dose of castor oil. Shakespeare suggested the same idea when Beatrice says, in reply to Don Pedro's proposal. 'No, my lord, unless I might have another for workingdays: your grace is too costly to wear every day.' Jemima, intellectually, is good for every-day wear, and Magnus knows this; Orinthia is the splendid Sunday relaxation. Married people will get on better after they have seen the second act of 'The Apple Cart.'"

★ ★ ★ ★ ★

We might have gone on for hours if Cedric Hardwicke had not suddenly remembered that in an hour or two he would be acting the King (instead of talking about him) on the stage of the Birmingham Repertory Theatre.

After he had waved us farewell it occurred to me that the author of "The Apple Cart" did not know that he was being "interviewed." When he sees this totally inadequate account of the talk in print he may blame Hardwicke for taking me over to Malvern. Mr. Shaw will not be too severe, I feel, because he admires the actor's performance as King Magnus tremendously.

Bernard Shaw's Denial

(Statement to the press, *The Star*, London,
30 September 1929)

The report of a conversation I had with a prominent
Polish journalist which has been sent by Reuter and
published in several papers, makes it necessary for me
to offer one or two elucidations.

I seem to have conveyed to my distinguished
foreign visitor that the Prime Minister discussed 'The
Apple Cart' with me after the performance, and that I
intended to base King Magnus on the personality of
Marshal Pilsudski, but refrained lest it should be said
that the Marshal had paid me to do so.

I also seem to have conveyed that the play has not
been received here with the enthusiasm it evoked in
Poland.

This is not precisely what I meant to say. I have
not spoken to the Prime Minister since he was present
on the first night, when we exchanged a few words
before the rise of the curtain.

I cannot claim the privilege of personal acquaintance with Marshal Pilsudski. I never dreamt of
using him, or any other living person, as a model,
though every living ruler in the world will find a
melancholy resemblance between his predicament
and that of King Magnus.

I cannot avoid the suggestion that I have been paid
by him, because it has already been made, and will
probably be repeated, mutatis mutandis in every
country where the play is produced.

Finally, as to the alleged more enthusiastic reception of 'The Apple Cart' in Poland than in London,
all I can say is that the reception in London has

reached its box-office limit, and that Polish enthusiasm, however frenzied, can go no further from
the author's point of view.

Naturally I am glad to learn that King Magnus's
Crown fits the heads of all the rulers and that his
subjects in all lands vie with one another in appreci-
ation of my picture of their political situation. That is
all I need say at present.

Mr Shaw and Democracy

(Interview by G. W. Bishop, based on written
statement by Shaw, *The Observer*, London,
23 March 1930)

"'The Apple Cart' is laid in the future. There seems
to be confusion about the approximate date. Is it—as
was suggested before the play was produced—at a time
when all people now living are dead?"

"Yes."

"Do you seriously think that democracy may drift
into the state of things shown in the play?"

"It has already drifted into it."

"Is not the tendency in this country towards a
bigger percentage of voting and a more enlightened
use of the franchise?"

"The tendency to disuse the franchise is so strong
that in some countries it is a punishable offence not to
vote. People vote in times of great social strain for
which the government is blamed. The newly en-
franchised (the women, for instance) vote whilst the
novelty lasts. But in a condition of general satisfaction,
or of general disgust at the failure of political parties

to make good their promises, people will not vote. In the old vestries, for which anybody could vote, a little ring of men used to meet and elect one another without the interference of a single general elector. Shareholders' meetings are very much the same. Do *you* ever vote ? "

THE IDEAL RULER

"You do not believe, I assume, that a benevolent monarchy is a better form of government than a democracy ? Do you think the veto of a hereditary ruler is a valuable safeguard in any self-governing country ? Is the ideal government when the two work smoothly together ? "

"Benevolent monarchies and democracies are idealisations which have never been realised. Even government itself is a very imperfectly realised ideal. Benevolence is not a qualification for rulership at all: capable rulers have often been infernal scoundrels, and benevolent monarchs hopelessly incapable rulers.

"The veto of a hereditary ruler has no value as a safeguard. The veto of a capable ruler, whether he be hereditary monarch, dictator, president, prime minister, or chief constable of a county, has the value of his capacity.

"The desideratum is a method of government in which the governed choose their rulers and can change them, but in which only capable persons are eligible for choice or change. Hereditary monarchy obviously cannot supply this. The notion that adult suffrage can supply it has been reduced to absurdity by experience. It is worse than hereditary monarchy, which may accidentally and occasionally produce a capable ruler, whereas adult suffrage, through the general dislike of capable rulers, and the popularity of agreeable and extravagant ne'er-do-weels (compare William the Conqueror with King Stephen), positively prevents capable rulers from entering politics, and exalts Titus Oateses to commanding positions."

THE ENGLISH-SPEAKING PEOPLES

"Would the United States be better off with a hereditary monarchy?"

"What sort of monarchy? Constitutional or Autocratic. The question in a practical form would be, 'Are the United States better off than the British Commonwealth?' The useless but only possible answer is, 'In some respects, yes; in others, no.' Evidently the difference is not great enough to produce a demand in either country for the form of government used in the other."

"Is America gradually annexing Great Britain? Can you conceive that a day will come when there will be an Empire of the English—or American—speaking peoples?"

"America is certainly Americanising Great Britain more than Europe is Europeanising it. In fact, America is Americanising Europe, whilst remaining itself blatantly American. Asia and Africa are not in the running. Russia is America's only rival as a basic civilising influence.

"Whether the United States will ever include all the States and Dominions in which English is the language of the people, is still a matter for speculation. It is not impossible. But, so far, it cannot be said that the bond of Western European civilisation is weaker than the bond of language. And do not forget that the Marxian dream of a world-wide proletarian revolution, though it is not now practical politics, may yet upset all our conceptions of international relations. The Reformation did not seem practicable in the Middle Ages; but it happened for all that."

GERMAN OBJECTIONS

"You told me when we met a short time ago that the most violent objections to 'The Apple Cart' came from the Social Democrats in Germany. Would you care to reply to those objections?"

"I don't know what they are. The idea seems to be that as a democrat I should have made the King the villain of the piece. Even if I were a democrat in the sense of believing that good government is secured by giving Jack and Jill a vote, which I am not and have never pretended to be, the idea would still seem childish to me. My business is not to satirise the vices of an autocracy which does not exist, but those of the pseudo-democracy which does exist."

"Were the members of the Cabinet dressed in fancy dress in the English production to meet the requirements of the Lord Chamberlain?"

"No. The Lord Chamberlain made no requirements. The play was licensed without demur at the first asking, quite unconditionally. The fancy dresses, in so far as they are not purely decorative, were prescribed by the author to remove the play as far as possible from the Cabinet and Court of to-day."

"When I saw the play for the third time recently, I thought that the curtain should have come down when the King is left alone on the stage? I felt that the entrance of the Queen was an anti-climax."

"Max Reinhardt, in Berlin, thought so, too, and did what you in your masculine idiocy suggest. Ask any woman what she thinks of your brains and Max's."

NO NEW PLAY AT PRESENT

"Is it true that 'The Apple Cart' is the first of a trilogy and that a new play by you may be seen at the Malvern festival this year?"

"No, there is no question of a trilogy. I will write another play for Malvern if I can; but as I am under contract to complete certain literary work involving prolonged labour this spring, it seems almost impossible that I can be in time for the Festival with a new play this year. It will have to be a very hasty one, in any case. I have not had time to give a thought to it yet."

"Has the play a special message for American audiences?"

"It has a special message for all audiences—even American ones."

The Apple-Cart Again

(Replies to a questionnaire by John Rintoul Hunt, *Courier*, London, Autumn 1943)

In The Apple-Cart, *Mr. Shaw, you dramatised in prophetic fashion the prospect of the British Empire and the United States of America re-uniting at no very distant date. That was in 1928–9, some fifteen years ago. Now, under the pressure of world catastrophes, and in spite of the handicap of a common history and a common language (more or less), the two countries are closer in spirit as well as in material matters than they have been for more than a century and a half. What do you imagine is the likeliest next move?*

The imagined next move never takes place: so I do not waste my time imagining it. The situation in The Apple-Cart made a good last act for a comedy;

but if I had wanted one for the first act of a tragedy I should have made England renew the old alliance with Japan made by the late Lord Lansdowne, followed by the immediate secession of New Zealand, Australia, South Africa, and Canada from the British Commonwealth and their federation with the United States in a defensive combination against Japan. Nobody who has not been to the Pacific has the faintest notion of what Japan means there.

Of course, as you realised at the time, some pretty constitutional problems would be set if ever the subject came up for debate by statesmen and lawyers, those wise but unpractical dreamers. Your "King Magnus" was put in the very devil of embarrassment when Vanhattan, the U.S. Ambassador, came bounding in with his demand, or ultimatum, that the U.S.A. be received back in the Empire and the Declaration of Independence and the Acts relating thereto be cancelled. Have you any idea how the lawyers would get round such difficulties as the American Constitution and the Statute of Westminster?

Not at all. There would be no trouble about that if both sides meant business. If they did not, then of course the lawyers and diplomatists would have no difficulty in proving that the thing is utterly impossible, or would take fifty years to work out. But if the two Governments were in earnest, they would just do it, and leave the rearrangements to follow the event, as they would have to, difficulties or no difficulties. The Statute of Westminster and the American Constitution are only scraps of paper; but facts are facts.

On the other hand, Americans—or quite a number of them—might prefer that the United Kingdom were admitted to the Union as the 49th State? And the self-governing Dominions as the 50th, 51st, 52nd and so on. With the Crown Colonies and India given a similar status to that of the Philippines.

The old nomenclatures need not be preserved. Why should they, seeing that they will only make trouble?

Where would you fit Ireland into the new scheme of things, Mr Shaw? In The Apple-Cart, *the Queen was so shocked at the whole proposal that she could only envisage the Court taking refuge in Dublin. That, I venture, was not suggested in all seriousness, was it? Would Belfast take Dublin's place? Or perhaps as a compromise the ancient glories of Tara or Galway be revived?*

Eire will have to fit itself into any change as best it can. Its military forces are too small to be considered by the big powers who will dominate the situation. It owes its present neutrality to the Partition, which gives England a foothold in the island, that would otherwise have had to be taken by force by either England or America. Ireland must live by her wits, which means that she must have alliances; but as she cannot ally herself with Japan or Germany her choice is restricted practically to England and America. And England is much more easily humbugged or bullied or coaxed than America. As to Dublin, which is within half an hour of the most enchanting mountain and seaside scenery, it is in these days of air transit one of the pleasantest seats of Government in the world. There is nothing wrong with it except its slums with their shocking vital statistics, and the perpetual derisive gabble of its inhabitants.

There is one aspect, referred to in The Apple-Cart, *which we have not touched on here—the attitude of the British Dominions. On a Gallup Poll taken in Canada this year slightly more than 20 per cent. of those canvassed for their views opted for inclusion in the United States. Opinion in Australia seems to favour closer links with the U.S. and to feel that Britain is too distant to afford permanent protection against the Japs. South Africa, after Smuts, may experience a reaction and desire a change of allegiance. What do you think, Mr. Shaw?*

These are talking points. The Dominions will have to take what they can get, which will be by no means all they want.

Finally, what of Moscow? This is a little aside from the main discussion. My excuse for troubling you is not merely that Moscow cannot be left out of any discussion anyway but also that in your play Moscow through your character, Boanerges, came prominently into it. Our statesmen, willy-nilly, have blundered into co-operation with Soviet Russia as well as perilously close to Anglo-American reunion—ought we not to see they don't blunder out of it again?

When the war is over Moscow will be cock of the walk, but at the cost of internal damage that will keep her too busy at home to make trouble for herself abroad, provided always that her Western frontiers are accepted as they stood before the German attack. Stalin has been explicit and emphatic about that from the beginning. Moscow will be strong enough to impose that condition. The question of whether Hong Kong is to be British or Chinese may prove more troublesome.

[393]

(Boanerges in the play was not a Russian; he was a vivid caricature of the late John Burns.)

Thank you, Mr. Shaw. The world has been transformed in the past 50 years, chiefly through your plays, and perhaps in another 50 years we shall all be good sensible Shavians. Isn't it true that history is made from the 50–year plans of poets and philosophers rather than the 5–year plans of sanitary engineers and production experts?

Until the poets know all about sanitary engineering and the sanitary engineers all about poetry and philosophy neither of them will be of any use as planners. Our present way of giving votes to ignorance and calling it democracy will upset any plan. Wisdom, knowledge, and energy can save civilisation; electioneering can only wreck it.

Too True to be Good:
A Political Extravaganza

WITH

Preface

From the Malvern Festival Book, 1932

*Why "Too True to be Good" Failed: A Moral
in Favour of a National Theatre*

Composition begun 5 March 1931; completed 30 June 1931. First published in German translation, as *Zu Wahr um schön zu sein*, 1932. First publication in English in *Too True to be Good, Village Wooing & On the Rocks*, 1934. First presented by the Theatre Guild at the National Theatre, Boston, on 29 February 1932.

The Monster   *Julius Evans*
The Patient (Miss Mopply)   *Hope Williams*
The Elderly Lady (Mrs Mopply)   *Minna Phillips*
The Doctor   *Alexander Clark, Jr.*
The Nurse (Susan "Sweetie" Simpkins,
    alias the Countess Valbrioni)   *Beatrice Lillie*
The Burglar ("Popsy," *alias* the Honorable
    Aubrey Bagot)   *Hugh Sinclair*
Colonel Tallboys, V.C., D.S.O.   *Ernest Cossart*
Private Napoleon Alexander Trotsky Meek
    Leo G. Carroll
Sergeant Fielding   *Frank Shannon*
The Elder   *Claude Rains*

Period—The Present
ACT I   *One of the Best Bedrooms in one of the Best Suburban Villas in one of the Richest Cities in England*
ACT II   *A Sea Beach in a Mountainous Country*
ACT III   *A Narrow Gap leading down to the Beach*

Preface

Contents

MONEY AND HAPPINESS

Somehow my play, Too True To Be Good, has in performance excited an animosity and an enthusiasm which will hardly be accounted for by the printed text. Some of the spectators felt that they had had a divine revelation, and overlooked the fact that the eloquent gentleman through whose extremely active mouth they had received it was the most hopeless sort of scoundrel: that is, one whose scoundrelism consists in the absence of conscience rather than in any positive vices, and is masked by good looks and agreeable manners. The less intellectual journalist critics sulked as they always do when their poverty but not their will consents to their witnessing a play of mine; but over and above the resultant querulousness to which I have long been accustomed I thought I detected an unusual intensity of resentment, as if I had hit them in some new and unbearably sore spot.

Where, then, was the offence that so exceedingly disgruntled these unhappy persons? I think it must have been the main gist and moral of the play, which is not, as usual, that our social system is unjust to the poor, but that it is cruel to the rich. Our revolutionary writers have dwelt on the horrors of poverty. Our conventional and romantic writers have ignored those horrors, dwelling pleasantly on the elegances of an existence free from pecuniary care. The poor have been pitied for miseries which do not, unfortunately, make them unbearably miserable. But who has pitied the idle rich or really believed that they have a worse time of it than those who have to live on ten shillings a day or less, and earn it? My play is a story of three reckless young people who come into possession of, for the moment, unlimited riches, and set out to have a thoroughly good time with all the modern machinery of pleasure to aid them. The result is that they get nothing for their money but a multitude of worries and a maddening dissatisfaction.

THE VAMPIRE AND THE CALF

I doubt whether this state of things is ever intentionally produced. We see a man apparently slaving to place his children in the position of my three adventurers; but on closer investigation we generally find that he does not care twopence for his children, and is wholly wrapped up in the fascinating game of making money. Like other games it is enjoyable only by people with an irresistible and virtually exclusive fancy for it, and enough arithmetical ability and flair for market values to play it well; but with these qualifications the poorest men can make the most astounding fortunes. They accumulate nothing but powers of extracting money every six months from their less acquisitive neighbors; and their children accumulate nothing but obligations to spend it. As between these two processes of bleeding and being bled, bleeding is the better fun. The vampire has a better time than the calf hung up by the heels with its throat cut. The moneygetter spends less on his food, clothes, and amusements than his clerks do, and is happy. His wife and sons and daughters, spending fabulous sums on themselves, are no happier than their housemaids, if so happy; for the routine of fashion is virtually as compulsory as the routine of a housemaid, its dressing is as much dictated as her uniform, its snubbings are as humiliating, and its monotony is more tedious because more senseless and useless, not to mention that it must be pleasanter to be tipped than to tip. And, as I surmise, the housemaid's day off or evening off is really off: in those hard earned hours she ceases to be a housemaid and can be herself; but the lady of fashion never has a moment off: she has to be fashionable even in her little leisure, and dies without ever having had any self at all. Here and there you find rich ladies taking up occupations and interests which keep them so busy doing professional or public work that they might as well have five hundred a year as fifty thousand "for all the good it does them" as the poor say in their amazement when they see people who could afford to be fashionable and extravagant working hard and dressing rather plainly. But that requires a personal endowment of tastes and talents quite out of the common run.

I remember a soldier of the old never-do-well type drifting into a little Socialist Society which I happened to be addressing more than fifty years ago. As he had evidently blundered into the wrong shop and was half drunk, some of the comrades began to chaff him, and finally held me up to him as an example of the advantages of teetotalism. With the most complete conviction he denounced me as a hypocrite and a liar affirming it to be a well-known and inexorable law of nature that no man with money in his pocket could pass a public house without going in for a drink.

THE OLD SOLDIER AND THE PUBLIC HOUSE

I have never forgotten that soldier, because his delusion, in less crude forms, and his conception of happiness, seem to afflict everybody in England more or less. When I say less crude forms I do not mean truer forms; for the soldier, being half drunk, was probably happier than he would have been if quite sober, whereas the plutocrat who has spent a hundred pounds in a day in the search for pleasure is not happier than if he had spent only five shillings. For it must be admitted that a private soldier, outside that surprising centre of culture, the Red Army of Russia, has so little to be happy about when sober that his case is hardly a fair one. But it serves to illustrate the moral of my play, which is, that our capitalistic system, with its golden exceptions of idle richery and its leaden rule of anxious poverty, is as desperate a failure from the point of view of the rich as of the poor. We are all amazed and incredulous, like the soldier, when we hear of the multimillionaire passing the public house without going in and drinking himself silly; and we envy his sons and daughters who do go in and drink themselves silly. The vulgar pub may be in fact a Palace Hotel, and the pints of beer or glasses of whisky an elaborate dinner with many courses and wines culminating in cigars and liqueurs; but the illusion and the results are cognate.

I therefore plead for a science of happiness to cure us of the miserable delusion that we can achieve it by becoming richer than our neighbors. Modern colossal fortunes have demonstrated its vanity. When country parsons were "passing rich with forty pounds a year" there was some excuse for believing that to be rich was to be happy, as the conception of riches did not venture beyond enough to pay for the necessities of a cultivated life. A hundred years ago Samuel Warren wrote a famous novel about a man who became enormously rich. The title of the novel was Ten Thousand a Year; and this, to any resident Irish family in my boyhood, represented an opulence beyond which only Lords Lieutenant and their like could aspire. The scale has changed since then. I have just seen in the papers a picture of the funeral of a shipping magnate whose income, if the capital value of the property left by him be correctly stated, must have been over four thousand pounds a day or a million and a half a year. If happiness is to be measured by riches he must have been fourteen thousand times as happy as the laborer lucky enough to be earning two pounds a week. Those who believe that riches are the reward of virtue are bound to conclude that he was also fourteen thousand times as sober, honest, and industrious, which would lead to the quaint conclusion that if he drank a bottle of wine a day the laborer must have drunk fourteen thousand.

THE UNLOADING MILLIONAIRES

This is so obviously monstrous that it may now be dismissed as an illusion of the poor who know nothing of the lives of the rich. Poverty, when it involves continual privation and anxiety, is, like toothache, so painful that the victim can desire nothing happier than the cessation of the pain. But it takes no very extraordinary supply of money to enable a humble person to say "I want for nothing"; and when that modest point is reached the power of money to produce happiness vanishes, and the trouble which an excess of it brings begins to assert itself, and finally reaches a point at which the multimillionaires are seen frantically unloading on charitable, educational, scientific, religious, and even (though rarely) artistic and political "causes" of all kinds, mostly without stopping to examine whether the causes produce any effects, and if so what effects. And far from suffering a loss of happiness every time they give away a thousand pounds, they find themselves rather in the enviable state of mind of the reveller in The Pilgrim's Progress with his riddle "There was a man, though some did think him mad, the more he gave away the more he had."

DELUSIONS OF POVERTY

The notion that the rich must be happy is complemented by the delusion that the poor must be miserable. Our society is so constituted that most people remain all their lives in the condition in which they were born, and have to depend on their imagination for their notions of what it is like to be in the opposite condition. The upstarts and the downstarts, though we hear a great deal about them either as popular celebrities or criminals, are exceptional. The rich, it is said, do not know how the poor live; but nobody insists on the more mischievous fact that the poor do not know how the rich live. The rich are a minority; and they are not consumed with envy of the poor. But the poor are a huge majority and they are so demoralized by the notion that they would be happy if only they were rich, that they make themselves poorer, if hopefuller, by backing horses and buying sweepstake tickets on the chance of realizing their daydreams of unearned fortunes. Our penny newspapers now depend for their circulation, and consequently for their existence, on the sale of what are virtually lottery coupons. The real opposition to Socialism comes from the fear (well founded) that it would cut off the possibilities of becoming rich beyond those dreams of avarice which our capitalist system encourages. The odds against a poor person becoming a millionaire are of astronomical magnitude; but they are sufficient to establish and maintain the Totalisator as a national institution, and to produce unlimited daydreams of bequests from imaginary long lost uncles in Australia or a lucky ticket in the Calcutta or Irish Sweeps.

TRYING IT FOR AN HOUR

Besides, even quite poor people save up for holidays during which they can be idle and rich, if not for life, at least for an hour, an afternoon, or even a week. And for the poor these moments derive such a charm from the change from the monotony of daily toil and servitude, that the most intolerable hardships and discomforts and fatigues in excursion trains and over-crowded lodgings seem delightful, and leave the reveller with a completely false notion of what a life-time of such revelry would be.

I maintain that nobody with a sane sense of values can feel that the sole prize which our villainous capital-ist system has to offer, the prize of admission to the ranks of the idle rich, can possibly confer either happiness or health or freedom on its winner. No one can convict me of crying sour grapes; for during the last thirty-five years I have been under no compulsion to work nor had any material privation or social ostracism to fear as a consequence of not working. But, like all the intelligent rich people of my acquaint-ance, I have worked as hard, ate and drunk no more, and dressed no better than when I had to work or starve. When my pockets were empty I did not buy any of the luxuries in the London shops because I had no money to buy them with. When, later on, I had enough to buy anything that London could tempt me with, the result was the same: I returned home day after day without having made a single purchase. And I am no ascetic: no man alive is freer than I from the fancy that selfmortification will propitiate a spiteful deity or increase my balance in a salvation bank in a world beyond the grave. I would and could live the life of the idle rich if I liked it; and my sole reason for not living it is that I dont like it. I have every opportunity of observing it both in its daily practice and its remoter results; and I know that a year of it would make me more unhappy than anything else of an accepted kind that I can imagine. For, just as the beanfeaster can live like a lord for an afternoon, and the Lancashire factory operative have a gorgeous week at Blackpool when the wakes are on, so I have had my afternoons as an idle rich man, and know only too well what it is like. It makes me feel suicidal.

You may say that I am an exceptional man. So I am, in respect of being able to write plays and books; but as everybody is exceptional in respect of being able to do something that most other people cannot do, there is nothing in that. Where I am really a little exceptional is in respect of my having experienced both poverty and riches, servitude and selfgovernment, and also having for some reason or other (possibly when I was assured in my infancy that some nasty medicine was delicious) made up my mind early in life never to let myself be persuaded that I am enjoying myself gloriously when I am, as a matter of fact, being bored and pestered and plundered and worried and tired. You cannot humbug me on this point: I understand perfectly why Florence Nightingale fled from fashionable society in London to the horrors of the Crimean hospitals rather than behave like a lady, and why my neighbour Mr Apsley Cherry-Garrard, the sole survivor of what he calls with good reason "the worst journey in the world" through the Antarctic winter, was no poor sailorman driven by his need for daily bread to make a hard living before the mast, but a country gentleman opulent enough to choose the best that London society could offer him if he chose. Better the wards of the most terrible of

field hospitals than a drawingroom in Mayfair: better
the South Pole at its blackest six months winter night
and its most murderous extremities of cold than
Sunday by the Serpentine in the height of the season.

CONSOLATIONS OF THE LANDED GENTRY

To some extent this misery of riches is a new thing.
Anyone who has the run of our country houses, with
their great parks and gardens, their staffs of retainers,
indoor and outdoor, and the local public work that is
always available for the resident landed gentry, will
at once challenge the unqualified assertion that the
rich, in a lump, are miserable. Clearly they are nothing
of the sort, any more than the poor in a lump. But
then they are neither idle nor free. A lady with a big
house to manage, and the rearing of a family to super-
vise, has a reasonably busy time of it even without
counting her share in the routine of sport and entertainment and occasional travel which to people
brought up to it is a necessary and important part of
a well ordered life. The landed gentry have enough
exercise and occupation and sense of social importance and utility to keep them on very good terms with
themselves and their neighbors. If you suddenly
asked them whether they really enjoyed their routine
and whether they would not rather be Communists in
Russia they would be more sincerely scandalized than
if you had turned to them in Church and asked them
whether they really believed every clause in the
Apostles' Creed. When one of their ugly ducklings
becomes a revolutionist it is not because country-
house life is idle, but because its activities are un-
congenial and because the duckling has tastes or
talents which it thwarts, or a faculty for social

criticism which discovers that the great country house is not built on the eternal rock but on the sandy shore of an ocean of poverty which may at any moment pass from calm to tempest. On the whole, there is no reason why a territorial lady should not be as happy as her dairymaid, or her husband be as happy as his game-keeper. The riches of the county families are attached to property; and the only miserable county people are those who will not work at their job.

MISERIES OF THE VAGRANT ROOTLESS RICH

But the new thing is riches detached from real pro-perty: that is, detached from work, from responsibility, from tradition, and from every sort of prescribed routine, even from the routine of going to the village church every Sunday, paying and receiving calls, and having every month set apart for the killing of some particular bird or animal. It means being a tramp without the daily recurrent obligation to beg or steal your dinner and the price of your bed. In-stead, you have the daily question "What shall I do? Where shall I go?" and the daily answer "Do what you please: go where you like: it doesnt matter what you do or where you go." In short, the perfect liberty of which slaves dream because they have no experi-ence of its horrors. Of course the answer of outraged Nature is drowned for a time by the luxury merchants shouting "Come and shop, whether you need any-thing or not. Come to our palace hotels. Come round the world in our liners. Come and wallow in our swimming pools. Come and see our latest model automobile: we have changed the inventor's design for-better-for-worse solely to give you an excuse for buying a new one and selling your old one at scrap iron prices. Come and buy our latest fashions in dress: you cannot possibly be seen in last season's garments." And so on and so forth. But the old questions come home to the rich tourists in the palace hotels and luxury liners just as they do to the tramps on the highroad. They come up when you have the latest car and the latest wardrobe and all the rest of it. The only want that money can satisfy without satiating for more than a few hours is the need for food and drink and sleep. So from one serious meal a day and two very minor ones you go on to three serious meals a day and two minor ones. Then you work another minor one between breakfast and lunch "to sustain you"; and you soon find that you cannot tackle any meal without a cocktail, and that you cannot sleep. That obliges you to resort to the latest soporific drug, guaranteed in the advertisements to have none of the ruinous effects of its equally guaranteed forerunner. Then comes the doctor, with his tonics, which are simply additional cocktails, and his sure knowledge that if he tells you the truth about yourself and refuses to prescribe the tonics and the drugs, his children will starve. If you indulge in such a luxury as a clerical spiritual adviser it is his duty to tell you what is the matter with you is that you are an idle useless glutton and drunkard and that you are going to hell; but alas! he, like the doctor, cannot afford this, as he may have to ask you for a subscription tomorrow to keep his church going. And that is "Liberty: thou choicest treasure."

This sort of life has been made possible, and indeed inevitable, by what William Cobbett, who had a sturdy sense of vital values, denounced as The Funding System. It was a product of war, which obliged belligerent governments to obtain enormous sums

from all and sundry by giving them in exchange the
right to live for nothing on the future income of the
country until their money was returned: a system now
so popular among people with any money to spare
that they can be induced to part with it only on condition that the Government promises not to repay it
before a certain more or less remote day. When joint
stock companies were formed to run big industrial
concerns with money raised on the still more tempting
terms that the money is never to be repaid, the
system became so extensive that the idle upstart rich
became a definitely mischievous and miserable class
quite different in character from the old feudal rich.

THE REDEMPTION FROM PROPERTY

When I propose the abolition of our capitalistic
system to redeem mankind from the double curse of
poverty and riches, loud wailings arise. The most
articulate sounds in the hubbub are to the effect that
the wretched slaves of the curse will lose their liberty
if they are forced to earn their living honorably. The
retort that they have nothing to lose but their chains,
with the addition that the gold chains are as bad as
the iron ones, cannot silence them, because they think
they are free, and have been brought up to believe
that unless the country remains the private property
of irresponsible owners maintaining a parliament to
make any change impossible, with churches schools
and universities to inculcate the sacredness of private
property and party government disguised as religion
education and democracy, civilization must perish. I
am accused of every sort of reactionary extravagance
by the people who think themselves advanced, and

of every sort of destructive madness by people who thank God they are no wiser than their fathers.

Now I cannot profitably discuss politics religion and economics with terrified ignoramuses who understand neither what they are defending nor what they are attacking. But it happens that Mr Gilbert Chesterton, who is not an ignoramus and not in the least terrified, and whose very interesting conversion to Roman Catholicism has obliged him to face the problem of social organization fundamentally, discarding the Protestant impostures on English history which inspired the vigorous Liberalism of his salad days, has lately taken me to task for the entirely imaginary offence of advocating government by a committee of celebrities. To clear up the matter I have replied to Mr Chesterton very fully and in Catholic terms. Those who have read my reply in the magazines in which it appeared need read no further, unless they wish, as I should advise, to read it twice. For the benefit of the rest, and to put it on permanent record, here it is.

FUNDAMENTAL NATURAL CONDITIONS OF HUMAN SOCIETY

1. Government is necessary wherever two or three are gathered together—or two or three billions—for keeps.

2. Government is neither automatic nor abstract: it must be performed by human rulers and agents as best they can.

3. The business of the rulers is to check disastrously selfish or unexpected behaviour on the part of individuals in social affairs.

4. This business can be done only by devizing and enforcing rules of social conduct codifying the

greatest common measure of agreement as to the necessary sacrifice of individual liberty to the good of the community.

5. The paradox of government is that as the good of the community involves a maximum of individual liberty for all its members the rulers have at the same time to enslave everyone ruthlessly and to secure for everyone the utmost possible freedom.

6. In primitive communities people feed and lodge themselves without bothering the Government. In big civilizations this is impossible; so the first business of the Government is to provide for the production and distribution of wealth from day to day and the just sharing of the labor and leisure involved. Thus the individual citizen has to be compelled not only to behave himself properly, but to work productively.

7. The moral slavery of the compulsion to behave properly is a whole-time compulsion admitting of no liberty; but the personal slavery of the compulsion to work lasts only as many hours daily as suffice to discharge the economic duties of the citizen, the remaining hours (over and above those needed for feeding, sleeping, locomotion, etc.) being his leisure.

8. Leisure is the sphere of individual liberty: labor is the sphere of slavery.

9. People who think they can be honestly free all the time are idiots: people who seek whole-time freedom by putting their share of productive work on others are thieves.

10. The use of the word slavery to denote subjection to public government has grown up among the idiots and thieves, and is resorted to here only because it is expedient to explain things to fools according to their folly.

So much for the fundamental natural conditions of

social organization. They are as completely beyond argument as the precession of the equinoxes; but they present different problems to different people. To the thief, for instance, the problem is how to evade his share of the labor of production, to increase his share in the distribution of the product, and to corrupt the Government so that it may protect and glorify his chicaneries instead of liquidating him. To Mr Chesterton the Distributist (or Extreme Left Communist) and Catholic (or Equalitarian Internationalist) it is how to select rulers who will govern righteously and impartially in accordance with the fundamental natural conditions.

The history of civilization is the history of the conflict between these rival views of the situation. The Pirate King, the Robber Baron, and the Manchester Man produced between them a government which they called the Empire, the state, the Realm, the Republic, or any other imposing name that did not give away its central purpose. The Chestertonians produced a government which they called The Church; and in due time the Last of the Chestertons joined this Catholic Church, like a very large ship entering a very small harbor, to the great peril of its many rickety old piers and wharves, and the swamping of all the small craft in its neighborhood. So let us see what the Catholic Church made of its governmental problem.

THE CATHOLIC SOLUTION

To begin with, the Church, being catholic, was necessarily democratic to the extent that its aim was to save the souls of all persons without regard to their age, sex, nationality, class, or color. The nobleman who felt that God would not lightly damn a man of his quality received no countenance from the Church in that conviction. Within its fold all souls were equal before God.

But the Church did not draw the ridiculous conclusion that all men and women are equally qualified or equally desirous to legislate, to govern, to administer, to make decisions, to manage public affairs or even their own private affairs. It faced the fact that only about five per cent. of the population are capable of exercising these powers, and are certain to be corrupted by them unless they have an irresistible religious vocation for public work and a faith in its beneficence which will induce them to take vows to abstain from any profit that is not shared by all the rest, and from all indulgences which might blunt their consciences or subject them to the family influences so bitterly deprecated by Jesus.

This natural "called" minority was never elected in the scandalous way we call democratic. Its members were in the first instance self-elected: that is, they voluntarily lived holy lives and devoted themselves to the public welfare in obedience to the impulse of the Holy Ghost within them. This impulse was their vocation. They were called from above, not chosen by the uncalled. To protect themselves and obtain the necessary power, they organized themselves, and called their organization The Church. After that, the genuineness and sufficiency of the vocation of the new recruits were judged by The Church. If the judgment was favorable, and the candidates took certain vows, they were admitted to the official priesthood and set to govern as priests in the parish and spiritual directors in the family, all of them being eligible, if they had the requisite ability, for promotion to the work of governing the Church itself as bishops or cardinals, or to the supreme rank of Pope or Vicar of Christ on earth. And all this without the smallest reference to the opinions of the uncalled and unordained.

NEED FOR A COMMON FAITH

Now comes the question, why should persons of genuine vocation be asked to take vows before being placed in authority? Is not the vocation a sufficient guarantee of their wisdom?

No. Before priests can govern they must have a common faith as to the fundamental conditions of a stable human society. Otherwise the result might be an assembly of random men of genius unable to agree on a single legislative measure or point of policy. An ecumenical council consisting of Einstein and Colonel Lynch, Aquinas and Francis Bacon, Dante and Galileo, Lenin and Lloyd George, could seldom come to an unanimous decision, if indeed to any decision except in the negative against a minority of one, on any point beyond the capacity of a coroner's jury. The Pope must not be an eccentric genius presiding over a conclave of variously disposed cardinals: he must have an absolutely closed mind on what Herbert Spencer called Social Statics; and in this the cardinals must resemble and agree with him. What is more, they must to some extent represent the conscience of the common people; for it is evident that if they made laws and gave personal directions which would produce general horror or be taken as proofs of insanity their authority would collapse. Hence the need for vows committing all who take them to definite articles of faith on social statics, and to their logical consequences in law and custom. Such vows automatically exclude revolutionary geniuses, who, being uncommon, are not representative, more especially scientific geniuses, with whom it is a point of honor to have unconditionally open minds even on the most apparently sacred subjects.

RUSSIA REDISCOVERS THE CHURCH SYSTEM

A tremendous importance is given to a clear understanding of the Catholic system at this moment by the staggering fact that the biggest State in the modern world, having made a clean sweep of its Church by denouncing its religion as dope, depriving its priests and bishops of any greater authority than a quack can pick up at a fair, encouraging its most seriously minded children to form a League of the Godless, shooting its pious Tsar, turning its cathedrals into historical museums illustrating the infamies of ecclesiastical history and expressly entitling them anti-religious: in short, addressing itself solemnly and implacably to a root-and-branch extermination of everything that we associate with priesthood, has, under pressure of circumstances, unconsciously and spontaneously established as its system of government an as-close-as-possible reproduction of the hierarchy of the Catholic Church. The nomenclature is changed, of course: the Church is called the Communist Party; and the Holy Office and its familiars are known as the Komintern and the Gay Pay Oo. There is the popular safeguard of having the symptoms of the priestly vocation verified in the first instance by the group of peasants or industrial workers with whom the postulant's daily life has been passed, thus giving a genuine democratic basis to the system; and the hierarchy elected on this basis is not only up to date for the moment, but amenable to the daily lessons of trial and error in its practical operations and in no way pledged against change and innovation as such. But essentially the system is that of the old Christian Catholic Church, even to its fundamental vow of Communism and the death penalty on Ananias and Sapphira for violating it.

If our newspapers knew what is really happening in the world, or could discriminate between the news value of a bicycle accident in Clapham and that of a capsize of civilization, their columns would be full of this literally epoch-making event. And the first question they would address to Russia would be "Why, seeing that the Christian system has been such a hopeless failure, do you go back to it, and invite us to go back to it?"

WHY THE CHRISTIAN SYSTEM FAILED

The answer is that the Christian system failed, not because it was wrong in its psychology, its fundamental postulate of equality, or its anticipation of Lenin's principle that the rulers must be as poor as the ruled so that they can raise themselves only by raising their people, but because the old priests' ignorance of economics and political science blinded them to the mischief latent in the selfishness of private property in the physical earth. Before the Church knew where it was (it has not quite located itself yet) it found itself so prodigiously rich that the Pope was a secular Italian prince with armies and frontiers, enjoying not only the rent of Church lands, but selling salvation on such a scale that when Torquemada began burning Jews instead of allowing them to ransom their bodies by payments to the

Roman treasury, and leaving their souls to God, a first-rate quarrel between the Church and the Spanish Inquisition was the result.

But the riches of the Church were nothing compared to the riches of the Church's great rival, the Empire. And the poverty of the priest was opulence compared to the poverty of the proletarian. Whilst the Church was being so corrupted by its own property, and by the influence on it of the lay proprietors, that it lost all its moral prestige, the warriors and robbers of the Empire had been learning from experience that a pirate ship needs a hierarchy of officers and an iron discipline even more than police boats, and that the work of robbing the poor all the time involves a very elaborate system of government to ensure that the poor shall, like bees, continue to produce not only their own subsistence but the surplus that can be robbed from them without bringing on them the doom of the goose that lays the golden eggs. Naked coercion is so expensive that it became necessary to practise on the imaginations of the poor to the extent of making them believe that it is a pious duty to be robbed, and that their moment of life in this world is only a prelude to an eternity in which the poor will be blest and happy, and the rich horribly tortured.

Matters at last reached a point at which there was more law and order in the Empire than in The Church. Emperor Philip of Spain was enormously more respectable and pious, if less amiable, than Pope Alexander Borgia. The Empire gained moral prestige as The Church lost it until the Empire, virtuously indignant, took it on itself to reform The Church, all the more readily as the restoration of priestly poverty was a first-rate excuse for plundering it.

Now The Church could not with any decency allow itself to be reformed by a plutocracy of pirate kings, robber barons, commercial adventurers, money-lenders, and deserters from its own ranks. It reformed itself from within by its own saints and the Orders they founded, and thus "dished" the Reformation; whilst the Reformers set up national Churches and free Churches of their own under the general definition of Protestants, and thereby found themselves committed to a curious adulteration of their doctrine of Individualism, or the right of private judgment, with most of the ecclesiastical corruptions against which they had protested. And as neither Church nor Empire would share the government of mankind with the other nor allow the common people any say in the matter, the Catholics and Protestants set to work to exterminate one another with rack and stake, fire, sword, and gunpowder, aided by the poison gas of scurrilous calumny, until the very name of religion began to stink in the nostrils of all really charitable and faithful people.

GOVERNMENT BY EVERYBODY

The moral drawn from all this was that as nobody could be trusted to govern the people the people must govern themselves, which was nonsense. Nevertheless it was assumed that by inscribing every man's name on a register of voters we could realize the ideal of every man his own Solon and his own Plato, as to which one could only ask why not every man his own Shakespear and his own Einstein? But this assumption suited the plutocrats very well, as they had only to master the easy art of stampeding elections by their newspapers to do anything they liked in the name of the people. Votes for everybody (called for short, Democracy) ended in government neither of the best nor of the worst, but in an official government which could do nothing but talk, and an actual government of landlords, employers, and financiers at war with an Opposition of trade unionists, strikers, pickets, and—occasionally—rioters. The resultant disorder, indiscipline, and breakdown of distribution, produced a reaction of pure disappointment and distress in which the people looked wildly round for a Savior, and were ready to give a hopeful trial to anyone bold enough to assume dictatorship and kick aside the impotent official government until he had completely muzzled and subjugated it.

FAILURE ALL ROUND

That is the history of Catholicism and Protestantism. Church and Empire, Liberalism and Democracy, up to date. Clearly a ghastly failure, both positively as an attempt to solve the problem of government and negatively as an attempt to secure freedom of thought and facility of change to keep pace with thought.

Now this does not mean in the least that the original Catholic plan was wrong. On the contrary, all the disasters to which it has led have been demonstrations of the eternal need for it. The alternative to vocational government is a mixture of a haporth of very incompetent official government with an intolerable deal of very competent private tyranny. Providence, or Nature if you prefer that expression, has not ordained that all men shall have a vocation for being "servants of all the rest" as saints or rulers. Providence knows better than to provide armies consisting exclusively of commanders-in-chief or factories staffed exclusively with managing directors; and to that inexorable natural fact we shall always have to come back, just as the Russian revolutionists, who were reeking with Protestant Liberal superstitions at the beginning, have had to come back to it. But we have now thought out much more carefully than St Peter the basic articles of faith, without which the vocation of the priest is inevitably pushed out by the vocation of the robbers and the racketeers, self-elected as gentlemen and ladies. We know that private property distributes wealth, work, and leisure so unevenly that a wretchedly poor and miserably over-worked majority are forced to maintain a minority inordinately rich and passionately convinced that labor is so disgraceful to them that they dare not be seen carrying a parcel down Bond Street. We know that the strains set up by such a division of interests also destroys peace, justice, religion, good breeding, honor, reasonable freedom, and everything that government exists to secure, and that all this iniquity arises automatically when we thoughtlessly allow a person to own a thousand acres of land in the middle of London much more completely than he owns the pair of boots in which he walks over it; for he may not kick me out of my house into the street with his boots; but he may do so with his writ of ejectment. And so we are driven to the conclusion that the modern priesthood must utterly renounce, abjure, abhor, abominate and annihilate private property as the very worst of all the devil's inventions for the demoralization and damnation of mankind. Civilized men and women must live by their ordered and equal share in the work needed to support the community, and must find their freedom in their ordered and equal share of the leisure produced by scientific economy in producing that support. It still takes some conviction to repudiate an institution so well spoken of as private property; but the facts must be faced: our clandestine methods of violating it by income tax and surtax, which mean only "What a thief stole steal thou from the thief," will no longer serve; for a modern government, as the Russians soon found out, must not take money, even from thieves, until it is ready to employ it productively. To throw it away in doles as our governing duffers do, is to burn the candle at both ends and precipitate the catastrophe they are trying to avert.

OBSOLETE VOWS

As to the vows, some of the old ones must go. The Catholic Church and our Board of Education insist on celibacy, the one for priests and the other for schoolmistresses. That is a remnant of the cynical superstition of original sin. Married people have a right to married rulers; mothers have a right to have their children taught and handled by mothers; and priests and pastors who meddle with family affairs should know what they are talking about.

Another important modern discovery is that government is not a whole-time job for all its agents. A council of peasants derives its ancient wisdom from its normal day's work on the land, without which it would be a council of tramps and village idiots. It is not desirable that an ordinary parish priest should have no other occupation, nor an abnormal occupation, even that of a scholar. Nor is it desirable that his uniform should be too sacerdotal; for that is the method of idolatry, which substitutes for rational authority the superstitious awe produced by a contrived singularity. St Vincent de Paul knew thoroughly well what he was about when he constituted his Sisterhood of Charity on the rule that the sister should not be distinguishable from an ordinary respectable woman. Unfortunately, the costume prescribed under this rule has in the course of the centuries become as extraordinary as that of the Bluecoat boy; and St Vincent's idea is consequently lost; but modern industrial experience confirms it; for the latest rediscovery of the Vincentian principle has been made by Mr Ford, who has testified that if you want a staff of helpful persons who will turn their hands to anything at need you must not give them either title, rank, or uniform, as the immediate result will be their partial disablement by the exclusion from their activities of many of the most necessary jobs as beneath their dignity.

Another stipulation made by St Vincent, who already in the sixteenth century was far ahead of us, was that no sister may pledge herself for longer than a year at a time, however often she may renew her vows. Thus the sisters can never lose their freedom nor suffer from cold feet. If he were alive today St Vincent would probably propose a clean sweep of all our difficulties about marriage and divorce by forbidding people to marry for longer than a year, and make them renew their vows every twelve months. In Russia the members of the Communist Party cannot dedicate themselves eternally: they can drop out into the laity when they please, and if they do not please and nevertheless have become slack in their ministry, they are pushed out.

SUPERNATURAL PRETENSIONS

Furthermore, modern priests must not make

supernatural pretensions. They must not be impostors. A vocation for politics, though essentially a religious vocation, must be on the same footing as a vocation for music or mathematics or cooking or nursing or acting or architecture or farming or billiards or any other born aptitude. The authority which must attach to all public officials and councils must rest on their ability and efficiency. In the Royal Navy every mishap to a ship involves a court martial on the responsible officer: if the officer makes a mistake he forfeits his command unless he can convince the court that he is still worthy of it. In no other way can our hackneyed phrase "responsible government" acquire any real meaning. When a Catholic priest goes wrong (or too right) he is silenced: when a Russian Commissar goes wrong, he is expelled from the Party. Such responsibility necessarily makes official authority very authoritative and frightens off the unduly nervous. Stalin and Mussolini are the most responsible statesmen in Europe because they have no hold on their places except their efficiency; and their authority is consequently greater than that of any of the monarchs, presidents, and prime ministers who have to deal with them. Stalin is one of the higher functionaries with whom governing is necessarily a whole-time job. But he is no richer than his neighbors, and can "better himself" only by bettering them, not by buttering them like a British demagogue.

ECLECTIC DEMOCRACY

I think my views on intellectual aristocracy and democracy and all the rest of it are now plain enough. As between the intentions of The Church and the intentions of The Empire (unrealized ideals both) I am on the side of The Church. As to the evil done by The Church with the best intentions and the good done by The Empire with the worst, I am an Eclectic: there is much to be learnt from each. I harp on Russia because the Moscow experiment is the only really new departure from Tweedledum and Tweedledee: Fascism is still wavering between Empire and Church, between private property and Communism. Years ago, I said that what democracy needed was a trustworthy anthropometric machine for the selection of qualified rulers. Since then I have elaborated this by demanding the formation of panels of tested persons eligible for the different grades in the governmental hierarchy. Panel A would be for diplomacy and international finance, Panel B for national affairs, Panel C for municipal and county affairs, Panel D for the village councils and so forth. Under such a panel system the voters would lose their present liberty to return such candidates as the late Horatio Bottomley to parliament by enormous majorities; but they would gain the advantage of at least knowing that their rulers know how to read and write, which they do not enjoy at present.

Nobody ventured to disagree with me when I urged the need for such panels; but when I was challenged to produce my anthropometric machine or my endocrine or phrenological tests, I was obliged to confess that they had not yet been invented, and that such existing attempts at them as competitive examinations are so irrelevant and misleading as to be worse than useless as tests of vocation. But the Soviet system, hammered out under the sternest pressure of circumstances, supplies an excellent provisional solution, which turns out to be the solution of the old Catholic

Church purged of supernatural pretension, assumption of final perfection, and the poison of private property with its fatal consequences. Mr Stalin is not in the least like an Emperor, nor an Archbishop, nor a Prime Minister, nor a Chancellor; but he would be strikingly like a Pope, claiming for form's sake an apostolic succession from Marx, were it not for his frank method of Trial and Error, his entirely human footing, and his liability to removal at a moment's notice if his eminence should upset his mental balance. At the other end of the scale are the rank and file of the Communist Party, doing an ordinary day's work with the common folk, and giving only their leisure to the Party. For their election as representatives of the commons they must depend on the votes of their intimate and equal neighbors and workmates. They have no incentive to seek election except the vocational incentive; for success, in the first instance, means, not release from the day's ordinary work, but the sacrifice of all one's leisure to politics, and, if promotion to the whole-time-grades be achieved, a comparatively ascetic discipline and virtually no pecuniary gain.

If anyone can suggest a better practically tested plan, now is the time to do it; for it is all up with the old Anarchist-Liberal parliamentary systems in the face of thirty millions of unemployed, and World Idiotic Conferences at which each nation implores all the others to absorb its unemployed by a revival of international trade. Mr Chesterton says truly that a government, if it is to govern, "cannot select one ruler to do something and another to undo it, one intellectual to restore the nation and another to ruin the nation." But that is precisely what our parliamentary party system does. Mr Chesterton has put it in a nutshell; and I hope he will appreciate the sound Catholicism with which I have cracked it.

AYOT ST LAWRENCE, *1933*

$\begin{bmatrix} \text{ACT} & \text{I} \end{bmatrix}$

*Night. One of the best bedrooms in one of the best sub-
urban villas in one of the richest cities in England. A
young lady with an unhealthy complexion is asleep in the
bed. A small table at the head of the bed, convenient to
her right hand, and crowded with a medicine bottle, a
measuring glass, a pill box, a clinical thermometer in a
glass of water, a half read book with the place marked
by a handkerchief, a powder puff and handmirror, and
an electric bell handle on a flex, shews that the bed is a
sick bed and the young lady an invalid.*

*The furniture includes a very handsome dressing table
with silverbacked hairbrushes and toilet articles, a
dainty pincushion, a stand of rings, a jewel box of black
steel with the lid open and a rope of pearls heaped
carelessly half in and half out, a Louis Quinze writing
table and chair with inkstand, blotter, and cabinet of
stationery, a magnificent wardrobe, a luxurious couch,
and a tall screen of Chinese workmanship which, like the
expensive carpet and everything else in the room, proclaims that the owner has money enough to buy the best
things at the best shops in the best purchaseable taste.*

*The bed is nearly in the middle of the room, so that the
patient's nurses can pass freely between the wall and
the head of it. If we contemplate the room from the foot
of the bed, with the patient's toes pointing straight at us,
we have the door (carefully sandbagged lest a draught of
fresh air should creep underneath) level with us in the
righthand wall, the couch against the same wall farther
away, the window (every ray of moonlight excluded by
closed curtains and a dark green spring blind) in the*

middle of the left wall with the wardrobe on its right and the writing table on its left, the screen at right angles to the wardrobe, and the dressing table against the wall facing us halfway between the bed and the couch.

Besides the chair at the writing table there is an easy chair at the medicine table, and a chair at each side of the dressing table.

The room is lighted by invisible cornice lights, and by two mirror lights on the dressing table and a portable one on the writing table; but these are now switched off; and the only light in action is another portable one on the medicine table, very carefully subdued by a green shade.

The patient is sleeping heavily. Near her, in the easy chair, sits a Monster. In shape and size it resembles a human being; but in substance it seems to be made of a luminous jelly with a visible skeleton of short black rods. It drops forward in the chair with its head in its hands, and seems in the last degree wretched.

THE MONSTER. Oh! Oh!! Oh!!! I am so ill! so miserable! Oh, I wish I were dead. Why doesnt she die and release me from my sufferings? What right has she to get ill and make me ill like this? Measles: thats what she's got. Measles! German measles! And she's given them to me, a poor innocent microbe that never did her any harm. And she says that *I* gave them to her. Oh, is this justice? Oh, I feel so rotten. I wonder what my temperature is: they took it from under her tongue half an hour ago. [*Scrutinizing the table and discovering the thermometer in the glass*]. Here's the thermometer: theyve left it for the doctor to see instead of shaking it down. If it's over a hundred I'm done for: I darent look. Oh, can it be that I'm dying? I must look. [*It looks, and drops the thermometer back into the glass with a gasping scream*]. A hundred and three! It's all over. [*It collapses*].

The door opens; and an elderly lady and a young doctor come in. The lady steals along on tiptoe, full of the deepest concern for the invalid. The doctor is indifferent, but keeps up his bedside manner carefully, though he evidently does not think the case is so serious as the lady does. She comes to the bedside on the invalid's left. He comes to the other side of the bed and looks attentively at his patient.

THE ELDERLY LADY [*in a whisper sibilant enough to wake the dead*] She is asleep.

THE MONSTER. I should think so. This fool here, the doctor, has given her a dose of the latest fashionable opiate that would keep a cock asleep till half past eleven on a May morning.

THE ELDERLY LADY. Oh doctor, do you think there is any chance? Can she possibly survive this last terrible complication.

THE MONSTER. Measles! He mistook it for influenza.

THE ELDERLY LADY. It was so unexpected! such a crushing blow! And I have taken such care of her. She is my only surviving child: my pet: my precious one. Why do they all die? I have never neglected the smallest symptom of illness. She has had doctors in attendance on her almost constantly since she was born.

THE MONSTER. She has the constitution of a horse or she'd have died like the others.

THE ELDERLY LADY. Oh, dont you think, dear doctor—of course you know best; but I am so terribly anxious—dont you think you ought to change the prescription? I had such hopes of that last bottle; but you know it was after that that she developed measles.

THE DOCTOR. My dear Mrs Mopply, you may rest assured that the bottle had nothing to do with the measles. It was merely a gentle tonic—

THE MONSTER. Strychnine!

THE DOCTOR. —to brace her up.

THE ELDERLY LADY. But she got measles after it.

THE DOCTOR. That was a specific infection: a germ, a microbe.

THE MONSTER. Me! Put it all on me.

THE ELDERLY LADY. But how did it get in? I keep the windows closed so carefully. And there is a sheet steeped in carbolic acid always hung over the door.

THE MONSTER [*in tears*] Not a breath of fresh air for me!

THE DOCTOR. Who knows? It may have lurked here since the house was built. You never can tell. But you must not worry. It is not serious: a light rubeola: you can hardly call it measles. We shall pull her through, believe me.

THE ELDERLY LADY. It is such a comfort to hear you say so, doctor. I am sure I shall never be able to express my gratitude for all you have done for us.

THE DOCTOR. Oh, that is my profession. We do what we can.

THE ELDERLY LADY. Yes; but some doctors are dreadful. There was that man at Folkestone: he was impossible. He tore aside the curtain and let the blazing sunlight into the room, though she cannot bear it without green spectacles. He opened the windows and let in all the cold morning air. I told him he was a murderer; and he only said "One guinea, please". I am sure he let in that microbe.

THE DOCTOR. Oh, three months ago! No: it was not that.

THE ELDERLY LADY. Then what was it? Oh, are you quite quite sure that it would not be better to change the prescription?

THE DOCTOR. Well, I have already changed it.

THE MONSTER. Three times!

THE ELDERLY LADY. Oh, I know you have, doctor: nobody could have been kinder. But it really did not do her any good. She got worse.

THE DOCTOR. But, my dear lady, she was sickening for measles. That was not the fault of my prescription.

THE ELDERLY LADY. Oh, of course not. You mustnt think that I ever doubted for a moment that everything you did was for the best. Still—

THE DOCTOR. Oh, very well, very well: I will write another prescription.

THE ELDERLY LADY. Oh, thank you, thank you: I felt sure you would. I have so often known a change of medicine work wonders.

THE DOCTOR. When we have pulled her through this attack I think a change of air—

THE ELDERLY LADY. Oh no: dont say that. She must be near a doctor who knows her constitution. Dear old Dr Newland knew it so well from her very birth.

THE DOCTOR. Unfortunately, Newland is dead.

THE ELDERLY LADY. Yes; but you bought his practice. I should never be easy in my mind if you were not within call. You persuaded me to take her to Folkestone; and see what happened! No: never again.

THE DOCTOR. Oh, well! [*He shrugs his shoulders resignedly, and goes to the bedside table*]. What about the temperature?

THE ELDERLY LADY. The day nurse took it. I havnt dared to look.

THE DOCTOR [*looking at the thermometer*] Hm!

[433]

THE ELDERLY LADY [*trembling*] Has it gone up? Oh, doctor!

THE DOCTOR [*hastily shaking the mercury down*] No. Nothing. Nearly normal.

THE MONSTER. Liar!

THE ELDERLY LADY. What a relief!

THE DOCTOR. You must be careful, though. Dont fancy she's well yet: she isnt. She must not get out of bed for a moment. The slightest chill might be serious.

THE ELDERLY LADY. Doctor: are you sure you are not concealing something from me? Why does she never get well in spite of the fortune I have spent on her illnesses? There must be some deep-rooted cause. Tell me the worst: I have dreaded it all my life. Perhaps I should have told you the whole truth; but I was afraid. Her uncle's stepfather died of an enlarged heart. Is that what it is?

THE DOCTOR. Good gracious, NO! What put that into your head?

THE ELDERLY LADY. But even before this rash broke out there were pimples.

THE MONSTER. Boils! Too many chocolate creams.

THE DOCTOR. Oh, that! Nothing. Her blood is not quite what it should be. But we shall get that right.

THE ELDERLY LADY. You are sure it is not her lungs?

THE DOCTOR. My good lady, her lungs are as sound as a seagull's.

THE ELDERLY LADY. Then it must be her heart. Dont deceive me. She has palpitations. She told me the other day that it stopped for five minutes when that horrid nurse was rude to her.

THE DOCTOR. Nonsense! She wouldnt be alive now if her heart had stopped for five seconds. There is nothing constitutionally wrong. A little below par: that is all. We shall feed her up scientifically. Plenty

[434]

of good fresh meat. A half bottle of champagne at lunch and a glass of port after dinner will make another woman of her. A chop at breakfast, rather underdone, is sometimes very helpful.

THE MONSTER. I shall die of overfeeding. So will she too: thats one consolation.

THE DOCTOR. Dont worry about the measles. It's really quite a light case.

THE ELDERLY LADY. Oh, you can depend on me for that. Nobody can say that I am a worrier. You wont forget the new prescription?

THE DOCTOR. I will write it here and now [*he takes out his pen and book, and sits down at the writing table*].

THE ELDERLY LADY. Oh, thank you. And I will go and see what the new night nurse is doing. They take so long with their cups of tea [*she goes to the door and is about to go out when she hesitates and comes back*]. Doctor: I know you dont believe in inoculations; but I cant help thinking she ought to have one. They do so much good.

THE DOCTOR [*almost at the end of his patience*] My dear Mrs Mopply: I never said that I dont believe in inoculations. But it is no use inoculating when the patient is already fully infected.

THE ELDERLY LADY. But I have found it so necessary myself. I was inoculated against influenza three years ago; and I have had it only four times since. My sister has it every February. Do, to please me, give her an inoculation. I feel such a responsibility if anything is left undone to cure her.

THE DOCTOR. Oh very well, very well: I will see what can be done. She shall have both an inoculation and a new prescription. Will that set your mind at rest?

THE ELDERLY LADY. Oh, thank you. You have lifted such a weight from my conscience. I feel sure they will do her the greatest good. And now excuse me a moment while I fetch the nurse. [*She goes out*].

THE DOCTOR. What a perfectly maddening woman!

THE MONSTER [*rising and coming behind him*] Yes: aint she?

THE DOCTOR [*starting*] What! Who is that?

THE MONSTER. Nobody but me and the patient. And you have dosed her so that she wont speak again for ten hours. You will overdo that some day.

THE DOCTOR. Rubbish! She thought it was an opiate; but it was only an aspirin dissolved in ether. But who am I talking to? I must be drunk.

THE MONSTER. Not a bit of it.

THE DOCTOR. Then who are you? What are you? Where are you? Is this a trick?

THE MONSTER. I'm only an unfortunate sick bacillus.

THE DOCTOR. A sick bacillus!

THE MONSTER. Yes. I suppose it never occurs to you that a bacillus can be sick like anyone else.

THE DOCTOR. Whats the matter with you?

THE MONSTER. Measles.

THE DOCTOR. Rot! The microbe of measles has never been discovered. If there is a microbe it cannot be measles: it must be parameasles.

THE MONSTER. Great Heavens! what are parameasles?

THE DOCTOR. Something so like measles that nobody can see any difference.

THE MONSTER. If there is no measles microbe why did you tell the old girl that her daughter caught measles from a microbe?

THE DOCTOR. Patients insist on having microbes nowadays. If I told her there is no measles microbe she wouldnt believe me; and I should lose my patient. When there is no microbe I invent one. Am I to understand that you are the missing microbe of measles, and that you have given them to this patient here?

THE MONSTER. No: she gave them to me. These humans are full of horrid diseases: they infect us poor microbes with them; and you doctors pretend that it is we that infect them. You ought all to be struck off the register.

THE DOCTOR. We should be, if we talked like that.

THE MONSTER. Oh, I feel so wretched! Please cure my measles.

THE DOCTOR. I cant. I cant cure any disease. But I get the credit when the patients cure themselves. When she cures herself she will cure you too.

THE MONSTER. But she cant cure herself because you and her mother wont give her a dog's chance. You wont let her have even a breath of fresh air. I tell you she's naturally as strong as a rhinoceros. Curse your silly bottles and inoculations! Why dont you chuck them and turn faith healer?

THE DOCTOR. I am a faith healer. You dont suppose I believe the bottles cure people? But the patient's faith in the bottle does.

THE MONSTER. Youre a humbug: thats what you are.

THE DOCTOR. Faith is humbug. But it works.

THE MONSTER. Then why do you call it science?

THE DOCTOR. Because people believe in science. The Christian Scientists call their fudge science for the same reason.

THE MONSTER. The Christian Scientists let their patients cure themselves. Why dont you?

THE DOCTOR. I do. But I help them. You see, it's easier to believe in bottles and inoculations than in oneself and in that mysterious power that gives us our life and that none of us knows anything about. Lots of people believe in the bottles and wouldnt know what you were talking about if you suggested the real thing. And the bottles do the trick. My patients get well as often as not. That is, unless their number's up. Then we all have to go.

THE MONSTER. No girl's number is up until she's worn out. I tell you this girl could cure herself and cure me if youd let her.

THE DOCTOR. And I tell you that it would be very hard work for her. Well, why should she work hard when she can afford to pay other people to work for her? She doesnt black her own boots or scrub her own floors. She pays somebody else to do it. Why should she cure herself, which is harder work than blacking boots or scrubbing floors, when she can afford to pay the doctor to cure her? It pays her and it pays me. That's logic, my friend. And now, if you will excuse me, I shall take myself off before the old woman comes back and provokes me to wring her neck. [*Rising*] Mark my words: someday somebody will fetch her a clout over the head. Somebody who can afford to. Not the doctor. She has driven me mad already: the proof is that I hear voices and talk to them. [*He goes out*].

THE MONSTER. Youre saner than most of them, you fool. They think I have the keys of life and death in my pocket; but I have nothing but a horrid headache. Oh dear! oh dear!

The Monster wanders away behind the screen. The patient, left alone, begins to stir in her bed. She turns over and calls querulously for somebody to attend to her.

THE PATIENT. Nurse! Mother! Oh, is anyone there? [*Crying*] Selfish beasts! to leave me like this. [*She snatches angrily at the electric bell which hangs within her reach and presses the button repeatedly*].

The Elderly Lady and the night nurse come running in. The nurse is young, quick, active, resolute, and decidedly pretty. Mrs Mopply goes to the bedside table, the nurse going to the patient's left.

THE ELDERLY LADY. What is it, darling? Are you awake? Was the sleeping draught no good? Are you worse? What has happened? What has become of the doctor?

THE PATIENT. I am in the most frightful agony. I have been lying here ringing for ages and ages, and no one has come to attend to me. Nobody cares whether I am alive or dead.

THE ELDERLY LADY. Oh, how can you say such things, darling? I left the doctor here. I was away only for a minute. I had to receive the new night nurse and give her her instructions. Here she is. And oh, do cover up your arm, darling. You will get a chill; and then it will be all over. Nurse: see that she is never uncovered for a moment. Do you think it would be well to have another hot water bottle against her arm until it is quite warm again? Do you feel it cold, darling?

THE PATIENT [*angrily*] Yes, deadly cold.

THE ELDERLY LADY. Oh dont say that. And there is so much pneumonia about. I wish the doctor had not gone. He could sound your lungs—

NIGHT NURSE [*feeling the patient's arm*] She is quite warm enough.

THE PATIENT [*bursting into tears*] Mother: take this hateful woman away. She wants to kill me.

THE ELDERLY LADY. Oh no, dear: she has been so highly recommended. I cant get a new nurse at this hour. Wont you try, for my sake, to put up with her until the day nurse comes in the morning?

THE NURSE. Come! Let me arrange your pillows and

make you comfortable. You are smothered with all this bedding. Four thick blankets and an eiderdown! No wonder you feel irritable.

THE PATIENT [*screaming*] Dont touch me. Go away. You want to murder me. Nobody cares whether I am alive or dead.

THE ELDERLY LADY. Oh, darling, dont keep on saying that. You know it's not true; and it does hurt me so.

THE NURSE. You must not mind what a sick person says, madam. You had better go to bed and leave the patient to me. You are quite worn out. [*She comes to Mrs Mopply and takes her arm coaxingly but firmly*].

THE ELDERLY LADY. I know I am: I am ready to drop. How sympathetic of you to notice it! But how can I leave her at such a moment?

THE NURSE. She ought not to have more than one person in the room at a time. You see how it excites and worries her.

THE ELDERLY LADY. Oh, thats very true. The doctor said she was to be kept as quiet as possible.

THE NURSE [*leading her to the door*] You need a good night's sleep. You may trust me to do what is right and necessary.

THE ELDERLY LADY [*whispering*] I will indeed. How kind of you! You will let me know if anything—

THE NURSE. Yes, yes. I promise to come for you and wake you if anything happens. Good night, madam.

THE ELDERLY LADY [*sotto voce*] Good night. [*She steals out*].

The nurse, left alone with her patient, pays no attention to her, but goes to the window. She opens the curtains and raises the blind, admitting a flood of moonlight. She unfastens the sash and throws it right up. She then makes for the door where the electric switch is.

THE PATIENT [*huddling herself up in the bedclothes*] What are you doing? Shut that window and pull down that blind and close those curtains at once. Do you want to kill me?

The nurse turns all the lights full on.

THE PATIENT [*hiding her eyes*] Oh! Oh! I cant bear it: turn it off.

The nurse switches the lights off.

THE PATIENT. So inconsiderate of you!

The nurse switches the lights on again.

THE PATIENT. Oh, please, please. Not all that light.

The nurse switches off.

THE PATIENT. No, no. Leave me something to read by. My bedside lamp is not enough, you stupid idiot.

The nurse switches on again, and calmly returns to the bedside.

THE PATIENT. I cant imagine how anyone can be so thoughtless and clumsy when I am so ill. I am suffering horribly. Shut that window and switch off half those lights at once: do you hear?

The nurse snatches the eiderdown and one of the pillows rudely from the bed, letting the patient down with a jerk, and arranges them comfortably in the bedside chair.

THE PATIENT. How dare you touch my pillow? The audacity!

The nurse sits down; takes out a leaf from an illustrated journal; and proceeds to study it attentively.

THE PATIENT. Well! How much longer are you going to sit there neglecting me? Shut that window instantly.

THE NURSE [*insolently, in her commonest dialect*] Oh go to—to sleep [*she resumes her study of the document*].

THE PATIENT. Dont dare address me like that. I dont believe you are a properly qualified nurse.

THE NURSE [*calmly*] I should think not. I wouldnt take five thousand a year to be a nurse. But I know how to deal with you and your like, because I was once a patient in a hospital where the women patients were a rough lot, and the nurses had to treat them accordingly. I kept my eyes open there, and learnt a little of the game. [*She takes a paper packet from her pocket and opens it on the bedside table. It contains about half a pound of kitchen salt*]. Do you know what that is and what it's for?

THE PATIENT. Is it medicine?

THE NURSE. Yes. It's a cure for screaming and hysterics and tantrums. When a woman starts making a row, the first thing she does is to open her mouth. A nurse who knows her business just shoves a handful of this into it. Common kitchen salt. No more screaming. Understand?

THE PATIENT [*hardily*] No I dont [*she reaches for the bell*].

THE NURSE [*intercepting her quickly*] No you dont. [*She throws the bell cord with its button away on the floor behind the bed*]. Now we shant be disturbed. No bell. And if you open your mouth too wide, youll get the salt. See?

THE PATIENT. And do you think I am a poor woman in a hospital whom you can illtreat as you please? Do you know what will happen to you when my mother comes in the morning?

THE NURSE. In the morning, darling, I shall be over the hills and far away.

THE PATIENT. And you expect me, sick as I am, to stay here alone with you!

THE NURSE. We shant be alone. I'm expecting a friend.

THE PATIENT. A friend!

[442]

THE NURSE. A gentleman friend. I told him he might drop in when he saw the lights switched off twice.

THE PATIENT. So that was why—

THE NURSE. That was why.

THE PATIENT. And you calmly propose to have your young man here in my room to amuse yourself all night before my face.

THE NURSE. You can go to sleep.

THE PATIENT. I shall do nothing of the sort. You will have to behave yourself decently before me.

THE NURSE. Oh, dont worry about that. He's coming on business. He's my business partner, in fact: not my best boy.

THE PATIENT. And can you not find some more suitable place for your business than in my room at night?

THE NURSE. You see, you dont know the nature of the business yet. It's got to be done here and at night. Here he is, I think.

A burglar, well dressed, wearing rubber gloves and a small white mask over his nose, clambers in. He is still in his early thirties, and quite goodlooking. His voice is disarmingly pleasant.

THE BURGLAR. All right, Sweetie?

THE NURSE. All right, Popsy.

The burglar closes the window softly; draws the curtains; and comes past the nurse to the bedside.

THE BURGLAR. Damn it, she's awake. Didnt you give her a sleeping draught?

THE PATIENT. Do you expect me to sleep with you in the room? Who are you? and what are you wearing that mask for?

THE BURGLAR. Only so that you will not recognize me if we should happen to meet again.

THE PATIENT. I have no intention of meeting you again. So you may just as well take it off.

[443]

THE NURSE. I havnt broken to her what we are here for, Popsy.

THE PATIENT. I neither know nor care what you are here for. All I can tell you is that if you dont leave the room at once and send my mother to me, I will give you both measles.

THE BURGLAR. We have both had them, dear invalid. I am afraid we must intrude a little longer. [*To the nurse*] Have you found out where it is?

THE NURSE. No: I havnt had time. The dressing table's over there. Try that.

The burglar crosses to the other side of the bed, coming round by the foot of it, and is making for the dressing table when—

THE PATIENT. What do you want at my dressing table?

THE BURGLAR. Obviously, your celebrated pearl necklace.

THE PATIENT [*escaping from her bed with a formidable bound and planting herself with her back to the dressing table as a bulwark for the jewel case*] Not if I know it, you shant.

THE BURGLAR [*approaching her*] You really must allow me.

THE PATIENT. Take that.

Holding on to the table edge behind her, she lifts her foot vigorously waist high, and shoots it hard into his solar plexus. He curls up on the bed with an agonized groan and rolls off on to the carpet at the other side. The nurse rushes across behind the head of the bed and tackles the patient. The patient swoops at her knees; lifts her; and sends her flying. She comes down with a thump flat on her back on the couch. The patient pants hard; sways giddily; staggers to the bed and falls on it, exhausted. The nurse, dazed by the patient's very unexpected athleticism, but not hurt, springs up.

THE NURSE. Quick, Popsy: tie her feet. She's fainted.

THE BURGLAR [*utters a lamentable groan and rolls over on his face*]!!

THE NURSE. Be quick, will you?

THE BURGLAR [*trying to rise*] Ugh! Ugh!

THE NURSE [*running to him and shaking him*] My God, you are a fool, Popsy. Come and help me before she comes to. She's too strong for me.

THE BURGLAR. Ugh! Let me die.

THE NURSE. Are you going to lie there for ever? Has she killed you?

THE BURGLAR [*rising slowly to his knees*] As nearly as doesnt matter. Oh, Sweetie, why did you tell me that this heavyweight champion was a helpless invalid?

THE NURSE. Shut up. Get the pearls.

THE BURGLAR [*rising with difficulty*] I dont seem to want any pearls. She got me just in the wind. I am sorry to have been of so little assistance; but oh, my Sweetie-Weetie, Nature never intended us to be burglars. Our first attempt has been a hopeless failure. Let us apologize and withdraw.

THE NURSE. Fathead! Dont be such a coward. [*Looking closely at the patient*] I say, Popsy: I believe she's asleep.

THE BURGLAR. Let her sleep. Wake not the lioness's wrath.

THE NURSE. You maddening fool, dont you see that we can tie her feet and gag her before she wakes, and get away with the pearls. It's quite easy if we do it quick together. Come along.

THE BURGLAR. Do not deceive yourself, my pet: we should have about as much chance as if we tried to take a female gorilla to the Zoo. No: I am not going to steal those jewels. Honesty is the best policy. I have another idea, and a much better one. You leave this to me. [*He goes to the dressing table. She follows him*].

THE NURSE. Whatever have you got into your silly head now?

THE BURGLAR. You shall see. [*Handling the jewel case*] One of these safes that open by a secret arrangement of letters. As they are as troublesome as an automatic telephone nobody ever locks them. Here is the necklace. By Jove! If they are all real, it must be worth about twenty thousand pounds. Gosh! here's a ring with a big blue diamond in it. Worth four thousand pounds if it's worth a penny. Sweetie: we are on velvet for the rest of our lives.

THE NURSE. What good are blue diamonds to us if we dont steal them?

THE BURGLAR. Wait. Wait and see. Go and sit down in that chair and look as like a nice gentle nurse as you can.

THE NURSE. But—

THE BURGLAR. Do as you are told. Have faith—faith in your Popsy.

THE NURSE [*obeying*] Well, I give it up. Youre mad.

THE BURGLAR. I was never saner in my life. Stop. How does she call people? Hasnt she an electric bell? Where is it?

THE NURSE [*picking it up*] Here. I chucked it out of her reach when she was grabbing at it.

THE BURGLAR. Put it on the bed close to her hand.

THE NURSE. Popsy: youre off your chump. She—

THE BURGLAR. Sweetie: in our firm I am the brains: you are the hand. This is going to be our most glorious achievement. Obey me instantly.

THE NURSE [*resignedly*] Oh, very well. [*She places the handle of the bell as desired*]. I wash my hands of this job. [*She sits down doggedly*].

THE BURGLAR [*coming to the bedside*] By the way, she is hardly a success as The Sleeping Beauty. She has a wretched complexion; and her breath is not precisely ambrosial. But if we can turn her out to grass she may put up some good looks. And if her punch is anything like her kick she will be an invaluable bodyguard for us two weaklings—if I can persuade her to join us.

THE NURSE. Join us! What do you mean?

THE BURGLAR. Shshshshsh. Not too much noise: we must wake her gently. [*He stoops to the patient's ear and whispers*] Miss Mopply.

THE PATIENT [*in a murmur of protest*] Mmmmmmmm-mmmmmmmmm.

THE NURSE. What does she say?

THE BURGLAR. She says, in effect, "You have waked me too soon: I must slumber again." [*To the patient, more distinctly*] It is not your dear mother, Miss Mopply: it is the burglar. [*The patient springs half up, threateningly. He falls on his knees and throws up his hands*]. Kamerad, Miss Mopply: Kamerad! I am utterly at your mercy. The bell is on your bed, close to your hand: look at it. You have only to press the button to bring your mother and the police in upon me [*she seizes the handle of the bell*] and be a miserable invalid again for the rest of your life. [*She drops the bell thoughtfully*]. Not an attractive prospect, is it? Now listen. I have something to propose to you of the greatest importance: something that may make another woman of you and change your entire destiny. You can listen to me in perfect security: at any moment you can ring your bell, or throw us out of the window if you prefer it. I ask you for five minutes only.

THE PATIENT [*still dangerously on guard*] Well?

THE BURGLAR [*rising*] Let me give you one more

proof of my confidence. [*He takes off his mask*]. Look. Can you be afraid of such a face? Do I look like a burglar?

THE PATIENT [*relaxing, and even shewing signs of goodhumor*] No: you look like a curate.

THE BURGLAR [*a little hurt*] Oh, not a curate. I hope I look at least like a beneficed clergyman. But it is very clever of you to have found me out. The fact is, I am a clergyman. But I must ask you to keep it a dead secret: for my father, who is an atheist, would disinherit me if he knew. I was secretly ordained when I was up at Oxford.

THE PATIENT. Oh, this is ridiculous. I'm dreaming. It must be that new sleeping draught the doctor gave me. But it's delicious, because I'm dreaming that I'm perfectly well. Ive never been so happy in my life. Go on with the dream, Pops: the nicest part of it is that I am in love with you. My beautiful Pops, my own, my darling, you are a perfect film hero, only more like an English gentleman. [*She waves him a kiss*].

THE NURSE. Well I'll be da—

THE BURGLAR. Shshshshsh. Break not the spell.

THE PATIENT [*with a deep sigh of contentment*] Let nobody wake me. I'm in heaven. [*She sinks back blissfully on her pillows*]. Go on, Pops. Tell me another.

THE BURGLAR. Splendid. [*He takes a chair from beside the dressing table and seats himself comfortably at the bedside*]. We are going to have an ideal night. Now listen. Picture to yourself a heavenly afternoon in July: a Scottish loch surrounded by mirrored mountains, and a boat—may I call it a shallop?—

THE PATIENT [*ecstatically*] A shallop! Oh, Popsy!

THE BURGLAR.—with Sweetie sitting in the stern,

and I stretched out at full length with my head pillowed on Sweetie's knees.

THE PATIENT. You can leave Sweetie out, Pops. Her amorous emotions do not interest me.

THE BURGLAR. You misunderstand. Sweetie's thoughts were far from me. She was thinking about you.

THE PATIENT. Just like her impudence! How did she know about me?

THE BURGLAR. Simply enough. In her lily hand was a copy of The Lady's Pictorial. It contained an illustrated account of your jewels. Can you guess what Sweetie said to me as she gazed at the soft majesty of the mountains and bathed her soul in the beauty of the sunset?

THE PATIENT. Yes. She said "Popsy: we must pinch that necklace."

THE BURGLAR. Exactly. Word for word. But now can you guess what *I* said?

THE PATIENT. I suppose you said "Right you are, Sweetie" or something vulgar like that.

THE BURGLAR. Wrong. I said, "If that girl had any sense she'd steal the necklace herself."

THE PATIENT. Oh! This is getting interesting. How could I steal my own necklace?

THE BURGLAR. Sell it; and have a glorious spree with the price. See life. Live. You dont call being an invalid living, do you?

THE PATIENT. Why shouldnt I call it living? I am not dead. Of course when I am awake I am terribly delicate—

THE BURGLAR. Delicate! It's not five minutes since you knocked me out, and threw Sweetie all over the room. If you can fight like that for a string of pearls that you never have a chance of wearing, why not fight for freedom to do what you like, with your pocket full of money and all the fun in the wide world at your command? Hang it all, dont you want to be young and goodlooking and have a sweet breath and be a lawn tennis champion and enjoy everything that is to be enjoyed instead of frowsting here and being messed about by your silly mother and all the doctors that live on her folly? Have you no conscience, that you waste God's gifts so shamefully? You think you are in a state of illness. Youre not: youre in a state of sin. Sell the necklace and buy your salvation with the proceeds.

THE PATIENT. Youre a clergyman all right, Pops. But I dont know how to sell the necklace.

THE BURGLAR. I do. Let me sell it for you. You will of course give us a fairly handsome commission on the transaction.

THE PATIENT. Theres some catch in this. If I trust you with it how do I know that you will not keep the whole price for yourself?

THE BURGLAR. Sweetie: Miss Mopply has the makings of a good business woman in her. [*To the patient*] Just reflect, Mops (Let us call one another Mops and Pops for short). If I steal that necklace, I shall have to sell it as a burglar to a man who will know perfectly well that I have stolen it. I shall be lucky if I get a fiftieth of its value. But if I sell it on the square, as the agent of its lawful owner, I shall be able to get its full market value. The payment will be made to you; and I will trust you to pay me the commission. Sweetie and I will be more than satisfied with fifty per cent.

THE PATIENT. Fifty! Oh!

THE BURGLAR [*firmly*] I think you will admit that we deserve it for our enterprise, our risk, and the priceless boon of your emancipation from this wretched home. Is it a bargain, Mops?

THE PATIENT. It's a monstrous overcharge; but in dreamland generosity costs nothing. You shall have your fifty. Lucky for you that I'm asleep. If I wake up I shall never get loose from my people and my social position. It's all very well for you two criminals: you can do what you like. If you were ladies and gentlemen, youd know how hard it is not to do what everybody else does.

THE BURGLAR. Pardon me; but I think you will feel more at ease with us if I inform you that we are ladies and gentlemen. My own rank—not that I would presume on it for a moment—is, if you ask Burke or Debrett, higher than your own. Your people's money was made in trade: my people have always lived by owning property or governing Crown Colonies. Sweetie would be a woman of the highest position but for the unfortunate fact that her parents, though united in the sight of Heaven, were not legally married. At least so she tells me.

THE NURSE [*hotly*] I tell you what is true. [*To the patient*] Popsy and I are as good company as ever you kept.

THE PATIENT. No, Sweetie: you are a common little devil and a liar. But you amuse me. If you were a real lady you wouldnt amuse me. Youd be afraid to be so unladylike.

THE BURGLAR. Just so. Come! confess! we are better fun than your dear anxious mother and the curate and all the sympathizing relatives, arnt we? Of course we are.

THE PATIENT. I think it perfectly scandalous that you two, who ought to be in prison, are having all the fun while I, because I am respectable and a lady, might just as well be in prison.

THE BURGLAR. Dont you wish you could come with us?

THE PATIENT [*calmly*] I fully intend to come with you. I'm going to make the most of this dream. Do you forget that I love you, Pops. The world is before us. You and Sweetie have had a week in the land of the mountain and the flood for seven guineas, tips included. Now you shall have an eternity with your Mops in the loveliest earthly paradise we can find, for nothing.

THE NURSE. And where do I come in?

THE PATIENT. You will be our chaperone.

THE NURSE. Chaperone! Well, you have a nerve, you have.

THE PATIENT. Listen. You will be a Countess. We shall go abroad, where nobody will know the difference. You shall have a splendid foreign title. The Countess Valbrioni: doesnt that tempt you?

THE NURSE. Tempt me hell! I'll see you further first.

THE BURGLAR. Stop. Sweetie: I have another idea. A regular dazzler. Lets stage a kidnap.

THE NURSE. What do you mean? stage a kidnap.

THE BURGLAR. It's quite simple. We kidnap Mops: that is, we shall hide her in the mountains of Corsica or Istria or Dalmatia or Greece or in the Atlas or where you please that is out of reach of Scotland Yard. We shall pretend to be brigands. Her devoted mother will cough up five thousand to ransom her. We shall share the ransom fifty-fifty: fifty for Mops, twentyfive for you, twentyfive for me. Mops: you will realize not only the value of the pearls, but of yourself. What a stroke of finance!

THE PATIENT [*excited*] Greece! Dalmatia! Kidnapped! Brigands! Ransomed! [*Collapsing a little*] Oh, dont tantalize me, you two fools: you have forgotten the measles.

The Monster suddenly reappears from behind the screen. It is transfigured. The bloated moribund Caliban has become a dainty Ariel.

THE MONSTER [*picking up the last remark of the patient*] So have you. No more measles: that scrap for the jewels cured you and cured me. Ha ha! I am well, I am well, I am well. [*It bounds about ecstatically, and finally perches on the pillows and gets into bed beside the patient*].

THE NURSE. If you could jump out of bed to knock out Popsy and me you can jump out to dress yourself and hop it from here. Wrap yourself up well: we have a car waiting.

THE BURGLAR. It's no worse than being taken to a nursing home, Mops. Strike for freedom. Up with you!

They pull her out of bed.

THE PATIENT. But I cant dress myself without a maid.

THE NURSE. Have you ever tried?

THE BURGLAR. We will give you five minutes. If you are not ready we go without you [*he looks at his watch*].

The patient dashes at the wardrobe and tears out a fur cloak, a hat, a walking dress, a combination, a pair of stockings, black silk breeches, and shoes, all of which she flings on the floor. The nurse picks up most of them; the patient snatches up the rest; the two retire behind the screen. Meanwhile the burglar comes forward to the foot of the bed and comments oratorically, half auctioneer, half clergyman.

THE BURGLAR. Fur cloak. Seal. Old fashioned but worth forty-five guineas. Hat. Quiet and ladylike. Tailor made frock. Combination: silk and wool. Real silk stockings without ladders. Knickers: how daringly modern! Shoes: heels only two inches but no use for the mountains. What a theme for a sermon! The well brought up maiden revolts against her respectable life. The aspiring soul escapes from home, sweet home, which, as a wellknown author has said, is the girl's prison and the woman's workhouse. The intrusive care of her anxious parents, the officious concern of the family clergyman for her salvation and of the family doctor for her health, the imposed affection of uninteresting brothers and sisters, the outrage of being called by her Christian name by distant cousins who will not keep their distance, the invasion of her privacy and independence at every turn by questions as to where she has been and what she has been doing, the whispering behind her back about her chances of marriage, the continual violation of that sacred aura which surrounds every living soul like the halo surrounding the heads of saints in religious pictures: against all these devices for worrying her to death the innermost uppermost life in her rises like milk in a boiling saucepan and cries "Down with you! away with you! henceforth my gates are open to real life, bring what it may. For what sense is there in this world of hazards, disasters, elations and victories, except as a field for the adventures of the life everlasting? In vain do we disfigure our streets with scrawls of Safety First: in vain do the nations clamor for Security, security, security. They who cry Safety First never cross the street: the empires which sacrifice life to security find it in the grave. For me Safety Last; and Forward, Forward, always For—"

THE NURSE [*coming from behind the screen*] Dry up, Popsy: she's ready.

The patient, cloaked, hatted, and shoed, follows her breathless, and comes to the burglar, on his left.

THE PATIENT. Here I am, Pops. One kiss; and then
—Lead on.

THE BURGLAR. Good. Your complexion still leaves
something to be desired; but [*kissing her*] your breath
is sweet: you breathe the air of freedom.

THE MONSTER. Never mind her complexion: look
at mine!

THE BURGLAR [*releasing the patient and turning to
the nurse*] Did you speak?

THE NURSE. No. Hurry up, will you.

THE BURGLAR. It must have been your mother snor-
ing, Mops. It will be long before you hear that music
again. Drop a tear.

THE PATIENT. Not one. A woman's future is not
with her mother.

THE NURSE. If you are going to start preaching like
Popsy, the milkman will be here before we get away.
Remember, I have to take off this uniform and put
on my walking things downstairs. Popsy: there may
be a copper on his beat outside. Spy out and see.
Safety First [*she hurries out*].

THE BURGLAR. Well, for just this once, safety first
[*he makes for the window*].

THE PATIENT [*stopping him*] Idiot: the police cant
touch you if I back you up. It's I who run the risk of
being caught by my mother.

THE BURGLAR. True. You have an unexpectedly
powerful mind. Pray Heaven that in kidnapping you
I am not biting off more than I can chew. Come
along. [*He runs out*].

THE PATIENT. He's forgotten the pearls!!! Thank
Heaven he's a fool, a lovely fool: I shall be able to do
as I like with him. [*She rushes to the dressing table;
bundles the jewels into their case; and carries it out*].

THE MONSTER [*sitting up*] The play is now virtually

[455]

over; but the characters will discuss it at great length for two acts more. The exit doors are all in order. Goodnight. [*It draws up the bedclothes round its neck and goes to sleep*].

$\big[$ ACT II $\big]$

A sea beach in a mountainous country. Sand dunes rise to a brow which cuts off the view of the plain beyond, only the summits of the distant mountain range which bounds it being visible. An army hut on hither side, with a klaxon electric horn projecting from a board on the wall, shews that we are in a military cantoonment. Opposite the hut is a particolored canvas bathing pavilion with a folding stool beside the entrance. As seen from the sand dunes the hut is on the right and the pavilion on the left. From the neighborhood of the hut a date palm throws a long shadow; for it is early morning.

In this shadow sits a British colonel in a deck chair, peacefully reading the weekly edition of The Times, but with a revolver in his equipment. A light cane chair for use by his visitors is at hand by the hut. Though well over fifty, he is still slender, handsome, well set up, and every inch a commanding officer. His full style and title is Colonel Tallboys V.C., D.S.O. He won his cross as a company-officer, and has never looked back since then.

He is disturbed by a shattering series of explosions announcing the approach of a powerful and very imperfectly silenced motor bicycle from the side opposite to the huts.

TALLBOYS. Damn that noise!

The unseen rider dismounts and races his engine with a hideous clatter.

TALLBOYS [*angrily*] Stop that motorbike, will you?

The noise stops; and the bicyclist, having hoiked his

machine up on to its stand, taken off his goggles and gloves, and extracted a letter from his carrier, comes past the pavilion into the colonel's view with the letter in his hand.

He is an insignificant looking private soldier, dusty as to his clothes and a bit gritty as to his windbeaten face. Otherwise there is nothing to find fault with: his tunic and puttees are smart and correct, and his speech ready and rapid. Yet the colonel, already irritated by the racket of the bicycle and the interruption to his newspaper, contemplates him with stern disfavor; for there is something exasperatingly and inexplicably wrong about him. He wears a pith helmet with a pagri; and in profile this pagri suggests a shirt which he has forgotten to tuck in behind, whilst its front view as it falls on his shoulders gives a feminine air of having ringlets and a veil which is in the last degree unsoldierly. His figure is that of a boy of seventeen; but he seems to have borrowed a long head and Wellingtonian nose and chin from somebody else for the express purpose of annoying the colonel. Fortunately for him these are offences which cannot be stated on a charge sheet and dealt with by the provo-marshal; and of this the colonel is angrily aware. The dispatch rider seems conscious of his incongruities; for, though very prompt, concise, and soldierly in his replies, he somehow suggests that there is an imprescriptible joke somewhere by an invisible smile which unhappily produces at times an impression of irony.

He salutes; hands the letter to the colonel; and stands at attention.

TALLBOYS [*taking the letter*] Whats this?

THE RIDER. I was sent with a letter to the headman of the native village in the mountains, sir. That is his answer, sir.

TALLBOYS. I know nothing about it. Who sent you?

[458]

THE RIDER. Colonel Saxby, sir.

TALLBOYS. Colonel Saxby has just returned to the base, seriously ill. I have taken over from him. I am Colonel Tallboys.

THE RIDER. So I understand, sir.

TALLBOYS. Well, is this a personal letter to be sent on to him, or is it a dispatch?

THE RIDER. Dispatch, sir. Service document, sir. You may open it.

TALLBOYS [*turning in his chair and concentrating on him with fierce sarcasm*] Thank you. [*He surveys him from his instep to his nose*]. What is your name?

THE RIDER. Meek, sir.

TALLBOYS [*with disgust*] What!

THE RIDER. Meek, sir. M, double e, k.

The colonel looks at him with loathing, and tears open the letter. There is a painful silence whilst he puzzles over it.

TALLBOYS. In dialect. Send the interpreter to me.

MEEK. It's of no consequence, sir. It was only to impress the headman.

TALLBOYS. INNdeed. Who picked you for this duty?

MEEK. Sergeant, sir.

TALLBOYS. He should have selected a capable responsible person, with sufficient style to impress the native headman to whom Colonel Saxby's letter was addressed. How did he come to select you?

MEEK. I volunteered, sir.

TALLBOYS. Did you indeed? You consider yourself an impressive person, eh? You think you carry about with you the atmosphere of the British Empire, do you?

MEEK. No, sir. I know the country. I can speak the dialects a little.

TALLBOYS. Marvellous! And why, with all these accomplishments, are you not at least a corporal?

MEEK. Not educationally qualified, sir.

TALLBOYS. Illiterate! Are you not ashamed?

MEEK. No, sir.

TALLBOYS. Proud of it, eh?

MEEK. Cant help it, sir.

TALLBOYS. Where did you pick up your knowledge of the country?

MEEK. I was mostly a sort of tramp before I enlisted, sir.

TALLBOYS. Well, if I could get hold of the recruiting sergeant who enlisted you, I'd have his stripes off. Youre a disgrace to the army.

MEEK. Yessir.

TALLBOYS. Go and send the interpreter to me. And dont come back with him. Keep out of my sight.

MEEK [*hesitates*] Er—

TALLBOYS [*peremptorily*] Now then! Did you hear me give you an order? Send me the interpreter.

MEEK. The fact is, Colonel—

TALLBOYS [*outraged*] How dare you say Colonel and tell me that the fact is? Obey your order and hold your tongue.

MEEK. Yessir. Sorry, sir. *I* am the interpreter.

Tallboys bounds to his feet; towers over Meek, who looks smaller than ever; and folds his arms to give emphasis to a terrible rejoinder. On the point of delivering it, he suddenly unfolds them again and sits down resignedly.

TALLBOYS [*wearily and quite gently*] Very well. If you are the interpreter you had better interpret this for me. [*He proffers the letter*].

MEEK [*not accepting it*] No need, thank you, sir. The headman couldnt compose a letter, sir. I had to do it for him.

TALLBOYS. How did you know what was in Colonel Saxby's letter?

MEEK. I read it to him, sir.

TALLBOYS. Did he ask you to?

MEEK. Yessir.

TALLBOYS. He had no right to communicate the contents of such a letter to a private soldier. He cannot have known what he was doing. You must have represented yourself as being a responsible officer. Did you?

MEEK. It would be all the same to him, sir. He addressed me as Lord of the Western Isles.

TALLBOYS. You! You worm! If my letter was sent by the hands of an irresponsible messenger it should have contained a statement to that effect. Who drafted it?

MEEK. Quartermaster's clerk, sir.

TALLBOYS. Send him to me. Tell him to bring his note of Colonel Saxby's instructions. Do you hear? Stop making idiotic faces; and get a move on. Send me the quartermaster's clerk.

MEEK. The fact is—

TALLBOYS [*thundering*] Again!

MEEK. Sorry, sir. *I* am the quartermaster's clerk.

TALLBOYS. What! You wrote both the letter and the headman's answer?

MEEK. Yessir.

TALLBOYS. Then either you are lying now or you were lying when you said you were illiterate. Which is it?

MEEK. I dont seem to be able to pass the examination when they want to promote me. It's my nerves, sir, I suppose.

TALLBOYS. Your nerves! What business has a soldier with nerves? You mean that you are no use for fighting, and have to be put to do anything that can be done without it.

MEEK. Yessir.

TALLBOYS. Well, next time you are sent with a letter I hope the brigands will catch you and keep you.

MEEK. There are no brigands, sir.

TALLBOYS. No brigands! Did you say no brigands?

MEEK. Yessir.

TALLBOYS. You are acquainted with the Articles of War, are you not?

MEEK. I have heard them read out, sir.

TALLBOYS. Do you understand them?

MEEK. I think so, sir.

TALLBOYS. You think so! Well, do a little more thinking. You are serving on an expeditionary force sent out to suppress brigandage in this district and to rescue a British lady who is being held for ransom. You know that. You dont think it: you know it, eh?

MEEK. So they say, sir.

TALLBOYS. You know also that under the Articles of War any soldier who knowingly does when on active service any act calculated to imperil the success of his Majesty's forces or any part thereof shall be liable to suffer death. Do you understand? Death!

MEEK. Yessir. Army Act, Part One, Section Four, Number Six. I think you mean Section Five, Number Five, sir.

TALLBOYS. Do I? Perhaps you will be good enough to quote Section Five, Number Five.

MEEK. Yessir. "By word of mouth spreads reports calculated to create unnecessary alarm or despondency."

TALLBOYS. It is fortunate for you, Private Meek, that the Act says nothing about private soldiers who create despondency by their personal appearance. Had it done so your life would not be worth half an hour's purchase.

MEEK. No, sir. Am I to file the letter and the reply with a translation, sir?

TALLBOYS [*tearing the letter to pieces and throwing them away*] Your folly has made a mockery of both. What did the headman say?

MEEK. Only that the country has very good roads now, sir. Motor coaches ply every day all the year round. The last active brigand retired fifteen years ago, and is ninety years old.

TALLBOYS. The usual tissue of lies. That headman is in league with the brigands. He takes a turn himself occasionally, I should say.

MEEK. I think not, sir. The fact is—

TALLBOYS. Did I hear you say "The fact is"?

MEEK. Sorry, sir. That old brigand was the headman himself. He is sending you a present of a sheep and six turkeys.

TALLBOYS. Send them back instantly. Take them back on your damned bicycle. Inform him that British officers are not orientals, and do not accept bribes from officials in whose districts they have to restore order.

MEEK. He wont understand, sir. He wont believe you have any authority unless you take presents. Besides, they havnt arrived yet.

TALLBOYS. Well, when his messengers arrive pack them back with their sheep and their turkeys and a note to say that my favor can be earned by honesty and diligence, but not purchased.

MEEK. They wont dare take back either the presents or the note, sir. Theyll steal the sheep and turkeys and report gracious messages from you. Better keep the meat and the birds, sir: they will be welcome after a long stretch of regulation food.

TALLBOYS. Private Meek.

MEEK. Yessir.

TALLBOYS. If you should be at any future time entrusted with the command of this expedition you will no doubt give effect to your own views and moral standards. For the present will you be good enough to obey my orders without comment?

MEEK. Yessir. Sorry, sir.

As Meek salutes and turns to go, he is confronted by the nurse, who, brilliantly undressed for bathing under a variegated silk wrap, comes from the pavilion, followed by the patient in the character of a native servant. All traces of the patient's illness have disappeared: she is sunburnt to the color of terra cotta; and her muscles are hard and glistening with unguent. She is disguised en belle sauvage *by headdress, wig, ornaments, and girdle proper to no locality on earth except perhaps the Russian ballet. She carries a sun umbrella and a rug.*

TALLBOYS [*rising gallantly*] Ah, my dear Countess, delighted to see you. How good of you to come!

THE COUNTESS [*giving him her finger tips*] How do, Colonel? Hot, isnt it? [*Her dialect is now a spirited amalgamation of the foreign accents of all the waiters she has known*].

TALLBOYS. Take my chair. [*He goes behind it and moves it nearer to her*].

THE COUNTESS. Thanks. [*She throws off her wrap, which the patient takes, and flings herself with careless elegance into the chair, calling*] Mr Meek. Mr Mee-e-e-eek!

Meek returns smartly, and touches the front of his cap.

THE COUNTESS. My new things from Paris have arrived at last. If you could be so very sweet as to get them to my bungalow somehow. Of course I will pay anything necessary. And could you get a letter of credit cashed for me. I'd better have three hundred pounds to go on with.

MEEK [*quite at his ease: unconsciously dropping the soldier and assuming the gentleman*] How many boxes, Countess?

THE COUNTESS. Six, I am afraid. Will it be a lot of trouble?

MEEK. It will involve a camel.

THE COUNTESS. Oh, strings of camels if necessary. Expense is no object. And the letter of credit?

MEEK. Sorry, Countess: I have only two hundred on me. You shall have the other hundred tomorrow. [*He hands her a roll of notes; and she gives him the letter of credit*].

THE COUNTESS. You are never at a loss. Thanks. So good of you.

TALLBOYS. Chut! Dismiss.

Meek comes to attention, salutes, left-turns, and goes out at the double.

TALLBOYS [*who has listened to this colloquy in renewed stupefaction*] Countess: that was very naughty of you.

THE COUNTESS. What have I done?

TALLBOYS. In camp you must never forget discipline. We keep it in the background; but it is always there and always necessary. That man is a private soldier. Any sort of social relation—any hint of familiarity with him—is impossible for you.

THE COUNTESS. But surely I may treat him as a human being.

TALLBOYS. Most certainly not. Your intention is natural and kindly; but if you treat a private soldier as a human being the result is disastrous to himself. He presumes. He takes liberties. And the consequence of that is that he gets into trouble and has a very bad time of it until he is taught his proper place by appropriate disciplinary measures. I must ask you to be particularly careful with this man Meek. He is only half-witted: he carries all his money about with him. If you have occasion to speak to him, make him feel by your tone that the relation between you is one of a superior addressing a very distant inferior. Never let him address you on his own initiative, or call you anything but "my lady." If there is anything we can do for you we shall be delighted to do it; but you must always ask me.

The patient, greatly pleased with the colonel for snubbing Sweetie, deposits her rug and umbrella on the sand, and places a chair for him on the lady's right with grinning courtesy. She then seats herself on the rug, and listens to them, hugging her knees and her umbrella, and trying to look as indigenous as possible.

TALLBOYS. Thank you. [*He sits down*].

THE COUNTESS. I am so sorry. But if I ask anyone else they only look helpless and say "You had better see Meek about it."

TALLBOYS. No doubt they put everything on the poor fellow because he is not quite all there. Is it understood that in future you come to me, and not to Meek ?

THE COUNTESS. I will indeed, Colonel. I am so sorry, and I thoroughly understand. I am scolded and forgiven, arnt I ?

TALLBOYS [*smiling graciously*] Admonished, we call it. But of course it is not your fault: I have no right to scold you. It is I who must ask your forgiveness.

THE COUNTESS. Granted.

THE PATIENT [*in waiting behind them, coughs significantly*]!!

THE COUNTESS [*hastily*] A vulgar expression, Colonel, isnt it ? But so simple and direct. I like it.

[466]

TALLBOYS. I didnt know it was vulgar. It is concise.

THE COUNTESS. Of course it isnt really vulgar. But a little lower middle class, if you follow me.

THE PATIENT [*pokes the chair with the sun umbrella*]!

THE COUNTESS [*as before*] Any news of the brigands, Colonel?

TALLBOYS. No; but Miss Mopply's mother, who is in a distracted condition—very naturally of course, poor woman!—has actually sent me the ransom. She implores me to pay it and release her child. She is afraid that if I make the slightest hostile demonstration the brigands will cut off the girl's fingers and send them in one by one until the ransom is paid. She thinks they may even begin with her ears, and disfigure her for life. Of course that is a possibility: such things have been done; and the poor lady points out very justly that I cannot replace her daughter's ears by exterminating the brigands afterwards, as I shall most certainly do if they dare lay a hand on a British lady. But I cannot countenance such a concession to deliberate criminality as the payment of a ransom. [*The two conspirators exchange dismayed glances*]. I have sent a message to the old lady by wireless to say that the payment of a ransom is out of the question, but that the British Government is offering a substantial reward for information.

THE COUNTESS [*jumping up excitedly*] Wotjesoy? A reward on top of the ransom?

THE PATIENT [*pokes her savagely with the umbrella*]!!!

TALLBOYS [*surprised*] No. Instead of the ransom.

THE COUNTESS [*recollecting herself*] Of course. How silly of me! [*She sits down and adds, reflectively*] If this native girl could find out anything would she get the reward?

TALLBOYS. Certainly she would. Good idea that: what?

THE COUNTESS. Yes, Colonel, isnt it?

TALLBOYS. By the way, Countess, I met three people yesterday who know you very well.

THE PATIENT [*forgetting herself and scrambling forward to her knees*] But you—

THE COUNTESS [*stopping her with a backhand slap on the mouth*] Silence, girl. How dare you interrupt the colonel? Go back to your place and hold your tongue.

The Patient obeys humbly until the Colonel delicately turns his head away, when she shakes her fist threateningly at the smiter.

TALLBOYS. One of them was a lady. I happened to mention your brother's name; and she lit up at once and said "Dear Aubrey Bagot! I know his sister intimately. We were all three children together."

THE COUNTESS. It must have been dear Florence Dorchester. I hope she wont come here. I want to have an absolute holiday. I dont want to see anybody —except you, Colonel.

TALLBOYS. Haw! Very good of you to say so.

The Burglar comes from the bathing tent, very elegant in black and white bathing costume and black silken wrap with white silk lapels: a clerical touch.

TALLBOYS [*continuing*] Ah, Bagot! Ready for your dip? I was just telling the Countess that I met some friends of yours yesterday. Fancy coming on them out here of all places! Shews how small the world is, after all. [*Rising*] And now I am off to inspect stores. There is a shortage of maroons that I dont understand.

THE COUNTESS. What a pity! I love maroons. They have such nice ones at that confectioner's near the Place Vendôme.

TALLBOYS. Oh, youre thinking of marrons glacés.

No: maroons are fireworks: things that go off with a bang. For signalling.

THE COUNTESS. Oh! the things they used to have in the war to warn us of an air raid?

TALLBOYS. Just so. Well, au revoir.

THE COUNTESS. Au revoir. Au revoir.

The Colonel touches his cap gallantly and bustles off past the hut to his inspection.

THE PATIENT [*rising vengefully*] You dare smack me in the face again, my girl, and I'll lay you out flat, even if I have to give away the whole show.

THE COUNTESS. Well, you keep that umbrella to yourself next time. What do you suppose I'm made of? Leather?

AUBREY [*coming between them*] Now! now! now! Children! children! Whats wrong?

THE PATIENT. This silly bitch—

AUBREY. Oh no, no, no, Mops. Damn it, be a lady. Whats the matter, Sweetie?

THE COUNTESS. You shouldnt talk like that, dearie. A low girl might say a thing like that; but youre expected to know better.

AUBREY. Mops: youve shocked Sweetie.

THE PATIENT. Well: do you think she never shocks me? She's a walking earthquake. And now what are we to do if these people the colonel has met turn up? There must be a real Countess Valbrioni.

THE COUNTESS. Not much there isnt. Do you suppose we three are the only liars in the world? All you have to do is to give yourself a swell title, and all the snobs within fifty miles will swear that you are their dearest friend.

AUBREY. The first lesson a crook has to learn, darling, is that nothing succeeds like lying. Make any statement that is so true that it has been staring us in the face all our lives, and the whole world will rise up and passionately contradict you. If you dont withdraw and apologize, it will be the worse for you. But just tell a thundering silly lie that everyone knows is a lie, and a murmur of pleased assent will hum up from every quarter of the globe. If Sweetie had introduced herself as what she obviously is: that is, an ex-hotel chambermaid who became a criminal on principle through the preaching of an ex-army chaplain—me!— with whom she fell in love deeply but transitorily, nobody would have believed her. But she has no sooner made the impossible statement that she is a countess, and that the ex-chaplain is her half step-brother the Honorable Aubrey Bagot, than clouds of witnesses spring up to assure Colonel Tallboys that it is all gospel truth. So have no fear of exposure, darling; and do you, my Sweetie, lie and lie and lie until your imagination bursts.

THE PATIENT [*throwing herself moodily into the deck chair*] I wonder are all crooks as fond of preaching as you are.

AUBREY [*bending affectionately over her*] Not all, dearest. I dont preach because I am a crook, but because I have a gift—a divine gift—that way.

THE PATIENT. Where did you get it ? Is your father a bishop ?

AUBREY [*straightening himself up to declaim*] Have I not told you that he is an atheist, and, like all atheists, an inflexible moralist ? He said I might become a preacher if I believed what I preached. That, of course, was nonsense: my gift of preaching is not confined to what I believe: I can preach anything, true or false. I am like a violin, on which you can play all sorts of music, from jazz to Mozart. [*Relaxing*] But the old man never could be brought to see it. He said the proper profession for me was the bar. [*He snatches up the rug; replaces it on the patient's left; and throws himself down lazily on it*].

THE COUNTESS. Aint we going to bathe?

AUBREY. Oh, dash it, dont lets go into the water. Lets sunbathe.

THE COUNTESS. Lazy devil! [*She takes the folding stool from the pavilion, and sits down discontentedly*].

THE PATIENT. Your father was right. If you have no conscience about what you preach, your proper job is at the bar. But as you have no conscience about what you do, you will probably end in the dock.

AUBREY. Most likely. But I am a born preacher, not a pleader. The theory of legal procedure is that if you set two liars to expose one another, the truth will emerge. That would not suit me. I greatly dislike being contradicted; and the only place where a man is safe from contradiction is in the pulpit. I detest argument: it is unmannerly, and obscures the preacher's message. Besides, the law is too much concerned with crude facts and too little with spiritual things; and it is in spiritual things that I am interested: they alone call my gift into full play.

THE PATIENT. You call preaching things you dont believe spiritual, do you?

AUBREY. Put a sock in it, Mops. My gift is divine: it is not limited by my petty personal convictions. It is a gift of lucidity as well as of eloquence. Lucidity is one of the most precious of gifts: the gift of the teacher: the gift of explanation. I can explain anything to anybody; and I love doing it. I feel I must do it if only the doctrine is beautiful and subtle and exquisitely put together. I may feel instinctively that it is the rottenest nonsense. Still, if I can get a moving dramatic effect out of it, and preach a really splendid sermon about it,

my gift takes possession of me and obliges me to sail
in and do it. Sweetie: go and get me a cushion for my
head: there's a dear.

THE PATIENT. Do nothing of the kind, Sweetie. Let
him wait on himself.

THE COUNTESS [*rising*] He'd only mess everything
about looking for it. I like to have my rooms left tidy.
[*She goes into the pavilion*].

THE PATIENT. Isnt that funny, Pops? She has a
conscience as a chambermaid and none as a woman.

AUBREY. Very few people have more than one point
of honor, Mops. And lots of them havnt even one.

THE COUNTESS [*returning with a silk cushion, which
she hurls hard at Aubrey's head*] There! And now I
give you both notice. I'm getting bored with this
place.

AUBREY [*making himself comfortable with his cushion*]
Oh, you are always getting bored.

THE PATIENT. I suppose that means that you are
tired of Tallboys.

THE COUNTESS [*moving restlessly about*] I am fed up
with him to that degree that I sometimes feel I could
almost marry him, just to put him on the list of the
inevitables that I must put up with willynilly, like
getting up in the morning, and washing and dressing
and eating and drinking: things you darent let yourself get tired of because if you did theyd drive you
mad. Lets go and have a bit of real life somewhere.

THE PATIENT. Real life! I wonder where thats to be
found! Weve spent nearly six thousand pounds in
two months looking for it. The money we got for the
necklace wont last for ever.

AUBREY. Sweetie: you will have to stick it in this spot
until we touch that ransom; and that's all about it.

THE COUNTESS. I'll do as I like, not what you tell

me. And I tell you again—the two of you—you can take a week's notice. I'm bored with this business. I need a change.

AUBREY. What are we to do with her, Mops? Always change! change! change!

THE COUNTESS. Well, I like to see new faces.

AUBREY. I could be happy as a Buddha in a temple, eternally contemplating my own middle and having the same old priest to polish me up every day. But Sweetie wants a new face every fortnight. I have known her fall in love with a new face twice in the same week. [*Turning to her*] Woman: have you any sense of the greatness of constancy?

COUNTESS. I might be constant if I were a real countess. But I'm only a hotel chambermaid; and a hotel chambermaid gets so used to new faces that at last they become a necessity. [*She sits down on the stool*].

AUBREY. And the oftener the faces change the more the tips come to, eh?

COUNTESS. Oh, it's not that, though of course that counts. The real secret of it is that though men are awfully nice for the first few days, it doesnt last. You get the best out of men by having them always new. What I say is that a love affair should always be a honeymoon. And the only way to make sure of that is to keep changing the man; for the same man can never keep it up. In all my life I have known only one man that kept it up til he died.

THE PATIENT [*interested*] Ah! Then the thing is possible?

COUNTESS. Yes: it was a man that married my sister: that was how I came to know about it.

AUBREY. And his ardor never palled? Day in and day out, until death did them part, he was the same

[473]

as on the wedding day? Is that really true, Sweetie?

THE COUNTESS. It is. But then he beat her on their wedding day; and he beat her just as hard every day afterwards. I made her get a separation order; but she went back to him because nobody else paid her any attention.

AUBREY. Why didnt you tell me that before? I'd have beaten you black and blue sooner than lose you. [*Sitting up*] Would you believe it, Mops, I was in love with this woman: madly in love with her. She was not my intellectual equal; and I had to teach her table manners. But there was an extraordinary sympathy between our lower centres; and when after ten days she threw me over for another man I was restrained from murder and suicide only by the most resolute exercise of my reasoning powers, my determination to be a civilized man, and fear of the police.

THE COUNTESS. Well, I gave you a good time for the ten days, didnt I? Lots of people dont get that much to look back on. Besides, you know it was for your own good, Popsy. We werent really suited, were we?

AUBREY. You had acquired an insatiable taste for commercial travellers. You could sample them at the rate of three a week. I could not help admiring such amazing mobility of the affections. I had heard operatic tenors bawling Woman is Fickle; but it always seemed to me what was to be dreaded in women was their implacable constancy. But you! Fickle! I should think so.

THE COUNTESS. Well, the travellers were just as bad, you know.

AUBREY. Just as bad! Say just as good. Fickleness means simply mobility, and mobility is a mark of civilization. You should pride yourself on it. If you dont you will lose your self-respect; and I cannot endure a woman who has no self-respect.

THE COUNTESS. Oh, whats the use of us talking about self-respect? You are a thief and so am I. I go a little further than that, myself; and so would you if you were a woman. Dont you be a hypocrite, Popsy: at least not with me.

AUBREY. At least not with you! Sweetie: that touch of concern for my spiritual welfare almost convinces me that you still love me.

THE COUNTESS. Not me. Not much. I'm through with you, my lad. And I cant quite fancy the colonel: he's too old, and too much the gentleman.

AUBREY. He's better than nobody. Who else is there?

THE COUNTESS. Well, there's the sergeant. I daresay I have low tastes; but he's my sort, and the colonel isnt.

THE PATIENT. Have you fallen in love with Sergeant Fielding, Sweetie?

THE COUNTESS. Well, yes; if you like to call it that.

AUBREY. May I ask have you sounded him on the subject?

THE COUNTESS. How can I? I'm a countess; and he's only a sergeant. If I as much as let on that I'm conscious of his existence I give away the show to the colonel. I can only look at him. And I cant do even that when anyone else is looking. And all the time I want to hug him [*she breaks down in tears*].

AUBREY. Oh for Heaven's sake dont start crying.

THE PATIENT. For all you know, Sweetie, the sergeant may be a happily married man.

THE COUNTESS. What difference does that make to my feelings? I am so lonely. The place is so dull. No pictures. No dances. Nothing to do but be ladylike. And the one really lovable man going to waste! I'd rather be dead.

THE PATIENT. Well, it's just as bad for me.

THE COUNTESS. No it isnt. Youre a real lady: youre broken in to be dull. Besides, you have Popsy. And youre supposed to be our servant. That gives you the run of the whole camp when youre tired of him. You can pick up a private when you like. Whats to prevent you?

THE PATIENT. My ladylike morals, I suppose.

THE COUNTESS. Morals your grandmother! I thought youd left all that flapdoodle behind you when you came away with us.

THE PATIENT. I meant to. Ive tried to. But you shock me in spite of myself every second time you open your mouth.

THE COUNTESS. Dont you set up to be a more moral woman than I am, because youre not.

THE PATIENT. I dont pretend to be. But I may tell you that my infatuation for Popsy, which I now see was what really nerved me to this astonishing break-away, has been, so far, quite innocent. Can you believe that, you clod?

THE COUNTESS. Oh yes I can: Popsy's satisfied as long as you let him talk. What I mean is—and I tell it to you straight—that with all my faults I'm content with one man at a time.

THE PATIENT. Do you suggest that I am carrying on with two men?

THE COUNTESS. I dont suggest anything. I say what I mean straight out; and if you dont like it you can lump it. You may be in love with Popsy; but youre interested in Private Meek, though what you see in that dry little worm beats me.

THE PATIENT. Have you noticed, my Sweetie, that your big strapping splendid sergeant is completely under the thumb of that dry little worm?

THE COUNTESS. He wont be when I get him under my thumb. But you just be careful. Take this tip from me: one man at a time. I am advising you for your good, because youre only a beginner; and what you think is love, and interest, and all that, is not real love at all: three quarters of it is only unsatisfied curiosity. Ive lived at that address myself; and I know. When I love a man now it's all love and nothing else. It's the real thing while it lasts. I havnt the least curiosity about my lovely sergeant: I know just what he'll say and what he'll do. I just want him to do it.

THE PATIENT [*rising, revolted*] Sweetie: I really cannot bear any more of this. No doubt it's perfectly true. It's quite right that you should say it frankly and plainly. I envy and admire the frightful coolness with which you plump it all out. Perhaps I shall get used to it in time. But at present it knocks me to pieces. I shall simply have to go away if you pursue the subject. [*She sits down in the cane chair with her back to them*].

AUBREY. Thats the worst of Sweetie. We all have—to put it as nicely as I can—our lower centres and our higher centres. Our lower centres act: they act with terrible power that sometimes destroys us; but they dont talk. Speech belongs to the higher centres. In all the great poetry and literature of the world the higher centres speak. In all respectable conversation the higher centres speak, even when they are saying nothing or telling lies. But the lower centres are there all the time: a sort of guilty secret with every one of us, though they are dumb. I remember asking my tutor at college whether, if anyone's lower centres began to talk, the shock would not be worse than the one Balaam got when his donkey began talking to him. He only told me half a dozen improper stories to shew how openminded he was. I never mentioned the subject again until I met Sweetie. Sweetie is Balaam's ass.

THE COUNTESS. Keep a civil tongue in your head, Popsy. I—

AUBREY [*springing to his feet*] Woman: I am paying you a compliment: Balaam's ass was wiser than Balaam. You should read your Bible. That is what makes Sweetie almost superhuman. Her lower centres speak. Since the war the lower centres have become vocal. And the effect is that of an earthquake. For they speak truths that have never been spoken before— truths that the makers of our domestic institutions have tried to ignore. And now that Sweetie goes shouting them all over the place, the institutions are rocking and splitting and sundering. They leave us no place to live, no certainties, no workable morality, no heaven, no hell, no commandments, and no God.

THE PATIENT. What about the light in our own souls that you were so eloquent about the day before yester-day at lunch when you drank a pint of champagne?

AUBREY. Most of us seem to have no souls. Or if we have them, they have nothing to hang on to. Meanwhile, Sweetie goes on shouting. [*He takes refuge in the deck chair*].

THE COUNTESS [*rising*] Oh, what are you gassing about? I am not shouting. I should be a good woman if it wasnt so dull. If youre goodnatured, you just get put upon. Who are the good women? Those that enjoy being dull and like being put upon. Theyve no appetites. Life's thrown away on them: they get nothing out of it.

THE PATIENT. Well, come, Sweetie! What do you get out of it?

THE COUNTESS. Excitement: thats what I get out of it. Look at Popsy and me! We're always planning robberies. Of course I know it's mostly imagination; but the fun is in the planning and the expectation. Even if we did them and were caught, there would be the excitement of being tried and being in all the papers. Look at poor Harry Smiler that murdered the cop in Croydon! When he came and told us what he'd done Popsy offered to go out and get him some cyanide to poison himself; for it was a dead sure thing that he'd be caught and bumped off. "What!" says Harry; "and lose the excitement of being tried for my life! I'd rather be hanged" he says; and hanged he was. And I say it must have been almost worth it. After all, he'd have died anyhow: perhaps of something really painful. Harry wasnt a bad man really; but he couldnt bear dullness. He had a wonderful collection of pistols that he had begun as a boy: he picked up a lot in the war. Just for the romance of it, you know: he meant no harm. But he'd never shot anyone with them; and at last the temptation was too great and he went out and shot the cop. Just for nothing but the feeling that he'd fired the thing off and done somebody in with it. When Popsy asked him why he'd done it, all he could say was that it was a sort of fulfilment. But it gives you an idea, doesnt it, of what I mean? [*She sits down again, relieved by her outburst*].

AUBREY. All it means is a low vitality. Here is a man with all the miracles of the universe to stagger his imagination and all the problems of human destiny to employ his mind, and he goes out and shoots an innocent policeman because he can think of nothing more interesting to do. Quite right to hang him. And all the people who can find nothing more exciting to do than to crowd into the court to watch him being sentenced to death should have been hanged too. You will be hanged someday, Sweetie, because you have

not what people call a richly stored mind. I have tried
to educate you—

THE COUNTESS. Yes: you gave me books to read. But
I couldnt read them: they were as dull as ditchwater.
Ive tried crossword puzzles to occupy my mind and
keep me off planning robberies; but what crossword
puzzle is half the fun and excitement of picking
somebody's pocket, let alone that you cant live by it?
You wanted me to take to drink to keep me quiet. But
I dont like being drunk; and what would become of
my good looks if I did? Ten bottles of champagne
couldnt make you feel as you do when you walk past a
policeman who has only to stop you and search you
to put you away for three years.

THE PATIENT. Pops: did you really try to set her
drinking? What a thoroughpaced blackguard you are!

AUBREY. She is much better company when she's half
drunk. Listen to her now, when she is sober.

THE PATIENT. Sweetie: are you really having such a
jolly time after all? You began by threatening to give
up our exciting enterprise because it is so dull.

AUBREY. She is free. There is the sergeant. And there
is always the hope of something turning up and the
sense of being ready for it without having to break
all the shackles and throw down all the walls that
imprison a respectable woman.

THE PATIENT. Well, what about me?

AUBREY [*puzzled*] Well, what about you? You are
free, arnt you?

THE PATIENT [*rising very deliberately, and going
behind him to his left hand, which she picks up and
fondles as she sermonizes, seated on the arm of his chair*]
My angel love, you have rescued me from respectability so completely that I have for a month past been
living the life of a mountain goat. I have got rid of

[480]

my anxious worrying mother as completely as a weaned kid, and I no longer hate her. My slavery to cooks stuffing me with long meals of fish, flesh, and fowl is a thing of the miserable past: I eat dates and bread and water and raw onions when I can get them; and when I cant get them I fast, with the result that I have forgotten what illness means; and if I ran away from you two neither of you could catch me; and if you did I could fight the pair of you with one hand tied behind me. I revel in all your miracles of the universe: the delicious dawns, the lovely sunsets, the changing winds, the cloud pictures, the flowers, the animals and their ways, the birds and insects and reptiles. Every day is a day of adventure with its cold and heat, its light and darkness, its cycles of exultant vigor and exhaustion, hunger and satiety, its longings for action that change into a longing for sleep, its thoughts of heavenly things that change so suddenly into a need for food.

AUBREY. What more could any mortal desire?

THE PATIENT [*seizing him by the ears*] Liar.

AUBREY. Thank you. You mean, I presume, that these things do not satisfy you: you want me as well.

THE PATIENT. You!! You!!! you selfish lazy sugary tongued blackguard. [*Releasing him*] No: I included you with the animals and their ways, just as I included Sweetie and the sergeant.

THE COUNTESS. You let Sweetie and her sergeant alone: d'y'hear? I have had enough of that joke on me.

THE PATIENT [*rising and taking her by the chin to turn her face up*] It is no joke, Sweetiest: it is the dead solemn earnest. I called Pops a liar, Sweetie, because all this is not enough. The glories of nature dont last any decently active person a week, unless theyre professional naturalists or mathematicians or a painter or something. I want something sensible to do. A beaver has a jolly time because it has to build its dam and bring up its family. I want my little job like the beaver. If I do nothing but contemplate the universe there is so much in it that is cruel and terrible and wantonly evil, and so much more that is oppressively astronomical and endless and inconceivable and impossible, that I shall just go stark raving mad and be taken back to my mother with straws in my hair. The truth is, I am free; I am healthy; I am happy; and I am utterly miserable. [*Turning on Aubrey*] Do you hear? Utterly miserable.

AUBREY [*losing his temper*] And what do you suppose I am? Here with nothing to do but drag about two damn' silly women and talk to them.

THE COUNTESS. It's worse for them. They have to listen to you.

THE PATIENT. I despise you. I hate you. You—you—you—you gentleman thief. What right has a thief to be a gentleman? Sweetie is bad enough, heaven knows, with her vulgarity and her low cunning: always trying to get the better of somebody or to get hold of a man; but at least she's a woman; and she's real. Men are not real: theyre all talk, talk, talk—

THE COUNTESS [*half rising*] You keep a civil tongue in your head: do you hear?

THE PATIENT. Another syllable of your cheek, Sweetie; and I'll give you a hiding that will keep you screaming for half an hour. [*Sweetie subsides*]. I want to beat somebody: I want to kill somebody. I shall end by killing the two of you. What are we, we three glorious adventurers? Just three inefficient fertilizers.

AUBREY. What on earth do you mean by that?

THE PATIENT. Yes: inefficient fertilizers. We do nothing but convert good food into bad manure. We are walking factories of bad manure: thats what we are.

THE COUNTESS [*rising*] Well, I am not going to sit here and listen to that sort of talk. You ought to be ashamed of yourself.

AUBREY [*rising also, shocked*] Miss Mopply: there are certain disgusting truths that no lady would throw in the teeth of her fellow creatures—

THE PATIENT. I am not a lady: I am free now to say what I please. How do you like it?

THE COUNTESS [*relenting*] Look here, dearie. You mustnt go off at the deep end like this. You— [*The patient turns fiercely on her: she screams*]. Ah-a-a-ah! Popsy: she's mad. Save me. [*She runs away, out past the pavilion*].

AUBREY. What is the matter with you? Are you out of your senses? [*He tries to hold her; but she sends him sprawling*].

THE PATIENT. No. I am exercising my freedom. The freedom you preached. The freedom you made possible for me. You dont like to hear Sweetie's lower centres shouting. Well, now you hear my higher centres shouting. You dont seem to like it any better.

AUBREY. Mops: youre hysterical. You felt splendid an hour ago; and you will feel splendid again an hour from now. You will always feel splendid if you keep yourself fit.

THE PATIENT. Fit for what? A lost dog feels fit: thats what makes him stray; but he's the unhappiest thing alive. I am a lost dog: a tramp, a vagabond. Ive got nothing to do. Ive got nowhere to go. Sweetie's miserable; and youre miserable; and I'm miserable; and I shall just kick you and beat you to a jelly.

She rushes at him. He dodges her and runs off past the hut. At that moment Tallboys returns with Meek

[483]

past the other side of the hut; and the patient, unable to check herself, crashes into his arms.

TALLBOYS [*sternly*] Whats this? What are you doing here? Why are you making this noise? Dont clench your fists in my presence. [*She droops obsequiously*]. Whats the matter?

THE PATIENT [*salaaming and chanting*] Bmal elttil a dah yram, Tuan.

TALLBOYS. Can you speak English?

THE PATIENT. No Engliss.

TALLBOYS. Or French?

THE PATIENT. No Frenns, Tuan. Wons sa etihw saw eceelf sti.

TALLBOYS. Very well: dont do it again. Now off with you.

She goes out backward into the pavilion, salaaming. Tallboys sits down in the deck chair.

TALLBOYS [*to Meek*] Here, you. You say youre the interpreter. Did you understand what that girl said to me?

MEEK. Yessir.

TALLBOYS. What dialect was it? It didnt sound like what the natives speak here.

MEEK. No sir. I used to speak it at school. English back slang, sir.

TALLBOYS. Back slang? What do you mean?

MEEK. English spelt backwards. She reversed the order of the words too, sir. That shews that she has those two little speeches off by heart.

TALLBOYS. But how could a native girl do such a thing? I couldnt do it myself.

MEEK. That shews that she's not a native girl, sir.

TALLBOYS. But this must be looked into. Were you able to pick up what she said?

[484]

MEEK. Only bmal elttil, sir. That was quite easy. It put me on to the rest.

TALLBOYS. But what does bmal elttil mean?

MEEK. Little lamb, sir.

TALLBOYS. She called me a little lamb!

MEEK. No sir. All she said was "Mary had a little lamb." And when you asked her could she speak French she said, of course, "Its fleece was white as snow."

TALLBOYS. But that was insolence.

MEEK. It got her out of her difficulty, sir.

TALLBOYS. This is very serious. The woman is passing herself off on the Countess as a native servant.

MEEK. Do you think so, sir?

TALLBOYS. I dont think so: I know so. Dont be a fool, man. Pull yourself together, and dont make silly answers.

MEEK. Yessir. No sir.

TALLBOYS [*angrily bawling at him*] "Ba Ba black sheep: have you any wool? Yes sir, no sir, three bags full." Dont say yessir no sir to me.

MEEK. No sir.

TALLBOYS. Go and fetch that girl back. Not a word to her about my finding her out, mind. When I have finished with her you will explain to me about those maroons.

MEEK. Yessir. [*He goes into the pavilion*].

TALLBOYS. Hurry up. [*He settles himself comfortably and takes out his cigarette case*].   •

The Countess peers round the corner of the pavilion to see whether she may safely return. Aubrey makes a similar reconnaissance round the corner of the hut.

THE COUNTESS. Here I am again, you see. [*She smiles fascinatingly at the Colonel and sits down on her stool*].

[485]

AUBREY. Moi aussi. May I— [*he stretches himself on the rug*].

TALLBOYS [*sitting up and putting the cigarette case back in his pocket*] Just in the nick of time. I was about to send for you. I have made a very grave discovery. That native servant of yours is not a native. Her lingo is a ridiculous fraud. She is an Englishwoman.

AUBREY. You dont say so!

THE COUNTESS. Oh, impossible.

TALLBOYS. Not a doubt of it. She's a fraud: take care of your jewels. Or else—and this is what I suspect —she's a spy.

AUBREY. A spy! But we are not at war.

TALLBOYS. The League of Nations has spies everywhere. [*To the Countess*] You must allow me to search her luggage at once, before she knows that I have found her out.

THE COUNTESS. But I have missed nothing. I am sure she hasnt stolen anything. What do you want to search her luggage for?

TALLBOYS. For maroons.

THE COUNTESS ⎱ [*together*] ⎰ Maroons!
AUBREY ⎰   ⎱ Maroons!

TALLBOYS. Yes, maroons. I inspected the stores this morning; and the maroons are missing. I particularly wanted them to recall me at lunch time when I go sketching. I am rather a dab at watercolors. And there is not a single maroon left. There should be fifteen.

AUBREY. Oh, I can clear that up. It's one of your men: Meek. He goes about on a motor bicycle with a sack full of maroons and a lot of wire. He said he was surveying. He was evidently very anxious to get rid of me; so I did not press my inquiries. But that accounts for the maroons.

TALLBOYS. Not at all. This is very serious. Meek is a

half witted creature who should never have been enlisted. He is like a child: this woman could do anything she pleases with him.

THE COUNTESS. But what could she possibly want
with maroons?

TALLBOYS. I dont know. This expedition has been
sent out without the sanction of the League of Nations.
We always forget to consult it when there is anything
serious in hand. The woman may be an emissary of
the League. She may be working against us.

THE COUNTESS. But even so, what harm can she do us?

TALLBOYS [*tapping his revolver*] My dear lady, do you
suppose I am carrying this for fun? Dont you realize
that the hills here are full of hostile tribes who may
try to raid us at any moment? Look at that electric
horn there. If it starts honking, look out; for it will
mean that a body of tribesmen has been spotted
advancing on us.

THE COUNTESS [*alarmed*] If I'd known that, you
wouldnt have got me here. Is that so, Popsy?

AUBREY. Well, yes; but it doesnt matter: theyre
afraid of us.

TALLBOYS. Yes, because they dont know that we are
a mere handful of men. But if this woman is in communication with them and has got hold of that idiot
Meek, we may have them down on us like a swarm of
hornets. I dont like this at all. I must get to the bottom
of it at once. Ah! here she comes.

*Meek appears at the entrance to the pavilion. He
stands politely aside to let the patient pass him, and
remains there.*

MEEK. The colonel would like a word with you, Miss.

AUBREY. Go easy with her, Colonel. She can run like
a deer. And she has muscles of iron. You had better
turn out the guard before you tackle her.

TALLBOYS. Pooh! Here, you!

The patient comes to him past the Countess with an air of disarming innocence; falls on her knees; lifts her palms, and smites the ground with her forehead.

TALLBOYS. They tell me you can run fast. Well, a bullet can run faster. [*He taps his revolver*]. Do you understand that?

THE PATIENT [*salaaming*] Bmal elttil a dah yram wons sa etihw saw eceelf tsi—

TALLBOYS [*tonitruant*] And everywhere that Mary went—

THE PATIENT [*adroitly cutting in*] That lamb was sure to go. Got me, Colonel. How clever of you! Well, what of it?

TALLBOYS. That is what I intend to find out. You are not a native.

THE PATIENT. Yes, of Somerset.

TALLBOYS. Precisely. Well, why are you disguised? Why did you try to make me believe that you dont understand English?

THE PATIENT. For a lark, Colonel.

TALLBOYS. Thats not good enough. Why have you passed yourself off on this lady as a native servant? Being a servant is no lark. Answer me. Dont stand there trying to invent a lie. Why did you pretend to be a servant?

THE PATIENT. One has so much more control of the house as a servant than as a mistress nowadays, Colonel.

TALLBOYS. Very smart, that. You will tell me next that one controls a regiment much more effectively as a private than as a colonel, eh?

The klaxon sounds stridently. The Colonel draws his revolver and makes a dash for the top of the sandhill, but is outraced by Meek, who gets there first and takes the word of command with irresistible authority, leaving him stupent. Aubrey, who has scrambled to his feet, moves towards the sand dunes to see what is happening. Sweetie clutches the patient's arm in terror and drags her towards the pavilion. She is fiercely shaken off; and Mops stands her ground defiantly and runs towards the sound of the guns when they begin.

MEEK. Stand to. Charge your magazines. Stand by the maroons. How many do you make them, sergeant? How far off?

SERGEANT FIELDING [*invisible*] Forty horse. Nine hundred yards, about, I make it.

MEEK. Rifles at the ready. Cut-offs open. Sights up to eighteen hundred, right over their heads: no hitting. Ten rounds rapid: fire. [*Fusillade of rifles*]. How is that?

SERGEANT'S VOICE. Theyre coming on, sir.

MEEK. Number one maroons: ready. Contact. [*Formidable explosions on the right*]. How is that?

SERGEANT'S VOICE. Theyve stopped.

MEEK. Number two maroons ready. Contact. [*Explosions on the left*]. How is that?

SERGEANT'S VOICE. Bolted, sir, every man of them.

Meek returns from the hill in the character of an insignificant private, followed by Aubrey, to the Colonel's left and right respectively.

MEEK. Thats all right, sir. Excuse interruption.

TALLBOYS. Oh! You call this an interruption?

MEEK. Yessir: theres nothing in it to trouble you about. Shall I draw up the report, sir? Important engagement: enemy routed: no British casualties. D.S.O. for you, perhaps, sir.

TALLBOYS. Private Meek: may I ask—if you will pardon my presumption—who is in command of this expedition, you or I?

[489]

MEEK. You, sir.

TALLBOYS [*repouching the revolver*] You flatter me. Thank you. May I ask, further, who the devil gave you leave to plant the entire regimental stock of maroons all over the hills and explode them in the face of the enemy?

MEEK. It was the duty of the intelligence orderly, sir. I'm the intelligence orderly. I had to make the enemy believe that the hills are bristling with British cannon. They think that now, sir. No more trouble from them.

TALLBOYS. Indeed! Quartermaster's clerk, interpreter, intelligence orderly. Any further rank of which I have not been informed?

MEEK. No sir.

TALLBOYS. Quite sure youre not a fieldmarshal, eh?

MEEK. Quite sure, sir. I never was anything higher than a colonel.

TALLBOYS. You a colonel? What do you mean?

MEEK. Not a real colonel, sir. Mostly a brevet, sir, to save appearances when I had to take command.

TALLBOYS. And how do you come to be a private now?

MEEK. I prefer the ranks, sir. I have a freer hand. And the conversation in the officers' mess doesnt suit me. I always resign a commission and enlist again.

TALLBOYS. Always! How many commissions have you held?

MEEK. I dont quite remember, sir. Three, I think.

TALLBOYS. Well, I am dashed!

THE PATIENT. Oh, Colonel! And you mistook this great military genius for a half wit!!!

TALLBOYS [*with aplomb*] Naturally. The symptoms are precisely the same. [*To Meek*] Dismiss.

Meek salutes and trots smartly out past the hut.

AUBREY. By Jove!!

THE COUNTESS. Well I ne— [*Correcting herself*] Tiens, tiens, tiens, tiens!

THE PATIENT. What are you going to do about him, Colonel?

TALLBOYS. Madam: the secret of command, in the army and elsewhere, is never to waste a moment doing anything that can be delegated to a subordinate. I have a passion for sketching in watercolors. Hitherto the work of commanding my regiment has interfered very seriously with its gratification. Henceforth I shall devote myself almost entirely to sketching, and leave the command of the expedition to Private Meek. And since you all seem to be on more intimate terms with him than I can claim, will you be good enough to convey to him—casually, you understand—that I already possess the D.S.O. and that what I am out for at present is a K.C.B. Or rather, to be strictly accurate, that is what my wife is out for. For myself, my sole concern for the moment is whether I should paint that sky with Prussian blue or with cobalt.

THE COUNTESS. Fancy you wasting your time on painting pictures!

TALLBOYS. Countess: I paint pictures to make me feel sane. Dealing with men and women makes me feel mad. Humanity always fails me: Nature never.

$$\boxed{\text{ACT III}}$$

*A narrow gap leading down to the beach through masses
of soft brown sandstone, pitted with natural grottoes.
Sand and big stones in the foreground. Two of the grottoes are accessible from the beach by mounting from the
stones, which make rough platforms in front of them. The
soldiers have amused themselves by hewing them into a
rude architecture and giving them fancy names. The one
on your right as you descend the rough path through the
gap is taller than it is broad, and has a natural pillar and
a stone like an altar in it, giving a Gothic suggestion which
has been assisted by knocking the top of the opening into
something like a pointed arch, and surmounting it with
the inscription* SN PAULS. *The grotto to the left is much
wider. It contains a bench long enough to accommodate
two persons; its recesses are illuminated rosily by bulbs
wrapped in pink paper; and some scholarly soldier has
carved above it in Greek characters the word* Αγαπεμουε,
beneath which is written in red chalk THE ABODE OF
LOVE, *under which again some ribald has added in white
chalk,* NO NEED TO WASTE THE ELECTRIC LIGHT.*

*For the moment The Abode of Love has been taken
possession of by the sergeant, a wellbuilt handsome man,
getting on for forty. He is sitting on the bench, and is
completely absorbed in two books, comparing them with
rapt attention.*

*St Pauls is also occupied. A very tall gaunt elder, by
his dress and bearing a well-to-do English gentleman,
sits on a stone at the altar, resting his elbows on it with*

[492]

his chin in his hands. He is in the deepest mourning; and his attitude is one of hopeless dejection.

Sweetie, now fully and brilliantly dressed, comes slowly down the path through the gap, moody and bored. On the beach she finds nothing to interest her until the sergeant unconsciously attracts her notice by finding some remarkable confirmation or contradiction between his two books, and smiting one of them appreciatively with his fist. She instantly brightens up; climbs to the mouth of the grotto eagerly; and posts herself beside him, on his right. But he is so rapt in his books that she waits in vain to be noticed.

SWEETIE [*contemplating him ardently*] Ahem!

The Sergeant looks up. Seeing who it is, he springs to his feet and stands to attention.

SWEETIE [*giving herself no airs*] You neednt stand up for me, you know.

THE SERGEANT [*stiffly*] Beg pardon, your ladyship. I was not aware of your ladyship's presence.

SWEETIE. Can all that stuff, Sergeant. [*She sits on the bench on his right*]. Dont lets waste time. This place is as dull for me as it is for you. Dont you think we two could amuse ourselves a bit if we were friends?

THE SERGEANT [*with stern contempt*] No, my lady, I dont. I saw a lot of that in the war: pretty ladies brightening up the hospitals and losing their silly heads, let alone upsetting the men; and I dont hold with it. Keep to your class: I'll keep to mine.

SWEETIE. My class! Garn! I'm no countess; and I'm fed up with pretending to be one. Didnt you guess?

THE SERGEANT [*resuming his seat and treating her as one of his own class*] Why should I trouble to start

guessing about you? Any girl can be a countess nowadays if she's goodlooking enough to pick up a count.

SWEETIE. Oh! You think I'm goodlooking, do you?

THE SERGEANT. Come! If youre not a countess what
are you? Whats the game, eh?

SWEETIE. The game, darling, is that youre my fancy.
I love you.

THE SERGEANT. Whats that to me? A man of my
figure can have his pick.

SWEETIE. Not here, dear. Theres only one other
white woman within fifty miles; and she's a real lady.
She wouldnt look at you.

THE SERGEANT. Well, thats a point. Thats a point,
certainly.

SWEETIE [*snuggling to him*] Yes, isnt it?

THE SERGEANT [*suffering the advance but not responding*] This climate plays the devil with a man, no
matter how serious minded he is.

SWEETIE [*slipping her arm through his*] Well, isnt it
natural? Whats the use of pretending?

THE SERGEANT. Still, I'm not a man to treat a
woman as a mere necessity. Many soldiers do: to
them a woman is no more than a jar of marmalade, to
be consumed and put away. I dont take that view. I
admit that there is that side to it, and that for people
incapable of anything better—mere animals as you
might say—thats the beginning and the end of it. But
to me thats only the smallest part of it. I like getting
a woman's opinions. I like to explore her mind as well
as her body. See these two little books I was deep in
when you accosted me? I carry them with me wherever
I go. I put the problems they raise for me to every
woman I meet.

SWEETIE [*with growing misgiving*] What are they?

THE SERGEANT [*pointing to them successively*] The

Bible. The Pilgrim's Progress from this world to that which is to come.

SWEETIE [*dismayed, trying to rise*] Oh, my God!

SERGEANT [*holding her ruthlessly in the crook of his elbow*] No you dont. Sit quiet; and dont take the name of the Lord your God in vain. If you believe in him, it's blasphemy: if you dont, it's nonsense. You must learn to exercise your mind: what is a woman without an active mind to a man but a mere convenience?

SWEETIE. I have plenty to exercise my mind looking after my own affairs. What I look to you for, my lad, is a bit of fun.

THE SERGEANT. Quite. But when men and women pick one another up just for a bit of fun, they find theyve picked up more than they bargained for, because men and women have a top storey as well as a ground floor; and you cant have the one without the other. Theyre always trying to; but it doesnt work. Youve picked up my mind as well as my body; and youve got to explore it. You thought you could have a face and a figure like mine with the limitations of a gorilla. Youre finding out your mistake: thats all.

SWEETIE. Oh, let me go: I have had enough of this. If I'd thought you were religious I'd have given you a wide berth, I tell you. Let me go, will you?

THE SERGEANT. Wait a bit. Nature may be using me as a sort of bait to draw you to take an interest in things of the mind. Nature may be using your pleasant animal warmth to stimulate my mind. I want your advice. I dont say I'll take it; but it may suggest something to me. You see, I'm in a mess.

SWEETIE. Well, of course. Youre in the sergeants' mess.

THE SERGEANT. Thats not the mess I mean. My

mind's in a mess—a muddle. I used to be a religious man; but I'm not so clear about it as I was.

SWEETIE. Thank goodness for that, anyhow.

THE SERGEANT. Look at these two books. I used to believe every word of them because they seemed to have nothing to do with real life. But war brought those old stories home quite real; and then one starts asking questions. Look at this bit here [*he points to a page of the Pilgrim's Progress*]. It's on the very first page of it. "I am for certain informed that this our city will be burned with fire from heaven, in which fearful overthrow both myself, with thee my wife, and you my sweet babes, shall miserably come to ruin, except some way of escape can be found whereby we may be delivered." Well, London and Paris and Berlin and Rome and the rest of them will be burned with fire from heaven all right in the next war: thats certain. Theyre all Cities of Destruction. And our Government chaps are running about with a great burden of corpses and debts on their backs, crying "What must we do to be saved?" There it is: not a story in a book as it used to be, but God's truth in the real actual world. And all the comfort they get is "Flee from the wrath to come." But where are they to flee to? There they are, meeting at Geneva or hob-nobbing at Chequers over the weekend, asking one another, like the man in the book, "Whither must we flee?" And nobody can tell them. The man in the book says "Do you see yonder shining light?" Well, today the place is blazing with shining lights: shining lights in parliament, in the papers, in the churches, and in the books that they call Outlines—Outlines of History and Science and what not—and in spite of all their ballyhoo here we are waiting in the City of Destruction like so many sheep for the wrath to come.

This uneducated tinker tells me the way is straight before us and so narrow that we cant miss it. But he starts by calling the place the wilderness of this world. Well, theres no road in a wilderness: you have to make one. All the straight roads are made by soldiers; and the soldiers didnt get to heaven along them. A lot of them landed up in the other place. No, John: you could tell a story well; and they say you were a soldier; but soldiers that try to make storytelling do for service end in the clink; and thats were they put you. Twelve years in Bedford Gaol, he got. He used to read the Bible in gaol; and—

SWEETIE. Well, what else was there to read there? It's all they give you in some gaols.

THE SERGEANT. How do you know that?

SWEETIE. Never you mind how I know it. It's nothing to do with you.

THE SERGEANT. Nothing to do with me! You dont know me, my lass. Some men would just order you off; but to me the most interesting thing in the world is the experience of a woman thats been shut up in a cell for years at a time with nothing but a Bible to read.

SWEETIE. Years! What are you talking about? The longest I ever did was nine months; and if anyone says I ever did a day longer she's a liar.

THE SERGEANT [*laying his hand on the bible*] You could read that book from cover to cover in nine months.

SWEETIE. Some of it would drive you melancholy mad. It only got me into trouble: it did. The chaplain asked me what I was in for. Spoiling the Egyptians, I says; and heres chapter and verse for it. He went and reported me, the swine; and I lost seven days remission for it.

THE SERGEANT. Serve you right! I dont hold with

spoiling the Egyptians. Before the war, spoiling the Egyptians was something holy. Now I see plainly it's nothing but thieving.

SWEETIE [*shocked*] Oh, you shouldnt say that. But what I say is, if Moses might do it why maynt I?

THE SERGEANT. If thats the effect it had on your mind, it's a bad effect. Some of this scripture is all right. Do justice; love mercy; and walk humbly before your God. That appeals to a man if only it could be set out in plain army regulations. But all this thieving, and slaughtering your enemies without giving quarter, and offering up human sacrifices, and thinking you can do what you like to other people because youre the chosen people of God, and you are in the right and everyone else is in the wrong: how does that look when you have had four years of the real thing instead of merely reading about it. No: damn it, we're civilized men; and though it may have gone down with those old Jews it isnt religion. And, if it isnt, where are we? Thats what I want to know.

SWEETIE. And is this all you care about? Sitting here and thinking of things like that?

THE SERGEANT. Well, somebody must think about them, or whats going to become of us all? The officers wont think about them. The colonel goes out sketching: the lootnants go out and kill the birds and animals, or play polo. They wont flee from the wrath to come, not they. When they wont do their military duties I have to do them. It's the same with our religious duties. It's the chaplain's job, not mine; but when you get a real religious chaplain you find he doesnt believe any of the old stuff; and if you get a gentleman, all he cares about is to shew you that he's a real sport and not a mealy mouthed parson. So I have to puzzle it out for myself.

SWEETIE. Well, God help the woman that marries you: thats all I have to say to you. I dont call you a man. [*She rises quickly to escape from him*].

THE SERGEANT [*also rising, and seizing her in a very hearty embrace*] Not a man, eh? [*He kisses her*] How does that feel, Judy?

SWEETIE [*struggling, but not very resolutely*] You let me go, will you. I dont want you now.

THE SERGEANT. You will if I kiss you half a dozen times, more than you ever wanted anything in your life before. Thats a hard fact of human nature; and its one of the facts that religion has to make room for.

SWEETIE. Oh, well, kiss me and have done with it. You cant kiss and talk about religion at the same time.

THE ELDER [*springing from his cell to the platform in front of it*] Forbear this fooling, both of you. You, sir, are not an ignorant man: you know that the universe is wrecked.

SWEETIE [*clinging to the sergeant*] He's mad.

THE ELDER. I am sane in a world of lunatics.

THE SERGEANT [*putting Sweetie away*] It's a queer thing, isnt it, that though there is a point at which I'd rather kiss a woman than do anything else in the world, yet I'd rather be shot than let anyone see me doing it?

THE ELDER. Sir: women are not, as they suppose, more interesting than the universe. When the universe is crumbling let women be silent; and let men rise to something nobler than kissing them.

The Sergeant, interested and overawed, sits down quietly and makes Sweetie sit beside him as before. The Elder continues to declaim with fanatical intensity.

THE ELDER. Yes, sir: the universe of Isaac Newton, which has been an impregnable citadel of modern civilization for three hundred years, has crumbled

[499]

like the walls of Jericho before the criticism of Einstein. Newton's universe was the stronghold of rational Determinism: the stars in their orbits obeyed immutably fixed laws; and when we turned from surveying their vastness to study the infinite littleness of the atoms, there too we found the electrons in their orbits obeying the same universal laws. Every moment of time dictated and determined the following moment, and was itself dictated and determined by the moment that came before it. Everything was calculable: everything happened because it must: the commandments were erased from the tables of the law; and in their place came the cosmic algebra: the equations of the mathematicians. Here was my faith: here I found my dogma of infallibility: I, who scorned alike the Catholic with his vain dream of responsible Free Will, and the Protestant with his pretence of private judgment. And now—now—what is left of it? The orbit of the electron obeys no law: it chooses one path and rejects another: it is as capricious as the planet Mercury, who wanders from his road to warm his hands at the sun. All is caprice: the calculable world has become incalculable: Purpose and Design, the pretexts for all the vilest superstitions, have risen from the dead to cast down the mighty from their seats and put paper crowns on presumptuous fools. Formerly, when differences with my wife, or business worries, tried me too hard, I sought consolation and reassurance in our natural history museums, where I could forget all common cares in wondering at the diversity of forms and colors in the birds and fishes and animals, all produced without the agency of any designer by the operation of Natural Selection. Today I dare not enter an aquarium, because I can see nothing in those grotesque monsters of the deep but the caricatures of

some freakish demon artist: some Zeus-Mephisto-
pheles with paintbox and plasticine, trying to surpass
himself in the production of fantastic and laughable
creatures to people a Noah's ark for his baby. I have
to rush from the building lest I go mad, crying, like
the man in your book, "What must I do to be saved?"
Nothing can save us from a perpetual headlong fall
into a bottomless abyss but a solid footing of dogma;
and we no sooner agree to that than we find that the
only trustworthy dogma is that there is no dogma. As I
stand here I am falling into that abyss, down, down,
down. We are all falling into it; and our dizzy brains
can utter nothing but madness. My wife has died
cursing me. I do not know how to live without her:
we were unhappy together for forty years. My son,
whom I brought up to be an incorruptible Godfearing
atheist, has become a thief and a scoundrel; and I can
say nothing to him but "Go, boy: perish in your
villainy; for neither your father nor anyone else
can now give you a good reason for being a man of
honor."

*He turns from them and is rushing distractedly away
when Aubrey, in white tropicals, comes strolling along
the beach from the St Pauls side, and hails him non-
chalantly.*

AUBREY. Hullo, father, is it really you? I thought I
heard the old trombone: I couldnt mistake it. How
the dickens did you turn up here?

THE ELDER [*to the sergeant*] This is my prodigal son.

AUBREY. I am not a prodigal son. The prodigal son
was a spendthrift and neer-do-weel who was reduced
to eating the husks that the swine did eat. I am not
ruined: I am rolling in money. I have never owed a
farthing to any man. I am a model son; but I regret to
say that you are very far from being a model father.

THE ELDER. What right have you to say that, sir? In what way have I fallen short?

AUBREY. You tried to thwart my manifest destiny. Nature meant me for the Church. I had to get ordained secretly.

THE ELDER. Ordained! You dared to get ordained without my knowledge!

AUBREY. Of course. You objected. How could I have done it with your knowledge? You would have stopped my allowance.

THE ELDER [*sitting down on the nearest stone, overwhelmed*] My son a clergyman! This will kill me.

AUBREY [*coolly taking another stone, on his father's right*] Not a bit of it: fathers are not so easily killed. It was at the university that I became what was then called a sky pilot. When the war took me it seemed natural that I should pursue that avocation as a member of the air force. As a flying ace I won a very poorly designed silver medal for committing atrocities which were irreconcilable with the profession of a Christian clergyman. When I was wounded and lost my nerve for flying, I became an army chaplain. I then found myself obliged to tell mortally wounded men that they were dying in a state of grace and were going straight to heaven when as a matter of fact they were dying in mortal sin and going elsewhere. To expiate this blasphemy I kept as much under fire as possible; but my nerve failed again: I had to take three months leave and go into a nursing home. In that home I met my doom.

THE ELDER. What do you mean by your doom? You are alive and well, to my sorrow and shame.

AUBREY. To be precise, I met Sweetie. Thats Sweetie.

SWEETIE. Very pleased to meet Popsy's father, I'm sure.

THE ELDER. My son was called Popsy in his infancy,
I put a stop to it, on principle, when he entered on his
sixth year. It is strange to hear the name from your
lips after so long an interval.

SWEETIE. I always ask a man what his mother called
him, and call him that. It takes the starch out of him,
somehow.

AUBREY [*resuming his narrative*] Sweetie was quite
the rottenest nurse that ever raised the mortality of a
hospital by ten per cent. But—

SWEETIE. Oh, what a lie! It was the other nurses that
killed the men: waking them up at six in the morning
and washing them! Half of them died of chills.

AUBREY. Well, you will not deny that you were the
prettiest woman in the place.

SWEETIE. You thought so, anyhow.

THE ELDER. Oh, cease—cease this trifling. I cannot
endure this unending sex appeal.

AUBREY. During the war it was found that sex appeal
was as necessary for wounded or shellshocked soldiers
as skilled nursing; so pretty girls were allowed to pose
as nurses because they could sit about on beds and
prevent the men from going mad. Sweetie did not
prevent me going mad: on the contrary, she drove
me mad. I saw in Sweetie not only every charm, but
every virtue. And she returned my love. When I left
that nursing home, she left it too. I was discharged as
cured on the third of the month: she had been kicked
out on the first. The trained staff could stand a good
deal; but they could not stand Sweetie.

SWEETIE. They were jealous; and you know it.

AUBREY. I daresay they were. Anyhow, Sweetie and I
took the same lodgings; and she was faithful to me
for ten days. It was a record for her.

SWEETIE. Popsy: are you going to give the whole

show away, or only part of it? The Countess Valbrioni would like to know.

AUBREY. We may as well be frank up to the point at which we should lose money by it. But perhaps I am boring the company.

THE ELDER. Complete your confession, sir. You have just said that you and this lady took the same lodging. Am I to understand that you are husband and wife.

SWEETIE. We might have been if we could have depended on you for a good time. But how could I marry an army chaplain with nothing but his pay and an atheist for his father?

AUBREY. So that was the calculation, Sweetie, was it? I never dreamt that the idea of marriage had occurred to either of us. It certainly never occurred to me. I went to live with you quite simply because I felt I could not live without you. The improbability of that statement is the measure of my infatuation.

SWEETIE. Dont you be so spiteful. Did I give you a good time or did I not?

AUBREY. Heavenly. That also seems improbable; but it is gospel truth.

THE ELDER. Wretched boy: do not dare to trifle with me. You said just now that you owe no man anything, and that you are rolling in money. Where did you get that money?

AUBREY. I stole a very valuable pearl necklace and restored it to the owner. She rewarded me munificently. Hence my present opulence. Honesty is the best policy—sometimes.

THE ELDER. Worse even than a clergyman! A thief!

AUBREY. Why make such a fuss about nothing?

THE ELDER. Do you call the theft of a pearl necklace nothing?

AUBREY. Less than nothing, compared to the things

I have done with your approval. I was hardly more than a boy when I first dropped a bomb on a sleeping village. I cried all night after doing that. Later on I swooped into a street and sent machine gun bullets into a crowd of civilians: women, children, and all. I was past crying by that time. And now you preach to me about stealing a pearl necklace! Doesnt that seem a little ridiculous?

THE SERGEANT. That was war, sir.

AUBREY. It was me, sergeant: ME. You cannot divide my conscience into a war department and a peace department. Do you suppose that a man who will commit murder for political ends will hesitate to commit theft for personal ends? Do you suppose you can make a man the mortal enemy of sixty millions of his fellow creatures without making him a little less scrupulous about his next door neighbour?

THE ELDER. I did not approve. Had I been of military age I should have been a conscientious objector.

AUBREY. Oh, you were a conscientious objector to everything, even to God. But my mother was an enthusiast for everything: that was why you never could get on with her. She would have shoved me into the war if I had needed any shoving. She shoved my brother into it, though he did not believe a word of all the lies we were stuffed with, and didnt want to go. He was killed; and when it came out afterwards that he was right, and that we were all a parcel of fools killing one another for nothing, she lost the courage to face life, and died of it.

THE SERGEANT. Well, sir, I'd never let a son of mine talk to me like that. Let him have a bit of your Determinism, sir.

THE ELDER [*rising impulsively*] Determinism is gone, shattered, buried with a thousand dead religions, evaporated with the clouds of a million forgotten winters. The science I pinned my faith to is bankrupt: its tales were more foolish than all the miracles of the priests, its cruelties more horrible than all the atrocities of the Inquisition. Its spread of enlightenment has been a spread of cancer: its counsels that were to have established the millennium have led straight to European suicide. And I—I who believed in it as no religious fanatic has ever believed in his superstition! For its sake I helped to destroy the faith of millions of worshippers in the temples of a thousand creeds. And now look at me and behold the supreme tragedy of the atheist who has lost his faith—his faith in atheism, for which more martyrs have perished than for all the creeds put together. Here I stand, dumb before my scoundrel of a son; for that is what you are, boy, a common scoundrel and nothing else.

AUBREY. Well, why not? If I become an honest man I shall become a poor man; and then nobody will respect me: nobody will admire me: nobody will say thank you to me. If on the contrary I am bold, unscrupulous, acquisitive, successful and rich, everyone will respect me, admire me, court me, grovel before me. Then no doubt I shall be able to afford the luxury of honesty. I learnt that from my religious education.

THE ELDER. How dare you say that you had a religious education. I shielded you from that, at least.

AUBREY. You thought you did, old man; but you reckoned without my mother.

THE ELDER. What!

AUBREY. You forbad me to read the Bible; but my mother made me learn three verses of it every day, and whacked me if I could not repeat them without misplacing a word. She threatened to whack me still worse if I told you.

THE ELDER [*thunderstruck*] Your mother!!!

AUBREY. So I learnt my lesson. Six days on the make, and on the seventh shalt thou rest. I shall spend another six years on the make, and then I shall retire and be a saint.

THE ELDER. A saint! Say rather the ruined son of an incorrigibly superstitious mother. Retire now—from the life you have dishonored. There is the sea. Go. Drown yourself. In that graveyard there are no lying epitaphs. [*He mounts to his chapel and again gives way to utter dejection*].

AUBREY [*unconcerned*] I shall do better as a saint. A few thousands to the hospitals and the political party funds will buy me a halo as large as Sweetie's sun hat. That is my program. What have any of you to say against it?

THE SERGEANT. Not the program of a gentleman, as I understand the word, sir.

AUBREY. You cannot be a gentleman on less than fifty thousand a year nowadays, sergeant.

THE SERGEANT. You can in the army, by God.

AUBREY. Yes: because you drop bombs on sleeping villages. And even then you have to be an officer. Are you a gentleman?

THE SERGEANT. No, sir: it wouldnt pay me. I couldnt afford it.

Disturbance. A voice is heard in complaint and lamentation. It is that of the Elderly Lady, Mrs Mopply. She is pursuing Colonel Tallboys down the path through the gap, the lady distracted and insistent, the colonel almost equally distracted: she clutching him and stopping him: he breaking loose and trying to get away from her. She is dressed in black precisely as if she were in Cheltenham, except that she wears a sun helmet. He is equipped with a box of sketching materials slung over his shoulder, an easel, which he has tucked under his left arm, and a sun umbrella, a substantial affair of fawn lined with red, podgily rolled up, which he carries in his right hand.

MRS MOPPLY. I wont be patient. I wont be quiet. My child is being murdered.

TALLBOYS. I tell you she is not being murdered. Will you be good enough to excuse me whilst I attend to my business.

MRS MOPPLY. Your business is to save my child. She is starving.

TALLBOYS. Nonsense. Nobody starves in this country. There are plenty of dates. Will you be good enough—

MRS MOPPLY. Do you think my child can live on dates? She has to have a sole for breakfast, a cup of nourishing soup at eleven, and a nice chop and a sweetbread for lunch, a pint of beef-tea with her ordinary afternoon tea, and a chicken and some lamb or veal—

TALLBOYS. Will you be good enough—

MRS MOPPLY. My poor delicate child with nothing to eat but dates! And she is the only one I have left: they were all delicate—

TALLBOYS. I really must— [*He breaks away and hurries off along the beach past the Abode of Love*].

MRS MOPPLY [*running after him*] Colonel, Colonel: you might have the decency to listen to a distracted mother for a moment. Colonel: my child is dying. She may be dead for all I know. And nobody is doing anything: nobody cares. Oh dear, wont you listen— [*Her voice is lost in the distance*].

Whilst they are staring mutely after the retreating pair, the patient, still in her slave girl attire, but with some brilliant variations, comes down the path.

THE PATIENT. My dream has become a nightmare.

My mother has pursued me to these shores. I cannot shake her off. No woman can shake off her mother. There should be no mothers: there should be only women, strong women able to stand by themselves, not clingers. I would kill all the clingers. Mothers cling: daughters cling: we are all like drunken women clinging to lamp posts: none of us stands upright.

THE ELDER. There is great comfort in clinging, and great loneliness in standing alone.

THE PATIENT. Hallo! [*She climbs to the St Pauls platform and peers into the cell*]. A sententious anchorite! [*To Aubrey*]. Who is he?

AUBREY. The next worst thing to a mother: a father.

THE ELDER. A most unhappy father.

AUBREY. My father, in fact.

THE PATIENT. If only I had had a father to stand between me and my mother's care. Oh, that I had been an orphan!

THE SERGEANT. You will be, miss, if the old lady drives the colonel too hard. She has been at him all the morning, ever since she arrived; and I know the colonel. He has a temper; and when it gives way, it's a bit of high explosive. He'll kill her if she pushes him too far.

THE PATIENT. Let him kill her. I am young and strong: I want a world without parents: there is no room for them in my dream. I shall found a sisterhood.

AUBREY. All right, Mops. Get thee to a nunnery.

THE PATIENT. It need not be a nunnery if men will come in without spoiling everything. But all the women must be rich. There must be no chill of poverty. There are plenty of rich women like me who hate being devoured by parasites.

AUBREY. Stop. You have the most disgusting mental

pictures. I really cannot stand intellectual coarseness. Sweetie's vulgarity I can forgive and even enjoy. But you say perfectly filthy things that stick in my mind, and break my spirit. I can bear no more of it. [*He rises angrily and tries to escape by the beach past the Abode of Love*].

SWEETIE. Youre dainty, arnt you? If chambermaids were as dainty as you, youd have to empty your own slops.

AUBREY [*recoiling from her with a yell of disgust*] You need not throw them in my teeth, you beast. [*He sits in his former place, sulking*].

THE ELDER. Silence, boy. These are home truths. They are good for you. [*To the patient*] May I ask young woman, what are the relations between you and my son, whom you seem to know.

THE PATIENT. Popsy stole my necklace, and got me to run away with him by a wonderful speech he made about freedom and sunshine and lovely scenery. Sweetie made me write it all down and sell it to a tourist agency as an advertisement. And then I was devoured by parasites: by tourist agencies, steamboat companies, railways, motor car people, hotel keepers, dressmakers, servants, all trying to get my money by selling me things I dont really want; shoving me all over the globe to look at what they call new skies, though they know as well as I do that it is only the same old sky everywhere; and disabling me by doing all the things for me that I ought to do for myself to keep myself in health. They preyed on me to keep themselves alive: they pretended they were making me happy when it was only by drinking and drugging—cocktails and cocaine—that I could endure my life.

AUBREY. I regret to have to say it, Mops; but you have

not the instincts of a lady. [*He sits down moodily on a stone a little way up the path*].

THE PATIENT. You fool, there is no such thing as a lady. I have the instincts of a good housekeeper: I want to clean up this filthy world and keep it clean. There must be other women who want it too. Florence Nightingale had the same instinct when she went to clean up the Crimean war. She wanted a sisterhood; but there wasnt one.

THE ELDER. There were several. But steeped in superstition, unfortunately.

THE PATIENT. Yes, all mixed up with things that I dont believe. Women have to set themselves apart to join them. I dont want to set myself apart. I want to have every woman in my sisterhood, and to have all the others strangled.

THE ELDER. Down! down! down! Even the young, the strong, the rich, the beautiful, feel that they are plunging into a bottomless pit.

THE SERGEANT. Your set, miss, if you will excuse me saying so, is only a small bit of the world. If you dont like the officers' mess, the ranks are open to you. Look at Meek! That man could be an emperor if he laid his mind to it: but he'd rather be a private. He's happier so.

THE PATIENT. I dont belong to the poor, and dont want to. I always knew that there were thousands of poor people; and I was taught to believe that they were poor because God arranged it that way to punish them for being dirty and drunken and dishonest, and not knowing how to read and write. But I didnt know that the rich were miserable. I didnt know that I was miserable. I didnt know that our respectability was uppish snobbery and our religion gluttonous selfishness, and that my soul was starving on them. I know

now. I have found myself out thoroughly—in my dream.

THE ELDER. You are young. Some good man may cure you of this for a few happy years. When you fall in love, life will seem worth living.

THE PATIENT. I did fall in love. With that thing. And though I was never a hotel chambermaid I got tired of him sooner than Sweetie did. Love gets people into difficulties, not out of them. No more lovers for me: I want a sisterhood. Since I came here I have been wanting to join the army, like Joan of Arc. It's a brotherhood, of a sort.

THE SERGEANT. Yes, miss: that is so; and there used to be a peace of mind in the army that you could find nowhere else. But the war made an end of that. You see, miss, the great principle of soldiering, I take it, is that the world is kept going by the people who want the right thing killing the people who want the wrong thing. When the soldier is doing that, he is doing the work of God, which my mother brought me up to do. But thats a very different thing from killing a man because he's a German and he killing you because youre an Englishman. We were not killing the right people in 1915. We werent even killing the wrong people. It was innocent men killing one another.

THE PATIENT. Just for the fun of it.

THE SERGEANT. No, miss: it was no fun. For the misery of it.

THE PATIENT. For the devilment of it, then.

THE SERGEANT. For the devilment of the godless rulers of this world. Those that did the killing hadnt even the devilment to comfort them: what comfort is there in screwing on a fuse or pulling a string when the devilment it makes is from three to forty miles off, and you dont know whether you have only made a harmless hole in the ground or blown up a baby in its cradle that might have been your own? That wasnt devilment: it was damnation. No, miss: the bottom has come out of soldiering. What the gentleman here said about our all falling into a bottomless pit came home to me. I feel like that too.

THE ELDER. Lost souls, all of us.

THE PATIENT. No: only lost dogs. Cheer up, old man: the lost dogs always find their way home. [*The voice of the Elderly Lady is heard returning*]. Oh! here she comes again!

Mrs Mopply is still pursuing the colonel, who is walking doggedly and steadily away from her, with closed lips and a dangerous expression on his set features.

MRS MOPPLY. You wont even speak to me. It's a disgrace. I will send a cable message home to the Government about it. You were sent out here to rescue my daughter from these dreadful brigands. Why is nothing being done? What are the relations between yourself and that disgraceful countess who ought to have her coronet stripped off her back? You are all in a conspiracy to murder my poor lost darling child. You are in league with the brigands. You are—

The Colonel turns at bay, and brings down his umbrella whack on poor Mrs Mopply's helmet.

MRS MOPPLY. Oh! Oh! Oh! Oh! [*With a series of short, dry, detached screams she totters and flutters back along the beach out of sight like a wounded bird*].

General stupefaction. All stare at the Colonel aghast. The Sergeant rises in amazement, and remains standing afterwards as a matter of military etiquette.

THE PATIENT. Oh, if only someone had done that to her twenty years ago, how different my childhood would have been! But I must see to the poor old dear. [*She runs after her mother*].

[513]

AUBREY. Colonel: you have our full, complete, unreserved sympathy. We thank you from the bottom of our hearts. But that does not alter the fact that the man who would raise his hand to a woman, save in the way of kindness, is unworthy the name of Briton.

TALLBOYS. I am perfectly aware of that, sir. I need no reminder. The lady is entitled to an apology. She shall have it.

THE ELDER. But have you considered the possibility of a serious injury—

TALLBOYS [*cutting him short*] My umbrella is quite uninjured, thank you. The subject is now closed. [*He sits down on the stone below St Pauls recently vacated by Aubrey. His manner is so decisive that nobody dares carry the matter further*].

As they sit uneasily seeking one another's eyes and avoiding them again, dumbfounded by the violence of the catastrophe, a noise like that of a machine gun in action reaches their ears from afar. It increases to shattering intensity as it approaches. They all put their fingers to their ears. It diminishes slightly, then suddenly rises to a climax of speed and uproar, and stops.

TALLBOYS. Meek.

AUBREY. Meek.

SWEETIE. Meek.

THE ELDER. What is this? Why do you all say Meek?

Meek, dusty and gritty, but very alert, comes down the path through the gap with a satchel of papers.

TALLBOYS. My dear Meek, can you not be content with a motor cycle of ordinary horse power? Must you always travel at eighty miles an hour?

MEEK. I have good news for you, Colonel; and good news should travel fast.

TALLBOYS. For me?

MEEK. Your K.C.B., sir. [*Presenting a paper*] Honors list by wireless.

TALLBOYS [*rising joyously to take the paper*] Ah! Congratulate me, my friends. My dear Sarah is Lady Tallboys at last. [*He resumes his seat and pores over the paper*].

AUBREY ⎫
THE SERGEANT ⎬ [*together*] ⎨ Splendid!
 ⎭ You deserve it, sir, if I
  may say so.
SWEETIE Delighted, I am sure.

THE ELDER. May I crave to know the nature of the distinguished service which has won this official recognition, sir?

TALLBOYS. I have won the battle of the maroons. I have suppressed brigandage here. I have rescued a British lady from the clutches of the brigands. The Government is preparing for a general election, and has had to make the most of these modest achievements.

THE ELDER. Brigands! Are there any here?

TALLBOYS. None.

THE ELDER. But—? The British lady? In their clutches?

TALLBOYS. She has been in my clutches, and perfectly safe, all the time.

THE ELDER [*more and more puzzled*] Oh! Then the battle of the—

TALLBOYS. Won by Private Meek. I had nothing whatever to do with it.

AUBREY. I invented the brigands and the British lady. [*To Tallboys*] By the way, Colonel, the impressive old party in the shrine is my father.

TALLBOYS. Indeed! Happy to meet you, sir, though I cannot congratulate you on your son, except in so far as you have brought into the world the most abandoned liar I have ever met.

THE ELDER. And may I ask sir, is it your intention not only to condone my son's frauds, but to take advantage of them to accept a distinction which you have in no way earned?

TALLBOYS. I have earned it, sir, ten times over. Do you suppose, because the brigandage which I am honored for suppressing has no existence, that I have never suppressed real brigands? Do you forget that though this battle of which I am crowned victor was won by a subordinate, I, too, have won real battles, and seen all the honors go to a brigadier who did not even know what was happening? In the army these things average themselves out: merit is rewarded in the long run. Justice is none the less justice though it is always delayed, and finally done by mistake. My turn today: Private Meek's tomorrow.

THE ELDER. And meanwhile Mr Meek—this humble and worthy soldier—is to remain in obscurity and poverty whilst you are strutting as a K.C.B.

TALLBOYS. How I envy him! Look at me and look at him! I, loaded with responsibilities whilst my hands are tied, my body disabled, my mind crippled because a colonel must not do anything but give orders and look significant and profound when his mind is entirely vacant! he, free to turn his hand to everything and to look like an idiot when he feels like one! I have been driven to sketching in watercolors because I may not use my hands in life's daily useful business. A commanding officer must not do this, must not do that, must not do the other, must not do anything but tell other men to do it. He may not even converse with them. I see this man Meek doing everything that is natural to a complete man: carpentering, painting, digging, pulling and hauling, fetching and carrying, helping himself and everybody else, whilst I, with a bigger body to exercise and quite as much energy, must loaf and loll, allowed to do nothing but read the papers and drink brandy and water to prevent myself going mad. I should have become a drunkard had it not been for the colors.

THE SERGEANT. Ah yes, sir, the colors. The fear of disgracing them has kept me off the drink many a time.

TALLBOYS. Man: I do not mean the regimental colors, but the water colors. How willingly would I exchange my pay, my rank, my K.C.B., for Meek's poverty, his obscurity!

MEEK. But, my dear Colonel—sorry, sir: what I mean to say is that you can become a private if you wish. Nothing easier: I have done it again and again. You resign your commission; take a new and very common name by deed poll; dye your hair and give your age to the recruiting sergeant as twenty-two; and there you are! You can select your own regiment.

TALLBOYS. Meek: you should not tantalize your commanding officer. No doubt you are an extraordinary soldier. But have you ever passed the extreme and final test of manly courage?

MEEK. Which one is that, sir?

TALLBOYS. Have you ever married?

MEEK. No, sir.

TALLBOYS. Then do not ask me why I do not resign my commission and become a free and happy private. My wife would not let me.

THE COUNTESS. Why dont you hit her on the head with your umbrella?

TALLBOYS. I dare not. There are moments when I wish some other man would. But in my presence I should kill him.

THE ELDER. We are all slaves. But at least your son is an honest man.

7]

TALLBOYS. Is he? I am glad to hear it. I have not spoken to him since he shirked military service at the beginning of the war and went into trade as a contractor. He is now so enormously rich that I cannot afford to keep up his acquaintance. Neither need you keep up that of your son. By the way, he passes here as the half step-brother of this lady, the Countess Valbrioni.

SWEETIE. Valbrioni be blowed! My name is Susan Simpkins. Being a countess isnt worth a damn. There's no variety in it: no excitement. What I want is a month's leave for the sergeant. Wont you give it to him, Colonel?

TALLBOYS. What for?

SWEETIE. Never mind what for. A fortnight might do; but I dont know for certain yet. There's something steadying about him; and I suppose I will have to settle down some day.

TALLBOYS. Nonsense! The sergeant is a pious man, not your sort. Eh, Sergeant?

SERGEANT. Well, sir, a man should have one woman to prevent him from thinking too much about women in general. You cannot read your Bible undisturbed if visions and wandering thoughts keep coming between you and it. And a pious man should not marry a pious woman: two of a trade never agree. Besides, it would give the children a onesided view of life. Life is very mixed, sir: it is not all piety and it is not all gaiety. This woman has no conscience; but I have enough for two. Mind: I am not committing myself so far as to say that I am not dead set against it. I have no money; but she seems to have enough. I am not committing myself to the vanities—and we have to live in it, you know, sir—the plane of this world and its this world and its she appeals to me.

AUBREY. Take care, sergeant. Constancy is not Sweetie's strong point.

THE SERGEANT. Neither is it mine. As a single man and a wandering soldier I am fair game for every woman. But if I settle down with this girl she will keep the others off. I'm a bit tired of adventures.

SWEETIE. Well, if the truth must be told, so am I. We were made for one another, Sergeant. What do you say?

THE SERGEANT. Well, I dont mind keeping company for a while, Susan, just to see how we get along together.

The voice of Mrs Mopply is again heard. Its tone is hardy and even threatening; and its sound is approaching rapidly.

MRS MOPPLY'S VOICE. You just let me alone, will you? Nobody asked you to interfere. Get away with you.

General awe and dismay. Mrs Mopply appears striding resolutely along the beach. She walks straight up to the Colonel, and is about to address him when he rises firmly to the occasion and takes the word out of her mouth.

TALLBOYS. Mrs Mopply: I have a duty to you which I must discharge at once. At our last meeting, I struck you.

MRS MOPPLY. Struck me! You bashed me. Is that what you mean?

TALLBOYS. If you consider my expression inadequate I am willing to amend it. Let us put it that I bashed you. Well, I apologize without reserve, fully and amply. If you wish, I will give it to you in writing.

MRS MOPPLY. Very well. Since you express your regret, I suppose there is nothing more to be said.

TALLBOYS [*darkening ominously*] Pardon me. I apologized. I did not express my regret.

AUBREY. Oh, for heaven's sake, Colonel, dont start her again. Dont qualify your apology in any way.

MRS MOPPLY. You shut up, whoever you are.

TALLBOYS. I do not qualify my apology in the least. My apology is complete. The lady has a right to it. My action was inexcusable. But no lady—no human being—has a right to impose a falsehood on me. I do not regret my action. I have never done anything which gave me more thorough and hearty satisfaction. When I was a company officer I once cut down an enemy in the field. Had I not done so he would have cut me down. It gave me no satisfaction: I was half ashamed of it. I have never before spoken of it. But this time I struck with unmixed enjoyment. In fact I am grateful to Mrs Mopply. I owe her one of the very few delightfully satisfactory moments of my life.

MRS MOPPLY. Well, thats a pretty sort of apology, isnt it?

TALLBOYS [*firmly*] I have nothing to add, madam.

MRS MOPPLY. Well, I forgive you, you peppery old blighter.

Sensation. They catch their breaths, and stare at one another in consternation. The patient arrives.

THE PATIENT. I am sorry to say, Colonel Tallboys, that you have unsettled my mother's reason. She wont believe that I am her daughter. She's not a bit like herself.

MRS MOPPLY. Isnt she? What do you know about myself? my real self? They told me lies; and I had to pretend to be somebody quite different.

TALLBOYS. Who told you lies, madam? It was not with my authority.

MRS MOPPLY. I wasnt thinking of you. My mother told me lies. My nurse told me lies. My governess told me lies. Everybody told me lies. The world is not a bit like what they said it was. I wasnt a bit like what they said I ought to be. I thought I had to pretend. And I neednt have pretended at all.

THE ELDER. Another victim! She, too, is falling through the bottomless abyss.

MRS MOPPLY. I dont know who you are or what you think you mean; but you have just hit it: I dont know my head from my heels. Why did they tell me that children couldnt live without medicine and three meat meals a day? Do you know that I have killed two of my children because they told me that? My own children! Murdered them, just!

THE ELDER. Medea! Medea!

MRS MOPPLY. It isnt an idea: it's the truth. I will never believe anything again as long as I live. I'd have killed the only one I had left if she hadnt run away from me. I was told to sacrifice myself—to live for others; and I did it if ever a woman did. They told me that everyone would love me for it; and I thought they would; but my daughter ran away when I had sacrificed myself to her until I found myself wishing she would die like the others and leave me a little to myself. And now I find it was not only my daughter that hated me but all my friends, all the time they were pretending to sympathize, were just longing to bash me over the head with their umbrellas. This poor man only did what all the rest would have done if theyd dared. When I said I forgave you I meant it: I am greatly obliged to you. [*She kisses him*]. But now what am I to do? How am I to behave in a world thats just the opposite of everything I was told about it?

THE PATIENT. Steady, mother! steady! steady! Sit down. [*She picks up a heavy stone and places it near the Abode of Love for Mrs Mopply to sit on*].

MRS MOPPLY [*seating herself*] Dont you call me mother. Do you think my daughter could carry rocks about like that? she that had to call the nurse to pick

up her Pekingese dog when she wanted to pet it! You
think you can get round me by pretending to be my
daughter; but that just shews what a fool you are; for
I hate my daughter and my daughter hates me, because I sacrificed myself to her. She was a horrid
selfish girl, always ill and complaining, and never
satisfied, no matter how much you did for her. The
only sensible thing she ever did was to steal her own
necklace and sell it and run away to spend the money
on herself. I expect she's in bed somewhere with a
dozen nurses and six doctors all dancing attendance
on her. Youre not a bit like her, thank goodness: thats
why Ive taken a fancy to you. You come with me,
darling. I have lots of money, and sixty years of a
misspent life to make up for; so you will have a good
time with me. Come with me as my companion; and
lets forget that there are such miserable things in the
world as mothers and daughters.

THE PATIENT. What use shall we be to one another?

MRS MOPPLY. None, thank God. We can do without
one another if we dont hit it off.

THE PATIENT. Righto! I'll take you on trial until Ive
had time to look about me and see what I'm going to
do. But only on trial, mind.

MRS MOPPLY. Just so, darling. We'll both be on trial.
So thats settled.

THE PATIENT. And now, Mr Meek, what about the
little commission you promised to do for me? Have
you brought back my passport?

THE COUNTESS. Your passport! Whatever for?

AUBREY. What have you been up to, Mops? Are you
going to desert me?

*Meek advances and empties a heap of passports from
his satchel on the sand, kneeling down to sort out the
patient's.*

TALLBOYS. What is the meaning of this? Whose passports are these? What are you doing with them? Where did you get them?

MEEK. Everybody within fifty miles is asking me to get a passport visa'd.

TALLBOYS. Visa'd! For what country?

MEEK. For Beotia, sir.

TALLBOYS. Beotia?

MEEK. Yessir. The Union of Federated Sensible Societies, sir. The U.F.S.S. Everybody wants to go there now, sir.

THE COUNTESS. Well I never!

THE ELDER. And what is to become of our unhappy country if all its inhabitants desert it for an outlandish place in which even property is not respected?

MEEK. No fear, sir: they wont have us. They wont admit any more English, sir: they say their lunatic asylums are too full already. I couldnt get a single visa, except [*to the Colonel*] for you, sir.

TALLBOYS. For me! Damn their impudence! I never asked for one.

MEEK. No, sir; but their people have so much leisure that they are at their wits' end for some occupation to keep them out of mischief. They want to introduce the only institution of ours that they admire.

THE ELDER. And pray which one is that?

MEEK. The English school of watercolor painting, sir. Theyve seen some of the Colonel's work; and theyll make him head of their centres of repose and culture if he'll settle there.

TALLBOYS. This cannot be true, Meek. It indicates a degree of intelligence of which no Government is capable.

MEEK. It's true, sir, I assure you.

TALLBOYS. But my wife—

MEEK. Yessir: I told them. [*He repacks his satchel*].

TALLBOYS. Well, well: there is nothing for it but to return to our own country.

THE ELDER. Can our own country return to its senses, sir? that is the question.

TALLBOYS. Ask Meek.

MEEK. No use, sir: all the English privates want to be colonels: there's no salvation for snobs. [*To Tallboys*] Shall I see about getting the expedition back to England, sir?

TALLBOYS. Yes. And get me two tubes of rose madder and a big one of Chinese White, will you?

MEEK [*about to go*] Yessir.

THE ELDER. Stop. There are police in England. What is to become of my son there?

SWEETIE [*rising*] Make Popsy a preacher, old man. But dont start him until weve gone.

THE ELDER. Preach, my son, preach to your heart's content. Do anything rather than steal and make your military crimes an excuse for your civil ones. Let men call you the reverend. Let them call you anything rather than thief.

AUBREY [*rising*] If I may be allowed to improve the occasion for a moment—

General consternation. All who are seated rise in alarm, except the patient, who jumps up and claps her hands in mischievous encouragement to the orator.

MRS MOPPLY		You hold your tongue, young man.
SWEETIE		Oh Lord! we're in for it now.
THE ELDER	[*together*]	Shame and silence would better become you, sir.
THE PATIENT		Go on, Pops. It's the only thing you do well.

[524]

AUBREY [*continuing*]—it is clear to me that though we seem to be dispersing quietly to do very ordinary things: Sweetie and the Sergeant to get married [*the Sergeant hastily steals down from his grotto, beckoning to Sweetie to follow him. They both escape along the beach*] the colonel to his wife, his watercolors, and his K.C.B. [*the colonel hurries away noiselessly in the opposite direction*] Napoleon Alexander Trotsky Meek to his job of repatriating the expedition [*Meek takes to flight up the path through the gap*] Mops, like Saint Teresa, to found an unladylike sisterhood with her mother as cook-housekeeper [*Mrs Mopply hastily follows the sergeant, dragging with her the patient, who is listening to Aubrey with signs of becoming rapt in his discourse*] yet they are all, like my father here, falling, falling, falling endlessly and hopelessly through a void in which they can find no footing. [*The Elder vanishes into the recesses of St Pauls, leaving his son to preach in solitude*]. There is something fantastic about them, something unreal and perverse, something profoundly unsatisfactory. They are too absurd to be believed in: yet they are not fictions: the newspapers are full of them: what storyteller, however reckless a liar, would dare to invent figures so improbable as men and women with their minds stripped naked? Naked bodies no longer shock us: our sunbathers, grinning at us from every illustrated summer number of our magazines, are nuder than shorn lambs. But the horror of the naked mind is still more than we can bear. Throw off the last rag of your bathing costume; and I shall not blench nor expect you to blush. You may even throw away the outer garments of your souls: the manners, the morals, the decencies. Swear; use dirty words; drink cocktails; kiss and caress and cuddle until girls who are like roses at eighteen are like battered demireps at twenty-two: in all these ways the bright young things of the victory have scandalized their dull old prewar elders and left nobody but their bright young selves a penny the worse. But how are we to bear this dreadful new nakedness: the nakedness of the souls who until now have always disguised themselves from one another in beautiful impossible idealisms to enable them to bear one another's company. The iron lighting of war has burnt great rents in these angelic veils, just as it has smashed great holes in our cathedral roofs and torn great gashes in our hillsides. Our souls go in rags now; and the young are spying through the holes and getting glimpses of the reality that was hidden. And they are not horrified: they exult in having found us out: they expose their own souls; and when we their elders desperately try to patch our torn clothes with scraps of the old material, the young lay violent hands on us and tear from us even the rags that were left to us. But when they have stripped themselves and us utterly naked, will they be able to bear the spectacle? You have seen me try to strip my soul before my father; but when these two young women stripped themselves more boldly than I—when the old woman had the mask struck from her soul and revelled in it instead of dying of it—I shrank from the revelation as from a wind bringing from the unknown regions of the future a breath which may be a breath of life, but of a life too keen for me to bear, and therefore for me a blast of death. I stand midway between youth and age like a man who has missed his train: too late for the last and too early for the next. What am I to do? What am I? A soldier who has lost his nerve, a thief who at his first great theft has found honesty the best policy and restored his booty to its owner. Nature

never intended me for soldiering or thieving: I am by
nature and destiny a preacher. I am the new Ecclesiastes. But I have no Bible, no creed: the war has shot
both out of my hands. The war has been a fiery
forcing house in which we have grown with a rush like
flowers in a late spring following a terrible winter. And
with what result? This: that we have outgrown our
religion, outgrown our political system, outgrown our
own strength of mind and character. The fatal word
NOT has been miraculously inserted into all our creeds:
in the desecrated temples where we knelt murmuring
"I believe" we stand with stiff knees and stiffer necks
shouting "Up, all! the erect posture is the mark of the
man: let lesser creatures kneel and crawl: we will not
kneel and we do not believe." But what next? Is NO
enough? For a boy, yes: for a man, never. Are we
any the less obsessed with a belief when we are denying it than when we were affirming it? No: I must
have affirmations to preach. Without them the young
will not listen to me; for even the young grow tired of
denials. The negativemonger falls before the soldiers,
the men of action, the fighters, strong in the old uncompromising affirmations which give them status,
duties, certainty of consequences; so that the pugna-
cious spirit of man in them can reach out and strike
deathblows with steadfastly closed minds. Their way
is straight and sure; but it is the way of death; and
the preacher must preach the way of life. Oh, if I
could only find it! [*A white sea fog swirls up from the
beach to his feet, rising and thickening round him*]. I am
ignorant: I have lost my nerve and am intimidated:
all I know is that I must find the way of life, for myself and all of us, or we shall surely perish. And meanwhile my gift has possession of me: I must preach and
preach and preach no matter how late the hour and

[527]

how short the day, no matter whether I have nothing to say—

The fog has enveloped him; the gap with its grottoes is lost to sight; the ponderous stones are wisps of shifting white cloud; there is left only fog: impenetrable fog; but the incorrigible preacher will not be denied his peroration, which, could we only hear it distinctly, would probably run—

—or whether in some pentecostal flame of revelation the Spirit will descend on me and inspire me with a message the sound whereof shall go out unto all lands and realize for us at last the Kingdom and the Power and the Glory for ever and ever. Amen.

The audience disperses (or the reader puts down the book) impressed in the English manner with the Pentecostal flame and the echo from the Lord's Prayer. But fine words butter no parsnips. A few of the choicer spirits will know that the Pentecostal flame is always alight at the service of those strong enough to bear its terrible intensity. They will not forget that it is accompanied by a rushing mighty wind, and that any rascal who happens to be also a windbag can get a prodigious volume of talk out of it without ever going near enough to be shrivelled up. The author, though himself a professional talk maker, does not believe that the world can be saved by talk alone. He has given the rascal the last word; but his own favorite is the woman of action, who begins by knocking the wind out of the rascal, and ends with a cheerful conviction that the lost dogs always find their own way home. So they will, perhaps, if the women go out and look for them.

From the Malvern Festival Book, 1932

Too True to be Good was written for Malvern; but
as the Malvern Festival comes only once a year, the
Theatre Guild of the United States captured the first
performance, with Poland a good second. The American critics (whom you must carefully distinguish from
the American public) on the whole disliked the play.
I am used to that; but this time they annoyed me by
taking the young gentleman-soldier-burglar-chaplain
in the play to be the mouthpiece of my own opinions
and the mirror of my own temperament, and inform-
ing the world that I am finishing my life in a condition
of pitiable but theatrically very tiresome disillusion
and despair, having recanted all my professions, renounced all my convictions, abandoned all my hopes,
and demolished all my Utopias.

Many people are like that, both in America and
here: if you hint that there is not a paradise they call
you a pessimist, though they never stop grumbling
at the abominable way in which they are being treated
by their own Governments. They also never tire of
repeating that I point out evils without suggesting
remedies, and am therefore not a practical man. Lest
our English critics should start all that over again when
they come down to Malvern—and many of them are
quite capable of it—let me hasten to assure them that
I have not recanted, renounced, abandoned, nor demolished anything whatever, and that extremely practical and precise remedies, including a complete
political reconstitution, a credible and scientific
religion, and a satisfactory economic scheme, are
discoverable by anyone under thirty (the older ones
are past praying for) who will take the trouble to bring

his or her education up to date by retiring into a House of Study and Contemplation and reading my works carefully through from beginning to end. I wrote them with a view to that; for though my trade is that of a playwright, my vocation is that of a prophet, with occasional lapses into what uncivil people call buffoonery. If my admirers dislike these lapses they should take care not to make me laugh, and to remember that there are others who think that I am endurable only when I indulge my unfortunate sense of humor.

In Poland, where criticism seems better equipped culturally, the success of the play so terrified the authorities, that they sacked the censor who had, in deference to my reputation, passed the play without reading it. Do not, however, waste sympathy on this enlightened official: he was reinstated three days later, presumably to avert a pro-Shavian revolution; and the play was allowed to proceed subject to the excision of all the disparagements of war in the last act. I invite the attention of the League of Nations, and of all Pacifist leagues and conferences, to this gesture by the Polish Government, and the light it throws on the real views of Poland as to the moral respectability—not to say glory—of war. Not that I would suggest for a moment that those views are a jot different from the views of the other imperialist States; but none of them have been quite so candid about it as the Polish Government in this instance.

The moral of my play, or rather the position illustrated by it, is simple enough. When wars were waged by professional armies, the reversal of morality which they involved was kept in a conscience-tight compartment: a civilian population might talk wickedly enough in its patriotic fervor; but it did not know what it was talking about: the actual slaughter and sack and rapine was only a story in the newspapers, not a real experience. But a war like that of 1914–18, in which the whole male population of military age was forced to serve, hosts of women volunteered for work under fire, and the new feature of aerial bombardment brought the bloody part of the business crash into the civilians' bedrooms, was quite another matter. The shock to common morals was enormously greater and more general. So was the strain on the nerves. This time all the old romantic pretences of "fearlessness" were dropped: nobody pretended to be immune either from actual funk under the barrage or from the wild reaction into security and hero-worship when at home on leave. When terror had gone to its limit, subsequent indulgence for everything, from the pitch and tone of a night at The Byng Boys to the manslaughter of a correspondent, obeyed the law that action and reaction are equal. And so, for four years, it was taken as a matter of course that young people, when they were not under fire, must be allowed a good time.

Now I do not at all object to young people having a good time. I think they should have a good time all the time, at peace as well as in war. I think that their having a good time is one of the tests of civilization. But I very strenuously warn both young and old against the monstrous folly of supposing that a good time has any resemblance to those wartime reactions after paroxysms of horror and terror, when the most childish indulgence seemed heavenly and the most reckless excesses excusable on the plea of "Let us eat and drink (especially drink), for tomorrow we die." Our difficulty now is that what the bright young things after the war tried to do, and what their wretched survivors are still trying to do, is to get the reaction without the terror, to go on eating cocaine and drinking cocktails as if they had only a few hours' expectation of life instead of forty years.

In my play the ex-war nurse and the ex-airman-ace persuade a respectable young lady, too respectable to have ever had a good time, to come with them and enjoy the sort of good time they had in the nightmare of 1914–18. My stage picture of the result of the experiment will, I hope, deter any respectable young lady who witnesses it from relieving the tedium and worthlessness of idle gentility in that way.

The demonstration is rather funny at first; but I know my business as a playwright too well to fall into the common mistake of believing that because it is pleasant to be kept laughing for an hour, it must be trebly pleasant to be kept laughing for three hours. When people have laughed for an hour, they want to be serio-comically entertained for the next hour; and when that is over they are so tired of not being wholly serious that they can bear nothing but a torrent of sermons.

My play is arranged accordingly.

July 1932   G. B. S.

Why "Too True to be Good" Failed: A Moral in Favour of a National Theatre

(*Everyman*, London, 5 November 1932)

The opportunity is rather a good one to draw a moral in favour of a National Theatre. You may remember that after the old experiment made by Vedrenne and Barker at the Court Theatre in 1904, which was finally pushed as far as it would go, and ended a bit further, Granville-Barker came to the conclusion that he could make a west end London theatre, playing Shakespear and highbrow repertory, pay its way if it were rent free and rate free. An endowment to that extent would solve the money problem.

In those days, remember, rents and salaries and production expenses were so much lower than at present that George Alexander, running the most expensive theatre of its size in London, complained to me that he could not carry on unless his receipts were £1,000 a week.

Now it happens that this is the exact figure at which *Too True* was withdrawn last Saturday. Alexander would have run the play for six months at such business; but Barry Jackson has to throw in his hand unless the receipts are £1,600.

When Cochran gallantly produced O'Casey's *Silver Tassie* he had to take it off, because his expenses were £1,700 a week.

Too True filled the cheaper seats and moved people as no play of mine has moved them before; the houses in Birmingham were crowded out for three weeks; and the tour is all right. But because the people who can afford to pay thirteen shillings for a stall do not care for that sort of play in sufficient quantities, and left the box office £50 short of "Stalls full" every night at the end, the play is described as a failure and has to give place to musical comedy. And meanwhile at the Old Vic and Sadler's Wells, *Cæsar and Cleopatra* fills these big houses with their reasonable prices.

Thus the case for a National Theatre grows stronger as the commercial theatres and cinemas flourish more and more and raise the standard of expenditure to a pitch undreamt of at the beginning of the century.

Here am I, expected to force intellectual drama to the utmost limits of human endurance—"as far as thought can reach," in fact—rebuked austerely by every saphead in the critics' circle if I humanely venture to give my audiences the least scrap of fun; and the reward I get is that when I have increased the takings more than sevenfold in thirty years, and had a success which in point of money would have ranked before the war as a silver mine, the play has to be withdrawn, leaving me hammered like an insolvent broker on the Stock Exchange. I must have a public pension of at least £10,000 a year if I am to carry on. *Too True* failed, as they call it, in America also. That means that after twelve weeks' roaring business, the receipts dropped in the last week to $6,500. Well, if the vanguard of the drama cannot live on the drama when the plunder amounts to $6,500 a week, it must perish unless governments and municipalities come to the rescue with endowed theatres. If this National Government will only pay the rent of the New Theatre, Sir Barry Jackson will run *Too True* for another year cheerfully. Neither he nor I can say any fairer than that, can we?

Village Wooing:
A Comedietta for Two Voices

Composition begun 2 January 1933; completed 27 July 1933. First published in German translation, as *Ländliche Werbung*, in the *Neue Freie Presse* (Vienna), 24 December 1933. First published in English in *Too True to be Good, Village Wooing & On the Rocks*, 1934. First presented at the Little Theatre, Dallas, on 16 April 1934.

A Passenger, "Z"   *Keith Woolley*
An Author, "A"   *Charles Meredith*
Deck Steward   (Not Named)
Period—The Present
First Conversation: *The Lounge Deck of the* Empress of Patagonia, *a Pleasure Ship*
Second Conversation: *In a Village Shop and Post Office on the Wiltshire Downs*
Third Conversation: *In the Same*

FIRST CONVERSATION

The lounge deck of the Empress of Patagonia, a pleasure ship. Two of the deck chairs are occupied by A, a literary looking pale gentleman under forty in green spectacles, a limp black beard, and a tropical suit of white silk, who is writing and does not wish to be disturbed, and z, a young woman, presentable but not aristocratic, who is bored with her book. She is undressed for bathing, but is very modestly covered up with a not too flamboyant wrap.

z. Excuse me. Could you tell me the time?

A. [*curtly*] Eleven.

z. My watch makes it half past ten.

A. The clocks were put on half an hour last night. We are going east.

z. I always think it adds to the interest of a voyage having to put on your watch.

A. I am glad you are so easily interested [*he resumes his writing pointedly*].

z. The steward will be round with the soup in half an hour. I thought we should have to wait an hour.

A. I never take it. It interrupts my work.

z. Why do you work all the time? It's not what one comes on a pleasure cruise for, is it?

A. Work is my only pleasure.

z. Oh, thats not good sense, is it? It gives me the pip to see you always sitting there over your writing, and never enjoying yourself, nor even taking a drop of soup. You should get up and have a game of deck quoits: you will feel ever so much better after it.

A. I feel perfectly well, thank you. And I loathe deck games, especially deck quoits. The slapping of those silly things on the deck destroys the quiet of the ship.

z. Oh, I see. That is why you select this end of the deck. I often wondered why.

a. Within the last fortnight you have inspected the priceless antiquities of Naples, Athens, Egypt, and the Holy Land. Please occupy your mind with them until the soup comes.

z. I never cared much for geography. Where are we now?

a. We are on the Red Sea.

z. But it's blue.

a. What did you expect it to be?

z. Well, I didnt know what color the sea might be in these parts. I always thought the Red Sea would be red.

a. Well, it isnt.

z. And isnt the Black Sea black?

a. It is precisely the color of the sea at Margate.

z. [*eagerly*] Oh, I am so glad you know Margate. Theres no place like it in the season, is there?

a. I dont know: I have never been there.

z. [*disappointed*] Oh, you ought to go. You could write a book about it.

a. [*shudders, sighs, and pretends to write very hard*]!
   A pause.

z. I wonder why they call it the Red Sea.

a. Because their fathers did. Why do you call America America?

z. Well, because it is America. What else would you call it?

a. Oh, call it what you like, dear lady; but I have five hundred words to write before lunch; and I cannot do that if I talk to you.

z. [*sympathetically*] Yes: it is awful to have to talk to people, isnt it? Oh, that reminds me: I have something really interesting to tell you. I believe the man in the cabin next mine beats his wife.

A. I feel a little like him myself. Some women would provoke any men to beat them.

Z. I will say this for him, that she always begins it.

A. No doubt.

Z. I hate a nagger: dont you?

A. It is your privilege as a woman to have the last word. Please take it and dont end all your remarks with a question.

Z. You are funny.

A. Am I? I never felt less funny in my life.

Z. I can't make you out at all. I am rather good at making out people as a rule; but I cant make head or tail of you.

A. I am not here to be made out. You are not here to make people out, but to revel in the enjoyments you have paid for. Deck tennis, deck quoits, shuffleboard, golf, squash rackets, the swimming pool, the gymnasium all invite you.

Z. I am no good at games: besides, theyre silly. I'd rather sit and talk.

A. Then for heaven's sake talk to somebody else. I have no time for talk. I have to work my passage.

Z. What do you mean: work your passage? You are not a sailor.

A. No. I make a precarious living on board ship by writing the Marco Polo Series of Chatty Guide Books. Unless I complete two thousand words a day I am bankrupt. I cannot complete them if you persist in talking to me.

Z. Do you mean you are writing a book about this cruise?

A. I am trying to—under great difficulties.

Z. Will I be in it?

A. [*grimly*] You will.

z. How thrilling! I have never been put in a book before. You will read me what you have written about me, wont you?

A. When the book is published you can read it to your heart's content.

z. But I should like you to get me right. After all, what do you know about me? I will tell you the whole of my life if you like.

A. Great heavens, NO. Please dont.

z. Oh, I dont care who knows it.

A. Evidently. You would hardly offer to tell it to a perfect stranger if you cared, or if it was of the smallest interest.

z. Oh, I'd never think of you as a stranger. Here we are on the same ship, arnt we? And most people would think my life quite a romance. Wouldnt you really like to hear it?

A. No, I tell you. When I want romances I invent them for myself.

z. Oh, well, perhaps you wouldnt think it very wonderful. But it was a regular treat for me. You may think because I am well dressed and travelling de lucks and all that, that I am an educated lady. But I'm not.

A. I never supposed for a moment that you were.

z. But how could you know? How did you find out?

A. I didnt find out. I knew.

z. Who told you?

A. Nobody told me.

z. Then how did you know?

A. [*exasperated*] How do I know that a parrot isnt a bird of paradise?

z. Theyre different.

A. Precisely.

z. There you are, you see. But what would you take me for if you met me in a third class carriage?

A. I should not notice you.

z. I bet you would. I maynt be a beauty; but when I get into a railway carriage every man in it has a look at me.

A. I am not Everyman. Everyman thinks that every woman that steps into a railway carriage may be the right woman. But she is always a disappointment.

z. Same with the women, isnt it? If you were a woman youd know.

A. I am a woman; and you are a man, with a slight difference that doesnt matter except on special occasions.

z. Oh, what a thing to say! I never could bring myself to believe that. I know, of course, that men have their weaknesses and their tempers; but all the same there is something wonderful you can get from a man that you never could get from a woman. Dont you think so?

A. Inexperienced men think there is something wonderful you can get from a woman that you never could get from a man. Hence many unhappy marriages.

z. Are you married?

A. Widower. Are you?

z. Oh, thats the first time youve asked me a question. We're getting on, arnt we?

A. No. I am not getting on with my work.

z. Youre an intellectual, arnt you?

A. What do you think you mean by an intellectual?

z. Only that you consider me no better than an idiot, and that you were a bad husband, most likely.

A. You are quite right on both points.

z. I thought so.

A. And now, please, may I go on with my work?

z. Please yourself. I'm not hindering you.

A. Thank you [*he resumes his writing*].

A pause.

z. What books would you recommend me to read to improve my mind?

A. [*shouting furiously*] Steward.

z. Oh, you shouldnt trouble the steward now. He's busy getting the soup.

A. I want him to remove my chair to the very furthest extremity of this ship.

z. I always say it's fresher under the awning at the end. You dont mind if I move too, do you?

A. If you persecute me any more I shall go overboard. Dont you see that I want to be left alone to work, and that your chatter is preventing me from working?

z. [*sympathetically*] It is annoying to have somebody talking to you all the time when you dont want to. But it's just as bad when you want to talk, and the other person wont, isnt it?

A. There are three or four hundred persons on this ship. Cannot you find one of them with the same insatiable thirst for conversation as yourself?

z. Well; but we all have to make ourselves agreeable, havnt we?

A. Not at oneanother's expense. You are not making yourself agreeable to me at present: you are driving me mad.

z. My father used to say that men and women are always driving oneanother mad.

A. That sounds literary. Was your father a man of letters?

z. Yes: I should think he was. A postman.

A. A what?

z. A postman. A village postman.

A. Ha ha! Ha ha ha!

z. What is there funny in that?

A. I dont know. Ha ha! The postman's daughter hath ripe red lips: butter and eggs and a pound of cheese! Ha ha ha!

z. Well, I'm glad Ive amused you. But I dont think it's very polite of you to laugh at my father.

A. [*punctiliously—recovering himself*] You are right. I was rude. But a good laugh is worth a hundred pounds to me. I feel a different man. Forgive me. You see, you quoted a remark of your father's—almost an epigram—which suggested that he must have been a man of genius.

z. Well, so he was. He had a genius for walking.

A. For what?

z. For walking. When he was a child, he won a prize as The Infant Pedestrian. And would you believe it, my mother was that indoory that she grudged having to go out and do her marketing. After we had a telephone put in she never went out at all.

A. Thats strange. As she was never out and he was never in, the household should have been a quiet one; but that remark of his about men and women driving oneanother mad rather suggests the opposite.

z. So it was the opposite. She was always complaining of being lonely; and he was always at her to take more exercise. When they were not quarrelling about that, they were quarrelling about me. You see, they had great ambitions for me. She wanted me to be a parlormaid in a great house. He wanted me to be a telephone operator. He said there is no future for the great houses and a great future for telephones.

A. And you? Had you no ambition for yourself?

z. Oh, I wanted to be something romantic, like an acrobat in a circus.

A. And what actually happened?

z. I became shop assistant and telephone operator in the village shop.

a. Do village shop assistants and telephone girls—

z. Operators.

a. Pardon: operators. Do they earn enough to take cruises round the world in pleasure ships?

z. Not they. I won the first prize in a newspaper competition. My mother wanted me to save it: she said it would help me to get a thrifty husband. My father told me to blue it all in a lump while I had the chance. "You will be poor all your life," he said; "but now you have the chance of living at the rate of five thousand a year for four months. Dont miss it," he said: "see what it's like. Have your fling" he said; "for they never can take that away from you once youve had it." His idea was a walking tour, spending the nights in the best hotels; but I chose the ship because it's more dressy and more people to look at. Besides, I can get all the walking I want round the deck. At the end of the cruise back I go to the village shop without a penny.

a. Have they found out here that you are not a lady?

z. The Americans dont know the difference: they think my telephone talk is aristocratic; and the English wont speak to anyone anyhow. And lots of them are just like me.

a. Well, how do you like living at the rate of five thousand a year? Is it worth it?

z. It is while the novelty lasts. You see, when youre at home you get tired of doing the same thing every day: the same places! the same faces! the same old round. When you get a holiday you go off in a crowded hot excursion train to the seaside and make yourself tired and miserable just because it's a change; and youd do anything for a change. But here it's change all the time until you begin to realize what it is to have a settled home and belong somewhere. I shant be sorry to get home to the shop and the telephone. I get such a dreadful lost dog feeling sometimes. Other times it seems such a foolish waste of money. And I hate wasting money.

A. Thats an extremely attractive point in your character. My wife used to waste my money. Stick to that and you will get married in no time.

z. Oh, I have had plenty of offers. But you know it's a terrible thing to be a poor man's wife when you have been accustomed to a clean decent job. I have seen so many bright jolly girls turn into dirty old drudges through getting married.

A. Dont be afraid of dirt. Mine is a clean job; but I often wish I had a dirty one to exercise me and keep me in health. Women are so set on clean collars that they make their sons clerks when they would be stronger and earn more money as navvies. I wish I was a navvy instead of writing guide books.

z. Well, whats to prevent you?

A. I am not trained to manual work. Half an hour of it would make me wish myself dead. And five minutes of my work would produce a strike among the navvies. I am only a writing machine, just as a navvy is a digging machine.

z. I dont think the world is rightly arranged: do you?

A. We must take the world as we find it. It's we that are not rightly arranged.

z. Thats what I mean. Well, I suppose I mustnt interrupt your work.

A. You mean that the steward is coming round with the soup at last.

z. Well, it's half past eleven, isnt it?

The steward appears with the soup and offers it to Z, *who seizes it eagerly; then to* A.

A. No, thank you. No soup.

He buries himself in his work, unmolested.

She buries herself in the soup.

In a village shop and post office on the Wiltshire Downs on a fine summer morning. The counter is for general shopping for most of its length; but one end is reserved and railed in for postal business. A couple of chairs are available for customers. The goods for sale include ginger beer in stone bottles, tablets of milk chocolate, glass jars of sweets containing (inter alia) sugared almonds, all on the counter; cheese, butter, and Hovis bread handy to the scales; and, in front of the counter, a sack of apples on the floor and some string bags hanging from the rafters.

z. [*invisible*] Th-reee ni-nnn. Sorry: no such number. Whoommm do you want? Doctor Byles? One fi-fff. You are through.

A. *comes in. He is in hiking costume, with stick and rucksack, but wears well cut breeches (not plus fours) instead of shorts. Seeing nobody to attend to him he raps loudly on the counter with his stick. z emerges.*

A. I want a packet of milk chocolate—

z. Thanks very much.

A. [*continuing*]—a couple of hard apples—

z. Thanks very much. [*She comes out through the counter to get them from the sack*].

A. [*continuing*]—quarter of a pound of Cheddar cheese—

z. Thanks very much.

A. Dont interrupt me. You can express your gratitude for the order when I have finished. Quarter of a pound of your best butter, a small loaf of Hovis, and two-pennyworth of sugared almonds.

z. Anything else?

A. No, thank you.

z. Thanks very much [*she goes back through the counter to cut and weigh the butter and cheese*].

He sits down watching her deft but leisurely proceedings.

A. Do you sell baskets?

z. We sell everything. Hadnt you better have a string bag? It's handier; and it packs away almost to nothing when it's empty.

A. What is a string bag? Shew me one.

z. [*coming out and taking one down*] This is the cheapest. Or would you like a better quality with a Zip fastening?

A. Certainly not. I should have the trouble of opening and shutting it, and the worry of wondering whether it would open or shut, with no compensatory advantage whatever.

z. Thats just like you. Youre not a bit changed.

A. What do you mean? I have been in this shop for less than two minutes. Why should I have changed in that time?

z. Excuse me: I shouldnt have mentioned it. Will you take a string bag?

A. Yes.

z. Thanks very much. Shall I put the rest of the order into it?

A. Of course. What else do you suppose I am buying it for? Have you any buttermilk?

z. Sorry. We dont stock it.

A. Any ginger beer?

z. Yes. We have a very good local brew.

A. Shove a bottle into the string bag.

z. Thanks very much.

A. How many times a day do you say thanks very much?

z. Depends on the number of orders.

A. Dont say it to me again, if you dont mind. It gets on my nerves.

z. It used to get on mine, at first. But I am used to it.

A. Have you a guide book of this village?

z. Sorry. Theres a leaflet in the church, written by the vicar. You are expected to put tuppence in the box for it. Excuse me; but the chocolates are tuppence, sixpence, and a shilling. Which size would you run to?

A. It is a poor heart that never rejoices. I will have a shilling one.

z. Thanks very much.

A. Dont.

z. Excuse me: I cant help it. I say it without thinking: same as if you touched a button.

The telephone rings.

A. Someone has touched the button.

z. [*vanishing into the post office section*] What number please? Whitehall on-n-n-e two on-n-n-e two. I will ring you. Whitehall one two one two. Yes. [*She reappears*] Thats a police call.

A. You need not point the information at me. I am not the criminal.

z. Oh, it isnt a criminal. Somebody thats been broadcasted on the wireless as lost. You know the sort of thing. Missing from his home since January the first. Last seen in a deck chair on the Empress of Patagonia talking to a female. Suffering from loss of memory.

A. How extraor— [*the telephone rings again*].

z. Excuse me. [*She vanishes*]. You are through to Whitehall. [*She reappears*].

A. You have hit on an extraordinary coincidence. I wonder whether you will believe me when I tell you

[549]

that in January last I was sitting on the deck of a ship named the Empress of Patagonia, and that I was talking to a female—or rather she was talking to me. How that woman did talk!

z. And are you suffering from loss of memory?

a. Certainly not. I never forget anything.

z. Oh, then it cant be you, can it?

a. There! Can it? That woman always finished up with can it? wont it? isnt it? so that you had to answer her out of common politeness. Take care never to pick up that trick or you will be murdered some day.

z. Some people are like that. It often goes with orange colored eyes [*or whatever color her eyes happen to be*]. Did you notice the color of her eyes?

a. No: I never notice things like that. I am not a detective. It is people's characters that impress me; I cant tell you the color of her hair or the shape of her nose; but I can tell you that she was a most fearful nuisance. How much does all that come to?

z. The string bag sixpence, chocolates a shilling: one and sixpence. The ginger beer is—

a. Spare me the details. Will ten shillings cover it?

z. Oh yes, of course. You shouldnt be so careless about money.

a. [*presenting a Treasury note*] Cease preaching. Take it; and give me the change.

z. Let me see. Eighteenpence, and fourpence for the ginger beer is one and tenpence, isnt it?

a. Have I denied it?

z. Cheese threepence: two and a penny; butter sixpence: two and sevenpence; apples we sell by the pound. Hadnt you better have a pound?

a. How many to the pound?

z. Three.

a. I cannot eat more than two apples at a time. Charge me for a pound; and eat the odd one yourself.

z. Oh well, say threepence for two: thats two and tenpence, isnt it?

a. I dont know.

z. Hovis, tuppence halfpenny. Three shillings and a halfpenny. Do you happen to have a halfpenny to save having to take fippence halfpenny in coppers?

a. I hate halfpennies: I always throw them away. Stop. I have one. Here.

z. Thanks very much. [*Handing him his change coin by coin*] Three, four, five, seven and six, ten. Thanks very much.

a. [*pocketing his change, but remaining comfortably seated*] Dont you find it rather dull in this village shop saying thanks very much all day?

z. Well, no matter where you are you are doing the same thing all day and every day, arnt you? The only way to get it off your mind is to live in the same place and stick at the same job. Then you never have to think about it. Thats the way the people live here; and they live for ever so long: eighty's no age here. Grandfather will be a hundred and two in August. Thats because he's never had to worry about what he'll do or where he'll go. He just imagines and imagines. It's the only way to be happy and longlived.

a. But if your imagination has only one village in it it must be pretty bare. How would you like to live in a room with only one chair in it.

z. Well, if you have only one seat what more do you want than one chair? Up at the castle there are thirty-six chairs of one sort or another in the big drawing-room; but Lady Flopping cant flop on more than one, can she?

A. [*pointing to the vacant chair*] May I suggest that you flop on that one while we talk?

z. [*sitting down*] Thanks very much.

A. I am not interrupting your work, I hope. There is nothing so maddening as to be talked to when you want to work.

z. Talking is part of the work in a village shop.

A. Tell me: do you ever read?

z. I used to read travels and guide books. We used to stock the Marco Polo series. I was mad about travelling. I had daydreams about the glory that was Greece, the grandeur that was Rome, and all that flapdoodle.

A. Flapdoodle!

z. Well, I suppose I shouldnt call it that; but it ended in my going to Rome and Athens. They were all right; but the old parts were half knocked down; and I couldnt see any glory or grandeur different to Cheltenham. I was glad to be home again. And I had so wanted to meet the Marco Polo man and walk about with him in the ruins by moonlight and hear him go on about them!

A. The Marco Polo man! The milkman! the postman! the muffin man! the Marco Polo man! Some frustrated poet, earning his crust by quoting scraps of verse to bring the Call of the East to dreaming telephone girls.

z. Operators.

A. Operators dont dream. Girls! girls of the golden west. Did that poor devil never bring you the Call of the East?

z. I'd read about it in novels and seen it on the films. They were all about moony drunkards and sheeks and the sort of girls that go dotty about them. I went right round the world to see the reality. Pretty places, of course; but the heat! and the mosquitoes! and the smells!! Travelling just destroyed the world for me as I imagined it. Give me this village all the time.

A. Had you no thrill when you stood somewhere where a poet had said "Stop; for thy tread is on an empire's dust"?

z. A guide, you mean. Theyd take the poetry out of anything; and all the time youre thinking what you ought to give them. If you fancy empires' dusts and all that sort of thing you should meet our vicar and start him talking about our standing stones, and the barrows on the downs, and the Mound. Every grain of our dust, he says, is full of history. Same everywhere, I expect.

A. Are you married?

z. No. Why? Have you any intentions?

A. Dont be in a hurry. Weve known each other less than ten minutes.

z. How much better do you think you will know me when we have talked for twenty years?

A. That is profoundly true. Still, I must think it over.

z. Nobody would ever marry if they thought it over. Youve got to take your chance, no matter how long you think.

A. You are in a hurry.

z. Well, I am past the age at which girls marry here, though I'm the pick of this village. Thats because I thought all my offers over. So I have made up my mind to take the next man that asks me, provided he's reasonably suitable.

A. Do I strike you as being reasonably suitable?

z. Well, I think I have the sort of commonsense you need to keep you straight. And you being a widower know what to expect from a woman. An inexperienced man expects the earth.

A. How do you know that I am a widower?

z. You told me.

a. Did I? When did I tell you?

z. Never mind. You did. I have noticed you have a bad memory; but I have a very good one; so it wont matter.

a. Steady. Steady. I have not yet made myself liable to an action for breach of promise.

z. Dont be afraid. I'm not that sort. We dont consider it respectable here.

a. Should I get any money with you? Do you own the shop?

z. No. All the money I ever had I blued on a trip round the world. But Mrs Ward is getting too old for the business: she couldnt run it now without me. If you could afford to buy her an annuity she'd sell it.

a. I dont know how much annuities cost.

z. You will find it in Whitaker's almanac.

a. This is rather upsetting. Somehow I have always taken it for granted that when I married again I'd marry a woman with money.

z. Oh, that wouldnt suit you at all. She'd want to spend it going into society and travelling about. How could you bear that sort of life? you that never spoke to anyone on the ship and wouldnt take any part in their games and dances! When it got about that you were the Marco Polo man—the man of all our dreams as you might say—I made a bet that I'd get you to talk to me; and I had all the trouble in the world to win it.

a. Do you mean to say that we have met before? That you were on that trip round the world?

z. Of course I do. But you never notice anything. Youre always reading or writing. The world doesnt exist for you. You never looked at me really. Youre shy with strangers, arnt you?

A. I am absolutely certain I never spoke to any woman on that ship. If I talk to women they always want to marry me.

z. Well, there you are, you see! The moment I set eyes on you I said to myself, "Now thats the sort of man that would suit me as a husband." I'd have said it even if you hadnt been the Marco Polo man.

A. Love at first sight: what?

z. Oh no. You know, if I fell in love with a man I'd never marry him: he could make me so miserable. But there was something about you: I dont exactly know what; but it made me feel that I could do with you in the house; and then I could fall in love with anyone I liked without any fear of making a fool of myself. I suppose it was because you are one of the quiet sort and dont run after women.

A. How do you know I dont run after women?

z. Well, if you want to know, it's because you didnt run after me. You mightnt believe it; but men do run after me.

A. Why?

z. Oh, how do I know? They dont know, themselves. But the lot of money they spend on things they dont want merely to come in and have a look at me and a word with me, you wouldnt believe. It's worth at least twenty pounds a year to the business.

A. [*putting on his glasses and looking at her attentively for the first time*] I shouldnt call you a pretty woman.

z. Oh, I'm not pretty. But what you might call desirable, dont you think?

A. [*alarmed*] No I dont think. May I explain? I am a man of letters and a gentleman. I am accustomed to associate with ladies. That means that I am accustomed to speak under certain well understood reserves

[555]

which act as a necessary protection to both parties. You are not a lady: you are a villager; but somebody has educated you—probably the Church or the local authority—to a point at which you can impose on unobservant and unwary travellers. You have had finishing lessons on the telephone which give you a distinguished articulation: you can say Th-reee fiv-v-v-v-e ni-n-n-n instead of theree fauv nawn. But you have not acquired any of the reserves. You say what you think. You announce all the plans that well-bred women conceal. You play with your cards on the table instead of keeping them where a lady should keep them: up your sleeve.

z. Well, wheres the harm?

a. Oh, no harm. Quite the contrary. But I feel rushed.

z. What do you mean? rushed?

a. Rushed. Precipitated. Carried to lengths I had no intention of going to.

z. Well, it gets you somewhere: doesnt it?

a. Yes; but where?

z. Here. Theres no mystery about it. Here, in a good business in a village shop in a quiet place, with me to keep it straight and look after you.

a. May I ask how much that expression "looking after me" includes? Let me be clear on the point. As a matter of fact I possess a small property which I could sell for enough to purchase an annuity for old Mrs Williams—

z. Ward.

a. I believe I have enough to purchase annuities for both Mrs Ward and Mrs Williams, as they are presumably both centenarians. But why on earth should I complicate the transaction by marrying you? I could pay you your present wages—

z. Salary.

A. I beg your pardon: salary. You will retain your present position as my shopgirl.

z. Shop assistant.

A. I beg your pardon: shop assistant. You can then make your own matrimonial arrangements, and leave me to make mine.

z. Oh, I'll make my own matrimonial arrangements all right enough. You may depend on that.

A. Excuse me: I added "and leave me to make mine." Can I depend on you for that also?

z. Well, we'll see.

A. [*angrily*] No: you will not see.

z. Well, what?

A. I dont know what. I will not commit myself. We'll see.

z. Just so: we'll see. It's a bargain then?

A. No: it most certainly is not a bargain. When I entered this shop half an hour ago I had not the faintest notion of buying a village shop or marrying a village maiden or any of the things you have put into my head. Have you ever read the fable of the spider and the fly?

z. No; but I used to sing a song called the honeysuckle and the bee.

A. [*resolutely*] Good morning. [*He makes for the door*].

z. [*following him with the string bag*] You are forgetting your things.

A. [*taking it*] Thank you.

z. Thanks very much.

She tempts him to kiss her.

A. No!!! [*he strides out*].

A *is now the proprietor of the shop with* Z *as his hired assistant. The counter has been fitted with a desk at the opposite end to the post-office section. At this* A *sits writing. He wears pepper-and-salt trousers of country cut, with an apron. He is in his shirtsleeves, and looks every inch a shopkeeper.* Z *comes in through the post office, very fresh and matutinal.*

Z. Morning, boss.

A. Good morning, slave.

Z. I havnt begun slaving yet. You have been at it for half an hour. Whatever on earth are you working at so hard?

A. I am making out my balance sheet.

Z. Oh, you neednt do that. The accountant's clerk from Salisbury does all that when he makes out the income tax return. Youre not expected to do figures in this village. Fancy old Mrs Ward doing such a thing!

A. When I bought this shop from Mrs Ward for an annuity I found she was much cleverer at figures than I was. She should have been a moneylender.

Z. She was. She lent a shilling for a penny a week.

A. That must have been between four and five hundred per cent per annum. Shylock would have blushed.

Z. Whats the good of it when you have to give credit at the shop, and then lend the customers the money to pay you?

A. Mrs Ward should have gone to Geneva. International finance would have come naturally to her.

Z. Thats too clever for me. Anyhow, you neednt worry over a balance sheet. The accountant will do all that for you.

A. [*rising and waving the balance sheet proudly as he comes through the counter into the public part of the shop*] This is not an accountant's balance sheet. It is a Robinson Crusoe balance sheet.

Z. [*following him*] Whatever's that?

A. Crusoe drew up a balance sheet of the advantages and disadvantages of being cast away on a desert island. I am cast away in a village on the Wiltshire Downs. I am drawing up a similar balance sheet. I propose to read it to you as far as I have got. [*He takes one of the customer's chairs*] You can remind me of anything I have forgotten.

Z. Lets have it. [*She takes the other chair*].

A. I begin with the credit entries.

Z. Things to your own credit, you mean?

A. No, to the credit of village shopkeeping as a way of life.

Z. Oh, you are a silly, boss.

A. That is a disrespectful remark. As such, it should not be made to a boss by his slave. The understanding on which I raised your salary when I engaged you as my assistant was that our relations should be completely conventional and businesslike on your side, however I might occasionally forget myself.

Z. [*rising*] Very well: you can keep your balance sheet to yourself. I will go on with the telephone call book.

A. You will do nothing of the sort. You will do what I tell you to do. That is what I pay you for. Sit down again. [*She does so*]. Now listen. [*He takes up his manuscript and reads*]. Item: I have sharpened my faculties, and greatly improved in observation and mathematics.

Z. Couldnt you put it into shorter words? What does it mean?

A. It means that formerly I always took what money

was given me without condescending to count it or attempting to calculate it. I can now both calculate and count quite rapidly. Formerly I made no distinctions between grades of butter and eggs. To me an egg was an egg: butter was butter. I now make critical distinctions of the greatest subtlety, and value them in terms of money. I am forced to admit that the shopkeeper is enormously superior to the Marco Polo man, and that I have learnt more in three months in this shop than I learnt in three years in Oxford.

z. I cant believe that about the learning. But see how your manners have improved!

a. My manners!!

z. Yes. Why, on that ship you hadnt a word to throw to a dog; and if anyone came near you you shrank up into yourself like a hedgehog, afraid that they didnt belong to your class and wanted to speak to you without an introduction. Now it's a pleasure to hear you say "Good morning; and what can I do for you today, Mrs Burrell?" and "Have you noticed the cauliflowers today, maam? Not a touch of frost on them!" and "Sparrowgrass very good today, my lady, if you would be wanting some."

a. I positively deny that I have ever in my life called asparagus sparrowgrass to an educated customer. Of course, when people are too ignorant to know the names of what they eat, that is another matter.

z. Well, anyhow, your manners have improved, havnt they?

a. I dont know. I know that they are no longer disinterested and sincere.

z. No more they never used to be. Never easy with anybody. Now you are hail fellow well met, as you might say, with everybody.

a. The world has become a world of customers. Let

me write that down. [*He pencils on the back of his balance sheet*] "Manners will never be universally good until every person is every other person's customer."

z. Youre not a real shopkeeper yet, boss. All you want is to find something clever to write.

A. Well, why not? Find enough clever things to say, and you are a Prime Minister. Write them down, and you are a Shakespear.

z. Yes; but who wants to be a Prime Minister or a Shakespear? Youve got to make a living.

A. Well, am I not making a living? I am no poorer than when I bought the shop.

z. But if the money goes as fast as it comes you cant save anything.

A. I loathe saving. It turns human nature sour. "Cast your bread upon the waters; and it will return to you after many days."

z. And how are you to live for the many days with nothing to eat?

A. I dont know. One does, somehow. Stop asking questions; and let us get on with the balance sheet.

z. I speak for your good.

A. [*rising wrathfully*] The most offensive liberty one human being can possibly take with another. What business is it of yours?

z. [*rising and facing him*] If you wont think for yourself somebody else must think for you. It's my business as much as yours.

A. Oh, indeed! Who does this shop belong to? I mean to whom does this shop belong?

z. I get my living out of it, dont I. If it shuts up what becomes of me?

A. Well, if you come to that, what becomes of me? You can get another job. I very greatly doubt whether anyone would give me one. [*Calming down*] Can you not be content with the fact that the shop is making enough to support two people? [*He resumes his seat*].

z. Aye; but suppose it had to support three people!

a. Why suppose? It hasnt: thats all.

z. It's not all. If you marry a stranger there will be three. And what about the children?

a. The remedy is simple. I shall not marry.

z. You dont know.

a. Neither do you.

z. Yes I do. You have married once; and you will marry twice. Somebody will snap you up. You are that sort of man.

a. If a woman snaps me up she must take the consequences. She must assist in the shop. And you will get the sack.

z. Oh, you are tiresome. [*She sits down, discouraged*]. But you see my point, at all events.

a. No. What point?

z. Well, that it's really cheaper to keep a wife than to pay an assistant. Let alone that you dont have to live a single life.

a. You can get rid of an assistant if she doesnt suit. You cant get rid of a wife.

z. If people thought that way, theyd never get married.

a. Precisely.

z. In this life you have to take chances.

a. I have taken them, and escaped.

z. You wont escape here. We dont hold with bachelors here.

a. You cant do without a general shop here, nor a post office. While I command both I am in an impregnable strategic position.

z. Well, I dont like to say it; but people are beginning to talk.

A. Beginning! When did they ever stop?

Z. Oh, theres no use talking to you.

A. Not the slightest.

Z. Oh well then, take a month's notice. [*She rises*].

A. A month's notice!

Z. Yes: a month's notice.

A. A month's notice because I refuse to marry some ridiculous village maiden or illiterate widow with whom I could not hold a moment's conversation!

Z. Wives are not for conversation: thats for visitors. Youve had plenty of conversation with me.

A. Leave yourself out of this conversation, please.

Z. Oh, very well. A month's notice.

A. Dont say that again. Utter nonsense. What have you to complain of? You are quite well off here. I purposely pay you ten pounds a year more than you could get anywhere else.

Z. Why?

A. What do you mean, why?

Z. Why do you pay me ten pounds more than you could get another assistant for?

A. Heaven only knows!

Z. [*in a fury*] I'll go this very day. I'll go this very minute. You can keep my month. You dont know when youre well off. Youre selfish. I dont wonder your wife died. Did she die mad?

A. [*gravely*] As a matter of fact, she did. I am one of those unlucky men who draw the black chances in the lottery of marriage.

Z. [*remorsefully*] Oh, I didnt know: I didnt indeed. I was only joking. [*She sits again*] I wouldnt have said it for the world if I'd known.

A. Never mind: I know you didnt mean it. By the way, I made an inconsiderate remark which hurt you. I did not intend that. I should have told you seriously

[563]

that I pay you ten pounds more than the market rate because I value your services in the shop, and wish to offer you every inducement to stay here permanently.

z. Ten pounds extra, to stay all my life here as a single woman!

A. Not necessarily. You can get married if you wish.

z. Who to?

A. To whom? Oh, anyone.

z. Anyone in the village is good enough for me; but nobody in the village is good enough for you: is that it?

A. Dont lose your temper again.

z. I will if I like. And if you knew how near I was to putting a couple of extra words in, youd perhaps realize that a woman wants something more in life than a job and a salary.

A. I know that perfectly well. There is one thing we are all out for when we are young.

z. And what is that, pray?

A. Trouble, adventure, hardship, care, disappointment, doubt, misery, danger, and death.

z. Not me, thank you. All I want is a husband and the usual consequences.

A. The same thing. Marriage is the village form of all these adventures.

z. Oh, why dont you take a more cheerful view of life?

A. I have learnt not to expect too much from life. That is the secret of real cheerfulness, because I am always getting agreeable surprises instead of desolating disappointments.

z. Well, your second marriage may be an agreeable surprise, maynt it?

A. What, exactly, do you mean by my second marriage? I have only been married once. I mean I have been married only once.

z. Well, look here. Straight, now. Is there any man in this village that would be suitable to me now that I have got used to you?

A. My dear: men are all alike.

z. You mean it will make no difference to me who I marry.

A. Very little, I am afraid.

z. And women are all alike too, arnt they?

A. [*suspicious*] What are you getting at?

z. If it doesnt matter who anybody marries, then it doesnt matter who I marry and it doesnt matter who you marry.

A. Whom, not who.

z. Oh, speak English: youre not on the telephone now. What I mean is that if it doesnt matter to me it doesnt matter to you either.

A. You admit, then, that it doesnt matter?

z. No I dont. It's a lie.

A. Oh!

z. Dont "oh" me. All men are not alike to me. There are men—and good nice men, too—that I wouldnt let touch me. But when I saw you on the ship I said to myself "I could put up with him."

A. Not at all. You told me just now that you said something quite different. I believe you really said something much more rapturous. Being rather a futile sort of person I attract vigorous women like you.

z. When you looked at me out of the corner of your eye—you looked at all the women out of the corner of your eye in spite of your keeping yourself so much to yourself—did you never say "I could put up with her"?

A. No. I said "Damn that women: she wont stop talking to me and interrupting my work."

z. Well, I tell you we were made for oneanother. It

[565]

maynt be as plain to you as to me yet; but if it's plain to me there must be something in it; for I'm never wrong when I see a thing quite plain. I dont believe youd ever have bought this shop and given up being a gentleman if I hadnt been here.

A. Now that you mention it I believe that is true. You were one of the amenities of the estate.

z. Well, I might be one of the amenities of the estate of holy matrimony, mightnt I?

A. Take care. You may find what you are trying to do easier than you think. About five per cent of the human race consists of positive masterful acquisitive people like you, obsessed with some passion which they must gratify at all hazards. The rest let them have their own way because they have neither the strength nor the courage to resist, or because the things the masterful ones want seem trifling beside the starry heavens and the destiny of Man. I am not one of the masterful ones. I am not worth marrying. Any woman could marry me if she took trouble enough.

z. Thats just what I'm afraid of. If I let you out of my sight for a month I might find you married to someone else at the end of it. Well, I'm taking no chances. I dont set up to be masterful: I dont like selfish uppish domineering people any more than you do; but I must and will have you; and thats all about it.

A. Well, you already have me—as an employer. And you are independent of me, and can leave me if you are not satisfied.

z. How can I be satisfied when I cant lay my hands on you? I work for you like a slave for a month on end; and I would have to work harder as your wife than I do now; but there come times when I want to get hold of you in my arms, every bit of you; and when I do I'll give you something better to think about than the starry heavens, as you call them. Youll find that you have senses to gratify as well as fine things to say.

A. Senses! You dont know what youre talking about. Look around you. Here in this shop I have everything that can gratify the senses: apples, onions, and acid drops; pepper and mustard; cosy comforters and hot water bottles. Through the window I delight my eyes with the old church and market place, built in the days when beauty came naturally from the hands of mediaeval craftsmen. My ears are filled with delightful sounds, from the cooing of doves and the humming of bees to the wireless echoes of Beethoven and Elgar. My nose can gloat over our sack of fresh lavender or our special sixpenny Eau de Cologne when the smell of rain on dry earth is denied me. My senses are saturated with satisfactions of all sorts. But when I am full to the neck with onions and acid drops; when I am so fed up with the mediaeval architecture that I had rather die than look at another cathedral; when all I desire is rest from sensation, not more of it, what use will my senses be to me if the starry heavens still seem no more than a senseless avalanche of lumps of stone and wisps of gas—if the destiny of Man holds out no higher hope to him than the final extinction and annihilation of so mischievous and miserable a creature?

z. We dont bother about all that in the village.

A. Yes you do. Our best seller here is Old Moore's Almanack; and next to it comes Napoleon's Book of Fate. Old Mrs Ward would never have sold the shop to me if she had not become persuaded that the Day of Judgment is fixed for the seventh of August next.

z. I dont believe such nonsense. Whats it all got to do with you and me?

a. You are inexperienced. You dont know. You are the dupe of thoughtless words like sensuality, sensuousness, and all the rest of the twaddle of the Materialists. I am not a Materialist: I am a poet; and I know that to be in your arms will not gratify my senses at all. As a matter of mere physical sensation you will find the bodily contacts to which you are looking forward neither convenient nor decorous.

z. Oh, dont talk like that. You mustnt let yourself think about it like that.

a. You must always let yourself think about everything. And you must think about everything as it is, not as it is talked about. Your secondhand gabble about gratifying my senses is only your virgin innocence. We shall get quite away from the world of sense. We shall light up for oneanother a lamp in the holy of holies in the temple of life; and the lamp will make its veil transparent. Aimless lumps of stone blundering through space will become stars singing in their spheres. Our dull purposeless village existence will become one irresistible purpose and nothing else. An extraordinary delight and an intense love will seize us. It will last hardly longer than the lightning flash which turns the black night into infinite radiance. It will be dark again before you can clear the light out of your eyes; but you will have seen; and for ever after you will think about what you have seen and not gabble catchwords invented by the wasted virgins that walk in darkness. It is to give ourselves this magic moment that we feel that we must and shall hold oneanother in our arms; and when the moment comes, the world of the senses will vanish; and for us there will be nothing ridiculous, nothing uncomfortable, nothing unclean, nothing but pure paradise.

z. Well, I am glad you take a nice view of it; for now I come to think of it I never could bear to be nothing more to a man than a lollipop. But you mustnt expect too much.

a. I shall expect more than you have ever dreamt of giving, in spite of the boundless audacity of women. What great men would ever have been married if the female nobodies who snapped them up had known the enormity of their own presumption? I believe they all thought they were going to refine, to educate, to make real gentlemen of their husbands. What do you intend to make of me, I wonder?

z. Well, I have made a decent shopkeeper of you already, havnt I? But you neednt be afraid of my not appreciating you. I want a fancy sort of husband, not a common villager that any woman could pick up. I shall be proud of you. And now Ive nailed you, I wonder at my own nerve.

a. So do I.

z. I'm not a bit like that, you know, really. Something above me and beyond me drove me on. Thats why I know it will be all right. Dont be afraid. I cant make a fine speech about it like you; but it will be all right. I promise you that.

a. Very well. Go round to the rectory; and put up the banns. And tell the rector's wife that we got in some prime artichokes this morning. She's fond of artichokes.

z. You are sure you feel happy about it?

a. I dont know what I feel about it. Go and do as you are told; and dont ask ridiculous questions.

The telephone rings. She hastens to answer it.

z. Number, please? . . . Oh, an order. Thanks very

much. . . . Yes: we have some very fine artichokes just in this morning. . . . Thanks very much: they shall be sent round directly. Oh; and theres something else—are you there? . . . Sorry to detain you: could I speak to the rector? . . . Yes: it's rather particular. It's about banns . . . banns . . . BANNS: b for beauty, a for audacity, two enns for nonsense, and s for singing. . . . Yes, banns: thats right. . . . Who are the what? . . . Oh, the parties! Of course. Well, it's—

The curtain falls

In the Sunda Strait, 27th January 1933

On the Rocks: A Political Comedy

WITH

Preface

Shaw Answers Some Questions

Composition begun 6 February 1933; completed 4 July 1933. Published in *Too True to be Good, Village Wooing & On the Rocks*, 1934. First presented at the Winter Garden Theatre, London, on 25 November 1933.

Sir Arthur Chavender (Prime Minister) *Nicholas Hannen*

Hilda Hanways (His Secretary) *Phyllis Thomas*

Sir Broadfoot Basham (Chief Commissioner of Police) *Walter Hudd*

Flavia Chavender *Marjorie Playfair*

Lady Chavender *Margaret Macdona*

David Chavender *Lewis Shaw*

Tom Humphries (Mayor of the Isle of Cats) *Charles Sewell*

Alderwoman Aloysia Brollikins *Ellen Pollock*

Alderman Blee *George E. Bancroft*

Viscount Barking *Emerton Court*

Mr Hipney *Edward Rigby*

The Lady *Fay Davis*

Sir Dexter Rightside (Foreign Secretary) *Charles Carson*

Admiral Sir Bemrose Hotspot (First Lord of the Admiralty) *Matthew Boulton*

Mr Glenmorison (President of the Board of Trade) *Norman MacOwan*

Sir Jafna Pandranath *Lewis Casson*

The Duke of Domesday *Lawrence Hanray*

Period—The Present

ACT I *The Cabinet Room at No. 10 Downing Street, London, S.W.1. July*

ACT II *The Same. 10 November, 9.30 a.m.*

Preface

Contents

EXTERMINATION

In this play a reference is made by a Chief of Police to the political necessity for killing people: a necessity so distressing to the statesmen and so terrifying to the common citizen that nobody except myself (as far as I know) has ventured to examine it directly on its own merits, although every Government is obliged to practise it on a scale varying from the execution of a single murderer to the slaughter of millions of quite innocent persons. Whilst assenting to these proceedings, and even acclaiming and celebrating them, we dare not tell ourselves what we are doing or why we are doing it; and so we call it justice or capital punishment or our duty to king and country or any other convenient verbal whitewash for what we instinctively recoil from as from a dirty job. These childish evasions are revolting. We must strip off the whitewash and find out what is really beneath it. Extermination must be put on a scientific basis if it is ever to be carried out humanely and apologetically as well as thoroughly.

KILLING AS A POLITICAL FUNCTION

That killing is a necessity is beyond question by any thoughtful person. Unless rabbits and deer and rats and foxes are killed, or "kept down" as we put it, mankind must perish; and that section of mankind which lives in the country and is directly and personally engaged in the struggle with Nature for a living has no sentimental doubts that they must be killed. As to tigers and poisonous snakes, their incompatibility with human civilization is unquestioned. This does not excuse the use of cruel steel traps, agonizing poisons, or packs of hounds as methods of extermination. Killing can be cruelly or kindly done; and the deliberate choice of cruel ways, and their organization as popular pleasures, is sinful; but the sin is in the cruelty and the enjoyment of it, not in the killing.

THE SACREDNESS OF HUMAN LIFE

In law we draw a line between the killing of human animals and non-human ones, setting the latter apart as brutes. This was founded on a general belief that humans have immortal souls and brutes none. Nowadays more and more people are refusing to make this distinction. They may believe in The Life Everlasting and The Life to Come; but they make no distinction between Man and Brute, because some of them believe that brutes have souls, whilst others refuse to believe that the physical materializations and personifications of The Life Everlasting are themselves everlasting. In either case the mystic distinction between Man and Brute vanishes; and the murderer pleading that though a rabbit should be killed for being mischievous he himself should be spared because he has an immortal soul and a rabbit has none is as hopelessly out of date as a gentleman duellist pleading his clergy. When the necessity for killing a dangerous human being arises, as it still does daily, the only distinction we make between a man and a snared rabbit is that we very quaintly provide the man with a minister of religion to explain to him that we are not killing him at all, but only expediting his transfer to an eternity of bliss.

The political necessity for killing him is precisely like that for killing the cobra or the tiger: he is so ferocious or unscrupulous that if his neighbors do not kill him he will kill or ruin his neighbors; so that there is nothing for it but to disable him once for all by making an end of him, or else waste the lives of useful and harmless people in seeing that he does no mischief, and caging him cruelly like a lion in a show.

Here somebody is sure to interject that there is the alternative of teaching him better manners; but I am not here dealing with such cases: the real necessity arises only in dealing with untameable persons who are constitutionally unable to restrain their violent or acquisitive impulses, and have no compunction about sacrificing others to their own immediate convenience. To punish such persons is ridiculous: we might as reasonably punish a tile for flying off a roof in a storm and knocking a clergyman on the head. But to kill them is quite reasonable and very necessary.

PRESENT EXTERMINATIONS

All this so far is mere elementary criminology, already dealt with very fully by me in my Essay on Prisons, which I recommend to those readers who may feel impelled to ramble away at this point into the prosings about Deterrence beloved by our Prison commissioners and judges. It disposes of the dogma of the unconditional sacredness of human life, or any other incarnation of life; but it covers only a corner of the field opened up by modern powers of extermination. In Germany it is suggested that the Nordic race should exterminate the Latin race. As both these lingual stocks are hopelessly interbred by this time, such a sacrifice to ethnological sciolism is not practicable; but its discussion familiarizes the idea and clears the way for practicable suggestions. The extermination of whole races and classes has been not only advocated but actually attempted. The extirpation of the Jew as such figured for a few mad moments in the program of the Nazi party in Germany. The extermination of the peasant is in active progress in Russia, where the extermination of the class of ladies and gentlemen of so-called independent means has already been accomplished; and an attempt to exterminate the old Conservative professional class and the kulak or prosperous farmer class has been checked only by the discovery that they cannot as yet be done without. Outside Russia the extermination of Communists is widely advocated; and there is a movement in the British Empire and the United States for the extermination of Fascists. In India the impulse of Moslems and Hindus to exterminate one another is complicated by the impulse of the British Empire to exterminate both when they happen to be militant Nationalists.

PREVIOUS ATTEMPTS MISS THE POINT

The novelty and significance of these instances consists in the equal status of the parties. The extermination of what the exterminators call inferior races is as old as history. "Stone dead hath no fellow" said Cromwell when he tried to exterminate the Irish. "The only good nigger is a dead nigger" say the

Americans of the Ku-Klux temperament. "Hates any man the thing he would not kill?" said Shylock naïvely. But we white men, as we absurdly call ourselves in spite of the testimony of our looking glasses, regard all differently colored folk as inferior species. Ladies and gentlemen class rebellious laborers with vermin. The Dominicans, the watchdogs of God, regarded the Albigenses as the enemies of God, just as Torquemada regarded the Jews as the murderers of God. All that is an old story: what we are confronted with now is a growing perception that if we desire a certain type of civilization and culture we must exterminate the sort of people who do not fit into it. There is a difference between the shooting at sight of aboriginal natives in the back blocks of Australia and the massacres of aristocrats in the terror which followed the foreign attacks on the French Revolution. The Australian gunman pots the aboriginal natives to satisfy his personal antipathy to a black man with uncut hair. But nobody in the French Republic had this feeling about Lavoisier, nor can any German Nazi have felt that way about Einstein. Yet Lavoisier was guillotined; and Einstein has had to fly for his life from Germany. It was silly to say that the Republic had no use for chemists; and no Nazi has stultified his party to the extent of saying that the new National Socialist Fascist State in Germany has no use for mathematician-physicists. The proposition is that aristocrats (Lavoisier's class) and Jews (Einstein's race) are unfit to enjoy the privilege of living in a modern society founded on definite principles of social welfare as distinguished from the old promiscuous aggregations crudely [policed by chiefs who had no notion of social criticism and no time to invent it.

KING CHARLES'S HEAD

It was, by the way, the English Revolution which
introduced the category of Malignant or Man of Blood,
and killed the King as an affirmation that even kings
must not survive if they are malignant. This was much
more advanced than the execution in the following
century of Louis XVI as an ordinary traitor, or of the
Tsar in our own time to prevent his being captured
by the Tchekoslovakian contingent and used as a
standard to rally the royalist reaction. Charles affirmed
a divine personal right to govern as against the parliament and would keep no bargain with it. Parliament
denied his right, and set up against it a divine right of
election winners to govern. They fought it out; and
the victorious election winners exterminated the king,
very logically. Finding that their authority still
needed a royal disguise they drove a hard bargain for
a crown with his son, and, after ejecting the next king
who broke it, a still harder one with his Dutch grandson before they allowed the title of king, with nine
tenths of the meaning knocked out of it, to be used as
a matter of convenience again in England. Nobody
had a word to say against Charles's private character.
It was solely for incompatibility of politics that he was
eliminated, or "liquidated" as we say now. There was
a real novelty in the transaction. The Church had for
centuries before compelled the secular State to liquidate heretics; and the slaughter of rebels who tried to
substitute one dynasty for another, or to seize the
throne for themselves, was common routine. But
Charles was neither a heretic nor a rebel. He was the
assertor of a divine right to govern without winning
elections; and because that right could not co-exist
with the supremacy of a much richer and more powerful plutocracy off went his head.

Charles was only the first victim. After Culloden the defeated Highland chiefs and their clansmen were butchered like sheep on the field. Had they been merely prisoners of war, this would have been murder. But as they were also Incompatibles with British civilization, it was only liquidation.

RIGHT TO EXTERMINATE CONFERRED BY PRIVATE PROPERTY

Having disposed of the divine right of kings the political liquidators turned their attention slowly to its derivatory the divine right of landlords, which had gradually disguised itself as private property in land. For when a tract of land becomes the private property of an individual who has to depend on it for his subsistence, the relation between him and the inhabitants of that tract becomes an economic one; and if they become economically superfluous or wasteful, he must exterminate them. This is continually happening wherever private property in land exists. If I possess land and find it profitable to grow wheat on it, I need many agricultural laborers to enable me to do it; and I tolerate their existence accordingly. If I presently find that it is more profitable to cover my land with sheep and sell their wool, I have to tolerate the existence of the sheep; but I no longer need tolerate the existence of the laborers; so I drive them off my land, which is my legal method of extermination, retaining only a few to act as shepherds. Later on I find that it is more profitable to cover my land with wild deer, and collect money from gentlemen and ladies who enjoy shooting them. I then exterminate my shepherds and keep only a few gamekeepers. But I may do much better by letting my land to industrial-

ists for the erection of factories. They exterminate the
sheep and the deer; but they need far more men than
I needed even when I grew wheat. The driven-offs
crowd into the factories and multiply like rabbits;
and for the moment population grows instead of
diminishing. But soon machines come along and make
millions of proletarians economically superfluous. The
factory owner accordingly sacks them, which is his
legal method of extermination. During these developments the exterminated, or, as we call them, the evicted
and sacked, try to avoid starvation partly by emigration, but mostly by offering themselves for all sorts
of employment as soldiers, servants, prostitutes, police
officers, scavengers, and operators of the immense
machinery of amusement and protection for the idle
rich classes created by the private property system.
By organization in trade unions, municipal and parliamentary Labor Parties, and the like, and maintaining
a sort of continual civil war consisting of strikes and
riots, they extort from the proprietors enough to
reduce the rate of extermination (shewn by the actuar-
ial expectation of life of the unpropertied) for periods
described as progressive, until the proprietors, by
engaging in suicidal wars, are forced to intensify their
economies, and the rate of extermination rises again.

DISGUISES UNDER WHICH PRIVATE EXTERMINATION OPERATES

Note that during all this the Registrar General's
returns do not give us the deaths of the exterminated
as such, because the exterminated do not starve as
lost travellers starve in the desert. Their starvation
is more or less protracted; and when the final catastrophe arrives, it is disguised under an imposing

array of doctors' names for moribundity. The victims die mostly in their first year, and subsequently at all ages short of the age at which properly nourished people die. Sometimes they are starved into attaining an age at which people with well filled pockets eat themselves to death. Either way and all ways the extermination is a real and permanent feature of private property civilization, though it is never mentioned as such, and ladies and gentlemen are carefully educated to be unconscious of its existence and to talk nonsense about its facts when they are too obvious or become too scandalous to be ignored, when they often advocate emigration or Birth Control or war as remedies. And against the facts there is a chronic humanitarian revolt expressing itself either underground or overground in revolutionary movements; making our political constitutions very unstable; and imposing an habitual disingenuousness on conservative statesmen.

PRIVATE POWERS OF LIFE AND DEATH

Now the central fact of all these facts is that the private proprietors have irresponsible powers of life and death in the State. Such powers may be tolerated as long as the Government is in effect a committee of private proprietors; yet if such a committee be widened into or superseded by a Government acting in the interest of the whole people, that Government will not suffer any private class to hold the lives of the citizens at its mercy and thereby become their real masters. A popular Government, before it fully grasps the situation, usually begins by attempting to redistribute property in such a manner as to make everyone a petty proprietor, as in the French Revolution. But when the impossibility of doing this (except in the special case of agricultural land) becomes apparent, and the question is probed to the bottom by unpropertied political philosophers like Proudhon and Marx, private property is sooner or later excommunicated and abolished; and what was formerly called "real property" is replaced by ordinary personal property and common property administrated by the State.

All modern progressive and revolutionary movements are at bottom attacks on private property. A Chancellor of the Exchequer apologizing for an increase in the surtax, a Fascist dictator organizing a Corporate State, a Soviet Commissar ejecting a kulak and adding his acres to a collective farm, are all running the same race, though all of them except the Commissar may be extremely reluctant to win it. For in the long run the power to exterminate is too grave to be left in any hands but those of a thoroughly Communist Government responsible to the whole community. The landlord with his writ of ejectment and the employer with his sack, must finally go the way of the nobleman with his sword and his benefit of clergy, and of Hannibal Chollop with his bowie knife and pistol.

Let us then assume that private property, already maimed by factory legislation, surtax, and a good deal of petty persecution in England, and in Russia tolerated only provisionally as a disgraceful necessity pending its complete extirpation, is finally discarded by civilized communities, and the duty of maintaining it at all costs replaced by the duty of giving effect to the dogma that every ablebodied and ableminded and ablesouled person has an absolute right to an equal share in the national dividend. Would the practice of

[583]

extermination thereupon disappear? I suggest that, on the contrary, it might continue much more openly and intelligently and scientifically than at present, because the humanitarian revolt against it would probably become a humanitarian support of it; and there would be an end of the hypocrisy, the venal special pleading, and the concealment or ignoring of facts which are imposed on us at present because extermination for the benefit of a handful of private persons against the interests of the race is permitted and practised. The old doctrine of the sacredness of human life, which in our idiot asylums at Darenth and elsewhere still terrifies us into wasting the lives of capable people in preserving the lives of monsters, was a crude expedient for beginning civilization. At present we discard it in dealing with murderers, heretics, traitors, and (in Scotland) vitriol throwers, who can be legally killed. A runaway convict can also be summarily shot by a warder to save the trouble of pursuing and recapturing him; and although the convict is not under capital sentence and the case is therefore clearly one of wilful murder, coroners' juries persist in treating it as a harmless and necessary incident in prison routine.

Unfortunately the whole question is bedevilled by our anti-Christian vice of punishment, expiation, sacrifice, and all the cognate tribal superstitions which are hammered into us in our childhood by barbarous scripturists, irascible or sadist parents, and a hideous criminal code. When the horrors of anarchy force us to set up laws that forbid us to fight and torture one another for sport, we still snatch at every excuse for declaring individuals outside the protection of law and torturing them to our hearts content.

CRUELTY'S EXCUSES

There have been summits of civilization at which heretics like Socrates, who was killed because he was wiser than his neighbors, have not been tortured, but ordered to kill themselves in the most painless manner known to their judges. But from that summit there was a speedy relapse into our present savagery. For Wallace, whom the Scots adored as a patriot and the English executed as a traitor, the most cruel and obscene method of killing that the human imagination could conceive at its vilest was specially invented to punish him for being a traitor (or "larn him to be a toad"); and this sentence has been passed, though not carried out, within the memory of persons now living. John of Leyden, for being a Communist, was tortured so frightfully before being hung up in a cage on the church tower to starve to death in sight of all the citizens and their little children, that the bishop who was officially obliged to witness it died of horror. Joan of Arc, for wearing men's clothes and being a Protestant and a witch, was burnt alive, after a proposal to torture her had been barely defeated. The people who saw her burnt were quite accustomed to such spectacles, and regarded them as holiday attractions. A woman's sex was made an excuse for burning her instead of more mercifully hanging her. Male criminals were broken on the wheel: that is, battered to death with iron bars, until well into the nineteenth century. This was a public spectacle; and the prolongation of the victim's suffering was so elaborately studied and arranged that Cartouche, one of the kings of scoundrelism, was bribed to betray his accomplices by the promise that he should be killed by the sixth blow of the bar. The wheel and the stake have lately gone out of use; but the Sadist mania for flogging seems ineradicable; for after a partially successful attempt to discard it in Victorian times it has revived again with redoubled ferocity: quite recently a criminal was sentenced to a flogging and ten years penal servitude; and although the victim escaped his punishment and gave a sensational advertisement to its savagery by committing suicide, nobody protested, though thirty years ago there would have been a strenuous outcry against it, raised by the old Humanitarian League, and voiced in Parliament by the Irish Nationalists. Alas! the first thing the Irish did when they at last enjoyed self-government was to get rid of these sentimental Nationalists and put flogging on their statute book in a series of Coercion Acts that would have horrified Dublin Castle. In a really civilized state flogging would cease because it would be impossible to induce any decent citizen to flog another. Among us a perfectly respectable official will do it for half a crown, and probably enjoy the job.

LEADING CASE OF JESUS CHRIST

I dislike cruelty, even cruelty to other people, and should therefore like to see all cruel people exterminated. But I should recoil with horror from a proposal to punish them. Let me illustrate my attitude by a very famous, indeed far too famous, example of the popular conception of criminal law as a means of delivering up victims to the normal popular lust for cruelty which has been mortified by the restraint imposed on it by civilization. Take the case of the extermination of Jesus Christ. No doubt there was a strong case for it. Jesus was from the point of view of the High Priest a heretic and an impostor. From the point of view of the merchants he was a rioter and a Communist. From the Roman Imperialist point of view he was a traitor. From the commonsense point of view he was a dangerous madman. From the snobbish point of view, always a very influential one, he was a penniless vagrant. From the police point of view he was an obstructor of thoroughfares, a beggar, an associate of prostitutes, an apologist of sinners, and a disparager of judges; and his daily companions were tramps whom he had seduced into vagabondage from their regular trades. From the point of view of the pious he was a Sabbath breaker, a denier of the efficacy of circumcision and the advocate of a strange rite of baptism, a gluttonous man and a winebibber. He was abhorrent to the medical profession as an unqualified practitioner who healed people by quackery and charged nothing for the treatment. He was not anti-Christ: nobody had heard of such a power of darkness then; but he was startlingly anti-Moses. He was against the priests, against the judiciary, against the military, against the city (he declared that it was impossible for a rich man to enter the kingdom of heaven), against all the interests, classes, principalities and powers, inviting everybody to abandon all these and follow him. By every argument, legal, political, religious, customary, and polite, he was the most complete enemy of the society of his time ever brought to the bar. He was guilty on every count of the indictment, and on many more that his accusers had not the wit to frame. If he was innocent then the whole world was guilty. To acquit him was to throw over civilization and all its institutions. History has borne out the case against him; for no State has ever constituted itself on his principles or made it possible to live according to his commandments: those States who have taken his name have taken it as an alias to enable them to persecute his followers more plausibly.

It is not surprising that under these circumstances, and in the absence of any defence, the Jerusalem community and the Roman government decided to exterminate Jesus. They had just as much right to do so as to exterminate the two thieves who perished with him. But there was neither right nor reason in torturing him. He was entitled to the painless death of Socrates. We may charitably suppose that if the death could have been arranged privately between Pilate and Caiaphas Jesus would have been dispatched as quickly and suddenly as John the Baptist. But the mob wanted the horrible fun of seeing somebody crucified: an abominably cruel method of execution. Pilate only made matters worse by trying to appease them by having Jesus flogged. The soldiers, too, had to have their bit of sport, to crown him with thorns and, when they buffeted him, challenge him ironically to guess which of them had struck the blow.

"CROSSTIANITY"

All this was cruelty for its own sake, for the pleasure of it. And the fun did not stop there. Such was and is the attraction of these atrocities that the spectacle of them has been reproduced in pictures and waxworks and exhibited in churches ever since as an aid to piety. The chief instrument of torture is the subject of a special Adoration. Little models of it in gold and ivory are worn as personal ornaments; and big reproductions in wood and marble are set up in sacred places and on graves. Contrasting the case with that of Socrates, one is forced to the conclusion that if Jesus had been humanely exterminated his memory would have lost ninetynine per cent of its attraction for posterity. Those who were specially susceptible to his morbid attraction were not satisfied with symbolic crosses which hurt nobody. They soon got busy with "acts of faith" which consisted of great public shows at which Jews and Protestants or Catholics, and anyone else who could be caught out on a point of doctrine, were burnt alive. Cruelty is so infectious that the very compassion it rouses is infuriated to take revenge by still viler cruelties.

The tragedy of this—or, if you will, the comedy—is that it was his clearness of vision on this very point that set Jesus so high above his persecutors. He taught that two blacks do not make a white; that evil should not be countered by worse evil but by good; that revenge and punishment only duplicate wrong; that we should conceive God, not as an irascible and vindictive tyrant but as an affectionate father. No doubt many private amiabilities have been inspired by this teaching; but politically it has received no more quarter than Pilate gave it. To all Governments it has remained paradoxical and impracticable. A typical acknowledgement of it was the hanging of a crucifix above the seat of the judge who was sentencing evildoers to be broken on the wheel.

CHRISTIANITY AND THE SIXTH COMMANDMENT

Now it is not enough to satirize this. We must examine why it occurred. It is not enough to protest that evildoers must not be paid in their own coin by treating them as cruelly as they have treated others. We still have to stop the mischief they do. What is to be done with them? It is easy to suggest that they should be reformed by gentleness and shamed by non-resistance. By all means, if they respond to that treatment. But if gentleness fails to reform them and non-resistance encourages them to further aggression, what then? A month spent in a Tolstoyan community will convince anybody of the soundness of the nearest police inspector's belief that every normal human group contains not only a percentage of saints but also a percentage of irreclaimable scoundrels and good-for-noughts who will wreck any community unless they are expensively restrained or cheaply exterminated. Our Mosaic system of vindictive punishment, politely called "retributory" by Prison Commissioners, disposes of them temporarily; but it wastes the lives of honest citizens in guarding them; sets a horrible example of cruelty and malicious injury; costs a good deal of money that might be better spent; and, after all, sooner or later lets the scoundrel loose again to recommence his depredations. It would be much more sensible and less cruel to treat him as we treat mad dogs or adders, without malice or cruelty, and without reference to catalogues of particular crimes. The notion that persons should be safe from extermination as long as they do not commit wilful murder, or levy war against the Crown, or kidnap, or throw vitriol, is not only to limit social responsibility unnecessarily, and to privilege the large range of intolerable misconduct that lies outside them, but to divert attention from the essential justification for extermination, which is always incorrigible social incompatibility and nothing else.

THE RUSSIAN EXPERIMENT

The only country which has yet awakened to this

extension of social responsibility is Russia. When the
Soviet Government undertook to change over from
Capitalism to Communism it found itself without any
instruments for the maintenance of order except a
list of crimes and punishments administered through
a ritual of criminal law. And in the list of crimes the
very worst offences against Communist society had
no place: on the contrary they were highly honored
and rewarded. As our English doggerel runs, the
courts could punish a man for stealing the goose from
off the common, but not the man who stole the common from the goose. The idler, that common enemy
of mankind who robs everybody all the time, though
he is so carefully protected from having his own pocket
picked, incurred no penalty, and had actually passed
the most severe laws against any interference with his
idling. It was the business of the Soviet to make all
business public business and all persons public servants; but the view of the ordinary Russian citizen
was that a post in a public service was an exceptional
stroke of good luck for the holder because it was a
sinecure carrying with it the privilege of treating the
public insolently and extorting bribes from it. For
example, when the Russian railways were communized, some of the local stationmasters interpreted the
change as meaning that they might now be as lazy
and careless as they pleased, whereas in fact it was of
life-or-death importance that they should redouble
their activity and strain every nerve to make the
service efficient. The unfortunate Commissar who
was Minister of Transport found himself obliged to
put a pistol in his pocket and with his own hand shoot
stationmasters who had thrown his telegrams into the
dustbin instead of attending to them, so that he might
the more impressively ask the rest of the staff whether

they yet grasped the fact that orders are meant to be executed.

INADEQUACY OF PENAL CODES

Now being Minister of Transport, or Minister of any other public service, is a whole time job: it cannot be permanently combined with that of amateur executioner, carrying with it the reputation in all the capitalist papers of the west of being a ferocious and coldblooded murderer. And no conceivable extension of the criminal code nor of the service disciplines, with their lists of specific offences and specific penalties, could have provided for instant exemplary exterminations of this kind, any more than for the growing urgency of how to dispose of people who would not or could not fit themselves into the new order of things by conforming to its new morality. It would have been easy to specify certain offences and certain penalties in the old fashion: as, for instance, if you hoard money you will be shot; if you speculate in the difference in purchasing power of the rouble in Moscow and Berlin you will be shot; if you buy at the Co-operative to sell at the private trader's shop you will be shot; if you take bribes you will be shot; if you falsify farm or factory balance sheets you will be shot; if you exploit labor you will be shot; and it will be useless to plead that you have been brought up to regard these as normal business activities, and that the whole of respectable society outside Russia agrees with you. But the most elaborate code of this sort would still have left unspecified a hundred ways in which wreckers of Communism could have sidetracked it without ever having to face the essential questions: are you pulling your weight in the social boat? are you giving more trouble than you are worth? have you earned the privilege of living in a civilized community? That is why the Russians were forced to set up an Inquisition or Star Chamber, called at first the Cheka and now the Gay Pay Oo (Ogpu), to go into these questions and "liquidate" persons who could not answer them satisfactorily. The security against the abuse of this power of life and death was that the Cheka had no interest in liquidating anybody who could be made publicly useful, all its interests being in the opposite direction.

LIMITED LIABILITY IN MORALS

Such a novelty is extremely terrifying to us, who are still working on a system of limited liability in morals. Our "free" British citizens can ascertain exactly what they may do and what they may not do if they are to keep out of the hands of the police. Our financiers know that they must not forge share certificates nor overstate their assets in the balance sheets they send to their shareholders. But provided they observe a few conditions of this kind they are free to enter upon a series of quite legitimate but not the less nefarious operations. For example, making a corner in wheat or copper or any other cornerable commodity and forcing up prices so as to make enormous private fortunes for themselves, or making mischief between nations through the Press to stimulate the private trade in armaments. Such limited liability no longer exists in Russia, and is not likely to exist in the future in any highly civilized state. It may be quite impossible to convict a forestaller or regrator under a criminal code of having taken a single illegal step, but quite easy to convince any reasonable body of judges that he is what the people call "a wrong one." In Russia such a conviction would lead to his disappearance and the receipt by his family of a letter to say that they need not wait up for him, as he would not return home any more.* In our country he would enjoy his gains in high honor and personal security, and thank his stars that he lived in a free country and not in Communist Russia.

But as the new tribunal has been forced on Russia by pressure of circumstances and not planned and thought out at leisure, the two institutions, the Ogpu and the ordinary police administering the criminal code, work side by side, with the odd result that the surest way to escape the Ogpu is to commit an ordinary crime and take refuge in the arms of the police and the magistrate, who cannot exterminate you because capital punishment has been abolished in Russia (liquidation by the Ogpu is not punishment: it is only "weeding the garden"); and the sentence of imprisonment, though it may seem severe to us in view of the cruelty of our treatment of criminals, will be carried out with comparative leniency, and probably, if the culprit behaves well be remitted after a while. As four years imprisonment is considered enough for any reasonable sort of murder, a cornerer who finds himself in imminent danger of detection and liquidation by the Ogpu would be well advised to lose his temper and murder his mother-in-law, thereby securing a lease of life for at least four years.

Sooner or later this situation will have to be thoroughly studied and thought out to its logical conclusion in all civilized countries. The lists of crimes

* Note, however, that a sentence of extermination should never be so certain as to make it worth the delinquent's while to avoid arrest by murdering his or her pursuers.

and penalties will obsolesce like the doctors' lists of diseases and medicines; and it will become possible to be a judge without ceasing to be a Christian. And extermination, my present subject, will become a humane science instead of the miserable mixture of piracy, cruelty, vengeance, race conceit, and superstition it now is.

NATURAL LIMIT TO EXTERMINATION

Fortunately the more frankly and realistically it is faced the more it detaches itself from the associations with crude slaughter which now make it terrible. When Charlemagne founded the Holy Roman Empire (as far as anyone can be said to have founded it) he postulated that all its subjects must be Catholic Christians, and made an amateurish attempt to secure this condition of social stability by killing everyone who fell into his power and refused to be baptized. But he cannot ever have got very far with it, because there is one sort of bird you must not kill on any pretext whatever: namely, the goose that lays the golden eggs. In Russia the Soviet Government began by a Charlemagnesque attempt to exterminate the bourgeoisie by classing them as intelligentsia, restricting their rations, and putting their children at the foot of the overcrowded educational list. They also proscribed the kulak, the able, hardheaded, hardfisted farmer who was richer than his neighbors and liked to see them poorer than himself. Him they rudely took by the shoulders and threw destitute into the lane. There were plausible reasons for this beginning of selection in population; for the moral outlook of the bourgeoisie and the kulaks was dangerously antisocial. But the results were disastrous. The bourgeoisie contained the professional class and the organizing business class. Without professional men and business organizers nothing could be done in the industries; and the hope that picked members of the proletariat could take up professional and organizing work on the strength of their native talent in sufficient numbers was crushingly disappointed. When the kulak was thrown out of his farm, and his farming ability paralyzed, food ran short. Very soon the kulak had to be thrown back into his farm and told to carry on until his hour had come; and a pleasant convention was established whereby all educated persons, however obviously ladies or gentlemen, who were willing to assure the authorities that their fathers had "worked on the land with their hands" were accepted as genuine proletarians, and transferred from the infamous category of intelligentsia to the honourable one of "the intellectual proletariat." Even Lenin and his colleagues, all ultra-bourgeois (otherwise they would never have so absurdly overestimated the intellectual resources of the proletariat and been so contemptuous of the pretension of their own class to be indispensable), allowed their parents to be described as hornyhanded cultivators of the soil. The pretence has now become a standing joke; but you will still come up against it if you accuse any Russian of being a lady or gentleman.

INCOMPATIBILITY OF PEASANTRY WITH MODERN CIVILIZATION

These, however, are merely expedients of transition. The Russian proletariat is now growing its own professional and organizing class; and the ex-bourgeois is dying out, after seeing his children receive a sound

Communist education and being lectured by them on his oldfashioned prejudices. And the planners of the Soviet State have no time to bother about moribund questions; for they are confronted with the new and overwhelming necessity for exterminating the peasants, who still exist in formidable numbers. The notion that a civilized State can be made out of any sort of human material is one of our old Radical delusions. As to building Communism with such trash as the Capitalist system produces it is out of the question. For a Communist Utopia we need a population of Utopians; and Utopians do not grow wild on the bushes nor are they to be picked up in the slums: they have to be cultivated very carefully and expensively. Peasants will not do; yet without the peasants the Communists could never have captured the Russian Revolution. Nominally it was the Soviets of peasants and soldiers who backed Lenin and saved Communism when all Western Europe set on him like a pack of hounds on a fox. But as all the soldiers were peasants, and all the peasants hungry for property, the military element only added to the peasants' cry of Give us land, the soldiers' cry of Give us peace. Lenin said, in effect, Take the land; and if feudally minded persons obstruct you, exterminate them; but do not burn their houses, as you will need them to live in. And it was the resultant legions of petty landed proprietors that made Lenin's position impregnable, and provided Trotsky and Stalin with the Red soldiers who defeated the counter-revolutionists of 1918. For the counter-revolution, in which we, to our eternal shame, took part (England sets the example of revolution and then attacks all other countries which presume to follow it), meant bringing the old landlords back; and the peasant fought against that as the mercenaries and conscripts of the Capitalist armies would not fight in favour of it.

A PEASANT VICTORY IS A VICTORY FOR PRIVATE PROPERTY

So far so good for Lenin; but the war against the counter-revolutionists, when it ended in victory for the peasant proprietor, was really a victory for private property, and was therefore succeeded by a fiercer struggle between the fanatically Communist Government and the fiercely individualist peasant proprietor, who wanted the produce of his plot for himself, and had no notion of pooling it with anybody, least of all with the urban proletarians who seemed like another species to him. Left to themselves the moujiks would have reproduced Capitalist civilization at its American worst in ten years. Thus the most urgent task before the victorious Communist Government was the extermination of the moujik; and yet the moujik, being still the goose that laid the golden eggs, could not be exterminated summarily without incidentally exterminating the whole Russian nation.

The way out of this deadlock was obvious enough, though very expensive and tedious. You can exterminate any human class not only by summary violence but by bringing up its children to be different. In the case of the Russian peasantry the father lives in a lousy kennel, at no man's call but his own, and extracts a subsistence by primitive methods from a strip of land on which a tractor could hardly turn even if he could afford such a luxury, but which is his very own. His book is a book of Nature, from which all wisdom can be gathered by those who have been taught to read it by due practice on printed books; but he has not been so practised, and for cultural purposes has to be classed as ignorant, though he knows things that university professors do not know. He is brutalized by excessive muscular labor; he is dirty; his freedom from civilized control leaves him so unprotected from the tyranny of Nature that it becomes evident to his children that the highly regulated people in the nearest collectivist farm, where thousands of acres are cultivated by dozens of tractors, and nobody can put his foot on one of the acres or his hand on one of the tractors and say "This is my own to do what I like with," are better fed and housed, nicer, and much more leisured, and consequently free, than he ever is.

PREVENTIVE EXTERMINATION:
ITS DIFFICULTIES

In short, you exterminate the peasant by bringing up his children to be scientifically mechanized farmers and to live a collegiate life in cultivated society. It sounds simple; but the process requires better planning than is always forthcoming (with local famines and revolts as the penalty); for while the grass grows the steed starves; and when education means not only schools and teachers, but giant collective farms equipped with the most advanced agricultural machinery, which means also gigantic engineering works for the production of the machinery, you may easily find that you have spent too much on these forms of capitalization and are running short of immediately consumable goods, presenting the spectacle of the nation with the highest level of general culture running short of boots and tightening its belt for lack of sufficient food.

I must not suggest that this has occurred all over

Russia; for I saw no underfed people there; and the children were remarkably plump. And I cannot trust the reports; for I have no sooner read in The Times a letter from Mr Kerensky assuring me that in the Ukraine the starving people are eating one another, than M. Herriot, the eminent French statesman, goes to Russia and insists on visiting the Ukraine so that he may have ocular proof of the alleged cannibalism, but can find no trace of it. Still, between satiety and starvation mitigated by cannibalism there are many degrees of shortage; and it is no secret that the struggle of the Russian Government to provide more collective farms and more giant factories to provide agricultural machinery for them has to be carried on against a constant clamor from the workers for new boots and clothes, and more varied food and more of it: in short, less sacrifice of the present to the future. As Stalin said quaintly "They will be demanding silver watches next." The constant correction of the inevitable swerves towards one extreme or the other, analogous to the control of the Bank rate by the Bank of England (only enormously more laborious), strains all the wit and industry of the Russian rulers; and occasional sideslips must be inevitable during these years when the ablest and oldest Communists are still learners.

TEMPERAMENTAL DIFFICULTIES

Even when the extinction of the bourgeoisie and the kulaks and the old aristocracy is complete, and the Russian population consists of citizens educated as Communists, there will still be questions to settle which are bottom questions as to the sort of civilization that is desirable; and this involves a decision as to the sort of people that are desirable and undesirable. Some of us, believing that a more primitive life than ours would be happier and better, advocate "a return to nature." Others dream of a much more mechanized, specialized, and complicated life. Some of us value machinery because it makes a shorter working day possible for us: others value it because it enriches us by increasing the product per hour. Some of us would like to take things easy and retire at 60: others would like to work their utmost and retire at 40. Some of us will say Let us be content with £200 a year: others No: let us live at the rate of £20,000 a year and strain every faculty to earn it. Some of us want a minimum of necessary work and a maximum of liberty to think and discover and experiment in the extension of science and art, philosophy and religion, sport and exploration: others, caring for none of these things, and desiring nothing more than to be saved the trouble of thinking and to be told what to do at every turn, would prefer thoughtless and comfortable tutelage and routine, not knowing what to do with themselves when at liberty. A life filled with scientific curiosity would be hell for the people who would not cross the street to find out whether the earth is flat or round; and a person with no ear for music would strenuously object to work for the support of municipal bands, whilst people of Shakespear's tastes would agitate for the extermination of the unmusical.

IMPORTANCE OF LAZINESS FOR FALLOWING

Some of these differences could be settled on give-and-take lines. The division of society into classes with different tastes and capacities—different natures, as folks call it—would not shake social stability provided everyone had an equal share of the national dividend. It is not true that it takes all sorts to make a world; for there are some sorts that would destroy any world very soon if they were suffered to live and have their way; but it is true that in the generations of men continuous high cultivation is not expedient; there must be fallows, or at least light croppings, between the intense cultivations; for we cannot expect the very energetic and vital Napoleon to be the son of an equally energetic father or the father of an equally vital son. Nobody has yet calculated how many lazy ancestors it takes to produce an indefatigable prodigy; but it is certain that dynasties of geniuses do not occur, and that this is the decisive objection to hereditary rulers (though not, let me hasten to add, to hereditary figure heads). There is a large field for toleration here: the clever people must suffer fools gladly, and the easygoing ones find out how to keep the energetic ones busy. There may be as good biological reasons for the existence of the workshy as of the workmad. Even one and the same person may have spells of intense activity and slackness varying from weeks to years.

STANDARD RELIGION INDISPENSABLE

Nevertheless there will be conflicts to the death in the creation of artificial humanity. There is nothing that can be changed more completely than human nature when the job is taken in hand early enough. Such artificial products as our agricultural laborers and urban mechanics, our country gentlemen and city plutocrats, though they are from the same human stock, are so different that they cannot live together without great discomfort, and are practically not intermarriageable. It is possible to get rid of their social incompatibility by giving them all the same education and income, and ranking them all in the same class. For example, Lord Lonsdale is not in the least socially incompatible with Dean Inge, though a really critical naturalist would as soon class Shetland ponies with zebras as lump these two gentlemen under the same heading. But the question remains, what is this same education to be? The training of the scholar and the sportsman may split and diverge as they adolesce; but they must start from a common training and a common morality as children. And when the state has to prescribe a uniform moral curriculum the variety of our temperaments makes it impossible to please everybody. The Quaker and the Ritualist, the Fundamentalist and the Freethinker, the Vegetarian and the flesh eater, the missionary and the cannibal, the humanitarian and the sportsman-hunter, the military terrorist and the Christian, will not agree as to the faiths and habits to be inculcated upon the children of the community in order that they may be good citizens. Each temperament will demand the extermination of the other through the schools and nurseries, and the establishment of its temperamental faith and habits as standard in these factories of future citizens. All will agree to exterminate illiteracy by compulsory reading, writing, and arithmetic: indeed they have already done so. But all will not agree on a standard religion. Yet a standard religion is indispensable, however completely it may shed the old theologies. Every attempt to banish religion from the schools proves that in this respect Nature abhors a vacuum, and that the community must make up its mind, or have its mind made up for it by its official thinkers, as to what its children are to be taught to believe and how they should be trained to behave.

Compromise is ruled out by the nature of the case. What compromise is possible between myself, for instance, who believe in the religion of Creative Evolution, the economics of Socialism, and a diet from which the dead bodies of men, fish, fowls, and animals are rigidly excluded, and my Fundamentalist neighbors who believe that all Evolutionists go to hell; that children languish and die without beefsteaks; and that without private property civilization must perish? We cannot exterminate one another at present; but the time cannot be very far off when the education authorities will have to consider which set of beliefs is the better qualification for citizenship in Utopia.

ECLECTIC RELIGIONS

They will probably pigeon-hole both, and proceed eclectically to compile several creeds suitable to the several capacities and ages of the children. For there is clearly no sense in offering the religion of a mature and scholarly philosopher to a child of five, nor attempting to bring the cosmogonies of Dante and Aquinas, Hegel and Marx, within the comprehension of a village dunce. Nurses rule their little charges by threatening them with bogies in whose existence no nurse believes, exactly as Mahomet ruled his Arabs by promises of a paradise and threats of a hell the details of which he must have known to be his own invention even if he did believe generally in a post mortem life of rewards and punishments for conduct in this world. Therefore I do not suggest that the education authorities in Utopia will seek for absolute truth in order to inculcate it though the heavens fall. Nor do I advise a return to Queen Elizabeth's plan of

39 Articles to please everybody by alternately affirming and denying all the disputed beliefs. The likeliest outcome is an elaborate creed of useful illusions, to be discarded bit by bit as the child is promoted from standard to standard or form to form, except such of them as adults may be allowed to comfort themselves with for the sake of the docility they produce.

There would be nothing new in this: it is what our authorities do at present, except that they do it unsystematically and unconsciously, being mostly more or less duped themselves by the illusions. Unfortunately they allow the illusions to fall behind the times and become incredible, at which point they become exceedingly dangerous; for when people are brought up on creeds which they cannot believe, they are left with no creeds at all, and are apt to buy pistols and take to banditry bag snatching and racketeering when employment fails and they find themselves short of money. It is the importance of keeping our inculcated illusions up to date that throws our higher professional classes into wild alarm when the individual liberty of thought, speech, and conscience which they think they possess (this is one of their inculcated illusions) is threatened by the dictatorships which are springing up all over the world as our pseudo-democratic parliamentary institutions reduce themselves more and more disastrously to absurdity.

IMPORTANCE OF FREE THOUGHT

Let me try to straighten this out for them. It was very generally believed as lately as in Victorian times that religious education consisted in imparting to children certain eternal, final, and absolute truths. I, for instance, being the son of an Irish Protestant gentleman, found myself, at the dawn of my infant conscience, absolutely convinced that all Roman Catholics go to hell when they die, a conviction which involved not only a belief in the existence of hell but a whole series of implications as to the nature and character of God. Now that I am older I cannot regard this as anything more than a provisional hypothesis which, on consideration, I must definitely reject. As the more pious of my uncles would have put it, I have lost my religious faith and am in peril of damnation as an Apostate. But I do not present my creed of Creative Evolution as anything more than another provisional hypothesis. It differs from the old Dublin brimstone creed solely in its greater credibility: that is, its more exact conformity to the facts alleged by our scientific workers, who have somehow won that faith in their infallibility formerly enjoyed by our priests. No future education authority, unless it is as badly educated as our present ones, will imagine that it has any final and eternal truths to inculcate: it can only select the most useful working hypotheses and inculcate them very much as it inculcates standard behaviour throughout that vast field of civilized conduct in which it does not matter in the least how people act in particular situations provided they all act in the same way, as in the rule of the road. All the provisional hypotheses may be illusions; but if they conduce to beneficial conduct they must be inculcated and acted on by Governments until better ones arrive.

TOLERATION MOSTLY ILLUSORY

But, cry the professors, are the hypotheses never to be questioned? Is disillusion to be punished as a crime? That will always depend a good deal on circumstances.

One of the best religious brains in England has said
that the war of 1914–18 was foolish and unnecessary;
and nobody now dreams of prosecuting him; but he
would not have been allowed to go through the
trenches from platoon to platoon saying so just before
zero hour, with or without the addition "Sirs, ye are
brethren: why do ye wrong one to another?" I have
no illusion of being free to say and write what I please.
I went round the world lately preaching that if
Russia were thrust back from Communism into competitive Capitalism, and China developed into a predatory Capitalist State, either independently or as
part of a Japanese Asiatic hegemony, all the western
States would have to quintuple their armies and lie
awake at nights in continual dread of hostile aeroplanes, the obvious moral being that whether we
choose Communism for ourselves or not, it is our
clear interest, even from the point of view of our
crudest and oldest militarist diplomacy, to do everything in our power to sustain Communism in Russia
and extend it in China, where at present provinces
containing at the least of many conflicting estimates
eighteen millions of people, have adopted it. Now I
was not physically prevented from saying this, nor
from writing and printing it. But in a western world
suffering badly from Marxphobia, and frantically
making itself worse like a shrew in a bad temper, I
could not get a single newspaper to take up my point
or report my utterance. When I say anything silly,
or am reported as saying anything reactionary, it runs
like wildfire through the Press of the whole world.
When I say anything that could break the carefully
inculcated popular faith in Capitalism the silence is
so profound as to be almost audible. I do not complain, because I do not share the professorial illusion

that there is any more freedom for disillusionists in the British Empire and the United States of North America than in Italy, Germany, and Russia. I have seen too many newspapers suppressed and editors swept away, not only in Ireland and India but in London in my time, to be taken in by Tennyson's notion that we live in a land where a man can say the thing he will. There is no such country. But this is no excuse for the extravagances of censorship indulged in by jejune governments of revolutionists, and by Churches who imagine they possess the eternal truth about everything, to say nothing of hereditary autocrats who conceive that they are so by divine right. Our papers are silent about the suppression of liberty in Imperialist Japan, though in Japan it is a crime to have "dangerous thoughts." In my native Ireland, now nominally a Free State, one of my books is on the index; and I have no doubt all the rest will follow as soon as the clerical censorship discovers their existence. In Austria my chronicle play St Joan had to be altered to please Catholic authorities who know much less about Catholicism than I do. In America books which can be bought anywhere in Europe are forbidden. The concentration of British and American attention on the intolerances of Fascism and Communism creates an illusion that they do not exist elsewhere; but they exist everywhere, and must be met, not with ridiculous hotheaded attacks on Germany, Italy, and Russia, but by a restatement of the case for Toleration in general.

LEADING CASES: SOCRATES AND JESUS

It is a historical misfortune that the most world-famous victims of persecution made no valid defence.

Socrates and Jesus are the most talked of in Christian countries. Socrates at his trial was in full possession of his faculties, and was allowed to say everything he had to say in his defence; but instead of defending his right to criticize he infuriated his accusers by launching at them a damning contrast between their infamous corruption and mendacity and his own upright disinterestedness and blameless record as citizen and soldier. Jesus made no defence at all. He did not regard himself as a prisoner being tried for a vulgar offence and using all his wit to escape condemnation. He believed that he was going through a sacrificial rite in which he should be slain, after which he should rise from the dead and come again in glory to establish his kingdom on earth for ever. It does not matter to our present purpose whether this was the delusion of a madman or a hard and holy fact: in either case the question of toleration was not at issue for him; therefore he did not raise it.

THE CASE OF GALILEO

In the epoch which Jesus inaugurated, or at least in which his name was habitually taken in vain, we have Joan of Arc and John of Leyden, Giordano Bruno and Galileo, Servetus and John Hus and the heroes of Foxe's Book of Martyrs standing out in our imagination from thousands of forgotten martyrdoms. Galileo is a favoured subject with our scientists; but they miss the point because they think that the question at issue at his trial was whether the earth went round the sun or was the stationary centre round which the sun circled. Now that was not the issue. Taken by itself it was a mere question of physical fact without any moral significance, and therefore no concern of the Church. As Galileo was not burnt and certainly not abhorred, it is quite credible that both his immediate judges and the Pope believed with at least half their minds that he was right about the earth and the sun. But what they had to consider was whether the Christian religion, on which to the best of their belief not only the civilization of the world but its salvation depended, and which had accepted the Hebrew scriptures and the Greek testament as inspired revelations, could stand the shock of the discovery that many of its tales, from the tactics of Joshua in the battle of Gibeon to the Ascension, must have been written by somebody who did not know what the physical universe was really like. I am quite familiar with the pre-Galileo universe of the Bible and St Augustine. As a child I thought of the earth as being an immense ground floor with a star studded ceiling which was the floor of heaven, and a basement which was hell. That Jesus should be taken up into the clouds as the shortest way to heaven seemed as natural to me as that, at the Opera, Mephistopheles should come up from hell through a trap in the floor. But if instead of telling me that Jesus was taken up into the clouds and that the disciples saw him no more, which still makes me feel quite holy, you tell me that he went up like a balloon into the stratosphere, I do not feel holy: I laugh obstreperously. The exalting vision has suddenly become a ribald joke. That is what the Church feared; and that is what has actually happened. Is it any wonder that the Pope told Galileo that he really must keep his discoveries to himself, and that Galileo consented to deny them? Possibly it was the Pope who, to console him, whispered "E pur se muove."

FIGMENT OF THE SELFREGARDING ACTION

St Joan did not claim toleration: she was so far from believing in it that she wanted to lead a crusade of extermination against the Husites, though she was burnt for sharing their heresy. That is how all the martyrs have missed the point of their defence. They all claimed to possess absolute truth as against the error of their persecutors, and would have considered it their duty to persecute for its sake if they had had the power. Real toleration: the toleration of error and falsehood, never occurred to them as a principle possible for any sane government. And so they have left us no model defence. And there is no modern treatise known to me which quite supplies this need. Stuart Mill's Essay on Liberty satisfied the nineteenth century, and was my own first textbook on the subject; but its conclusion that selfregarding actions should not be interfered with by the authorities carries very little weight for socialists who perceive that in a complex modern civilization there are no purely self-regarding actions in the controversial sphere. The color of a man's braces or a woman's garters may concern the wearers alone; but people have never been burnt for wearing black underclothes instead of white; and the notion that preaching a sermon or publishing a pamphlet can be classed as a selfregarding action is manifestly absurd. All great Art and Literature is propaganda. Most certainly the heresies of Galileo were not selfregarding actions: his feat of setting the earth rolling was as startling as Joshua's feat of making the sun stand still. The Church's mistake was not in interfering with his liberty, but in imagining that the secret of the earth's motion could be kept, and fearing that religion could not stand the shock of its disclosure, or a thousand such. It was idiotic to try to adapt Nature to the Church instead of continually adapting the Church to Nature by changing its teaching on physical matters with every advance made in our knowledge of Nature. In treating the legend of Joshua's victory as a religious truth instead of insisting that it did not make the smallest difference to religion whether Joshua was any more real than Jack the Giant Killer, and that Galileo might play skittles with the whole solar system without moving the Eternal Throne and the Papal Chair which was its visible tangible symbol on earth a single inch, it lost a great opportunity, as it has since lost many others, leaving itself open to the reproach of stupidity in not understanding Galileo's argument, of pride in not having humility enough to admit that it had been wrong in its astronomy, and of feebleness of faith and confusion of the temporal with the spiritual as aforesaid, laying itself open to much damaging Protestant and scientific disparagement, both mostly open to precisely the same reproaches.

INCOMPLETENESS OF THE GREAT TRIALS

No doubt Galileo missed the real point at issue as completely as Socrates or Jesus. For this we need not blame him: he was a physicist and not a politician; and to him the only questions at issue were whether the earth moved or not, and whether a ten pound cannon ball would fall twice as fast as a five pound one or only just as fast and no faster. But Socrates was by vocation and habit a solver of problems of conduct, both personal and political; and Jesus, who had spent his life in propounding the most staggering paradoxes on the same subject, not by any means always in the abstract, but as personal directions to his followers, must, if he had any sense of moral responsibility, have been challenged by his own conscience again and again as to whether he had any right to set men on a path which was likely to lead the best of them to the cross and the worst of them to the moral destruction described by St Augustine. No man could expressly admit that his word would bring not peace but a sword without having satisfied himself that he was justified in doing so. He must have been told as frequently as I have been told that he was giving pain to many worthy people; and even with the fullest allowance for the strain of impishness with which the Life Force endows those of us who are destined by it to *épater le bourgeois*, he cannot have believed that the mere satisfaction of this Punchesque *Schadenfreude* could justify him in hurting anyone's feelings. What, then, would have been his defence if, at his trial, he had been his old self, defending himself as an accused man threatened with a horrible penalty, instead of a god going through an inevitable ordeal as a prelude to the establishment of his kingdom on earth ?

A MODERN PASSION PLAY IMPOSSIBLE

The question is of such importance at the present crisis, when the kingdoms are breaking up, and upstart rulers are sowing their wild oats by such grotesque persecutions that Galileo's great successor Einstein is a plundered fugitive from officially threatened extermination, that I must endeavor to dramatize the trial of Jesus as it might have proceeded had it taken place before Peter uttered his momentous exclamation "Thou art the Christ." I have been asked repeatedly to dramatize the Gospel story, mostly by admirers of my dramatization of the trial of St Joan. But the trial of a dumb prisoner, at which the judge who puts the crucial question to him remains unanswered, cannot be dramatized unless the judge is to be the hero of the play. Now Pilate, though perhaps a trifle above the average of colonial governors, is not a heroic figure. Joan tackled her judges valiantly and wittily: her trial was a drama ready made, only needing to be brought within theatrical limits of time and space to be a thrilling play. But Jesus would not defend himself. It was not that he had not a word to say for himself, nor that he was denied the opportunity of saying it. He was not only allowed but challenged to defend himself. He was an experienced public speaker, able to hold multitudes with his oratory, happy and ready in debate and repartee, full of the illustrative hypothetical cases beloved of lawyers (called parables in the Gospels), and never at a loss when plied with questions. If ever there was a full dress debate for the forensic championship to be looked forward to with excited confidence by the disciples of the challenged expert it was this trial of Christ. Yet their champion put up no fight: he went like a lamb to the slaughter, dumb. Such a spectacle is disappointing on the stage, which is the one thing that a drama must not be; and when the disappointment is followed by scourging and crucifixion it is unbearable: not even the genius of our Poet Laureate, with all the magic of Canterbury Cathedral for scenery, can redeem it except for people who enjoy horror and catastrophe for their own sake and have no intellectual expectations to be disappointed.

DIFFERENCE BETWEEN READER
AND SPECTATOR

It may be asked why the incident of the trial and execution must fail on the stage, seeing that the gospel narrative is so pathetic, and so many of us have read it without disappointment. The answer is very simple: we have read it in childhood; and children go on from horror to horror breathlessly, knowing nothing of the constitutional questions at issue. Some of them remain in this condition of intellectual innocence to the end of their lives, whilst the cleverer ones seldom reconsider the impressions they have received as little children. Most Christians, I suspect, are afraid to think about it critically at all, having been taught to consider criticism blasphemous when applied to Bible stories. Besides, there are a thousand things that will pass in a well told story that will not bear being brought to actuality on the stage. The evangelists can switch off our attention from Jesus to Peter hearing the cock crow (or the bugle blow) or to Pilate chaffering with the crowd about Barabbas; but on the stage the dumb figure cannot be got rid of: it is to him that we look for a speech that will take us up to heaven, and not to the weeping of Peter and the bawling of the mob, which become unbearable interruptions instead of skilful diversions.

For my part, when I read the story over again as an adult and as a professional critic to boot, I felt the disappointment so keenly that I have been ever since in the condition of the musician who, when he had gone to bed, heard somebody play an unresolved discord, and could not go to sleep until he had risen to play the resolution on his piano. What follows is my attempt to resolve Pilate's discord. I began with the narrative of St John, the only one of the four which represents Jesus as saying anything more than any crazy person might in the same circumstances.

PILATE. Are you the king of the Jews?

JESUS. Do you really want to know? or have those people outside put it into your head to ask me?

PILATE. Am I a Jew that I should trouble myself about you? Your own people and their priests have brought you to me for judgment. What have you done?

JESUS. My kingdom is not of this world: if it were, my followers would have fought the police and rescued me. But that sort of thing does not happen in my kingdom.

PILATE. Then you are a king?

JESUS. You say so. I came into this world and was born a common man for no other purpose than to reveal the truth. And everyone capable of receiving the truth recognizes it in my voice.

PILATE. What is truth?

JESUS. You are the first person I have met intelligent enough to ask me that question.

PILATE. Come on! no flattery. I am a Roman, and no doubt seem exceptionally intelligent to a Jew. You Jews are always talking about truth and righteousness and justice: you feed on words when you are tired of making money, or too poor to have anything else to feed on. They want me to nail you up on a cross; but as I do not yet see what particular harm you have done I prefer to nail you down to an argument. Fine words butter no parsnips in Rome. You say your vocation is to reveal the truth. I take your word for it; but I ask you what is truth?

JESUS. It is that which a man must tell even if he be stoned or crucified for telling it. I am not offering

[616]

you the truth at a price for my own profit: I am offering it freely to you for your salvation at the peril of my own life. Would I do that if I were not driven by God to do it against all the protests of my shrinking flesh?

PILATE. You Jews are a simple folk. You have found only one god. We Romans have found many; and one of them is a God of Lies. Even you Jews have to admit a Father of Lies whom you call the devil, deceiving yourselves with words as usual. But he is a very potent god, is he not? And as he delights not only in lies but in all other mischief such as stonings and crucifixions of innocent men, how am I to judge whether it is he who is driving you to sacrifice yourself for a lie, or Minerva driving you to be sacrificed for the truth? I ask you again, what is truth?

JESUS. It is what you know by your experience to be true or feel in your soul must be true.

PILATE. You mean that truth is a correspondence between word and fact. It is true that I am sitting in this chair; but I am not the truth and the chair is not the truth: we are only the facts. My perception that I am sitting here may be only a dream; therefore my perception is not the truth.

JESUS. You say well. The truth is the truth and nothing else. That is your answer.

PILATE. Aye; but how far is it discoverable? We agree that it is true that I am sitting in this chair because our senses tell us so; and two men are not likely to be dreaming the same dream at the same moment. But when I rise from my chair this truth is no longer true. Truth is of the present, not of the future. Your hopes for the future are not the truth. Even in the present your opinions are not the truth. It is true that I sit in this chair. But is it true that it is better for your people that I should sit in this chair and impose on them the peace of Rome than that they should be left to slaughter oneanother in their own native savagery, as they are now clamoring to me to slaughter you?

JESUS. There is the peace of God that is beyond our understanding; and that peace shall prevail over the peace of Rome when God's hour strikes.

PILATE. Very pretty, my friend; but the hour of the gods is now and always; and all the world knows what the peace of your Jewish God Means. Have I not read it in the campaigns of Joshua? We Romans have purchased the *pax Romana* with our blood; and we prefer it as a plain understandable thing which keeps men's knives off oneanother's throats to your peace which is beyond understanding because it slaughters man woman and child in the name of your God. But that is only our opinion. It is not yours. Therefore it is not necessarily the truth. I must act on it, because a governor must act on something: he cannot loaf round the roads and talk beautifully as you do. If you were a responsible governor instead of a poetic vagrant, you would soon discover that my choice must lie, not between truth and falsehood, neither of which I can ever ascertain, but between reasonable and well informed opinion and sentimental and ill informed impulse.

JESUS. Nevertheless, opinion is a dead thing and impulse a live thing. You cannot impose on me with your reasonable and well informed opinion. If it is your will to crucify me, I can find you a dozen reasons for doing so; and your police can supply you with a hundred facts to support the reasons. If it is your will to spare me I can find you just as many reasons for that; and my disciples will supply you with more facts than you will have time or patience to listen to. That is why your lawyers can plead as well for one side as another, and can therefore plead without dishonor for the side that pays them, like the hackney charioteer who will drive you north as readily as south for the same fare.

PILATE. You are cleverer than I thought; and you are right. There is my will; and there is the will of Cæsar to which my will must give way; and there is above Cæsar the will of the gods. But these wills are in continual conflict with oneanother; therefore they are not truth; for truth is one, and cannot conflict with itself. There are conflicting opinions and conflicting wills; but there is no truth except the momentary truth that I am sitting in this chair. You tell me that you are here to bear witness to the truth! You, a vagrant, a talker, who have never had to pass a sentence nor levy a tax nor issue an edict! What have you to say that I should not have the presumption scourged out of you by my executioners?

JESUS. Scourging is not a cure for presumption, nor is it justice, though you will perhaps call it so in your report to Cæsar: it is cruelty; and that cruelty is wicked and horrible because it is the weapon with which the sons of Satan slay the sons of God is part of the eternal truth you seek.

PILATE. Leave out cruelty: all government is cruel; for nothing is so cruel as impunity. A salutary severity—

JESUS. Oh please! You must excuse me, noble Governor; but I am so made by God that official phrases make me violently sick. Salutary severity is ipecacuanha to me. I have spoken to you as one man to another, in living words. Do not be so ungrateful as to answer me in dead ones.

PILATE. In the mouth of a Roman words mean something: in the mouth of a Jew they are a cheap substitute for strong drink. If we allowed you you would fill the whole world with your scriptures and psalms and talmuds; and the history of mankind would become a tale of fine words and villainous deeds.

JESUS. Yet the word came first, before it was made flesh. The word was the beginning. The word was with God before he made us. Nay, the word was God.

PILATE. And what may all that mean, pray?

JESUS. The difference between man and Roman is but a word; but it makes all the difference. The difference between Roman and Jew is only a word.

PILATE. It is a fact.

JESUS. A fact that was first a thought; for a thought is the substance of a word. I am no mere chance pile of flesh and bone: if I were only that, I should fall into corruption and dust before your eyes. I am the embodiment of a thought of God: I am the Word made flesh: that is what holds me together standing before you in the image of God.

PILATE. That is well argued; but what is sauce for the goose is sauce for the gander; and it seems to me that if you are the Word made flesh so also am I.

JESUS. Have I not said so again and again? Have they not stoned me in the streets for saying it? Have I not sent my apostles to proclaim this great news to the Gentiles and to the very ends of the world? The Word is God. And God is within you. It was when I said this that the Jews—my own people—began picking up stones. But why should you, the Gentile, reproach me for it?

PILATE. I have not reproached you for it. I pointed it out to you.

JESUS. Forgive me. I am so accustomed to be contradicted—

PILATE. Just so. There are many sorts of words; and they are all made flesh sooner or later. Go among my soldiers and you will hear many filthy words and witness many cruel and hateful deeds that began as thoughts. I do not allow those words to be spoken in my presence. I punish those deeds as crimes. Your truth, as you call it, can be nothing but the thoughts for which you have found words which will take effect in deeds if I set you loose to scatter your words broadcast among the people. Your own people who bring you to me tell me that your thoughts are abominable and your words blasphemous. How am I to refute them? How am I to distinguish between the blasphemies of my soldiers reported to me by my centurions and your blasphemies reported to me by your High Priest?

JESUS. Woe betide you and the world if you do not distinguish!

PILATE. So you think. I am not frightened. Why do you think so?

JESUS. I do not think: I know. I have it from God.

PILATE. I have the same sort of knowledge from several gods.

JESUS. In so far as you know the truth you have it from my God, who is your heavenly father and mine. He has many names and his nature is manifold. Call him what you will: he is still Our Father. Does a father tell his children lies?

PILATE. Yes: many lies. You have an earthly father and an earthly mother. Did they tell you what you are preaching?

JESUS. Alas! no.

PILATE. Then you are defying your father and

mother. You are defying your Church. You are breaking your God's commandments, and claiming a right
to do so. You are pleading for the poor, and declaring
that it is easier for a camel to pass through the eye of a
needle than for a rich man to enter your God's paradise. Yet you have feasted at the tables of the rich,
and encouraged harlots to spend on perfume for your
feet money that might have been given to the poor,
thereby so disgusting your treasurer that he has
betrayed you to the High Priest for a handful of silver.
Well, feast as much as you please: I do not blame you
for refusing to play the fakir and make yourself a
walking exhibition of silly austerities; but I must draw
the line at your making a riot in the temple and throwing the gold of the moneychangers to be scrambled
for by your partizans. I have a law to administer. The
law forbids obscenity, sedition, and blasphemy. You
are accused of sedition and blasphemy. You do not
deny them: you only talk about the truth, which turns
out to be nothing but what you like to believe. Your
blasphemy is nothing to me: the whole Jewish religion
is blasphemy from beginning to end from my Roman
point of view; but it means a great deal to the High
Priest; and I cannot keep order in Jewry except by
dealing with Jewish fools according to Jewish folly.
But sedition concerns me and my office very closely;
and when you undertook to supersede the Roman
Empire by a kingdom in which you and not Cæsar
are to occupy the throne, you were guilty of the uttermost sedition. I am loth to have you crucified; for
though you are only a Jew, and a half baked young one
at that, yet I perceive that you are in your Jewish way
a man of quality; and it makes me uneasy to throw a
man of quality to the mob, even if his quality be only
a Jewish quality. For I am a patrician and therefore

myself a man of quality; and hawks should not pick out hawks' eyes. I am actually condescending to parley with you at this length in the merciful hope of finding an excuse for tolerating your blasphemy and sedition. In defence you offer me nothing but an empty phrase about the truth. I am sincere in wishing to spare you; for if I do not release you I shall have to release that blackguard Barabbas, who has gone further than you and killed somebody, whereas I understand that you have only raised a Jew from the dead. So for the last time set your wits to work, and find me a sound reason for letting a seditious blasphemer go free.

JESUS. I do not ask you to set me free; nor would I accept my life at the price of Barabbas's death even if I believed that you could countermand the ordeal to which I am predestined. Yet for the satisfaction of your longing for the truth I will tell you that the answer to your demand is your own argument that neither you nor the prisoner whom you judge can prove that he is in the right; therefore you must not judge me lest you be yourself judged. Without sedition and blasphemy the world would stand still and the Kingdom of God never be a stage nearer. The Roman Empire began with a wolf suckling two human infants. If these infants had not been wiser than their fostermother your empire would be a pack of wolves. It is by children who are wiser than their fathers, subjects who are wiser than their emperors, beggars and vagrants who are wiser than their priests, that men rise from being beasts of prey to believing in me and being saved.

PILATE. What do you mean by believing in you?

JESUS. Seeing the world as I do. What else could it mean?

PILATE. And you are the Christ, the Messiah, eh?

JESUS. Were I Satan, my argument would still hold.

PILATE. And I am to spare and encourage every heretic, every rebel, every lawbreaker, every rapscallion lest he should turn out to be wiser than all the generations who made the Roman law and built up the Roman Empire on it?

JESUS. By their fruits ye shall know them. Beware how you kill a thought that is new to you. For that thought may be the foundation of the kingdom of God on earth.

PILATE. It may also be the ruin of all kingdoms, all law, and all human society. It may be the thought of the beast of prey striving to return.

JESUS. The beast of prey is not striving to return: the kingdom of God is striving to come. The empire that looks back in terror shall give way to the kingdom that looks forward with hope. Terror drives men mad: hope and faith give them divine wisdom. The men whom you fill with fear will stick at no evil and perish in their sin: the men whom I fill with faith shall inherit the earth. I say to you Cast out fear. Speak no more vain things to me about the greatness of Rome. The greatness of Rome, as you call it, is nothing but fear: fear of the past and fear of the future, fear of the poor, fear of the rich, fear of the High Priests, fear of the Jews and Greeks who are learned, fear of the Gauls and Goths and Huns who are barbarians, fear of the Carthage you destroyed to save you from your fear of it and now fear worse than ever, fear of imperial Cæsar, the idol you have yourself created, and fear of me, the penniless vagrant, buffeted and mocked, fear of everything except the rule of God: faith in nothing but blood and iron and gold. You, standing for Rome, are the universal coward: I, standing for the kingdom of God, have braved everything, lost everything, and won an eternal crown.

PILATE. You have won a crown of thorns; and you shall wear it on the cross. You are a more dangerous fellow than I thought. For your blasphemy against the god of the high priests I care nothing: you may trample their religion into hell for all I care; but you have blasphemed against Cæsar and against the Empire; and you mean it, and have the power to turn men's hearts against it as you have half turned mine. Therefore I must make an end of you whilst there is still some law left in the world.

JESUS. Law is blind without counsel. The counsel men agree with is vain: it is only the echo of their own voices. A million echoes will not help you to rule righteously. But he who does not fear you and shews you the other side is a pearl of the greatest price. Slay me and you go blind to your damnation. The greatest of God's names is Counsellor; and when your Empire is dust and your name a byword among the nations the temples of the living God shall still ring with his praise as Wonderful! Counsellor! the Everlasting Father, the Prince of Peace.

THE SACREDNESS OF CRITICISM

And so the last word remains with Christ and Handel; and this must stand as the best defence of Tolerance until a better man than I makes a better job of it.

Put shortly and undramatically the case is that a civilization cannot progress without criticism, and must therefore, to save itself from stagnation and putrefaction, declare impunity for criticism. This means impunity not only for propositions which, however novel, seem interesting, statesmanlike, and

respectable, but for propositions that shock the uncritical as obscene, seditious, blasphemous, heretical,
and revolutionary. That sound Catholic institution,
the Devil's Advocate, must be privileged as possibly
the Herald of the World to Come. The difficulty is to
distinguish between the critic and the criminal or
lunatic, between liberty of precept and liberty of
example. It may be vitally necessary to allow a person
to advocate Nudism; but it may not be expedient to
allow that person to walk along Piccadilly stark naked.
Karl Marx writing the death warrant of private property in the reading room of the British Museum was
sacred; but if Karl Marx had sent the rent of his villa
in Maitland Park to the Chancellor of the Exchequer,
and shot the landlord's agents when they came to
distrain on his furniture or execute a writ of ejectment,
he could hardly have escaped hanging by pleading his
right to criticize. Not until the criticism changes the
law can the magistrate allow the critic to give effect to
it. We are so dangerously uneducated in citizenship
that most of us assume that we have an unlimited right
to change our conduct the moment we have changed
our minds. People who have a vague notion that
Socialism is a state of society in which everyone gives
away everything he possesses to everybody else occasionally reproach me because I, being a Socialist, do
not immediately beggar myself in this fashion. People
who imagined, more specifically, that a Socialist could
not consistently keep a motor car, almost succeeded in
making a public question of the possession of such a
vehicle by a Prime Minister who at that time professed Socialism. But even if these idiots had really
understood what they were talking about, they would
have been wrong in supposing that a hostile critic of
the existing social order either could or should behave

as if he were living in his own particular Utopia. He may, at most, be a little eccentric at the cost of being indulged as slightly cracked.

On the other hand the Government, too, has not only a right but a duty of criticism. If it is to abandon once for all its savage superstition that whoever breaks the law is fair game for the torturers, and that the wrong wrought by the evildoer can be expiated and undone by a worse wrong done to him by judges and priests: if it is to substitute the doctrine of Jesus that punishment is only a senseless attempt to make a white out of two blacks, and to abolish the monstrous list of crimes and punishments by which these superstitions have been reduced to practice for routine officials, then there must be a stupendous extension of governmental criticism; for every crime will raise the essential critical question whether the criminal is fit to live at all, and if so whether he is fit to live under more or less tutelage and discipline like a soldier, or at normal liberty under an obligation to make good the damage he has cost.

For such functions as these we shall need critics educated otherwise than our judges of today; but the same may be said of all whose public functions transcend the application of a routine.

I have no doubt that the eradication of malice, vindictiveness, and Sadist libido on these terms from the personal contacts of citizens with their rulers, far from having a reassuring effect, is likely to be rather terrifying at first, as all people with any tenderness of conscience will feel the deepest misgivings as to whether they are really worth keeping alive in a highly civilized community; but that will wear off as standards of worth get established and known by practice. In the meantime the terror will act as a sort of social conscience which is dangerously lacking at present, and which none of our model educational establishments ever dreams of inculcating.

AYOT ST LAWRENCE, *22nd October, 1933*

$\lceil$ ACT I $\rceil$

The Cabinet Room in number ten Downing Street, Westminster, the official residence of the British Prime Minister. The illustrious holder of that office, Sir Arthur Chavender, is reading The Times on the hearth under the portrait of Walpole. The fireplace wall is covered with bookshelves; but one bit of it, on Walpole's right, is a masked door, painted with sham books and shelves, leading to the Minister's private apartments; and in the end of the same wall, on Walpole's left, is a door leading to the office of Sir Arthur's private secretary Miss Hilda Hanways. The main door is in the side wall on Walpole's right. In the opposite wall on his left are the spacious windows. Everything is on an imposing scale, including an oblong table across the middle of the room, with four-teen leather upholstered chairs, six at each side and one at each end, pushed in all along it. The presidential chair is the central one next the cold fireplace (it is mid-July); and there is a telephone and a switchboard on the table within reach of it. Sir Arthur has pulled it round and is making himself comfortable in it as he reads. At the end of the table nearest the window a silver tray, with coffee and milk for one person, indicates Sir Arthur's unofficial seat. In the corner farthest from Walpole, on his right, is a writing bureau and chair for the secretary. In the corresponding corner on his left, an armchair. There is a bluebook lying, neglected and dusty, on a half empty shelf of the bookcase within reach of the Prime Minister's seat.

Sir Arthur can hardly be much less than fifty; but his natural buoyancy makes him look younger. He has an orator's voice of pleasant tone; and his manners are very genial. In oldish clothes he has the proper aristocratic air of being carelessly but well dressed, an easy feat for him, as he is so trimly built that any clothes would look well cut on him. On the whole, a very engaging personality.

He reads The Times until his secretary hurries in from her office, with her notebook and a sheaf of letters in her hand. Her age is unknown; but she is made up to pass as reasonably young and attractive. She looks capable; but she does not carry the burden of State affairs as easily as the Prime Minister. Both are worried; but with a difference. She is worried not only by an excess of business but a sense of responsibility. He is equally worried by the excess of business; but in him enjoyment of his position leaves no doubt in his mind as to his own entire adequacy to it.

HILDA. I hear you have been asking for me, Sir Arthur. I'm so sorry to be late; but really the streets are becoming quite impassable with the crowds of unemployed. I took a taxi; but it was no use: we were blocked by a procession; and I had to get out and push my way through. [*She goes to her bureau*].

SIR ARTHUR [*rising*] What on earth good do they think they can do themselves by crowding aimlessly about Westminster and the public offices?

HILDA. Thank Goodness the police wont let them into Downing Street. [*She sits down*]. They would be all over the doorstep.

SIR ARTHUR. It's all so foolish—so ignorant, poor chaps! [*He throws The Times on the table and moves to the end chair, where his coffee is*]. They think because I'm Prime Minister I'm Divine Providence and can find jobs for them before trade revives. [*He sits down and fidgets with his papers*].

HILDA. Trafalgar Square's full. The Horse Guards parade is full. The Mall is full all the way down to Marlborough House and Buckingham Palace.

SIR ARTHUR. They have no right to be there. Trafalgar Square is not a public place: it belongs to the Commissioner of Woods and Forests. The Horse Guards parade is reserved for the military. The Mall is a thoroughfare: anyone stopping there is guilty of obstruction. What are the police thinking of? Why dont they clear them out?

HILDA. I asked the policeman who got me through to the gates why they didnt. He said "We're only too glad to have them where they cant break any windows, and where the mounted men can have a fair whack at the Hooligan Fringe when they get too obstreperous."

SIR ARTHUR. Hooligan Fringe! He got that out of the papers. It only encourages them to write them up like that.

HILDA. Sir Broadfoot Basham has come over from Scotland Yard. He is talking to Lady Chavender.

SIR ARTHUR [*rising and making for the telephone*] Yes: I telephoned for him. He really must do something to stop these meetings. It was a mistake to make a man with a name like that Chief Commissioner of Police. People think him a trampling, bashing, brutal terrorist no matter how considerately the police behave. What we need is a thoroughly popular figure. [*He takes up the telephone*] Ask Sir Broadfoot Basham to come up.

HILDA. I dont think any chief of police could be popular at present. Every day they are bludgeoning deputations of the unemployed. [*She sits down and busies herself with letters*].

SIR ARTHUR. Poor devils! I hate that part of the business. But what are the police to do? We cant have the sittings of the local authorities threatened by deputations. Deputations are frightful nuisances even in the quietest times; but just now they are a public danger.

The Chief Commissioner of Police enters by the main door. A capable looking man from the military point of view. He is a gentleman: and his manners are fairly pleasant; but they are not in the least conciliatory.

Hilda rises and pulls out a chair for him at the end of the table nearest to her and farthest from Sir Arthur; then returns to her work at her desk. Sir Arthur comes round to his side of the table.

SIR ARTHUR. Morning, Basham. Sit down. I'm devilishly busy; but you are always welcome to your ten minutes.

BASHAM [*coolly, sitting down*] Thank you. You sent for me. [*Anxiously*] Anything new?

SIR ARTHUR. These street corner meetings are going beyond all bounds.

BASHAM [*relieved*] What harm do they do? Crowds are dangerous when theyve nothing to listen to or look at. The meetings keep them amused. They save us trouble.

SIR ARTHUR. Thats all very well for you, Basham; but think of the trouble they make for me! Remember: this is a National Government, not a party one. I am up against my Conservative colleagues all the time; and they cant swallow the rank sedition that goes on every day at these meetings. Sir Dexter Rightside— you know what a regular old Diehard he is—heard a speaker say that if the police used tear gas the unemployed would give old Dexy something to cry for without any tear gas. That has brought matters to a head in the Cabinet. We shall make an Order in Council to enable you to put a stop to all street meetings and speeches.

BASHAM [*unimpressed—slowly*] If you dont mind, P.M., I had rather you didnt do that.

SIR ARTHUR. Why not?

BASHAM. Crowd psychology.

SIR ARTHUR. Nonsense! Really, Basham, if you are going to come this metaphysical rot over me I shall begin to wonder whether your appointment wasnt a mistake.

BASHAM. Of course it was a mistake. Dealing with the unemployed is not a soldier's job; and I was a soldier. If you want these crowds settled on soldierly lines, say so; and give me half a dozen machine guns. The streets will be clear before twelve o'clock.

SIR ARTHUR. Man: have you considered the effect on the bye-elections?

BASHAM. A soldier has nothing to do with elections. You shew me a crowd and tell me to disperse it. All youll hear is a noise like a watchman's rattle. Quite simple.

SIR ARTHUR. Far too simple. You soldiers never understand the difficulties a statesman has to contend with.

BASHAM. Well, whats your alternative?

SIR ARTHUR. I have told you. Arrest the sedition mongers. That will shut old Dexy's mouth.

BASHAM. So that Satan may find mischief still for idle hands to do. No, P.M.: the right alternative is mine: keep the crowd amused. You ought to know that, I think, better than most men.

SIR ARTHUR. I! What do you mean?

BASHAM. The point is to prevent the crowd doing anything, isnt it?

SIR ARTHUR. Anything mischievous: I suppose so. But—

BASHAM. An English crowd will never do anything, mischievous or the reverse, while it is listening to speeches. And the fellows who make the speeches can be depended on never to do anything else. In the first place, they dont know how. In the second, they are afraid. I am instructing my agents to press all the talking societies, the Ethical Societies, the Socialist societies, the Communists, the Fascists, the Anarchists, the Syndicalists, the official Labor Party, the Independent Labor Party, the Salvation Army, the Church Army and the Atheists, to send their best tub-thumpers into the streets to seize the opportunity.

SIR ARTHUR. What opportunity?

BASHAM. They dont know. Neither do I. It's only a phrase that means nothing: just what they are sure to rise at. I must keep Trafalgar Square going night and day. A few Labor M.P.s would help. You have a rare lot of gasbags under your thumb in the House. If you could send half a dozen of them down to the Yard, I could plant them where they would be really useful.

SIR ARTHUR [incensed] Basham: I must tell you that we are quite determined to put a stop to this modern fashion of speaking disrespectfully of the House of Commons. If it goes too far we shall not hesitate to bring prominent offenders to the bar of the House, no matter what their position is.

BASHAM. Arthur: as responsible head of the police, I am up against the facts all day and every day; and one of the facts is that nowadays nobody outside the party cliques cares a brass button for the House of Commons. [Rising] You will do what I ask you as to letting the speaking go on, wont you?

SIR ARTHUR. Well, I—er—

BASHAM. Unless you are game to try the machine guns.

SIR ARTHUR. Oh do drop that, Basham [*he returns to his chair and sits moodily*].

BASHAM. Righto! We'll let them talk. Thanks ever so much. Sorry to have taken up so much of your time: I know it's priceless. [*He hurries to the door; then hesitates and adds*] By the way, I know it's asking a lot; but if you could give us a turn in Trafalgar Square yourself—some Sunday afternoon would be best—it—

SIR ARTHUR [*springing up, thoroughly roused*] I!!!!

BASHAM [*hurriedly*] No: of course you couldnt. Only, it would do such a lot of good—keep the crowd quiet talking about it for a fortnight. However, of course it's impossible: say no more: so long. [*He goes out*].

SIR ARTHUR [*collapsing into his chair*] Well, really! Basham's losing his head. I wonder what he meant by saying that I ought to know better than most men. What ought I to know better than most men?

HILDA. I think he meant that you are such a wonderful speaker you ought to know what a magical effect a fine speech has on a crowd.

SIR ARTHUR [*musing*] Do you know, I am not at all sure that there is not something in his idea of my making a speech in Trafalgar Square. I have not done such a thing for many many years; but I have stood between the lions in my time; and I believe that if I were to tackle the unemployed face to face, and explain to them that I intend to call a conference in March next on the prospects of a revival of trade, it would have a wonderfully soothing effect.

HILDA. But it's impossible. You have a conference every month until November. And think of the time taken by the travelling! One in Paris! Two in Geneva!

One in Japan! You cant possibly do it: you will break down.

SIR ARTHUR. And shall I be any better at home here leading the House? sitting up all night in bad air listening to fools insulting me? I tell you I should have been dead long ago but for the relief of these conferences: the journeys and the change. And I look forward to Japan. I shall be able to pick up some nice old bric-a-brac there.

HILDA. Oh well! You know best.

SIR ARTHUR [*energetically*] And now to work. Work! work! work! [*He rises and paces the floor in front of the table*]. I want you to take down some notes for my speech this afternoon at the Church House. The Archbishop tells me that the Anglo-Catholics are going mad on what they call Christian Communism, and that I must head them off.

HILDA. There are those old notes on the economic difficulties of Socialism that you used at the British Association last year.

SIR ARTHUR. No: these parsons know too much about that. Besides, this is not the time to talk about economic difficulties: we're up to the neck in them. The Archbishop says "Avoid figures; and stick to the fact that Socialism would break up the family." I believe he is right: a bit of sentiment about the family always goes down well. Just jot this down for me. [*Dictating*] Family. Foundation of civilization. Foundation of the empire.

HILDA. Will there be any Hindus or Mahometans present?

SIR ARTHUR. No. No polygamists at the Church House. Besides, everybody knows that The Family means the British family. By the way, I can make a point of that. Put down in a separate line, in red capitals, "One man one wife." Let me see now: can I work that up? "One child one father." How would that do?

HILDA. I think it would be safer to say "One child one mother."

SIR ARTHUR. No: that might get a laugh—the wrong sort of laugh. I'd better not risk it. Strike it out. A laugh in the wrong place in the Church House would be the very devil. Where did you get that necklace? it's rather pretty. I havnt seen it before.

HILDA. Ive worn it every day for two months. [*Striking out the "one child" note*] Yes?

SIR ARTHUR. Then—er—what subject are we on? [*Testily*] I wish you wouldnt interrupt me: I had the whole speech in my head beautifully; and now it's gone.

HILDA. Sorry. The family.

SIR ARTHUR. The family? Whose family? What family? The Holy Family? The Royal Family? The Swiss Family Robinson? Do be a little more explicit, Miss Hanways.

HILDA [*gently insistent*] Not any particular family. THE family. Socialism breaking up the family. For the Church House speech this afternoon.

SIR ARTHUR. Yes yes yes, of course. I was in the House yesterday until three in the morning; and my brains are just so much tripe.

HILDA. Why did you sit up? The business didnt matter.

SIR ARTHUR [*scandalized*] Not matter! You really must not say these things, Miss Hanways. A full dress debate on whether Jameson or Thompson was right about what Johnson said in the Cabinet!

HILDA. Ten years ago.

SIR ARTHUR. What does that matter? The real

[637]

question: the question whether Jameson or Thompson is a liar, is a vital question of the first importance.

HILDA. But theyre both liars.

SIR ARTHUR. Of course they are; but the division might have affected their inclusion in the next Cabinet. The whole House rose at it. Look at the papers this morning! Full of it.

HILDA. And three lines about the unemployed, though I was twenty minutes late trying to shove my way through them. Really, Sir Arthur, you should have come home to bed. You will kill yourself if you try to get through your work and attend so many debates as well: you will indeed.

SIR ARTHUR. Miss Hanways: I wish I could persuade you to remember occasionally that I happen to be the leader of the House of Commons.

HILDA. Oh, what is the use of leading the House if it never goes anywhere? It just breaks my heart to see the state you come home in. You are good for nothing next morning.

SIR ARTHUR [*yelling at her*] Dont remind me of it: do you think I dont know? My brain is overworked: my mental grasp is stretched and strained to breaking point. I shall go mad. [*Pulling himself together*] However, it's no use grousing about it: I shall have a night off going to Geneva, and a week-end at Chequers. But it is hard to govern a country and do fifty thousand other things every day that might just as well be done by the Beadle of Burlington Arcade. Well, well, we mustnt waste time. Work! work! work! [*He returns to his chair and sits down resolutely*]. Get along with it. What were we talking about?

HILDA. The family.

SIR ARTHUR [*grasping his temples distractedly*] Oh

[638]

dear! Has Lady Chavender's sister-in-law been making a fuss again?

HILDA. No, no. The family. Not any real family. THE family. Socialism breaking up the family. Your speech this afternoon at the Church House.

SIR ARTHUR. Ah, of course. I am going dotty. Thirty years in Parliament and ten on the Front Bench would drive any man dotty. I have only one set of brains and I need ten. I—

HILDA [*urgently*] We must get on with the notes for your speech, Sir Arthur. The morning has half gone already; and weve done nothing.

SIR ARTHUR [*again infuriated*] How can the busiest man in England find time to do anything? It is you who have wasted the morning interrupting me with your silly remarks about your necklace. What do I care about your necklace?

HILDA. You gave it to me, Sir Arthur.

SIR ARTHUR. Did I? Ha ha ha! Yes: I believe I did. I bought it in Venice. But come along now. What about that speech?

HILDA. Yes. The family. It was about the family.

SIR ARTHUR. Well, I know that: I have not yet become a complete idiot. You keep saying the family, the family, the family.

HILDA. Socialism and the family. How Socialism will break up the family.

SIR ARTHUR. Who says Socialism will break up the family? Dont be a fool.

HILDA. The Archbishop wants you to say it. At the Church House.

SIR ARTHUR. Decidedly I am going mad.

HILDA. No: you are only tired. You were getting along all right. One man one wife: that is where you stopped.

SIR ARTHUR. One man one wife is one wife too many, if she has a lot of brothers who cant get on with the women they marry. Has it occurred to you, Miss Hanways, that the prospect of Socialism destroying the family may not be altogether unattractive?

HILDA [*despairingly*] Oh, Sir Arthur, we must get on with the notes: we really must. I have all the letters to do yet. Do try to pick up the thread. The family the foundation of the empire. The foundation of Christianity. Of civilization. Of human society.

SIR ARTHUR. Thats enough about the foundation: it wont bear any more. I must have another word to work up. Let me see. I have it. Nationalization of women.

HILDA [*remonstrating*] Oh, Sir Arthur!

SIR ARTHUR. Whats the matter now?

HILDA. Such bunk!

SIR ARTHUR. Miss Hanways: when a statesman is not talking bunk he is making trouble for himself; and Goodness knows I have trouble enough without making any more. Put this down. [*He rises and takes his platform attitude at the end of the table*]. "No, your Grace, my lords and gentlemen. Nationalize the land if you will; nationalize our industries if we must; nationalize education, housing, science, art, the theatre, the opera, even the cinema; but spare our women."

HILDA [*having taken it down*] Is that the finish?

SIR ARTHUR [*abandoning the attitude and pacing about*] No: write in red capitals under it "Rock of Ages."

HILDA. I think Rock of Ages will be rather a shock unless in connexion with something very sincere. May I suggest "The Church's One Foundation"?

SIR ARTHUR. Yes. Much better. Thank you. The family the Church's one foundation. Splendid.

Miss Flavia Chavender, 19, *bursts violently into the room through the masked door and dashes to her father.*

FLAVIA. Papa: I will not stand Mamma any longer. She interferes with me in every possible way out of sheer dislike of me. I refuse to live in this house with her a moment longer.

Lady Chavender follows her in, speaking as she enters, and comes between the Prime Minister and his assailant.

LADY CHAVENDER. I knew you were coming here to make a scene and disturb your father, though he has had hardly six hours sleep this week, and was up all night. I am so sorry, Arthur: she is uncontrollable.

David Chavender, 18, *slight, refined, rather small for his age, charges in to the table.*

DAVID [*in a childish falsetto*] Look here, Mamma. Cant you let Flavia alone ? I wont stand by and see her nagged at and treated like a child of six. Nag! nag! nag! everything she does.

LADY CHAVENDER. Nag!! I control myself to the limit of human endurance with you all. But Flavia makes a study of annoying me.

FLAVIA. It's not true: I have considered you and given up all the things I wanted for you until I have no individuality left. If I take up a book you want me to read something else. If I want to see anybody you want me to see somebody else. If I choose the color of my own dress you want something different and dowdy. I cant sit right nor stand right nor do my hair right nor dress myself right: my life here is a hell.

LADY CHAVENDER. Flavia!!

FLAVIA [*passionately*] Yes, hell.

DAVID. Quite true. [*Fortissimo*] Hell.

LADY CHAVENDER [*quietly*] Miss Hanways: would you mind—

HILDA. Yes, Lady Chavender [*she rises to go*]

FLAVIA. You neednt go, Hilda. You know what I have to endure.

DAVID. Damn all this paralyzing delicacy! Damn it!

LADY CHAVENDER. Arthur—

SIR ARTHUR [*patting her*] Never mind, dear. They must be let talk. [*He returns placidly to his chair*]. It's just like the House of Commons, except that the speeches are shorter.

FLAVIA. Oh, it's no use trying to make papa listen to anything. [*She throws herself despairingly into Basham's chair and writhes*].

DAVID [*approaching Sir Arthur with dignity*] I really think, father, you might for once in a way take some slight interest in the family.

SIR ARTHUR. My dear boy, at this very moment I am making notes for a speech on the family. Ask Miss Hanways.

HILDA. Yes. Mr Chavender: Sir Arthur is to speak this afternoon on the disintegrating effect of Socialism on family life.

FLAVIA [*irresistible amusement struggling with hysterics and getting the better of them*] Ha ha! Ha ha ha!

DAVID [*retreating*] Ha ha! Haw! Thats the best—ha ha ha!

SIR ARTHUR. I dont see the joke. Why this hilarity?

DAVID. Treat the House to a brief description of this family; and you will get the laugh of your life.

FLAVIA. Damn the family!

LADY CHAVENDER. Flavia!

FLAVIA [*bouncing up*] Yes: there you go. I mustnt say damn. I mustnt say anything I feel and think, only what you feel and think. Thats family life. Scold, scold, scold!

DAVID. Squabble, squabble, squabble!

FLAVIA. Look at the unbearable way you treat me!
Look at the unbearable way you treat Papa!

SIR ARTHUR [*rising in flaming wrath*] How dare you?
Silence. Leave the room.

*After a moment of awestruck silence Flavia, rather
dazed by the avalanche she has brought down on herself,
looks at her father in a lost way; then bursts into tears
and runs out through the masked door.*

SIR ARTHUR [*quietly*] Youd better go too, my boy.

*David, also somewhat dazed, shrugs his shoulders and
goes out. Sir Arthur looks at Hilda. She hurries out
almost on tiptoe.*

SIR ARTHUR [*taking his wife in his arms affectionately*]
Treat me badly! You!! I could have killed her, poor
little devil.

*He sits down; and she passes behind him and takes the
nearest chair on his right.*

*She is a nice woman, and goodlooking; but she is
bored; and her habitual manner is one of apology for
being not only unable to take an interest in people, but
even to pretend that she does.*

LADY CHAVENDER. It serves us right, dear, for letting
them bring themselves up in the post-war fashion instead of teaching them to be ladies and gentlemen.
Besides, Flavia was right. I do treat you abominably.
And you are so good!

SIR ARTHUR. Nonsense! Such a horrid wicked thing
to say. Dont you know, my love, that you are the
best of wives? the very best as well as the very
dearest?

LADY CHAVENDER. You are certainly the best of
husbands, Arthur. You are the best of everything. I
dont wonder at the country adoring you. But Flavia
was quite right. It is the first time I have ever known
her to be right about anything. I am a bad wife and a

bad mother. I dislike my daughter and treat her badly. I like you very much; and I treat you abominably.

SIR ARTHUR. No; no.

LADY CHAVENDER. Yes, yes. I suppose it's something wrong in my constitution. I was not born for wifing and mothering. And yet I am very very fond of you, as you know. But I have a grudge against your career.

SIR ARTHUR. My career! [*Complacently*] Well, theres not much wrong with that, is there? Of course I know it keeps me too much away from home. That gives you a sort of grudge against it. All the wives of successful men are a bit like that. But it's better to see too little of a husband than too much of him, isnt it?

LADY CHAVENDER. I am so glad that you really feel successful.

SIR ARTHUR. Well, it may sound conceited and all that; but after all a man cant be Prime Minister and go about with a modest cough pretending to be a nobody. Facts are facts; and the facts in my case are that I have climbed to the top of the tree; I am happy in my work; and—

LADY CHAVENDER. Your what?

SIR ARTHUR. You are getting frightfully deaf, dear. I said "my work."

LADY CHAVENDER. You call it work?

SIR ARTHUR. Brain work, dear, brain work. Do you really suppose that governing the country is not work, but a sort of gentlemanly diversion?

LADY CHAVENDER. But you dont govern the country, Arthur. The country isnt governed: it just slummocks along anyhow.

SIR ARTHUR. I have to govern within democratic limits. I cannot go faster than our voters will let me.

LADY CHAVENDER. Oh, your voters! What do they

know about government? Football, prizefighting, war: that is what they like. And they like war because it isnt real to them: it's only a cinema show. War is real to me; and I hate it, as every woman to whom it is real hates it. But to you it is only part of your game: one of the regular moves of the Foreign Office and the War Office.

SIR ARTHUR. My dear, I hate war as much as you do. It makes a Prime Minister's job easy because it brings every dog to heel; but it produces coalitions; and I believe in party government.

LADY CHAVENDER [*rising*] Oh, it's no use talking to you, Arthur. [*She comes behind him and plants her hands on his shoulders*]. You are a dear and a duck and a darling; but you live in fairyland and I live in the hard wicked world. Thats why I cant be a good wife and take an interest in your career.

SIR ARTHUR. Stuff! Politics are not a woman's business: thats all it means. Thank God I have not a political wife. Look at Higginbotham! He was just ripe for the Cabinet when his wife went into Parliament and made money by journalism. That was the end of him.

LADY CHAVENDER. And I married a man with a hopelessly parliamentary mind; and that was the end of me.

SIR ARTHUR. Yes, yes, my pettums. I know that you have sacrificed yourself to keeping my house and sewing on my buttons; and I am not ungrateful. I am sometimes remorseful; but I love it. And now you must run away, I am very very very busy this morning.

LADY CHAVENDER. Yes, yes, very very busy doing nothing. And it wears you out far more than if your mind had something sensible to work on! Youll have a nervous breakdown if you go on like this. Promise me that you will see the lady I spoke to you about—if you wont see a proper doctor.

SIR ARTHUR. But you told me this woman is a doctor! [*He rises and breaks away from her*]. Once for all, I wont see any doctor. I'm old enough to do my own doctoring; and I'm not going to pay any doctor, male or female, three guineas to tell me what I know perfectly well already: that my brain's overworked and I must take a fortnight off on the links, or go for a sea voyage.

LADY CHAVENDER. She charges twenty guineas, Arthur.

SIR ARTHUR [*shaken*] Oh! Does she? What for?

LADY CHAVENDER. Twenty guineas for the diagnosis and twelve guineas a week at her sanatorium in the Welsh mountains, where she wants to keep you under observation for six weeks. That would really rest you; and I think you would find her a rather interesting and attractive woman.

SIR ARTHUR. Has she a good cook?

LADY CHAVENDER. I dont think that matters.

SIR ARTHUR. Not matter!

LADY CHAVENDER. No. She makes her patients fast.

SIR ARTHUR. Tell her I'm not a Mahatma. If I pay twelve guineas a week I shall expect three meals a day for it.

LADY CHAVENDER. Then you will see her?

SIR ARTHUR. Certainly not, if I have to pay twenty guineas for it.

LADY CHAVENDER. No, no. Only a social call, not a professional visit. Just to amuse you, and gratify her curiosity. She wants to meet you.

SIR ARTHUR. Very well, dear, very well, very well. This woman has got round you, I see. Well, she shant get round me; but to please you I'll have a look at her.

And now you really must run away. I have a frightful mass of work to get through this morning.

LADY CHAVENDER. Thank you, darling. [*She kisses him*] May I tell Flavia she is forgiven?

SIR ARTHUR. Yes. But I havnt really forgiven her. I'll never forgive her.

LADY CHAVENDER [*smiling*] Dearest. [*She kisses his fingers and goes out, giving him a parting smile as she goes through the masked door*].

Sir Arthur, left alone, looks inspired and triumphant. He addresses an imaginary assembly.

SIR ARTHUR. "My lords and gentlemen: you are not theorists. You are not rhapsodists. You are no longer young"—no, damn it, old Middlesex wont like that. "We have all been young. We have seen visions and dreamt dreams. We have cherished hopes and striven towards ideals. We have aspired to things that have not been realized. But we are now settled experienced men, family men. We are husbands and fathers. Yes, my lords and gentlemen: husbands and fathers. And I venture to claim your unanimous consent when I affirm that we have found something in these realities that was missing in the ideals. I thank you for that burst of applause: which I well know is no mere tribute to my poor eloquence, but the spontaneous and irresistible recognition of the great natural truth that our friends the Socialists have left out of their fancy pictures of a mass society in which regulation is to take the place of emotion and economics of honest human passion." Whew! that took a long breath. "They never will, gentlemen, I say they never will. They will NOT [*he smites the table and pauses, glaring round at his imaginary hearers*]. I see that we are of one mind, my lords and gentlemen. I need not labor the point." Then labor it for the next ten minutes.

That will do. That will do. [*He sits down; rings the telephone bell; and seizes the milk jug, which he empties at a single draught*].

Hilda appears at the main door.

HILDA. Did you say you would receive a deputation from the Isle of Cats this morning? I have no note of it.

SIR ARTHUR. Oh, confound it, I believe I did. I totally forgot it.

HILDA. Theyve come.

SIR ARTHUR. Bother them!

HILDA. By all means. But how am I to get rid of them? What am I to say?

SIR ARTHUR [*resignedly*] Oh, I suppose I must see them. Why do I do these foolish things? Tell Burton to shew them in.

HILDA. Burton is in his shirt sleeves doing something to the refrigerator. I'd better introduce them.

SIR ARTHUR. Oh, bundle them in anyhow. And tell them I am frightfully busy.

She goes out, closing the door softly behind her. He pushes away the breakfast tray and covers it with The Times, which he opens out to its fullest extent for that purpose. Then he collects his papers into the vacant space, and takes up a big blue one, in the study of which he immerses himself profoundly.

HILDA [*flinging the door open*] The worshipful the Mayor of the Isle of Cats.

The Mayor, thick and elderly, enters, a little shyly, followed by (a) an unladylike but brilliant and very confident young woman in smart factory-made clothes after the latest Parisian models, (b) a powerfully built loud voiced young man fresh from Oxford University, defying convention in corduroys, pullover, and unshaven black beard, (c) a thin, undersized lower middle class

[648]

young man in an alderman's gown, evidently with a good conceit of himself, and (d) a sunny comfortable old chap in his Sunday best, who might be anything from a working man with a very sedentary job (say a watchman) to a city missionary of humble extraction. He is aggressively modest, or pretends to be, and comes in last with a disarming smile rather as a poor follower of the deputation than as presuming to form part of it. They group themselves at the door behind the Mayor, who is wearing his chain of office.

SIR ARTHUR [*starting from his preoccupation with important State documents, and advancing past the fireplace to greet the Mayor with charming affability*] What! My old friend Tom Humphries! How have you been all these years? Sit down. [*They shake hands, whilst Hilda deftly pulls out a chair from the end of the table nearest the door*].

The Mayor sits down, rather overwhelmed by the cordiality of his reception.

SIR ARTHUR [*continuing*] Well, well! fancy your being Mayor of—of—

HILDA [*prompting*] The Isle of Cats.

THE YOUNG WOMAN [*brightly, helping her out*] Down the river, Sir Arthur. Twenty minutes from your door by Underground.

THE OXFORD YOUTH [*discordantly*] Oh, he knows as well as you do, Aloysia. [*He advances offensively on Sir Arthur, who declines the proximity by retreating a step or two somewhat haughtily*]. Stow all this fo bunnum business, Chavender.

SIR ARTHUR. This what?

OXFORD YOUTH. Oh, chuck it. You know French as well as I do.

SIR ARTHUR. Oh, faux bonhomme, of course, yes. [*Looking him up and down*]. I see by your costume that

[649]

you represent the upper classes in the Isle of Cats.

OXFORD YOUTH. There are no upper classes in the Isle of Cats.

SIR ARTHUR. In that case, since it is agreed that there is to be no fo bunnum nonsense between us, may I ask what the dickens you are doing here?

OXFORD YOUTH. I am not here to bandy personalities. Whatever the accident of birth and the humbug of rank may have made me I am here as a delegate from the Borough Council and an elected representative of the riverside proletariat.

SIR ARTHUR [*suddenly pulling out a chair from the middle of the table—peremptorily*] Sit down. Dont break the chair. [*The Youth scowls at him and flings himself into the chair like a falling tree*]. You are all most welcome. Perhaps, Tom, you will introduce your young friends.

THE MAYOR [*introducing*] Alderwoman Aloysia Brollikins.

SIR ARTHUR [*effusively shaking her hand*] How do you do, Miss Brollikins? [*He pulls out a chair for her on the Oxford Youth's right*].

ALOYSIA. Nicely, thank you. Pleased to meet you, Sir Arthur. [*She sits*].

THE MAYOR. Alderman Blee.

SIR ARTHUR [*with flattering gravity, pressing his hand*] Ah, we have all heard of you, Mr Blee. Will you sit here? [*He indicates the presidential chair on the Oxford Youth's left*].

BLEE. Thank you. I do my best. [*He sits*].

THE MAYOR. Viscount Barking.

SIR ARTHUR [*triumphantly*] Ah! I thought so. A red Communist: what!

OXFORD YOUTH. Red as blood. Same red as the people's.

SIR ARTHUR. How did you get the blue out of it? The Barkings came over with the Conqueror.

OXFORD YOUTH [*rising*] Look here. The unemployed are starving. Is this a time for persiflage?

SIR ARTHUR. Camouflage, my lad, camouflage. Do you expect me to take you seriously in that get-up?

OXFORD YOUTH [*hotly*] I shall wear what I damn well please. I—

ALOYSIA. Shut up, Toffy. You promised to behave yourself. Sit down; and lets get to business.

BARKING [*subsides into his chair with a grunt of disgust*]!

SIR ARTHUR [*looking rather doubtfully at the old man, who is still standing*] Is this gentleman a member of your deputation?

THE MAYOR. Mr Hipney. Old and tried friend of the working class.

OXFORD YOUTH. Old Hipney. Why dont you call him by the name the East End knows him by? Old Hipney. Good old Hipney.

OLD HIPNEY [*slipping noiselessly into the secretary's chair at the bureau*] Dont mind me, Sir Arthur. I dont matter.

SIR ARTHUR. At such a crisis as the present, Mr Hipney, every public-spirited man matters. Delighted to meet you. [*He returns to his own chair and surveys them now that they are all seated, whilst Hilda slips discreetly out into her office*]. And now, what can I do for you, Miss Brollikins? What can I do for you, gentlemen?

THE MAYOR [*slowly*] Well, Sir Arthur, as far as I can make it out the difficulty seems to be that you cant do anything. But something's got to be done.

SIR ARTHUR [*stiffening suddenly*] May I ask why, if everything that is possible has already been done?

THE MAYOR. Well, the unemployed are—well, un-employed, you know.

SIR ARTHUR. We have provided for the unemployed. That provision has cost us great sacrifices; but we have made the sacrifices without complaining.

THE OXFORD YOUTH [*scornfully*] Sacrifices! What sacrifices? Are you starving? Have you pawned your overcoat? Are you sleeping ten in a room?

SIR ARTHUR. The noble lord enquires—

OXFORD YOUTH [*furiously*] Dont noble lord me: you are only doing it to rattle me. Well, you cant rattle me. But it makes me sick to see you rolling in luxury and think of what these poor chaps and their women folk are suffering.

SIR ARTHUR. I am not rolling, Toffy—I think that is what Miss Brollikins called you. [*To Aloysia*] Toffy is a diminutive of Toff, is it not, Miss Brollikins?

OXFORD YOUTH. Yah! Now you have something silly to talk about, youre happy. But I know what would make you sit up and do something.

SIR ARTHUR. Indeed? Thats interesting. May I ask what?

OXFORD YOUTH. Break your bloody windows.

THE MAYOR. Order! order!

ALOYSIA. Come, Toffy! you promised not to use any of your West End language here. You know we dont like it.

SIR ARTHUR. Thats right, Miss Brollikins: snub him. He is disgracing his class. As a humble representative of that class I apologize for him to the Isle of Cats. I apologize for his dress, for his manners, for his language. He must shock you every time he opens his mouth.

BLEE. We working folks know too much of bad language and bad manners to see any fun in them or think they can do any good.

THE MAYOR. Thats right.

ALOYSIA. We are as tired of bad manners as Toffy is tired of good manners. We brought Toffy here, Sir Arthur, because we knew he'd speak to you as a dock laborer would speak to you if his good manners would let him. And he's right, you know. He's rude; but he's right.

OXFORD YOUTH. Yours devotedly, Brolly. And what has his Right Honorable nibs to say to that?

SIR ARTHUR [*concentrating himself on his adversary in the House of Commons manner*] I will tell the noble lord what I have to say. He may marshal his friends the unemployed and break every window in the West End, beginning with every pane of glass in this house. What will he gain by it? Next day a score or so of his followers will be in prison with their heads broken. A few ignorant and cowardly people who have still any money to spare will send it to the funds for the relief of distress, imagining that they are ransoming their riches. You, ladies and gentlemen, will have to put your hands in your pockets to support the wives and children of the men in prison, and to pay cheap lawyers to put up perfectly useless defences for them in the police courts. And then, I suppose, the noble lord will boast that he has made me do something at last. What can I do? Do you suppose that I care less about the sufferings of the poor than you? Do you suppose I would not revive trade and put an end to it all tomorrow if I could? But I am like yourself: I am in the grip of economic forces that are beyond human control. What mortal men could do this Government has done. We have saved the people from starvation by stretching unemployment benefit to the utmost limit of our national resources. We—

OXFORD YOUTH. You have cut it down to fifteen bob

a week and shoved every man you could off it with your beastly means test.

SIR ARTHUR [*fiercely*] What do you propose? Will you take my place and put the dole up to five pounds a week without any means test?

THE MAYOR. Order! order! Why are we here? We are here because we are all sick of arguing and talking, and we want something doing. And here we are arguing and talking just as if it was an all night sitting of the Borough Council about an item of three-and-six for refreshments. If you, Sir Arthur, tell us that you cant find work for our people we are only wasting your time and our own, sitting here.

He rises. The rest, except Hipney, follow his example. Sir Arthur is only too glad to rise too.

SIR ARTHUR. At least I hope I have convinced you about the windows, Mr Mayor.

THE MAYOR. We needed no convincing. More crockery than windows will have to be broken if you gentlemen can do nothing to get us out of our present mess. But some people will say that a few thousand more to the relief funds is better than nothing. And some of the unemployed are glaziers.

SIR ARTHUR. Let us close our little talk on a more hopeful note. I assure you it has been intensely interesting to me; and I may tell you that signs of a revival of trade are not wholly wanting. Some of the best informed city authorities are of opinion that this year will see the end of the crisis. Some of them even hold that trade is already reviving. By the last returns the export of Spanish onions has again reached the 1913 level.

OXFORD YOUTH. Holy Jerusalem! Spanish onions! Come on, Brolly. [*He goes out*].

THE MAYOR. Weve got nothing out of this. We dont

run to Spanish in the Isle. [*Resignedly*] Good morning.
[*He goes out*].

SIR ARTHUR [*winningly*] And do you, Miss Brollikins,
feel that you have got nothing?

ALOYSIA. I feel what they feel. And I dont believe
you feel anything at all. [*She goes out, followed by Blee*].

BLEE [*turning at the door*] The Mayor's wrong. Weve
got something all right.

SIR ARTHUR [*brightening*] Indeed? What is it?

BLEE [*with intense contempt*] Your measure. [*He goes
out*].

    *The Prime Minister, nettled by this gibe, resumes his
seat angrily and pushes the bluebook out of his way. Then
he notices that old Hipney has not budged from his seat
at the secretary's bureau.*

SIR ARTHUR. The deputation has withdrawn. Mr
Hipney.

HIPNEY [*rising and coming to a chair at Sir Arthur's
elbow, in which he makes himself comfortable with a
disarmingly pleasant air of beginning the business instead
of ending it*] Yes: now we can talk a bit. I been at this
game now for fifty year.

SIR ARTHUR [*interested in spite of himself*] What
game? Deputations?

HIPNEY. Unemployed deputations. This is my
twelfth.

SIR ARTHUR. As many as that! But these crises dont
come oftener than every ten years, do they?

HIPNEY. Not what you would call a crisis, perhaps.
But unemployment is chronic.

SIR ARTHUR. It always blows over, doesnt it? Trade
revives.

HIPNEY. It used to. We was the workshop of the
world then. But you gentlemen went out of the workshop business to make a war. And while that was going

on our customers had to find out how to make things for themselves. Now we shall have to be their customers when weve any money to buy with.

SIR ARTHUR. No doubt that has occurred to some extent; but there is still an immense fringe of the human race growing up to a sense of the necessity for British goods.

HIPNEY. All goods is alike to that lot provided theyre the cheapest. They tell me the Italians are tapping their volcanoes for cheap power. We dont seem able to tap nothing. The east is chock full of volcanoes: they think no more of an earthquake there than you would of a deputation. A Chinese coolie can live on a penny a day. What can we do against labor at a penny a day and power for next to nothing out of the burning bowels of the earth?

SIR ARTHUR. Too true, Mr Hipney. Our workers must make sacrifices.

HIPNEY. They will if you drive em to it, Srarthur. But it's you theyll sacrifice.

SIR ARTHUR. Oh come, Mr Hipney! you are a man of sense and experience. What good would it do them to sacrifice me?

HIPNEY. Not a bit in the world, sir. But that wont stop them. Look at your self. Look at your conferences! Look at your debates! They dont do no good. But you keep on holding them. It's a sort of satisfaction to you when you feel helpless. Well, sir, if you come to helplessness there isnt on God's earth a creature more helpless than what our factories and machines have made of an English working man when nobody will give him a job and pay him to do it. And when he gets it what does he understand of it? Just nothing. Where did the material that he does his little bit of a job on come from? He dont know. What will

[656]

happen to it when it goes out of the factory after he and his like have all done their little bits of jobs on it? He dont know. Where could he buy it if it stopped coming to him? He dont know. Where could he sell it if it was left on his hands? He dont know. He dont know nothing of the business that his life depends on. Turn a cat loose and itll feed itself. Turn an English working man loose and he'll starve. You have to buy him off with a scrap of dole to prevent him saying "Well, if I'm to die I may as well have the satisfaction of seeing you die first."

SIR ARTHUR. But—I really must press the point— what good will that do him?

HIPNEY. What good does backing horses do him? What good does drinking do him? What good does going to political meetings do him? What good does going to church do him? Not a scrap. But he keeps on doing them all the same.

SIR ARTHUR. But surely you recognize, Mr Hipney, that all this is thoroughly wrong—wrong in feeling— contrary to English instincts—out of character, if I may put it that way.

HIPNEY. Well, Srarthur, whatever's wrong you and your like have taken on yourselves the job of setting it right. I havnt: I'm only a poor man: a nobody, as you might say.

SIR ARTHUR. I have not taken anything on myself, Mr Hipney. I have chosen a parliamentary career, and found it, let me tell you, a very arduous and trying one: I might almost say a heartbreaking one. I have just had to promise my wife to see a doctor for brain fag. But that does not mean that I have taken it on myself to bring about the millennium.

HIPNEY [*soothingly*] Just so, Srarthur: just so. It tries you and worries you, and breaks your heart and does no good; but you keep on doing it. Theyve often wanted me to go into Parliament. And I could win the seat. Put up old Hipney for the Isle of Cats and your best man wouldnt have a chance against him. But not me: I know too much. It would be the end of me, as it's been the end of all the Labor men that have done it. The Cabinet is full of Labor men that started as red-hot Socialists; and what change has it made except that theyre in and out at Bucknam Palace like peers of the realm?

SIR ARTHUR. You ought to be in Parliament, Mr Hipney. You have the making of a first-rate debater in you.

HIPNEY. Psha! An old street corner speaker like me can debate the heads off you parliamentary gentlemen. You stick your thumbs in your waistcoat holes and wait half an hour between every sentence to think of what to say next; and you call that debating. If I did that in the Isle not a man would stop to listen to me. Mind you, I know you mean it as a compliment that I'd make a good parliamentary debater. I appreciate it. But people dont look to Parliament for talk nowadays: that game is up. Not like it was in old Gladstone's time, eh?

SIR ARTHUR. Parliament, Mr Hipney, is what the people of England have made it. For good or evil we have committed ourselves to democracy. I am here because the people have sent me here.

HIPNEY. Just so. Thats all the use they could make of the vote when they got it. Their hopes was in you; and your hopes is in Spanish onions. What a world it is, aint it, Srarthur?

SIR ARTHUR. We must educate our voters, Mr Hipney. Education will teach them to understand.

HIPNEY. Dont deceive yourself, Srarthur: you cant teach people anything they dont want to know. Old Dr Marx—Karl Marx they call him now—my father knew him well—thought that when he'd explained the Capitalist System to the working classes of Europe theyd unite and overthrow it. Fifty years after he founded his Red International the working classes of Europe rose up and shot one another down and blew one another to bits, and turned millions and millions of their infant children out to starve in the snow or steal and beg in the sunshine, as if Dr Marx had never been born. And theyd do it again tomorrow if they was set on to do it. Why did you set them on? All they wanted was to be given their job, and fed and made comfortable according to their notion of comfort. If youd done that for them you wouldnt be having all this trouble. But you werent equal to it; and now the fat's in the fire.

SIR ARTHUR. But the Government is not responsible for that. The Government cannot compel traders to buy goods that they cannot sell. The Government cannot compel manufacturers to produce goods that the traders will not buy. Without demand there can be no supply.

HIPNEY. Theres a powerful demand just now, if demand is what you are looking for.

SIR ARTHUR. Can you point out exactly where, Mr Hipney?

HIPNEY. In our children's bellies, Srarthur. And in our own.

SIR ARTHUR. That is not an effective demand, Mr. Hipney. I wish I had time to explain to you the inexorable laws of political economy. I—

HIPNEY [interrupting him confidentially] No use, Srarthur. That game is up. That stuff you learnt at

[659]

college, that gave you such confidence in yourself, wont go down with my lot.

SIR ARTHUR [*smiling*] What is the use of saying that economic science and natural laws wont go down, Mr Hipney? You might as well say that the cold of winter wont go down.

HIPNEY. You see, you havnt read Karl Marx, have you?

SIR ARTHUR. Mr Hipney, when the Astronomer Royal tells me that it is twelve o'clock by Greenwich time I do not ask him whether he has read the nonsense of the latest flat earth man. I have something better to do with my time than to read the ravings of a half-educated German Communist. I am sorry you have wasted your own time reading such stuff.

HIPNEY. Me read Marx! Bless you, Srarthur, I am like you: I talk about the old doctor without ever having read a word of him. But I know what that man did for them as did read him.

SIR ARTHUR. Turned their heads, eh?

HIPNEY. Just that, Srarthur. Turned their heads. Turned them right round the other way to yours. I dont know whether what Marx said was right or wrong, because I dont know what he said. But I know that he puts into every man and woman that does read him a conceit that they know all about political economy and can look down on the stuff you were taught at college as ignorant oldfashioned trash. Look at that girl Aloysia Brollikins! Her father was a basket maker in Spitalfields. She's full of Marx. And as to examinations and scholarships and certificates and gold medals and the like, she's won enough of them to last your whole family for two generations. She can win them in her sleep. Look at Blee! His father was a cooper. But he managed to go through Ruskin College. You start him paying out Marx, and

proving by the materialist theory of history that
Capitalism is bound to develop into Communism, and
that whoever doesnt know it is an ignorant nobody or
a half-educated college fool; and youll realize that
your college conceit is up against a Marxist conceit
that beats anything you ever felt for cocksureness and
despising the people that havnt got it. Look across
Europe if you dont believe me. It was that conceit, sir,
that nerved them Russians to go through with their
Communism in 1917.

SIR ARTHUR. I must read Marx, Mr Hipney. I knew
I had to deal with a sentimental revolt against unemployment. I had no idea that it had academic pretensions.

HIPNEY. Lord bless you, Srarthur, the Labor movement is rotten with book learning; and your people
dont seem ever to read anything. When did an under-
secretary ever sit up half the night after a hard day's
work to read Karl Marx or anyone else? No fear.
Your hearts are not in your education; but our young
people lift themselves out of the gutter with it. Thats
how you can shoot and you can ride and you can play
golf; and some of you can talk the hind leg off a
donkey; but when it comes to book learning Aloysia
and Blee can wipe the floor with you.

SIR ARTHUR. I find it hard to believe that the Mayor
ever burnt the midnight oil reading Marx.

HIPNEY. No more he didnt. But he has to pretend to,
same as your people have to pretend to understand
the gold standard.

SIR ARTHUR [*laughing frankly*] You have us there, Mr
Hipney. I can make neither head nor tail of it; and I
dont pretend to.

HIPNEY. Did you know the Mayor well, Srarthur?
You called him your old friend Tom.

SIR ARTHUR. He took the chair for me once at an election meeting. He has an artificial tooth that looks as if it were made of zinc. I remembered him by that. [*Genially—rising*]. What humbugs we Prime Ministers have to be, Mr Hipney! You know: dont you? [*He offers his hand to signify that the conversation is over*].

MR HIPNEY [*rising and taking it rather pityingly*] Bless your innocence, Srarthur, you dont know what humbug is yet. Wait til youre a Labor leader. [*He winks at his host and makes for the door*].

SIR ARTHUR. Ha ha! Ha ha ha! Goodbye, Mr Hipney: goodbye. Very good of you to have given me so much of your time.

HIPNEY. Youre welcome to it, Srarthur. Goodbye. [*He goes out*].

Sir Arthur presses a button to summon Hilda. Then he looks at his watch, and whistles, startled to find how late it is. Hilda comes in quickly through the masked door.

SIR ARTHUR. Do you know how late it is? To work! work! work! work! Come along.

HILDA. I am afraid you cant do any work before you start for the Church House lunch. The whole morning is gone with those people from the Isle of Cats.

SIR ARTHUR. But I have mountains of work to get through. With one thing and another I havnt been able to do a thing for the last three weeks; and it accumulates and accumulates. It will crush me if I dont clear it off before it becomes impossible.

HILDA. But I keep telling you, Sir Arthur, that if you will talk to everybody for half an hour instead of letting me get rid of them for you in two minutes, what can you expect? You say you havent attended to anything for three weeks; but really you havnt attended to anything since the session began. I hate to say anything; but really, when those Isle of Cats people took themselves off your hands almost providentially, to let that ridiculous old man talk to you for an hour—! [*She sits down angrily*].

SIR ARTHUR. Nonsense! he didnt stay two minutes; and I got a lot out of him. What about the letters this morning?

HILDA. I have dealt with them: you neednt bother. There are two or three important ones that you ought to answer: I have put them aside for you when you have time.

Flavia and David dash into the room through the masked door even more excited and obstreperous than before, Flavia to her father's right, David to his left.

FLAVIA. Papa: weve been to a meeting of the unemployed with Aloysia and Toffy.

DAVID. Such a lark!

FLAVIA. We saw a police charge. David was arrested.

SIR ARTHUR. Do you mean to say that you went with those people who were here?

FLAVIA. Yes: theyve come back to lunch with us.

SIR ARTHUR. To lunch!!!

DAVID. Yes. I say: Aloysia's a marvellous girl.

SIR ARTHUR [*determinedly*] I dont mind the girl; but if that young whelp is coming to lunch here he must and shall change his clothes.

DAVID. He's gone home to change and shave: he's dotty on Flavia.

SIR ARTHUR. Why am I afflicted with such children? Tell me at once what you have been doing. What happened?

DAVID. The police brought the Chancellor of the Exchequer to make a speech to the unemployed to quiet them. The first thing we heard him say was "Gentlemen: be patient. I promise you you will soon

[663]

see the one thing that can revive our industries and save our beloved country: a rise in prices." The mob just gave one howl and went for him. Then the police drew their batons and charged.

FLAVIA. Davy couldnt stand the way the people were knocked about. He screamed to them to stand. The inspector collared him.

SIR ARTHUR. Of course he did. Quite right. Such folly! [*To David*] How do you come to be here if you were arrested? Who bailed you?

DAVID. I asked the inspector who in hell he thought he was talking to. Then Flavia cut in and told him who we were and that old Basham was like a father to us. All he said was "You go home, sir; and take your sister with you. This is no place for you." So as I was rather in a funk by that time we collected Aloysia and Toffy and bunked for home.

SIR ARTHUR. I have a great mind to have that inspector severely reprimanded for letting you go. Three months would have done you a lot of good. Go back to the drawing room, both of you, and entertain your new friends. You know you are not allowed to come in here when I am at work. Be off with you. [*He goes back to his seat*].

FLAVIA. Well, what are we to do? Mamma sends us in on purpose to interrupt you when she thinks you have done enough.

DAVID. She says it's all we're good for.

SIR ARTHUR. A Prime Minister should have no children. Will you get out, both of you; or must I ring for Burton to throw you out?

FLAVIA. Mamma says you are to lunch, Hilda. She wants another woman to make up the party.

HILDA. Oh dear! [*rising*] You must excuse me, Sir Arthur: I must telephone to put off some people who were coming to lunch with me at The Apple Cart. And I must change my frock.

FLAVIA [*squabbling*] You neednt dress up for Brollikins, need you?

DAVID. You let Aloysia alone. You dont want Hilda to dress up for Barking, I suppose.

SIR ARTHUR [*out of patience*] Get out. Do you hear? Get out, the lot of you.

HILDA. Do come, Miss Chavender. Your father is very busy.

SIR ARTHUR [*furious*] Get OUT.

They retreat precipitately through the masked door. Sir Arthur, left alone, rests his wearied head on the table between his arms.

SIR ARTHUR. At last, a moment's peace.

The word rouses the orator in him. He raises his head and repeats it interrogatively; then tries its effect sweetly and solemnly again and again.

SIR ARTHUR. Peace?... Peace. Peace. Peace. Peace. Peace. [*Now perfectly in tune*] "Yes, your Grace, my lords and gentlemen, my clerical friends. We need peace. We English are still what we were when time-honored Lancaster described us as 'This happy breed of men.' We are above all a domestic nation. On occasion we can be as terrible in war as we have always been wise and moderate in counsel. But here, in this Church House, under the banner of the Prince of Peace, we know that the heart of England is the English home. Not the battlefield but the fireside—yes, your Grace, yes, my lords and gentlemen, yes, my clerical friends, the fire—"

He starts violently as his eye, sweeping round the imaginary assembly, lights on a woman in grey robes contemplating him gravely and pityingly. She has stolen in noiselessly through the masked door.

[665]

SIR ARTHUR. Fffff!!! Who is that? Who are you?
Oh, I beg your pardon. You gave me such a— Whew!!
[*He sinks back into his chair*] I didnt know there was
anyone in the room.

The lady neither moves nor speaks. She looks at him
with deepening pity. He looks at her, still badly scared.
He rubs his eyes; shakes himself; looks again.

SIR ARTHUR. Excuse me; but are you real?

THE LADY. Yes.

SIR ARTHUR. I wish youd do something real. Wont
you sit down?

THE LADY. Thank you. [*She sits down, very uncannily*
as it seems to him, in Basham's chair].

SIR ARTHUR. Will you be so good as to introduce
yourself? Who are you?

THE LADY. A messenger.

SIR ARTHUR. Please do not be enigmatic. My nerves
are all in rags. I did not see you come in. You appeared
there suddenly looking like a messenger of death. And
now you tell me you are a messenger.

THE LADY. Yes: a messenger of death.

SIR ARTHUR. I thought so. [*With sudden misgiving*]
You mean my death, I hope. Not my wife nor any of
the children?

THE LADY [*smiling kindly*] No. Your death.

SIR ARTHUR [*relieved*] Well, thats all right.

THE LADY. You are going to die.

SIR ARTHUR. So are we all. The only question is, how
soon?

THE LADY. Too soon. You are half dead already. You
have been dying a long time.

SIR ARTHUR. Well, I knew I was overworking:
burning the candle at both ends: killing myself. It
doesnt matter. I have made my will. Everything
is provided for: my wife will be comfortably off;

and the children will have as much as is good for them.

THE LADY. You are resigned?

SIR ARTHUR. No; but I cannot help myself.

THE LADY. Perhaps I can help you. I am not only a messenger. I am a healer.

SIR ARTHUR. A what?

THE LADY. A healer. One who heals the sick. One who holds off death until he is welcome in his proper time.

SIR ARTHUR. You cannot help me. I am caught in the wheels of a merciless political machine. The political machine will not stop for you. It has ground many men to pieces before their time; and it will grind me.

THE LADY. My business is with life and death, not with political machinery.

SIR ARTHUR. In that case I am afraid you can be of no use to me; so will you think it very uncivil of me if I go on with my work?

THE LADY. Shall I vanish?

SIR ARTHUR. Not unless you have something else to do. As you are a ghost, and therefore not in time but in eternity, another ten minutes or so wont cost you anything. Somehow, your presence is helping me. A presence is a wonderful thing. Would you mind sitting there and reading The Times while I work?

THE LADY. I never read the newspapers. I read men and women. I will sit here and read you. Or will that make you self-conscious?

SIR ARTHUR. My dear ghost, a public man is so accustomed to people staring at him that he very soon has no self to be conscious of. You wont upset me in the least. You may even throw in a round of applause occasionally; so that I may find out the effective bits to work up.

THE LADY. Go on. I will wait as long as you like.

SIR ARTHUR. Thank you. Now let me see where I was when you appeared. [*He takes up a scrap of paper on which he has made a memorandum*]. Ah yes: Ive got it. Peace. Yes: peace. [*Trying to make out a word*] Ence —ence—what? Oh, ensue! Of course: a good word. "My friends, lay and clerical, we must ensue peace. Yes, ensue peace. Peace. Disarmament." A burst of Pacifist applause there, perhaps. "Who says that we need a hundred battleships, gentlemen? Christian brotherhood is a safer defence than a thousand battleships. You have my pledge that the Government will be quite content with—with—" oh, well, my secretary will fill that in with whatever number of ships the Japanese are standing out for. By the way, do you think battleships are any real use now? Kenworthy says theyre not: and he was in the navy. It would be such a tremendous score for us at Geneva if we offered to scrap all our battleships. We could make up for them in aeroplanes and submarines. I should like to have the opinion of an impartial and disinterested ghost.

THE LADY. As I listen to you I seem to hear a ghost preparing a speech for his fellow ghosts, ghosts from a long dead past. To me it means nothing, because I am a ghost from the future.

SIR ARTHUR. Thats a curious idea. Of course if there are ghosts from the past there must be ghosts from the future.

THE LADY. Yes: women and men who are ahead of their time. They alone can lead the present into the future. They are ghosts from the future. The ghosts from the past are those who are behind the times, and can only drag the present back.

SIR ARTHUR. What an excellent definition of a Conservative! Thank Heaven I am a Liberal!

THE LADY. You mean that you make speeches about Progress and Liberty instead of about King and Country.

SIR ARTHUR. Of course I make speeches: that is the business of a politician. Dont you like speeches?

THE LADY. On the Great Day of Judgment the speechmakers will stand with the seducers and the ravishers, with the traffickers in maddening drugs, with those who make men drunk and rob them, who entice children and violate them.

SIR ARTHUR. What nonsense! Our sermons and speeches are the glories of our literature, and the inspired voices of our religion, our patriotism, and—of course—our politics.

THE LADY. Sermons and speeches are not religion, not patriotism, not politics: they are only the gibbering of ghosts from the past. You are a ghost from a very dead past. Why do you not die your bodily death? Is it fair for a ghost to go about with a live body?

SIR ARTHUR. This is too personal. I am afraid I cannot get on with my speech while you are there ordering my funeral. Oblige me by vanishing. Go. Disappear. Shoo!

THE LADY. I cannot vanish. [*Merrily changing her attitude*]. Shall we stop playing at ghosts, and accept one another for convenience sake as real people?

SIR ARTHUR [*shaking off his dreaminess*] Yes, lets. [*He rises and comes to her*]. We have been talking nonsense. [*He pulls out a chair. They sit close together*]. You had me half hypnotized. But first, shake hands. I want to feel that you are real.

He offers his right hand. She seizes both his hands and holds them vigorously, looking straight into his eyes.

SIR ARTHUR [*brightening*] Well, I dont know whether this is real or not; but it's electric, and very soothing and jolly. Ah-a-a-ah! [*a deep sighing breath*]. And now my dear lady, will you be good enough to tell me who the devil you are?

THE LADY [*releasing him*] Only your wife's lady doctor. Did she not tell you to expect me?

SIR ARTHUR. Of course, of course. How stupid of me! Yes, yes, yes, yes, yes, to be sure. And now I am going to be frank with you. I dont believe in doctors. Neither does my wife; but her faith in quacks is unlimited. And as I am on the verge of a nervous breakdown, she is planting every possible variety of quack on me—you will excuse the expression?—

THE LADY. I excuse everything from my patients. Go on.

SIR ARTHUR. Well, I receive them all as I am receiving you, just to gratify her, or rather to prevent her from making my life miserable. They all say the same obvious thing; and they are none of them of the slightest use. You are going to say it all over again. Can you forgive me for saying flatly that I will not pay you twenty guineas for saying it: not if you said it twenty times over?

THE LADY. Not even if I shew you how to cure yourself? The twenty guineas is an important part of the cure. It will make you take it seriously.

SIR ARTHUR. I know perfectly well how to cure myself. The cure is as simple as abc. I am Prime Minister of Great Britain. That is, I am an overworked, overworried, overstrained, overburdened, overdriven man, suffering from late hours, irregular snatched meals, no time for digestion nor for enough sleep, and having to keep my mind at full stretch all the time struggling with problems that are no longer national problems but world problems. In short, I am suffering acutely from brain fag.

THE LADY. And the cure?

SIR ARTHUR. A fortnight's golf: thats the cure. I know it all by heart. So suppose we drop it, and part friends. You see, I am really frightfully busy.

THE LADY. That is not my diagnosis. [*She rises*]. Goodbye.

SIR ARTHUR [*alarmed*] Diagnosis! Have you been diagnosing me? Do you mean that there is something else the matter with me?

THE LADY. Not something else. Something different.

SIR ARTHUR. Sit down, pray: I can spare another two minutes. Whats wrong?

THE LADY [*resuming her seat*] You are dying of an acute want of mental exercise.

SIR ARTHUR [*unable to believe his ears*] Of—of—of WHAT, did you say?

THE LADY. You are suffering from that very common English complaint, an underworked brain. To put it in one word, a bad case of frivolity, possibly incurable.

SIR ARTHUR. Frivolity! Did I understand you to say that frivolity is a common English failing?

THE LADY. Yes. Terribly common. Almost a national characteristic.

SIR ARTHUR. Do you realize that you are utterly mad?

THE LADY. Is it you or I who have piloted England on to the rocks?

SIR ARTHUR. Come come! No politics. What do you prescribe for me?

THE LADY. I take my patients into my retreat in the Welsh mountains, formerly a monastery, now much stricter and perfectly sanitary. No newspapers, no letters, no idle ladies. No books except in the afternoon as a rest from thinking.

SIR ARTHUR. How can you think without books?

THE LADY. How can you have thoughts of your own when you are reading other people's thoughts?

SIR ARTHUR [*groaning*] Oh, do talk sense. What about golf?

THE LADY. Games are for people who can neither read nor think. Men trifle with their business and their politics; but they never trifle with their games. Golf gives them at least a weekend of earnest concentration. It brings truth home to them. They cannot pretend that they have won when they have lost, nor that they made a magnificent drive when they foozled it. The Englishman is at his best on the links, and at his worst in the Cabinet. But what your country needs is not your body but your mind. And I solemnly warn you that unless you exercise your mind you will lose it. A brain underexercised is far more injurious to health than an underexercised body. You know how men become bone lazy for want of bodily exercise. Well, they become brain lazy for want of mental exercise; and if nature meant them to be thinkers the results are disastrous. All sorts of bodily diseases are produced by half used minds; for it is the mind that makes the body: that is my secret, and the secret of all the true healers. I am sorry you will not allow me to take you a little on the way back to health with me. Good morning. [*She rises*].

SIR ARTHUR. Must you go?

THE LADY. Well, you are so busy—

SIR ARTHUR [*rising*] Ah yes: I forgot. I am frightfully busy. Still, if you could spare another minute—

THE LADY. If you wish. [*She sits down*].

SIR ARTHUR [*sitting down*] You see, what makes your diagnosis so pricelessly funny to me is that as a matter of fact my life has been a completely intellectual life, and my training the finest intellectual training in the world. First rate preparatory school. Harrow. Oxford. Parliament. An Undersecretaryship. The Cabinet. Finally the Leadership of the House as Prime Minister. Intellect, intellect, all the time.

THE LADY. At Harrow you wrote Latin verses, did you not?

SIR ARTHUR. Yes, of course.

THE LADY. Do you write any now?

SIR ARTHUR. No, of course not. You dont understand. We learnt to write Latin verses not because the verses are any good—after all, it's only a trick of stringing old tags together—but because it's such a splendid training for the mind.

THE LADY. Have all the boys who made Latin verses at Harrow splendidly trained minds?

SIR ARTHUR. Yes. I unhesitatingly say yes. I dont mean, of course, that they are all geniuses; but if you go into the best society you will see that their minds are far superior to those of persons who have had no classical training.

THE LADY. You mean that they can all be trusted to say the same thing in the same way when they discuss public affairs.

SIR ARTHUR. Precisely. They are an educated class, you see.

THE LADY [*coldly, rising*] Yes: I see. I have really nothing more to say, Sir Arthur. [*She takes a card from her bag and puts it on the table*] That is the address of my retreat in Wales.

SIR ARTHUR [*rising, rather disappointed at having produced no effect*] But surely you cannot deny that a

[673]

man is the better for having been put through the mill of our great educational system.

THE LADY. If a man is born with a hopelessly bad set of teeth I think it is better for him, and kinder to him, to pull them all out and replace them with a good set of artificial teeth. If some of your political colleagues had not been provided with artificial political minds in the manner you described they would have been left without any political minds at all. But in that case they would not have meddled in politics; and that, I think, would have been a public advantage. May I reserve a bedroom and a private study for you?

SIR ARTHUR. Pooh! I am not going to your retreat.

THE LADY [steadfastly] I think you are.

SIR ARTHUR. I give you up. You are factproof. I am lazy; I am idle; and I am breaking down from overwork. How logical!

THE LADY. All the idlest and laziest of my patients slave from morning to midnight trifling and tittle-tattling about great things. To a retreat, Sir Arthur: get thee to a retreat. I am never mistaken in my diagnosis. I shall telephone to ask whether my number one suite, with private bath and meditation parlor, is vacant.

SIR ARTHUR. No: I wont be rushed. Do you hear? I wont be rushed. [She is quite unshaken; and he proceeds, much less resolutely] Of course I shall have to go somewhere for a rest; and if you could really recommend it as a bracing place—

THE LADY. Bracing? What for?

SIR ARTHUR. Well, bracing, you know. Bracing.

THE LADY. Curious, how idle people are always clamouring to be braced! Like trousers.

SIR ARTHUR. Idle people! How you stick to your point! And what a humbug you are! Dont think you

[674]

can impose on me with your meditation parlor and your dignified airs: I do that sort of thing myself occasionally; and you know it's no use giving tracts to a missionary. But I feel somehow that you are good for me. You are a dear delightful bighearted wrongheaded half-educated crazyboots; but a woman may be all that and yet have the right instinct as to how to flirt intellectually with a tired thinker. Will you promise to talk to me if I come?

THE LADY. I will even let you talk to me. I guarantee that in a fortnight you will begin to think before you talk. Your dead mind will come to life. I shall make a man of you. Goodbye. [*She goes out quickly through the main door*].

SIR ARTHUR [*calling after her gaily*] Ha ha! Incorrigible, incorrigible. [*He takes her card from the table, and contemplates it*]. Oh! I forgot to ask her how much a week she wants for that meditation parlor. [*He looks tragic*].

HILDA [*emerging from her office*] Anything the matter, Sir Arthur?

SIR ARTHUR. I am going into a retreat. Because my brain is underworked. Do you grasp that idea? Have you ever heard of a retreat for the mentally underworked?

HILDA. There is a very nice one at Sevenoaks that my aunt was sent to. But that is for inebriates.

SIR ARTHUR. The one I'm going to is for the mentally underworked, the thoughtless and brainless, the inveterately lazy and frivolous. Yes; the frivolous: your ears do not deceive you.

HILDA [*going to her desk*] Oh, well, theyll amuse you: you always get on well with people of that sort. Shall I pack your usual holiday books? some detective stories and Wordsworth?

SIR ARTHUR. No. You will procure all the books you can find by a revolutionary German Jew named Harry Marks—

HILDA. Dont you mean Karl Marx?

SIR ARTHUR. Thats the man. Karl Marx. Get me every blessed book by Karl Marx that you can find translated into English; and have them packed for the retreat.

HILDA. There are much newer books by Marxists: Lenin and Trotsky and Stalin and people like that.

SIR ARTHUR. Get them all. Pack the lot. By George, I'll teach Alderwoman Aloysia Brollikins to give herself airs. I'll teach her and her rabble of half-baked half-educated intellectual beggars-on-horseback that any Oxford man can beat them at their own silly game. I'll just turn Karl Marx inside-out for them. [*The household gong sounds*]. Lunch! Come on: that woman's given me an appetite. [*He goes out impetuously through the masked door*].

HILDA [*rushing after him*] No, no, Sir Arthur: the Church House! the Church House! youve forgotten that you have to lunch at [*her voice is lost in the distance*].

$\left[\text{ACT II}\right]$

The same scene on the 10th November at 9.30 in the morning. There is a generous fire in the grate; and the visitors wear winter clothes. Basham is on the hearthrug, warming his back and reading The Daily Herald.

BASHAM [*amazed by what he reads*] Gosh! [*He reads further*] Wh-e-e-ew!! [*He reads still further*] Well I'll be dashed!!!

Hilda enters through the main door, and announces an explosive elderly gentleman, evidently a person of consequence, who follows her.

HILDA. Sir Dexter Rightside.

SIR DEXTER [*joining Basham on the hearth*] Ah! That you, Basham? Have you come to arrest him?

BASHAM. You may well ask. He isnt up yet. Miss Hanways: is there any sign of his getting a move on?

HILDA [*much worried*] Lady Chavender wont allow him to be disturbed. She says his speech last night at the Guildhall banquet quite tired him out. People have been ringing up and calling all the morning; but she just puts her back to his door and says that anyone who makes noise enough to waken him leaves her service that minute.

SIR DEXTER. Nonsense! He must see me. Does Lady Chavender suppose that a Prime Minister can stand the country on its head without a word of warning to his colleagues and then go to bed as if he was tired out by a day's fishing?

HILDA [*desperate*] Well, what can *I* do, Sir Dexter? [*She goes to her bureau*].

SIR DEXTER. Basham: go and break open his bedroom door.

BASHAM. I cant. I'm a policeman: I mustnt do it without a warrant. Go and do it yourself.

SIR DEXTER. I have a devilish good mind to. Can you conceive anything more monstrous, Basham? [*He sits down in the chair next the end chair*]. But I said that this would happen. I said so. When we made this damned coalition that they call a National Government I was entitled to the Prime Ministership. I was the Leader of the Conservative Party. I had an enormous majority in the country: the election proved that we could have done quite well without Chavender. But I had to give way. He humbugged us. He pretended that without his old guard of Liberals and his ragtag and bobtail of Labor men and Socialists and lawyers and journalists-on-the-make and used-up trade union secretaries, and all the rest of the democratic dregs of human society, we couldnt be sure of a majority. His golden voice was to do the trick. He was the popular man, the safe man: I was the unpopular Die Hard who couldnt be trusted to keep my temper. So I stood down. I sacrificed myself. I took the Foreign Secretaryship. Well, what price your safe man now? How do you like your Bolshy Premier? Who was right? the funkers and compromisers or the old Die Hard?

BASHAM. It's amazing. I could have sworn that if there was a safe man in England that could be trusted to talk and say nothing, to thump the table and do nothing, Arthur Chavender was that man. Whats happened to him? What does it mean? Did he go mad at the sanatorium, do you think? Or was he mad before that woman took him there?

SIR DEXTER. Mad! Not a bit of it. But you had better

look up that woman's record: there may be money from Moscow behind this.

BASHAM. Arthur take money! Thats going too far.

SIR DEXTER. The woman took the money. It would be waste of money to bribe Chavender: you could always trust him to say whatever he thought would please his audience without being paid for it: damned mountebank.

BASHAM. But he didnt try to please his audience at the Guildhall. They wanted some of his best soothing syrup about law and order after the attack on the Lord Mayor's Show in the afternoon by the unemployed; but according to The Daily Herald here he gave them a dose of boiling Socialism instead.

SIR DEXTER [*nervously*] By the way, Basham, I hope you have the unemployed well in hand today.

BASHAM. Quiet as lambs. Theyre all reading the papers. New editions every half-hour. Like 1914 over again.

Sir Arthur's voice is heard, singing scales. Hilda looks in.

HILDA. I think I hear Sir Arthur singing. He must have got up.

SIR DEXTER. Singing! Is this a moment for minstrelsy?

HILDA. He always sings scales after his bath [*she vanishes*].

After a final burst of solfeggi the masked door is opened vigorously and Chavender enters beaming.

SIR ARTHUR. Ah, here you are, Dexy [*he proffers his hand*].

SIR DEXTER [*like a baited bull*] Dont attempt to shake hands with me. Dont dare call me Dexy.

SIR ARTHUR. What on earth's the matter? Got out at the wrong side of the bed this morning, eh? Frightfully sorry to have kept you waiting, Basham. Whats wrong with the Foreign Secretary this time?

SIR DEXTER. This time! What do you mean by this time?

SIR ARTHUR. Well theres nothing very novel about your turning up before breakfast in a blazing rage, is there? What is it, Basham?

BASHAM. Oh come, P.M.! If you were too drunk last night at the Guildhall to know what you were saying, youd better read the papers [*he offers his paper*].

SIR ARTHUR [*keeping his hands behind his back to warm them*] I remember perfectly well what I said last night. And I drank nothing but barley water.

BASHAM [*insisting*] But look at it man. [*Quoting the headlines*] New program for winter session. Nationalization of ground rents. Nationalization of banks. Nationalization of collieries. Nationalization of transport.

SIR DEXTER [*moaning*] Nationalization of women. Why omit it? Why omit it?

BASHAM. No: nothing about women. Municipalization of urban land and the building trade, and consequent extinction of rates.

SIR DEXTER. Apostate!

BASHAM. No: nothing about the Church. Abolition of tariffs and substitution of total prohibition of private foreign trade in protected industries. State imports only, to be sold at State regulated prices.

SIR DEXTER. Rot! Incomprehensible and unheard-of rot.

BASHAM. Compulsory public service for all, irrespective of income, as in war time.

SIR DEXTER. Slavery. Call it by its proper name. Slavery.

BASHAM. Restoration of agriculture. Collective farming. Nationalization of fertilizer industries. Nitrogen from the air. Power from the tides. Britain self-supporting and blockade proof.

SIR DEXTER. Madness. Ruin to our foreign trade.

BASHAM. Ruthless extinction of parasitism.

SIR DEXTER. You dont even know the present law. You have the Verminous Persons Act. What more do you want?

BASHAM. Doubling of the surtax on unearned incomes.

SIR DEXTER. Yes: take our last penny! And when the little that the present ruinous taxation has left us is gone; when we have closed our accounts with the last tradesman and turned the last servant into the streets, where are they to find employment? Who is to pay their wages? What is to become of religion when nobody can afford pewrents or a penny to put in the plate? Even sport will not be safe: our breed of horses will be doomed; our packs of hounds sold or slaughtered; and our masters of hounds will be caddies on motor bicycles. That is to be England's future!

SIR ARTHUR. But is that all the papers have reported?

SIR DEXTER. All!!!

BASHAM. Oh come! All! Isnt that about enough?

SIR ARTHUR. But have they said nothing about our promise to restore the cuts made in the pay of the army and navy and police?

SIR DEXTER. Our promise! Whose promise?

BASHAM [*interested*] What was that you said? Are you going to put my men's wages up to the old figure?

SIR ARTHUR. We shall give you another five thousand men; pay the old wages with a rise of ten per cent; and double your salary.

BASHAM. Whew! That alters the case a bit.

SIR DEXTER [*rising*] Basham: you are not going to allow yourself to be corrupted like this! Are you such a dupe as to imagine that free Englishmen will tolerate such a monstrous waste of public money?

BASHAM. If I have another five thousand men and a rise on the old wages, I'll answer for the free Englishmen. If they dont like it they can lump it.

SIR DEXTER. You really believe he can keep all the monstrous promises he has made?

BASHAM. No: of course he cant. But he can keep this one. He can raise the pay of the ranks and double my salary; and that is all that concerns me. I'm a policeman, not a politician.

SIR DEXTER. Youre a mercenary gangster and a damned fool: thats what you are. [*He flings himself into the end chair*].

BASHAM [*calmly*] You seem ruffled, Sir Dexter.

Before Sir Dexter can reply, Hilda returns and announces a new visitor.

HILDA. Admiral Sir Bemrose Hotspot. [*She goes out*].

Sir Bemrose is a halfwitted admiral; but the half that has not been sacrificed to his profession is sound and vigorous.

SIR BEMROSE [*in the breeziest spirits*] Morning, Dexy. Morning, Basham. [*Slapping Sir Arthur on the back*] Splendid, Arthur! Never heard you in better form. Thats the stuff to give em. [*They shake hands cordially*].

SIR DEXTER [*sobered by his astonishment*] Rosy: have you gone mad too? Have you forgotten that you are a Conservative, and that it was as a Conservative that you were made First Lord of the Admiralty, at my personal suggestion and insistence, in this so-called National Government, which now, thank Heaven, wont last one day after the next meeting of Parliament?

SIR BEMROSE. Wont it, by Jove! It's safe for the next five years. What the country wants is straight orders, discipline, character, pluck, a big navy, justice for the British sailor, no sham disarmaments, and absolute command of the sea. If that isnt Conservatism what is Conservatism? But mind, Arthur, I must have twelve new aeroplane-carrying battleships. I have my eye on Japan. And theres America. And, of course, Russia.

SIR ARTHUR. You shall have them, Rosy. Twenty-four if you say the word.

SIR BEMROSE. Good! Then I'll answer for the House of Commons.

SIR DEXTER. Dont be silly. What can you do with the House of Commons, except empty it whenever you get up to speak?

SIR BEMROSE. I leave the speaking to Arthur: it's his job, not mine. But if there is any further attempt to starve the navy it can give you a little surprise at Westminster. How will you feel when you see a submarine come to the surface off the terrace, and the commander sends in word that he gives you just five minutes before he torpedoes the whole damned Front Bench?

SIR DEXTER. You are talking ridiculous nonsense. Do you suppose for a moment that the navy would be allowed to interfere in politics?

SIR BEMROSE. Who's to stop it? Where would Lenin and Stalin and Trotsky and all that Bolshy lot have been without the Baltic fleet and the Kronstadt sailors? Do you suppose the British navy, with its discipline and its respectable Conservative commanders, couldnt do what these Communist scoundrels did?

SIR DEXTER. How long would the British navy survive the abolition of property in this country? tell me that.

SIR BEMROSE. Dont talk to the navy about property. We dont live by property: we live by service. [*He takes the chair next to the presidential one, and pursues his personal grievance angrily*]. You and your confounded property owners grudge us a clerk's salary for commanding a battleship, and then dock a quarter off it for income tax. We cant set foot on shore without being rented and rated until we can hardly afford to educate our children. Thanks to Arthur, you are pledged now to give us our pay honestly free of income tax and make these lazy idle lubbers of landlords sweat for it. I call that the essence of Conservatism. Thats the way to dish these Labor chaps and Red flaggers and all the rest of the scum you have been pandering to ever since you gave them the vote. Give them whats good for them; and put their ballot papers behind the fire: thats what this country needs.

SIR ARTHUR. You see, Dexy: we have the navy and the police on our side.

SIR DEXTER. May I ask who are "we"?

SIR ARTHUR. Why, the National Government, of course. You and I, Dexy: you and I.

SIR DEXTER. It makes me sick to hear you couple my name with yours. It always did.

HILDA [*announcing*] The President of the Board of Trade. Mr Glenmorison.

Glenmorison is an easy mannered Scottish gentleman, distinctly the youngest of the party.

SIR ARTHUR. Hallo, Sandy. Sit down. Lets all sit down and have it out.

They settle themselves at the table with their backs to the fire, Sir Arthur in the middle, Glenmorison on his left, Sir Bemrose on his right, and Sir Dexter and Basham right and left respectively.

GLENMORISON. Well, Sir Arthur, when you were

letting yourself go so recklessly you might have said a word about Home Rule for Scotland. We may as well be hanged for a sheep as for a lamb.

SIR DEXTER. We! we! we! Who are we? If you mean the Cabinet, it is not responsible for the Prime Minister's frantic proceedings. He acted without consulting us. Do you suppose that if I had heard a word of this outburst of Bolshevism I should have consented to it?

SIR ARTHUR. That was why I didnt consult you.

SIR DEXTER. Psha!

SIR ARTHUR. The responsibility is mine and mine alone.

SIR BEMROSE. Not at all. I claim my share, Arthur. You got the part about the navy from me.

GLENMORISON. Same here, Sir Dexter. I claim at least two items.

SIR DEXTER. Much good may they do you. Arthur's seat is safe: anybody named Chavender can get in unopposed in this constituency because his cunning old father-in-law has every voter in the place bribed up to the neck. But your majority at the last election was seventeen: there were three recounts. Your seat's gone, anyhow.

GLENMORISON. On the contrary, Sir Dexter, it's safe for the first time in the history of Scotland.

SIR DEXTER. Safe! How? You will get the boot as a crazy Bolshevik unless you come out with me and repudiate Chavender promptly and decisively.

GLENMORISON. Oh, I'm afraid I cant do that, Sir Dexter. You see, the balance is held in my constituency by the tradesmen and shopkeepers. Their great grievance is the heavy rates. And though they are all doing middling well they think they could do better if they could raise enough capital to extend their businesses a bit. But the financiers and promoters wont look at small businesses. They are thinking in millions while my people are thinking in thousands, and mostly in only four figures at that. It's easy enough to get a couple of hundred thousand pounds if you are willing to call it a quarter of a million and pay interest on that sum. But what good is that to a man in the High Street in my constituency who wants from five to twenty thousand to extend his little business ?

SIR DEXTER. Nonsense! The bank will give him an overdraft if his credit is good.

GLENMORISON. Yes; and call it in at the next slump and panic on the Stock Exchange. I can shew you half a dozen men who were forced into bankruptcy in the last panic, though they were as solvent as you or I. But Sir Arthur's proposal of panic-proof national and municipal banks, as ready and eager to find five thousand for the five thousand man as the financiers are to find a million on condition that enough of it sticks to their own fingers, is just the thing for my people. I darent say a word against it. It's an inspiration as far as my constituents are concerned. Theyre a canny lot, my people: theyd vote for the devil if he'd promise to abolish the rates and open a municipal bank. My majority fell to seventeen last time because I went to them with empty hands and a bellyful of advice to economize and make sacrifices. This bank nationalization is good business for them: theyll just jump at it.

SIR DEXTER. In short, you will make Utopian promises that you know very well will never be carried out.

GLENMORISON. You made a lot of Utopian promises, Sir Dexter, when you formed this National Government. Instead of carrying them out you told the voters to tighten their belts and save the Bank of England. They tightened their belts; and now the Bank of England is paying twelve and sixpence in the pound. Still, I admit, you pulled down my Liberal majority over my Conservative opponent from four thousand to seventeen. Ive got to pull that up again. I say nothing about the rest of the program; but I represent the small man; and on this bank business I am with Sir Arthur all the time.

HILDA [*announcing*] Sir Jafna Pandranath. [*She withdraws*].

This announcement creates a marked sensation. All five gentlemen rise as if to receive a royal personage. Sir Jafna is an elderly Cingalese plutocrat, small and slender to the verge of emaciation, elegantly dressed, but otherwise evidently too much occupied and worried by making money to get any fun out of spending it. One guesses that he must make a great deal of it; for the reverence with which he is received by the five Britons, compared with their unceremonious handling of one another, is almost sycophantic.

SIR JAFNA. Hallo! Am I breaking into a Cabinet meeting?

SIR ARTHUR. No: not a bit. Only a few friendly callers. Pray sit down.

SIR DEXTER [*offering the end chair to the visitor*] You are welcome, Sir Jafna: most welcome. You represent money; and money brings fools to their senses.

SIR JAFNA. Money! Not at all. I am a poor man. I never know from one moment to another whether I am worth thirteen millions or only three. [*He sits down. They all sit down*].

SIR BEMROSE. I happen to know, Sir Jafna, that

your enterprises stand at twenty millions today at the very least.

GLENMORISON. Fifty.

SIR JAFNA. How do you know? How do you know? The way I am plundered at every turn! [*To Sir Dexter*] Your people take the shirt off my back.

SIR DEXTER. My people! What on earth do you mean?

SIR JAFNA. Your land monopolists. Your blackmailers. Your robber barons. Look at my Blayport Docks reconstruction scheme! Am I a public benefactor or am I not? Have I not enough to live on and die on without troubling myself about Blayport? Shall I be any the happier when it has ten square miles of docks instead of a tuppeny-hapeny fishing harbor? What have I to gain except the satisfaction of seeing a big publicly useful thing well done, and the knowledge that without me it could not be done? Shall I not be half ruined if it fails?

SIR BEMROSE. Well, whats wrong with it, old chap?

SIR JAFNA. Rosy: you make me puke. What is wrong with it is that the owners of all the miles of land that are indispensable to my scheme, and that without it would not be worth fifteen pounds an acre, are opening their mouths so wide that they will grab sixty per cent of the profit without lifting a finger except to pocket the wealth that I shall create. I live, I work, I plan, I shatter my health and risk all I possess only to enrich these parasites, these vampires, these vermin in the commonwealth. [*Shrieking*] Yes: vermin! [*Subsiding*] You were quite right at the Guildhall last night, Arthur: you must nationalize the land and put a stop to this shameless exploitation of the financiers and entrepreneurs by a useless, idle, and predatory landed class.

[688]

SIR ARTHUR [*chuckling*]. Magnificent! I have the support of the City.

SIR JAFNA. To the last vote, to the last penny. These pirates think nothing of extorting a million an acre for land in the city. A man cannot have an address in London for his letters until he has agreed to pay them from five hundred to a thousand a year. He cant even die without paying them for a grave to lie in. Make them disgorge, Arthur. Skin them alive. Tax them twenty shillings in the pound. Make them earn their own living, damn them. [*He wipes his brow and adds, rather hysterically*] Excuse me, boys; but if you saw the Blayport estimates—! [*he can no more*].

SIR DEXTER. May I ask you to address yourself to this question not as an emotional oriental [*Sir Jafna chokes convulsively*] but as a sane man of business. If you destroy the incomes of our landed gentry where will you find the capital that exists solely through their prudent saving—their abstinence?

SIR JAFNA. Bah pooh! Pooh bah! I will find it where they find it, in the product of the labor I employ. At present I have to pay exorbitant and unnecessary wages. Why? Because out of those wages the laborer has to pay half or quarter as rent to the landlord. The laborer is ignorant: he thinks he is robbed by the landlord; but the robbed victim is me—ME! Get rid of the landlord and I shall have all the capital he now steals. In addition I shall have cheap labor. That is not oriental emotion: it is British Commonsense. I am with you, Arthur, to the last drop of my oriental blood. Nationalized land: compulsory labor: abolition of rates: strikes made criminal: I heartily endorse them all in the name of Capital and private enterprise. I say nothing about the rest of your program, Arthur;

[689]

but on these points no true Liberal can question your magnificent statesmanship.

SIR ARTHUR [*delighted*] You hear that, Dexy. Put that in your pipe and smoke it.

HILDA [*announcing*] His Grace the Duke of Domesday. [*She goes out*].

An elderly delicately built aristocrat comes in. Well preserved, but nearer 70 than 60.

THE DUKE [*surprised to see so many people*] Do I intrude, Arthur? I thought you were disengaged.

SIR ARTHUR. Not at all. Only a talk over last night. Make yourself at home.

SIR DEXTER. You come in the nick of time. Sir Jafna here has just been qualifying you as a bloodsucker, a pirate, a parasite, a robber baron and finally as vermin. Vermin! How do you like it?

THE DUKE [*calmly taking the end chair nearest the window, on Basham's left*] I wonder why the epithet robber is applied only to barons. You never hear of robber dukes; yet my people have done plenty of robbery in their time. [*With a sigh of regret*] Ah, thats all over now. The robbers have become the robbed. I wish you would create some immediate class of honest folk. I dislike your calling me vermin, Arthur.

SIR ARTHUR. I didnt. It was Jafna.

THE DUKE. Ungrateful Jafna! He is buying up my Blayport estate for next to nothing.

SIR JAFNA. Next to nothing! Holy Brahma!

THE DUKE [*continuing*] He will make millions out of it. After paying off the mortgages I shall get three and a half per cent on what is left to me out of the beggarly price he offers; and on that three and a half I shall be income-taxed and surtaxed. Jafna's grandsons will go to Eton. Mine will go to a Polytechnic.

SIR BEMROSE. Send them to Dartmouth, old chap.

Theres a career for them in the navy now that Arthur is at the helm.

SIR DEXTER. A lieutenant's pay and pension for the future Duke of Domesday! Thats the proposition, is it?

THE DUKE. He will be lucky to have any pay at all. But I shall support you in any case, Arthur. You have at last publicly admitted that the death duties are unsound in principle, and promised to abolish them. That will save us from utter extinction in three generations; and the landed classes are with you to the last man for it. Accept the humble gratitude of a pauperized duke.

SIR DEXTER. And the rest of the program. Do you swallow that too?

THE DUKE. I doubt if the rest of the program will come off. Besides, I dont pretend to understand it. By the way, Sir Jafna, I wish you would take Domesday Towers off my hands for a while. I cant afford to live in it. I cant afford even to keep it dusted. You can have it for a hundred a year.

SIR JAFNA. Too far from town.

THE DUKE. Not by aeroplane. Do think it over.

Sir Jafna shrugs his shoulders and intimates that it is hopeless. The Duke resigns himself to the expected.

SIR ARTHUR. Dexy: you are in a minority of one. The landlords are on my side. The capitalists, big and little, are on my side. The fighting services are on my side. The police are on my side. If you leave us you go out into the wilderness alone. What have you to say?

SIR DEXTER. I have to say that you are a parcel of blind fools. You are trying to scuttle the ship on the chance of each of you grabbing a share of the insurance money. But the Country will deal with you. The

Country does not want change. The Country never has wanted change. The Country never will want change. And because I will resist change while I have breath in my body I shall not be alone in England. You have all deserted me and betrayed your party; but I warn you that though I am utterly alone in this room . . .

HILDA [*reappearing*] The deputation, Sir Arthur. Theyve come back. [*She vanishes*].

The deputation enters. Hipney is not with them. Barking shaved, brilliantly dressed, and quite transfigured, is jubilant. Aloysia glows indignation. Blee and the Mayor, doggedly wearing their hats and overcoats, are gloomy, angry, and resolute. They group themselves just inside the door, glowering at the Prime Minister and his colleagues.

SIR ARTHUR [*beaming*] Gentlemen: a Labor deputation from the Isle of Cats. The one element that was lacking in our councils. You have heard the voice of the peerage, of the city, of the King's forces. You will now hear the voice of the proletariat. Sit down, ladies and gentlemen.

THE MAYOR [*rudely*] Who are you calling the proletariat? Do you take us for Communists? [*He remains standing*].

ALOYSIA. What you are going to hear, Sir Arthur, is the voice of Labor. [*She remains standing*].

BLEE. The verdict of democracy. [*He remains standing*].

EARL OF BARKING. The bleating of a bloody lot of fools. I am with you, Chavender. [*He detaches himself from the group and flings himself into Hilda's chair with intense disgust*].

SIR ARTHUR [*surprised*] Am I to understand that your colleagues are against me?

THE MAYOR. Of course we're against you. Do you expect me to go back to my people and tell them they should vote for compulsory labor and doing away with strikes?

BLEE. Arnt the workers enslaved enough already without your depriving them of that last scrap of their liberty? the only weapon they have against the capitalists?

SIR ARTHUR. My dear Mr Mayor, what is the right to strike? The right to starve on your enemy's doorstep and set the whole public against you. Which of you starves first when it comes to the point?

THE MAYOR. I am not going to argue. You can beat me at that. But if you think that the British workingman will listen to compulsory labor and putting down strikes you dont know the world youre living in; and thats all about it.

SIR ARTHUR. But we need not compel the workers to work: they are working already. We shall compel the idlers. Not only your idlers but our idlers: all the idle young gentlemen who do nothing but waste their own time and your labor.

BLEE. We know. Keep all the soft jobs for your lot and the hard ones for us. Do you take us for fools?

BARKING. He does. And you are fools.

SIR ARTHUR. I am glad to have your lordship's support.

ALOYSIA. Support your grandparents! He wants to marry your daughter.

BARKING [springing up] Oh! You can hit below the belt, Aloysia. But as a matter of fact, I do want to marry your daughter, Chavender.

SIR ARTHUR. Hardly the moment to go into that now, is it?

BARKING. It was Aloysia and not I who let the cat

[693]

out of the bag. Being a cat herself she had a fellow-feeling for the animal. [*He resumes his seat*].

BLEE. Youre an aristocrat, young-fellow-me-lad. I always said that when things got serious youd turn on us and side with your own.

BARKING. Rot! Youre always bragging that you are descended from the Blee of Blayport, whoever he may have been. I shouldnt have tuppence in my pocket if my grandfather hadnt made a fortune in pork pies and bought my father's Norman title for his daughter with it. The blue blood is in your skimpy little veins: the proletarian red's in mine.

ALOYSIA. Youve too much money, Toffy.

BARKING. I havnt had all the pluck taken out of me by poverty, like you chaps. And what good will it do me to have a lot of money when I have to work like anyone else?

SIR DEXTER. Why should a man work like anyone else if he has money?

BARKING. My brother had heaps of money; but he had to go into the trenches and fight like anyone else in the war. Thats how I came into the property.

BLEE. So we're all to be slaves for the sake of setting a few loafers to work. The workers will die sooner than put up with it. I want my liberty—

BARKING. Liberty to work fourteen hours a day and bring up three children on thirtyfour shillings a week, like your brother the shopman. To hell with your filthy liberty!

BLEE [*hotly*] I—

THE MAYOR. Order! order! Dont argue with him, Blee. No good ever comes of arguing with college men. I'm not arguing with Sir Arthur: I'm telling him. The long and the short of it is that if he dont withdraw that silly new program he'll lose every vote in the Isle of Cats. And what the Isle of Cats thinks to-day, all England thinks tomorrow.

SIR JAFNA. May I speak to this gentleman? Will you introduce me, Arthur?

SIR ARTHUR [*introducing*] Sir Jafna Pandranath. The Mayor of the Isle of Cats.

SIR JAFNA. You have heard of me, Mr Mayor. You know that I am a man who knows what he is talking about. Well, I tell you that the fundamental question is not the Labor question but the Land Question.

THE MAYOR. Yes: we all know that.

SIR JAFNA. Then you will vote for Sir Arthur because he will nationalize the land for you.

BLEE [*scornfully*] Yes, with compensation! Take the land with one hand and give back its cash value to the landlords with the other! Not likely. I ask again, do you take us for fools?

SIR ARTHUR [*introducing*] Mr Alderman Blee.

THE DUKE. Enchanted. I happen to be a landlord—a duke, in fact—and I can assure you, Mr Alderman, that as the compensation will come out of my own pocket and that of my unfortunate fellow landlords in the form of income tax, surtax, and estate duties—what you call death duties—you will get all your cash back and the land as well.

THE MAYOR. Blee: I tell you, dont argue. Stick to your point. No compensation.

BLEE. Not a penny, by God.

THE DUKE. You believe in God, Mr Alderman. I am charmed to hear it.

Here the Duke is astonished to find Aloysia towering over him and pointing an accusing finger at him. At the moment of his introduction of himself as a duke, her eyes lighted up; and she has moved menacingly across the hearth towards him until she is now standing behind the vacant chair between him and Basham.

ALOYSIA. Have you ever heard of the Domesday clearances?

THE DUKE. Clearances? Which clearances do you refer to? The latest cleared me out of Domesday Towers. I can no longer afford to live there.

ALOYSIA. Dont prevaricate. You know very well what I mean. It is written in blood and tears on the pages of working class history.

SIR ARTHUR [*introducing*] Alderwoman Aloysia Brollikins. The Duke of Domesday.

THE DUKE [*rising courteously*] Wont you sit down?

ALOYSIA [*sternly*] You shall not put me out by these tricks and ceremonies. My Lord Duke: I would rather touch the hand of the most degraded criminal in London than touch yours.

THE DUKE [*collapsing into his chair*] Great heavens! Why?

ALOYSIA. Do you forget how your family drove a whole countryside of honest hardworking Scotch crofters into the sea, and turned their little farms into deer forests because you could get more shooting rents out of them in that way? Do you forget that women in childbirth were carried out by your bailiffs to die by the roadside because they clung to their ancient homesteads and ignored your infamous notices to quit? Would it surprise you to learn that I am only one of thousands of young women who have read the hideous story of this monstrous orgy of housebreaking and murder, and sworn to ourselves that never, if we can help it, will it again be possible for one wicked rich man to say to a whole population "Get off the earth."

SIR JAFNA. Admirable! What did I tell you? Hear hear!

ALOYSIA. I thank you, Sir Jafna, for shewing this man that even hardened capitalist millionaires shudder when that story is told. You will not find it in your school histories; but in the new histories, the histories of the proletariat, it has been written, not by the venal academic triflers you call historians, but by the prophets of the new order: the men in whom the word is like a burning fire shut up in their bones so that they are weary of forbearing and must speak.

THE MAYOR. Aye: in the Bible, that is.

ALOYSIA. The Domesday Clearances filled your pockets with gold to console you for the horror and remorse of your dreams: but the vengeance they cried to God for in vain is upon you now that Labor is coming to its own; and it is your turn now to get off the earth.

BLEE. And in the face of all this, you come whining for compensation! Compensation!! Compensation from us to you! From the oppressed to the oppressor! What a mockery!

ALOYSIA. It is from you that we shall exact compensation: aye, to the uttermost farthing. You are conspiring here with these capitalist bloodsuckers to rob us again of the value of what you have already stolen— to make us give you gilt edged securities in exchange for the land that no longer brings you in shooting rents; and you think we cannot see through the plot. But in vain is the net spread in sight of the bird. We shall expose you. We shall tell the story of the Domesday Clearances until the country rings with it if you dare to lift your dishonored head again in English politics. Your demand for compensation is dismissed, turned down: we spit it back in your face. The crofters whom you drove from their country to perish in a foreign land would turn in their graves at the chink of a single penny of public money in your hungry pocket. [*She tears out a chair from under the table and flops into it, panting with oratorical emotion*].

BLEE

SIR JAFNA 〉 Good for you, Brolly!

SIR BEMROSE 〉 [*enthused*] Hear hear! [*They hammer on the table with their knuckles*].

GLENMORISON

THE DUKE [*very appreciative*] What a magnificent speech, Miss Brollikins! I really must insist on your shaking hands with me before we part.

ALOYSIA. Never. How dare you ask me? [*She sweeps away from him and sits down in the opposite chair at the other side of the table*].

THE DUKE [*taking the armchair*] May I not have the privilege of telling my grandchildren how I once met and shook hands with the greatest orator of my time? I assure you all these shocking things happened before I was born.

BLEE [*bawling at him*] Yes; but you still pocket the shooting rents.

THE DUKE [*brusquely*] Of course I do; and so would you too if you were in my place. [*Tenderly, to Aloysia*] I assure you, Miss Brollikins, the people make much more money out of my shooting tenants than they could as crofters: they would not go back to croftering for worlds. Wont you let bygones be bygones—except when you are exercising your wonderful gift of eloquence on the platform? Think of what your ancestors were doing in those ruthless old days!

BARKING. Grabbing all they could get, like yours or mine. Whats the good of tubthumping at these johnnies, Brolly? Theyve been doing it themselves all their lives. Cant you see that compensation makes them share the loss fairly between them?

SIR BEMROSE. It's no use. These damned Liberals cant understand anything but virtuous indignation.

THE MAYOR. Who are you calling a Liberal? I represent the Labor Party.

SIR BEMROSE. Youre a No Compensation man, arnt you?

THE MAYOR. Of course I am.

SIR BEMROSE. Then youre a Liberal.

THE MAYOR. Call me what you like. I'm not arguing. I'm telling you that the Labor Party of the Isle of Cats puts down its foot and says No Compensation. Is that plain?

SIR DEXTER. I am glad we have arrived at the same conclusion from our opposite points of view, Mr Mayor. The Party I represent, the Conservative Party, will withdraw from the Coalition if there is the slightest wobbling on this point. We shall defend our property—and yours: yours, Mr Mayor, to the last drop of our blood.

BASHAM [*incisively re-entering the conversation; they had forgotten him, and now turn to him in some surprise*] Our blood, you mean, dont you?

SIR DEXTER [*puzzled*] Whose blood?

BASHAM. The police's blood. You landed gentlemen never do a thing yourselves: you only call us in. I have twenty thousand constables, all full of blood, to shed it in defence of whatever the Government may decide to be your property. If Sir Arthur carries his point theyll shed it for land nationalization. If you carry yours theyll stand by your rent collectors as usual.

BLEE. The police come from the ranks of labor: dont forget that.

BASHAM. Thats not how they look at it, Blee. They feel that theyve escaped from the ranks of labor; and theyre proud of it. They have a status which they feel to be a part of the status of the Duke here.

THE DUKE. I suppose that is why they are always so civil to me.

BASHAM. In short, Mister Blee, the police are what you Socialists call class-conscious. You will find that out if you are foolish enough to fall out with them.

BLEE. Who cut their pay? Tell me that.

SIR ARTHUR. I shall restore the cuts, Mr Alderman, with a premium.

THE MAYOR. There! Now you see what comes of arguing, Blee. It only gives him his chance.

ALOYSIA. You need not warn us, Sir Broadfoot Basham, D.S.O., K.C.M.G., O.B.E. In the Class War your myrmidons will be well paid.

THE DUKE. Myrmidons!

ALOYSIA. We know too well what we have to expect from your Janissaries.

BLEE. Your bludgeoning Bashi-Bazouks.

ALOYSIA. The Class War is a fact. We face it. What we want we shall have to take; and we know it. The good of the community is nothing to you: you care only for surplus value. You will never give up your privileges voluntarily. History teaches us that: the history you never read.

THE DUKE. I assure you, my dear Héloise?

ALOYSIA. Héloise! Who are you calling Héloise?

THE DUKE. Pardon. I could not resist the French form of your charming name.

ALOYSIA [*interjects*] The cheek!

THE DUKE [*continuing*] I was merely going to point out, as between one student of history and another, that in the French Revolution it was the nobility who voluntarily abolished all their own privileges at a single sitting, on the sentimental principles they had acquired from reading the works of Karl Marx's revolutionary predecessor Rousseau. That bit of history is repeating itself today. Here is Sir Arthur offering us a program of what seems to me to be first rate Platonic Communism. I, a Conservative Duke, embrace it. Sir Jafna Pandranath here, a Liberal capitalist whose billions shame my poverty, embraces it. The Navy embraces it with the sturdy arms of Sir Bemrose Hotspot. The police are enthusiastic. The Army will be with Sir Arthur to the last man. He has the whole propertied class on his side. But the proletariat rises against him and spews out his Socialism through the eloquent lips of its Aloysia. I recall the warning my dear old father gave me when I was five years old. Chained dogs are the fiercest guardians of property; and those who attempt to unchain them are the first to be bitten.

ALOYSIA. Your Grace calls us dogs. We shall not forget that.

THE DUKE. I have found no friends better than faithful dogs, Miss Brollikins. But of course I spoke figuratively. I should not dream of calling you a dog.

ALOYSIA. No. As I am a female dog I suppose you will call me something shorter when my back is turned.

THE DUKE. Oh! Think of the names you have called me!

THE MAYOR. Well, if you will argue, Alderwoman Brollikins, there's no use my staying here. I wish I could stop your mouth as easy as I can stop my ears. Sir Arthur: youve planked down your program and weve planked down our answer. Either you drop compulsory labor and drop compensation or never shew your face in the Isle of Cats again. [*He goes out resolutely*].

BLEE. Take this from me. I am no Communist: I am a respectable Labor man, as law abiding as any man here. I am what none of you has mentioned yet: a democrat. I am just as much against Cabinet dictatorship as individual dictatorship. What I want done is the will of the people. I am for the referendum. I am for the initiative. When a majority of the people are in favour of a measure then I am for that measure.

SIR BEMROSE. Rot! The majority is never in favour of any measure. They dont know what a measure is. What they want is their orders, and as much comfort as they are accustomed to. The lower deck doesnt want to give orders, it looks to the bridge for them. If I asked my men to do my job theyd chuck me overboard; and serve me jolly well right! You just know nothing about it, because youve never had to command; and you havnt sense enough to obey and be thankful to those who have saved you the trouble of thinking for yourself and keeping you off the rocks.

BLEE. You havnt kept us off the rocks. We're on the rocks, the whole lot of us. So long, Rosy. [*He goes out*].

BARKING. Silly swine! When they are offered what they want they wont have it just because you fellows want it too. They think there must be a catch in it somewhere.

THE DUKE. There generally is. That is how you feel, Miss Brollikins, isnt it?

ALOYSIA. You dont know how I feel; and you never will. We are going to save ourselves and not be saved by you and your class. And I prefer Sir Dexter Rightside's downright outspoken opposition to your silly-clever cynicism and your sickening compliments.

THE DUKE. It is only in middle class books, Miss

Brollikins, that noblemen are always cynical and insincere. I find you a most brilliant and delightful woman. May I not tell you so? And WHAT a speaker! Will you spend a quiet week-end with me in some out-of-the-way place in the country, and let me try to convince you that a duke is a human being like yourself?

ALOYSIA [*rearing*] Are you trying to seduce me?

THE DUKE. That would be exquisite, Miss Brollikins; but I am an old and very poor man. You are young, beautiful, and probably opulent. Can you find anything seductive about me?

ALOYSIA. Yes. Youre a duke. And you have the charm of a majestic ruin, if you understand me.

BARKING [*rising*] Come on out of this, Brolly: youre only making a fool of yourself listening to that old bird buttering you up. You just dont know when to go.

ALOYSIA [*moving to the hearthrug, behind Sir Arthur*] You can go if you like. I have some business with Sir Arthur that doesnt concern you. Get out.

SIR ARTHUR. Some business with me! Public business?

ALOYSIA. Not exactly.

SIR ARTHUR. Oh! Private business?

ALOYSIA. I dont care who knows it. But perhaps you would.

BARKING. She means to marry your son David. One below the belt for you, Brolly. Ha ha! Ha ha ha ha ha! [*He goes out roaring with laughter*].

SIR ARTHUR [*after a moment of shock*] I congratulate David, Miss Brollikins. Have you arranged the date?

ALOYSIA. I havnt mentioned it to him yet. I hope all you gentlemen will remember that I was not the one that blurted this out: it was your noble viscount.

However, now it's out, I stand by it: David is a good boy; and his class is not his fault. Goodbye all. [*She goes to the door*].

THE DUKE [*rising*] And that week-end, Miss Brollikins? Or has David cut me out?

ALOYSIA. Right you are. Your Grace! I will call for you at Domesday House on Friday at half past four. As I shall bring a few friends we shall hire an omnibus from the London Transport; so you neednt trouble about a car. You wont mind my publishing an account of what happens as a special interview: you know that we Labor intelligentsia have to live by our brains. Au revoir. [*She goes out*].

THE DUKE. There is a frightful unexpectedness about these people. Where on earth shall I borrow the money to pay for the omnibus and entertain them all? [*He goes back to his chair at the end of the table and sits down*].

BASHAM. Your share will only be a few shillings, Duke; and she will reckon on having to pay for you. What girl in her class wouldnt foot the bill if she had a duke to walk out with?

THE DUKE. You reassure me, Sir Broadfoot. Thank you.

SIR DEXTER [*triumphant*] Well, Chavender? What have you to say now? When these people came in I was saying that though I was alone in this room, the people of England were on my side and always would be when it came to the point. Was I right or wrong?

SIR BEMROSE. We never meant to desert you, Dexy. You mustnt think that.

SIR ARTHUR. As you have no more intention of consulting the people of England than I have, the situation is unaltered.

SIR DEXTER. Than you have! What do you mean?

Do you think you can govern in this country without the consent of the English people?

SIR ARTHUR. No country has ever been governed by the consent of the people, because the people object to be governed at all. Even you, who ought to know better, are always complaining of the income tax.

THE DUKE. But five shillings in the pound, Arthur! Five shillings in the pound!!

SIR DEXTER. Never mind my income tax. If what you said just now means anything it means that you are going to play fast and loose with democracy: that is, you think you are going to do something that both the people and the governing class of this country are determined you shall not do. The Conservative Party, which is ten times more really democratic than you Liberals have ever been, will carry the people with it against you. How do you propose to get over that? What are you banking on? Put your cards on the table if you really have any.

SIR ARTHUR. Well, here is my ace of trumps. The people of this country, and of all the European countries, and of America, are at present sick of being told that, thanks to democracy, they are the real government of the country. They know very well that they dont govern and cant govern and know nothing about Government except that it always supports profiteering, and doesnt really respect anything else, no matter what party flag it waves. They are sick of twaddle about liberty when they have no liberty. They are sick of idling and loafing about on doles when they are not drudging for wages too beggarly to pay the rents of anything better than overcrowded one-room tenements. They are sick of me and sick of you and sick of the whole lot of us. They want to see something done that will give them decent employment. They want to eat and drink the wheat and coffee that the profiteers are burning because they cant sell it at a profit. They want to hang people who burn good food when people are going hungry. They cant set matters right themselves; so they want rulers who will discipline them and make them do it instead of making them do the other thing. They are ready to go mad with enthusiasm for any man strong enough to make them do anything, even if it is only Jew baiting, provided it's something tyrannical, something coercive, something that we all pretend no Englishman would submit to, though weve known ever since we gave them the vote that theyd submit to anything.

SIR DEXTER [*impatiently*] Yes, yes: we know the cant of all the tuppeny-hapeny dictators who think themselves Mussolinis. Come down to tin tacks. How are you going to get it through Parliament?

SIR ARTHUR. I am not going to get it through Parliament: I am going to prorogue Parliament and then do it. When it is done I shall call a meeting of Parliament to pass an Act of Indemnity for all my proceedings.

SIR DEXTER. You cannot prorogue Parliament. Only the King can prorogue Parliament.

SIR ARTHUR. Precisely. Kings always have prorogued Parliament and governed without them until money ran short.

GLENMORISON. But, man alive, it is not His Majesty alone that you have to consider. The law courts will not enforce your decisions if they are illegal. The civil servants will sabotage you even if they dont flatly disobey you.

SIR ARTHUR. We shall sidetrack them quite easily by setting up new tribunals and special commissions manned by officials we can depend on.

SIR DEXTER. That was how Cromwell cut off King Charles's head. His commissioners found out afterwards that they were doing it with ropes round their rascally necks.

SIR ARTHUR. A rope round a statesman's neck is the only constitutional safeguard that really safeguards. But never fear the rope. As long as we give the people an honest good time we can do just what seems good to us. The proof of the pudding will be in the eating. That will be really responsible government at last.

SIR DEXTER. So that is your game, is it? Has it occurred to you that two can play at it? What can you do that I cannot do if you drive me to it: tell me that.

SIR ARTHUR. Nothing, if you are willing to take on my job. Are you?

SIR DEXTER. The job of ruining the country and destroying the empire? My job is to prevent you from doing that. And I will prevent you.

SIR ARTHUR. Your job is to prevent me or anybody else from doing anything. Your job is to prevent the world from moving. Well, it is moving; and if you dont get out of the way something will break; and it wont be the world.

SIR DEXTER. Nothing has broken so far except the heads of the unemployed when they are encouraged by your seditious rot to rebel against the laws of nature. England is not breaking. She stands foursquare where she always stood and always will stand: the strongest and greatest land, and the birthplace of the noblest imperial race, that ever God created.

SIR ARTHUR. Loud and prolonged cheering. Come! let us both stop tub thumping and talk business. The real master of the situation is Basham here, with his fifteen thousand police.

BASHAM. Twenty thousand.

[707]

SIR ARTHUR. Well, twenty thousand. They dont stop functioning when Parliament is prorogued, do they?

BASHAM. No. At Scotland Yard we look to the Home Secretary as far as we look to anybody.

SIR ARTHUR. I can make myself Home Secretary. So that will be all right.

SIR DEXTER. Will it, by George? If you and Basham dare to try your twenty thousand police on me, do you know what I will do?

SIR ARTHUR. What?

SIR DEXTER. I will put fifty thousand patriotic young Londoners into Union Jack shirts. You say they want discipline and action. They shall have them. They shall have machine guns and automatic pistols and tear gas bombs. My Party has the money. My Party has the newspapers. My Party has the flag, the traditions, the glory that is England, the pluck, the breed, the fighting spirit. One of us is worth ten of your half starved guttersnipes and their leaders that never could afford more than a shilling for a dinner until they voted themselves four hundred a year out of our pockets.

SIR BEMROSE [*carried away*] Thats the stuff, Dexy. Now you are talking, by Jiminy.

BASHAM [*taking command of the discussion coolly*] You are all talking through your hats. The police can do nothing unless the people are on the side of the police. The police cant be everywhere: there arnt enough of them. As long as the people will call the police when anything goes wrong, and stop the runaway criminal and give evidence against him, then twenty thousand constables can keep eight million citizens in order. But if the citizens regard the policeman as their enemy—if the man who snipes a policeman in the back is not given in charge by the bystanders—if he is helped to get away—if the police cannot get a single citizen to go into the box and witness against him, where are you then? You have to double your force because the police must patrol in pairs: otherwise the men will be afraid to patrol at all. Your twenty thousand have to be reinforced up to forty thousand for their own protection; but that doesnt protect you. You would have to put two policemen standing over every ablebodied man and woman in the town to see that they behaved themselves as you want them to behave. You would need not thousands of constables but millions.

SIR DEXTER. My Union Jack men would keep order, or theyd know the reason why.

BASHAM. And who would keep them in order, I should like to know: silly amateurs. And let me remind you of one thing. It seems easy to buy a lot of black shirts, or brown shirts, or red shirts, and give one to every hooligan who is out for any sort of mischief and every suburban out-of-work who fancies himself a patriot. But dont forget that the colored shirt is a uniform.

GLENMORISON. What harm is there in that? It enables a man to recognize his friends.

BASHAM. Yes; but it marks him out as an enemy in uniform; and to kill an enemy in uniform at sight is not murder: it's legitimate warfare.

SIR DEXTER. Monstrous! I should give no quarter to such an outrageous piece of sophistry.

BASHAM. In war you have to give quarter because you have to ask for it as often as to give it. It's easy to sit here and think of exterminating your opponents. But a war of extermination is a massacre. How long do you think a massacre would last in England today? Just as long as it takes a drunken man to get sick and sober.

GLENMORISON. Easy, Sir Broadfoot, easy, easy. Who is talking of extermination? I dont think you will ever induce respectable Britons to wear red-white-and-blue shirts; but surely you can have volunteers, special constables, auxiliary forces—

BASHAM [*flinching violently*] Auxiliary forces! I was in command of them in Ireland when you tried that game on the Irish, who were only a little handful of peasants in their cabbage patch. I have seen these things. I have done them. I know all about it: you know nothing about it. It means extermination; and when it comes to the point you cant go through with it. I couldnt. I resigned. You couldnt: you had to back down. And I tell you, Dexy, if you try any colored shirt hooliganism on me, I'll back the P.M. and shew you what Scotland Yard can do when it's put to it.

SIR DEXTER. Traitor!

BASHAM. Liar! Now weve called one another names how much farther has it got us?

GLENMORISON. Easy, easy: dont let us quarrel. I must support the Prime Minister, Sir Dexter, to secure my seat in Parliament. But I am a Liberal, and, as such, bound by Liberal principles. Whatever we do must be done through Parliament if I am to be a party to it. I am all for the new program; but we must draw up a parliamentary timetable for it. To carry out the program will involve the introduction of at least twelve bills. They are highly controversial bills: everyone of them will be resisted and obstructed to the very last clause. You may have to go to the country on several of them. The committee stages will last for weeks and weeks, no matter how hard you work the guillotine: there will be thousands of amendments. Then, when you have got through what is left of your

Bill and carried it, the House of Lords will turn it down; and you will have to wait two years and go through the whole job again before you can get your Bill on the statute book as an Act of Parliament. This program is not a matter of today or tomorrow. I calculate that at the very least it will take fifty years to get it through.

SIR ARTHUR. And you think the world will wait for that, Sandy?

GLENMORISON [*naïvely*] What else can it do?

SIR ARTHUR. It wont wait. Unless we can find a shorter way, the program will be fought out in the streets.

SIR DEXTER. And you think that in the streets you will win? You think the mob will be on your side? "Ye are many: they are few" eh? The Class War! Well, you will find out your mistake.

SIR ARTHUR. I dont believe in the Class War any more than you do, Dexy. I know that half the working class is slaving away to pile up riches, only to be smoked out like a hive of bees and plundered of everything but a bare living by our class. But what is the other half doing? Living on the plunder at second hand. Plundering the plunderers. As fast as we fill our pockets with rent and interest and profits theyre emptied again by West End tradesmen and hotel keepers, fashionable doctors and lawyers and parsons and fiddlers and portrait painters and all sorts, to say nothing of huntsmen and stablemen and gardeners, valets and gamekeepers and jockeys, butlers and housekeepers and ladies' maids and scullery maids and deuce knows who not.

THE DUKE. How true, Arthur! how profoundly true! I am with you there to the last drop of my blood.

SIR ARTHUR. Well, these parasites will fight for the

rights of property as they would fight for their own skins. Can you get a Labor member into Parliament in the places where they are in a majority? No: there is no class war: the working class is hopelessly divided against itself. But I will tell you what there is. There is the gulf between Dexy's view of the world and mine. There is the eternal war between those who are in the world for what they can get out of it and those who are in the world to make it a better place for everybody to live in.

SIR DEXTER [*rising*] I will not sit here listening to this disgusting ungentlemanly nonsense. Chavender: the coalition is dissolved. I resign. I shall take with me three quarters of the Cabinet. I shall expose the shamelessly corrupt motives of those who have supported you here today. Basham: you will get the sack the day after the King sends for me. Domesday: you have gone gaga: go home to bed and drivel where your dotage can do no harm. Rosy: you are a damned fool; and you ought to know it by this time. Pandranath: you are only a silly nigger pretending to be an English gentleman: you are found out. Good afternoon, gentlemen.

He goes out, leaving an atmosphere of awe behind him, in which the Indian is choking with indignation, and for the moment inarticulate.

SIR BEMROSE. This is awful. We cannot do without him.

SIR JAFNA [*finding his tongue*] I am despised. I am called nigger by this dirty faced barbarian whose forefathers were naked savages worshipping acorns and mistletoe in the woods whilst my people were spreading the highest enlightenment yet reached by the human race from the temples of Brahma the thousandfold who is all the gods in one. This primitive savage dares to accuse me of imitating him: me, with the blood in my veins of conquerors who have swept through continents vaster than a million dogholes like this island of yours. They founded a civilization compared to which your little kingdom is no better than a concentration camp. What you have of religion came from the east; yet no Hindu, no Parsee, no Jain, would stoop to its crudities. Is there a mirror here? Look at your faces and look at the faces of my people in Ceylon, the cradle of the human race. There you see Man as he came from the hand of God, who has left on every feature the unmistakeable stamp of the great original creative artist. There you see Woman with eyes in her head that mirror the universe instead of little peepholes filled with faded pebbles. Set those features, those eyes, those burning colors beside the miserable smudged lumps of half baked dough, the cheap commercial copies of a far away gallery of masterpieces that you call western humanity, and tell me, if you dare, that you are the original and I the imitation. Do you not fear the lightning? the earthquake? the vengeance of Vishnu? You call me nigger, sneering at my color because you have none. The jackdaw has lost his tail and would persuade the world that his defect is a quality. You have all cringed to me, not for my greater nearness to God, but for my money and my power of making money and ever more money. But today your hatred, your envy, your insolence has betrayed itself. I am nigger. I am bad imitation of that eater of unclean foods, never sufficiently washed in his person or his garments, a British islander. I will no longer bear it. The veil of your hypocrisy is rent by your own mouths: I should dishonor my country and my race by remaining here where both have been insulted. Until now I have supported the connection between India and England because I knew that in the course of nature and by the justice of Brahma it must end in India ruling England just as I, by my wealth and my brains, govern this roomful of needy imbeciles. But I now cast you off. I return to India to detach it wholly from England, and leave you to perish in your ignorance, your vain conceit, and your abominable manners. Good morning, gentlemen. To hell with the lot of you. [*He goes out and slams the door*].

SIR ARTHUR. That one word nigger will cost us India. How could Dexy be such a fool as to let it slip!

SIR BEMROSE [*very serious—rising solemnly*] Arthur: I feel I cannot overlook a speech like that. After all, we are white men.

SIR ARTHUR. You are not, Rosy, I assure you. You are walnut color, with a touch of claret on the nose. Glenmorison is the color of his native oatmeal: not a touch of white on him. The fairest man present is the Duke. He's as yellow as a Malayan headhunter. The Chinese call us Pinks. They flatter us.

SIR BEMROSE. I must tell you, Arthur, that frivolity on a vital point like this is in very bad taste. And you know very well that the country cannot do without Dexy. Dexy was at school with me before I went to Dartmouth. To desert him would be for me not only an act of political bad faith but of personal bad feeling. I must go and see him at once. [*He goes very sadly to the door*].

SIR ARTHUR. Make my apologies to Sir Jafna if you overtake him. How are we to hold the empire together if we insult a man who represents nearly seventy per cent of its population?

SIR BEMROSE. I dont agree with you, Arthur. It is for Pandy to apologize. Dexy really shares the premiership with you; and if a Conservative Prime Minister of England may not take down a heathen native when he forgets himself there is an end of British supremacy.

SIR ARTHUR. For Heaven's sake dont call him a native. You are a native.

SIR BEMROSE [*very solemnly*] Of Kent, Arthur: of Kent. Not of Ceylon. [*He goes out*].

GLENMORISON. I think I'd better clear out too. I can make allowances for Sir Dexter: he is an Englishman, and has not been trained to use his mind like us in Scotland. But that is just what gives him such a hold on the Country. We must face it: he's indispensable. I'll just go and assure him that we have no intention of breaking with him. Ta ta. Good morning, Duke. [*He goes out*].

SIR ARTHUR [*rising and strolling round to the other side of the table like a cleaned-out gambler*] That finishes me, I'm afraid.

He throws himself into the middle chair. Basham rises moodily and goes to the window to contemplate the street. The Duke comes sympathetically to Sir Arthur and sits down beside him.

THE DUKE. Oh Arthur, my dear Arthur, why didnt you play golf on your holiday instead of thinking? Didnt you know that English politics wont bear thinking about? Didnt you know that as a nation we have lost the trick of thinking? Hadnt you noticed that though in our great British Constitution there is a department for everything else in the world almost —for agriculture and health and fisheries, for home affairs and foreign affairs and education, for the exchequer and the Treasury and even the Chiltern Hundreds and the Duchy of Lancaster—we have no department for thinking? The Russians have a special Cabinet for it; and it has knocked the whole place to

pieces. Where should you and I be in Russia today?
[*He resumes his seat with a hopeless shrug*].

SIR ARTHUR. In our proper place, the dustbin. Yet
they got their ideas from us. Karl Marx thought it all
out in Bloomsbury. Lenin learnt his lesson in Holford
Square, Islington. Why can we never think out anything, nor learn any lessons? I see what has to be
done now; but I dont feel that I am the man to do it.

THE DUKE. Of course not. Not a gentleman's job.

SIR ARTHUR. It might be a duke's job, though. Why
not have a try at it?

THE DUKE. For three reasons, Arthur. First, I'm not
built that way. Second, I'm so accustomed as a duke
to be treated with the utmost deference that I simply
dont know how to assert myself and bully people.
Third, I'm so horribly hard up for pocket money
without knowing how to do without it that Ive lost all
my self-respect. This job needs a man with nothing
to lose, plenty of hard driving courage, and a complete incapacity for seeing any side of a question but
his own. A mere hereditary duke would be no use.
When Domesday Towers is sold to an American I
shall have no family seat left, and must fall back on
my political seat, which is at present on the fence.
From that eminence I shall encourage the dictator
when he arrives as far as I can without committing
myself dangerously. Sorry I can be of no use to you,
my dear Arthur.

SIR ARTHUR. What about you, Basham? You are a
man of action.

BASHAM. I have a jolly good mind to go to the King
and make him take the bit between his teeth and
arrest the lot of you.

SIR ARTHUR. Do, Basham, do. You couldnt make a
worse hash of things than we have.

THE DUKE. Theres nothing to prevent you. Look at Kemal Pasha! Look at Mussolini! Look at Hitler! Look at De Valera! Look at Franklin Roosevelt!

BASHAM. If only I had ambition enough I'd think very seriously over it. As it is, I'll go back quietly to Scotland Yard. [*He is going out when he is confronted in the doorway by Hipney*] Hallo! What the devil are you doing here?

SIR ARTHUR. I am afraid you are late, Mr Hipney. The deputation has been here. They have all gone.

HIPNEY [*seating himself beside Sir Arthur with his usual calm*] I came with them, Srarthur. I been listening on the quiet as you might say. I just came in to tell you not to mind that parliamentary lot. Theyre all the same, west end or east end, parkside or riverside. Theyll never do anything. They dont want to do anything.

BASHAM [*sitting down again in Hilda's chair*] Hipney: I may as well tell you that I have had my eye on you for some time. Take care I have no objection to your calling yourself a revolutionary Socialist: they all do that. But I suspect you of really meaning business.

HIPNEY. I do, Sir Broadfoot: I do. And if Srarthur means business, then let him come out of Parliament and keep out. It will take the life out of him and leave him a walking talking shell of a man with nothing inside. The only man that ever had a proper understanding of Parliament was old Guy Fawkes.

SIR ARTHUR. But even if he had blown that Parliament up, they would just have elected another.

HIPNEY. Yes; but it was a sort of gesture as you might say. Symbolic, I call it. Mark my words: some day there will be a statue to old Guy in Westminster on the site of the present House of Commons.

THE DUKE. Democracy, Arthur, democracy. This is
what it ends in.

SIR ARTHUR [*introducing*] His Grace the Duke of
Domesday, Mr Hipney.

HIPNEY. Bless you, I know his Grace. About town,
as you might say, though weve never been introduced.

THE DUKE. Very much honored, Mr Hipney.

HIPNEY. No great honor, your Grace. But old Hipney
can tell you something about Democracy at first hand.
Democracy was a great thing when I was young and
we had no votes. We talked about public opinion and
what the British people would stand and what they
wouldnt stand. And it had weight, I tell you, sir:
it held Governments in check: it frightened the stout-
est of the tyrants and the bosses and the police: it
brought a real reverence into the voices of great
orators like Bright and Gladstone. But that was when
it was a dream and a vision, a hope and a faith and
a promise. It lasted until they dragged it down to
earth, as you might say, and made it a reality by giving
everybody votes. The moment they gave the working
men votes they found that theyd stand anything.
They gave votes to the women and found they were
worse than the men; for men would vote for men—
the wrong men, but men all the same—but the
women wouldnt even vote for women. Since then
politics have been a laughing stock. Parliamentary
leaders say one thing on Monday and just the opposite
on Wednesday; and nobody notices any difference.
They put down the people in Egypt, in Ireland, and in
India with fire and sword, with floggings and hangings,
burning the houses over their heads and bombing
their little stores for the winter out of existence; and
at the next election theyd be sent back to Parliament
by working class constituencies as if they were plaster

[718]

saints, while men and women like me, that had spent
their lives in the service of the people, were booted out
at the polls like convicted criminals. It wasnt that the
poor silly sheep did it on purpose. They didnt notice:
they didnt remember: they couldnt understand: they
were taken in by any nonsense they heard at the
meetings or read in the morning paper. You could
stampede them by crying out that the Russians were
coming, or rally them by promising them to hang the
Kaiser, or Lord knows what silliness that shouldnt
have imposed on a child of four. That was the end of
democracy for me; though there was no man alive
that had hoped as much from it, nor spoke deeper
from his heart about all the good things that would
happen when the people came to their own and had
votes like the gentry. Adult suffrage: that was what
was to save us all. My God! It delivered us into the
hands of our spoilers and oppressors, bound hand and
foot by our own folly and ignorance. It took the heart
out of old Hipney; and now I'm for any Napoleon or
Mussolini or Lenin or Chavender that has the stuff in
him to take both the people and the spoilers and
oppressors by the scruffs of their silly necks and just
sling them into the way they should go with as many
kicks as may be needful to make a thorough job of it.

BASHAM. A dictator: eh? Thats what you want.

HIPNEY. Better one dictator standing up responsible
before the world for the good and evil he does than a
dirty little dictator in every street responsible to nobody, to turn you out of your house if you dont pay
him for the right to exist on the earth, or to fire you
out of your job if you stand up to him as a man and
an equal. You cant frighten me with a word like
dictator. Me and my like has been dictated to all our
lives by swine that have nothing but a snout for

money, and think the world is coming to an end if anybody but themselves is given the power to do anything.

SIR ARTHUR. Steady, Mr Hipney, steady! Dont empty the baby out with the bath. If the people are to have no voice in the government and no choice of who is to govern them, it will be bad for the people.

HIPNEY. Let em have a voice. Let em have a choice. Theyve neither at present. But let it be a voice to squeal with when theyre hurt, and not to pretend they know more than God Almighty does. Give em a choice between qualified men: there's always more than one pebble on the beach; but let them be qualified men and not windbags and movie stars and soldiers and rich swankers and lawyers on the make. How are they to tell the difference between any cheap Jack and Solomon or Moses? The Jews didnt elect Moses: he just told them what to do and they did it. Look at the way they went wrong the minute his back was turned! If you want to be a leader of the people, Srarthur, youve got to elect yourself by giving us a lead. Old Hipney will follow anyone that will give him a good lead; and to blazes with your elections and your Constitution and your Democracy and all the rest of it!

THE DUKE. The police wont let him, Mr Hipney.

BASHAM [*rising and planting himself between Hipney and Sir Arthur*] Ha ha ha! Dont be too sure of that. I might come down on your side, Arthur, if I spotted you as a winner. Meanwhile, Hipney, I have my eye on you as a dangerous character.

SIR ARTHUR. And on me?

BASHAM. You dont matter: he does. If the proletariat comes to the top things will be more comfortable for Hipney; but they wont be more comfortable for you.

His heart is in the revolution: you have only your head in it. Your wife wouldnt like it: his would, if he has one.

HIPNEY. Not me. I'm under no woman's thumb. She's dead; and the children are grown up and off my hands. I'm free at last to put my neck in a noose if I like.

BASHAM. I wonder should I find any bombs in your house if I searched it.

HIPNEY. You would if you put them there first, Sir Broadfoot. What good would a police chief be if he couldnt find anything he wanted to find?

BASHAM. Thats a suggestion, Hipney, certainly. Isnt it rather rash of you to put it into my head?

HIPNEY. There's plenty to put it into your head if I didnt. You could do it if you liked; and you know it, Sir Broadfoot. But perhaps your conscience wouldnt let you.

BASHAM. Perhaps.

HIPNEY [*rising with a chuckle*] Aha! [*Impressively*] You take it from me, you three gentlemen: all this country or any country has to stand between it and blue hell is the consciences of them that are capable of governing it.

THE DUKE [*rising*] Mr Hipney: I find myself in complete agreement with you. Will you lunch with me at the Carlton?

HIPNEY. No: them big clubs is too promiscuous for the like of you and me. You come and lunch with me: I know a nice little place where the cooking's good and the company really select. You wont regret it: come along. Morning, Srarthur. Morning, Boss. [*He goes out, greatly pleased*].

SIR ARTHUR AND BASHAM [*simultaneously*] Morning. Morning.

THE DUKE. You would never have got rid of him, Arthur, if I hadnt made that move. Goodbye. Goodbye, Sir Broadfoot. [*He goes to the door*]

BASHAM. Goodbye. I wish you joy of your host.

THE DUKE. You dont appreciate him. He is absolutely unique.

BASHAM. In what way, pray?

THE DUKE. He is the only politician I ever met who had learnt anything from experience [*he goes out*].

BASHAM [*making for the door*] Well, I must be off to the Yard. The unemployed are going to have a general election to amuse them. I suppose youll be off to your constituency right away.

SIR ARTHUR [*rising*] No. I am not going to stand.

BASHAM [*returning to him in amazement*] Not stand! What do you mean? You cant chalk up a program like that and then run away.

SIR ARTHUR. I am through with parliament. It has wasted enough of my life.

BASHAM. Dont tell me you are going to take your politics into the street. You will only get your head broken.

SIR ARTHUR. Never fear: your fellows wont break my head: they have too much respect for an ex-Prime Minister. But I am not going into the streets. I am not a man of action, only a talker. Until the men of action clear out the talkers we who have social consciences are at the mercy of those who have none; and that, as old Hipney says, is blue hell. Can you find a better name for it?

BASHAM. Blackguardocracy. I should call it.

SIR ARTHUR. Do you believe in it? I dont.

BASHAM. It works all right up to a point. Dont run your head against it until the men of action get you past that point. Bye bye.

SIR ARTHUR. Bye bye. I wont.

Basham goes out through the main door. Sir Arthur drops into his chair again and looks rather sick, with his elbows on his knees and his temples on his fists. Barking and Miss Brollikins break into the room simultaneously by the private door, struggling for precedence, Sir Arthur straightens up wearily.

BARKING. I was here first. You get out and wait for your turn.

ALOYSIA. Ladies first, if you please. Sir Arthur—

BARKING [*barring her way with an arm of iron*] Ladies be damned! youre no lady. [*He comes past the table to Sir Arthur's right*]. Sir Arthur: I have proposed for the hand of your daughter Flavia; and all I can get out of her is that she is not a gold digger, and wouldnt be seen at a wedding with a lousy viscount. She wants to marry a poor man. I said I'd go over her head straight to you. You cant let her miss so good a match. Exert your authority. Make her marry me.

SIR ARTHUR. Certainly. I'll order her to marry you if you think that will get you any further. Go and tell her so, like a good boy. I'm busy.

BARKING. Righto! [*he dashes out through the masked door*].

SIR ARTHUR. Sit down, Miss Brollikins. [*She comes round to Hipney's chair; and Sir Arthur takes the Duke's chair*]. Have you consulted David?

ALOYSIA [*sitting down rather forlornly*] Of course I have. But he's obstinate. He wont look at it the right way.

SIR ARTHUR. Did he object? He should have jumped at it.

ALOYSIA. Its very nice of you to say so if you really mean it, Sir Arthur. But he has no sense. He objects to my name. He says it's ridiculous.

SIR ARTHUR. But your marriage will change it.

ALOYSIA. Yes; but he says it would be in The Times in the births marriages and deaths: Chavender and Brollikins. My name's not good enough for him. You should have heard what he said about it.

SIR ARTHUR. I hope he did not use the adjective his sister applied to poor young Barking's title.

ALOYSIA. Yes he did. The language you West End people use! I'm sure I dont know where you pick it up.

SIR ARTHUR. It doesnt mean anything, Miss Brollikins. You mustnt mind.

ALOYSIA. Would you mind calling me Aloysia, Sir Arthur? You can call me Brolly if you like; but I prefer Aloysia.

SIR ARTHUR. Certainly, Aloysia.

ALOYSIA. Thank you. I wish I could get rid of Brollikins. I'd never stoop to be ashamed of my name; but I cant deny there's something funny about it. I'm not to blame for that, am I?

SIR ARTHUR. But you can get rid of it quite easily. You can take a new name: any name you like, by deed poll. It costs only ten pounds; and David would have to pay it if it was on his account you changed. What about Bolingbroke [*he pronounces it Bullingbrook*]? Bolingbroke would be rather a nice name for The Times; and you wouldnt have to change your initials. No bother about your clothes at the laundry, for instance.

ALOYSIA. Thank you, Sir Arthur: thats a practical suggestion. At any rate it will shut David up if he talks about my name again.

SIR ARTHUR. Well, now you can run off and marry him.

ALOYSIA. But thats not all, Sir Arthur. He's such a

queer boy. He says he's never loved anyone but his sister, and that he hates his mother.

SIR ARTHUR. He had no right to tell you that he hates his mother, because as a matter of fact he doesnt. Young people nowadays read books about psycho-analysis and get their heads filled with nonsense.

ALOYSIA. Of course I know all about psycho-analysis. I explained to him that he was in love with his mother and was jealous of you. The Edipus complex, you know.

SIR ARTHUR. And what did he say to that?

ALOYSIA. He told me to go to Jericho. But I shall teach him manners.

SIR ARTHUR. Do, Aloysia. Did he make any further objection?

ALOYSIA. Well, he says his people couldnt stand my relatives.

SIR ARTHUR. Tut! the young snob! Still, snobbery is a very real thing: he made a point there, Aloysia. How did you meet it?

ALOYSIA. I said my people couldnt stand his relatives; and no more they could. I said I wasnt asking him to marry my relatives; nor was I proposing to marry his.

SIR ARTHUR. And what did he say to that?

ALOYSIA. He told me to go to hell. He's like that, you know.

SIR ARTHUR. Yes, a hasty boy.

ALOYSIA. He is, just that. But I shall cure him of it.

SIR ARTHUR [*gravely*] Take care, Aloysia. All young women begin by believing they can change and reform the men they marry. They cant. If you marry David he will remain David and nobody else til death do you part. If he tells you to go to hell today instead of try-ing to argue with you, he will do the same on the morning of your silver wedding.

ALOYSIA [*grimly*] We shall see.

SIR ARTHUR. May I ask whether this match is your idea or David's? So far I do not gather that he has expressed any strong feeling of—of—shall I say devotion?—to you.

ALOYSIA. We have discussed all that.

SIR ARTHUR. Satisfactorily?

ALOYSIA. I suppose so. You see, Sir Arthur, I am not like David. I am a reading thinking modern woman; and I know how to look at these things objectively and scientifically. You know the way you meet thousands of people and they mean nothing to you sexually: you wouldnt touch one of them with a barge pole. Then all of a sudden you pick out one, and feel sexy all over. If he's not nice you feel ashamed of yourself and run away. But if he is nice you say "Thats the man for me." You have had that experience yourself, havnt you?

SIR ARTHUR. Quite. The moment I saw Lady Chavender I said "Thats the woman for me."

ALOYSIA. Well, the moment I laid eyes on David I went all over like that. You cant deny that he is a nice boy in spite of his awful language. So I said—

SIR ARTHUR. "David's the man for me"?

ALOYSIA. No. I said "Evolution is telling me to marry this youth." That feeling is the only guide I have to the evolutionary appetite.

SIR ARTHUR. The what??

ALOYSIA. The evolutionary appetite. The thing that wants to develop the race. If I marry David we shall develop the race. And thats the great thing in marriage, isnt it?

SIR ARTHUR. My dear Aloysia, the evolutionary appetite may be a guide to developing the race; but it doesnt care a rap for domestic happiness. I have known the most remarkable children come of the most dreadfully unsuitable and unhappy marriages.

ALOYSIA. We have to take our chance of that, Sir Arthur. Marriage is a lottery. I think I can make David as happy as anybody ever is in this—

SIR ARTHUR. In this wicked world. Ah yes. Well, I wont press that.

ALOYSIA. I was about to say "in the capitalist phase of social development." I dont talk like your grandmother, if you will excuse me saying so.

SIR ARTHUR. I beg your pardon. I suppose I do. Have you explained this evolutionary view of the situation to David?

ALOYSIA. Of course I have. I dont treat him as a child.

SIR ARTHUR. And what did he say?

ALOYSIA. He told me to go and— Oh, I really cannot repeat what he told me to go and do. But you see how familiar we are together. I couldnt bear his being distant with me. He talks just as if we were married already.

SIR ARTHUR. Quite. But does he feel about you as you feel about him? Has he picked you out from among the thousand ladies to whom he is indifferent? To use your own expression, does he come all over like that in your presence?

ALOYSIA. He does when I get hold of him. He needs educating in these matters. I have to awaken David. But he's coming along nicely.

SIR ARTHUR. Well, if it must be it must be. I shall not withhold my blessing. That is all I can say. [*He rises: she does the same and prepares to go*]. You see, Aloysia, the effete society in which I move is based on the understanding that we shall speak and behave in the manner in which we are expected to behave.

We are hopeless when this understanding is violated. We dont know what to say or what to do. Well, you have violated it recklessly. What you have said has been unexpected to the last possible degree—

ALOYSIA. It has been true.

SIR ARTHUR. That is the climax of unexpectedness in polite society. Therefore I am at a loss. Apparently my son was not at a loss. He knows how to deal with you: I do not. I must really refer you back to him for further consideration and report.

They are about to shake hands when Lady Chavender comes in through the masked door.

LADY CHAVENDER. Still here, Miss Brollikins! I thought you had gone. [*She comes past the table to Sir Arthur's right*].

SIR ARTHUR. She wants to marry David, my dear.

LADY CHAVENDER [*calmly*] Very naturally. I think if I were in Miss Brollikins' position I should want to marry David.

ALOYSIA. I know your class point of view, Lady Chavender. You think it would be a big catch for me and a come-down for him.

LADY CHAVENDER. We both know that point of view, Miss Brollikins; but it is you, not I, that have mentioned it. Wont you sit down? [*She sits down herself in the nearest chair*].

ALOYSIA [*murmurs*] I was just going. [*She resumes her seat*].

Sir Arthur also sits.

LADY CHAVENDER. I daresay a match with you might be a very good thing for David. You seem to have all the qualities in which he is deficient. And he has been declaring for some months past that if he ever marries he will marry a factory girl.

ALOYSIA. Well, I have been a factory girl. I started

as a school teacher; but when they cut my salary I went into the factory. I organized the girls there, and became a trade union secretary. Wherever I went I rose because I couldnt keep down. But I am proletarian, bone and blood, if thats what David wants.

LADY CHAVENDER. Nobody is that in England, Miss Brollikins. We have never had a noble caste: our younger sons have always been commoners.

SIR ARTHUR. Yes, Aloysia: all British blood is blue.

ALOYSIA. Well, call it what you like. All I say is that I belong to the common working people and am proud of it; and that is what David wants, isnt it?

LADY CHAVENDER. What I said was that he wants to marry a factory girl. But I do not know what his attitude will be when a factory girl wants to marry him. Have you proposed to him?

SIR ARTHUR. Yes. He told her to go to hell.

LADY CHAVENDER. David has rather a habit of telling people to go to hell when he is too lazy to think of anything better to say. Miss Brollikins is a resolute and successful young woman. David is an irresolute and unsuccessful young man. If she has made up her mind to marry him she will probably succeed. She will have to support him; but I daresay she can do that as easily as she can support herself.

ALOYSIA. I shall expect him to work for his living.

LADY CHAVENDER. Marriage seldom fulfils all our expectations. You dont know David yet.

ALOYSIA. I will find him a job and see that he does it. I will interest him in it.

SIR ARTHUR. Splendid!

ALOYSIA [*puzzled*] But I cant make out you two. You havnt flared up as I thought you might; but are you for me or against me?

LADY CHAVENDER. Miss Brollikins: I am sorry; but

there are two things that I cannot bring myself to take the smallest interest in: parliamentary affairs and love affairs. They both bore me to distraction.

ALOYSIA [*to Sir Arthur*] Well, dont you take an interest in David?

SIR ARTHUR. David is at the age at which young men have to break loose from their fathers. They are very sensitive about being interfered with at that age. He would regard my taking an interest in him as parental tyranny. Therefore I am particularly careful not to take any interest in him.

ALOYSIA [*rising*] Well, you preach at me because my conversation is unexpected; but you two are the most unexpected lot I have ever been up against. What am I to understand. Will you play fair and let David take his own way?

SIR ARTHUR [*rising*] We will even let him take your way if he wishes, Aloysia.

LADY CHAVENDER [*rising*] You may leave me out of the question, Miss Brollikins. It is not my business, but my son's. I am neither his enemy nor yours.

ALOYSIA [*perplexed*] But do you think I ought to marry him?

LADY CHAVENDER. Nobody ought to marry anybody, Aloysia. But they do.

ALOYSIA. Well, thank you for calling me Aloysia, anyhow. It's about all the satisfaction I have got here.

She is about to go when David breaks in obstreperously through the masked door, and strides between the table and the window to Aloysia's left.

DAVID. Look here, Aloysia. What are you up to here? If you think you can get round me by getting round my parents, youre very much mistaken. My parents dont care a damn what I do as long as I take myself off their hands. And I wont be interfered with. Do you hear? I wont be interfered with.

ALOYSIA. Your parents are too good for you, you uncivilized lout. Youve put me right off it by talking that way in front of your mother. If I was your mother I'd smack some manners into you.

DAVID [*appalled and imploring*] Aloysia! [*He tries to take her in his arms*].

ALOYSIA. Take your dirty hands off me [*she flings him off*]. It's off, I tell you, off. Goodbye all. [*She storms out through the main door*].

DAVID [*in loud lament to his mother*] Youve ruined my whole life. [*He goes in pursuit, crying*] Aloysia, Aloysia, wait a moment. [*With anguished intensity*] Aloysia. [*His cries recede in the distance*].

| LADY CHAVENDER | | He might do worse. |
| SIR ARTHUR | [*simultaneously*] | He might do worse. |

LADY CHAVENDER. I beg your pardon. What did you say?

SIR ARTHUR. I said he might do worse.

LADY CHAVENDER. That is what I said. David is overbred: he is so fine-drawn that he is good for nothing; and he is not strong enough physically. Our breed needs to be crossed with the gutter or the soil once in every three or four generations. Uncle Theodore married his cook on principle; and his wife was my favourite aunt. Brollikins may give me goose flesh occasionally; but she wont bore me as a lady daughter-in-law would. I shall be always wondering what she will say or do next. If she were a lady I'd always know. I am so tired of wellbred people, and party politics, and the London season, and all the rest of it.

SIR ARTHUR. I sometimes think you are the only really revolutionary revolutionist I have ever met.

LADY CHAVENDER. Oh, lots of us are like that. We were born into good society; and we are through with it: we have no illusions about it, even if we are fit for nothing better. I dont mind Brollikins one bit.

SIR ARTHUR. What about Barking?

LADY CHAVENDER. I—

Barking enters through the masked door, jubilant. He comes between the pair as they rise, and claps them both on the shoulders right and left simultaneously. They flinch violently, and stare at him in outraged amazement.

BARKING. Good news, old dears! It's all right about Flavia. We may put up the banns. Hooray! [*He rubs hands gleefully*].

SIR ARTHUR. May I ask how you have got over her craze for marrying a poor man?

BARKING. Oh, that was a girlish illusion. You see, she had a glimpse today, at the unemployment meeting, of what poor men are really like. They were awfully nice to her. That did the trick. You see, what she craved for before was their rough manners, their violence, their brutality and filthy language, their savage treatment of their women folk. That was her ideal of a delightful husband. She found today that the working man doesnt realize it. I do. I am a real he-man. I called her the foulest names until she gave in. She's a dear. We shall be perfectly happy. Good old mother-in-law. [*He kisses Lady Chavender, who is too astounded to resist or speak*]. Tootle loo, Chavender. [*He slaps him on the shoulder*]. I am off to buy her a lot of presents. [*He dashes out through the main door*].

SIR ARTHUR. So thats that.

LADY CHAVENDER. The brute! How dare he kiss me? [*She rubs the place with her handkerchief*].

SIR ARTHUR. Do you realize that we two are free at last? Free, dearest: think of that! No more children. Free to give up living in a big house and to spend the remainder of our lives as we please. A cottage near a good golf links seems to be indicated. What would you like?

LADY CHAVENDER. But your political career? Are you really going to give up that?

SIR ARTHUR. It has given me up, dearest. Arnt you glad?

LADY CHAVENDER. Arthur: I cant bear this.

SIR ARTHUR. Cant bear what?

LADY CHAVENDER. To see you discouraged. You have never been discouraged before: you have always been so buoyant. If this new departure is to do nothing for you but take away your courage and high spirits and selfconfidence, then in Heaven's name go back to your old way of life. I will put up with anything rather than see you unhappy. That sort of unhappiness kills; and if you die I'll die too. [*She throws herself into a chair and hides her face on the table*].

SIR ARTHUR. Dont fuss, dearest: I'm not unhappy. I am enjoying the enormous freedom of having found myself out and got myself off my mind. That looks like despair; but it is really the beginning of hope, and the end of hypocrisy. Do you think I didnt know, in the days of my great speeches and my roaring popularity, that I was only whitewashing the slums? I did it very well—I dont care who hears me say so—and there is always a sort of artistic satisfaction in doing a thing very well, whether it's getting a big Bill through the House, or carrying a big meeting off its feet, or winning a golf championship. It was all very jolly;

and I'm still a little proud of it. But even if I had not had you here to remind me that it was all hot air, I couldnt help knowing as well as any of those damned Socialists that though the West End of London was chockful of money and nice people all calling one another by their Christian names, the lives of the millions of people whose labor was keeping the whole show going were not worth living. I knew it quite well; but I was able to put it out of my mind because I thought it couldnt be helped and I was doing the best that could be done. I know better now: I know that it can be helped, and how it can be helped. And rather than go back to the old whitewashing job, I'd seize you tight round the waist and make a hole in the river with you.

LADY CHAVENDER [*rising*] Then why, dearest love, dont you—

SIR ARTHUR. Why dont I lead a revolt against it all? Because I'm not the man for the job, darling; and nobody knows that better than you. And I shall hate the man who will carry it through for his cruelty and the desolation he will bring on us and our like.

Shouting, as of an excited mob suddenly surging into the street; and a sound of breaking glass and police whistling.

LADY CHAVENDER. What on earth is that?

Hilda comes from her office and runs to the window.

LADY CHAVENDER [*joining her*] What is going on, Hilda?

HILDA. The unemployed have broken into Downing Street; and theyre breaking the windows of the Colonial Office. They think this side is only private houses.

SIR ARTHUR [*going to see*] Yes: they always break the wrong windows, poor devils!

HILDA. Oh! here come the mounted police.

SIR ARTHUR. Theyve splendid horses, those fellows.

HILDA. The people are all running away. And they cant get out: theyre in a cul-de-sac. Oh, why dont they make a stand, the cowards?

LADY CHAVENDER. Indeed I hope they wont. What are you thinking of, Hilda?

SIR ARTHUR. Men are like that, Hilda. They always run away when they have no discipline and no leader.

HILDA. Well, but cant the police let them run away without breaking their heads? Oh look: that policeman has just clubbed a quite old man.

SIR ARTHUR. Come away: it's not a nice sight. [*He draws her away, placing himself between her and the window*].

HILDA. It's all right when you only read about it in the papers; but when you actually see it you want to throw stones at the police.

Defiant singing through the tumult.

LADY CHAVENDER [*looking out*] Someone has opened the side gate and let them through into the Horse Guards Parade. They are trying to sing.

SIR ARTHUR. What are they singing? The Red Flag?

LADY CHAVENDER. No. I dont know the tune. I caught the first two words. "England, arise."

HILDA [*suddenly hysterical*] Oh, my God! I will go out and join them [*she rushes out through the main door*].

LADY CHAVENDER. Hilda! Hilda!

SIR ARTHUR. Never mind, dear: the police all know her: she'll come to no harm. She'll be back for tea. But what she felt just now other girls and boys may feel tomorrow. And just suppose—!

LADY CHAVENDER. What?

SIR ARTHUR. Suppose England really did arise!

Unemployed England, however, can do nothing but continue to sing, as best it can to a percussion accompaniment of baton thwacks, Edward Carpenter's verses

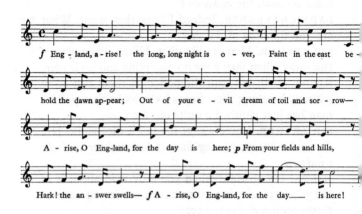

England, arise! the long, long night is over, Faint in the east behold the dawn appear; Out of your evil dream of toil and sorrow— Arise, O England, for the day is here; From your fields and hills, Hark! the answer swells— Arise, O England, for the day is here!

Shaw Answers Some Questions

(Replies to a questionnaire by Andrew E. Malone, from the holograph manuscript in the Humanities Research Center of the University of Texas at Austin. Published as an interview in the *Sunday Chronicle*, Manchester, 19 August 1934)

In On The Rocks, *which was staged a few weeks ago at the Abbey Theatre, The Prime Minister capitulates when he had, apparently, won over all his more important colleagues in the Cabinet to his programme. If Prime Ministers consistently behaved like this government, as we know it now, political power must inevitably pass to militant Dictators everywhere. Do you believe that Militant Dictatorship is the only form of government which will get the nations off the rocks?*

The P.M. in On the Rocks did not win over anybody. The proletarians attacked and repudiated him at once; and the Conservatives, though quite approving of the items in his program which favored their private affairs, deserted him and followed their Die Hard leader the moment he called them to heel.

As to militant Dictatorship, it means no more than Gas and Gaiters. At present all the countries which are not, like England, merely sticking in the mud, are dominated by dictators: Stalin, Hitler, Mussolini, Kemal, Roosevelt, Pilsudski, and De Valera. But none of these dictatorships is like any of the others. The only feature they have in common is the abolition of party government and of Oppositions. The notion that the only alternative to the party system is a Tsardom masquerading as a Republican Dictatorship is only a symptom of political ignorance and thoughtlessness, which is unfortunately an almost universal disease at present.

Do you believe that your stage Prime Minister's way, of conceding everything to the powerful ones, or that of your King Magnus, of threatening to make an appeal to the country, is the better way of preserving and continuing the system of Representative Government?

A Prime Minister cannot help himself within the limits of the Constitution. Power is to the powerful. King Magnus outwitted his ministers at the party game, but was left entirely helpless in the face of Big Business and the threatened absorption of England by the United States under cover of Re-Union. Representative government is not at stake. It existed before party government (a dodge hit upon by a Scottish adviser of William III of glorious, pious and immortal memory) existed; and it will exist long after party government has ceased in England as completely as in Russia.

Do you think that a limitation of the franchise to those who really desire it, and take some trouble to secure it, would be of assistance in making parliamentary government really effective?

There should be no limitation of the franchise. Everybody who is capable of suffering by misgovernment must have a means of squealing loudly when he is hurt. Otherwise the Government cannot possibly tell whether it is doing harm or good. It is only when fools and robbers pretend that the man in the street can legislate and administer and govern that it becomes necessary to bind the man in the street hand and foot and gag him, which is exactly what the robbers want. Parliament is for the ventilation of grievances. An organ for that purpose is an indispensable part of any stable political structure; and it should be available for everybody, even for children—perhaps especially for children.

F. S. Oliver holds that a parliament "Where none was for a party, But all were for the State" would be "no more than an impotent Babel of virtuous voices." What is your opinion on the subject?

What is wanted is a parliament in which no one is for a party and everyone for his own fireside. Then the Government will be able to find out what is wrong with the firesides. If it is an honest Government it will set its wits to work to right the wrong. If it is a Gombeen Government it will study to maintain the wrong and, if possible, to intensify it.

In Ireland Mr. de Valera has expressed the opinion that when once the electorate has given a decision by electing a majority of any party to be the government all opposition to the policy of the victorious party should cease. All vocal opposition is then merely factious, and all active opposition treachery. Would you agree that this should be so?

Of course Mr de Valera is only talking the plainest common sense. He is exactly and finally right. The business of an Opposition is to oppose, even when it is opposing measures of the desirability of which it is so convinced that it passes them itself when it gets into power. How could any sane business be conducted on such a principle? Let the Irish people by all means choose whether they will be governed by Mr A or Mr B, or if you prefer it, by Mr de V. or Mr O'D (or their wives); but to ask Mr A to govern the country and then send in Mr B. to prevent his doing it is an act of political lunacy which can be advocated by people who want to prevent the country being governed at all. Mr de Valera is forced by the very nature of things to refuse to govern under such impossible conditions.

Do you think that Ireland, or the Irish Free State, is on the rocks? Or, Is it heading for the rocks? Or, Do you think that it has escaped the rocks?

Yes: of course she is on the rocks, the same old rocks. And when a Catholic Irishman tries to get her off, a Protestant Irishman immediately tries to keep her on; and *vice versa.* Contrairyness is the curse of Ireland, as fatheaded snobbery is the curse of England.

If we are on the rocks, with most of the world, do you think we are on the same rocks? Or, Have we struck a specially national reef of our own?

Just the same old rock, on which idleness and parasitism are idolized, subsidized, and glorified, whilst useful labor and honest self-support are starved and despised. . . .

If we are all on the rocks—What must we do to get refloated? What must we do to be saved? You cannot, like your Prime Minister, just wave your hands ineffectively and vanish from the stage.

My Prime Minister vanished because he was fit for nothing but being Prime Minister in a party government. But his program remains. There is no longer any doubt or obscurity or indefiniteness as to what needs to be done. Of course it is not clear to muddleheads: nothing is clear to muddleheads. And it is not known to invincible ignorance. But the muddleheads and incurable ignoramuses will have to do just what they are told or they will be the ruin of us. Good morning.

G. BERNARD SHAW
Great Malvern
25th July 1934

The Simpleton of the Unexpected Isles:
A Vision of Judgment

Preface on Days of Judgment
The Simple Truth of the Matter

THE SIMPLETON
OF THE UNEXPECTED ISLES

Composition begun 16 February 1934; completed 26 April 1934. First published in German translation, as *Die Insel der Überraschungen*, 1935 (the first scene of the Prologue had earlier appeared in the *Berliner Tageblatt*, 12 February 1935). First published in English in *The Simpleton, The Six, and The Millionairess*, 1936. First presented by the Theatre Guild at the Guild Theatre, New York, on 18 February 1935.

Emigration Officer (Hugo Hyering) *Rex O'Malley*

Wilks *Lionel Pape*

Young Woman (Mrs Hyering) *Patricia Calvert*

Station Master *Reginald Malcolm*

Pra, a Priest *McKay Morris*

Prola, a Priestess *Alla Nazimova*

Lady Farwaters *Viola Roache*

Sir Charles Farwaters *Lawrence Grossmith*

Reverend Phosphor Hammingtap *Romney Brent*

Janga *Leon Janney*

Kanchin *Franklin Gray*

Maya *Alma Lloyd*

Vashti *Rita Vale*

The Angel *Louis Hector*

Period—Approaching Judgment Day

Prologue:

Scene 1 *The Emigration Office at a Tropical Port in the British Empire*

Scene 2 *A Grassy Cliff-top overhanging the Sea*

Scene 3 *A Shelf of Rock halfway down the Cliff*

ACT I *The Lawn of a Stately House on the North Coast of a Tropical Island in the Pacific. About 20 years later*
ACT II *The Same. A Fine Forenoon Some Years Later. (During this act the lights are dimmed to denote the passage of time)*

Preface on Days of Judgment

The increasing bewilderment of my journalist critics as to why I should write such plays as The Simpleton culminated in New York in February 1935, when I was described as a dignified old monkey throwing coco-nuts at the public in pure senile devilment. This is an amusing and graphic description of the effect I produce on the newspapers; but as a scientific criticism it is open to the matter-of-fact objection that a play is not a coco-nut nor I a monkey. Yet there is an analogy. A coco-nut is impossible without a suitable climate; and a play is impossible without a suitable civilization. If author and journalist are both placid Panglossians, convinced that their civilization is the best of all possible civilizations, and their countrymen the greatest race on earth: in short, if they have had a university education, there is no trouble: the press notices are laudatory if the play is entertaining. Even if the two are pessimists who agree with Jeremiah that the heart of man is deceitful above all things and desperately wicked, and with Shakespear that political authority only transforms its wielders into angry apes, there is still no misunderstanding; for that dismal view, or a familiar acquaintance with it, is quite common.

Such perfect understanding covers much more than nine hundred and ninety cases out of every thousand new plays. But it does not cover the cases in which the author and the journalist are not writing against the same background. The simplest are those in which the journalist is ignorant and uncultivated, and the author is assuming a high degree of knowledge and culture in his audience. This occurs oftener than it should; for some newspaper editors think that any

[745]

reporter who has become stage struck by seeing half a dozen crude melodramas is thereby qualified to deal with Sophocles and Euripides, Shakespear and Goethe, Ibsen and Strindberg, Tolstoy and Tchekov, to say nothing of myself. But the case with which I am concerned here is one in which a reasonably well equipped critic shoots wide because he cannot see the target nor even conceive its existence. The two parties have not the same vision of the world. This sort of vision varies enormously from individual to individual. Between the superstatesman whose vision embraces the whole politically organized world, or the astronomer whose vision of the universe transcends the range of our utmost telescopes, and the peasant who fiercely resists a main drainage scheme for his village because others as well as he will benefit by it, there are many degrees. The Abyssinian Danakil kills a stranger at sight and is continually seeking for an excuse to kill a friend to acquire trophies enough to attract a wife. Livingstone risked his life in Africa every day to save a black man's soul. Livingstone did not say to the sun colored tribesman "There is between me and thee a gulf that nothing can fill": he proposed to fill it by instructing the tribesman on the assumption that the tribesman was as capable mentally as himself, but ignorant. That is my attitude when I write prefaces. My newspaper critics may seem incapable of anything better than the trash they write; but I believe they are capable enough and only lack instruction.

I wonder how many of them have given serious thought to the curious changes that take place in the operation of human credulity and incredulity. I have pointed out on a former occasion that there is just as much evidence for a law of the Conservation of Credulity as of the Conservation of Energy. When we refuse to believe in the miracles of religion for no better reason fundamentally than that we are no longer in the humor for them we refill our minds with the miracles of science, most of which the authors of the Bible would have refused to believe. The humans who have lost their simple childish faith in a flat earth and in Joshua's feat of stopping the sun until he had finished his battle with the Amalekites, find no difficulty in swallowing an expanding boomerang universe.

They will refuse to have their children baptized or circumcized, and insist on their being vaccinated, in the teeth of overwhelming evidence that vaccination has killed thousands of children in quite a horrible way whereas no child has ever been a penny the worse for baptism since John the Baptist recommended it. Religion is the mother of scepticism: Science is the mother of credulity. There is nothing that people will not believe nowadays if only it be presented to them as Science, and nothing they will not disbelieve if it be presented to them as religion. I myself began like that; and I am ending by receiving every scientific statement with dour suspicion whilst giving very respectful consideration to the inspirations and revelations of the prophets and poets. For the shift of credulity from religious divination to scientific invention is very often a relapse from comparatively harmless romance to mischievous and even murderous quackery.

Some credulities have their social uses. They have been invented and imposed on us to secure certain lines of behavior as either desirable for the general good or at least convenient to our rulers. I learned this early in life. My nurse induced me to abstain from certain troublesome activities by threatening that if I indulged in them the cock would come down the chimney. This event seemed to me so apocalyptic that

I never dared to provoke it nor even to ask myself in what way I should be the worse for it. Without this device my nurse could not have ruled me when her back was turned. It was the first step towards making me rule myself.

Mahomet, one of the greatest of the prophets of God, found himself in the predicament of my nurse in respect of having to rule a body of Arab chieftains whose vision was not co-extensive with his own, and who therefore could not be trusted, when his back was turned, to behave as he himself would have behaved spontaneously. He did not tell them that if they did such and such things the cock would come down the chimney. They did not know what a chimney was. But he threatened them with the most digusting penances in a future life if they did not live according to his word, and promised them very pleasant times if they did. And as they could not understand his inspiration otherwise than as a spoken communication by a personal messenger he allowed them to believe that the angel Gabriel acted as a celestial postman between him and Allah, the fountain of all inspiration. Except in this way he could not have made them believe in anything but sacred stones and the seven deadly sins.

The Christian churches and the Christian Kings were driven to the same device; and when I evolved beyond the cock and chimney stage I found myself possessed with a firm belief that all my Roman Catholic fellow children would inevitably burn in blazing brimstone to all eternity, and even that I myself, in spite of my Protestant advantages, might come to the same endless end if I were not careful. The whole civilized world seemed to be governed that way in those days. It is so to a considerable extent still. A friend of mine lately asked a leading Irish statesman why he did not resort to a rather soulless stroke of diplomacy. Because, replied the statesman, I happen to believe that there is such a place as hell.

Anywhere else than in Ireland the obsolescence of this explanation would have been startling. For somehow there has been a shift of credulity from hell to perishing suns and the like. I am not thinking of the humanitarian revolt against everlasting brimstone voiced by the late Mrs Bradlaugh Bonner, nor of Tolstoy's insistence on the damnation on earth of the undetected, unpunished, materially prosperous criminal. I am leaving out of the question also the thoughtful, sentimental, honorable, conscientious people who need no hell to intimidate them into considerate social behaviour, and who have naturally outgrown the devil with his barbed tail and horns just as I outgrew the cock in the chimney.

But what of the people who are capable of no restraint except that of intimidation? Must they not be either restrained or, as the Russians gently put it, liquidated. No State can afford the expense of providing policemen enough to watch them all continually; consequently the restraint must, like the fear of hell, operate when nobody is looking. Well, a shift of credulity has destroyed the old belief in hell. How then is the social work previously done by that belief to be taken up and carried on? It is easy to shirk the problem by pointing out that the belief in hell did not prevent even the most superstitious people from committing the most damnable crimes. But though we know of these failures of infernal terrorism we have no record of its successes. We know that naïve attempts to bribe divine justice led to a trade in absolutions, pardons, and indulgences which proved by the hardness of the cash the sinners put down and the cost of the cathedrals they put up that there was a continual overdrawing of salvation accounts by firm believers in the brimstone; but we do not know, and never shall know, how many crimes were refrained from that would have been committed but for the dread of damnation. All we can do is to observe and grapple with the effect of the shift of credulity which has robbed hell of its terrors.

No community, however devout, has ever trusted wholly to damnation and excommunication as deterrents. They have been supplemented by criminal codes of the most hideous barbarity (I have been contemporary with Europeans whose amusements included seeing criminals broken on the wheel). Therefore their effect on conduct must be looked for in that very extensive part of it which has not been touched by the criminal codes, or in which the codes actually encourage anti-social action and penalize its opposite, as when the citizen is forced by taxation or compulsory military service to become an accomplice in some act of vulgar pugnacity and greed disguised as patriotism.

Unless and until we get a new column in the census papers on the point we can only guess how far the shift of credulity has actually taken place in countries like our own in which children, far from being protected against the inculcation of the belief in brimstone, are exposed to it in every possible way, and are actually, when they have been confirmed, legally subject to ruinous penalties for questioning it. It happens, however, that in one of the largest States in the world, Russia, the children are protected from proselytizing (otherwise than by the State itself) not only by the negative method called Secular Education, but by positive instruction that there is no personal life after death for the individual, the teaching being that of Ecclesiastes in our own canon "Whatsoever thy hand findeth to do, do it with thy might; for there is no work, nor device, nor knowledge, nor wisdom, in the grave whither thou goest." We may take it that no civilized Russian born within the last twenty years has any apprehension of having to suffer after death for sins committed before it. At the same time the list of activities blacklisted by the Russian State as felonious has been startlingly extended; for the Russian Government has turned the country's economic morals down-side up by breaking away from our Capitalist Utopia and adopting instead the views of the Bolshevist prophets whose invectives and warnings fill the last books of the Old Testament, and the Communist principles of Jesus, Peter, and Paul. Not that the Soviet Republic allows the smallest authority to Jesus or Peter, Jeremiah or Micah the Morasthite. They call their economic system, not Bolshevik Christianity, but Scientific Socialism. But as their conclusions are the same, they have placed every Russian under a legal obligation to earn his own living, and made it a capital crime on his part to compel anyone else to do it for him. Now outside Russia the height of honor and success is to be a gentleman or lady, which means that your living is earned for you by other people (mostly untouchables), and that, far from being under an obligation to work, you are so disgraced by the mere suggestion of it that you dare not be seen carrying a parcel along a fashionable thoroughfare. Nobody has ever seen a lady or gentleman carrying a jug of milk down Bond Street or the *rue de la Paix*. A white person doing such a thing in Capetown would be socially ruined.

The physical activities called Sport, which are needed to keep the gentry in health, must be unpaid and unproductive: if payment is accepted for such activities the payee loses caste and is no longer called Mister. Labor is held to be a cross and a disgrace; and the lowest rank known is that of laborer. The object of everyone's ambition is an unearned income; and hundreds of millions of the country's income are lavished annually on ladies and gentlemen whilst laborers are underfed, ill clothed, and sleeping two or three in a bed and ten in a room.

Eighteen years ago this anti-labor creed of ours was the established religion of the whole civilized world. Then suddenly, in one seventh of that world, it was declared a damnable heresy, and had to be rooted out like any other damnable heresy. But as the heretics were carefully taught at the same time that there is no such thing as damnation, how were they to be dealt with? The well-to-do British Liberal, clamoring for freedom of conscience, objects to heretics being restrained in any way: his panacea for that sort of difficulty is Toleration. He thinks that Quakers and Ritualists should tolerate one another; and this solution works quite well because it does not now matter a penny to the State or the individual whether a citizen belongs to one persuasion or the other. But it was not always so. George Fox, the heroic founder of the Quakers, could not hear a church bell without dashing into the church and upsetting the service by denouncing the whole business of ritual religion as idolatrous. The bell, he said, "struck on his heart." Consequently it was not possible for the Churches to tolerate George Fox, though both Cromwell and Charles II liked the man and admired him.

Now the heretic in Russia is like Fox. He is not

content with a quiet abstract dissent from the State religion of Soviet Russia: he is an active, violent, venomous saboteur. He plans and carries out breakages of machinery, falsifies books and accounts to produce insolvencies, leaves the fields unsown or the harvests to rot unreaped, and slaughters farm stock in millions even at the cost of being half starved (sometimes wholly starved) by the resultant "famine" in his fanatical hatred of a system which makes it impossible for him to become a gentleman. Toleration is impossible: the heretic-saboteur will not tolerate the State religion; consequently the State could not tolerate him even if it wanted to.

This situation, though new to our generation of Liberal plutocrats, is not new historically. The change from paganism and Judaism to Christianity, from the worship of consecrated stones to an exalted monotheism under Mahomet, and from world catholicism to national individualism at the Reformation, all led to the persecution and virtual outlawry of the heretics who would not accept the change. The original official Roman Catholic Church, which had perhaps the toughest job, was compelled to develop a new judicial organ, called the Inquisition or Holy Office, to deal with heresy; and though in all the countries in which the Reformation triumphed the Inquisition became so unpopular that its name was carefully avoided when similar organs were developed by the Protestant and later on by the Secularist governments, yet the Holy Office cropped up again under all sorts of disguises. Protestant England would never have tolerated the Star Chamber if it had called itself an Inquisition and given Laud the official title borne by Torquemada. In the end all the specific Inquisitions petered out, not in the least through a growth of real tolerance, but because, as the world settled down into the new faiths, and the heretics stopped sabotaging and slaughtering, it was found that the ordinary courts could do all the necessary persecution, such as transporting laborers for reading the works of Thomas Paine, or imprisoning poor men for making sceptical jokes about the parthenogenesis of Jesus.

Thus the Inquisition came to be remembered in England only as an obsolete abomination which classed respectable Protestants with Jews, and burned both. Conceive, then, our horror when the Inquisition suddenly rose up again in Russia. It began as the Tcheka; then it became the Gay-pay-oo (Ogpu); now it has settled down as part of the ordinary police force. The worst of its work is over: the heretics are either liquidated, converted, or intimidated. But it was indispensable in its prime. The Bolsheviks, infected as they were with English Liberal and Agnostic notions, at first tried to do without it; but the result was that the unfortunate Commissars who had to make the Russian industries and transport services work, found themselves obliged to carry pistols and execute saboteurs and lazy drunkards with their own hands. Such a Commissar was Djerjinsky, now, like Lenin, entombed in the Red Square. He was not a homicidally disposed person; but when it fell to his lot to make the Russian trains run at all costs, he had to force himself to shoot a station master who found it easier to drop telegrams into the waste paper basket than to attend to them. And it was this gentle Djerjinsky who, unable to endure the duties of an executioner (even had he had time for them), organized the Tcheka.

Now the Tcheka, being an Inquisition and not an ordinary police court dealing under written statutes and established precedents with defined offences, and sentencing the offenders to prescribed penalties, had to determine whether certain people were public spirited enough to live in a Communist society, and, if not, to blow their brains out as public nuisances. If you would not work and pull your weight in the Russian boat, then the Tcheka had to make you do it by convincing you that you would be shot if you persisted in your determination to be a gentleman. For the national emergencies were then desperate; and the compulsion to overcome them had to be fiercely in earnest.

I, an old Irishman, am too used to Coercion Acts, suspension of the Habeas Corpus Act, and the like, to have any virtuous indignation left to spare for the blunders and excesses into which the original Tcheka, as a body of well intentioned amateurs, no doubt fell before it had learnt the limits of its business by experience. My object in citing it is to draw attention to the legal novelty and importance of its criterion of human worth. I am careful to say legal novelty because of course the criterion must have been used in the world long before St Paul commanded that "if any would not work, neither should he eat." But our courts have never taken that Communist view: they have always upheld unconditional property, private property, real property, do-what-you-like-with-your-own property, which, when it is insanely extended to the common earth of the country, means the power to make landless people earn the proprietors' livings for them. Such property places the social value of the proprietor beyond question. The propertyless man may be challenged as a rogue and a vagabond to justify himself by doing some honest work; but if he earns a gentleman's living for him he is at once vindicated and patted on the back. Under such conditions we have lost the power of conceiving ourselves as responsible to society for producing a full equivalent of what we consume, and indeed more. On the contrary, every inducement to shirk that primary duty is continually before us. We are taught to think of an Inquisition as a tribunal which has to decide whether we accept the divinity of Christ or are Jews, whether we believe in transubstantiation or merely in the Supper, whether we are prelatists or Presbyterians, whether we accept the authority of the Church or the conclusions of our private judgments as the interpreters of God's will, whether we believe in a triune godhead or a single one, whether we accept the 39 Articles or the Westminster Confession, and so on. Such were the tests of fitness to live accepted by the old Inquisitions. The public never dreams of an economic test except in the form of a Means Test to baffle the attempts of the very poor to become sinecurists like ladies and gentlemen.

My own acquaintance with such a possibility began early in life and shocked me somewhat. My maternal grandfather, a country gentleman who was an accomplished sportsman, was out shooting one day. His dog, growing old, made a mistake: its first. He instantly shot it. I learnt that he always shot his sporting dogs when they were past their work. Later on I heard of African tribes doing the same with their grandparents. When I took seriously to economic studies before electric traction had begun I found that tramway companies had found that the most profitable way of exploiting horses was to work them to death in four years. Planters in certain districts had found the like profitable term for slaves to be eight years. In fully civilized life there was no provision except a savagely penal Poor Law for workers thrown out of our industrial establishments as "too old at forty."

As I happen to be one of those troublesome people who are not convinced that whatever is is right these things set me thinking. My thoughts would now be attributed to Bolshevik propaganda; and pains would be taken by our rulers to stop the propaganda under the impression that this would stop the thoughts; but there was no Bolshevik propaganda in those days; and I can assure the Foreign Office that the landed gentry in the person of my grandfather, the tramway companies, and the capitalist planters, made the question of whether individual dogs and men are worth their salt familiar to me a whole generation before the Tcheka ever existed.

It still seems to me a very pertinent question, as I have to pay away about half my earnings in tribute to the lady-and-gentleman business in order to get permission to live on this earth; and I consider it money very ill spent. For if the people who live on my earnings were changed by some Arabian Nights magician into dogs, and handed over to the sporting successors of my grandfather, they would be shot; and if they were changed into horses or slaves they would be worn out by overwork before their natural time. They are now worn out by underwork.

Nevertheless I do not plead a personal grievance, because though I still amuse myself with professional pursuits and make money by them, I also have acquired the position of a gentleman, and live very comfortably on other people's earnings to an extent which more than compensates me for the depredations of which I am myself the victim. Now my grandfather's dog had no such satisfaction. Neither had the tramway horses nor the slaves, nor have the discarded "too old at forty." In their case there was no proper account keeping. In the nature of things a human creature must incur a considerable debt for its nurture and education (if it gets any) before it becomes productive. And as it can produce under modern conditions much more than it need consume it ought to be possible for it to pay off its debt and provide for its old age in addition to supporting itself during its active period. Of course if you assume that it is no use to itself and is there solely to support ladies and gentlemen, you need not bother about this: you can just leave it to starve when it ceases to be useful to its superiors. But if, discarding this view, you assume that a human creature is created for its own use and should have matters arranged so that it shall live as long as it can, then you will have to go into people's accounts and make them all pay their way. We need no Bolshevik propaganda to lead us to this obvious conclusion; but it makes the special inquisitionary work of the Tcheka intelligible. For the Tcheka was simply carrying out the executive work of a constitution which had abolished the lady and gentleman exactly as the Inquisition carried out the executive work of a catholic constitution which had abolished Jupiter and Diana and Venus and Apollo.

Simple enough; and yet so hard to get into our genteel heads that in making a play about it I have had to detach it altogether from the great Russian change, or any of the actual political changes which threaten to raise it in the National-Socialist and Fascist countries, and to go back to the old vision of a day of reckoning by divine justice for all mankind.

Now the ordinary vision of this event is almost pure

bugaboo: we see it as a colossal Old Bailey trial, with the good people helped up into heaven and the bad ones cast headlong into hell; but as to what code of law will govern the judgment and classify the judged as sheep or goats as the case may be we have not troubled to ask. We are clear about Judas Iscariot going to hell and Florence Nightingale to heaven; but we are not so sure about Brutus and Cromwell. Our general knowledge of mankind, if we dare bring it into play, would tell us that an immense majority of the prisoners at the bar will be neither saints nor scoundrels, but borderland cases of extreme psychological complexity. It is easy to say that to divine justice nothing is impossible; but the more divine the justice the more difficult it is to conceive how it could deal with every case as one for heaven or hell. But we think we need not bother about it; for the whole affair is thought of as a grand finish to the human race and all its problems, leaving the survivors in a condition of changeless unprogressive bliss or torment for the rest of eternity.

To me this vision is childish; but I must take people's minds as I find them and build on them as best I can. It is no use my telling them that their vision of judgment is a silly superstition, and that there never will be anything of the kind. The only conclusion the pious will draw is that I, at all events, will go to hell. As to the indifferent and the sceptical, I may do them the mischief against which Jesus vainly warned our missionaries. I may root out of their minds the very desirable conception that they are all responsible to divine justice for the use they make of their lives, and put nothing in its place except a noxious conceit in their emancipation and an exultant impulse to abuse it. The substitution of irresponsibility for responsibility may present itself as an advance; but it is in fact a retreat which may leave its victim much less eligible as a member of a civilized community than the crudest Fundamentalist. A prudent banker would lend money on personal security to Bunyan rather than to Casanova. Certainly I should if I were a banker.

Who shall say, then, that an up-to-date Vision of Judgment is not an interesting subject for a play, especially as events in Russia and elsewhere are making it urgently desirable that believers in the Apocalypse should think out their belief a little? In a living society every day is a day of judgment; and its recognition as such is not the end of all things but the beginning of a real civilization. Hence the fable of The Simpleton of the Unexpected Isles. In it I still retain the ancient fancy that the race will be brought to judgment by a supernatural being, coming literally out of the blue; but this inquiry is not whether you believe in Tweedledum or Tweedledee but whether you are a social asset or a social nuisance. And the penalty is liquidation. He has appeared on the stage in the person of Ibsen's button moulder. And as history always follows the stage, the button moulder came to life as Djerjinsky. My Angel comes a day after the fair; but time enough for our people, who know nothing of the button moulder and have been assured by our gentleman-ladylike newspapers that Djerjinsky was a Thug.

The button moulder is a fiction; and my Angel is a fiction. But the pressing need for bringing us to the bar for an investigation of our personal social values is not a fiction. And Djerjinsky is not a fiction. He found that as there are no button moulders and no angels and no heavenly tribunals available, we must set up earthly ones, not to ascertain whether Mr

Everyman in the dock has committed this or that act or holds this or that belief, but whether he or she is a creator of social values or a parasitical consumer and destroyer of them

Unfortunately the word tribunal immediately calls up visions not only of judgment but of punishment and cruelty. Now there need be no more question of either of these abominations than there was in the case of my grandfather's dog. My grandfather would have been horribly ashamed of himself if the dog's death had not been instantaneous and unanticipated. And the idea of punishment never entered either his mind or the dog's. (Djerjinsky, by the way, is believed to have devised a similar method of painless liquidation.) It may be expedient that one man should die for the people; but it does not follow in the least that he should be tortured or terrified. Public savagery may demand that the law shall torment a criminal who does something very provoking; for the Sermon on The Mount is still a dead letter in spite of all the compliments we pay it. But to blow a man's brains out because he cannot for the life of him see why he should not employ labor at a profit, or buy things solely to sell them again for more than he gave for them, or speculate in currency values: all of them activities which have for centuries enjoyed the highest respectability, is an innovation which should be carried out with the utmost possible delicacy if public opinion is to be quite reconciled to it. We have also to reckon with the instinctive shrinking from outright killing which makes so many people sign petitions for the reprieve of even the worst murderers, and take no further interest if a reprieve decrees that their lives shall be taken by the slow torture of imprisonment. Then we have a mass of people who think that murderers should be judicially killed, but that the lives of the most mischievous criminals should be held sacred provided they do not commit murder. To overcome these prejudices we need a greatly increased intolerance of socially injurious conduct and an uncompromising abandonment of punishment and its cruelties, together with a sufficient school inculcation of social responsibility to make every citizen conscious that if his life costs more than it is worth to the community the community may painlessly extinguish it.

The result of this, however, will finally be a demand for codification. The citizen will say "I really must know what I may do and what I may not do without having my head shot off." The reply "You must keep a credit balance always at the national bank" is sufficiently definite if the national accountancy is trustworthy and compulsory unemployment made impossible. In fact it is so definite that it finally takes the matter out of the hands of the Inquisition and makes an overdraft an ordinary offence to be dealt with by the police. But police measures are not enough. Any intelligent and experienced administrator of the criminal law will tell you that there are people who come up for punishment again and again for the same offence, and that punishing them is a cruel waste of time. There should be an Inquisition always available to consider whether these human nuisances should not be put out of their pain, or out of their joy as the case may be. The community must drive a much harder bargain for the privilege of citizenship than it now does; but it must also make the bargain not only practicable but in effect much easier than the present very imperfect bargain. This involves a new social creed. A new social creed involves a new heresy. A new heresy involves an Inquisition. The precedents established by the Inquisition furnish the material for a new legal code. Codification enables the work of the Inquisition to be done by an ordinary court of law. Thereupon the Inquisition, as such, disappears, precisely as the Tcheka has disappeared. Thus it has always been; and thus it ever shall be.

The moral of the dramatic fable of The Simpleton is now clear enough. With amateur Inquisitions under one name or another or no name at work in all directions, from Fascist *autos-da-fé* to American Vigilance Committees with lynching mobs as torturers and executioners, it is time for us to reconsider our Visions of Judgment, and see whether we cannot change them from old stories in which we no longer believe and new stories which are only too horribly true to serious and responsible public tribunals.

By the way, I had better guard myself against the assumption that because I have introduced into my fable a eugenic experiment in group marriage I am advocating the immediate adoption of that method of peopling the world for immediate practice by my readers. Group marriage is a form of marriage like any other; and it is just as well to remind our western and very insular Imperialists that marriage in the British Empire is startlingly different in the east from marriage in the British Isles; but I have introduced it only to bring into the story the four lovely phantasms who embody all the artistic, romantic, and military ideals of our cultured suburbs. On the Day of Judgment not merely do they cease to exist like the useless and predatory people: it becomes apparent that they never did exist. And, enchanting as they may be to our perfumers, who give us the concentrated odor of the flower without the roots or the clay or even the leaves, let us hope they never will.

ON THE INDIAN OCEAN, *April 1935*

⌐PROLOGUE⌐

The emigration office at a tropical port in the British Empire. The office is an annex of the harbor and customs sheds on one side and of the railway station on the other. Placards direct passengers TO THE CUSTOMS and TO THE TRAINS through the open doors right and left respectively. The emigration officer, an unsatisfactory young man of unhealthy habits, is sitting writing at his table in the middle of the room. His clerk is at a standing desk against the wall on the customs side. The officer wears tropical clothes, neither too tidy nor too clean. The clerk is in a shabby dark lounge suit.

THE E. O. [*finishing his writing*] Is that the lot?

CLERK. It's the lot from the French ship; but there is that case standing over from the Liverpool one.

THE E. O. [*exasperated*] Now look here, Wilks. Are you the emigration officer here or am I? Did I tell you that that girl was to be sent back or did I not?

WILKS. Well I thought—

THE E. O. What business had you to think? I told you she was to go back. I suppose she tipped you to let her come here and make a scene on the chance of getting round me.

WILKS [*hotly*] Youll either take that back or prove it.

THE E. O. I will neither take it back nor prove it until you explain why you are letting this girl bother me again, though she has no papers, no passports, and is in excess of the quota without any excuse for it.

WILKS. Who's letting her bother you again? She told the High Commissioner that you turned her down; and he told her she had better see you again.

THE E. O. And why the devil didnt you tell me that at first, instead of blithering about her as if she was a common case?

WILKS. The High Commissioner's daughter was on the ship coming back from school. He came down to meet her. This girl had made friends with her or taken care of her or something.

THE E. O. Thats no good. We cant let her through on that.

WILKS. Well, will you see her?

THE E. O. Is she waiting to see me?

WILKS. She says she's waiting to see what will happen to her.

THE E. O. Same thing, isnt it?

WILKS. I suppose so. But she put it as if there was a difference. I think she's a bit mad. But the Medical Officer says she passes all his tests of sanity, though I could see that he has his doubts.

THE E. O. Oh, shut up. You need a medical test yourself, I think. Fetch her in.

Wilks goes out sulkily through the customs door and returns with a young woman. He leads her to the table and then goes back to his desk.

THE Y. W. Good morning, sir. You dont look as well as you did yesterday. Did you stay up too late?

THE E. O. [*nonplussed for the moment*] I—er— [*Collecting himself*] Look here, young lady. You have to answer questions here, not to ask them.

THE Y. W. You have been drinking.

THE E. O. [*springing up*] What the hell do you mean?

THE Y. W. You have. I smell it.

THE E. O. Very well. Back you go by the next boat, my lady.

THE Y. W. [*unmoved*] At this hour of the morning too! Dont you know you shouldnt?

[766]

THE E. O. [*to Wilks*] Take her away, you. [*To the young woman*] Out you go.

THE Y. W. I ought to speak to somebody about it. And look at the state the office is in! Whose business is it to see that it's properly dusted? Let me talk to them for you.

THE E. O. What concern is it of yours?

THE Y. W. I hate to see dust lying about. Look! You could write your name in it. And it's just awful to see a young man drinking before eleven in the morning.

WILKS [*propitiatory*] Dont say anything about it, Miss: I will see to the dust. Everybody starts the day with a drink here. Dont go talking, Miss, will you?

THE E. O. [*suddenly breaking down in tears*] You can go and tell who you damn well please. For two pins I'd chuck myself into the harbor and have done with it. This climate is hell: you cant stand it unless you drink til you see blue monkeys.

WILKS. Never mind him, Miss: he has nerves. We all have them here sooner or later, off and on. Here! I'll give you a landing ticket; and you just clear off and say nothing. [*He takes a ticket from the table and gives it to her*].

THE E. O. [*weeping*] A man's a slave here worse than a nigger. Spied on, reported on, checked and told off til he's afraid to have a pound note in his pocket or take a glass in his hand for fear of being had up for bribery or drinking. I'm fed up with it. Go and report me and be damned to you: what do I care? [*He sniffs and blows his nose, relieved by his outburst*].

WILKS. Would you have the kindness to clear out, Miss. We're busy. Youre passed all right: nothing to do but shew the ticket. You wont have to go back: we was only joking.

THE Y. W. But I want to go back. If this place is what he says, it is no place for me. And I did so enjoy the voyage out: I ask nothing better than to begin it all over again.

THE E. O. [*with the calm of despair*] Let her have her own way, Wilks. Shew her the way to the ship and shew her the way to the dock gate. She can take which she pleases. But get her out of this or I shall commit suicide.

THE Y. W. Why? Arnt you happy? It's not natural not to be happy. I'd be ashamed not to be happy.

THE E. O. What is there to make a man happy here?

THE Y. W. But you dont need to be made happy. You ought to be happy from the inside. Then you wouldnt need things to make you happy.

THE E. O. My inside! Oh Lord!

THE Y. W. Well, you can make your inside all right if you eat properly and stop drinking and keep the office dusted and your nice white clothes clean and tidy. You two are a disgrace.

THE E. O. [*roaring with rage*] Chuck that woman out.

WILKS. Chuck her yourself. What can *I* do? [*Imploringly to her*] If youd only have the goodness to go, Miss. We're so busy this morning.

THE Y. W. But I am a stranger here: I have nobody else to talk to. And you have nothing to do until the next boat comes in.

THE E. O. The next boat is due the day after tomorrow at five in the afternoon. Do you expect us to sit here talking to you until then?

THE Y. W. Well, it's I who have to do most of the talking, isnt it? Couldnt you shew me round the town? I'll pay for the taxi.

THE E. O. [*feebly rebellious*] Look here: you cant go on like this, you know.

THE Y. W. What were you going to do with yourself this morning if I hadnt come?

THE E. O. I—I—Whats that to you?

THE Y. W. I see you hadnt made up your mind. Let me make it up for you. Put on your hat and come along and shew me round. I seem to spend my life making up other people's minds for them.

THE E. O. [*helplessly*] All right, all right, all right. You neednt make a ballyhoo about it. But I ask myself—

THE Y. W. Dont ask yourself anything, my child. Let life come to you. March.

THE E. O. [*at the railway door, to Wilks, in a last effort to assert himself*] Carry on, you. [*He goes*].

THE Y. W. Wouldnt you like to come too?

WILKS. Yes, Miss; but somebody must stay in the office; and it had better be me than him. I am indispensable.

THE Y. W. What a word! Dispensables and indispensables: there you have the whole world. I wonder am I a dispensable or an indispensable. [*She goes out through the railway door*].

WILKS [*alone*] Let life come to you. Sounds all right, that. Let life come to you. Aye; but suppose life doesnt come to you! Look at me! What am I? An empire builder: thats what I am by nature. Cecil Rhodes: thats me. Why am I a clerk with only two shirts to my back, with that young waster wiping his dirty boots on me for doing the work he cant do himself, though he gets all the praise and all the pudding? Because life never came to me like it came to Rhodes. Found his backyard full of diamonds, he did; and nothing to do but wash the clay off them and be a millionaire. I had Rhodes's idea all right. Let the whole earth be England, I said to the school teacher; and let Englishmen govern it. Nobody put that into

my head: it came of itself. But what did I find in my
backyard? Next door's dead cat. Could I make myself head of a Chartered Company with a dead cat?
And when I threw it back over the wall my mother
said "You have thrown away your luck, my boy" she
says "you shouldnt have thrown it back: you should
have passed it on, like a chain letter. Now you will
never have no more luck in this world." And no more
I have. I says to her "I'll be in the papers yet some
day" I says "like Cecil Rhodes: you see if I'm not."
"Not you, my lad" she says. "Everything what comes
to you you throw it back." Well, so I do. Look at this
girl here. "Come with me" she says. And I threw the
cat back again. "Somebody must be left in the
office" I says. "I am indispensable" I says. And all
the time I knew that nobody neednt be in the office,
and that any Jew boy could do all I do here and do it
better. But I promised my mother I'd get into the
papers; and I will. I have that much of the Rhodes
touch in me. [*He sits at the table and writes on a
luggage label; then reads what he has written*] "Here
lies a man who might have been Cecil Rhodes if he
had had Rhodes's luck. Mother, farewell: your son has
kept his word." [*He ties the label to the lapel of his
coat*] Wheres that fool's gun? [*He opens a drawer and
takes out a brandy flask and an automatic pistol,
which he throws on the table*]. I'll damned well shew
em whether I'm an empire builder or not. That lassie
shant say that I didnt leave the place tidy either,
though she can write in the dust of it with her finger.
[*He shuts the drawer, and places the chair trimly at the
table. Then he goes to his desk and takes out a duster,
with which he wipes first the desk and then the table. He
replaces the duster in the desk, and takes out a comb and
a hand mirror. He tidies his hair; replaces the comb and*

glass in the desk; closes it and sets the stool in its place before it. He then returns to the table, and empties the flask at a draught]. Now for it. The back of the head: thats the Russian touch. [*He takes the pistol and presents it over his shoulder to his occiput*]. Let the whole earth be England; and let Englishmen rule it. [*Singing*] Rule Britannia: Britannia rules the wa—

He blows his brains out and falls dead. The Station Master enters.

THE STATION MASTER. Here! Who's been shooting here? [*He sees the body*] Wilks!! Dear! dear! dear! What a climate! The fifth this month. [*He goes to the door*]. Hallo there, Jo. Bring along the stretcher and two or three with you. Mr Wilks has shot himself.

JO [*without, cheerfully*] Right you are, sir.

THE STATION MASTER. What a climate! Poor old Wilks!

SCENE II

A grassy cliff top overhanging the sea. A seat for promenaders. The young woman and the emigration officer stand on the brink.

THE Y. W. Pity theres no beach. We could bathe.

THE E. O. Not us. Not likely. Theres sharks there. And killer whales, worse than any sharks.

THE Y. W. It looks pretty deep.

THE E. O. I should think it is. The biggest liners can get close up. Like Plymouth. Like Lulworth Cove. Dont stand so close. Theres a sort of fascination in it; and you might get giddy.

They come away from the edge and sit on the seat together: she on his left, he nearest the sea.

THE Y. W. It's lovely here. Better than the town.

THE E. O. Dont deceive yourself. It's a horrible place. The climate is something terrible. Do you know that if you hadnt come in this morning I'd have done myself in.

THE Y. W. Dont talk nonsense. Why should you do yourself in?

THE E. O. Yes I should. I had the gun ready in the drawer of that table. I'd have shot Wilks and then shot myself.

THE Y. W. Why should you shoot poor Wilks? What has he done?

THE E. O. I hate him. He hates me. Everybody here hates everybody else. And the fellow is so confoundedly smug and happy and satisfied: it drives me mad when I can hardly bear my own life. No fear of him shooting himself: not much. So I thought I'd save him the trouble.

THE Y. W. But that would be murder.

THE E. O. Not if I shot myself after. That would make us quits.

THE Y. W. Well, I am surprised to hear a young man like you, in the prime of life as you might say, talking like that. Why dont you get married?

THE E. O. My salary's too small for a white woman. Theyre all snobs; and they want a husband only to take them home out of this.

THE Y. W. Why, it's an earthly paradise.

THE E. O. Tell them so; and see what theyll say to you.

THE Y. W. Well, why not marry a colored woman?

THE E. O. You dont know what youre talking about. Ive tried. But now theyre all educated they wont look at a white man. They tell me I'm ignorant and that I smell bad.

THE Y. W. Well, so you do. You smell of drink and

indigestion and sweaty clothes. You were quite disgusting when you tried to make up to me in the taxi. Thats why I got out, and made for the sea air.

THE E. O. [*rising hurriedly*] I cant stand any more of this. [*He takes a wallet of papers from his breast pocket and throws them on the seat*]. Hand them in at the office, will you: theyll be wanted there. I am going over.

He makes for the edge of the cliff. But there is a path down the cliff face, invisible from the seat. A native priest, a handsome man in the prime of life, beautifully dressed, rises into view by this path and bars his way.

PRIEST. Pardon, son of empire. This cliff contains the temple of the goddess who is beyond naming, the eternal mother, the seed and the sun, the resurrection and the life. You must not die here. I will send an acolyte to guide you to the cliff of death, which contains the temple of the goddess's brother, the weeder of the garden, the sacred scavenger, the last friend on earth, the prolonger of sleep and the giver of rest. It is not far off: life and death dwell close together: you need prolong your unhappiness only a bare five minutes. The priest there will attend to your remains and see they are disposed of with all becoming rites.

THE E. O. [*to the young woman*] Is he real; or is it the drink?

THE Y. W. He's real. And, my word! isnt he jolly good looking? [*To the priest*] Youll excuse this young man, sir, wont you? He's been drinking pretty hard.

THE PRIEST [*advancing between them*] Blame him not, sweet one. He comes from a strange mad country where the young are taught languages that are dead and histories that are lies, but are never told how to meat and drink and clothe themselves and reproduce their species. They worship strange ancient gods; and they play games with balls marvellously well; but of the great game of life they are ignorant. Here, where they are in the midst of life and loveliness, they die by their own hands to escape what they call the horrors. We do not encourage them to live. The empire is for those who can live in it, not for those who can only die in it. Take your friend to the cliff of death; and bid him farewell tenderly; for he is very unhappy.

THE E. O. Look here: I am an Englishman; and I shall commit suicide where I please. No nigger alive shall dictate to me.

THE PRIEST. It is forbidden.

THE E. O. Who's to stop me? Will you?

The priest shakes his head and makes way for him.

THE Y. W. Oh, you are not going to let him do it, are you?

THE PRIEST [*holding her back*] We never offer violence to the unhappy. Do not interfere with his destiny.

THE E. O. [*planting himself on the edge and facing the abyss*] I am going to do it: see? Nobody shall say that I lived a dog's life because I was afraid to make an end of it. [*He bends his knees to spring, but cannot*]. I WILL. [*He makes another effort, bending almost to his haunches, but again fails to make the spring-up a spring-over*].

THE PRIEST. Poor fellow! Let me assist you. [*He shoots his foot against the E. O.'s posterior and sends him over the cliff*].

THE E. O. [*in a tone of the strongest remonstrance as he is catapulted into the void*] Oh! [*A prodigious splash*].

THE Y. W. Murderer!

THE PRIEST. Not quite. There are nets below, and a palisade to keep out the sharks. The shock will do him good.

THE Y. W. Well, I never!

THE PRIEST. Come, young rose blossom, and feast with us in the temple.

THE Y. W. Not so much rose blossom, young man. Are there any priestesses down there?

THE PRIEST. Of course. How can men feast without women?

THE Y. W. Well, let life come to you I always say; and dont cry out until youre hurt. After you, sir.

They descend.

SCENE III

A shelf of rock half way down the cliff forms an esplanade between the sea and a series of gigantic images of oriental deities in shallow alcoves cut in the face of the wall of rock. A feast of fruit and bread and soft drinks is spread on the ground. The young woman is sitting at it between the priest on her right nearest the sea and a very handsome young native priestess in robes of dusky yellow silk on her left nearest the images.

THE Y. W. You know, to me this is a funny sort of lunch. You begin with the dessert. We begin with the entrées. I suppose it's all right; but I have eaten so much fruit and bread and stuff that I dont feel I want any meat.

THE PRIEST. We shall not offer you any. We dont eat it.

THE Y. W. Then how do you keep up your strength?

THE PRIEST. It keeps itself up.

THE Y. W. Oh, how could that be? [*To the priestess*] You wouldnt like a husband that didnt eat plenty of

[775]

meat, would you? But then youre a priestess; so I suppose it doesnt matter to you, as you cant marry.

THE PRIESTESS. I am married.

THE Y. W. Oh! And you a priestess!

THE PRIESTESS. I could not be a priestess if I were not married. How could I presume to teach others without a completed human experience? How could I deal with children if I were not a mother?

THE Y. W. But that isnt right. My sister was a teacher; but when she married they took her job away from her and wouldnt let her teach any more.

THE PRIESTESS. The rulers of your country must be mad.

THE Y. W. Oh no. Theyre all right: just like other people. [*To the priest*] I say, reverend. What about the poor lad you kicked over the cliff? Is he really safe? I dont feel easy about him.

THE PRIEST. His clothes are drying in the sun. They will lend him some clothes and send him up here as soon as he has recovered from his ducking.

An English lady tourist, Baedeker in hand, has wandered in, trying to identify the images with the aid of her book. She now comes behind the seated group and accosts the priest.

THE L. T. Excuse me; but can you tell me which of these figures is the principal god?

THE PRIEST [*rising courteously*] The principal one? I do not understand.

THE L. T. I get lost among all these different gods: it is so difficult to know which is which.

THE PRIEST. They are not different gods. They are all god.

THE L. T. But how can that be? The figures are different.

THE PRIEST. God has many aspects.

THE L. T. But all these names in the guide book?

THE PRIEST. God has many names.

THE L. T. Not with us, you know.

THE PRIEST. Yes: even with you. The Father, the Son, the Spirit, the Immaculate Mother—

THE L. T. Excuse me. We are not Catholics.

THE PRIESTESS [*sharply*] Are your temples then labelled "For men only"?

THE L. T. [*shocked*] Oh, really! So sorry to have troubled you. [*She hurries away*].

THE PRIEST [*resuming his seat*] You should not be rude to the poor lady. She is English, and doesnt understand.

THE PRIESTESS. I find these heathen idolaters very trying. Is it really kind to treat them according to their folly instead of to our wisdom?

THE Y. W. Here! Steady on, you. Who are you calling heathen idolaters? Look at all those images. I should say, if you ask me, that the boot is on the other leg.

THE PRIEST. Those images are not idols: they are personifications of the forces of nature by which we all live. But of course to an idolater they are idols.

THE Y. W. You talk a lot about religion here. Cant you think of something livelier? I always say let life come to you; and dont bother about religion.

THE PRIESTESS. An excellent rule. But the more you let life come to you, the more you will find yourself bothering about religion.

The Emigration Officer rises into view in a spotless white robe. He is clean and rather pale, but looks regenerated.

THE Y. W. Oh boy, you do look the better for your dip. Why, he's an angel, a lamb. What have you done to him?

THE E. O. [*seating himself at the end of the table with his*

[777]

back to the sea] Well, if you want to know, this blighter kicked me into the sea; and when I'd swallowed a ton or two of your best salt water they fished me out in a net and emptied me out. I brought up my immortal soul. They gave me what I thought was a nice cup of their tea to settle my stomach; but it made me ten times as sick as I was before. Theres nothing of the man you met this morning left except his skin and bones. You may regard me as to all intents and purposes born again.

THE PRIEST. Do you still wish to kill yourself?

THE E. O. When you have been through what I have been through since they fished me out of the water you wont worry about trifles as I used to, old man.

THE Y. W. Thats right. Let life come to you, I always say.

THE E. O. Yes, let life come. The premises are quite empty.

THE LADY TOURIST [*returning and addressing the priest*] Excuse me; but I have been thinking so much about you since you spoke to me. Would you mind accepting and reading this little tract?

THE PRIEST [*rising and coming forward to her, meanwhile reading the title with a polite show of interest*] "Where will you spend eternity?"

THE L. T. [*strangely moved*] I have been haunted by your face. I could not bear to think of your spending eternity in torment. I feel sure it is a Christian face.

THE PRIEST. It is very kind of you. I will read the tract with the greatest attention. Thank you.

The lady, having no excuse for staying, moves away reluctantly towards the images.

THE PRIESTESS [*calling after her imperiously*] Where have you spent eternity so far, may I ask? That which has no end can have no beginning?

[778]

THE L. T. Excuse me: I have no desire to speak to you.

THE Y. W. [*indicating the priest*] Fallen in love with him, have you? Well, let yourself rip. Let life come to you.

THE L. T. Oh! How dare you? Really! Really!! [*She goes out indignantly*].

THE PRIESTESS. Another conquest, Pra?

THE Y. W. Is his name Pra?

THE PRIESTESS. He has many names; but he answers to Pra when you call him.

THE Y. W. Oh, what a way to put it! The man isnt a dog, is he?

THE PRIESTESS. He inspires a doglike devotion in women. He once did in me; so I know.

THE PRIEST. Dont be vindictive, Prola. I dont do it on purpose. [*He sits down again, this time next to her on her left*].

THE PRIESTESS. No: you do it by instinct. That, also, is rather doglike.

THE PRIEST. No matter: I shall soon get the poor lady beyond the doglike stage.

THE E. O. [*who has been unable to take his eyes off the priestess*] Is your name Prola?

THE PRIEST. She has many names: some of them terrible ones; but she answers to Prola when you call her.

THE PRIESTESS. Young man: are my eyes like the fishpools of Heshbon?

THE E. O. Well, I have never seen the fishpools of Heshbon; but your eyes make me feel like that.

THE Y. W. Seems to me theres some sort of magic about this old cave thats dangerous. If you dont mind, I'll bid you all good morning. I always say let life come to you; but here it's coming a bit too thick for me. [*She rises*].

THE PRIESTESS. Wait. We can share him.

THE Y. W. Well I never! [*She flops back into her seat, flabbergasted*].

THE PRIESTESS. Hush. Look.

The Lady Tourist returns and again goes to the priest.

THE L. T. Excuse me; but could I have a word with you alone?

THE PRIEST [*rising*] Certainly. Come with me.

They go into the caves together.

THE E. O. What about a word with me alone, Prola?

THE Y. W. [*with redoubled emphasis*] Well I NEVER!!

THE PRIESTESS [*to the Officer*] You are not yet sufficiently regenerated. But you may hope.

THE Y. W. You take care, boy. I think youve got a touch of the sun. You cant be too careful in the tropics.

An English male tourist enters from among the images. He is on the young side of middle age, with pleasant aristocratic appearance and manners.

THE M. T. Excuse me: I have mislaid my wife. English lady with a guide book. Wears glasses. Bi-focals.

THE Y. W. Her husband! Oh, I say!

THE E. O. [*rising deferentially*] Just left us, Sir Charles.

THE M. T. Hallo! Weve met before, I think, havnt we?

THE E. O. When you landed, Sir Charles. I am the emigration officer.

SIR CHARLES. Ah, of course: yes. You know Lady Farwaters by sight. Which way did she go?

THE E. O. I am sorry: I didnt notice.

SIR CHARLES [*worried*] I wonder what she can be doing.

THE Y. W. So do I.

SIR CHARLES. I beg your pardon?

THE Y. W. Granted.

THE PRIESTESS [*rising and coming to him*] May I shew you round the temple, Sir Charles? We shall probably find her there.

SIR CHARLES [*who has not yet hitherto looked particularly at her*] No thank you, no, no.

THE PRIESTESS. It is interesting. I am not a professional guide: I am a priestess; and I will see that you are not asked for anything. You had better come with me.

SIR CHARLES. No: I— [*he looks at her. His tone changes instantly*]. Well, yes, if you will be so good. Certainly. Thank you.

They go into the alcoves together.

THE Y. W. [*leaving the table*] Oh boy, what do you think of this abode of love? Lady Farwaters, as white as Canterbury veal, has fallen for a brown bishop; and her husband, the whitest English west-end white, has been carried off to her den by an amber colored snake charmer. Lets get out of it while we're safe.

THE E. O. I feel quite safe, thank you. I have been cleaned up. You havnt.

THE Y. W. What do you mean, I havnt?

THE E. O. I mean that you were quite right to object to me half an hour ago. Your offensive personal remarks were fully justified. But now the tables are turned. I havnt gone through the fire; but Ive gone through the water. And the water has gone through me. It is for me now to object and to make personal remarks.

THE Y. W. Make as much as one; and you will get your face smacked.

THE E. O. [*seizing her by the wrist and the back of her collar*] Go and get cleaned up, you disgusting little devil. [*He rushes her to the edge*].

THE Y. W. [*screaming*] No.

THE E. O. Yes. [*He hurls her over*].

A scream cut short by a splash. The E. O. sits down at the table and attacks the remains of the feast ravenously.

THE PROLOGUE ENDS

$\begin{bmatrix} \text{ACT I} \end{bmatrix}$

The lawn of a stately house on the north coast of a trop-
ical island in the Pacific commands a fine view of the
ocean and of a breakwater enclosing a harbor, large
enough to accommodate a fleet, but at present shipless.
The western face of the house is reached by a terrace and
a flight of steps. The steps lead down to a crescent formed
by two curved stone seats separated by a patch of sward
surrounding a circular well with a low marble parapet.
This parapet, like the stone seats, has silk cushions
scattered about it.

Behind the crescent the lawn is banked to a higher
level and becomes a flower garden, sheltered from the
wind by shrubberies. To the west of the flower garden
the lawn falls away to the sea, but not to sea level, all
that is visible of the port being the top of the lighthouse.
There are trees enough in all directions to provide shade
everywhere.

However, the raised flower garden is the centre of
interest; for in it are four shrines marking the corners
of a square. In the two foremost shrines two girl-
goddesses sit crosslegged. In the two further ones two
youthful gods are sitting in the same fashion. The ages
of the four appear to be between 17 and 20. They are
magically beautiful in their Indian dresses, softly
brilliant, making the tropical flowers of the garden seem
almost crude beside them. Their expressions are intent,
grave, and inscrutable. They face south with their
backs to the sea. The goddess to the east has raven black
hair, a swarthy skin, and robes of a thousand shades of
deep carnation, in contrast to the younger one on her

right, who is a ravishing blonde in a diaphanous white and gold sari. There is a parallel contrast between the two youths, the one on the west being the younger and more delicate, and the one on his left older and more powerfully framed.

The four figures give the garden a hieratic aspect which has its effect on a young English clergyman, who wanders into the grounds at the north west corner, looking curiously and apprehensively about him with the air of a stranger who is trespassing. When he catches sight of the four figures he starts nervously and whips off his hat; then approaches them on tiptoe. He has a baby complexion, and a childish expression, credulous and disarmingly propitiatory. His age is at most 24.

Down the steps at this moment comes Pra, about twenty years older than when we saw him last, but splendidly preserved. His approach is dignified and even courteous, though not warmly so. He evidently wants to know what the stranger is doing in his garden.

THE CLERGYMAN [*nervously, hat in hand*] I beg your pardon. I fear I am trespassing. I am a stranger here; and I could not find a road up from the beach. I thought I might cut across through your grounds. [*Indicating the figures*] But I assure you I had no idea I was intruding on consecrated ground.

PRA. You are not on conscrated ground, except in so far as all ground is consecrated.

THE CLERGYMAN. Oh, excuse me. I thought— those idols—

PRA. Idols!

THE CLERGYMAN. No, of course not idols. I meant those gods and goddesses—

PRA. They are very beautiful, are they not? [*He speaks without awe or enthusiasm, with a touch of pity for the parson and weariness on his own part*].

THE CLERGYMAN. They are most beautiful. Quite marvellous even to me, an English clergyman. I can hardly wonder at your worshipping them, though of course you shouldnt.

PRA. Beauty is worshipful, within limits. When you have worshipped your fill may I shew you the shortest way out? It is through the house. Where do you wish to go, by the way?

THE CLERGYMAN. I dont know. I am lost.

PRA. Lost?

THE CLERGYMAN. Yes, quite lost. I dont know where I am. I mean I dont even know what country I am in.

PRA. You are in the Unexpected Isles, a Crown Colony of the British Empire.

THE CLERGYMAN. Do you mean the isles that came up out of the sea when I was a baby.

PRA. Yes. [*Pointing to the breakwater*] That is the harbor of the port of Good Adventure.

THE CLERGYMAN. They put me on shore there.

PRA. Who put you on shore?

THE CLERGYMAN. The pirates.

PRA. Pirates!

THE CLERGYMAN. Yes. I was their chaplain.

PRA. You were their—! [*He turns to the house and calls*] Prola. Prola.

PROLA'S VOICE. Yes. What is it?

PRA. Come out here.

Prola comes down the steps. She, like Pra, is twenty years older; but the years have only made her beauty more impressive.

THE CLERGYMAN [*gaping at her in an undisguised*

[785]

awe and admiration] Oh dear! Is this the lady of the house?

PROLA [*coming past Pra to the Clergyman*] Who is this gentleman?

PRA. He does not seem to know. I think he has escaped from the asylum.

THE CLERGYMAN [*distressed*] Oh, dear beautiful lady, I am not mad. Everybody thinks I am. Nobody believes what I say, though it is the simple truth. I know it is very hard to believe.

PROLA. In the Unexpected Isles nothing is unbelievable. How did you get in here?

THE CLERGYMAN. I lost my way trying to find a short cut up from the beach. I climbed the fence. I am so sorry.

PROLA. Really sorry?

THE CLERGYMAN. I did not mean to intrude. I apologize most sincerely.

PROLA. I did not ask you to apologize: you are quite welcome. I asked were you really sorry. Do you regret finding yourself in this garden?

THE CLERGYMAN. Oh no. It's like the Garden of Eden: I should like to stay here forever. [*Suddenly breaking down to the verge of tears*] I have nowhere to go.

PROLA. Perhaps he is weak with hunger.

THE CLERGYMAN. No: it's not that. I have been under a great strain for a long time; and now that I have escaped—and the beauty of those four—and your lovely awfulness—and—oh [*collapsing on the stone seat*] I am making a fool of myself. I always make a fool of myself. Dont mind me.

PRA. He thinks he has been chaplain in a pirate ship.

THE CLERGYMAN [*rising in desperate protest*] But I have. I have. They kidnapped me at Weston Super

Mare where I was doing locum tenens for the Rector of Saint Biddulphs. It was on a Sunday afternoon: I had my clerical clothes on after taking the afternoon service. "You look so innocent and respectable" they said. "Just what we want!" They took me all over the world, where I couldnt speak the language and couldnt explain.

PRA. And they wanted you to minister to them spiritually?

THE CLERGYMAN. No no: that was what was so dreadful. They were crooks, racketeers, smugglers, pirates, anything that paid them. They used me to make people believe that they were respectable. They were often so bored that they made me hold a service and preach; but it was only to make themselves ill laughing at me. Though perhaps I shouldnt say that. Some of them were such dear nice fellows: they assured me it did them no end of good. But they got tired of me and put me ashore here. [*He again resorts to the stone seat, clasping his temples distractedly*] Oh dear! oh dear! nothing ever happens to me that happens to other people. And all because I was not a natural baby. I was a nitrogen baby.

PROLA. A nitrogen baby!

PRA [*to Prola*] Steady. There may be something in this. [*He goes to the clergyman and sits down beside him*] What do you mean by a nitrogen baby?

THE CLERGYMAN. You see, my father is a famous biological chemist.

PROLA. I do not see. Your father may be a biological chemist; but biological chemists' children are like other people's children.

THE CLERGYMAN. No. No, I assure you. Not my father's children. You dont know my father. Even my Christian name is Phosphor.

PRA. Is what?

THE CLERGYMAN. Phosphor. [*He spells it*] P.H.O.S. P.H.O.R. The name of the morning star. Phosphorus, you know. The stuff they make matches with. Such a name to baptize a boy by! Please dont call me by it.

PRA. Come come! Neither your father nor your god-fathers and godmothers could change your human nature by giving you an unusual name in baptism.

THE CLERGYMAN. But it wasnt only the name. My father fed our cows on nitrogen grass.

PRA. Nitrogen gas, you mean.

THE CLERGYMAN. No: nitrogen grass. Some sort of grass that came up when he sprinkled our fields with chemicals. The cows ate it; and their butter was very yellow and awfully rich. So was the milk. I was fed on that sort of milk and butter. And the wheat in my bread was grown from special nitrates that my father made.

PRA [*to Prola*] I believe he is not mad after all.

THE CLERGYMAN. I assure you I am not. I am weakminded; but I am not mad.

PRA. I have read some very interesting articles about this by an English chemist named Hammingtap.

THE CLERGYMAN. Thats my father. My name is Hammingtap. The old family name is Hummingtop; but my grandfather changed it when he was at Oxford.

PRA. Prola: our young friend here may really be a new sort of man. Shall we go in and tell the others about him? We might take him into the family for a while, as an experiment.

THE CLERGYMAN [*alarmed*] Oh please, no. Why does everyone want to make an experiment of me?

PROLA. All men and women are experiments. What is your religion?

THE CLERGYMAN. The Christian religion, of course. I am a clergyman.

PROLA. What is the Christian religion?

THE CLERGYMAN. Well, it is—well, I suppose it is the Christian religion. I thought everybody knew. But then of course you are a heathen.

PROLA. What does the Christian religion mean to you?

THE CLERGYMAN. Oh, to me it means everything that is good and lovely and kind and holy. I dont profess to go any further than that.

PROLA. You need not. You had better not. Wait here until we return. We may find some use for you. Come, Pra.

She goes up the steps into the house, followed by Pra. The Clergyman, left with the four figures, looks at them, looks round to make sure that nobody is watching. Then he steals up to the fair goddess.

THE CLERGYMAN. Oh, how lovely you are! How I wish you were alive and I could kiss your living lips instead of the paint on a hard wooden image. I wonder is it idolatry to adore you? St Peter in Rome is only a bronze image; but his feet have been worn away by the kisses of Christian pilgrims. You make me feel as I have never felt before. I must kiss you. [*He does so and finds that she is alive. She smiles as her eyes turn bewitchingly towards him*]. Oh!!! [*He stands gasping, palpitating*].

THE ELDER YOUTH. Beware.

THE YOUNGER. On guard.

THE FAIR GIRL. Let him worship. His lips are sweet and pure.

THE DARK ONE. "For he on honey dew hath fed"—

THE FAIR ONE.—"and drunk the milk of paradise."

THE DARK ONE. I, Vashti, can see his aura. It is violet.

THE FAIR ONE. I, Maya, can see his halo. It is silvery.

VASHTI. Blessed are the shining ones!

MAYA. Blessed are the simple ones!

THE ELDER YOUTH. Beware. I, Janga, warn thee.

THE YOUNGER YOUTH. On guard. I, Kanchin, shew thee the red light.

JANGA. Their eyebrows are drawn bows.

KANCHIN. Their arrows feel sweet in the heart—

JANGA. —but are deadly.

KANCHIN. The ground within reach of their arms is enchanted.

JANGA. Vashti is lovely even to her brothers.

KANCHIN. Little children would die for Maya.

JANGA. Beware.

KANCHIN. On guard.

JANGA. Trust them not.

KANCHIN. They will break thy spear.

JANGA. They will pierce thy shield.

VASHTI. Fear not, beginner: I will strengthen thee.

MAYA. Strive not, beloved: I will keep thy soul for thee.

THE 2 YOUTHS [*together, fortissimo*] Beware.

The two girl-goddesses suddenly and simultaneously spring from their shrines and march down upon him, Vashti to his left, Maya to his right.

VASHTI. Dare you tread the plains of heaven with us, young pilgrim?

MAYA. We are waves of life in a sea of bliss. Dare you breast them, young swimmer?

THE CLERGYMAN. Oh, I dont know whether you are gods and goddesses or real people. I only know that you fill my heart with inexpressible longings.

MAYA. We are the awakening.

VASHTI. We are the way.

MAYA. We are the life.

VASHTI. I am the light. Look at me. [*She throws her arm round him and turns his face to hers*].

MAYA. I am the fire. Feel how it glows [*She also throws her arm round him*].

LADY FARWATERS *comes from the house, and pauses at the top of the steps to take in what is going on.*

THE CLERGYMAN. Oh, one at a time, please.

VASHTI. Perfect love casteth out choice.

MAYA. In love there is neither division nor measure.

LADY FARWATERS [*rushing to him and dragging him away from them*] Stop it, children: you are driving the man mad. Go away, all of you.

The two youths spring from their pedestals and whirl the girls away through the shrubberies.

VASHTI [*invisible, calling*] I will return in dreams.

MAYA [*similarly*] I leave my arrow in your heart.

LADY FARWATERS. You musnt mind them.

Prola and Pra come down the steps, followed by Sir Charles Farwaters and by Hugo Hyering C.B. and Mrs Hyering. Hyering is the former emigration officer, now an elderly and very different man, disciplined, responsible and well groomed. His wife is the emigrant girl twenty years older and better drilled socially, but still very much her old self. Lady Farwaters, once a gaunt and affected tourist visiting cave temples and distributing tracts to the heathen, is now a bland and attractive matron.

PRA. Mr Hammingtap: let me introduce you to the Governor of the Unexpected Isles, Sir Charles Farwaters.

SIR CHARLES [*offering his hand*] How do you do, Mr Hammingtap?

THE CLERGYMAN [*jerkily nervous*] Very pleased. [*They shake hands*].

   Sir Charles sits down in the middle of the stone seat nearest the steps.

PRA. Lady Farwaters.

LADY FARWATERS [*smiles and proffers her hand*]!

THE CLERGYMAN. Most kind— er. [*He shakes*].

   Lady Farwaters sits down in the middle of the other stone seat.

PRA. This is Mr Hugo Hyering, political secretary to the Isles.

THE CLERGYMAN. How do you do, Sir Hugo?

HYERING [*shaking hands*] Not Sir Hugo. [*Introducing*] Mrs Hyering.

MRS HYERING [*shaking hands*] C.B., in case you are addressing a letter. [*She sits down on Sir Charles's left*].

THE CLERGYMAN. Oh, I am so sorry.

HYERING. Not at all. [*He sits on Lady Farwaters' right*].

PRA [*indicating the parapet of the well*] You had better sit here.

THE CLERGYMAN [*sitting down as directed*] Thank you.

   Prola sits down on Sir Charles's left, and Pra on Lady Farwaters' left.

LADY FARWATERS. You have made the acquaintance of our four children, Mr Hammingtap?

THE CLERGYMAN. I couldnt help it. I mean—

PROLA. We know what you mean. You need not explain.

THE CLERGYMAN. But I assure you I—that is—

MRS HYERING. Dont apologize, Mr Hammingtap. We know quite well what our daughters are capable of when they are attracted by a young stranger.

THE CLERGYMAN. I did not understand. They are so sunburnt, and their dresses are so eastern: I thought they were orientals.

SIR CHARLES. They are half orientals. You see, the family is a mixed one. This lady, whom you may address as Prola, and this gentleman, known as Pra, are both entirely oriental, and very dominant personalities at that; so that naturally our children would have a strong oriental strain, would they not?

THE CLERGYMAN [*hastily*] Oh, of course. Quite. Certainly. [*He looks piteously at their gracious unconcerned faces, which tell him nothing*]. I beg your pardon. I am frightfully sorry; but my nerves are in rags; and I cannot follow what you are saying.

HYERING. Oh yes you can. It's all right: you have understood perfectly.

MRS HYERING. Buck up, Mr Hammingtap. Let life come to you.

LADY FARWATERS. Our family arrangements are not those usual in England. We are making a little domestic experiment—

THE CLERGYMAN. Oh, not an experiment, I hope. Chemical experiments are bad enough: I am one myself; but they are scientific. I dont think I could countenance a domestic experiment. And in spite of what you say I am not sure that I am not going mad.

SIR CHARLES. We are distracting you. Let us change the subject. Would you like to be a bishop?

THE CLERGYMAN. Oh dear! Can you make me one?

SIR CHARLES. Well, my recommendation would probably be decisive. A bishop is needed here: a bishop in partibus infidelium. Providence seems to have thrown you on this shore for the purpose, like Jonah. Will you undertake it?

THE CLERGYMAN. I should like to have a bishop's

salary, certainly. But unfortunately I am weak-minded.

SIR CHARLES. Many bishops are; and they are the best sort. A strongminded bishop is a horror.

THE CLERGYMAN. I am too young.

SIR CHARLES. You will not remain so. Most bishops are too old.

THE CLERGYMAN [*tempted*] It would be rather a lark, wouldnt it?

MRS HYERING. Thats right, Mr Hammingtap: let life come to you.

PRA. What objection have you to be a bishop?

THE CLERGYMAN. Oh, none, I assure you. Of course no clergyman could object to be a bishop. But why do you want to make me one?

SIR CHARLES. I will be quite frank with you, Mr Hammingtap. Twenty years ago my wife and I, with Mr and Mrs Hyering, joined this eastern gentleman and his colleague in a eugenic experiment. Its object was to try out the result of a biological blend of the flesh and spirit of the west with the flesh and spirit of the east. We formed a family of six parents.

THE CLERGYMAN. Six?

SIR CHARLES. Yes, six. The result has been a little disappointing from the point of view of numbers; but we have produced four children, two of each sex, and educated them in the most enlightened manner we were capable of. They have now grown up; consequently the time has arrived when the family group must be extended by young persons of their own age, so that the group may produce a second generation. Now sooner or later this extension of the family group will set people talking.

THE CLERGYMAN. It would strike my people dumb, if I grasp your meaning rightly.

SIR CHARLES. You do. I mean exactly what I say. There will be a struggle with public opinion in the empire. We shall not shirk it: it is part of our plan to open people's minds on the subject of eugenics and the need for mixing not only western and eastern culture but eastern and western blood. Still, we do not want to be stopped, as the Mormons were, or as the Oneida Community would have been if it had not voluntarily broken up. We want to set the intelligent people talking, and to strike the stupid people dumb. And we think we could do both by adding a bishop to the family.

MRS HYERING. And that is where you come in, young man.

PRA. There is another consideration that weighs with us: at least with me. I am convinced that there is something lacking in the constitution of the children. It may be a deficiency of nitrogen. It certainly is a deficiency of something that is essential to a complete social human being.

THE CLERGYMAN. Oh, I cannot believe that. They seemed to me to be quite perfect. I cannot imagine anyone more perfect than Maya.

PRA. Well, what did you think of Maya's conscience, for example?

THE CLERGYMAN [*bewildered*] Her conscience? I suppose—I dont know—I—

PRA. Precisely. You dont know. Well, we do know. Our four wonderful children have all sorts of talents, all sorts of accomplishments, all sorts of charms. And we are heartily tired of all their attractions because, though they have artistic consciences, and would die rather than do anything ugly or vulgar or common, they have not between the whole four of them a scrap of moral conscience. They have been very carefully fed: all the vitamins that the biological chemists have discovered are provided in their diet. All their glands are scientifically nourished. Their physical health is perfect. Unfortunately the biological chemists have not yet discovered either the gland that produces and regulates the moral conscience or the vitamins that nourish it. Have you a conscience, Mr Hammingtap?

THE CLERGYMAN. Oh yes: I wish I hadnt. It tortures me. You know, I should have enjoyed being a pirate's chaplain sometimes if it hadnt been for my terrible conscience. It has made my life one long remorse; for I have never had the strength of mind to act up to it.

PRA. That suggests very strongly that the conscientious man is, chemically speaking, the nitrogenic man. Here, then, we have four young adults, insufficiently nitrogenized, and therefore deficient in conscience. Here also we have a young adult saturated with nitrogen from his cradle, and suffering from a morbid excess of conscience. A union between him and our girls is clearly indicated.

THE CLERGYMAN. You mean that I ought to marry one of them?

PRA. Not at all. They would regard that as an invidious proceeding.

THE CLERGYMAN. Invidious! I dont understand.

LADY FARWATERS [*goodnaturedly*] Let me try to break it to you, Mr Hammingtap. The two girls attract you very much, dont they?

THE CLERGYMAN. How can one help being attracted, Lady Farwaters? Theyre quite beautiful.

LADY FARWATERS. Both of them?

THE CLERGYMAN. Oh, as a clergyman I could not

be attracted by more than one at a time. Still, some-how, I seem to love them all in an inexpressible sort of way. Only, if there were any question of marriage, I should have to choose.

PROLA. And which would you choose?

THE CLERGYMAN. Oh, I should choose Maya.

PROLA. Maya would at once reject you.

THE CLERGYMAN [*much dejected*] I suppose so. I know I am no catch for Maya. Still, she was very kind to me. In fact—but perhaps I oughtnt to tell you this—she kissed me.

SIR CHARLES. Indeed? That shews that she con-templates a union with you.

LADY FARWATERS. You must not think she would reject you on the ground of any personal unworthiness on your part.

THE CLERGYMAN. Then on what ground? Oh, I shouldnt have kissed her.

MRS HYERING. Oho! You said it was she who kissed you.

THE CLERGYMAN. Yes: I know I should have ex-plained that. But she let me kiss her.

MRS HYERING. That must have been a thrill, Mr Hammingtap. Life came to you that time, didnt it?

THE CLERGYMAN. Oh please, I cant speak of it. But why should she reject me if I make her an honorable proposal?

LADY FARWATERS. Because she will consider your honorable proposal dishonorable, Mr Hammingtap, unless it includes all the ladies of the family. You will not be allowed to pick and choose and make distinc-tions. You marry all or none.

THE CLERGYMAN. Oh dear! My poor little brain is giving way. I cant make sense of what you are saying. I know that your meaning must be perfectly right and respectable, Lady Farwaters; but it sounds like a dreadful sort of wickedness.

LADY FARWATERS. May I try to explain?

THE CLERGYMAN. Please do, Lady Farwaters. But I wish you wouldnt call me Mr Hammingtap. I am accustomed to be called Iddy among friends.

MRS HYERING. What does Iddy stand for?

THE CLERGYMAN. Well, in our home I was known as the idiot.

MRS HYERING. Oh! I am sorry: I didnt know.

THE CLERGYMAN. Not at all. My sister was the Kiddy; so I became the Iddy. Do please call me that. And be kind to me. I am weakminded and lose my head very easily; and I can see that you are all wonderfully clever and strongminded. That is why I could be so happy here. I can take in anything if you will only tell it to me in a gentle hushabyebaby sort of way and call me Iddy. Now go on, Lady Farwaters. Excuse me for interrupting you so long.

LADY FARWATERS. You see, Iddy—

IDDY. Oh, thanks!

LADY FARWATERS [*continuing*] —our four children are not like European children and not like Asiatic children. They have the east in their brains and the west in their blood. And at the same time they have the east in their blood and the west in their brains. Well, from the time when as tiny tots they could speak, they invented fairy stories. I thought it silly and dangerous, and wanted to stop them; but Prola would not let me: she taught them a game called the heavenly parliament in which all of them told tales and added them to the general stock until a fairyland was built up, with laws and religious rituals, and finally a great institution which they called the Superfamily. It began by my telling them in my old

conventional English way to love oneanother; but
they would not have that at all: they said it was vulgar
nonsense and made them interfere with oneanother
and hate oneanother. Then they hit out for themselves the idea that they were not to love oneanother,
but that they were to be oneanother.

IDDY. To be oneanother! I dont understand.

SIR CHARLES. Neither do I. Pra and Prola think they
understand it; but Lady Farwaters and I dont; and
we dont pretend to. We are too English. But the
practical side of it—the side that concerns you—is
that Vashti and Maya are now grown up. They must
have children. The boys will need a young wife.

IDDY. You mean two wives.

LADY FARWATERS. Oh, a dozen, if so many of the
right sort can be found.

IDDY. But—but—but that would be polygamy.

PROLA. You are in the east, Mr Iddy. The east is
polygamous. Try to remember that polygamists form
an enormous majority of the subjects of the British
Empire, and that you are not now in Clapham.

IDDY. How dreadful! I never thought of that.

LADY FARWATERS. And the girls will need a young
husband.

IDDY [imploringly] Two young husbands, Lady
Farwaters. Oh please, two.

LADY FARWATERS. I think not, at first.

IDDY. Oh! But I am not an oriental. I am a clergyman
of the Church of England.

HYERING. That means nothing to Vashti.

PRA. And still less to Maya.

IDDY. But—but—oh dear! dont you understand? I
want to marry Maya. And if I marry Maya I cannot
marry Vashti. An English clergyman could not marry
two women.

LADY FARWATERS. From their point of view they are not two women: they are one. Vashti is Maya; and Maya is Vashti.

IDDY. But even if such a thing were possible how could I be faithful to Vashti without being unfaithful to Maya? I couldnt bear to be unfaithful to Maya.

LADY FARWATERS. Maya would regard the slightest unfaithfulness to Vashti as a betrayal of herself and a breach of your marriage vow.

IDDY. But thats nonsense: utter nonsense. Please dont put such things into my head. I am trying so hard to keep sane; but you are terrifying me. If only I could bring myself never to see Maya again I should rush out of this garden and make for home. But it would be like rushing out of heaven. I am most unhappy; and yet I am dreadfully happy. I think I am under some sort of enchantment.

MRS HYERING. Well, stick to the enchantment while it lasts. Let life come to you.

PRA. May I remind you that not only Vashti and Maya, but all the ladies here, are included in the super-family compact.

IDDY. Oh, how nice and comfortable that would be! They would be mothers to me.

PROLA [*rebuking Pra*] Let him alone, Pra. There is such a thing as calf love. Vashti and Maya are quite enough for him to begin with. Maya has already driven him half mad. There is no need for us old people to drive him quite out of his senses. [*She rises*] This has gone far enough. Wait here alone, Mr Hammingtap, to collect your thoughts. Look at the flowers; breathe the air; open your soul to the infinite space of the sky. Nature always helps.

IDDY [*rising*] Thank you, Lady Prola. Yes: that will be a great help.

PROLA. Come [*She goes up the steps and into the house*].

They all rise and follow her, each bestowing a word of counsel or comfort on the distracted clergyman.

PRA. Relax. Take a full breath and then relax. Do not strangle yourself with useless anxieties. [*He goes*].

LADY FARWATERS. Cast out fear, Iddy. Warm heart. Clear mind. Think of having a thousand friends, a thousand wives, a thousand mothers. [*She pats him on the shoulder and goes*].

SIR CHARLES. Stand up to it, my boy. The world is changing. Stand up to it. [*He goes*].

MRS HYERING. Dont let that conscience of yours worry you. Let life come to you. [*She goes*].

HYERING. Try to sleep a little. The morning has been too much for you. [*He goes*].

IDDY. Sleep! I will not sleep. They want me to disgrace my cloth; but I wont. I wont relax: I wont disobey my conscience: I wont smell those flowers: I wont look at the sky. Nature is not good for me here. Nature is eastern here: it's poison to an Englishman. I will think of England and tighten myself up and pull myself together. England! The Malverns! the Severn plain! the Welsh border! the three cathedrals! England that is me: I that am England! Damn and blast all these tropical paradises: I am an English clergyman; and my place is in England. Floreat Etona! Back to England and all that England means to an Englishman! In this sign I shall conquer. [*He turns resolutely to go out as he came in, and finds himself face to face with Maya, who has stolen in and listened gravely and intently to his exhortation.*

IDDY [*collapsing in despair on the parapet of the well*] Oh, Maya, let me go, let me go.

MAYA [*sinking beside him with her arm round his neck*]

Speak to me from your soul, and not with words that you have picked up in the street.

IDDY. Respect my cloth, Miss Farwaters.

MAYA. Maya. Maya is my name. I am the veil of the temple. Rend me in twain.

IDDY. I wont. I will go home and marry some honest English girl named Polly Perkins. [*Shuddering in her embrace*] Oh, Maya, darling: speak to me like a human being.

MAYA. That is how I speak to you; but you do not recognize human speech when you hear it: you crave for slang and small talk, and for readymade phrases that mean nothing. Speak from your soul; and tell me: do you love Vashti? Would you die for Vashti?

IDDY. No.

MAYA [*with a flash of rage, springing up*] Wretch! [*Calmly and conclusively*] You are free. Farewell [*She points his way through the house*].

IDDY [*clutching at her robe*] No, no. Do not leave me. I love you—you. I would die for you. That sounds like a word picked up in the street; but it is true. I would die for you ten times over.

MAYA. It is not true. Words, words, words out of the gutter. Vashti and Maya are one: you cannot love me if you do not love Vashti: you cannot die for me without dying for Vashti.

IDDY. Oh, I assure you I can.

MAYA. Lies, lies. If you can feel one heart throb for me that is not a throb for Vashti: if for even an instant there are two women in your thoughts instead of one, then you do not know what love can be.

IDDY. But it's just the contrary. I—

VASHTI [*who has entered silently, sits beside him and throws an arm round his shoulders*] Do you not love me? Would you not die for me?

[802]

IDDY. [*mesmerized by her eyes*] Oh DEAR!!! Yes: your eyes make my heart melt: your voice opens heaven to me: I love you. I would die a thousand times for you.

VASHTI. And Maya? You love Maya. You would die a million times for Maya?

IDDY. Yes, yes. I would die for either, for both: for one, for the other—

MAYA. For Vashti Maya?

IDDY. For Vashti Maya, for Maya Vashti.

VASHTI. Your lives and ours are one life.

MAYA [*sitting down beside him*] And this is the Kingdom of love.

The three embrace with interlaced arms and vanish in black darkness.

$\lceil$ ACT II $\rceil$

*A fine forenoon some years later. The garden is un-
changed; but inside the distant breakwater the harbor is
crowded with cruisers; and on the lawn near the steps is
a writing table littered with papers and furnished with
a wireless telephone. Sir Charles is sitting at the end of
it with his back to the house. Seated near him is Pra.
Both are busy writing. Hyering enters.*

SIR CHARLES. Morning, Hyering.

HYERING. Morning. [*He sits at the other end of the
table after waving an acknowledgment of Pra's
indication of a salaam*]. Anything fresh?

SIR CHARLES [*pointing to the roadstead*] Look! Five
more cruisers in last night. The papers say it is the
first time the fleets of the British Empire have ever
assembled in one place.

HYERING. I hope it will never happen again. If we
dont get rid of them quickly there will be the biggest
naval battle on record. They are quarrelling already
like Kilkenny cats.

SIR CHARLES. What about?

HYERING. Oh, about everything. About moorings,
about firing salutes: which has the right to fire first?
about flags, about shore parties, about nothing. We
shall never be able to keep the peace between them.
The Quebec has got alongside the Belfast. The
Quebec has announced Mass at eleven on All Saints
Day; and the Belfast has announced firing practice
at the same hour. Do you see that sloop that came in
last night?

SIR CHARLES. What is it?

HYERING. The Pitcairn Island fleet. They are Seventh Day Adventists, and are quite sure the Judgment Day is fixed for five o'clock this afternoon. They propose to do nothing until then but sing hymns. The Irish Free State admiral threatens to sink them if they dont stop. How am I to keep them quiet?

PRA. Dont keep them quiet. Their squabbles will make them forget what they were sent here for.

HYERING. Forget! not they. I have six ultimatums from their admirals, all expiring at noon today. Look. [*He takes a batch of letters from his pocket and throws them on the table*].

SIR CHARLES [*pointing to the letters on the table*] Look at these!

PRA. All about Iddy.

SIR CHARLES. Iddy has got into the headlines at home. The cables are humming with Iddy. Iddy has convulsed the Empire, confound him!

HYERING. Anything fresh from London or Delhi?

SIR CHARLES. The same old songs. The Church of England wont tolerate polygamy on any terms, and insists on our prosecuting Iddy if we cannot whitewash him. Delhi declares that any attempt to persecute polygamy would be an insult to the religions of India.

PRA. The Cultural Minister at Delhi adds a postscript to say that as he has been married two hundred and thirtyfour times, and could not have lived on his salary without the dowries, the protest of the Church of England shews a great want of consideration for his position. He has a hundred and seventeen children surviving.

SIR CHARLES. Then there's a chap I never heard of, calling himself the Caliph of British Islam. He demands that Iddy shall put away all his wives except four.

HYERING. What does the Foreign Office say to that?

PRA. The Foreign Office hails it as a happy solution of a difficulty that threatened to be very serious.

HYERING. What do you think about it all yourself, Pra?

PRA. Think! Thought has no place in such discussions. Each of them must learn that its ideas are not everybody's ideas. Here is a cablegram from the League of British Imperial Womanhood, Vancouver and Pretoria. "Burn him alive and his hussies with him." Do you expect me to think about such people?

HYERING. Nobody has made any practical suggestion, I suppose?

PRA. The United States intervene with a friendly suggestion that the parties should be divorced. But the Irish Free State will not hear of divorce, and points out that if the parties become Catholics their marriages can be annulled with the greatest ease.

HYERING. Oh, the west! the west! the west!

PRA. Oh, the east! the east! the east! I tried to reconcile them; and I had only two successes: you and Lady Farwaters.

HYERING. You kicked me into the sea.

SIR CHARLES. You made love to Lady Farwaters.

PRA. I had to use that method with very crude novices; and Lady Farwaters, with her English ladylike bringing-up, was so crude that she really could not understand any purely intellectual appeal. Your own mind, thanks to your public school and university, was in an even worse condition; and Prola had to convert you by the same elementary method. Well, it has worked, up to a point. The insight you obtained into eastern modes of thought has enabled

you to govern the eastern crown colonies with extraordinary success. Downing Street hated you; but
Delhi supported you; and since India won Dominion
status Delhi has been the centre of the British Empire.
You, Hyering, have had the same diplomatic success
in the east for the same reason. But beyond this we
have been unable to advance a step. Our dream of
founding a millennial world culture: the dream which
united Prola and Pra as you first knew them, and then
united us all six, has ended in a single little household
with four children, wonderful and beautiful, but
sterile. When we had to find a husband for the blos-
soming girls, only one man was found capable of
merging himself in the unity of the family: a man fed
on air from his childhood. And how has this paragon
turned out? An impotent simpleton. It would be
impossible to conceive a human being of less consequence in the world. And yet, look! There is the
Imperial Armada, in which every petty province
insists on its separate fleet, every trumpery islet its
battleship, its cruiser, or at least its sloop or gunboat!
Why are they here, armed to the teeth, threatening
what they call their sanctions? a word that once meant
the approval of the gods, and now means bombs full
of poison gas. Solely on account of the simpleton. To
reform his morals, half of them want to rain destruction on this little household of ours, and the other
half is determined to sink them if they attempt it.

HYERING. They darent use their bombs, you
know.

PRA. True; but what is to prevent them from taking
to their fists and coming ashore to fight it out on the
beach with sticks and bottles and stones, or with
their fists? What do the ultimatums say, Hyering?

HYERING [*reading them*] Number one from the

English admiral. "If the polygamist-adulterer Hammingtap is not handed over by noon tomorrow" that is today "I shall be obliged to open fire on Government House." Number two, from the commander of the Bombay Squadron. "Unless an unequivocal guarantee of the safety and liberty of Mr Hammingtap be in my hands by noon today" that came this morning "I shall land a shore party equipped with machine guns and tear gas bombs to assist the local police in the protection of his person." Number three: "I have repeatedly informed you that the imperial province of Holy Island demands the immediate and exemplary combustion of the abominable libertine and damnable apostate known as Phosfor Hammingtap. The patience of the Holy Island fleet will be exhausted at noon on the 13th" today "and the capital of the Unexpected Islands must take the consequences." Number four—

SIR CHARLES. Oh, bother number four! They are all the same: not one of them has originality enough to fix half-past-eleven or a quarter-to-one.

HYERING. By the way, Pra, have you taken any steps? I havnt.

PRA. Yes I have. Dont worry. I have sent a message.

SIR CHARLES. What message?

PRA. The Mayor of the Port earnestly begs the commanders of the imperial fleet to suspend action for another day, as his attention is urgently occupied by a serious outbreak of smallpox in the harbor district.

SIR CHARLES. Good [*The boom of a cannon interrupts him*] There goes the noonday cannon!

HYERING. I hope they got the message in time.

The garden and its occupants vanish. When they reappear, the harbor is empty: not a ship is visible. The writing table, with its chairs and papers, has been re-

moved and replaced by a small tea-table. Tea is ready.
The wireless telephone is still there.

Vashti and Maya are in their shrines. Lady Far-
waters is sitting on the western stone seat, with Mrs
Hyering beside her on her right. Prola is sitting on the
eastern seat. All five ladies are taking tea.

Pra comes from the house with Sir Charles and
Hyering. They help themselves to tea. Pra abstains.

SIR CHARLES. Not a blessed ship left in the harbor!
Your message certainly did the trick, Pra. [*He sits
down beside Prola, on her left*].

PRA [*sitting down between the two British ladies*] They
may come back.

HYERING [*sitting beside Prola, on her right*] Not a bit
of it. By the time the fleet realizes that it has been
humbugged the Empire will be tired of Iddy.

VASHTI. The world is tired of Iddy.

MAYA. *I* am tired of Iddy.

VASHTI. Iddy is a pestilence.

MAYA. Iddy is a bore.

VASHTI. Let us throw ourselves into the sea to escape
from Iddy.

MAYA. Let us throw Iddy into the sea that he may
escape from himself.

VASHTI. You are wise, Prola. Tell us how to get rid of
Iddy.

MAYA. We cannot endure Iddy for ever, Prola.

PROLA. You two chose him, not I.

MAYA. We were young: we did not know.

VASHTI. Help us, Pra. You have lost faith in us; but
your wits are still keen.

MAYA. Pra: we beseech thee. Abolish the incubus.

VASHTI. Give him peace that we may have rest.

MAYA. Give him rest that we may have peace.

VASHTI. Let him be as he was before we knew him.

MAYA. When we were happy.

VASHTI. When he was innocent.

PRA. You raised this strange spirit. I cannot exorcise him.

VASHTI. Rather than endure him I will empty the heavens of their rain and dew.

MAYA. Silence him, O ye stars.

Iddy comes from the house in a condition of lazy self-complacence. He is received in dead silence. Nobody looks at him. He pours himself out a cup of tea. The silence becomes grim. He sits down on the grass at Prola's feet, and sips his tea. The silence continues.

IDDY [*at last*] I am a futile creature.

They all turn as if stung and look at him. Then they resume their attitudes of deadly endurance.

IDDY. It is a terrible thing to be loved. I dont suppose any man has ever been loved as I have been loved, or loved as I have loved. But there's not so much in it as people say. I am writing a sermon about it. It is a sermon on Eternity.

They look at him as before.

IDDY. The line I am going to take is this. We have never been able to imagine eternity properly. St John of Patmos started the notion of playing harps and singing praises for ever and ever. But the organist tells me that composers have to use the harp very sparingly because, though it makes a very pretty effect at first, you get tired of it so soon. You couldnt go on playing the harp for ever; and if you sang "Worthy is the Lamb" for ever you would drive the Lamb mad. The notion is that you cant have too much of a good thing; but you can: you can bear hardship much longer than you could bear heaven. Love is like music. Music is very nice: the organist says that when the wickedness of mankind tempts him to despair he comforts himself by remembering that the human race produced Mozart; but a woman who plays the piano all day is a curse. A woman who makes love to you all day is much worse; and yet nothing is lovelier than love, up to a point. We all love one another here in a wonderful way: I love Vashti, I love Maya, I love Prola; and they all love me so wonderfully that their three loves are only one love. But it is my belief that some day we'll have to try something else. If we dont we'll come to hate one another.

VASHTI. If it is any consolation to you, Iddy, I can assure you that I already hate you so intensely that if it were in my nature to kill anything I should kill you.

IDDY. There now! I ought to be wounded and horrified; but I'm not: I feel as if youd given me a strawberry ice. Thank you, dear Vashti, thank you. You give me hope that even Maya will get tired of me someday.

MAYA. I have been on the point of beating you to a jelly for ever so long past; but just as my fists were clenched to do it you always managed to come out with some stroke of idiocy that was either so funny or so piteous that I have kissed you instead.

IDDY. You make me happier than I have been for months. But, you know, that does not settle my difficulties. I dont know whether other people are like me or not—

LADY FARWATERS. No, Iddy: you are unique.

IDDY. Anyhow, I have made a discovery as regards myself.

VASHTI. Enough is known already.

MAYA. Seek no further: there is nothing there.

VASHTI. There never has been anything.

IDDY. Shut up, you two. This is something really interesting. I am writing a second sermon.

ALL THE REST [*gasp*] !!!!!!!

PRA. Was eternity not long enough for one sermon?

IDDY. This one is on love.

VASHTI [*springing up*] I will cast myself down from a precipice.

MAYA [*springing up*] I will gas myself.

IDDY. Oh, not until you have heard my sermon, please.

PROLA. Listen to him, children. Respect the wisdom of the fool.

VASHTI [*resuming her goddess-in-a-shrine attitude*] The oracles of the wise are unheeded. Silence for the King of Idiots.

MAYA [*also enshrining herself*] Speak, Solomon.

IDDY. Well, the discovery I have made is that we were commanded to love our enemies because loving is good for us and dreadfully bad for them. I love you all here intensely; and I enjoy loving you. I love Vashti; I love Maya; and I adore Prola with a passion that grows and deepens from year to year.

PROLA. Dolt! I am too old.

IDDY. You were never young and you will never be old. You are the way and the light for me. But you have never loved me and never will love me. You have never loved anything human: why should you? Nothing human is good enough to be loved. But every decent human creature has some capacity for loving. Look at me! What a little worm I am! My sermons are wretched stuff, except these last two, which I think really have something in them. I cannot bear being loved, because I know that I am a worm, and that nobody could love me unless they were completely deluded as to my merits. But I can love, and delight in loving. I love Vashti for hating me, because she is quite right to hate me: her hatred is a proof of her beautiful clear judgment. I love Maya for being out of all patience with me, because I know that I am enough to drive anybody mad, and she is wise enough to know how worthless I am. I love Prola because she is far above loving or hating me; and there is something about her dark beauty that—

PROLA [*kicking him*] Silence, simpleton. Let the unspeakable remain unspoken.

IDDY. I dont mind your kicking me, Prola: you understand; and that is enough for me. And now you see what a jolly fine sermon it will be, and why I shall be so happy here with you from this day on. For I have the joy of loving you all without the burden of being loved in return, or the falsehood of being idolized.

MAYA. Solomon has spoken.

VASHTI. Stupendous.

LADY FARWATERS. Do not mock, darlings. There is something in what he says.

MAYA [*desperately*] But how are we to get rid of him? He is settling down with us for life.

VASHTI. We have brought him on ourselves.

MAYA. We cannot make him hate us.

VASHTI. He will go with us to heaven.

MAYA. In the depths of hell he will find us.

Kanchin and Janga enter processionally, reading newspapers.

KANCHIN. News!

JANGA. News!

They sit enshrined, foursquare with their sisters.

KANCHIN. By wireless.

JANGA. Tomorrow's three o'clock edition.

KANCHIN. The land that brought forth Iddy begins the Apocalypse.

HYERING. What do you mean? Has anything happened in England?

KANCHIN. England has broken loose.

SIR CHARLES. What do you mean? broken loose. Read the news, man. Out with it.

KANCHIN [*reading the headlines*] Dissolution of the British Empire.

JANGA [*reading*] Withdrawal of England from the Empire.

KANCHIN. England strikes for independence.

JANGA. Downing Street declares for a right little tight little island.

KANCHIN. The British Prime Minister cuts the cable and gives the new slogan.

JANGA. Back to Elizabeth's England; and to hell with the empire!

KANCHIN. Ireland to the rescue!

JANGA. Free State President declares Ireland cannot permit England to break the unity of the Empire. Ireland will lead the attack on treason and disruption.

KANCHIN. The Prime Minister's reply to the President suppressed as unprintable.

JANGA. Canada claims position of premier Dominion left vacant by the secession of England.

KANCHIN. Australia counterclaims as metropolitan dominion.

JANGA. New Zealand proclaims a butter blockade until its claim to precedence is recognized by Australia.

KANCHIN. South Africa renames Capetown Empire City, and gives notice to all Britishers to clear out of Africa within ten days.

JANGA. His Holiness the Pope calls on all Christendom to celebrate the passing away of the last vain dream of earthly empire, and the unity of all living souls in the Catholic Kingdom of God and his Church.

LADY FARWATERS. That sounds like the voice of a

grown-up man through the whooping of a pack of schoolboys.

JANGA [*prosaically*] So far, there have been no disturbances and little popular interest.

KANCHIN. The various international Boards are carrying on as usual.

JANGA. Today's football—

PROLA. No, Janga: certainly not.

SIR CHARLES. But what becomes of our jobs as Governor and political secretary, Hyering? Will this affect our salaries?

HYERING. They will stop: that is all. We had better proclaim the Unexpected Isles an independent republic and secure the new jobs for ourselves.

VASHTI. The world is tired of republics and their jobberies. Proclaim a kingdom.

MAYA. Or a queendom.

IDDY. Oh yes: let us make Prola queen. And I shall be her chaplain.

PRA. By all means, as far as I am concerned. Prola has always been the real ruler here.

VASHTI. Prola is she who decides.

MAYA. Prola is she who unites.

VASHTI. Prola is she who knows.

MAYA. No one can withstand Prola.

PROLA. Be quiet, you two. You shall not make an idol of me.

KANCHIN. We shall make you Empress of the Isles.

JANGA. Prola the First.

VASHTI. Homage, Prola.

MAYA. Love, Prola.

KANCHIN. Obedience, Prola.

JANGA. Absolute rule, Prola.

PROLA. All your burdens on me. Lazy idle children.

KANCHIN. Hurrah! All burdens on Prola.

JANGA. The burden of thought.

VASHTI. The burden of knowledge.

MAYA. The burden of righteousness.

VASHTI. The burden of justice.

MAYA. The burden of mercy.

PROLA. Cease, cease: these are not burdens to me: they are the air I breathe. I shall rule you as I have always done because you are too lazy to rule yourselves.

HYERING. You can rule us, Prola. But will the public ever understand you?

PRA. They will obey her. They would not do that if they understood.

IDDY. I have just been thinking—

MAYA. Solomon has been thinking.

VASHTI. Thoughts without brains.

IDDY. Will the Antiphonal Quartet, if it wants to give another concert, kindly remove itself out of hearing.

KANCHIN. Silence for the Prophet.

JANGA. Mum!

VASHTI. Dumb.

MAYA. Tiddy iddy um. Carry on, darling.

IDDY. Prola can rule this house because she knows what is happening in it. But how is she to be an Empress if she doesnt know what is happening everywhere?

MRS HYERING. She can read the newspapers, cant she, silly?

IDDY. Yes; but fifteen years later, when the statesmen write their memoirs and autobiographies and publish them, we shall find that it never happened at all and what really happened was quite different. We dont know the truth about any of our statesmen until they are dead and cant take libel actions. Nobody knows the sort of people we really are. The papers have been full of us for weeks past; and not a single word they say about us is true. They think I am a sort of Mahdi or Mad Mullah, and that Prola and Vashti and Maya are a troop of immoral dancing girls, and that Sir Charles is a voluptuous sultan and Hyering a co-respondent. They dont live in a world of truth: they live in a world of their own ideas, which have nothing to do with our ideas. Consequently—Therefore—er—er— What was I going to say, Pra? My brain is not strong enough to keep the thread of my remarks. I ought to have written it down.

PRA. What you have arrived at is that we cannot live in a world of political facts, because we shall not know the political facts for years to come. We must therefore live in a world of original ideas, created by ourselves out of our own nature.

IDDY. Yes. We musnt pretend to be omniscient. Even God would not be omniscient if He read the newspapers. We must have an ideal of a beautiful and good world. We must believe that to establish that beautiful and good world on earth is the best thing we can do, and the only sort of religion and politics that is worth bothering about.

PROLA. What about the people who have no original ideas, Iddy?

PRA. The great majority of mankind?

IDDY. Theyll be only too glad to do what you tell them, Prola, if you can make them feel that it's right.

PROLA. And if they are incapable of feeling it?

JANGA. Kill.

KANCHIN. Kill.

VASHTI. Kill.

MAYA. Kill.

PROLA. They can do that as easily as I. Any fool can. And there are more of them.

JANGA. Set them to kill one another; and rule.

KANCHIN. Divide and govern.

VASHTI. Feed them on splendid words.

MAYA. Dazzle them with our beauty.

MRS HYERING. Well I never!

IDDY [*rising*] Excuse me. I'm going into the house to get the field glass. [*He goes up the steps*].

MRS HYERING. Whatever do you want the field glass for?

IDDY [*pointing to the sky*] There's a strange bird flying about there. I think it's an albatross. [*He goes into the house*].

VASHTI, MAYA, KANCHIN, JANGA [*hissing after him*] Liar. Baby. Dastard. Hypocrite.

SIR CHARLES [*laughing*] An albatross! Now would anybody in the world, over the age of six, except Iddy, invent such a ridiculous excuse for going to his room to indulge in his poor little secret vice of cigaret smoking?

MAYA. Faugh! The unkissable.

VASHTI. The air poisoner.

KANCHIN. The albatrocity.

MAYA. VASHTI. JANGA [*shocked by the pun*] Oh!!

LADY FARWATERS. Cant you four darlings do something useful instead of sitting there deafening us with your slogans?

KANCHIN [*springing erect*] Yes, action. Action!

JANGA [*rising similarly*] No more of this endless talk! talk! talk!

VASHTI. Yes, action! daring! Let us rob.

MAYA. Let us shoot.

KANCHIN. Let us die for something.

JANGA. For our flag and for our Empress.

VASHTI. For our country, right or wrong.

MAYA. Let there be sex appeal. Let the women make the men brave.

KANCHIN. We must defend our homes.

JANGA. Our women.

VASHTI. Our native soil.

MAYA. It is sweet to die for one's country.

VASHTI. It is glorious to outface death.

ALL FOUR. Yes. Death! death! Glory! glory!

PROLA. Hold your tongues, you young whelps. Is this what we have brought you up for?

PRA. Stop screaming about nothing, will you. Use your minds.

MAYA. We have no minds.

VASHTI. We have imaginations.

KANCHIN. We have made this house a temple.

JANGA. We have made Prola its goddess.

MAYA. We have made it a palace.

VASHTI. A palace for Queen Prola.

KANCHIN. She shall reign.

JANGA. For ever and ever.

VASHTI AND MAYA [*in unison*] Hail, Prola, our goddess!

KANCHIN AND JANGA [*in unison*] Hail, Prola, our empress!

ALL FOUR [*rushing down to the lawn and throwing themselves on their knees before her*] Hail!

PROLA. Will you provoke me to box your ears, you abominable idolaters. Get up this instant. Go and scrub the floors. Do anything that is dirty and grubby and smelly enough to shew that you live in a real world and not in a fool's paradise. If I catch you grovelling to me, a creature of the same clay as yourselves, but fortunately for you with a little more common sense, I will beat the slavishness out of your bones.

MAYA. Oh, what ecstasy to be beaten by Prola!

VASHTI. To feel her rule in the last extremity of pain!

KANCHIN. To suffer for her!

JANGA. To die for her!

PROLA. Get out, all four. My empire is not of such as you. Begone.

MAYA. How lovely is obedience! [*She makes an obeisance and runs away through the garden*].

VASHTI. Obedience is freedom from the intolerable fatigue of thought. [*She makes her obeisance and sails away, disappearing between the garden and the house*].

KANCHIN. You speak as an empress should speak. [*He salaams and bounds off after Maya*].

JANGA. The voice of authority gives us strength and unity. Command us always thus: it is what we need and love. [*He strides away in Vashti's footsteps*].

PROLA. An excuse for leaving everything to me. Lazy, lazy, lazy! Someday Heaven will get tired of lazy people; and the Pitcairn Islanders will see their Day of Judgment at last.

A distant fusillade of shotguns answers her.

SIR CHARLES. Shooting! What can the matter be?

They all rise and listen anxiously.

A trumpet call rings out from the sky.

HYERING. Where on earth did that come from? There is not such a thing as a trumpet in the island.

The four come rushing back into the garden, wildly excited.

KANCHIN. Look, look, quick! The albatross.

PRA [*rising*] The albatross!!

MAYA. Yes: Iddy's albatross. Look!

JANGA. Flying over the town.

VASHTI [*pointing*] There it goes. See.

A second fusillade of shotguns, much nearer.

MAYA. Oh, theyre all trying to shoot it. Brutes!

KANCHIN. They havnt hit it. Here it comes.

MAYA. It's flying this way.

VASHTI. It's swooping down.

Iddy comes from the house and trots down the steps with a field glass in his hand.

IDDY. Ive been looking at it through the window for the last five minutes. It isnt an albatross. Look at it through this. [*He hands the glass to Pra*].

KANCHIN. Then what is it?

IDDY. I think it's an angel.

JANGA. Oh get out, you silly idiot.

PRA [*looking through the glass*] That is no bird.

An angel flies down into the middle of the garden. General stupefaction. He shakes himself. Quantities of bullets and small shot fall from his wings and clothes.

THE ANGEL. Really, your people ought to know better than to shoot at an angel.

MAYA. Are you an angel?

THE ANGEL. Well, what do you suppose I am?

VASHTI. Of course he is an angel. Look at his wings.

THE ANGEL. Attention, please! Have you not heard the trumpet? This is the Judgment Day.

ALL THE REST. The what???!!!

THE ANGEL. The Judgment Day. The Day of Judgment.

SIR CHARLES. Well I'll be damned!

THE ANGEL. Very possibly.

HYERING. Do you mean that the Pitcairn Islanders were right after all?!

[821]

THE ANGEL. Yes. You are all now under judgment, in common with the rest of the English speaking peoples. Dont gape at me as if you had never seen an angel before.

PROLA. But we never have.

THE ANGEL [*relaxing*] True. Ha ha ha! Well, you thoroughly understand, dont you, that your records are now being looked into with a view to deciding whether you are worth your salt or not.

PRA. And suppose it is decided that we are not worth our salt?

THE ANGEL [*reassuring them in a pleasantly off-handed manner*] Then you will simply disappear: that is all. You will no longer exist. Dont let me keep you all standing. Sit down if you like. Never mind me: sitting and standing are all alike to an angel. However —[*he sits down on the parapet of the well*].

They sit as before, the four superchildren enshrining themselves as usual.

The telephone rings. Hyering rises and takes it.

HYERING [*to the angel*] Excuse me. [*To the telephone*] Yes? Hyering speaking . . . Somebody what? . . . Oh! somebody fooling on the wireless. Well, theyre not fooling: an angel has just landed here to tell us the same thing. . . . An angel. A for arrowroot, N for nitrogen, G for—thats it: an angel. . . . Well, after all, the Judgment Day had to come some day, hadnt it? Why not this day as well as another? . . . I'll ask the angel about it and ring you later. Goodbye. [*He rings off*]. Look here, angel. The wireless has been on all over Europe. London reports the Judgment Day in full swing; but Paris knows nothing about it; Hilversum knows nothing about it; Berlin, Rome, Madrid, and Geneva know nothing about it; and Moscow says the British bourgeoisie has been driven mad by its superstitions. How do you account for that? If it is the Judgment Day in England it must be the Judgment Day everywhere.

THE ANGEL. Why?

HYERING [*sitting down*] Well, it stands to reason.

THE ANGEL. Does it? Would it be reasonable to try cases in hundreds of different lands and languages and creeds and colors on the same day in the same place? Of course not. The whole business will last longer than what you call a year. We gave the English speaking folk the first turn in a compliment to one of your big guns—a dean—name of Inge, I think. I announced it to him last night in a dream, and asked him whether the English would appreciate the compliment. He said he thought they would prefer to put it off as long as possible, but that they needed it badly and he was ready. The other languages will follow. The United States of America will be tried tomorrow, Australasia next day, Scotland next, then Ireland—

LADY FARWATERS. But excuse me: they do not speak different languages.

THE ANGEL. They sound different to us.

SIR CHARLES. I wonder how they are taking it in England.

THE ANGEL. I am afraid most of them are incapable of understanding the ways of heaven. They go motoring or golfing on Sundays instead of going to church; and they never open a Bible. When you mention Adam and Eve, or Cain and Abel, to say nothing of the Day of Judgment, they dont know what you are talking about. The others—the pious ones—think we have come to dig up all the skeletons and put them through one of their shocking criminal trials. They actually expect us to make angels of them for ever and ever.

[823]

MRS HYERING. See here, angel. This isnt a proper sort of Judgment Day. It's a fine day. It's like Bank Holiday.

THE ANGEL. And pray why should the Day of Judgment not be a fine day?

MRS HYERING. Well, it's hardly what we were led to expect, you know.

JANGA. "The heavens shall pass away with a great noise."

KANCHIN. "The elements shall melt with fervent heat."

JANGA. "The earth also and the works that are therein shall be burnt up."

VASHTI. The stars are fixed in their courses. They have not fallen to the earth.

MAYA. The heavens are silent. Where are the seven thunders?

VASHTI. The seven vials full of the wrath of God?

JANGA. The four horses?

KANCHIN. The two witnesses?

THE ANGEL. My good people, if you want these things you must provide them for yourselves. If you want a great noise, you have your cannons. If you want a fervent heat to burn up the earth you have your high explosives. If you want vials of wrath to rain down on on you, they are ready in your arsenals, full of poison gases. Some years ago you had them all in full play, burning up the earth and spreading death, famine, and pestilence. But the spring came and created life faster than you could destroy it. The birds sang over your trenches; and their promise of summer was fulfilled. The sun that shone undisturbed on your pitiful Day of Wrath shines today over Heaven's Day of Judgment. It will continue to light us and warm us;

and there will be no noise nor wrath nor fire nor thunder nor destruction nor plagues nor terrors of any sort. I am afraid you will find it very dull.

LADY FARWATERS [*politely*] Not at all. Pray dont think that.

MRS HYERING. Well, a little good manners never does any harm; but I tell you straight, Mister Angel, I cant feel as if there was anything particular happening, in spite of you and your wings. Ive only just had my tea; and I cant feel a bit serious without any preparation or even an organ playing.

THE ANGEL. You will feel serious enough presently when things begin to happen.

MRS HYERING. Yes; but what things?

THE ANGEL. What was foretold to you. "His angels shall gather together his elect. Then shall two be in the field: the one shall be taken and the other left. Two women shall be grinding at the mill. The one shall be taken and the other left."

MRS HYERING. But which? Thats what I want to know.

PROLA. There is nothing new in this taking of the one and leaving the other: natural death has always been doing it.

THE ANGEL. Natural death does it senselessly, like a blind child throwing stones. We angels are executing a judgment. The lives which have no use, no meaning, no purpose, will fade out. You will have to justify your existence or perish. Only the elect shall survive.

MRS HYERING. But where does the end of the world come in?

THE ANGEL. The Day of Judgment is not the end of the world, but the end of its childhood and the beginning of its responsible maturity. So now you know; and my business with you is ended. [*He rises*].

[825]

Is there any way of getting out on the roof of this house?

SIR CHARLES [*rising*] Certainly: it is a flat roof where we often sit. [*He leads the way to the house*].

KANCHIN. In theory.

JANGA. In fact we never sit there.

THE ANGEL. That does not matter. All I want is a parapet to take off from. Like the albatross, I cannot rise from the ground without great difficulty. An angel is far from being the perfect organism you imagine. There is always something better.

VASHTI. Excelsior.

ALL FOUR [*rising and singing vociferously*] Eck-cel-see-orr! Eck-cel-see-or!

THE ANGEL [*putting his fingers in his ears*] Please, no. In heaven we are tired of singing. It is not done now. [*He follows Sir Charles out*].

KANCHIN. Lets see him take off.

The four rush up the garden and look up at the roof. The others rise and watch.

JANGA [*calling up*] Start into the wind, old man. Spring off hard, from the ball of the foot. Dont fall on us.

KANCHIN. Oopsh! Off he goes.

The beating of the angel's wings is heard.

VASHTI. He makes a noise like a vacuum cleaner.

MAYA [*wafting kisses*] Goodbye, silly old Excelsior.

The noise stops.

JANGA. His wings have stopped beating. He is soaring up the wind.

KANCHIN. He is getting smaller and smaller. His speed must be terrific.

MAYA. He is too small for an albatross.

VASHTI. He is smaller than a canary.

KANCHIN. He is out of sight.

MAYA. There! One last glint of the sun on his wings. He is gone.

The four troop back and resume their seats. The others sit as before, except that Iddy deserts Prola and sits on the well parapet. Sir Charles returns from the house with a batch of wireless messages in his hand.

SIR CHARLES [*sitting in his former place*] Well, my dears: the Judgment Day is over, it seems.

IDDY. I cant believe it was really the Judgment Day.

PRA. Why?

IDDY. Well, I thought some special notice would have been taken of the clergy. Reserved seats or something like that. But he treated me as if I were only the organ blower.

SIR CHARLES. There are such a lot of priests in the world, Iddy. It would be impossible to reserve seats for them all.

IDDY. Oh, I meant only the clergy of the Church of England, of course.

MRS HYERING. What I cant get over is their sending along just one angel to judge us, as if we didnt matter.

LADY FARWATERS. He actually went away and forgot to judge us.

PRA. I am not so sure of that.

IDDY. Well, are we sheep or goats? tell me that.

MAYA. You are a sheep, Iddy, my sweet: there can be no doubt about that.

IDDY [*bursting into tears*] I love you, Maya; and you always say unkind things to me. [*He rushes away through the garden, sobbing*].

MAYA. Oh, poor Iddy! I'll go and soothe him with a thousand kisses. [*She runs after him*].

HYERING [*to Sir Charles*] What have you got there? Any news from London?

SIR CHARLES. Yes: Exchange Telegraph and Reuters. Copyright reserved.

HYERING. Lets have it.

SIR CHARLES [*reading*] "Judgment Day. Widespread incredulity as to anything having really happened. Reported appearance of angels in several quarters generally disbelieved. Several witnesses are qualifying or withdrawing their statements in deference to the prevailing scepticism."

HYERING. We shall have to be careful too, Charles. Who will believe us if we tell this yarn of an angel flying down into the garden?

SIR CHARLES. I suppose so. I never thought of it in that way. Still, listen to this. [*Reading*] "Policeman who attempted to arrest angel in Leicester Square removed to mental hospital. Church Assembly at Lambeth Palace decides by a large majority that there has been a Visitation. Dissenting minority, led by the Bishop of Edgbaston, denounces the reports as nonsense that would not impose even on the Society for Psychical Research. His Holiness the Pope warns Christendom that supernatural communications reaching the earth otherwise than through the Church are contrary to the Catholic faith, and, if authentic, must be regarded as demoniacal. Cabinet hastily summoned to discuss the situation. Prime Minister, speaking in emergency meeting at the Mansion House, declares that reports of utterances by angels are hopelessly contradictory, and that alleged verbatim reports by shorthand writers contain vulgar expressions. The Government could not in any case allow the British Empire to be placed in the position of being judged by a commission of a few angels instead of by direct divine authority. Such a slight to the flag would never be tolerated by Englishmen; and the Cabinet was unanimous in refusing to believe that such an outrage had occurred. The Prime Minister's speech was received with thunderous applause, the audience rising spontaneously to sing the National Anthem."

PRA. They would.

SIR CHARLES [*looking at another paper*] Hallo! Whats this? [*Reading*] "Later. During the singing of the second verse of the National Anthem at the Mansion House the proceedings were interrupted by the appearance of an angel with a flaming sword who demanded truculently what they meant by ordering God about to do their dirty political work. He was accompanied by unruly cherubim who floated about tweaking the Lord Mayor's nose, pouring ink into the Prime Minister's hat, and singing derisively Con-Found their Poll-It-Ticks. Part of the audience fell to their knees, repeating the Confession. Others rushed frantically to the doors. Two Salvation lasses stemmed the rush, at great personal danger to themselves, by standing in the doorway and singing Let Angels Prostrate Fall. Order was restored by the Prime Minister, who offered the angel an unreserved apology and an undertaking that the offending verse should not be sung again. A new one is to be provided by the Poet Laureate. The Premier's last words were lost through the misconduct of a cherub who butted him violently in the solar plexus. A wave of the angel's sword and a terrible thunderclap then threw the entire audience prone to the floor. When they rose to their feet the angel and the cherubs had disappeared."

HYERING. Oh, an invention. We cant swallow those cherubs, really.

SIR CHARLES [*taking up a third paper*] This sounds a little more plausible. "A representative of the Fascist Press has called at the War Office to ask whether any steps are being taken to defend the right of public meeting, and to deal with the angelic peril. The Commander-in-Chief, whilst denying that there is any such thing as a right of public meeting by undisciplined and irresponsible persons, declared that the Mansion House incident was quite incomprehensible to him, as he could not conceive how the only really practical part of the National Anthem could give any offence. Any suggestion that it was not the plain duty of the Ruler of the Universe to confound England's enemies could only lead to widespread atheism. The First Lord of the Admiralty, interviewed last night, said that he could not make head or tail of the reports, but that he could assure the public that whatever had really happened, the British Navy would not take it lying down. Later. A Hyde Park orator was thrown into the Serpentine for saying that the British Empire was not the only pebble on the beach. He has been fined thirty shillings for being in unlawful possession of a life buoy, the property of the Royal Humane Society. There can be no doubt that the disparaging remarks and assumed superiority of the angels has started a wave of patriotism throughout the country which is bound to lead to action of some sort."

PRA. Which means, if it means anything, that England's next war will be a war with heaven.

PROLA. Nothing new in that. England has been at war with heaven for many a long year.

VASHTI [*inspired*] The most splendid of all her wars!

KANCHIN. The last conquest left to her to achieve!

VASHTI. To overcome the angels!

JANGA. To plant the flag of England on the ramparts of Heaven itself! that is the final glory.

PROLA. Oh go away, children: go away. Now that

Maya has gone to kiss somebody, there is nothing left for you to glorify but suicide.

VASHTI [*rising*] I rebel.

JANGA [*rising*] We rebel against Prola, the goddess empress.

KANCHIN [*rising*] Prola has turned back from the forlorn hope.

VASHTI. Prola is a coward. She fears defeat and death.

KANCHIN. Without death there can be no heroism.

JANGA. Without faith unto death there can be no faith.

VASHTI. Prola has failed us in the great Day of Judgment.

KANCHIN. Our souls have been called to their final account.

ALL THREE [*marching away through the garden*] Guilty, Prola: guilty. Adieu, Prola!

PROLA. Oh, adieu until you all want your tea.

PRA. We have taught them everything except common sense.

LADY FARWATERS. We have taught them everything except how to work for their daily bread instead of praying for it.

PROLA. It is dangerous to educate fools.

PRA. It is still more dangerous to leave them uneducated.

MRS HYERING. There just shouldnt be any fools. They wernt born fools: we made fools of them.

PRA. We must stop making fools.

Iddy returns alone. Something strange has happened to him. He stares at them and tries to speak; but no sound comes from his lips.

LADY FARWATERS. What on earth is the matter with you, Iddy? Have you been drinking?

IDDY [*in a ghastly voice*] Maya.

PROLA. What has happened to Maya?

IDDY. Heaven and earth shall pass away; but I shall not pass away. That is what she said. And then there was nothing in my arms. Nothing. Nothing in my arms. Heaven and earth would pass away; but the love of Maya would never pass away. And there was nothing. [*He collapses on the well parapet, overcome, not in tears but in a profound awe*].

PRA. Do you mean that she died in your arms?

IDDY. Died? No. I tell you there was nothing. Dont you understand? Where she had just been there was nothing. There never had been anything.

PROLA. And the others? Quick, Pra: go and find the others.

PRA. What others?

PROLA. The other three: our children. I forget their names.

IDDY. They said "Our names shall live forever." What were their names?

HYERING. They have gone clean out of my head.

SIR CHARLES. Most extraordinary. I cant for the life of me remember. How many of them did you say there were, Prola?

PROLA. Four. Or was it four hundred?

IDDY. There were four. Their names were Love, Pride, Heroism and Empire. Love's pet name was Maya. I loved Maya. I loved them all; but it was through love of Maya that I loved them. I held Maya in my arms. She promised to endure for ever; and suddenly there was nothing in my arms. I have searched for the others; but she and they were one: I found nothing. It is the Judgment.

PROLA. Has she left a great void in your heart, Iddy, that girl who turned to nothing in your arms?

IDDY. No. This is a beautiful climate; and you are beautiful people; but you are not real to me; and the sun here is not what it is in the valley of the Severn. I am glad I am an English clergyman. A village and a cottage: a garden and a church: these things will not turn to nothing. I shall be content with my little black coat and my little white collar and my little treasure of words spoken by my Lord Jesus. Blessed be the name of the Lord: I shall not forget it as I shall forget Maya's. [*He goes out seaward like a man in a trance*].

LADY FARWATERS [*troubled, half rising*] But, Iddy,—

PROLA. Let him go. The pigeon knows its way home.

Lady Farwaters sinks back into her seat. There is a moment of rather solemn silence. **Then** *the telephone rings.*

PRA [*taking up the receiver*] Yes? . . . What? . . . Yes: amazing news: we know all about that. What is the latest? . . . Yes: "plot to destroy our most valuable citizens": I got that; but what was the first word? What plot? . . . Oh, Russian plot. Rubbish! havnt you some sensible reports? . . . Special news broadcast just coming in? . . . Good: put me on to it. [*To the others*] Im through to London Regional. Listen: I'll repeat it as it comes. [*He echoes the news*] Extraordinary disappearances. Indescribable panic. Stock Exchange closes: only two members left. House of Commons decimated: only fourteen members to be found: none of Cabinet rank. House of Lords still musters fifty members; but not one of them has ever attended a meeting of the Chamber. Mayfair a desert: six hotels left without a single guest. Fresh disappearances. Crowded intercession service at Westminster Abbey brought to a close by disappearance of the congregation at such a rate that the rest

[833]

fled leaving the dean preaching to the choir. At the Royal Institution Sir Ruthless Bonehead, Egregious Professor of Mechanistic Biology to the Rockefeller Foundation, drew a crowded audience to hear his address on "Whither have they gone?" He disappeared as he opened his mouth to speak. Noted Cambridge professor suggests that what is happening is a weeding-out of nonentities. He has been deprived of his Chair; and The Times, in a leading article, points out that the extreme gravity of the situation lies in the fact that not only is it our most important people who are vanishing, but that it is the most unquestionably useful and popular professions that are most heavily attacked, the medical profession having disappeared almost en bloc, whilst the lawyers and clergy are comparatively immune. A situation of terrible suspense has been created everywhere. Happy husbands and fathers disappear from the family dinner with the soup. Several popular leaders of fashion and famous beauties, after ringing their bells for their maids, have been found non-existent when the bells were answered. More than a million persons have disappeared in the act of reading novels. The Morning Post contains an eloquent protest by Lady Gushing, president of the Titled Ladies' League of Social Service, on the inequality of sacrifice as between the west end and the east, where casualties have been comparatively few. Lady Gushing has since disappeared. There is general agreement that our losses are irreparable, though their bad effects are as yet unfelt. But before long—

HYERING. Whats the use of going on, Pra? The angels are weeding the garden. The useless people, the mischievous people, the selfish somebodies and the noisy nobodies, are dissolving into space, which is the simplest form of matter. We here are awaiting our own doom.

MRS HYERING. What was it the angel said?

PROLA. The lives which have no use, no meaning, no purpose, will fade out. We shall have to justify our existences or perish. We shall live under a constant sense of that responsibility. If the angels fail us we shall set up tribunals of our own from which worthless people will not come out alive. When men no longer fear the judgment of God, they must learn to judge themselves.

SIR CHARLES. I seem to remember somebody saying "Judge not, that ye be not judged."

PROLA. That means "Punish not, that ye be not punished." This is not punishment, but judgment.

HYERING. What is judgment?

PRA. Judgment is valuation. Civilizations live by their valuations. If the valuations are false, the civilization perishes as all the ancient ones we know of did. We are not being punished today: we are being valued. That is the Newest Dispensation.

LADY FARWATERS. I feel an absolute conviction that I shall not disappear and that Charles will not disappear. We have done some queer things here in the east perhaps; but at bottom we are comfortable commonsense probable English people; and we shall not do anything so improbable as disappear.

SIR CHARLES [to his wife] Do not tempt the angels, my dear. Remember: you used to distribute tracts before you met Pra.

LADY FARWATERS. Ssh-sh-sh! Dont remind the angels of those tracts.

HYERING [rising] Look here. I have an uneasy feeling that we'd better get back to our work. I feel pretty sure that we shant disappear as long as we're doing something useful; but if we only sit here talking, either we shall disappear or the people who are listening to us will. What we have learnt here today is that the day of judgment is not the end of the world but the beginning of real human responsibility. Charles and I have still our duties: the Unexpected Islands have to be Governed today just as they had to be yesterday. Sally: if you have given your orders for the housework today, go and cook something or sew something or tidy up the books. Come on, Charles. Lets get to work. [*He goes into the house*].

SIR CHARLES [*to his wife, rising*] You might take a turn in the garden, dear: gardening is the only unquestionably useful job. [*He follows Hyering into the house*].

LADY FARWATERS [*rising*] Prola: shall I bring you some knitting to occupy you?

PROLA. No, thank you. I have some thinking to do.

LADY FARWATERS. Well, dear: I hope that will count as work. I shall feel safer with my gardening basket. [*She goes into the house*].

MRS HYERING. J'you think itll be all right if I go and do some crossword puzzles? It cultivates the mind so, dont you think?

PROLA. Does it? Well, do the puzzles and see what will happen. Let life come to you. Goodbye.

MRS HYERING [*alarmed*] Why do you say goodbye? Do you think I am going to disappear?

PROLA. Possibly. Or possibly *I* may.

MRS HYERING. Oh then for heaven's sake dont do it in my presence. Wait til Ive gone.

She scuttles up the steps into the house, leaving Prola and Pra alone together.

PRA. Tell me the truth, Prola. Are you waiting for me to disappear? Do you feel that you can do better without me? Have you always felt that you could do better without me?

PROLA. That is a murderer's thought. Have you ever let yourself think it? How often have you said to yourself "I could do better alone, or with another woman"?

PRA. Fairly often, my dear, when we were younger. But I did not murder you. Thats the answer. And you?

PROLA. All that stuff belongs to the past: to the childhood of our marriage. We have now grown together until we are each of us a part of the other. I no longer think of you as a separate possibility.

PRA. I know. I am part of the furniture of your house. I am a matter of course. But was I always that? Was I that in the childhood of our marriage?

PROLA. You are still young enough and manlike enough to ask mischievous questions.

PRA. No matter: we shall both disappear presently; and I have still some curiosity left. Did you ever really care for me? I know I began as a passion and have ended as a habit, like all husbands; but outside that routine there is a life of the intellect that is quite independent of it. What have I been to you in that life? A help or a hindrance?

PROLA. Pra: I always knew from the very beginning that you were an extraordinarily clever fool.

PRA. Good. That is exactly what I am.

PROLA. But I knew also that nobody but a fool would be frivolous enough to join me in doing all the mad things I wanted to do. And no ordinary fool would have been subtle enough to understand me, nor clever enough to keep off the rocks of social ruin. Ive grown fond enough of you for all practical purposes;—

PRA. Thank you.

PROLA. —but Ive never allowed you or any other man to cut me off my own stem and make me a parasite on his. That sort of love and sacrifice is not the consummation of a capable woman's existence: it is the temptation she must resist at all costs.

PRA. That temptation lies in the man's path too. The worst sacrifices I have seen have been those of men's highest careers to women's vulgarities and follies.

PROLA. Well, we two have no reproaches and no regrets on that score.

PRA. No. We are awaiting judgment here quite simply as a union of a madwoman with a fool.

PROLA. Who thought they had created four wonderful children. And who are now brought to judgment and convicted of having created nothing. We have only repeated the story of Helen and Faust and their beautiful child Euphorion. Euphorion also vanished, in his highest flight.

PRA. Yes; but Helen was a dream. You are not a dream. The children did not vanish like Euphorion in their infancy. They grew up to bore me more intensely than I have ever been bored by any other set of human creatures. Come, confess: did they not bore you?

PROLA. Have I denied it? Of course they bored me. They must have bored one another terribly in spite of all their dressing up and pretending that their fairyland was real. How they must have envied the gardener's boy his high spirits!

PRA. The coming race will not be like them. Meanwhile we are face to face with the fact that we two have made a precious mess of our job of producing the coming race by a mixture of east and west. We are failures. We shall disappear.

PROLA. I do not feel like that. I feel like the leader of

a cavalry charge whose horse has been shot through the head and dropped dead under him. Well, a dead hobby horse is not the end of the world. Remember: we are in the Unexpected Isles; and in the Unexpected Isles all plans fail. So much the better: plans are only jigsaw puzzles: one gets tired of them long before one can piece them together. There are still a million lives beyond all the Utopias and the Millenniums and the rest of the jigsaw puzzles: I am a woman and I know it. Let men despair and become cynics and pessimists because in the Unexpected Isles all their little plans fail: women will never let go their hold on life. We are not here to fulfil prophecies and fit ourselves into puzzles, but to wrestle with life as it comes. And it never comes as we expect it to come.

PRA. It comes like a thief in the night.

PROLA. Or like a lover. Never will Prola go back to the Country of the Expected.

PRA. There is no Country of the Expected. The Unexpected Isles are the whole world.

PROLA. Yes, if our fools only had vision enough to see that. I tell you this is a world of miracles, not of jigsaw puzzles. For me every day must have its miracle, and no child be born like any child that ever was born before. And to witness this miracle of the children I will abide the uttermost evil and carry through it the seed of the uttermost good.

PRA. Then I, Pra, must continue to strive for more knowledge and more power, though the new knowledge always contradicts the old, and the new power is the destruction of the fools who misuse it.

PROLA. We shall plan commonwealths when our empires have brought us to the brink of destruction; but our plans will still lead us to the Unexpected

Isles. We shall make wars because only under the strain of war are we capable of changing the world; but the changes our wars will make will never be the changes we intended them to make. We shall clamor for security like frightened children; but in the Unexpected Isles there is no security; and the future is to those who prefer surprise and wonder to security. I, Prola, shall live and grow because surprise and wonder are the very breath of my being, and routine is death to me. Let every day be a day of wonder for me and I shall not fear the Day of Judgment. [*She is interrupted by a roll of thunder*]. Be silent: you cannot frighten Prola with stage thunder. The fountain of life is within me.

PRA. But you have given the key of it to me, the Man.

PROLA. Yes: I need you and you need me. Life needs us both.

PRA. All hail, then, the life to come!

PROLA. All Hail. Let it come.

They pat hands eastern fashion.

The Simple Truth of the Matter

(A reply to the assertion of Joseph Wood Krutch in *The Nation*, New York, 6 March 1935, that Shaw's recent plays were merely vaudeville, quite devoid of meaning. *Malvern Festival Book*, 1935)

Mr Krutch's article comes to me as a very welcome surprise from America. He found my play entertaining, and said so. Only those who have read the torrent of abuse with which the New York Press assailed and overwhelmed The Simpleton can appreciate Mr Krutch's courage in confessing that he enjoyed himself when sitting at it. The kindest thing his colleagues had to say was a description of me as "a dignified monkey shying coco-nuts at a bewildered public." It was really nice to call me dignified, though how a monkey shying coco-nuts can preserve the dignity of Jove hurling thunderbolts is beyond even my ingenuity as a stage-manager. Still, the softening adjective was kindly meant; and I was duly touched by it.

My heart goes out specially to Mr Krutch when he says, "I insist that Mr Shaw's text is diverting; and the only way in which an intelligent spectator can prevent himself from enjoying it is by doing what intelligent spectators at Shaw plays have always been told to do: namely, try to discover its serious meaning." This is excellent. People come to a play as they come to all forms of art, to have their minds agreeably occupied in their hours of leisure. That is what they pay their money for; and my first duty as an honest theatrical tradesman is to give them their money's worth. As to their being "told to" look further and bother themselves with speculations about myself,

I can only say that I object to it strenuously, and hereby curse to all eternity the officious duffers who do the telling. If I have ulterior designs, if in occupying the playgoer's mind agreeably I take advantage of his preoccupation to extirpate his worn-out convictions and substitute fresh ones: in short, if I not only occupy his mind but change it, then the last thing I desire is that he should be conscious of the operation. The pickpocket does not want to be caught in the act. The burglar, however proud of his skill and daring, does not whistle for the police. I like my patients to leave the hospital without a suspicion that they have been operated on and are leaving it with a new set of glands.

But what takes place in a theatre is not always a simple matter of you please me and I'll pay you. If the playgoer is to keep up his (or her) power of enjoyment he must not stick in the same groove all his life. He must be prepared to come across from time to time a sort of play that quite upsets his notions of what a play should be. He may not like it at first; but if it takes a grip of the stage, he must go on enduring it until he does like it, or else give up going to the theatre and be derided by the young as a back number. When a play or a picture or a musical composition or a piece of sculpture is disagreeable at first sight, it is a mistake to run away from it, and revile its author for ever after. Of course, if there is nothing new in it, and its disagreeableness is due to mere folly and incompetence on the part of its maker, there is nothing more to be said. But if he is evidently a capable and skilled workman, and therefore must have made his work what it is on purpose and actually liked it, the chances are that you will like it too when you get used to it; for as he is a human being, built just as you are, his peculiar taste is a human taste and may therefore be acquired by any other human being at the same stage of civilized development. I can remember when Wagner's music was generally considered horribly discordant and quite destitute of melody. I can remember when Ibsen was denounced as an obscene and malignant lunatic. Plays of my own, popular enough now, were forbidden by the censorship for many years; and even today, when I am 79, the New York critics can see nothing in my latest play but the antics of a monkey. But they will get used to it in time; and when they shriek out their dislike of my next play, they will deplore it as an ignominious fall from the heights on which I produced that masterpiece, The Simpleton. All my plays are masterpieces except the last one. They always were. The donkey, no matter how fast he scampers, never overtakes the carrot.

There is, in fact, a force in nature which impels all born leaders in the arts continually to extend the scope of their works beyond the established and familiar form and content of such things. And, what is less often recognized, this same force impels audiences to come and endure this pioneering until they first discover that their old favorites have become stale and unbearable, and then that the new ones are not half bad when you get the hang of them.

As Malvern is, I hope, a much more cultivated centre of culture than New York, I have no hesitation in introducing The Simpleton to the British public at the Malvern Festival, though no doubt the London critics will make all their old mistakes about it as if they had not made them every time before. I can assure Mr Krutch that there has not been, as he suggests, any reckless new departure on my part: I have written The Simpleton exactly as I have written all my earlier plays, just as it came into my head. Naturally, it is more far-fetched than its forerunners, because I have already written plays on all the subjects that lay near to hand. I cannot go on repeating Back to Methuselah and Saint Joan, as musical comedy librettists go on repeating their old plots with nothing changed but the names and the tunes. I must go ever further and further afield except when I am coming nearer and nearer home; and it happens that in The Simpleton I am going further and further afield. And if you don't like it you must lump it—for a while—until you get used to the taste.

What I miss in Mr Krutch is a proper respect for the Apocalypse. As a child I was taught to fear the Day of Judgment, which was presented to my young imagination in so clear a fashion that once when I dreamt of it, I thought I had stepped into our garden in the middle of the night and seen above the gloom of the garden wall a great silver radiance in the sky, and in the middle of it a black equestrian statue like that of King William in College Green, Dublin, whom I immediately identified with God, come to judge the world. I did not call on the mountains to hide me; but I slipped back very quickly into the house and fastened the door noiselessly before the all-seeing eye lighted on me; for you cannot get it out of the head of a Christian child, or a Christian adult either, that God cannot be dodged and cheated like an earthly father.

That vision of judgment of mine was not more unlike any conceivable possible event than the great fresco by Michael Angelo in the Sistine Chapel in Rome, or that other one by Tintoretto in the ducal palace in Venice, or than the more compact painting by Albrecht Dürer. Such visions and pictures do not impose on the children in this age of science; and I should as soon think of dramatizing Jack and the Beanstalk as Michael Angelo's picture. But in rejecting all this imagery, we are apt to make the usual blunder of emptying the baby out with the bath. By all means dismiss the scenes painted by Tintoretto, Albrecht Dürer, and the rest as having no more reality than a Red Lion on a signboard. Cancel the authority of the Book of Revelation as the hallucinations of a drug addict which should never have been included in the canon. But do not think you have got rid of the idea of a judgment to which all human lives must finally come, and without which life has no meaning. On the contrary, the burning up of the old stage scenery and the exorcism of the old spectres only brings into clearer reality the need for justifying one's existence as well as merely enjoying or suffering it. The question "What good are you?" cannot be disposed of by the simple retort, "Mind your own business!" Even if it were not everybody's business in a civilized society, it is a question which people with properly trained social consciences cannot help asking themselves. In Russia, if the answer is not satisfactory, they occasionally go so far as to shoot you.

You may now declare that if this terrifying judgment is the theme of The Simpleton, you will take care to keep away from it. But you need not fear: you can depend on me to get plenty of fun out of the most dismal subjects and to improve your mind into the bargain. Even if you have to see beauty, chivalry, military heroism, and patriotic madness vanish like the phantasms of a long delirium, they will not pass away in a horror of September massacres, but in a very matter-of-fact and quite amusing manner. So take your courage in both hands, and face its first performance in England like a Briton.

One more word to Mr Krutch. I find it hard to forgive him for saying that I announced, in my last Malvern play, Too True to be Good, that world affairs are now irremediable, and that mankind is damned beyond hope and redemption. I affirm, on the contrary, that never before during my lifetime has the lot of mankind seemed more hopeful, and the beginnings of a new civilization more advanced. The despair of the shell-shocked young gentleman-burglar-clergyman who made such a pitiful attempt to be happy by spending a lump of unearned money, is not my despair, though I share his opinion of the utter unsatisfactoriness of that popular receipt for a good life. I made him a good preacher to warn the world against mere fluency, and the result was that his talking took Mr Krutch in. He must be more careful next time.

The Millionairess

WITH

Preface on Bosses

Composition begun 27 April 1934; completed 10 May 1934. First published in German translation, as *Die Millionärin*, 1936 [1935]. First published in English in *The Simpleton, The Six, and The Millionairess*, 1936. First presented in German by the Burgtheater at the Akademie Theater, Vienna, on 4 January 1936. First presented in English by the McMahon Players at the King's Theatre, Melbourne, on 7 March 1936. First presented in England by the Matthew Forsyth Repertory Company at the De La Warr Pavilion, Bexhill-on-Sea, on 17 November 1936. First professional West End production at the New Theatre, London, on 27 June 1952.

Julius Sagamore   *Campbell Cotts*
Epifania Ognisanti di Parerga Fitzfassenden
    Katharine Hepburn
Alastair Fitzfassenden   *Peter Dynley*
Patricia Smith   *Meriel Forbes*
Adrian Blenderbland   *Cyril Ritchard*
The Doctor   *Robert Helpmann*
The Man (Joe)   *Bertram Shuttleworth*
The Woman (His Wife)   *Nora Nicholson*
Hotel Manager   *Vernon Greeves*

Period—The Present

ACT I *Mr Julius Sagamore's Office in Lincoln's Inn Fields. A Spring Morning*
ACT II *The Coffee-room of the Pig and Whistle, a Riverside Inn. That Evening*
ACT III *A Basement Sweatshop in the Commercial Road. The Following Morning*
ACT IV *The Pig and Whistle (now the Cardinal's Hat). Five Months Later*

[848]

Preface on Bosses

Though this play of The Millionairess does not pretend to be anything more than a comedy of humorous and curious contemporary characters such as Ben Jonson might write were he alive now, yet it raises a question that has troubled human life and moulded human society since the creation.

The law is equal before all of us; but we are not all equal before the law. Virtually there is one law for the · rich and another for the poor, one law for the cunning and another for the simple, one law for the forceful and another for the feeble, one law for the ignorant and another for the learned, one law for the brave and another for the timid, and within family limits one law for the parent and no law at all for the child.

In the humblest cabin that contains a family you may find a *maitresse femme* who rules in the household by a sort of divine right. She may rule amiably by being able to think more quickly and see further than the others, or she may be a tyrant ruling violently by intensity of will and ruthless egotism. She may be a grandmother and she may be a girl. But the others find they are unable to resist her. Often of course the domestic tyrant is a man; but the phenomenon is not so remarkable in his case, as he is by convention the master and lawgiver of the hearthstone.

In every business street you will find a shopkeeper who is always in difficulties and ends his business adventures in the bankruptcy court. Hard by you will find another shopkeeper, with no greater advantages to start with, or possibly less, who makes larger and larger profits, and inspires more and more confidence in his banker, until he ends as the millionaire head of a giant multiple shop.

How does the captain of a pirate ship obtain his position and maintain his authority over a crew of scoundrels who are all, like himself, outside the law? How does an obscure village priest, the son of humble fisherfolk, come to wear the triple crown and sit in the papal chair? How do common soldiers become Kings, Shahs, and Dictators? Why does a hereditary peer find that he is a nonentity in a grand house organized and ruled by his butler?

Questions like these force themselves on us so continually and ruthlessly that many turn in despair from Socialism and political reform on the ground that to abolish all the institutional tyrannies would only deliver the country helplessly into the hands of the born bosses. A king, a prelate, a squire, a capitalist, a justice of the peace may be a good kind Christian soul, owing his position, as most of us do, to being the son of his father; but a born boss is one who rides roughshod over us by some mysterious power that separates him from our species and makes us fear him: that is, hate him.

What is to be done with that section of the possessors of specific talents whose talent is for moneymaking? History and daily experience teach us that if the world does not devise some plan of ruling them, they will rule the world. Now it is not desirable that they should rule the world; for the secret of moneymaking is to care for nothing else and to work at nothing else; and as the world's welfare depends on operations by which no individual can make money, whilst its ruin by war and drink and disease and drugs and debauchery is enormously profitable to moneymakers, the supremacy of the moneymaker is the destruction of the State. A society which depends on the incentive of private profit is doomed.

And what about ambitious people who possess commanding business ability or military genius or both? They are irresistible unless they are restrained by law; for ordinary individuals are helpless in their hands. Are they to be the masters of society or its servants?

What should the nineteenth century have done in its youth with Rothschild and Napoleon? What is the United States to do with its money kings and bosses? What are we to do with ours? How is the mediocre private citizen to hold his own with the able bullies and masterful women who establish family despotisms, school despotisms, office despotisms, religious despotisms in their little circles all over the country? Our boasted political liberties are a mockery to the subjects of such despotisms. They may work well when the despot is benevolent; but they are worse than any political tyranny in the selfish cases.

It is much more difficult to attack a personal despotism than an institutional one. Monarchs can be abolished: they have been abolished in all directions during the last century and a half, with the result, however, of sometimes replacing a personally amiable and harmless monarch, reigning under strict constitutional and traditional restraints, by energetic dictators and presidents who, having made hay of constitutions and traditions, are under no restraints at all. A hereditary monarch, on the throne because he is the son of his father, may be a normal person, amenable to reasonable advice from his councils, and exercising no authority except that conferred on him (or her) by the Constitution. Behead him, as we beheaded our Charles, or the French their Louis, and the born despot Cromwell or Napoleon (I purposely avoid glaring contemporary examples because I am not quite sure where they will be by the time this book is published) takes his place. The same mysterious personal force that makes the household tyrant, the school tyrant, the office tyrant, the brigand chief and the pirate captain, brings the born boss to the top by gravitation that ordinary people cannot resist.

The successful usurpers of thrones are not the worst cases. The political usurper may be an infernal scoundrel, ruthless in murder, treachery, and torture; but once his ambition is achieved and he has to rule a nation, the magnitude and difficulty of his job, and the knowledge that if he makes a mess of it he will fall as suddenly as he has risen, will civilize him with a ruthlessness greater than his own. When Henry IV usurped the English crown he certainly did not intend to die of political overwork; but that is what happened to him. No political ruler could possibly be as wickedly selfish and cruel as the tyrant of a private house. Queen Elizabeth was a *maitresse femme;* but she could have had her own way much more completely as landlady of the Mermaid Tavern than she had as sovereign of England. Because Nero and Paul I of Russia could not be made to understand this, they were killed like mad dogs by their own courtiers. But our petty fireside tyrants are not killed. Christina of Sweden would not have had to abdicate if her realm had been a ten-roomed villa. Had Catherine II reigned over her husband only, she need not nor could not have had him murdered; but as Tsarina she was forced to liquidate poor Peter very much against her own easy good nature, which prevented her from scolding her maids properly.

Modern Liberal democracy claims unlimited opportunities for tyranny: qualification for rule by heredity and class narrows it and puts it in harness and blinkers. Especially does such democracy favour money rule. It is in fact not democracy at all, but unashamed plutocracy. And as the meanest creature can become rich if he devotes his life to it, and the people with wider and more generous interests become or remain poor with equal certainty, plutocracy is the very devil socially, because it creates a sort of Gresham law by which the baser human currency drives out the nobler coinage. This is quite different from the survival of the fittest in the contests of character and talent which are independent of money. If Moses is the only tribesman capable of making a code of laws, he inevitably becomes Lawgiver to all the tribes, and, equally inevitably, is forced to add to what he can understand of divine law a series of secular regulations designed to maintain his personal authority. If he finds that it is useless to expect the tribesmen to obey his laws as a matter of common sense, he must persuade them that his inspiration is the result of direct and miraculous communication with their deity. Moses and Mahomet and Joseph Smith the Mormon had to plead divine revelations to get them out of temporary and personal difficulties as well as out of eternal and impersonal ones. As long as an individual of their calibre remains the indispensable man (or woman) doing things that the common man can neither do without nor do for himself, he will be, up to a point, the master of the common man in spite of all the democratic fudge that may be advanced to the contrary.

Of course there are limits. He cannot go to the lengths at which the common man will believe him to be insane or impious: when measures of that complexion are necessary, as they very often are, he must either conceal them or mask them as follies of the sort the common man thinks splendid. If the ruler thinks it well to begin a world war he must persuade his people that it is a war to end war, and that the people he wants them to kill are diabolical scoundrels; and if he is forced to suspend hostilities for a while, and does so by a treaty which contains the seeds of half a dozen new wars and is impossible enough in its conditions to make its violation certain, he must create a general belief that it is a charter of eternal peace and a monument of retributive justice.

In this way the most honest ruler becomes a tyrant and a fabricator of legends and falsehoods, not out of any devilment in himself, but because those whom he rules do not understand his business, and, if they did, would not sacrifice their own immediate interests to the permanent interests of the nation or the world. In short, a ruler must not only make laws, and rule from day to day: he must, by school instruction and printed propaganda, create and maintain an artificial mentality which will endorse his proceedings and obey his authority. This mentality becomes what we call Conservatism; and the revolt against it when it is abused oppressively or becomes obsolete as social conditions change, is classed as sedition, and reviled as Radicalism, Anarchism, Bolshevism, or what you please.

When a mentality is created and a code imposed, the born ruler, the Moses or Lenin, is no longer indispensable: routine government by dunderheads becomes possible and in fact preferable as long as the routine is fairly appropriate to the current phase of social development. The assumption of the more advanced spirits that revolutionists are always right is as questionable as the conservative assumption that they are always wrong. The industrious dunderhead who always does what was done last time because he is incapable of conceiving anything better, makes the best routineer. This explains the enormous part played by dunderheads as such in the history of all nations, provoking repeated explanations of surprise at the littleness of the wisdom with which the world is governed.

But what of the ambitious usurper? the person who has a capacity for kingship but has no kingdom and must therefore acquire a readymade one which is getting along in its own way very well without him? It cannot be contended with any plausibility that William the Conqueror was indispensable in England: he wanted England and grabbed it. He did this by virtue of his personal qualities, entirely against the will of the people of England, who, as far as they were politically conscious at all, would have greatly preferred Harold. But William had all the qualities that make an individual irresistible: the physical strength and ferocity of a king of beasts, the political genius of a king of men, the strategic cunning and tactical gumption of a military genius; and nothing that France or England could say or do prevailed against him. What are we to do with such people?

When an established political routine breaks down and produces political chaos, a combination of personal ambition with military genius and political capacity in a single individual gives that individual his opportunity. Napoleon, if he had been born a century earlier, would have had no more chance of becoming emperor of the French than Marshal Saxe had of supplanting Louis XV. In spite of the French Revolution, he was a very ordinary snob in his eighteenth-century social outlook. His assumption of the imperial diadem, his ridiculous attempt to establish the little Buonaparte family on all the thrones under his control, his re-manufacture of a titular aristocracy to make a court for himself, his silly insistence on imperial etiquette when he was a dethroned and moribund prisoner in St Helena, shew that, for all his genius, he was and always had been behind the times. But he was for a time irresistible because, though he could fight battles on academic lines only, and was on that point a routineer soldier, he could play the war game on the established procedure so superbly that all the armies of Europe crumpled up before him. It was easy for anti-Bonapartist writers, from Taine to Mr H. G. Wells, to disparage him as a mere cad; but Goethe, who could face facts, and on occasion rub them in, said simply "You shake your chains in vain." Unfortunately for himself and Europe Napoleon was fundamentally a commonplace human fool. In spite of his early failure in the east he made a frightful draft on the manhood of France for his march to Moscow, only to hurry back leaving his legions dead in the snow, and thereafter go from disaster to disaster. Bernadotte, the lawyer's son who enlisted as a common soldier and ended unconquered on the throne of Sweden (his descendants still hold it), made a far better job of his affairs. When for the first time Napoleon came up against a really original commander at Waterloo, he still made all the textbook moves he had learnt at the military academy, and did not know when he was beaten until it was too late to do anything but run away. Instead of making for America at all hazards he threw himself on the magnanimity of the Prince Regent, who obviously could not have spared him even if he had wanted to. His attempt to wedge himself and his upstart family into the old dynasties by his divorce and his Austrian marriage ended in making him a notorious cuckold.

But the vulgarer fool and the paltrier snob you prove Napoleon to have been, the more alarming becomes the fact that this shabby-genteel Corsican subaltern (and a very unsatisfactory subaltern at that) dominated Europe for years, and placed on his own head the crown of Charlemagne. Is there really nothing to be done with such men but submit to them until, having risen by their specialities, they ruin themselves by their vulgarities?

It was easy for Napoleon to make a better job of restoring order after the French Revolution than Sieyès, who tried to do it by writing paper constitutions, or than a plucky bully like Barras, who cared for nothing except feathering his own nest. Any tidy and public spirited person could have done as much with the necessary prestige. Napoleon got that prestige by feeding the popular appetite for military glory. He could not create that natural appetite; but he could feed it by victories; and he could use all the devices of journalism and pageantry and patriotic braggadocio to make La Gloire glorious. And all this because, like William the Conqueror, he had the group of talents that make a successful general and democratic ruler. Had not the French Revolution so completely failed to produce a tolerable government to replace the monarchy it overthrew, and thereby reduced itself to desperation, Napoleon would have been only a famous general like Saxe or Wellington or Marlborough, who under similar circumstances could and indeed must have become kings if they had been ungovernable enough to desire it. Only the other day a man without any of the social advantages of these commanders made himself Shah of Iran.

Julius Cæsar and Cromwell also mounted on the débris of collapsing political systems; and both of them refused crowns. But no crown could have added to the power their military capacity gave them. Cæsar bribed enormously; but there were richer men than he in Rome to play that game. Only, they could not have won the battle of Pharsalia. Cromwell proved invincible in the field—such as it was.

It is not, however, these much hackneyed historical figures that trouble us now. Pharsalias and Dunbars and Waterloos are things of the past: battles nowadays last several months and then peter out on barbed wire under the fire of machine guns. Suppose Ludendorff had been a Napoleon, and Haig a Marlborough, Wellington, and Cromwell rolled into one, what more could they have done than either declare modern war impossible or else keep throwing masses of infantry in the old fashion against slaughtering machinery like pigs in Chicago? Napoleon's booklearnt tactics and the columns that won so many battles for him would have no more chance nowadays than the ragged Irish pikemen on Vinegar Hill; and Wellington's thin red line and his squares would have vanished in the fumes of T.N.T. on the Somme. "The Nelson touch" landed a section of the British fleet at the bottom of the Dardanelles. And yet this war, which, if it did not end civilized war (perhaps it did, by the way, though the War Office may not yet have realized it) at least made an end of the supremacy of the glory virtuoso who can play brilliant variations on the battle of Hastings, has been followed by such a group of upstart autocrats as the world had ceased to suppose possible. Mussolini, Hitler, Kemal and Riza Khan began in the ranks, and have no Marengos to their credit; yet there they are at the top!

Here again the circumstances gave the men their opportunity. Neither Mussolini nor Hitler could have achieved their present personal supremacy when I was born in the middle of the nineteenth century, because the prevailing mentality of that deluded time was still hopefully parliamentary. Democracy was a dream, an ideal. Everything would be well when all men had votes. Everything would be better than well when all women had votes. There was a great fear of public opinion because it was a dumb phantom which every statesman could identify with his own conscience and dread as the Nemesis of unscrupulous ambition. That was the golden age of democracy: the phantom was a real and beneficent force. Many delusions are. In those days even our Conservative rulers agreed that we were a liberty loving people: that, for instance, Englishmen would never tolerate compulsory military service as the slaves of foreign despots did.

It was part of the democratic dream that Parliament was an instrument for carrying out the wishes of the voters, absurdly called its constituents. And as, in the nineteenth century, it was still believed that British individual liberty forbad Parliament to do anything that it could possibly leave to private enterprise, Parliament was able to keep up its reputation by simply maintaining an effective police force and enforcing private contracts. Even Factory Acts and laws against adulteration and sweating were jealously resisted as interferences with the liberty of free Britons. If there was anything wrong, the remedy was an extension of the franchise. Like Hamlet, we lived on the chameleon's dish "air, promise crammed."

But you cannot create a mentality out of promises without having to face occasional demands for their materialization. The Treasury Bench was up for auction at every election, the bidding being in promises. The political parties, finding it much less troublesome to give the people votes than to carry out reforms, at last established adult suffrage.

The result was a colossal disappointment and disillusion. The phantom of Democracy, *alias* Public Opinion, which, acting as an artificial political conscience, had restrained Gladstone and Disraeli, vanished. The later parliamentary leaders soon learnt from experience that they might with perfect impunity tell the nation one thing on Tuesday and the opposite on Friday without anyone noticing the discrepancy. The donkey had overtaken the carrots at last; and instead of eating them he allowed them to be snatched away from him by any confidence trickster who told him to look up into the sky.

The diplomatists immediately indulged themselves with a prodigiously expensive war, after which the capitalist system, which had undertaken to find employment for everybody at subsistence wages, and which, though it had never fulfilled that undertaking, had at least found employment for enough of them to leave the rest too few to be dangerous, defaulted in respect of unprecedented millions of unemployed, who had to be bought off by doles administered with a meanness and cruelty which revived all the infamies of the Poor Law of a century ago (the days of Oliver Twist) and could not be administered in any kinder way without weakening the willingness of its recipients to prefer even the poorliest paid job to its humiliations.

The only way of escape was for the government to organize the labor of the unemployed for the supply of their own needs. But Parliament not only could not do this, but could and did prevent its being done. In vain did the voters use their votes to place a Labor

Government, with a Cabinet of Socialists, on the Treasury Bench. Parliament took these men, who had been intransigent Socialists and revolutionists all their lives, and reduced them to a condition of political helplessness in which they were indistinguishable except by name from the most reactionary members of the House of Lords or the military clubs. A Socialist Prime Minister, after trying for years to get the parliamentary car into gear for a move forward, and finding that though it would work easily and smoothly in neutral the only gear that would engage was the reverse gear (popularly called "the axe" because it could do nothing but cut down wages), first formed what he called a national government by a coalition of all parties, and then, having proved by this experiment that it did not make the smallest difference whether members of the Cabinet were the reddest of Bolsheviks or the bluest of Tories, made things easier by handing over his premiership to a colleague who, being a Conservative, and popular and amiable into the bargain, could steal a horse where a Socialist dare not look over a hedge. The voters rejected him at the next election; but he retained his membership of the Cabinet precisely as if he had been triumphantly returned. Bismarck could have done no more.

These events, helped by the terrific moral shock of war, and the subsequent exposure of the patriotic lying by which the workers of Europe had been provoked to slaughter one another, made an end of the nineteenth century democratic mentality. Parliament fell into contempt; ballot papers were less esteemed than toilet papers; the men from the trenches had no patience with the liberties that had not saved them from being driven like sheep to the shambles.

Of this change our parliamentarians and journalists had no suspicion. Creatures of habit, they went on as if nothing had occurred since Queen Victoria's death except a couple of extensions of the franchise and an epochmaking revolution in Russia which they poohpoohed as a transient outburst of hooliganism fomented by a few bloodthirsty scoundrels, exactly as the American revolution and the French revolution had been poohpoohed when they, too, were contemporary.

Here was clearly a big opportunity for a man psychologist enough to grasp the situation and bold enough to act on it. Such a man was Mussolini. He had become known as a journalist by championing the demobilized soldiers, who, after suffering all the horrors of the war, had returned to find that the men who had been kept at home in the factories comfortably earning good wages, had seized those factories according to the Syndicalist doctrine of "workers' control", and were wrecking them in their helpless ignorance of business. As one indignant master-Fascist said to me "They were listening to speeches round red flags and leaving the cows unmilked."

The demobilized fell on the Syndicalists with sticks and stones. Some, more merciful, only dosed them with castor oil. They carried Mussolini to Rome with a rush. This gave him the chance of making an irreparable mistake and spending the next fifteen years in prison. It seemed just the occasion for a grand appeal for liberty, for democracy, for a parliament in which the people were supreme: in short, for nineteenth century resurrection pie. Mussolini did not make that mistake. With inspired precision he denounced Liberty as a putrefying corpse. He declared that what people needed was not liberty but discipline, the sterner the better. He said that he would not tolerate Oppositions: he called for action and silence. The people, instead of being shocked like good Liberals, rose to him. He was able to organize a special constabulary who wore black shirts and applied the necessary coercion.

Such improvised bodies attracted young men of military tastes and old soldiers, inevitably including a percentage of ruffians and Sadists. This fringe of undesirables soon committed outrages and a couple of murders, whereupon all the Liberal newspapers in Europe shrieked with horror as if nothing else was happening in Italy. Mussolini refused to be turned aside from his work like a parliamentary man to discuss "incidents." All he said was "I take the responsibility for everything that has happened." When the Italian Liberals joined in the shrieking he seized the shriekers and transported them to the Lipari Isles. Parliament, openly flouted, chastised, and humiliated, could do nothing. The people were delighted; for that was just how they wanted to see Parliament treated. The doctrinaires of liberty fled to France and England, preferring them to Lipari, and wrote eloquent letters to the papers demanding whether every vestige of freedom, freedom of speech, freedom of the press, freedom of Parliament, was to be trampled under the heel of a ruthless dictator merely because the Italian trains were running punctually and travellers in Italy could depend on their luggage not being stolen without actually sitting on it. The English editors gave them plenty of space, and wrote sympathetic articles paraphrasing John Stuart Mill's Essay on Liberty. Mussolini, now Il Duce, never even looked round: he was busy sweeping up the elected municipalities, and replacing them with efficient commissioners of his own choice, who had to do their job or get out. The editors had finally to accord him a sort of Pragmatic Sanction by an admission that his plan worked better than the old plan; but they were still blind to the fact staring them in the face that Il Duce, knowing what the people wanted and giving it to them, was responding to the real democratic urge whilst the cold tealeaves of the nineteenth century were making them sick. It was evident that Mussolini was master of Italy as far as such mastership is possible; but what was not evident to Englishmen who had had their necks twisted the other way from their childhood was that even when he deliberately spat in the face of the League of Nations at Corfu, and defiantly asked the Powers whether they had anything to say about it, he was delighting his own people by the spectacle of a great Italian bullying the world, and getting away with it triumphantly. Parliaments are supposed to have their fingers always on the people's pulse and to respond to its slightest throb. Mussolini proved that parliaments have not the slightest notion of how the people are feeling, and that he being a good psychologist and a man of the people himself to boot, was a true organ of democracy.

I, being a bit of a psychologist myself, also understood the situation, and was immediately denounced by the refugees and their champions as an anti-democrat, a hero worshipper of tyrants, and all the rest of it.

Hitler's case was different; but he had only one quality in common with Il Duce: he knew what the victorious Allies would fight for and what they would only bluster about. They had already been forced to recognize that their demands for plunder had gone far beyond Germany's utmost resources. But there re-

mained the clauses of the Versailles treaty by which
Germany was to be kept in a condition of permanent,
decisive, and humiliating military inferiority to the
other Powers, and especially to France. Hitler was
political psychologist enough to know that the time
had arrived when it would be quite impossible for the
Allies to begin the war over again to enforce these
clauses. He saw his opportunity and took it. He violated the clauses, and declared that he was going to
go on violating them until a fully re-armed Germany
was on equal terms with the victors. He did not soften
his defiance by any word of argument or diplomacy.
He knew that his attitude was safe and sure of success;
and he took care to make it as defiant as that of Ajax
challenging the lightning. The Powers had either to
renew the war or tear up the impossible clauses with a
good grace. But they could not grasp the situation,
and went on nagging pitifully about the wickedness of
breaking a treaty. Hitler said that if they mentioned
that subject again Germany would withdraw from
the League of Nations and cut the Powers dead. He
bullied and snubbed as the man who understands a
situation can always bully and snub the nincompoops
who are only whining about it. He at once became a
popular idol, and had the regular executive forces so
completely devoted to him that he was able to disband
the brownshirted constabulary he had organized on
the Mussolini model. He met the conventional democratic challenge by plebiscites of ninety per cent in his
favor. The myopia of the Powers had put him in a
position so far stronger than Mussolini's that he was
able to kill seventy-seven of his most dangerous opponents at a blow and then justify himself completely
before an assembly fully as representative as the
British Parliament, the climax being his appointment

as absolute dictator in Germany for life, a stretch of
Cæsarism no nineteenth century Hohenzollern would
have dreamt of demanding.

Hitler was able to go further than Mussolini because
he had a defeated, plundered, humiliated nation to
rescue and restore, whereas Mussolini had only an
irritated but victorious one. He carried out a persecution of the Jews which went to the scandalous length
of outlawing, plundering, and exiling Albert Einstein,
a much greater man than any politician, but great in
such a manner that he was quite above the heads of
the masses and therefore so utterly powerless economically and militarily that he depended for his very existence on the culture and conscience of the rulers of
the earth. Hitler's throwing Einstein to the Antisemite
wolves was an appalling breach of cultural faith. It
raised the question which is the root question of this
preface: to wit, what safeguard have the weaponless
great against the great who have myrmidons at their
call? It is the most frightful betrayal of civilization
for the rulers who monopolize physical force to withhold their protection from the pioneers in thought.
Granted that they are sometimes forced to do it because intellectual advances may present themselves
as quackery, sedition, obscenity, or blasphemy, and
always present themselves as heresies. Had Einstein
been formally prosecuted and sentenced by the
German National Socialist State, as Galileo was prosecuted by the Church, for shaking the whole framework of established physical science by denying the
infallibility of Newton, introducing fantastic factors
into mathematics, destroying human faith in absolute
measurement, and playing an incomprehensible trick
with the sacred velocity of light, quite a strong case
could have been made out by the public prosecutor.

But to set the police on him because he was a Jew could be justified only on the ground that the Jews are the natural enemies of the rest of the human race, and that as a state of perpetual war necessarily exists between them any Gentile has the same reason for killing any Jew at sight as the Roman soldier had for killing Archimedes.

Now no doubt Jews are most obnoxious creatures. Any competent historian or psycho-analyst can bring a mass of incontrovertible evidence to prove that it would have been better for the world if the Jews had never existed. But I, as an Irishman, can, with patriotic relish, demonstrate the same of the English. Also of the Irish. If Herr Hitler would only consult the French and British newspapers and magazines of the latter half of 1914, he would learn that the Germans are a race of savage idolaters, murderers, liars, and fiends whose assumption of the human form is thinner than that of the wolf in Little Red Riding Hood.

We all live in glass houses. Is it wise to throw stones at the Jews? Is it wise to throw stones at all?

Herr Hitler is not only an Antisemite, but a believer in the possibility and desirability of a pure bred German race. I should like to ask him why. All Germans are not Mozarts, nor even Mendelssohns and Meyerbeers, both of whom, by the way, though exceptionally desirable Germans, were Jews. Surely the average German can be improved. I am told that children bred from Irish colleens and Chinese laundry-men are far superior to inbred Irish or Chinese. Herr Hitler is not a typical German. I should not be at all surprised if it were discovered that his very mixed blood (all our bloods today are hopelessly mixed) got fortified somewhere in the past by that of King David.

He cannot get over the fact that the lost tribes of Israel expose us all to the suspicion (sometimes, as in Abyssinia, to the boast) that we are those lost tribes, or at least that we must have absorbed them.

One of my guesses in this matter is that Herr Hitler in his youth was fascinated by Houston Chamberlain's Foundations of the XIX Century, an interesting book which at the time of its appearance I recommended everybody to read. Its ethnology was not wholly imaginary. A smattering of Mendelism is all that one needs to know that the eternal fusion of races does not always blend them. The Jews often throw up an apparently purebred Hittite or a pure-bred Philistine. The Germans throw up out-and-out blond beasts side by side with dark Saturnine types like the Führer himself. I am a blond, much less an antique Roman than a Dane. One of my sisters was a brunette: the other had hair of a flaming red seen only in the Scottish Highlands, to which my ancestry has been traced. All these types with which writers like Chamberlain play: the Teutons and Latins, the Apollonians and Dionysians, the Nordics and Southics, the Dominants and Recessives, have existed and keep cropping up as individuals, and exciting antipathies or affinities quite often enough to give substance to theories about them; but the notion that they can be segregated as races or species is bosh. We have nations with national characteristics (rapidly fading, by the way), national languages, and national customs. But they deteriorate without cross fertilization; and if Herr Hitler could put a stop to cross fertilization in Germany and produce a population of brainless Bismarcks Germany would be subjugated by cross-fertilized aliens, possibly by cosmopolitan Jews. There is more difference between a Catholic Bavarian and a

Lutheran Prussian, between a tall fair Saxon and a stocky Baltic Celt, than there is between a Frankfort Jew and a Frankfort Gentile. Even in Africa, where pink emigrants struggle with brown and black natives for possession of the land, and our Jamaican miscegenation shocks public sentiment, the sun sterilizes the pinks to such an extent that Cabinet ministers call for more emigration to maintain the pink population. They do not yet venture to suggest that the pinks had better darken their skins with a mixture of Bantu or Zulu blood; but that conclusion is obvious. In New Zealand, in Hawaii, there are pure-bred pinks and yellows; but there are hardly any pure-bred Maories or South Sea Islanders left. In Africa the intelligent pink native is a Fusionist as between Dutch and British stock. The intelligent Jew is a Fusionist as between Jew and Gentile stock, even when he is also a bit of a Zionist. Only the stupidest or craziest ultra-Nationalists believe the people corralled within the same political frontier are all exactly alike, and that they improve by continuous inbreeding.

Now Herr Hitler is not a stupid German. I therefore urge upon him that his Antisemitism and national exclusiveness must be pathological: a craze, a complex, a bee in his bonnet, a hole in his armor, a hitch in his statesmanship, one of those lesions which sometimes prove fatal. As it has no logical connection with Fascism or National Socialism, and has no effect on them except to bring them into disrepute, I doubt whether it can survive its momentary usefulness as an excuse for plundering raids and *coups d'état* against inconvenient Liberals or Marxists. A persecution is always a man hunt; and man hunting is not only a very horrible sport but socially a dangerous one, as it revives a primitive instinct incompatible with civilization: indeed civilization rests fundamentally on the compact that it shall be dropped.

And here comes the risk we run when we allow a dominant individual to become a despot. There is a story told of a pious man who was sustained through a lifetime of crushing misfortune by his steady belief that if he fought the good fight to the end he would at last stand in the presence of his God. In due course he died, and presented himself at the gates of heaven for his reward. St Peter, who was for some reason much worried, hastily admitted him and bade him go and enjoy himself. But the good man said that he did not want to enjoy himself: he wanted to stand in the presence of God. St Peter tried to evade the claim, dwelling on the other delights of heaven, coaxing, bullying, arguing. All in vain: he could not shake the claimant and could not deny his right. He sent for St Paul, who was as worried and as evasive as his colleague; but he also failed to induce the newcomer to forgo his promised privilege. At last they took him by the arms and led him to a mighty cathedral, where, entering by the west door, he saw the Ancient of Days seated in silent majesty on a throne in the choir. He sprang forward to prostrate himself at the divine feet, but was held back firmly by the apostles. "Be quiet" said St Paul. "He has gone mad; and we dont know what to do." "Dont tell anybody" added St Peter. And there the story ends.

But that is not how the story ends on earth. Make any common fellow an autocrat and at once you have the Beggar on Horseback riding to the devil. Even when, as the son of his father, he has been trained from infancy to behave well in harness and blinkers, he may go as mad sadistically as a Roman emperor or a Russian Tsar. But that is only the extreme case.

Uncommon people, promoted on their merits, are by no means wholly exempt from megalomania. Morris's simple and profound saying that "no man is good enough to be another man's master" holds good unless both master and man regard themselves as equally the fellow servants of God in States where God still reigns, or, in States where God is dead, as the subjects and agents of a political constitution applying humane principles which neither of them may violate. In that case autocrats are no longer autocrats. Failing any such religious or political creed all autocrats go more or less mad. That is a plain fact of political pathology.

Judged in this light our present predicament is lamentable. We no longer believe in the old "sanctions" (as they are called nowadays) of heaven and hell; and except in Russia there is not in force a single political constitution that enables and enjoins the citizen to earn his own living as a matter of elementary honesty, or that does not exalt vast personal riches and the organization of slaughter and conquest above all other conditions and activities. The financier and the soldier are the cocks of the walk; and democracy means that their parasites and worshippers carry all before them.

Thus when so many other tyrannies have been swept away by simple Liberalism, the tyranny of the talented individuals will remain. Again I ask what are we to do with them in self-defence? Mere liquidation would be disastrous, because at present only about five per cent of the population are capable of making decisions of any importance; and without many daily decisions civilization would go to pieces. The problem is how to make sure that the decisions shall be made in the general interest and not solely in the immediate personal interest of the decider. It was argued by our classical political economists that there is a divine harmony between these two interests of such a nature that if every decider does the best for himself the result will also be the best for everybody. In spite of a century of bitter experience of the adoption of these excuses for laziness in politics, shameless selfishness in industry, and glorification of idle uselessness in the face of the degrading misery of the masses, they are still taught in our universities, and, what is worse, broadcast by university professors by wireless, as authentic political economy instead of what they really are: that is, the special pleading put forward in defence of the speculators, exploiters, and parasitic property owners in whose grossly antisocial interests the country is misgoverned. Since Karl Marx and Friedrich Engels exposed the horrible condition of the working classes that underlies the pursepride and snobbery of the upper middle classes and the prestige of the landed gentry and peerage there has been no substantial excuse for believing in the alleged harmony of interests. Nothing more diabolical can be conceived than the destiny of a civilization in which the material sources of the people's subsistence are privately owned by a handful of persons taught from childhood that every penny they can extort from the propertyless is an addition to the prosperity of their country and an enrichment of the world at large.

But private property is not the subject of my demonstration in The Millionairess. Private property can be communized. Capitalists and landlords can be pressed into the service of the community, or, if they are idle or incorrigibly recalcitrant, handed over to the police. Under such circumstances the speculator would find his occupation gone. With him would disappear the routine exploiter. But the decider, the dominator, the organizer, the tactician, the mesmerizer would remain; and if they were still educated as ladies and gentlemen are educated today, and consequently had the same sort of consciences and ambitions, they would, if they had anything like our present proletariat to deal with, re-establish industrial anarchy and heritable private property in land with all their disastrous consequences and Gadarene destiny. And their rule, being that of able persons and not of nincompoops born with silver spoons in their mouths, would at first produce some striking improvements in the working of the public services, including the elimination of dud dignitaries and the general bracing up of plodders and slackers. But when dominators die, and are succeeded by persons who can only work a routine, a relapse is inevitable; and the destruction by the dominators of the organizations by which citizens defend themselves against oppression (trade unions, for example) may be found to leave society less organized than it was before the hand of the master had risen from the dust to which it has returned. For it is obvious that a business organized for control by an exceptionally omnipotent and omniscient head will go to pieces when that head is replaced by a commonplace numskull. We need not go back to Richard Cromwell or the Duke of Reichstadt to illustrate this. It is occurring every day in commercial business.

Now the remedy lies, not in the extermination of all dominators and deciders, but on the contrary in their multiplication to what may be called their natural minority limit, which will destroy their present scarcity value. But we must also eliminate the mass of ignorance, weakness, and timidity which force them to treat fools according to their folly. Armies, fanatical sects and mobs, and the blackshirts complained of today by their black and blue victims, have consisted hitherto mostly of people who should not exist in civilized society. Titus Oates and Lord George Gordon owed their vogue to the London mob. There should not have been any London mob. The soldiers of Marlborough and Wellington were never-do-wells, mental defectives, and laborers with the minds and habits of serfs. Military geniuses could hunt with such products more easily than with a pack of hounds. Our public school and university education equips armies of this kind with appropriate staffs of officers. When both are extinct we shall be able to breathe more freely.

Let us therefore assume that the soldier and his officer as we know them, the Orange and Papist rioters of Belfast, the Moslem and Hindu irreconcilables of the east and the Ku-Klux-Klans and lynching mobs of the west, have passed away as the less dangerous prehistoric monsters have passed, and that all men and women are meeting on equal terms as far as circumstances and education are concerned. Let us suppose that no man can starve or flog his fellows into obeying him, or force upon them the alternative of risking their lives for him in battle or being shot at dawn. Let us take for granted armies intelligent enough to present their officers at any moment with the alternative of organizing a return home or being superseded out of hand. Let us narrow the case to the mysterious precedence into which certain people get pushed even when they lack ambition and are far too intelligent to believe that eminence and its responsibilities are luxuries. To be "greatest among you" is a distinction dearly bought at the price of being "servant to all the rest." Plato was quite right in taking reluctance to govern as a leading symptom of supreme fitness for it. But if we insisted on this qualification in all cases, we should find ourselves as short of governors as the churches would be if they insisted on all their parish priests or rectors being saints. A great deal of the directing and organizing work of the world will still have to be done by energetic and capable careerists who are by no means void of vulgar ambition, and very little troubled by the responsibilities that attend on power. When I said that Napoleon was fundamentally a fool and a snob I did not mean for a moment to question his extraordinary capacity as a ruler of men. If we compare him with his valet-secretary Bourrienne we find that there were no external circumstances to prevent Bourrienne becoming the emperor and Napoleon the valet. They quarrelled and parted with an exchange of epithets unprintable in polite English. Bourrienne was as much a Man of Destiny as Buonaparte. But it was his destiny to be ruled and Buonaparte's to rule; and so Buonaparte became Napoleon Bonaparte, First Consul and Emperor, as inevitably as Bourrienne remained a speculator, litterateur and diplomatist. I am not forgetting that Bourrienne saw Napoleon come and go, and had a much more comfortable and finally a more successful career than his quondam master; but the point is that Napoleon was master whilst their personal relations lasted. And please note that Napoleon did not and could not impose on Bourrienne and Talleyrand, nor even on the more cultivated of his marshals (all planetary Napoleons) as he could and did on the soldiery and peasantry. They turned against him very promptly when his fortunes changed and he could no longer be of any use to them.

Now if a ruler can command men only as long as he is efficient and successful his rule is neither a tyranny nor a calamity: it is a very valuable asset. But suppose the nation is made up for the most part of people too ignorant to understand efficient government, and taught, as far as they are taught at all, to measure greatness by pageantry and the wholesale slaughter called military glory. It was this ignorance and idolatry that first exalted Napoleon and then smashed him. From Toulon to Austerlitz Napoleon did what good he did by stealth, and had no occasion to "blush to find it fame," as nobody gave him the least credit for anything but killing. When the glory turned to shame on the road back from Moscow his good works availed him nothing, and the way was open to St Helena. Catherine of Russia, when she was faced with a revolt against the misery of her people, said, not "Let us relieve their misery by appropriate reforms," but "Let us give them a little war to amuse them." Every tottering regime tries to rally its subjects to its support in the last resort by a war. It was not only the last card of Napoleon III before he lost the game: it played a considerable part in the capitalist support of Hohenzollern sabre rattling which made the desperate onslaught of Germany in 1914 possible. Patriotism, roused to boiling point by an enemy at the gate, is not only the last refuge of a scoundrel in Dr. Johnson's sense, it is far more dangerously the everyday resort of capitalism and feudalism as a red herring across the scent of Communism. Under such circumstances it is fortunate that war on the modern scale is so completely beyond the capacity of private capitalism that, as in 1915, it forces the belligerents into national factory production, public discipline, and rationed distribution: in short into Socialism. Not only did national factories spring up like mushrooms, but the private factories had to be brought up to the mark by public control of prices and dictation of scientific business methods, involving such an exposure of the obsolescence and inefficiency of profitmongering methods that it took years of reckless lying from Press and platform to make the silly public believe the contrary. For war is like the seven magic bullets which the devil has ready to sell for a human soul. Six of them may hit the glory-monger's mark very triumphantly; but the seventh plays some unexpected and unintended trick that upsets the gunman's apple cart. It seemed an astute stroke of German imperial tactics to send Lenin safely through Germany to Russia so that he might make trouble for the Tsar. But the bullet was a number seven: it killed the Tsar very efficiently; but it came back like a boomerang and laid the Hohen-zollerns beside the Romanoffs.

Pageantry will lose its black magic when it becomes a local popular amusement; so that the countryside may come to know it from behind the scenes, when, though it will still please, it will no longer impose. For mere iconoclasm is a mistake: the Roundhead folly (really a Thickhead one) of destroying the power of the pageant by forbidding all theatrical displays and dressings-up, and making everybody wear ugly clothes, ended in the flamboyant profligacy of the Restoration; and the attempt to enforce the second commandment by smashing the images soon smashed the second commandment. Give away the secret that the dressed-up performers are only amateurs, and the images works of art, and the dupes and worshippers will become undeluded connoisseurs.

Unfortunately it is easier to produce a nation of

artistic than of political connoisseurs. Our schools and universities do not concern themselves with fine art, which they despise as an unmanly pursuit. It is possible for a young gentleman to go through the whole educational mill of preparatory school, public school, and university with the highest academic honors without knowing the difference between a chanty and a symphony, a tavern sign and a portrait by Titian, a ballad by Macaulay and a stanza by Keats. But at least he is free to find out all this for himself if he has a fancy that way.

Not so in political science. Not so in religion. In these subjects he is proselytized from the beginning in the interests of established institutions so effectually that he remains all his life firmly convinced that his greatest contemporaries are rascally and venal agitators, villainous blasphemers, or at best seditious cads. He will listen to noodles' orations, read pompous leading articles, and worship the bloodthirsty tribal idols of Noah and Samuel with a gravity and sincerity that would make him infinitely pitiable if they did not also make him infinitely dangerous. He will feed his mind on empty phrases as Nebuchadnezzar fed his body on grass; and any boss who has mastered these phrases can become his dictator, his despot, his evangelist, and in effect his god-emperor.

Clearly we shall be bossridden in one form or another as long as education means being put through this process, or the best imitation of it that our children's parents can afford. The remedy is another Reformation, now long and perilously overdue, in the direction and instruction of our children's minds politically and religiously. We should begin well to the left of Russia, which is still encumbered with nineteenth century superstitions. Communism is the fairy godmother who can transform Bosses into "servants to all the rest"; but only a creed of Creative Evolution can set the souls of the people free. Then the dominator will still find himself face to face with subordinates who can do nothing without him; but that will not give him the inside grip. A late rich shipowner, engaged in a quarrel with his workmen in which he assumed that I was on their side, rashly asked me what his men could do without him. Naturally I asked him what he could do without them, hoping to open his eyes to the fact that apart from the property rights he had bought or borrowed he was as dependent on them as they on him. But I fear I impressed him most by adding, quite untruly, that no gentleman would have asked that question.

Save for my allusion to the persecution and exile of Einstein I have not said a word here about the miserable plight of the great men neglected, insulted, starved, and occasionally put to death, sometimes horribly, by the little ones. Their case is helpless because nothing can defend them against the might of overwhelming numbers unless and until they develop the Vril imagined by Bulwer-Lytton which will enable one person to destroy a multitude, and thereby make us more particular than we are at present about the sort of persons we produce. I am confining myself to the power wielded by the moneymakers and military geniuses in political life and by the dominant personalities in private life. Lytton's Vril was a fiction only in respect of its being available for everybody, and therefore an infallible preventive of any attempt at oppression. For that individuals here and there possess a power of domination which others are unable to resist is undeniable; and since this power is as yet nameless we may as well call it Vril as

anything else. It is the final reality of inequality. It is
easy to equalize the dominators with the common-
placers economically: you just give one of them half-
a-crown and the other two-and-sixpence. Nelson was
paid no more than any other naval captain or admiral
and the poverty of Mozart or Marx was worse than
the voluntary holy poverty of the great heads of the
religious orders. Dominators and dominated are
already equalized before the law: shall not I, a playwright of Shakesperean eminence, be hanged if I
commit a murder precisely as if I were the most
illiterate call boy? Politically we all have at least the
symbol of equality in our votes, useless as they are to
us under political and economic institutions made to
encourage William the Conqueror to slay Harold and
exploit Hodge. But, I repeat, when all these perfectly
feasible equalizations are made real, there still remains Epifania, shorn of her millions and unable to
replace them, but still as dominant as Saint Joan,
Saint Clare, and Saint Teresa. The most complete
Communism and Democracy can only give her her
chance far more effectively than any feudal or capitalist society.

And this, I take it, is one of the highest claims of
Communism and Democracy to our consideration,
and the explanation of the apparently paradoxical fact
that it is always the greatest spirits, from Jesus to
Lenin, from St Thomas More to William Morris,
who are communists and democrats, and always the
commonplace people who weary us with their blither-
ings about the impossibility of equality when they
are at a loss for any better excuse for keeping other
people in the kitchen and themselves in the drawing
room. I say cheerfully to the dominators "By all
means dominate: it is up to us to so order our institu-

tions that you shall not oppress us, nor bequeath any of your precedence to your commonplace children." For when ambition and greed and mere brainless energy have been disabled, the way will be clear for inspiration and aspiration to save us from the fat-headed stagnation of the accursed Victorian snobbery which is bringing us to the verge of ruin.

MALVERN, *28th August 1935*

$\begin{bmatrix} ACT & I \end{bmatrix}$

Mr Julius Sagamore, a smart young solicitor, is in his office in Lincoln's Inn Fields. It is a fine morning in May. The room, an old panelled one, is so arranged that Mr Sagamore, whom we see sitting under the window in profile with his back to it and his left side presented to us, is fenced off by his writing table from excessive intimacy with emotional clients or possible assault by violent or insane ones. The door is on his right towards the farther end of the room. The faces of the clients are thus illuminated by the window whilst his own countenance is in shadow. The fireplace, of Adams design, is in the wall facing him. It is surmounted by a dingy portrait of a judge. In the wall on his right, near the corner farthest from him, is the door, with a cleft pediment enshrining a bust of some other judge. The rest of this wall is occupied by shelves of calf-bound law books. The wall behind Mr Sagamore has the big window as aforesaid, and beside it a stand of black tin boxes inscribed with clients' names.

So far, the place proclaims the eighteenth century; but as the year is 1935, and Mr Sagamore has no taste for dust and mould, and requires a room which suggests opulence, and in which lady clients will look their best, everything is well dusted and polished; the green carpet is new, rich, and thick; and the half dozen chairs, four of which are arranged under the bookshelves, are Chippendales of the very latest fake. Of the other two one is occupied by himself, and the other stands half way between his table and the fireplace for the accommodation of his clients.

The telephone, on the table at his elbow, rings.

SAGAMORE [*listening*] Yes?... [*Impressed*] Oh! Send her up at once.

A tragic looking woman, athletically built and expensively dressed, storms into the room. He rises obsequiously.

THE LADY. Are you Julius Sagamore, the worthless nephew of my late solicitor Pontifex Sagamore?

SAGAMORE. I do not advertize myself as worthless; but Pontifex Sagamore was my uncle; and I have returned from Australia to succeed to as much of his business as I can persuade his clients to trust me with.

THE LADY. I have heard him speak of you; and I naturally concluded that as you had been packed off to Australia you must be worthless. But it does not matter, as my business is very simple. I desire to make my will, leaving everything I possess to my husband. You can hardly go wrong about that, I suppose.

SAGAMORE. I shall do my best. Pray sit down.

THE LADY. No: I am restless. I shall sit down when I feel tired.

SAGAMORE. As you please. Before I draw up the will it will be necessary for me to know who your husband is.

THE LADY. My husband is a fool and a blackguard. You will state that fact in the will. You will add that it was his conduct that drove me to commit suicide.

SAGAMORE. But you have not committed suicide.

THE LADY. I shall have, when the will is signed.

SAGAMORE. Of course, quite so: stupid of me. And his name?

THE LADY. His name is Alastair Fitzfassenden.

SAGAMORE. What! The amateur tennis champion and heavy weight boxer?

THE LADY. Do you know him?

SAGAMORE. Every morning we swim together at the club.

THE LADY. The acquaintance does you little credit.

SAGAMORE. I had better tell you that he and I are great friends, Mrs Fitzfassen—

THE LADY. Do not call me by his detestable name. Put me in your books as Epifania Ognisanti di Parerga.

SAGAMORE [*bowing*] Oh! I am indeed honored. Pray be seated.

EPIFANIA. Sit down yourself; and dont fuss.

SAGAMORE. If you prefer it, certainly. [*He sits*] Your father was a very wonderful man, madam.

EPIFANIA. My father was the greatest man in the world. And he died a pauper. I shall never forgive the world for that.

SAGAMORE. A pauper! You amaze me. It was reported that he left you, his only child, thirty millions.

EPIFANIA. Well, what was thirty millions to him? He lost a hundred and fifty millions. He had promised to leave me two hundred millions. I was left with a beggarly thirty. It broke his heart.

SAGAMORE. Still, an income of a million and a half—

EPIFANIA. Man: you forget the death duties. I have barely seven hundred thousand a year. Do you know what that means to a woman brought up on an income of seven figures? The humiliation of it!

SAGAMORE. You take away my breath, madam.

EPIFANIA. As I am about to take my own breath away, I have no time to attend to yours.

SAGAMORE. Oh, the suicide! I had forgotten that.

EPIFANIA. Had you indeed? Well, will you please give your mind to it for a moment, and draw up a will for me to sign, leaving everything to Alastair.

SAGAMORE. To humiliate him?

EPIFANIA. No. To ruin him. To destroy him. To

make him a beggar on horseback so that he may ride to the devil. Money goes to his head. I have seen it at work on him.

SAGAMORE. I also have seen that happen. But you cannot be sure. He might marry some sensible woman.

EPIFANIA. You are right. Make it a condition of the inheritance that within a month from my funeral he marries a low female named Polly Seedystockings.

SAGAMORE [*making a note of it*] A funny name.

EPIFANIA. Her real name is Patricia Smith. But her letters to Alastair are signed Polly Seedystockings, as a hint, I suppose, that she wants him to buy her another dozen.

SAGAMORE [*taking another sheet of paper and writing*] I should like to know Polly.

EPIFANIA. Pray why?

SAGAMORE [*talking as he writes*] Well, if Alastair prefers her to you she must be indeed worth knowing. I shall certainly make him introduce me.

EPIFANIA. You are hardly tactful, Julius Sagamore.

SAGAMORE. That will not matter when you have taken this [*he hands her what he has written*]

EPIFANIA. Whats this?

SAGAMORE. For the suicide. You will have to sign the chemist's book for the cyanide. Say it is for a wasp's nest. The tartaric acid is harmless: the chemist will think you want it to make lemonade. Put the two separately in just enough water to dissolve them. When you mix the two solutions the tartaric and potash will combine and make tartrate of potash. This, being insoluble, will be precipitated to the bottom of the glass; and the supernatant fluid will be pure hydrocyanic acid, one sip of which will kill you like a thunderbolt.

EPIFANIA [*fingering the prescription rather discon-certedly*] You seem to take my death very coolly, Mr Sagamore.

SAGAMORE. I am used to it.

EPIFANIA. Do you mean to tell me that you have so many clients driven to despair that you keep a prescription for them?

SAGAMORE. I do. It's infallible.

EPIFANIA. You are sure that they have all died painlessly and instantaneously?

SAGAMORE. No. They are all alive.

EPIFANIA. Alive! The prescription is a harmless fraud!

SAGAMORE. No. It's a deadly poison. But they dont take it.

EPIFANIA. Why?

SAGAMORE. I dont know. But they never do.

EPIFANIA. I will. And I hope you will be hanged for giving it to me.

SAGAMORE. I am only acting as your solicitor. You say you are going to commit suicide; and you come to me for advice. I do my best for you, so that you can die without wasting a lot of gas or jumping into the Serpentine. Six and eightpence I shall charge your executors.

EPIFANIA. For advising me how to kill myself?

SAGAMORE. Not today. Tomorrow.

EPIFANIA. Why put it off until tomorrow?

SAGAMORE. Well, it will do as well tomorrow as to-day. And something amusing may happen this evening. Or even tomorrow evening. Theres no hurry.

EPIFANIA. You are a brute, a beast, and a pig. My life is nothing to you: you do not even ask what has driven me to this. You make money out of the death of your clients.

SAGAMORE. I do. There will be a lot of business connected with your death. Alastair is sure to come to me to settle your affairs.

EPIFANIA. And you expect me to kill myself to make money for you?

SAGAMORE. Well, it is you who have raised my expectations, madam.

EPIFANIA. O God, listen to this man! Has it ever occurred to you that when a woman's life is wrecked she needs a little sympathy and not a bottle of poison?

SAGAMORE. I really cant sympathize with suicide. It doesnt appeal to me, somehow. Still, if it has to be done, it had better be done promptly and scientifically.

EPIFANIA. You dont even ask what Alastair has done to me?

SAGAMORE. It wont matter what he has done to you when you are dead. Why bother about it?

EPIFANIA. You are an unmitigated hog, Julius Sagamore.

SAGAMORE. Why worry about me? The prescription will cure everything.

EPIFANIA. Damn your prescription. There! [*She tears it up and throws the pieces in his face*].

SAGAMORE [*beaming*] It's infallible. And now that you have blown off steam, suppose you sit down and tell me all about it.

EPIFANIA. You call the outcry of an anguished heart blowing off steam, do you?

SAGAMORE. Well, what else would you call it?

EPIFANIA. You are not a man: you are a rhinoceros. You are also a fool.

SAGAMORE. I am only a solicitor.

EPIFANIA. You are a rotten solicitor. You are not a gentleman. You insult me in my distress. You back up my husband against me. You have no decency, no understanding. You are a fish with the soul of a black-beetle. Do you hear?

SAGAMORE. Yes: I hear. And I congratulate myself on the number of actions for libel I shall have to defend if you do me the honor of making me your solicitor.

EPIFANIA. You are wrong. I never utter a libel. My father instructed me most carefully in the law of libel. If I questioned your solvency, that would be a libel. If I suggested that you are unfaithful to your wife, that would be a libel. But if I call you a rhinoceros—which you are: a most unmitigated rhinoceros—that is only vulgar abuse. I take good care to confine myself to vulgar abuse; and I have never had an action for libel taken against me. Is that the law, or is it not?

SAGAMORE. I really dont know. I will look it up in my law books.

EPIFANIA. You need not. I instruct you that it is the law. My father always had to instruct his lawyers in the law whenever he did anything except what everybody was doing every day. Solicitors know nothing of law: they are only good at practice, as they call it. My father was a great man: every day of his life he did things that nobody else ever dreamt of doing. I am not, perhaps, a great woman; but I am his daughter; and as such I am an unusual woman. You will take the law from me and do exactly what I tell you to do.

SAGAMORE. That will simplify our relations considerably, madam.

EPIFANIA. And remember this. I have no sense of humor. I will not be laughed at.

SAGAMORE. I should not dream of laughing at a client with an income of three quarters of a million.

EPIFANIA. Have you a sense of humor?

SAGAMORE. I try to keep it in check; but I am afraid I have a little. You appeal to it, somehow.

EPIFANIA. Then I tell you in cold blood, after the most careful consideration of my words, that you are a heartless blackguard. My distress, my disgrace, my humiliation, the horrible mess and failure I have made of my life seem to you merely funny. If it were not that my father warned me never to employ a solicitor who had no sense of humor I would walk out of this office and deprive you of a client whose business may prove a fortune to you.

SAGAMORE. But, my dear lady, I dont know anything about your distress, your disgrace, the mess you have made of your life and all the rest of it. How can I laugh at things I dont know? If I am laughing—and am I really laughing?—I assure you I am laughing, not at your misfortunes, but at you.

EPIFANIA. Indeed? Am I so comic a figure in my misery?

SAGAMORE. But what is your misery? Do, pray, sit down.

EPIFANIA. You seem to have one idea in your head, and that is to get your clients to sit down. Well, to oblige you. [*She sits down with a flounce. The back of the chair snaps off short with a loud crack. She springs up*]. Oh, I cannot even sit down in a chair without wrecking it. There is a curse on me.

SAGAMORE [*collapses on the table, shaking with uncontrollable laughter*]!!!!!!

EPIFANIA. Ay: laugh, laugh, laugh. Fool! Clown!

SAGAMORE [*rising resolutely and fetching another chair from the wall*] My best faked Chippendale gone. It cost me four guineas. [*Placing the chair for her*] Now will you please sit down as gently as you can, and stop calling me names? Then, if you wish, you can tell me what on earth is the matter. [*He picks up the broken-off back of the chair and puts it on the table*].

EPIFANIA [*sitting down with dignity*] The breaking of that chair has calmed and relieved me, somehow. I feel as if I had broken your neck, as I wanted to. Now listen to me. [*He comes to her and looks down gravely at her*]. And dont stand over me like that. Sit down on what is left of your sham Chippendale.

SAGAMORE. Certainly [*he sits*]. Now go ahead.

EPIFANIA. My father was the greatest man in the world. I was his only child. His one dread was that I should make a foolish marriage, and lose the little money he was able to leave me.

SAGAMORE. The thirty millions. Precisely.

EPIFANIA. Dont interrupt me. He made me promise that whenever a man asked me to marry him I should impose a condition on my consent.

SAGAMORE [*attentive*] So? What condition?

EPIFANIA. I was to give him one hundred and fifty pounds, and tell him that if within six months he had turned that hundred and fifty pounds into fifty thousand, I was his. If not, I was never to see him again. I saw the wisdom of this. Nobody but my father could have thought of such a real, infallible, unsentimental test. I gave him my sacred promise that I would carry it out faithfully.

SAGAMORE. And you broke that promise. I see.

EPIFANIA. What do you mean—broke that promise?

SAGAMORE. Well, you married Alastair. Now Alastair is a dear good fellow—one of the best in his way—but you are not going to persuade me that he made fifty thousand pounds in six months with a capital of one hundred and fifty.

EPIFANIA. He did. Wise as my father was, he sometimes forgot the wise things he said five minutes after he said them. He warned me that ninety per cent of our selfmade millionaires are criminals who have taken a five hundred to one chance and got away with it by pure luck. Well, Alastair was that sort of criminal.

SAGAMORE. No no: not a criminal. That is not like Alastair. A fool, perhaps, in business. But not a criminal.

EPIFANIA. Like all solicitors you think you know more about my husband than I do. Well, I tell you that Alastair came back to me after six months probation with fifty thousand pounds in his pocket instead of the penal servitude he richly deserved. That man's luck is extraordinary. He always wins. He wins at tennis. He wins at boxing. He won me, the richest heiress in England.

SAGAMORE. But you were a consenting party. If not, why did you put him to the test? Why did you give him the hundred and fifty to try his luck with?

EPIFANIA. Boxing.

SAGAMORE. Boxing?

EPIFANIA. His boxing fascinated me. My father held that women should be able to defend themselves. He made me study Judo.

SAGAMORE. Judo? Do you mean Hebrew?

EPIFANIA. Hebrew! Nonsense! Judo is what ignorant people call jujitsu. I could throw you through that window as easily as you handed me that rotten chair.

SAGAMORE. Oh! Japanese wrestling. Rather a rough sport for a lady, isnt it?

EPIFANIA. How dare you call Judo a sport? It is a religion.

SAGAMORE [*collapsing*] Forgive me. Go on with your story. And please break it to me as gently as you can. I have never had a client like you before.

EPIFANIA. You never will again.

[891]

SAGAMORE. I dont doubt it for a moment. Now tell me: where does Alastair come in?

EPIFANIA. I saw him win an amateur heavy weight championship. He has a solar plexus punch that no other boxer can withstand.

SAGAMORE. And you married a man because he had a superlative solar plexus punch!

EPIFANIA. Well, he was handsome. He stripped well, unlike many handsome men. I am not insusceptible to sex appeal, very far from it.

SAGAMORE [*hastily*] Oh quite, quite: you need not go into details.

EPIFANIA. I will if I like. It is your business as a solicitor to know the details. I made a very common mistake. I thought that this irresistible athlete would be an ardent lover. He was nothing of the kind. All his ardor was in his fists. Never shall I forget the day —it was during our honeymoon—when his coldness infuriated me to such a degree that I went for him with my fists. He knocked me out with that abominable punch in the first exchange. Have you ever been knocked out by a punch in the solar plexus?

SAGAMORE. No, thank heaven. I am not a pugilist.

EPIFANIA. It does not put you to sleep like a punch on the jaw. When he saw my face distorted with agony and my body writhing on the floor, he was horrified. He said he did it automatically—that he always countered that way, by instinct. I almost respected him for it.

SAGAMORE. Then why do you want to get rid of him?

EPIFANIA. I want to get rid of myself. I want to punish myself for making a mess of my life and marrying an imbecile. I, Epifania Ognisanti di Parerga, saw myself as the most wonderful woman in England marrying the most wonderful man. And I was only a goose marrying a buck rabbit. What was there for me but death? And now you have put me off it with your fooling; and I dont know what I want. That is a horrible state of mind. I am a woman who must always want something and always get it.

SAGAMORE. An acquisitive woman. Precisely. How splendid! [*The telephone rings. He rises*]. Excuse me. [*He goes to the table and listens*] Yes?... [*Hastily*] One moment. Hold the line. [*To Epifania*] Your husband is downstairs, with a woman. They want to see me.

EPIFANIA [*rising*] That woman! Have them up at once.

SAGAMORE. But can I depend on you to control yourself?

EPIFANIA. You can depend on Alastair's fists. I must have a look at Seedystockings. Have them up I tell you.

SAGAMORE [*into the telephone*] Send Mr Fitzfassenden and the lady up.

EPIFANIA. We shall see now the sort of woman for whom he has deserted ME!

SAGAMORE. I am thrilled. I expect something marvellous.

EPIFANIA. Dont be a fool. Expect something utterly common.

Alastair Fitzfassenden and Patricia Smith come in. He is a splendid athlete, with most of his brains in his muscles. She is a pleasant quiet little woman of the self-supporting type. She makes placidly for the table, leaving Alastair to deal with his wife.

ALASTAIR. Eppy! What are you doing here? [*To Sagamore*] Why didnt you tell me?

EPIFANIA. Introduce the female.

PATRICIA. Patricia Smith is my name, Mrs Fitzfassenden.

EPIFANIA. That is not how you sign your letters, I think.

ALASTAIR. Look here, Eppy. Dont begin making a row—

EPIFANIA. I was not speaking to you. I was speaking to the woman.

ALASTAIR [*losing his temper*] You have no right to call her a woman.

PATRICIA. Now, now, Ally: you promised me—

EPIFANIA. Promised you! What right had he to promise you? How dare he promise you? How dare you make him promise you?

ALASTAIR. I wont have Polly insulted.

SAGAMORE [*goodhumoredly*] You dont mind, Miss Smith, do you?

PATRICIA [*unconcerned*] Oh, I dont mind. My sister goes on just like that.

EPIFANIA. Your sister! You presume to compare your sister to me!

PATRICIA. Only when she goes off at the deep end. You mustnt mind me: theres nothing like letting yourself go if you are built that way. Introduce me to the gentleman, Ally.

ALASTAIR. Oh, I forgot. Julius Sagamore, my solicitor. An old pal. Miss Smith.

EPIFANIA. Alias Polly Seedystockings.

PATRICIA. Thats only my pet name, Mr Sagamore. Smith is the patronymic, as dear wise old father says.

EPIFANIA. She sets up a wise father! This is the last straw.

SAGAMORE. Do sit down, Miss Smith, wont you? [*He goes to fetch a chair from the wall*].

PATRICIA [*contemplating the wrecked chair*] Hallo! Whats happened to the chair?

EPIFANIA. *I* have happened to the chair. Let it be a warning to you.

Sagamore places the chair for Patricia next the table. Alastair shoves the broken chair back out of the way with his foot; fetches another from the wall, and is about to sit on it next Patricia when Epifania sits on it and motions him to her own chair, so that she is seated between the two, Patricia on her left, Alastair on her right. Sagamore goes back to his official place at the table.

PATRICIA. You see, Mr Sagamore, it's like this. Alastair—

EPIFANIA. You need not explain. I have explained everything to Mr Sagamore. And you will please have the decency in his presence and in mine to speak of my husband as Mr Fitzfassenden. His Christian name is no business of yours.

ALASTAIR [*angry*] Of course, Eppy, if you wont let anybody speak—

EPIFANIA. I am not preventing you nor anybody from speaking. If you have anything to say for yourself, say it.

PATRICIA. I am sorry. But it's such a long name. In my little circle everyone calls him just Ally.

EPIFANIA [*her teeth on edge*] You hear this, Mr Sagamore! My husband is called "Ally" by these third rate people! What right have they to speak of him at all? Am I to endure this?

PATRICIA [*soothingly*] Yes: we know you have to put up with a lot, deary;—

EPIFANIA [*stamping*] Deary!!!

PATRICIA [*continuing*]—but thats what the world is like.

EPIFANIA. The world is like that to people who are like that. Your world is not my world. Every woman

[895]

has her own world within her own soul. Listen to me, Mr Sagamore. I married this man. I admitted him to my world, the world which my imagination had peopled with heroes and saints. Never before had a real man been permitted to enter it. I took him to be hero, saint, lover all in one. What he really was you can see for yourself.

ALASTAIR [*jumping up with his fists clenched and his face red*] I am damned if I stand this.

EPIFANIA [*rising and facing him in the pose of a martyr*] Yes: strike me. Shew your knock-out punch. Let her see how you treat women.

ALASTAIR [*baffled*] Damn! [*He sits down again*].

PATRICIA. Dont get rattled, Ally: you will only put yourself in the wrong before Mr Sagamore. I think youd better go home and leave me to have it out with her.

EPIFANIA. Will you have the goodness not to speak of me as "her"? I am Mrs Fitzfassenden. I am not a pronoun. [*She resumes her seat haughtily*].

PATRICIA. Sorry; but your name is such a tongue-twister. Mr Sagamore: dont you think Ally had better go? It's not right that we should sit here arguing about him to his face. Besides, he's worn out: he's hardly slept all night.

EPIFANIA. How do you know that, pray?

PATRICIA. Never mind how I know it. I do.

ALASTAIR. It was quite innocent; but where could I go to when you drove me out of the house by your tantrums?

EPIFANIA [*most unexpectedly amused*] You went to her?

ALASTAIR. I went to Miss Smith: she's not a pronoun, you know. I went where I could find peace and kindness, to my good sweet darling Polly. So there!

EPIFANIA. I have no sense of humor; but this strikes me as irresistibly funny. You actually left ME to spend the night in the arms of Miss Seedystockings!

ALASTAIR. No, I tell you. It was quite innocent.

EPIFANIA [*to Patricia*] Was he in your arms or was he not?

PATRICIA. Well, yes, of course he was for a while. But not in the way you mean.

EPIFANIA. Then he is even more a sexless fish than I took him for. But really a man capable of flouncing out of the house when I was on the point of pardoning him and giving him a night of legitimate bliss would be capable of any imbecility.

ALASTAIR. Pardoning me! Pardoning me for what? What had I done when you flew out at me?

EPIFANIA. I did not fly out at you. I have never lost my dignity even under the most insufferable wrongs.

ALASTAIR. You hadnt any wrongs. You drove me out of the house—

EPIFANIA. I did not. I never meant you to go. It was abominably selfish of you. You had your Seedystockings to go to; but I had nobody. Adrian was out of town.

SAGAMORE. Adrian! This is a new complication. Who is Adrian?

PATRICIA. Adrian is Mrs Fitzfassenden's Sunday husband, Mr Sagamore.

EPIFANIA. My what, did you say?

PATRICIA. Your Sunday husband. You understand. What Mr Adrian Blenderbland is to you, as it were. What Ally is to me.

SAGAMORE. I dont quite follow. What is Mr Blenderbland to you, Mrs Fitzfassenden, if I may ask?

EPIFANIA. Well, he is a gentleman with whom I

discuss subjects that are beyond my husband's mental grasp, which is extremely limited.

ALASTAIR. A chap that sets up to be an intellectual because his father was a publisher! He makes up to Eppy and pretends to be in love with her because she has a good cook; but I tell her he cares for nothing but his food. He always calls at mealtimes. A bellygod, I call him. And I am expected to put up with him. But if I as much as look at Polly! Oh my!

EPIFANIA. The cases are quite different. Adrian worships the ground I tread on: that is quite true. But if you think that Seedystockings worships the ground you tread on, you flatter yourself grossly. She endures you and pets you because you buy stockings for her, and no doubt anything else she may be short of.

PATRICIA. Well, I never contradict anyone, because it only makes trouble. And I am afraid I do cost him a good deal; for he likes me to have nice things that I cant afford.

ALASTAIR [affectionately] No, Polly: you dont. Youre as good as gold. I'm always pressing things on you that you wont take. Youre a jolly sight more careful of my money than I am myself.

EPIFANIA. How touching! You are the Sunday wife, I suppose.

PATRICIA. No: I should say that you are the Sunday wife, Mrs Fitzfassenden. It's I that have to look after his clothes and make him get his hair cut.

EPIFANIA. Surely the creature is intelligent enough to do at least that much for himself.

PATRICIA. You dont understand men: they get interested in other things and neglect themselves unless they have a woman to look after them. You see, Mr Sagamore, it's like this. There are two sorts of people in the world: the people anyone can live with and the people that no one can live with. The people that no one can live with may be very goodlooking and vital and splendid and temperamental and romantic and all that; and they can make a man or woman happy for half an hour when they are pleased with themselves and disposed to be agreeable; but if you try to live with them they just eat up your whole life running after them or quarrelling or attending to them one way or another: you cant call your soul your own. As Sunday husbands and wives, just to have a good tearing bit of lovemaking with, or a blazing row, or mostly one on top of the other, once a month or so, theyre all right. But as everyday partners theyre just impossible.

EPIFANIA. So I am the Sunday wife. [*To Patricia, scornfully*] And what are you, pray?

PATRICIA. Well, I am the angel in the house, if you follow me.

ALASTAIR [*blubbering*] You are, dear: you are.

EPIFANIA [*to Patricia*] You are his doormat: thats what you are.

PATRICIA. Doormats are very useful things if you want the house kept tidy, dear.

The telephone rings. Sagamore attends to it.

SAGAMORE. Yes? . . . Did you say Blenderbland?

EPIFANIA. Adrian! How did he know I was here?

SAGAMORE. Ask the gentleman to wait [*He hangs up the receiver*]. Perhaps you can tell me something about him, Mrs Fitzfassenden. Is he the chairman of Blenderbland's Literary Pennyworths?

EPIFANIA. No. That is his father, who created the business. Adrian is on the board; but he has no business ability. He is on fifteen boards of directors on the strength of his father's reputation, and has never, as far as I know, contributed an idea to any of them.

ALASTAIR. Be fair to him, Eppy. No man in London knows how to order a dinner better. Thats what keeps him at the top in the city.

SAGAMORE. Thank you: I think I have his measure sufficiently. Shall I have him up?

EPIFANIA. Certainly. I want to know what he is doing here.

ALASTAIR. I dont mind. You understand, of course, that I am not supposed to know anything of his relations with my wife, whatever they may be.

EPIFANIA. They are perfectly innocent, so far. I am not quite convinced that I love Adrian. He makes himself agreeable: that is all.

SAGAMORE [*into the telephone*] Send Mr Blenderbland up. [*He hangs up the instrument*].

ALASTAIR [*to Patricia*] You will now see the blighter who has cut me out with Eppy.

PATRICIA. I cant imagine any man cutting you out with any woman, dear.

EPIFANIA. Will you be good enough to restrain your endearments when he comes in?

Adrian Blenderbland, an imposing man in the prime of life, bearded in the Victorian literary fashion, rather handsome, and well dressed, comes in. Sagamore rises. Adrian is startled when he sees the company, but recovers his aplomb at once, and advances smiling.

ADRIAN. Hallo! Where have we all come from? Good morning, Mrs Fitzfassenden. How do, Alastair? Mr Sagamore, I presume. I did not know you were engaged.

SAGAMORE. Your arrival is quite opportune, sir. Will

you have the goodness to sit down? [*He takes a chair from the wall and places it at the table, on his own right and Patricia's left*].

ADRIAN [*sitting down*] Thank you. I hope I am not interrupting this lady.

PATRICIA. Not at all. Dont mind me.

SAGAMORE [*introducing*] Miss Smith, an intimate friend of Mr Fitzfassenden.

PATRICIA. Pleased to meet you, I'm sure.

Adrian bows to her; then turns to Sagamore.

ADRIAN. The fact is, Mrs Fitzfassenden mentioned your name to me in conversation as her choice of a new solicitor. So I thought I could not place myself in better hands.

SAGAMORE [*bowing*] Thank you, sir. But—excuse me —had you not a solicitor of your own?

ADRIAN. My dear Mr Sagamore: never be content with a single opinion. When I feel ill I always consult at least half a dozen doctors. The variety of their advice and prescriptions convinces me that I had better cure myself. When a legal point arises I consult six solicitors, with much the same—

EPIFANIA. Adrian: I have no sense of humor; and you know how it annoys me when you talk the sort of nonsense that is supposed to be funny. Did you come here to consult Mr Sagamore about me?

ADRIAN. I did. But of course I expected to find him alone.

SAGAMORE. Has the matter on which you wish to consult me any reference to Mr Fitzfassenden's family circle?

ADRIAN. It has.

SAGAMORE. Is it of such a nature that sooner or later it will have to be discussed with all the adult members of that circle?

ADRIAN. Well, yes: I suppose so. But hadnt we better talk it over a little in private first.

EPIFANIA. You shall do nothing of the sort. I will not have my affairs discussed by anybody in public or in private. They concern myself alone.

ADRIAN. May I not discuss my own affairs?

EPIFANIA. Not with my solicitor. I will not have it.

ALASTAIR. Now she is off at the deep end again. We may as well go home.

EPIFANIA [*restlessly rising*] Oh, the deep end! the deep end! What is life if it is not lived at the deep end? Alastair: you are a tadpole. [*She seizes his head and ruffles his hair as she passes him*].

ALASTAIR. Dont do that. [*He tries to smooth his hair*].

EPIFANIA [*to Patricia*] Smooth it for him, angel in the house.

PATRICIA [*moving to Epifania's chair and doing so*] You shouldnt make a sight of him like that.

SAGAMORE. Mr Fitzfassenden: why did you marry Mrs Fitzfassenden?

EPIFANIA. Why!!! Does that require any explanation? I have told you why *I* married him.

ALASTAIR. Well, though you mightnt think it, she can be frightfully fascinating when she really wants to be.

EPIFANIA. Why might he not think it? What do you mean?

ALASTAIR. He knows what I mean.

EPIFANIA. Some silly joke, I suppose.

ADRIAN. Dont be absurd, Fitzfassenden. Your wife is the most adorable woman on earth.

EPIFANIA. Not here, Adrian. If you are going to talk like that, take me away to some place where we can be alone.

[902]

ALASTAIR. Do, for heaven's sake, before she drives us all crazy.

SAGAMORE. Steady! steady! I hardly know where I am. You are all consulting me; but none of you has given me any instructions. Had you not better all be divorced?

EPIFANIA. What is the creature to live on? He has nothing: he would have had to become a professional boxer or tennis player if his uncle had not pushed him into an insurance office, where he was perfectly useless.

ALASTAIR. Look here, Eppy: Sagamore doesnt want to hear all this.

EPIFANIA. He does. He shall. Be silent. When Alastair proposed to me—he was too great an idiot to comprehend his own audacity—I kept my promise to my father. I handed him a cheque for a hundred and fifty pounds. "Make that into fifty thousand within six months" I said "and I am yours."

ADRIAN. You never told me this.

EPIFANIA. Why should I? It is a revolting story.

ALASTAIR. What is there revolting about it? Did I make good or did I not? Did I go through hell to get that money and win you or did I not?

ADRIAN [amazed] Do I understand you to say, Alastair, that you made fifty thousand pounds in six months?

ALASTAIR. Why not?

EPIFANIA. You may well look incredulous, Adrian. But he did. Yes: this imbecile made fifty thousand pounds and won Epifania Ognisanti di Parerga for his bride. You will not believe me when I tell you that the possession of all that money, and the consciousness of having made it himself, gave him a sort of greatness. I am impulsive: I kept my word and married him

[903]

instantly. Then, too late, I found out how he had made it.

ALASTAIR. Well, how did I make it? By my own brains.

EPIFANIA. Brains! By your own folly, your ignorance, your criminal instincts, and the luck that attends the half-witted. You won my hand, for which all Europe was on its knees to me. What you deserved was five years penal servitude.

ALASTAIR. Five years! Fifteen, more likely. That was what I risked for you. And what did I get by it? Life with you was worse than any penal servitude.

EPIFANIA. It would have been heaven to you if Nature had fitted you for such a companionship as mine. But what was it for me? No man had been good enough for me. I was like a princess in a fairy tale offering all men alive my hand and fortune if they could turn my hundred and fifty pound cheque into fifty thousand within six months. Able men, brilliant men, younger sons of the noblest families either refused the test or failed. Why? Because they were too honest or too proud. This thing succeeded; and I found myself tied for life to an insect.

ALASTAIR. You may say what you like; but you were just as much in love with me as I was with you.

EPIFANIA. Well, you were young; you were well shaped; your lawn tennis was outstanding; you were a magnificent boxer; and I was excited by physical contact with you.

SAGAMORE. Is it necessary to be so very explicit, Mrs Fitzfassenden?

EPIFANIA. Julius Sagamore: you may be made of sawdust; but I am made of flesh and blood. Alastair is physically attractive: that is my sole excuse for having married him. Will you have the face to pretend that he has any mental charm?

ADRIAN. But how did he make fifty thousand pounds? Was it on the Stock Exchange?

EPIFANIA. Nonsense! the creature does not know the difference between a cumulative preference and a deferred ordinary. He would not know even how to begin.

ADRIAN. But how did he begin? My bank balance at present is somewhere about a hundred and fifty. I should very much like to know how to make it up to fifty thousand. You are so rich, Epifania, that every decent man who approaches you feels like a needy adventurer. You dont know how a man to whom a hundred pounds is a considerable sum feels in the arms of a woman to whom a million is mere pin money.

EPIFANIA. Nor do you know what it feels like to be in the arms of a man and know that you could buy him up twenty times over and never miss the price.

ADRIAN. If I give you my hundred and fifty pounds, will you invest it for me?

EPIFANIA. It is not worth investing. You cannot make money on the Stock Exchange until your weekly account is at least seventy thousand. Do not meddle with money, Adrian: you do not understand it. I will give you all you need.

ADRIAN. No, thank you: I should lose my self-respect. I prefer the poor man's luxury of paying for your cabs and flowers and theatre tickets and lunches at the Ritz, and lending you all the little sums you have occasion for when we are together.

The rest all stare at this light on Epifania's habits.

EPIFANIA. It is quite true: I never have any pocket money: I must owe you millions in odd five pound notes. I will tell my bankers that you want a thousand on account.

ADRIAN. But I dont. I love lending you fivers. Only, as they run through my comparatively slender resources at an appalling rate, I should honestly like a few lessons from Alastair in the art of turning hundreds into tens of thousands.

EPIFANIA. His example would be useless to you, Adrian, because Alastair is one of Nature's marvels; and there is nothing marvellous about you except your appetite. Listen. On each of his birthdays his aunt had presented him with a gramophone record of the singing of the celebrated tenor Enrico Caruso. Now it so happens that Nature, in one of her most unaccountable caprices, has endowed Alastair with a startlingly loud singing voice of almost supernatural range. He can sing high notes never before attained by mortal man. He found that he could imitate gramophone records with the greatest facility; and he became convinced that he could make a fortune as an operatic tenor. The first use he made of my money was to give fifty pounds to the manager of some trumpery little opera company which was then on its last legs in the suburbs to allow him to appear for one night in one of Caruso's most popular roles. He actually took me to hear his performance.

ALASTAIR. It wasnt my fault. I can sing Caruso's head off. It was a plot. The regular tenor of the company: a swine that could hardly reach B flat without breaking his neck, paid a lot of blackguards to go into the gallery and boo me.

EPIFANIA. My dear Alastair, the simple truth is that Nature, when she endowed you with your amazing voice, unfortunately omitted to provide you with a musical ear. You can bellow loudly enough to drown ten thousand bulls; but you are always at least a quarter tone sharp or flat as the case may be. I laughed until I fell on the floor of my box in screaming hysterics. The audience hooted and booed; but they could not make themselves heard above your roaring. At last the chorus dragged you off the stage; and the regular tenor finished the performance only to find that the manager had absconded with my fifty pounds and left the whole company penniless. The prima donna was deaf in the left ear, into which you had sung with all your force. I had to pay all their salaries and send them home.

ALASTAIR. I tell you it was a plot. Why shouldnt people like my singing? I can sing louder than any tenor on the stage. I can sing higher.

EPIFANIA. Alastair: you cannot resist a plot when the whole world is a party to it.

ADRIAN. Still, this does not explain how Alastair made the fifty thousand pounds.

EPIFANIA. I leave him to tell that disgraceful tale himself. I believe he is proud of it. [*She sits down disdainfully in the vacant chair*].

ALASTAIR. Well, it worked out all right. But it was a near thing, I tell you. What I did was this. I had a hundred pounds left after the opera stunt. I met an American. I told him I was crazy about a woman who wouldnt marry me unless I made fifty thousand in six months, and that I had only a hundred pounds in the world. He jumped up and said "Why, man alive, if you have a hundred you can open a bank account and get a cheque book." I said "What good is a cheque book?" He said "Are we partners, fifty fifty?" So I said yes: what else could I say? That very day we started in. We lodged the money and got a book of a hundred cheques. We took a theatre. We engaged a first rate cast. We got a play. We got a splendid production: the scenery was lovely: the girls were lovely: the principal woman was an angry-eyed creature with a queer foreign voice and a Hollywood accent, just the sort the public loves. We never asked the price of anything: we just went in up to our necks for thousands and thousands.

ADRIAN. But how did you pay for all these things?

ALASTAIR. With our cheques, of course. Didnt I tell you we had a cheque book?

ADRIAN. But when the hundred was gone the cheques must have been dishonored.

ALASTAIR. Not one of them. We kited them all. But it was a heartbreaking job.

ADRIAN. I dont understand. What does kiting mean?

SAGAMORE. It is quite simple. You pay for something with a cheque after the banks have closed for the day: if on Saturday or just before a bank holiday all the better. Say the cheque is for a hundred pounds and you have not a penny at the bank. You must then induce a friend or a hotel manager to cash another cheque for one hundred pounds for you. That provides for the previous cheque; but it obliges you, on pain of eighteen months hard labor, to induce another friend or hotel manager to cash another cheque for you for two hundred pounds. And so you go on spending and kiting from hundreds to thousands and from risks of eighteen months imprisonment to five years, ten years, fourteen years even.

ALASTAIR. If you think that was an easy job, just try it yourself: thats all. I dream of it sometimes: it's my worst nightmare. Why, my partner and I never saw that theatre! never saw that play! until the first night: we were signing cheques and kiting them all the time. Of course it was easier after a while, because as we paid our way all right we found it easier to get credit; and the biggest expenses didnt come until after the play was produced and the money was coming in. I could have done it for half the money; but the American could only keep himself up to the excitement of it by paying twice as much as we needed for everything and shoving shares in it on people for nothing but talk. But it didnt matter when the money began to come in. My! how it did come in! The whole town went mad about the angry-eyed woman. It rained money in bucketsful. It went to my head like drink. It went to the American's head. It went to the head of the American's American friends. They bought all the rights: the film rights, the translation rights, the touring rights, all sorts of rights that I never knew existed, and began selling them to one another until everybody in London and New York and Hollywood had a rake-off on them. Then the American bought all the rights back for five hundred thousand dollars, and sold them to an American syndicate for a million. It took six more Americans to do it; and every one of them had to have a rake-off; but all I wanted was fifty thousand pounds; and I cleared out with that and came swanking back to claim Eppy's hand. She thought I was great. I was great: the money made me great: I tell you I was drunk with it: I was another man. You may believe it or not as you like; but my hats were really too small for me.

EPIFANIA. It is quite true. The creature was not used to money; and it transfigured him. I, poor innocent, had no suspicion that money could work such miracles; for I had possessed millions in my cradle; and it meant no more to me than the air I breathed.

SAGAMORE. But just now, when I suggested a divorce,

you asked how he was to live. What has become of the fifty thousand pounds?

EPIFANIA. He lost it all in three weeks. He bought a circus with it. He thought everything he touched would turn into gold. I had to liquidate that circus a month later. He was about to turn the wild beasts loose and run away when I intervened. I was down four hundred and thirty pounds sixteen and seven-pence by the transaction.

ALASTAIR. Was it my fault? The elephant got influenza. The Ministry of Health closed me down and wouldnt let me move on because the animals might carry foot-and-mouth disease.

EPIFANIA. At all events, the net result was that instead of his being fifty thousand pounds to the good I was four hundred and thirty pounds to the bad. Instead of bringing me the revenues of a prince and a hero he cost me the allowance of a worm. And now he has the audacity to ask for a divorce.

ALASTAIR. No. I dont. It was Sagamore who suggested that. How can I afford to let you divorce me? As your husband I enjoy a good deal of social consideration; and the tradesmen give me unlimited credit.

EPIFANIA. For stockings, among other things.

PATRICIA. Oh [*she weeps*]! Does she pay for them, Ally?

ALASTAIR. Never mind, dear: I have shewn that I can make money when I am put to it; and I will make it again and buy you all the stockings you need out of my own earnings. [*He rises and goes behind her chair to take her cheeks in his hands*]. There, darling: dont cry.

EPIFANIA. There! They think they are married already!

SAGAMORE. But the matter is not in your hands, Mr Fitzfassenden. Mrs Fitzfassenden can divorce you whether you like it or not. The evidence is that on a recent occasion you left your wife and took refuge in the arms of Miss Smith. The Court will give Mrs Fitzfassenden a decree on that.

PATRICIA [*consoled and plucky*] Well, let it. I can support Alastair until he has time to make another fortune. You all think him a fool; but he's a dear good boy; and it just disgusts me the way you all turn against him, and the way his wife treats him as if he were dirt under her feet. What would she be without her money, I'd like to know?

EPIFANIA. Nobody is anybody without money, Seedystockings. My dear old father taught me that. "Stick to your money" he said "and all the other things shall be added unto you." He said it was in the Bible. I have never verified the quotation; but I have never forgotten it. I have stuck to my money; and I shall continue to stick to it. Rich as I am, I can hardly forgive Alastair for letting me down by four hundred and thirty pounds.

ALASTAIR. Sixteen and sevenpence! Stingy beast. But I will pay it.

PATRICIA. You shall, dear. I will sell out my insurance and give it to you.

EPIFANIA. May I have that in writing, Miss Smith?

ALASTAIR. Oh, you ought to be ashamed of yourself, you greedy pig. It was your own fault. Why did you let the elephant go for thirty pounds? He cost two hundred.

SAGAMORE. Do not let us wander from the point.

EPIFANIA. What is the point, pray?

SAGAMORE. The point is that you can obtain a divorce if you wish.

EPIFANIA. I dont wish. Do you think I am going to be dragged through the divorce court and have my picture in the papers with that thing? To have the story of my infatuation told in headlines in every rag in London! Besides, it is convenient to be married. It is respectable. It keeps other men off. It gives me a freedom that I could not enjoy as a single woman. I have become accustomed to a husband. No: decidedly I will not divorce Alastair—at least until I can find a substitute whom I really want.

PATRICIA. You couldnt divorce him unless he chose to let you. Alastair's too much the gentleman to mention it; but you know very well that your own behavior hasnt been so very nunlike that you dare have it shewn up in court.

EPIFANIA. Alastair was the first man I ever loved; and I hope he will not be the last. But legal difficulties do not exist for people with money. At all events, as Alastair cannot afford to divorce me, and I have no intention of divorcing him, the question does not arise. What o'clock is it?

ALASTAIR. I really think, Eppy, you might buy a wrist watch. I have told you so over and over again.

EPIFANIA. Why should I go to the expense of buying a wrist watch when everyone else has one; and I have nothing to do but ask? I have not carried a watch since I lost the key of my father's old repeater.

PATRICIA. It is ten minutes past twelve.

EPIFANIA. Gracious! I have missed my lesson. How annoying!

ALASTAIR. Your lesson? What are you learning now, may I ask?

EPIFANIA. All-in wrestling. When you next indulge in your favourite sport of wife beating, look out for a surprise. What did I come here for, Mr Sagamore?

SAGAMORE. To give me instructions about your will.

ALASTAIR. She makes a new will every time she

loses her temper, Sagamore. Jolly good business for you.

EPIFANIA. Do be quiet, Alastair. You forget the dignity of your position as my husband. Mr Sagamore: I have changed my mind about my will. And I shall overlook your attempt to poison me.

SAGAMORE. Thank you.

EPIFANIA. What do I owe you for this abortive consultation?

SAGAMORE. Thirteen and fourpence, if you please.

EPIFANIA. I do not carry money about with me. Adrian: can you lend me thirteen and fourpence?

ADRIAN [*puts his hand in his pocket*]——

EPIFANIA. Stop. Mr Sagamore: you had better be my family solicitor and send me your bill at the end of the year.

ALASTAIR. Send a County Court summons with it, Sagamore; or you may go whistle for your money.

EPIFANIA. Do hold your tongue, Alastair. Of course I always wait for a summons. It is a simple precaution against paying bills sent in twice over.

SAGAMORE. Quite, Mrs Fitzfassenden. An excellent rule.

EPIFANIA. You are a man of sense, Mr Sagamore. And now I must have some fresh air: this orgy of domesticity has made the room stuffy. Come along, Adrian: we'll drive out into the country somewhere, and lunch there. I know the quaintest little place up the river. Goodbye, Mr Sagamore. Goodbye, Seedy: take care of Alastair for me. His good looks will give you a pleasing sensation down your spine. [*She goes out*].

SAGAMORE [*as Adrian is following her out*] By the way, Mr Blenderbland, what did you come for?

ADRIAN. I totally forget. I dont feel equal to any more

this morning. [*He goes out without further salutations*].

SAGAMORE [*to Alastair*] Your wife is a most extraordinary lady.

ALASTAIR [*utters a stifled howl*]!

PATRICIA. He cant find words for her, poor dear.

SAGAMORE. And now, Mr Fitzfassenden, may I ask what you came to consult me about?

ALASTAIR. I dont know. After ten minutes of Eppy I never do know whether I am standing on my head or on my heels.

PATRICIA. It was about a separation. Pull yourself together a bit, dear.

ALASTAIR. Separation! You might as well try to separate yourself from a hurricane. [*He becomes sententious*]. Listen to me, Sagamore. I am one of those unfortunate people—you must know a lot of them—I daresay many of them have sat in this chair and talked to you as I am talking to you—

SAGAMORE [*after waiting in vain for a completion of the sentence*] Yes? You were saying—?

PATRICIA. Dont wander, Ally. Tell Mr Sagamore what sort of people.

ALASTAIR. The people that have bitten off more than they can chew. The ordinary chaps that have married extraordinary women. The commonplace women that have married extraordinary men. They all thought it was a splendid catch for them. Take my advice, Sagamore: marry in your own class. Dont misunderstand me: I dont mean rank or money. What I mean —what I mean—

PATRICIA [*coming to the rescue*] What he means is that people who marry should think about the same things and like the same things. They shouldnt be over oneanother's heads, if you follow me.

SAGAMORE. Perfectly. May I take it that Alastair

made that mistake, and that later on (too late, unfortunately) he discovered in you a—shall I say a soul
mate?

ALASTAIR. No: that sounds silly. Literary, you know.

PATRICIA. More of a mind mate. I should call it.

SAGAMORE. Precisely. Thank you. A mind mate with
whom he could be thoroughly comfortable.

ALASTAIR [*grasping Sagamore's hand fervently*] Thank
you, Sagamore: you are a real friend. Youve got it
exactly. Think over it for us. Come on, Seedy darling:
we mustnt waste a busy man's time.

*He goes out, leaving Patricia and Sagamore alone
together. She rises and goes to the table.*

PATRICIA. Mr Sagamore: youll stand by us, wont
you? Youll save Ally from that awful woman. Youll
save him for me.

SAGAMORE. I'm afraid I cant control her, Miss Smith.
Whats worse, I'm afraid she can control me. It's not
only that I cant afford to offend so rich a client. It's
that her will paralyzes mine. It's a sort of genius some
people have.

PATRICIA. Dont you be afraid of her, Mr Sagamore.
She has a genius for making money. It's in her family.
Money comes to her. But I have my little bit of genius
too; and she cant paralyze me.

SAGAMORE. And what have you a genius for, Miss
Smith, if I may ask?

PATRICIA. For making people happy. Unhappy people
come to me just as money comes to her.

SAGAMORE [*shaking his head*] I cant think that your
will is stronger than hers, Miss Smith.

PATRICIA. It isnt, Mr Sagamore. I have no will at all.
But I get what I want, somehow. Youll see.

ALASTAIR [*outside, shouting*] Seedy! Come on!

PATRICIA. Coming, darling. [*To Sagamore*] Goodbye,

Mr Sagamore [*they shake hands quickly. She hurries to the door*]. Youll see. [*She goes out*].

SAGAMORE [*to himself*] I think I shall wait and see.

He resumes his morning's work.

$\begin{bmatrix} \text{ACT II} \end{bmatrix}$

A dismal old coffee room in an ancient riverside inn. An immense and hideous sideboard of the murkiest mahogany stretches across the end wall. Above it hang, picturewise, two signboards, nearly black with age: one shewing the arms of the lord of the manor, and the other a sow standing upright and playing a flageolet. Underneath the sow is inscribed in tall letters THE PIG & WHISTLE. Between these works of art is a glass case containing an enormous stuffed fish, certainly not less than a century old.

At right angles to the sideboard, and extending nearly the whole length of the room, are two separate long tables, laid for lunch for about a dozen people each. The chairs, too close together, are plain wooden ones, hard and uncomfortable. The cutlery is cheap kitchen ware, with rickety silver cruets and salt cellars to keep up appearances. The table cloths are coarse, and are not fresh from the laundry.

The walls are covered with an ugly Victorian paper which may have begun as a design of dull purple wreaths on a dark yellow background, but is now a flyblown muck of no describable color. On the floor a coarse drugget, very old. The door, which stands wide open and has COFFEE ROOM inscribed on it, is to the right of anyone contemplating the sideboard from the opposite end of the room. Next the door an old fashioned hatstand flattens itself against the wall; and on it hang the hat and light overcoat of Mr Adrian Blenderbland.

He, with Epifania, is seated at the end of the table farthest from the door. They have just finished a meal.

*The cheese and biscuits are still on the table. She looks
interested and happy. He is in the worst of tempers.*

EPIFANIA. How jolly!

ADRIAN [*looking round disparagingly*] I must be a very
attractive man.

EPIFANIA [*opening her eyes wide*] Indeed! Not that
I am denying it; but what has it to do with what I
have just said?

ADRIAN. You said "How jolly!" I look round at this
rotten old inn trying to pretend that it's a riverside
hotel. We have just had a horrible meal of tomato tea
called soup, the remains of Sunday's joint, sprouts,
potatoes, apple tart and stale American synthetic
cheese. If you can suffer this and say "How jolly!"
there must be some irresistible attraction present; and
I can see nothing that is not utterly repulsive except
myself.

EPIFANIA. Dont you like these dear old-world places?
I do.

ADRIAN. I dont. They ought all to be rooted up,
pulled down, burnt to the ground. Your flat on the
Embankment in London cost more to furnish than
this place did to build from the cellar to the roof. You
can get a decent lunch there, perfectly served, by a
word through the telephone. Your luxurious car will
whisk you out to one of a dozen first rate hotels in
lovely scenery. And yet you choose this filthy old inn
and say "How jolly!" What is the use of being a
millionairess on such terms?

EPIFANIA. Psha! When I was first let loose on the
world with unlimited money, how long do you think
it took me to get tired of shopping and sick of the
luxuries you think so much of? About a fortnight.

My father, when he had a hundred millions, travelled third class and never spent more than ten shillings a day on himself except when he was entertaining people who were useful to him. Why should he? He couldnt eat more than anyone else. He couldnt drink more than anyone else. He couldnt wear more than anyone else. Neither can I.

ADRIAN. Then why do you love money and hate spending it?

EPIFANIA. Because money is power. Money is security. Money is freedom. It's the difference between living on the slope of a volcano and being safe in the garden of the Hesperides. And there is the continual pleasure of making more of it, which is quite easy if you have plenty to start with. I can turn a million into two million much more easily than a poor woman can turn five pounds into ten, even if she could get the five pounds to begin with. It turns itself, in fact.

ADRIAN. To me money is a vulgar bore and a soul destroying worry. I need it, of course; but I dont like it. I never think of it when I can possibly help it.

EPIFANIA. If you dont think about money what do you think about? Women?

ADRIAN. Yes, of course; but not exclusively.

EPIFANIA. Food?

ADRIAN. Well, I am not always thinking about my food; but I am rather particular about it. I confess I looked forward to a better lunch than [*indicating the table*] that.

EPIFANIA. Oho! So that is what has put you out of temper, is it?

ADRIAN [*annoyed*] I am not out of temper, I hope. But you promised me a very special treat. You said you had found out the most wonderful place on the river, where we could be ourselves and have a delicious

[919]

cottage meal in primitive happiness. Where is the charm of this dismal hole? Have you ever eaten a viler lunch? There is not even a private sitting room: anybody can walk in here at any moment. We should have been much more comfortable at Richmond or Maidenhead. And I believe it is raining.

EPIFANIA. Is that my fault?

ADRIAN. It completes your notion of a happy day up the river. Why is it that the people who know how to enjoy themselves never have any money, and the people who have money never know how to enjoy themselves?

EPIFANIA. You are not making yourself agreeable, Adrian.

ADRIAN. You are not entertaining me very munificently, Epifania. For heaven's sake let us get into the car and drive about the country. It is much more luxurious than this hideous coffee room, and more private.

EPIFANIA. I am tired of my car.

ADRIAN. I am not. I wish I could afford one like it.

EPIFANIA. I thought you would enjoy sitting in this crazy out-of-way place talking to me. But I find you are a spoilt old bachelor: you care about nothing but your food and your little comforts. You are worse than Alastair; for at least he could talk about boxing and tennis.

ADRIAN. And you can talk about nothing but money.

EPIFANIA. And you think money uninteresting! Oh, you should have known my father!

ADRIAN. I am very glad I did not.

EPIFANIA [*suddenly dangerous*] Whats that you say?

ADRIAN. My dear Epifania, if we are to remain friends, I may as well be quite frank with you. Everything you have told me about your father convinces me that though he was no doubt an affectionate parent and amiable enough to explain your rather tiresome father fixation, as Dr Freud would call it, he must have been quite the most appalling bore that ever devastated even a Rotary club.

EPIFANIA [*stunned for a moment by this blasphemy*] My father! You infinite nothingness! My father made a hundred and fifty millions. You never made even half a million.

ADRIAN. My good girl, your father never made anything. I have not the slightest notion of how he contrived to get a legal claim on so much of what other people made; but I do know that he lost four fifths of it by being far enough behind the times to buy up the properties of the Russian nobility in the belief that England would squash the Soviet revolution in three weeks or so. Could anyone have made a stupider mistake? Not I.

EPIFANIA [*springing up*] You rotten thing. [*He rises apprehensively*]. Take that for calling my father a bore. [*She throws him*].

ADRIAN [*picking himself up painfully*] Oh! Restrain yourself. You might have hurt me very seriously.

EPIFANIA. I will hurt you until you wish yourself dead. Scum! Filth! Take that for saying he never made anything. [*She throws him again*].

ADRIAN. Help! help! There is a madwoman here: I shall not be able to hold her single handed. Help! [*He comes behind her and seizes her round the waist*].

EPIFANIA. Vermin! [*She throws him over her shoulder*].

ADRIAN. Police! She is murdering me. She is mad. Help! help! [*He scrambles up and is flying to the door when she overtakes him*].

EPIFANIA. Dirt! Carrion! [*She throws him out head over heels and flings his hat and overcoat after him*].

[921]

ADRIAN [*outside, rolling downstairs with appalling bumps*] Oh! Oh! Help! Murder! Police! Oh! [*He faints. Silence*].

EPIFANIA. You brute! You have killed me. [*She totters to the nearest chair and sinks into it, scattering the crockery as she clutches the table with her outstretched arms and sprawls on it in convulsions*].

A serious looking middleaged Egyptian gentleman in an old black frock coat and a tarboosh, speaking English too well to be mistaken for a native, hurries in.

THE EGYPTIAN [*peremptorily*] Whats the matter? What is going on here?

EPIFANIA [*raising her head slowly and gazing at him*] Who the devil are you?

THE EGYPTIAN. I am an Egyptian doctor. I hear a great disturbance. I hasten to ascertain the cause. I find you here in convulsions. Can I help?

EPIFANIA. I am dying.

THE DOCTOR. Nonsense! You can swear. The fit has subsided. You can sit up now: you are quite well. Good afternoon.

EPIFANIA. Stop. I am not quite well: I am on the point of death. I need a doctor. I am a rich woman.

THE DOCTOR. In that case you will have no difficulty in finding an English doctor. Is there anyone else who needs my help? I was upstairs. The noise was of somebody falling downstairs. He may have broken some bones. [*He goes out promptly*].

EPIFANIA [*struggling to her feet and calling after him*] Never mind him: if he has broken every bone in his body it is no more than he deserves. Come back instantly. I want you. Come back. Come back.

THE DOCTOR [*returning*] The landlord is taking the gentleman to the Cottage Hospital in your car.

EPIFANIA. In my car! I will not permit it. Let them get an ambulance.

THE DOCTOR. The car has gone. You should be very glad that it is being so useful.

EPIFANIA. It is your business to doctor me, not to lecture me.

THE DOCTOR. I am not your doctor: I am not in general practice. I keep a clinic for penniless Mahometan refugees; and I work in the hospital. I cannot attend to you.

EPIFANIA. You can attend to me. You must attend to me. Are you going to leave me here to die?

THE DOCTOR. You are not dying. Not yet, at least. Your own doctor will attend to you.

EPIFANIA. You are my own doctor. I tell you I am a rich woman: doctors' fees are nothing to me: charge me what you please. But you must and shall attend to me. You are abominably rude; but you inspire confidence as a doctor.

THE DOCTOR. If I attended all those in whom I inspire confidence I should be worn out in a week. I have to reserve myself for poor and useful people.

EPIFANIA. Then you are either a fool or a Bolshevik.

THE DOCTOR. I am nothing but a servant of Allah.

EPIFANIA. You are not: you are my doctor: do you hear? I am a sick woman: you cannot abandon me to die in this wretched place.

THE DOCTOR. I see no symptoms of any sickness about you. Are you in pain?

EPIFANIA. Yes. Horrible pain.

THE DOCTOR. Where?

EPIFANIA. Dont cross-examine me as if you didnt believe me. I must have sprained my wrist throwing that beast all over the place.

THE DOCTOR. Which hand?

EPIFANIA [*presenting a hand*] This.

THE DOCTOR [*taking her hand in a businesslike way, and pulling and turning the fingers and wrist*] Nothing whatever the matter.

EPIFANIA. How do you know? It's my hand, not yours.

THE DOCTOR. You would scream the house down if your wrist were sprained. You are shamming. Lying. Why? Is it to make yourself interesting?

EPIFANIA. Make myself interesting! Man: I am interesting.

THE DOCTOR. Not in the least, medically. Are you interesting in any other way?

EPIFANIA. I am the most interesting woman in England. I am Epifania Ognisanti di Parerga.

THE DOCTOR. Never heard of her. Italian aristocrat, I presume.

EPIFANIA. Aristocrat! Do you take me for a fool? My ancestors were moneylenders to all Europe five hundred years ago: we are now bankers to all the world.

THE DOCTOR. Jewess, eh?

EPIFANIA. Christian, to the last drop of my blood. Jews throw half their money away on charities and fancies like Zionism. The stupidest di Parerga can just walk round the cleverest Jew when it comes to moneymaking. We are the only real aristocracy in the world: the aristocracy of money.

THE DOCTOR. The plutocracy, in fact.

EPIFANIA. If you like. I am a plutocrat of the plutocrats.

THE DOCTOR. Well, that is a disease for which I do not prescribe. The only known cure is a revolution; but the mortality rate is high; and sometimes, if it is the wrong sort of revolution, it intensifies the disease.

[924]

I can do nothing for you. I must go back to my work. Good morning.

EPIFANIA [*holding him*] But this is your work. What else have you to do?

THE DOCTOR. There is a good deal to be done in the world besides attending the rich imaginary invalids.

EPIFANIA. But if you are well paid?

THE DOCTOR. I make the little money I need by work which I venture to think more important.

EPIFANIA [*throwing him away and moving about distractedly*] You are a pig and a beast and a Bolshevik. It is the most abominable thing of you to leave me here in my distress. My car is gone. I have no money. I never carry money about.

THE DOCTOR. I have none to carry. Your car will return presently. You can borrow money from your chauffeur.

EPIFANIA. You are an unmitigated hippopotamus. You are a Bashibazouk. I might have known it from your ridiculous tarboosh. You should take it off in my presence. [*She snatches it from his head and holds it behind her back*]. At least have the manners to stay with me until my chauffeur comes back.

The motor horn is heard honking.

THE DOCTOR. He has come back.

EPIFANIA. Damn! Cant you wait until he has had his tea and a cigarette?

THE DOCTOR. No. Be good enough to give me back my fez.

EPIFANIA. I wanted to see what you looked like without it [*She puts it tenderly on his head*]. Listen to me. You are having an adventure. Have you no romance in you? Havnt you even common curiosity? Dont you want to know why I threw that beast downstairs? Dont you want to throw your wretched work to the devil for once and have an afternoon on the river with an interesting and attractive woman?

THE DOCTOR. Women are neither interesting nor attractive to me except when they are ill. I know too much about them, inside and out. You are perfectly well.

EPIFANIA. Liar. Nobody is perfectly well, nor ever has been, nor ever will be. [*She sits down, sulking*].

THE DOCTOR. That is true. You must have brains of a sort. [*He sits down opposite to her*]. I remember when I began as a young surgeon I killed several patients by my operations because I had been taught that I must go on cutting until there was nothing left but perfectly healthy tissue. As there is no such thing as perfectly healthy tissue I should have cut my patients entirely away if the nurse had not stopped me before they died on the table. They died after they left the hospital; but as they were carried away from the table alive I was able to claim a successful operation. Are you married?

EPIFANIA. Yes. But you need not be afraid. My husband is openly unfaithful to me and cannot take you into court if you make love to me. I can divorce him if necessary.

THE DOCTOR. And the man you threw downstairs: who was he? One does not throw one's husband downstairs. Did he make love to you?

EPIFANIA. No. He insulted my father's memory because he was disappointed with his lunch here. When I think of my father all ordinary men seem to me the merest trash. You are not an ordinary man. I should like to see some more of you. Now that you have asked me confidential questions about my family, and I have answered them, you can no longer pretend that you are not my family doctor. So that is settled.

THE DOCTOR. A father fixation, did you say?

EPIFANIA [*nods*]!

THE DOCTOR. And an excess of money?

EPIFANIA. Only a beggarly thirty millions.

THE DOCTOR. A psychological curiosity. I will consider it.

EPIFANIA. Consider it! You will feel honored, gratified, delighted.

THE DOCTOR. I see. Enormous self-confidence. Reckless audacity. Insane egotism. Apparently sexless.

EPIFANIA. Sexless! Who told you that I am sexless?

THE DOCTOR. You talk to me as if you were a man. There is no mystery, no separateness, no sacredness about men to you. A man to you is only a male of your species.

EPIFANIA. My species indeed! Men are a different and very inferior species. Five minutes conversation with my husband will convince you that he and I do not belong to the same species. But there are some great men, like my father. And there are some good doctors, like you.

THE DOCTOR. Thank you. What does your regular doctor say about you?

EPIFANIA. I have no regular doctor. If I had I should have an operation a week until there was nothing left of me or of my bank balance. I shall not expect you to maul me about with a stethoscope, if that is what you are afraid of. I have the lungs of a whale and the digestion of an ostrich. I have a clockwork inside. I sleep eight hours like a log. When I want anything I lose my head so completely about it that I always get it.

THE DOCTOR. What things do you want mostly?

EPIFANIA. Everything. Anything. Like a lightning flash. And then there is no stopping me.

THE DOCTOR. Everything and anything is nothing.

EPIFANIA. Five minutes ago I wanted you. Now I have got you.

THE DOCTOR. Come! You cannot bluff a doctor. You may want the sun and the moon and the stars; but you cannot get them.

EPIFANIA. That is why I take good care not to want them. I want only what I can get.

THE DOCTOR. Good. A practical intellect. And what do you want at present, for instance?

EPIFANIA. That is the devil of it. There is nothing one can get except more money.

THE DOCTOR. What about more men?

EPIFANIA. More Alastairs! More Blenderblands! Those are not deep wants. At present I want a motor launch.

THE DOCTOR. There is no such thing in this little place.

EPIFANIA. Tell the landlord to stop the first one that comes along and buy it.

THE DOCTOR. Tcha! People will not sell their boats like that.

EPIFANIA. Have you ever tried?

THE DOCTOR. No.

EPIFANIA. I have. When I need a car or a motor boat or a launch or anything like that I buy straight off the road or off the river or out of the harbor. These things cost thousands when they are new; but next day you cannot get fifty pounds for them. Offer £300 for any of them, and the owner dare not refuse: he knows he will never get such an offer again.

THE DOCTOR. Aha! You are a psychologist. This is very interesting.

EPIFANIA. Nonsense! I know how to buy and sell, if that is what you mean.

THE DOCTOR. That is how good psychologists make money.

EPIFANIA. Have you made any?

THE DOCTOR. No. I do not care for money: I care for knowledge.

EPIFANIA. Knowledge is no use without money. Are you married?

THE DOCTOR. I am married to Science. One wife is enough for me, though by my religion I am allowed four.

EPIFANIA. Four! What do you mean?

THE DOCTOR. I am what you call a Mahometan.

EPIFANIA. Well, you will have to be content with two wives if you marry me.

THE DOCTOR. Oh! Is there any question of that between us?

EPIFANIA. Yes. I want to marry you.

THE DOCTOR. Nothing doing, lady. Science is my bride.

EPIFANIA. You can have Science as well: I shall not be jealous of her. But I made a solemn promise to my father on his deathbed—

THE DOCTOR [*interrupting*] Stop. I had better tell you that I made a solemn promise to my mother on her deathbed.

EPIFANIA. What!!!

THE DOCTOR. My mother was a very wise woman. She made me swear to her that if any woman wanted to marry me, and I felt tempted, I would hand the woman two hundred piastres and tell her that unless she would go out into the world with nothing but that and the clothes she stood in, and earn her living alone and unaided for six months, I would never speak to her again.

EPIFANIA. And if she stood the test?

THE DOCTOR. Then I must marry her even if she were the ugliest devil on earth.

EPIFANIA. And you dare ask me—me, Epifania Ognisanti di Parerga! to submit myself to this test—to any test!

THE DOCTOR. I swore. I have a mother fixation. Allah has willed it so. I cannot help myself.

EPIFANIA. What was your mother?

THE DOCTOR. A washerwoman. A widow. She brought up eleven children. I was the youngest, the Benjamin. The other ten are honest working folk. With their help she made me a man of learning. It was her ambition to have a son who could read and write. She prayed to Allah; and he endowed me with the necessary talent.

EPIFANIA. And you think I will allow myself to be beaten by an old washerwoman?

THE DOCTOR. I am afraid so. You could never pass the test.

EPIFANIA. Indeed! And my father's test for a husband worthy of me?

THE DOCTOR. Oh! The husband is to be tested too! That never occurred to me.

EPIFANIA. Nor to your mother either, it seems. Well, you know better now. I am to give you a hundred and fifty pounds. In six months you are to increase it to fifty thousand. How is that for a test?

THE DOCTOR. Quite conclusive. At the end of six months I shall not have a penny of it left, praise be to Allah.

EPIFANIA. You confess yourself beaten?

THE DOCTOR. Absolutely. Completely.

EPIFANIA. And you think I am beaten too.

THE DOCTOR. Hopelessly. You do not know what

homeless poverty is; and Allah the Compassionate will take care that you never do.

EPIFANIA. How much is two hundred piastres?

THE DOCTOR. At the rate of exchange contemplated by my mother, about thirtyfive shillings.

EPIFANIA. Hand it over.

THE DOCTOR. Unfortunately my mother forgot to provide for this contingency. I have not got thirtyfive shillings. I must borrow them from you.

EPIFANIA. I have not a penny on me. No matter: I will borrow it from the chauffeur. He will lend you a hundred and fifty pounds on my account if you dare ask him. Goodbye for six months. [*She goes out*].

THE DOCTOR. There is no might and no majesty save in Thee, O Allah; but, oh! most Great and Glorious, is this another of Thy terrible jokes?

A basement in the Commercial Road. An elderly man, anxious, poor, and ratlike, sits at a table with his wife. He is pouring over his accounts. She, on his left, is sewing buttons on a coat, working very fast. There is a pile of coats on the table to her right waiting to have buttons sewn on, and another to her left which she has finished. The table is draped down to the ground with an old cloth. Some daylight comes in down the stone stairs; but does not extend to the side where the couple sit, which is lighted by a small electric bulb on a wire. Between the stairs and the table a dirty old patched curtain hangs in front of an opening into a farther compartment.

A bell tinkles. The woman instantly stops sewing and conceals the piles of coats under the table. Epifania, her dress covered by an old waterproof, and wearing an elaborately damaged hat, comes down the stairs. She looks at the pair; then looks round her; then goes to the curtain and looks through. The old man makes a dash to prevent her, but is too late. He snatches the curtain from her and bars her passage.

THE MAN. What do you want? What are you doing here?

EPIFANIA. I want employment. A woman told me I should find it here. I am destitute.

THE MAN. Thats not the way to get employment: poking your nose into places that dont concern you. Get out. There are no women employed here.

EPIFANIA. You lie. There are six women working in there. Who employs them?

THE MAN. Is that the way to talk to me? You think a lot of yourself, dont you? What do you take me for?

EPIFANIA. A worm.

THE MAN [*making a violent demonstration*]!!

EPIFANIA. Take care. I can use my fists. I can shoot, if necessary.

THE WOMAN [*hurrying to the man and holding him*] Take care, Joe. She's an inspector. Look at her shoes.

EPIFANIA. I am not an inspector. And what is the matter with my shoes, pray?

THE WOMAN [*respectfully*] Well maam, could a woman looking for work at tuppence hapeny an hour afford a west end shoe like that? I assure you we dont employ any women here. We're only caretakers.

EPIFANIA. But I saw six women—

THE MAN [*throwing open the curtain*] Where? Not a soul. Search the whole bloody basement.

THE WOMAN. Hush, hush, Joe: dont speak to the lady like that. You see, maam: theres not a soul.

EPIFANIA. Theres a smell. You have given them a signal to hide. You are breaking the law. Give me some work or I will send a postcard to the Home Office.

THE MAN. Look here, lady. Cant we arrange this? What good will it do you to get me into trouble and shut up my little shop?

EPIFANIA. What good will it do me to say nothing?

THE MAN. Well, what about half a crown a week?

EPIFANIA. I cannot live on half a crown a week.

THE MAN. You can if you look round a bit. There are others, you know.

EPIFANIA. Give me the address of the others. If I am to live by blackmail I must have an extended practice.

THE MAN. Well, if I have to pay I dont see why the others shouldnt too. Will you take half a crown? [*He holds up half a crown*]. Look here! Look at it! Listen to it! [*He rings it on the table*]. It's yours, and another every Wednesday if you keep the inspector off me.

EPIFANIA. It's no use ringing half crowns at me: I am accustomed to them. And I feel convinced that you will pay five shillings if I insist.

THE WOMAN. Oh, maam, have some feeling for us. You dont know the struggle we have to live.

THE MAN [*roughly*] Here: we're not beggars. I'll pay what the business can afford and not a penny more. You seem to know that it can afford five shillings. Well, if you know that, you know that it cant afford any more. Take your five shillings and be damned to you. [*He flings two half crowns on the table*].

THE WOMAN. Oh, Joe, dont be so hasty.

THE MAN. You shut up. You think you can beg a shilling or two off: but you cant. I can size up a tough lot without looking at her shoes. She's got us; and she knows she's got us.

EPIFANIA. I do not like this blackmailing business. Of course if I must I must; but can you not give me some manual work?

THE MAN. You want to get a little deeper into our business, dont you?

EPIFANIA. I am as deep as I can go already. You are employing six women in there. The thing in the corner is a gas engine: that makes you a workshop under the Act. Except that the sanitary arrangements are probably abominable, there is nothing more for me to know. I have you in the hollow of my hand. Give me some work that I can live by or I will have you cleared out like a wasp's nest.

THE MAN. I have a good mind to clear out now and take some place where you wont find me so easy. I am used to changing my address.

EPIFANIA. That is the best card in your hand. You have some business ability. Tell me why you cannot give me work to live by just as you give it, I suppose, to the women I saw in there.

THE MAN. I dont like the people I employ to know too much.

EPIFANIA. I see. They might call in the inspector.

THE MAN. Call in the inspector! What sort of fool are you? They dread the inspector more than I do.

EPIFANIA. Why? Dont they want to be protected?

THE WOMAN. The inspector wouldnt protect them, maam: he'd only shut up the place and take away their job from them. If they thought youd be so cruel as to report them theyd go down on their knees to you to spare them.

THE MAN. You that know such a lot ought to know that a business like this cant afford any luxuries. It's a cheap labor business. As long as I get women to work for their natural wage, I can get along; but no luxuries, mind you. No trade union wages. No sanitary arrangements as you call them. No limewashings every six months. No separate rooms to eat in. No fencing in of dangerous machinery or the like of that: not that I care; for I have nothing but the old gas engine that wouldnt hurt a fly, though it brings me under the blasted Workshop Act as you spotted all right. I have no big machinery; but I have to undersell those that have it. If I put up my prices by a farthing theyd set their machinery going and drop me. You might as well ask me to pay trade union wages as do all that the inspector wants: I should be out of business in a week.

EPIFANIA. And what is a woman's natural wage?

THE MAN. Tuppence hapeny an hour for twelve hours a day.

EPIFANIA. Slavery!

THE WOMAN. Oh no, maam: nobody could call that slavery. A good worker can make from twelve to fifteen shillings a week at it, week in and week out.

THE MAN. Isnt it what the Government paid at the beginning of the war when all the women were called on to do their bit? Do you expect me to pay more than the British Government?

THE WOMAN. I assure you it's the regular and proper wage and always has been, maam.

THE MAN. Like five per cent at the Bank of England it is. This is a respectable business, whatever your inspectors may say.

EPIFANIA. Can a woman live on twelve shillings a week?

THE MAN. Of course she can. Whats to prevent her?

THE WOMAN. Why, maam, when I was a girl in a match factory I had five shillings a week, and it was a godsend to my mother. And a girl who had no family of her own could always find a family to take her in for four and sixpence, and treat her better than if she had been in her father's house.

THE MAN. I can find you a family what'll do it today, in spite of all the damned doles and wages boards that have upset everything and given girls ideas above their station without giving them the means to pamper themselves.

EPIFANIA. Well, I will work even for that, to prove that I can work and support myself. So give me work and have done talking.

THE MAN. Who started talking? You or I?

EPIFANIA. I did. I thank you for the information you have given me: it has been instructive and to the point. Is that a sufficient apology? And now to work, to work. I am in a hurry to get to work.

THE MAN. Well, what work can you do?

THE WOMAN. Can you sew? Can you make button-holes?

EPIFANIA. Certainly not. I dont call that work.

THE MAN. Well, what sort of work are you looking for?

EPIFANIA. Brain work.

THE MAN. She's dotty!

EPIFANIA. Your work. Managing work. Planning work. Driving work. Let me see what you make here. Tell me how you dispose of it.

THE MAN [*to his wife*] You had better get on with your work. Let her see it. [*To Epifania, whilst the woman pulls out the pile of coats from under the table and sits down resignedly to her sewing*] And when youve quite satisfied your curiosity, perhaps youll take that five shillings and go.

EPIFANIA. Why? Dont you find my arrival a pleasant sort of adventure in this den?

THE MAN. I never heard the like of your cheek, not from nobody. [*He sits down to his accounts*].

EPIFANIA [*to the woman, indicating the pile of coats*] What do you do with these when they are finished?

THE WOMAN [*going on with her work*] The man comes with his lorry and takes them away.

EPIFANIA. Does he pay you for them?

THE WOMAN. Oh no. He gives us a receipt for them. Mr Superflew pays us for the receipts at the end of the week.

EPIFANIA. And what does Mr Superflew do with the coats?

THE WOMAN. He takes them to the wholesaler that supplies him with the cloth. The lorry brings us the cloth when it takes away the finished clothes.

EPIFANIA. Why dont you deal directly with the wholesalers?

THE WOMAN. Oh no: that wouldnt be right. We dont know who they are; and Mr Superflew does. Besides, we couldnt afford a lorry.

EPIFANIA. Does Mr Superflew own the lorry?

THE WOMAN. Oh no: that wouldnt be right. He hires it by the hour from Bolton's.

EPIFANIA. Is the driver always the same man?

THE WOMAN. Yes, of course: always old Tim Goodenough.

EPIFANIA [*to the man*] Write those names for me: Superflew, Bolton's, Goodenough.

THE MAN. Here! I'm not your clerk, you know.

EPIFANIA. You will be, soon. Do as I tell you.

THE MAN. Well of all the cheek—! [*He obeys*].

EPIFANIA. When Goodenough comes round next tell him to tell Bolton's that he has found somebody who will buy the lorry for fourteen pounds. Tell him that if he can induce Bolton's to part from it at that figure you will give him a pound for himself and engage him at half a crown advance on his present wages to drive it just the same old round to the same places. He knows the wholesalers. Mr Superflew is superfluous. We shall collect not only our own stuff but that of all the other sweaters.

THE MAN. Sweaters! Who are you calling sweaters?

EPIFANIA. Man, know thyself. You sweat yourself; you sweat your wife; you sweat those women in there; you live on sweat.

THE MAN. Thats no way to talk about it. It isnt civil. I pay the right wages, same as everybody pays. I give employment that the like of them couldnt make for themselves.

EPIFANIA. You are sensitive about it. I am not. I am

going to sweat Mr Superflew out of existence. I am going to sweat Mr Timothy Goodenough instead of allowing Mr Superflew to sweat him.

THE MAN. See here. Does this business belong to me or to you?

EPIFANIA. We shall see. Dare you buy the lorry?

THE MAN. Wheres the money to come from?

EPIFANIA. Where does all money come from? From the bank.

THE MAN. You got to put it there first, havnt you?

EPIFANIA. Not in the least. Other people put it there; and the bank lends it to you if it thinks you know how to extend your business.

THE WOMAN [*terrified*] Oh, Joe, dont trust your money in a bank. No good ever comes out of banks for the likes of us. Dont let her tempt you, Joe.

EPIFANIA. When had you last a holiday?

THE WOMAN. Me! A holiday! We cant afford holidays. I had one on Armistice Day, eighteen years ago.

EPIFANIA. Then it cost a world war and the slaughter of twenty millions of your fellow creatures to give you one holiday in your lifetime. I can do better for you than that.

THE WOMAN. We dont understand that sort of talk here. Weve no time for it. Will you please take our little present and go away?

The bell tinkles.

THE MAN [*rising*] Thats Tim, for the clothes.

EPIFANIA [*masterfully*] Sit down. I will deal with Tim.

She goes out. The man, after a moment of irresolution sits down helplessly.

THE WOMAN [*crying*] Oh, Joe, dont listen to her: dont let her meddle with us. That woman would spend our little savings in a week, and leave us to slave to the end of our days to make it up again. I cant go on slaving for ever: we're neither of us as young as we were.

THE MAN [*sullen*] What sort of wife are you for a man? You take the pluck out of me every time. Dont I see other men swanking round and throwing money about that they get out of the banks? In and out of banks they are, all day. What do they do but smoke cigars and drink champagne? A five pound note is to them what a penny is to me. Why shouldnt I try their game instead of slaving here for pence and hapence?

THE WOMAN. Cause you dont understand it, Joe. We know our own ways; and though we're poor our ways have never let us down; and they never will if we stick to them. And who would speak to us? who would know us or give us a helping hand in hard times if we began doing things that nobody else does? How would you like to walk down Commercial Road and get nothing but black looks from all your friends and be refused a week's credit in the shops? Joe: Ive gone on in our natural ways all these years without a word of complaint; and I can go on long enough still to make us comfortable when we're too old to see what I'm sewing or you to count the pence. But if youre going to risk everything and put our money in a bank and change our ways I cant go on: I cant go on: itll kill me. Go up and stop her, Joe. Dont let her talk: just put her out. Be a man, darling: dont be afraid of her. Dont break my heart and ruin yourself. Oh, dont sit there dithering: you dont know what she may be doing. Oh! oh! oh! [*She can say no more for sobbing*].

THE MAN [*rising, but not very resolutely*] There! there! Hold your noise: I'm not going to let her interfere with us. I'll put her out all right. [*He goes to the stairs, Epifania comes down*]. Now, missis: lets have an understanding.

EPIFANIA. No understanding is necessary. Tim is sure that Bolton's will take ten pounds for the lorry. Tim is my devoted slave. Make that poor woman stop howling if you can. I am going now. There is not enough work here for me: I can do it all in half a day every week. I shall take a job as scullery maid at a hotel to fill up my time. But first I must go round to the address Tim has given me and arrange that we send them our stuff direct and collect just as Superflew did. When I have arranged everything with them I will come back and arrange everything for you. Meanwhile, carry on as usual. Good morning. [*She goes out*].

THE MAN [*stupefied*] It seems to me like a sort of dream. What could I do?

THE WOMAN [*who has stopped crying on hearing Epifania's allusion to her*] Do what she tells us, Joe. We're like children—[*She begins crying again softly*].

There is nothing more to be said.

⌈ACT IV⌉

*The coffee room of The Pig & Whistle, now trans-
mogrified into the lounge of The Cardinal's Hat, a very
attractive riverside hotel. The long tables are gone, replaced by several teatables with luxurious chairs round
them. The old sideboard, the stuffed fish, the signboards
are no more: instead there is an elegant double writing
desk for two sitters, divided by stationery cases and
electric lamps with dainty shades. Near it is a table with
all the illustrated papers and magazines to hand. Farther
down the room, towards the side next the door, there is a
long well cushioned seat, capable of accommodating three
persons. With three chairs at the other side it forms a
fireside circle. The old hatstand has gone to its grave
with the sideboard. The newly painted walls present an
attractive color scheme. The floor is parquetted and
liberally supplied with oriental rugs. All the appurten-
ances of a brand new first class hotel lounge are in
evidence.*

*Alastair, in boating flannels, is sprawling happily on
the long seat, reading an illustrated magazine. Patricia,
in her gladdest summer rags, is knitting in the middle
chair opposite, full of quiet enjoyment.*

*It is a fine summer afternoon; and the general effect is
that of a bank holiday paradise.*

ALASTAIR. I say, Seedy, isnt this jolly?
PATRICIA. Yes, darling: it's lovely.
ALASTAIR. Nothing beats a fine week-end on the
river. A pull on the water in the morning to give one
a good stretch and a good appetite. A good lunch, and

then a good laze. What more can any man desire on earth?

PATRICIA. You row so beautifully, Ally. I love to see you sculling. And punting too. You look so well standing up in the punt.

ALASTAIR. It's the quiet of it, the blessed quiet. You are so quiet: I'm never afraid of your kicking up a row about nothing. The river is so smooth. I dont know which is more comforting, you or the river, when I think of myself shooting Niagara three or four times a day at home.

PATRICIA. Dont think of it, darling. It isnt home: this is home.

ALASTAIR. Yes, dear: youre right: this is what home ought to be, though it's only a hotel.

PATRICIA. Well, what more could anyone ask but a nice hotel? All the housekeeping done for us: no trouble with the servants: no rates nor taxes. I have never had any peace except in a hotel. But perhaps a man doesnt feel that way.

The manager of the hotel, a young man, smartly dressed, enters. He carries the hotel register, which he opens and places on the newspaper table. He then comes obsequiously to his two guests.

MANAGER [*between them*] Good afternoon, sir. I hope you find everything here to your liking.

ALASTAIR. Yes, thanks. But what have you done to the old place? When I was here last, a year ago, it was a common pub called The Pig and Whistle.

THE MANAGER. It was so until quite lately, sir. My father kept The Pig and Whistle. So did his forefathers right back to the reign of William the Conqueror. Cardinal Wolsey stopped once for an hour at The Pig and Whistle when his mule cast a shoe and had to go to the blacksmith's. I assure you my forefathers

[943]

thought a lot of themselves. But they were uneducated men, and ruined the old place by trying to improve it by getting rid of the old things in it. It was on its last legs when you saw it, sir. I was ashamed of it.

ALASTAIR. Well, you have made a first rate job of it now.

THE MANAGER. Oh, it was not my doing, sir: I am only the manager. You would hardly believe it if I were to tell you the story of it. Much more romantic, to my mind, than the old tale about Wolsey. But I mustnt disturb you talking. You will let me know if theres anything I can do to make you quite comfortable.

PATRICIA. I should like to know about the old Pig if it's romantic. If you can spare the time, of course.

THE MANAGER. I am at your service, madam, always.

ALASTAIR. Fire ahead, old man.

THE MANAGER. Well, madam, one day a woman came here and asked for a job as a scullery maid. My poor old father hadnt the nerve to turn her out: he said she might just try for a day or two. So she started in. She washed two dishes and broke six. My poor old mother was furious: she thought the world of her dishes. She had no suspicion, poor soul, that they were ugly and common and old and cheap and altogether out of date. She said that as the girl had broken them she should pay for them if she had to stay for a month and have the price stopped out of her wages. Off went the girl to Reading and came back with a load of crockery that made my mother cry: she said we should be disgraced for ever if we served a meal on such old fashioned things. But the very next day an American lady with a boating party bought them right off the table for three times what they cost; and my poor mother never dared say another word. The scullery maid took things into her own hands in a way we could never have done. It was cruel for us; but we couldnt deny that she was always right.

PATRICIA. Cruel! What was there cruel in getting nice crockery for you?

THE MANAGER. Oh, it wasnt only that, madam: that part of it was easy and pleasant enough. You see all she had to do with the old crockery was to break it and throw the bits into the dustbin. But what was the matter with the old Pig and Whistle was not the old thick plates that took away your appetite. It was the old people it had gathered about itself that were past their work and had never been up to much according to modern ideas. They had to be thrown into the street to wander about for a few days and then go into the workhouse. There was the bar that was served by father and mother: she dressed up to the nines, as she thought, poor old dear, never dreaming that the world was a day older than when she was married. The scullery maid told them the truth about themselves; and it just cut them to pieces; for it was the truth; and I couldnt deny it. The old man had to give in, because he had raised money on his freehold and was at his wits' end to pay the mortgage interest. The next thing we knew, the girl had paid off the mortgage and got the whip hand of us completely. "It's time for you two to sell your freehold and retire: you are doing no good here" she said.

PATRICIA. But that was dreadful, to root them up like that.

THE MANAGER. It was hard; but it was the truth. We should have had the brokers in sooner or later if we had gone on. Business is business; and theres no room for sentiment in it. And then, think of the good she did. My parents would never have got the price for the freehold that she gave them. Here was I, ashamed of the place, tied to the old Pig and Whistle by my feeling for my parents, with no prospects. Now the house is a credit to the neighborhood and gives more employment than the poor old Pig did in its best days; and I am the manager of it with a salary and a percentage beyond anything I could have dreamt of.

ALASTAIR. Then she didnt chuck you, old man.

THE MANAGER. No, sir. You see, though I could never have made the change myself, I was intelligent enough to see that she was right. I backed her up all through. I have such faith in that woman, sir, that if she told me to burn down the hotel tonight I'd do it without a moment's hesitation. When she puts her finger on a thing it turns to gold every time. The bank would remind my father if he overdrew by five pounds; but the manager keeps pressing overdrafts on her: it makes him miserable when she has a penny to her credit. A wonderful woman, sir: one day a scullery maid, and the next the proprietress of a first class hotel.

PATRICIA. And are the old people satisfied and happy?

THE MANAGER. Well, no: the change was too much for them at their age. My father had a stroke and wont last long, I'm afraid. And my mother has gone a bit silly. Still, it was best for them; and they have all the comforts they care for.

ALASTAIR. Well, thats a very moving tale: more so than you think, old boy, because I happen to know a woman of that stamp. By the way, I telegraphed for a friend of mine to come and spend the week-end with us here: a Mr Sagamore. I suppose you can find a room for him.

THE MANAGER. That will be quite all right, sir, thank you.

PATRICIA. Have you many people in the house this week-end?

THE MANAGER. Less than usual, madam. We have an Egyptian doctor who takes his meals here: a very learned man I should think: very quiet: not a word to anybody. Then there is another gentleman, an invalid, only just discharged from the Cottage Hospital. The Egyptian doctor recommended our chef to him; and he takes his meals here too. And that is all, madam, unless some fresh visitors arrive.

ALASTAIR. Well, we must put up with them.

THE MANAGER. By the way, sir, I am sorry to trouble you; but you came up this morning without signing the register. I have brought it up. Would you be so good? [*He fetches the register from the table and presents it to Alastair with his fountain pen*].

ALASTAIR [*sitting up and taking it on his knees*] Oh, I am sorry: I forgot. [*He signs*]. There you are. [*He puts up his legs again*].

THE MANAGER. Thanks very much, sir. [*He glances at the register before shutting it. The signature surprises him*]. Oh, indeed, sir! We are honored.

ALASTAIR. Anything wrong?

THE MANAGER. Oh no, sir, nothing wrong: quite the contrary. Mr and Mrs Fitzfassenden. The name is so unusual. Have I the honor of entertaining the celebrated——

ALASTAIR [*interrupting*] Yes: it's all right: I am the tennis champion and the boxing champion and all the rest of it; but I am here for a holiday and I dont want to hear anything more about it.

THE MANAGER [*shutting the book*] I quite understand, sir. I should not have said anything if it were not that the proprietress of this hotel, the lady I told you of, is a Mrs Fitzfassenden.

ALASTAIR [*rising with a yell*] What! Let me out of this. Pack, up, Seedy. My bill, please, instantly.

THE MANAGER. Certainly, sir. But may I say that she is not on the premises at present and that I do not expect her this week-end.

PATRICIA. Dont fuss, darling. Weve a perfect right to be in her hotel if we pay our way just like anybody else.

ALASTAIR. Very well: have it your own way. But my week-end is spoilt.

THE MANAGER. Depend on it, she wont come, sir. She is getting tired of paying us unexpected visits now that she knows she can depend on me. [*He goes out, but immediately looks in again to say*] Your friend Mr Sagamore, sir, coming up with the invalid gentleman. [*He holds the door open for Sagamore and Adrian, who come in. Then he goes out, taking the register with him.*]

Adrian, who comes first, limps badly on two walking sticks; and his head is bandaged. He is disagreeably surprised at seeing Fitzfassenden and Patricia.

ADRIAN. Alastair! Miss Smith! What does this mean, Sagamore? You never told me who you were bringing me to see: you said two friends. Alastair: I assure you I did not know you were here. Sagamore said some friends who would be glad to see me.

PATRICIA. Well, we are glad to see you, Mr Blenderbland. Wont you sit down?

ALASTAIR. But whats happened to you, old chap? What on earth have you done to yourself?

ADRIAN [*exasperated*] Everyone asks me what I have done to myself. I havnt done anything to myself. I suppose you mean this and this [*he indicated his injuries*] Well, they are what your wife has done to me. That is why Sagamore should not have brought me here.

ALASTAIR. I say: I am frightfully sorry, old chap.

PATRICIA [*rising solicitously*] Do sit down, Mr Blenderbland. Rest yourself on that couch. [*Arranging cushions*] Dear! dear!

ALASTAIR. Eppy is like that, you know.

ADRIAN. Yes: I know now. But I ought not to be here: Sagamore should not have brought me here.

PATRICIA. But why not? I assure you we're delighted to see you. We dont mind what Mrs Fitzfassenden does.

ADRIAN. But I do. You are most kind; but I cannot claim the privilege of a friend and at the same time be the plaintiff in an action for assault and battery.

ALASTAIR. Yes you can, old chap. The situation is not new. The victims always come to us for sympathy. Make yourself comfortable.

ADRIAN [*reluctantly sitting down and disposing his damaged limbs along the couch*] Well, it's most kind of you; and I really cant stand any longer. But I dont understand why Sagamore should have played such a trick on me. And, of course, on you too.

Patricia returns to her chair, and resumes her knitting.

SAGAMORE [*taking a chair next Patricia on her left*] Well, the truth of the matter is that Blenderbland wont be reasonable; and I thought you two might help me to bring him to his senses.

ADRIAN [*obstinately*] It's no use, Sagamore. Two thousand five hundred. And costs. Not a penny less.

SAGAMORE. Too much. Ridiculous. A jury might give five hundred if there was a clear disablement from earning, or if the defendant had done something really womanly, like throwing vitriol. But you are only a sleeping partner in the firm your father founded: you dont really earn your income. Besides, hang it all! a man accusing a woman of assault!

ALASTAIR. Why didnt you give her a punch in the solar plexus?

ADRIAN. Strike a woman! Impossible.

ALASTAIR. Rot! If a woman starts fighting she must take what she gets and deserves.

PATRICIA. Look at the marks she's left on you, Mr Blenderbland! You shouldnt have put up with it: it only encourages her.

ALASTAIR. Search me for marks: you wont find any. Youd have found a big mark on her this first time she tried it on me. There was no second time.

ADRIAN. Unfortunately I have neither your muscle nor your knowledge of how to punch. But I will take lessons when I get well. And she shall pay for them. Two thousand five hundred. And medical expenses. And costs.

SAGAMORE. And cab fare to the Cottage Hospital, I suppose.

ADRIAN. No: I went in her own car. But now you remind me, I tipped the chauffeur. Now dont misunderstand me. It is not the money. But I wont be beaten by a woman. It's a point of honor: of self-respect.

SAGAMORE. Yes; but how do you arrive at the figure? Why is your honor and self-respect worth two thousand five hundred pounds and not two thousand five hundred millions?

ADRIAN. My brother got two thousand five hundred from the railway company when an electric truck butted into him on the platform at Paddington. I will not let Epifania off with less. It was an unprovoked, brutal, cowardly assault.

SAGAMORE. Was it quite unprovoked? You will not get a jury to swallow that without a peck of salt?

ADRIAN. I have told you over and over again that it

was absolutely unprovoked. But the concussion from which I suffered obliterated all consciousness of what happened immediately before the assault: the last thing I can recollect was a quite ordinary conversation about her father's money.

SAGAMORE. So much the worse for you. She can accuse you of anything she likes. And remember: no man can get damages out of a British jury unless he goes into court as a moral man.

ADRIAN. Do you suggest that I am not a moral man?

SAGAMORE. No; but Mrs Fitzfassenden's counsel will if you take her into court.

ADRIAN. Stuff! Would any jury believe that she and I were lovers on the strength of a sprained ankle, a dislocated knee, and a lump on my head the size of an ostrich's egg?

SAGAMORE. The best of evidence against you. It's only lovers that have lovers' quarrels. And suppose she pleads self-defence against a criminal assault!

ADRIAN. She dare not swear to such a lie.

SAGAMORE. How do you know it's a lie? You dont know what happened at the end. You had concussion of the brain.

ADRIAN. Yes: after the assault.

SAGAMORE. But it obliterated your consciousness of what happened before the assault. How do you know what you did in those moments?

ADRIAN. Look here. Are you my solicitor or hers?

SAGAMORE. Fate seems to have made me the solicitor of everybody in this case. If I am forced to throw up either her case or yours, I must throw up yours. How can I afford to lose a client with such an income and such a temper? Her tantrums are worth two or three thousand a year to any solicitor.

ADRIAN. Very well, Sagamore. You see my condition:

you know that right and justice are on my side. I shall not forget this.

The manager enters, looking very serious.

THE MANAGER [*to Alastair*] I am extremely sorry, sir. Mrs Fitzfassenden is downstairs with the Egyptian doctor. I really did not expect her.

EPIFANIA [*dashing into the room and addressing herself fiercely to the manager*] You have allowed my husband to bring a woman to my hotel and register her in my name. You are fired. [*She is behind the couch and does not see Adrian. Sagamore rises*].

THE MANAGER. I am sorry, madam: I did not know that the gentleman was your husband. However, you are always right. Do you wish me to go at once or to carry on until you have replaced me?

EPIFANIA. I do not wish you to go at all: you are re-engaged. Throw them both out, instantly.

ALASTAIR. Ha ha ha!

SAGAMORE. Your manager cannot throw Alastair out: Alastair can throw all of us out, if it comes to that. As to Miss Smith, this is a licensed house; and she has as much right to be here as you or I.

EPIFANIA. I will set fire to the hotel if necessary. [*She sees Adrian*] Hallo! What is this? Adrian here too! What has happened to your head? What are those sticks for? [*To the manager*] Send the doctor here at once. [*To Adrian*] Have you hurt yourself?

The manager hurries out, glad to escape from the mêlée.

ADRIAN. Hurt myself! Hurt myself!!

EPIFANIA. Has he been run over?

ADRIAN. This woman has half killed me; and she asks have I hurt myself! I fell down the whole flight of stairs. My ankle was sprained. My knee was twisted. The small bone of my leg was broken. I ricked my spine. I had to give them a subscription at the Cottage Hospital, where your man took me. I had to go from there to a nursing home: twelve guineas a week. I had to call in three Harley Street surgeons; and none of them knew anything about dislocated knees: they wanted to cut my knee open to see what was the matter with it. I had to take it to a bonesetter; and he charged me fifty guineas.

EPIFANIA. Well, why did you not walk downstairs properly? Were you drunk?

ADRIAN [*suffocating*] I—

SAGAMORE [*cutting in quickly*] He declares that his injuries were inflicted by you when you last met, Mrs Fitzfassenden.

EPIFANIA. By me! Am I a prizefighter? Am I a coal-heaver?

ADRIAN. Both.

SAGAMORE. Do you deny that you assaulted him?

EPIFANIA. Of course I deny it. Anything more monstrous I never heard. What happened was that he insulted my father grossly, without the slightest provocation, at a moment when I had every reason to expect the utmost tenderness from him. The blood rushed to my head: the next thing I remember is that I was lying across the table, trembling, dying. The doctor who found me can tell you what my condition was.

ADRIAN. I dont care what your condition was. What condition did your chauffeur find me in?

SAGAMORE. Then neither of you has the least notion of how this affair ended.

ADRIAN. I have medical evidence.

EPIFANIA. So have I.

ADRIAN. Well, we shall see. I am not going to be talked out of my case.

EPIFANIA. What do you mean by your case?

SAGAMORE. He is taking an action against you.

EPIFANIA. An action! Very well: you know my invariable rule. Fight him to the last ditch, no matter what it costs. Take him to the House of Lords if necessary. We shall see whose purse will hold out longest. I will not be blackmailed.

ADRIAN. You think your father's money places you above the law?

EPIFANIA [*flushing*] Again!

She makes for him. Alastair seizes her from behind and whirls her away towards Sagamore; then places himself on guard between her and the couch, balancing his fists warningly.

ALASTAIR. Now! now! now! None of that. Toko, my girl, toko.

SAGAMORE. Toko! What is toko?

ALASTAIR. She knows. Toko is an infallible medicine for calming the nerves. A punch in the solar plexus and a day in bed: thats toko.

EPIFANIA. You are my witness, Mr Sagamore, how I go in fear of my husband's brutal violence. He is stronger than I am: he can batter me, torture me, kill me. It is the last argument of the lower nature against the higher. My innocence is helpless. Do your worst. [*She sits down in Sagamore's chair with great dignity*].

ALASTAIR. Quite safe now, ladies and gentlemen. [*He picks up his illustrated paper, and retires with it to one of the remoter teatables, where he sits down to read as quietly as may be*].

ADRIAN [*to Epifania*] Now you know what I felt. It serves you right.

EPIFANIA. Yes: go on. Insult me. Threaten me. Blackmail me. You can all do it with impunity now.

SAGAMORE [*behind her chair*] Dont take it that way,

Mrs Fitzfassenden. There is no question of black-mailing or insulting you. I only want to settle this business of Mr Blenderbland's injuries before we go into the matrimonial question.

EPIFANIA. I want to hear no more of Mr Blender-bland and his ridiculous injuries.

SAGAMORE. Do be a little reasonable, Mrs Fitz-fassenden. How are we to discuss the compensation due to Mr Blenderbland without mentioning his injuries?

EPIFANIA. There is no compensation due to Mr Blenderbland. He deserved what he got, whatever that was.

SAGAMORE. But he will take an action against you.

EPIFANIA. Take one against him first.

SAGAMORE. What for?

EPIFANIA. For anything; only dont bother me about it. Claim twenty thousand pounds damages. I tell you I will not be blackmailed.

ADRIAN. Neither will I. I am entitled to compensation and I mean to have it.

SAGAMORE [*coming between them*] Steady! steady! please. I cannot advise either of you to go to law; but quite seriously, Mrs Fitzfassenden, Mr Blenderbland is entitled to some compensation. You can afford it.

EPIFANIA. Mr Sagamore: a woman as rich as I am cannot afford anything. I have to fight to keep every penny I possess. Every beggar, every blackmailer, every swindler, every charity, every testimonial, every political cause, every league and brotherhood and sister-hood, every church and chapel, every institution of every kind on earth is busy from morning to night trying to bleed me to death. If I weaken for a moment, if I let a farthing go, I shall be destitute by the end of the month. I subscribe a guinea a year to the Income

Tax Payers' Defence League; but that is all: absolutely all. My standing instructions to you are to defend every action and to forestall every claim for damages by a counterclaim for ten times the amount. That is the only way in which I can write across the sky "Hands off My Money."

SAGAMORE. You see, Mr Blenderbland, it's no use. You must withdraw your threat of an action.

ADRIAN. I wont.

SAGAMORE. You will. You must. Mrs Fitzfassenden: he can do nothing against you. Let me make an appeal on his behalf ad misericordiam.

EPIFANIA [*impatiently*] Oh, we are wasting time; and I have more important business to settle. Give him a ten pound note and have done with it.

ADRIAN. A ten pound note!!!

SAGAMORE [*remonstrant*] Oh, Mrs Fitzfassenden!

EPIFANIA. Yes: a ten pound note. No man can refuse a ten pound note if you crackle it under his nose.

SAGAMORE. But he wants two thousand five hundred.

EPIFANIA [*rising stupefied*] Two thou— [*She gasps*].

ADRIAN. Not a penny less.

EPIFANIA [*going past Sagamore to the couch*] Adrian, my child, I have underrated you. Your cheek, your gluttony, your obstinacy impose respect on me. I threw a half baked gentleman downstairs: and my chauffeur picked him up on the mat a magnificently complete Skunk.

ADRIAN [*furious*] Five thousand for that, Sagamore: do you hear?

SAGAMORE. Please! please! Do keep your temper.

ADRIAN. Keep your own temper. Has she lamed you for life? Has she raised a bump on your head? Has she called you a skunk?

SAGAMORE. No; but she may at any moment.

EPIFANIA [*flinging her arms round him with a whoop of delight*] Ha ha! Ha ha! My Sagamore! My treasure! Shall I give him five thousand on condition that he turns it into a million in six months?

ADRIAN. I will do what I like with it. I will have it unconditionally.

SAGAMORE [*extricating himself gently from Epifania's hug*] Mr Blenderbland: it is a mistake to go into court in the character of a man who has been called a skunk. It makes the jury see you in that light from the start. It is also very difficult for a plaintiff to get sympathy in the character of a man who has been thrashed by a woman. If Mrs Fitzfassenden had stabbed you, or shot you, or poisoned you, that would have been quite in order: your dignity would not have been compromised. But Mrs Fitzfassenden knows better. She knows the privileges of her sex to a hair's breadth and never oversteps them. She would come into court beautifully dressed and looking her best. No woman can be more ladylike—more feminine—when it is her cue to play the perfect lady. Long before we can get the case into the lists the bump on your head will have subsided; your broken bone will have set; and the color will have come back to your cheeks. Unless you can provoke Mrs Fitzfassenden to assault you again the day before the trial—and she is far too clever for that—the chances are a million to one against you.

ALASTAIR [*rising and coming from the other end of the room*] That is so, Blenderbland. You havnt a dog's chance. Next time you see her fist coming in your direction, duck and counter. If you dont get that satisfaction you wont get any. [*He sits down next Patricia, on her right*].

PATRICIA. Yes. Mr Blenderbland: Alastair's right.

Ask her nicely, and perhaps she'll pay your expenses.

ADRIAN [*sitting up and taking his head in his hands, shaken, almost lachrymose*] Is there any justice for a man against a woman?

SAGAMORE [*sitting beside him to console him*] Believe me: no. Not against a millionairess.

EPIFANIA. And what justice is there for a millionairess, I should like to know?

SAGAMORE. In the courts—

EPIFANIA. I am not thinking of the courts: there is little justice there for anybody. My millions are in themselves an injustice. I speak of the justice of heaven.

ALASTAIR. Oh Lord! Now we're for it. [*He deliberately puts his arm round Patricia's waist*].

EPIFANIA. Alastair: how can you jeer at me? Is it just that I, because I am a millionairess, cannot keep my husband, cannot keep even a lover, cannot keep anything but my money? There you sit before my very eyes, snuggling up to that insignificant little nothingness who cannot afford to pay for her own stockings; and you are happy and she is happy. [*She turns to Adrian*] Here is this suit of clothes on two sticks. What does it contain?

ADRIAN [*broken*] Let me alone, will you?

EPIFANIA. Something that once resembled a man, something that liked lending me five pound notes and never asked me to repay them. Why? Kindness to me? Love of me? No: the swank of a poor man lending to a millionairess. In my divine wrath I smashed him as a child smashes a disappointing toy; and when he was beaten down to his real self I found I was not a woman to him but a bank account with a good cook.

PATRICIA. Thats all very fine, deary; but the truth is that no one can live with you.

EPIFANIA. And anyone can live with you. And apparently you can live with anybody.

ALASTAIR. What Seedy says is God's truth. Nobody could live with you.

EPIFANIA. But why? Why? Why?

SAGAMORE. Do be reasonable, Mrs Fitzfassenden. Can one live with a tornado? with an earthquake? with an avalanche?

EPIFANIA. Yes. Thousands of people live on the slopes of volcanoes, in the track of avalanches, on land thrown up only yesterday by earthquakes. But with a millionairess who can rise to her destiny and wield the power her money gives her, no. Well, be it so. I shall sit in my lonely house, and be myself, and pile up millions until I find a man good enough to be to me what Alastair is to Seedystockings.

PATRICIA. Well, I hope you wont have to wait too long.

EPIFANIA. I never wait. I march on; and when I come upon the things I need I grab them. I grabbed your Alastair. I find that he does not suit me: he beats me—

ALASTAIR. In self-defence. I never raised a hand to you except in self-defence.

EPIFANIA. Yes: you are like the great European Powers: you never fight except in self-defence. But you are two stone heavier than I; and I cannot keep my head at infighting as you can. You do not suit. I throw you to Greedy-Seedy-Stockings: you can punch her to your heart's content. Mr Sagamore: arrange the divorce. Cruelty and adultery.

PATRICIA. But I dont like this: it's not fair to Alastair. Why is he to be divorced instead of you?

EPIFANIA. Mr Sagamore: take an action against

Patricia Smith for alienating my husband's affections. Damages twenty thousand pounds.

PATRICIA. Oh! Is such a thing possible, Mr Sagamore?

SAGAMORE. I am afraid it is, Miss Smith. Quite possible.

PATRICIA. Well, my dear old father used to say that in the law courts there is only one way to beat the people who have unlimited money; and that is to have no money at all. You cant get twenty thousand out of me. And call it vanity if you will; but I should rather like the world to know that in my little way I was able to take the best and dearest man in England from the richest woman.

EPIFANIA. Damn your dear old father!

ALASTAIR [*laughing boisterously*] Ha ha! One for you, Eppy. [*He kisses Patricia*].

SAGAMORE [*smiling*] I am afraid the laugh is with old Mr Smith, Mrs Fitzfassenden. Where there is nothing, the king loses his rights.

EPIFANIA. Oh, I can bear no more of this. I will not have my life dragged down to planes of vulgarity on which I cannot breathe. I will live in utter loneliness and keep myself sacred until I find the right man—the man who can stand with me on the utmost heights and not lose his head—the mate created for me in heaven. He must be somewhere.

THE DOCTOR [*appearing at the door*] The manager says I am wanted here. Who wants me?

EPIFANIA. *I* want you. Come here [*she stretches out her hand to him imperiously*].

THE DOCTOR [*coming to her and feeling her pulse*] Something wrong with your blood pressure, eh? [*Amazed*] Ooooh!! I have never felt such a pulse. It is like a slow sledge hammer.

EPIFANIA. Well, is my pulse my fault?

THE DOCTOR. No. It is the will of Allah. All our pulses are part of the will of Allah.

ALASTAIR. Look here, you know, Doc: that wont go down in this country. We dont believe in Allah.

THE DOCTOR. That does not disconcert Allah in the least, my friend. The pulse beats still, slow, strong. [*To Epifania*] You are a terrible woman; but I love your pulse. I have never felt anything like it before.

PATRICIA. Well, just fancy that! He loves her pulse.

THE DOCTOR. I am a doctor. Women as you fancy them are nothing to me but bundles of ailments. But the life! the pulse! is the heartbeat of Allah, save in Whom there is no majesty and no might. [*He drops her hand*].

EPIFANIA. My pulse will never change: this is the love I crave for. I will marry you. Mr Sagamore: see about a special licence the moment you have got rid of Alastair.

THE DOCTOR. It is not possible. We are bound by our vows.

EPIFANIA. Well, have I not passed your mother's test? You shall have an accountant's certificate. I learned in the first half hour of my search for employment that the living wage for a single woman is five shillings a week. Before the end of the week I had made enough to support me for a hundred years. I did it honestly and legitimately. I explained the way in which it was done.

THE DOCTOR. It was not the way of Allah, the Merciful, the Compassionate. Had you added a farthing an hour to the wages of those sweated women, that wicked business would have crashed on your head. You sold it to the man Superflew for the last penny of his savings; and the women still slave for him at one piastre an hour.

EPIFANIA. You cannot change the market price of labor: not Allah himself can do that. But I came to this hotel as a scullery maid: the most incompetent scullery maid that ever broke a dinner service. I am now its owner; and there is no tuppencehapney an hour here.

THE DOCTOR. The hotel looks well in photographs; and the wages you pay would be a fortune to a laborer on the Nile. But what of the old people whose natural home this place had become? the old man with his paralytic stroke? the old woman gone mad? the cast out creatures in the workhouse? Was not this preying on the poverty of the poor? Shall I, the servant of Allah, live on such gains? Shall I, the healer, the helper, the guardian of life and the counsellor of health, unite with the exploiter of misery?

EPIFANIA. I have to take the world as I find it.

THE DOCTOR. The wrath of Allah shall overtake those who leave the world no better than they found it.

EPIFANIA. I think Allah loves those who make money.

SAGAMORE. All the evidence is that way, certainly.

THE DOCTOR. I do not see it so. I see that riches are a curse; poverty is a curse; only in the service of Allah is there justice, righteousness, and happiness. But all this talk is idle. This lady has easily fulfilled the condition imposed by my mother. But I have not fulfilled the condition imposed by the lady's father.

EPIFANIA. You need not trouble about that. The six months have not expired. I will shew you how to turn your hundred and fifty pounds into fifty thousand.

THE DOCTOR. You cannot. It is gone.

EPIFANIA. Oh, you cannot have spent it all: you who live like a mouse. There must be some of it left.

THE DOCTOR. Not a penny. Not a piastre. Allah—

EPIFANIA. Oh, bother Allah! What did you do with it?

THE DOCTOR. Allah is never bothered. On that afternoon when you left me to earn your own living I called upon the Merciful, the Compassionate, to reveal to me whether you were not one of the strokes of his infinite humor. Then I sat down and took up a newspaper. And behold! a paragraph headed Wills and Bequests. I read a name that I cannot remember: Mrs Somebody of Clapham Park, one hundred and twenty two thousand pounds. She had never done anything but live in Clapham Park; and she left £122,000. But what was the next name? It was that of the teacher who changed my whole life and gave me a new soul by opening the world of science to me. I was his assistant for four years. He used to make his own apparatus for his experiments; and one day he needed a filament of metal that would resist a temperature that melted platinum like sealing wax.

EPIFANIA. Buy his patent for me if it has not been snapped up.

THE DOCTOR. He never took out a patent. He believed that knowledge is no man's property. And he had neither time nor money to waste in patent offices. Millions have been made out of that discovery of his by people who care nothing about science and everything about money. He left four hundred pounds and a widow: the good woman who had been a second mother to me. A shilling a day for her at most: not even one piastre an hour.

EPIFANIA. That comes of marrying an incompetent

[963]

dreamer. Are you going to beg for her? I warn you I am tired of destitute widows. I should be a beggar myself if I took them all on my shoulders.

THE DOCTOR. Have no fear. The Merciful, the Compassionate heard the prayer of the widow. Listen. I once cured a Prime Minister when he imagined himself to be ill. I went to him and told him that it was the will of Allah that the widow should have a civil list pension. She received it: a hundred pounds a year. I went to the great Metallurgical Trust which exploits his discovery, and told them that her poverty was a scandal in the face of Allah. They were rich and generous: they made a special issue of founders' shares for her, worth three hundred a year to her. They called it letting her in on the ground floor. May her prayers win them favour from Him save in whom there is no might and no majesty! But all this took time. The illness, the nurse, the funeral, the disposal of the laboratory, the change to a cheaper lodging, had left her without a penny, though no doctor and no lawyer took a farthing, and the shopkeepers were patient; for the spirit of Allah worked more strongly upon them than on the British Treasury, which clamored for its little death duty. Between the death and the pensions there was a gap of exactly one hundred and fifty pounds wide. He who is just and exact supplied that sum by your chauffeur's hands and by mine. It rejoiced my heart as money had never rejoiced it before. But instead of coming to you with fifty thousand pounds I am in arrear with my bill for my daily bread in your hotel, and am expecting every day to be told by your manager that this cannot go on: I must settle.

ALASTAIR. Well, old man, you may not have done a lot for yourself; but you have done damned well for the widow. And you have escaped Eppy. She wont marry you with your pockets empty.

EPIFANIA. Pray why? Fifty thousand pounds must have been made out of that discovery ten times over. The doctor, in putting my money into the widow's necessary expenses, may be said to have made a retrospective investment in the discovery. And he has shewn the greatest ability in the affair: has he not, Mr Sagamore?

SAGAMORE. Unquestionably. He has bowled out the Prime Minister. He has bowled out the Imperial Metallurgical Trust. He has settled the widow's affairs to perfection.

THE DOCTOR. But not my own affairs. I am in debt for my food.

EPIFANIA. Well, if you come to that, *I* am in debt for my food. I got a letter this morning from my purveyors to say that I have paid them nothing for two years, and unless I let them have something on account they will be obliged to resort to the premises.

THE DOCTOR. What does that mean?

EPIFANIA. Sell my furniture.

THE DOCTOR. You cannot sell mine, I am afraid. I have hardly any.

BLENDERBLAND. If you have a stick she will sell it. She is the meanest woman in England.

EPIFANIA. That is why I am also the richest. Mr Sagamore: my mind is made up: I will marry this doctor. Ascertain his name and make the necessary arrangements.

BLENDERBLAND. You take care, doctor. She is unfaithful to her husband in wanting to marry you. She flirted with me: took me down the river and made me believe I was to be Alastair's successor before ever she saw you. See what she has done to me! She will do it to you when the next man takes her fancy.

THE DOCTOR [*to Epifania*] What have you to say to that?

EPIFANIA. You must learn to take chances in this world. This disappointed philanderer tries to frighten you with my unfaithfulness. He has never been married: I have. And I tell you that in the very happiest marriages not a day passes without a thousand moments of unfaithfulness. You begin by thinking you have only one husband: you find you have a dozen. There is a creature you hate and despise and are tied to for life; and before breakfast is over the fool says something nice and becomes a man whom you admire and love; and between these extremes there are a thousand degrees with a different man and woman at each of them. A wife is all women to one man: she is everything that is devilish: the thorn in his flesh, the jealous termagant, the detective dogging all his movements, the nagger, the scolder, the worrier. He has only to tell her an affectionate lie and she is his comfort, his helper, at best his greatest treasure, at worst his troublesome but beloved child. All wives are all these women in one, all husbands all these men in one. What do the unmarried know of this infinitely dangerous heart tearing everchanging life of adventure that we call marriage? Face it as you would face a dangerous operation: have you not performed hundreds of them?

THE DOCTOR. Of a surety there is no wit and no wisdom like that of a woman ensnaring the mate chosen for her by Allah. Yet I am very well as I am. Why should I change? I shall be very happy as an old bachelor.

EPIFANIA [*flinging out her wrist at him*] Can you feel my pulse every day as an old bachelor?

THE DOCTOR [*taking her wrist and mechanically taking out his watch at the same time*] Ah! I had forgotten the pulse. One, two, three: it is irresistible: it is a pulse in a hundred thousand. I love it: I cannot give it up.

BLENDERBLAND. You will regret it to the last day of your life.

EPIFANIA. Mr Sagamore: you have your instructions.

SAGAMORE [*bows*].

PATRICIA. Congratulations, darling.

And that is how the story ends in capitalist countries. In Russia, however, and in countries with Communist sympathies, the people demand that the tale shall have an edifying moral. Accordingly, when the doctor, feeling Epifania's pulse, says that he loves it and cannot give it up. Blenderbland continues the conversation as follows.

BLENDERBLAND. Take care. Her hand is accursed. It is the hand of Midas: it turns everything it touches to gold.

THE DOCTOR. My hand is more deeply accursed. Gold flies away from it. Why am I always poor? I do not like being poor.

EPIFANIA. Why am I always rich? I do not like being rich.

ALASTAIR. Youd better both go to Russia, where there are neither rich nor poor.

EPIFANIA. Why not? I buy nothing but Russian stock now.

BLENDERBLAND. The Russians would shoot you as they would a mad dog. You are a bloated capitalist, you know.

EPIFANIA. I am a capitalist here; but in Russia I should be a worker. And what a worker! My brains are wasted here: the wealth they create is thrown away on idlers and their parasites, whilst poverty, dirt, disease, misery and slavery surround me like a black sea in which I may be engulfed at any moment by a turn of the money market. Russia needs managing women like me. In Moscow I shall not be a millionairess; but I shall be in the Sovnarkom within six months and in the Politbureau before the end of the year. Here I have no real power, no real freedom, and no security at all: we may all die in the workhouse. In Russia I shall have such authority! such scope for my natural powers! as the Empress Catharine never enjoyed. I swear that before I have been twenty years in Russia every Russian baby shall weigh five pounds heavier and every Russian man and woman live ten years longer. I shall not be an empress; and I may work myself to death; but in a thousand years from now holy Russia shall again have a patron saint, and her name shall be Saint Epifania.

BLENDERBLAND. The egotism of that woman!!

SAGAMORE. I am afraid there are no saints now in Russia.

THE DOCTOR. There are saints everywhere: they are the one species you cannot liquidate. Kings, emperors, conquerors, pontiffs and all the other idols are swept away sooner or later; and all the king's horses and all the king's men cannot set them up again; but the saints shall reign for ever and ever in the temple of the hammer and the sickle. But we must not go to Russia, because the Russians do not need us: they have stayed at home and saved their own souls. Ought not we to stay at home and save ours? Why not make the British Empire a Soviet republic?

EPIFANIA. By all means; but we shall have to liquidate all the adult inhabitants and begin with the newly born. And the first step to that is to get married. Mr Sagamore: make the necessary arrangements.

SAGAMORE [*bows*].

PATRICIA. Congratulations, darling.

The Six of Calais:
A Medieval War Story

WITH

Prefatory Note
Author's Note

Composition begun 13 May 1934; completed 16 May 1934. First published in German translation, as *Die Sechs von Calais*, in the *Neue Freie Presse* (Vienna), 25 December 1934. First published in English in *The Simpleton, The Six, and The Millionairess*, 1936. First presented at the Open Air Theatre, Regent's Park, London, on 17 July 1934.

The Black Prince	*Hubert Gregg*
John of Gaunt	*Leonard Thorne*
Edward III	*Charles Carson*
A Court Lady	*Greer Garson*
Queen Philippa of Hainault	*Phyllis Neilson-Terry*

Eustache de St Pierre		*Vincent Sternroyd*
Piers de Rosty		*Leonard Shepherd*
Piers de Wissant	The	*Clement Hamelin*
Jean d'Aire	Six	*Frank Tickle*
Gilles d'Oudebolle		*Derek Prentice*
Jacques de Wissant		*E. S. Kenney*

Also Sir Walter Manny, Lord Derby, Lord Northampton, Lord Arundel, and other noblemen, courtiers, three men-at-arms, soldiers, etc.

Period—A.D. 4th August 1347
Scene—*Before the Walls of Calais on the Last Day of the Siege. Camp of King Edward III*

Prefatory Note

The most amusing thing about the first performance of this little play was the exposure it elicited of the quaint illiteracy of our modern London journalists. Their only notion of a king was a pleasant and highly respectable gentleman in a bowler hat and Victorian beard, shaking hands affably with a blushing football team. To them a queen was a dignified lady, also Victorian as to her coiffure, graciously receiving bouquets from excessively washed children in beautiful new clothes. Such were their mental pictures of Great Edward's grandson and his queen Philippa. They were hurt, shocked, scandalized at the spectacle of a medieval soldier monarch publicly raging and cursing, crying and laughing, asserting his authority with thrasonic ferocity and the next moment blubbering like a child in his wife's lap or snarling like a savage dog at a dauntless and defiant tradesman: in short behaving himself like an unrestrained human being in a very trying situation instead of like a modern constitutional monarch on parade keeping up an elaborate fiction of living in a political vacuum and moving only when his ministers pull his strings. Edward Plantagenet the Third had to pull everybody else's strings and pull them pretty hard, his father having been miserably killed for taking his job too lightly. But the journalist critics knew nothing of this. A King Edward who did not behave like the son of King Edward the Seventh seemed unnatural and indecent to them, and they rent their garments accordingly.

They were perhaps puzzled by the fact that the play has no moral whatever. Every year or so I hurl at them a long play full of insidious propaganda, with a moral in every line. They never discover what I am driving at: it is always too plainly and domestically stated to be grasped by their subtle and far flung minds; but they feel that I am driving at something: probably something they had better not agree with if they value their livelihoods. A play of mine in which I am not driving at anything more than a playwright's direct business is as inconceivable by them as a medieval king.

Now a playwright's direct business is simply to provide the theatre with a play. When I write one with the additional attraction of providing the twentieth century with an up-to-date religion or the like, that luxury is thrown in gratuitously; and the play, simply as a play, is not necessarily either the better or the worse for it. What, then, is a play simply as a play?

Well, it is a lot of things. Life as we see it is so haphazard that it is only by picking out its key situations and arranging them in their significant order (which is never how they actually occur) that it can be made intelligible. The highbrowed dramatic poet wants to make it intelligible and sublime. The farce writer wants to make it funny. The melodrama merchant wants to make it as exciting as some people find the police news. The pornographer wants to make it salacious. All interpreters of life in action, noble or ignoble, find their instrument in the theatre; and all the academic definitions of a play are variations of this basic function.

Yet there is one function hardly ever alluded to now, though it was made much too much of from Shakespear's time to the middle of the nineteenth century. As I write my plays it is continually in my mind and very much to my taste. This function is to provide an exhibition of the art of acting. A good play with bad parts is not an impossibility; but it is a monstrosity. A bad play with good parts will hold the stage and be kept alive by the actors for centuries after the obsolescence of its mentality would have condemned it to death without them. A great deal of the British Drama, from Shakespear to Bulwer Lytton, is as dead as mutton, and quite unbearable except when heroically acted; yet Othello and Richelieu can still draw hard money into the pay boxes; and The School For Scandal revives again and again with unabated vigor. Rosalind can always pull As You Like It through in spite of the sententious futility of the melancholy Jaques; and Millamant, impossible as she is, still produces the usual compliments to the wit and style of Congreve, who thought that syphilis and cuckoldry and concupiscent old women are things to be laughed at.

The Six of Calais is an acting piece and nothing else. As it happened, it was so well acted that in the eighteenth century all the talk would have been about Siddons as Philippa. But the company got no thanks except from the audience: the critics were prostrated with shock, damn their eyes!

I have had to improve considerably on the story as told by that absurd old snob Froissart, who believed that "to rob and pill was a good life" if the robber was at least a baron. He made a very poor job of it in my opinion.

ON THE HIGH SEAS, *28th May 1935*

A.D. 4th August 1347. Before the walls of Calais on the last day of the siege. The pavilion of Edward III, King of England, is on your left as you face the walls. The pavilion of his consort Philippa of Hainault is on your right. Between them, near the King's pavilion, is a two-seated chair of state for public audiences. Crowds of tents cover the background; but there is a clear way in the middle through the camp to the great gate of the city with its drawbridge still up and its flag still flying.

The Black Prince, aged 17, arrives impetuously past the Queen's tent, a groom running after him.

THE PRINCE. Here is the King's pavilion without a single attendant to announce me. What can the matter be?

A child's scream is heard from the royal pavilion; and John of Gaunt, aged 7, dashes out and is making for his mother's tent when the Prince seizes him.

THE PRINCE. How now, Johnny? Whats the matter?

JOHN [*struggling*] Let me go. Father is in a frightful wax.

THE PRINCE. I shall be in a wax myself presently. [*Releasing him*] Off with you to mother. [*The child takes refuge in the Queen's pavilion*].

THE KING'S VOICE. Grrr! Yah! Why was I not told? Gogswoons, why was I not told? [*Edward III, aged 35, dashes from his pavilion foaming*]. Out! [*The groom flies for his life*]. How long have you been here? They never tell me anything. I might be a dog instead of a king.

THE PRINCE [*about to kneel*] Majesty—

THE KING. No no: enough of that. Your news. Anything from Scotland? Anything from Wales?

[976]

THE PRINCE. I—

THE KING [*not waiting for the answer*] The state of things here is past words. The wrath of God and all his saints is upon this expedition.

THE PRINCE. I hope not, sir. I—

THE KING [*raging on*] May God wither and blast this accursed town! You would have thought that these dogs would have come out of their kennels and grovelled for mercy at my summons. Am I not their lawful king, ha?

THE PRINCE. Undoubtedly, sir. They—

THE KING. They have held me up for twelve months! A whole year!! My business ruined! My plans upset! My money exhausted! Death, disease, mutiny, a dog's life here in the field winter and summer. The bitch's bastard who is in command of their walls came to demand terms from me! to demand terms!!! looked me straight in the eyes with his head up as if I—I, his king! were dirt beneath his feet. By God, I will have that head: I will kick it to my dogs to eat. I will chop his insolent herald into four quarters—

THE PRINCE [*shocked*] Oh no, sir: not a herald: you cannot do that.

THE KING. They have driven me to such extremity that I am capable of cutting all the heralds in Christendom into their quarterings. [*He sits down in his chair of state and suddenly becomes ridiculously sentimental*]. I have not told you the worst. Your mother, the Queen, my Philippa, is here: here! Edward, in her delicate state of health. Even that did not move them. They want her to die: they are trying to murder her and our innocent unborn child. Think of that, boy: Oh, think of that [*he almost weeps*].

THE PRINCE. Softly, father: that is not their fault: it is yours.

THE KING. Would you make a jest of this? If it is not their fault it shall be their misfortune; for I will have every man, woman, and child torn to pieces with red hot pincers for it.

THE PRINCE. Truly, dear Sir, you have great cause to be annoyed; but in sober earnest how does the matter stand? They must be suffering the last extremity of famine. Their walls may hold out; but their stomachs cannot. Cannot you offer them some sort of terms to end the business? Money is running short. Time is running short. You only make them more desperate by threatening them. Remember: it is good policy to build a bridge of silver for a flying foe.

THE KING. Do I not know it? Have I not been kind, magnanimous? Have I not done all that Christian chivalry could require of me? And they abuse my kindness: it only encourages them: they despise me for it.

THE PRINCE. What terms have you offered them?

THE KING. I have not threatened the life of a single knight. I have said that no man of gentle condition and noble blood shall be denied quarter and ransom. It was their knightly duty to make a show of arms against me. But [*rising wrathfully*] these base rascals of burgesses: these huckstering hounds of merchants who have made this port of Calais a nest of pirates: these usurers and tradesmen: these rebel curs who have dared to take up arms against their betters: am I to pardon their presumption? I should be false to our order, to Christendom, if I did not make a signal example.

THE PRINCE. By all means, sir. But what have you demanded?

THE KING. Six of the most purseproud of their

burgesses, as they call themselves—by God, they begin to give themselves the airs of barons—six of them are to come in their shirts with halters round their necks for me to hang in the sight of all their people. [*Raising his voice again and storming*] They shall die the dog's death they deserve. They shall—

A court lady comes in.

THE COURT LADY. Sir: the Queen. Sssh!

THE KING [*subsiding to a whisper*] The Queen! Boy: not a word here. Her condition: she must not be upset: she takes these things so amiss: be discreet, for heaven's sake.

Queen Philippa, aged 33, comes from her pavilion, attended.

THE QUEEN. Dear child: welcome.

THE PRINCE. How do you, lady mother? [*He kisses her hand*].

THE KING [*solicitously*] Madam: are you well wrapped up? Is it wise to come into the cold air here? Had they better not bring a brazier and some cushions, and a hot drink—a posset—

THE QUEEN [*curtseying*] Sir: beloved: dont fuss. I am very well; and the air does me good. [*To the Prince*] You must cheer up your father, my precious. He will fret about my health when it is his own that needs care. I have borne him eleven children; and St Anne be my witness they have cost less looking after than this one big soldier, the greatest baby of them all. [*To the King*] Have you put on your flannel belly band, dearest?

THE KING. Yes, yes, yes, my love: do not bother about me. Think of yourself and our child—

THE QUEEN. Oh, leave me to take care of myself and the child. I am no maternal malingreuse I promise you. And now, sir sonny, tell me all your news. I—

She is interrupted by a shrill trumpet call.

THE KING. What is that ? What now ?

John of Gaunt, who has been up to the town gates to see the fun, runs in excitedly.

JOHN OF GAUNT [*bending his knee very perfunctorily*] Sire: they have surrendered: the drawbridge is down. The six old men have come out in their shirts with ropes round their necks.

THE KING [*clouting him*] Sssh! Hold your tongue, you young devil.

THE QUEEN. Old men in their shirts in this weather!! They will catch cold.

THE KING. It is nothing, madam my love: only the ceremony of surrender. You must go in: it is not fitting that these half naked men should be in your presence. I will deal with them.

THE QUEEN. Do not keep them too long in the cold, dearest sir.

THE KING [*uxoriously waving her a kiss*] My love!

The Queen goes into her pavilion; and a group of noblemen attendant on the King, including Sir Walter Manny and the Lords Derby, Northampton, and Arundel, issue from their tents and assemble behind the chair of state, where they are joined by the Black Prince, who stands at the King's right hand and takes charge of John of Gaunt.

THE KING. Now for these swine, these bloodsuckers. They shall learn—[*shouting*] Fetch me these fellows in here. Drag them in. I'll teach them to hold me up here for twelve months. I'll—

The six burgesses, hustled by men-at-arms, enter in their shirts and halters, each carrying a bunch of massive iron keys. Their leader, Eustache de St Pierre, kneels at the King's feet. Four of his fellow victims, Piers de Wissant, Jacques de Wissant, Jean d'Aire, and Gilles d'Oudebolle, kneel in pairs behind him, and, following his example, lay their keys on the ground. They are deeply cast down, bearing themselves like condemned men, yet maintaining a melancholy dignity. Not so the sixth, Piers de Rosty (nicknamed Hardmouth), the only one without a grey or white beard. He has an extraordinary dogged chin with a few bristles on it. He deliberately separates himself from the rest by passing behind the royal chair to the King's right and planting himself stiffly erect in an attitude of intense recalcitrance. The King, scowling fiercely at St Pierre and the rest, does not notice this until Peter flings down his keys with a violence which suggests that he would very willingly have brained Edward with them.

THE KING. On your knees, hound.

PETER. I am a good dog, but not of your kennel, Neddy.

THE KING. Neddy!!!!

PETER. Order your own curs: I am a free burgess and take commands from nobody.

Before the amazed monarch can retort, Eustache appeals to Peter.

EUSTACHE. Master Peter: if you have no regard for yourself, remember that our people, our wives and children, are at the mercy of this great king.

PETER. You mistake him for his grandfather. Great! [*He spits*].

EUSTACHE. Is this your promise to be patient?

PETER. Why waste civilities on him, Master Mayor? He can do no worse than hang us; and as to the town, *I* would have burnt it to the last brick, and every man, woman and child along with it, sooner than surrender. I came here to make up the tale of six to be hanged. Well, he can hang me; but he shall not outface me. I am as good a dog as he, any day in the week.

THE PRINCE. Fie, fellow! is this a way for one of thy degree to speak to an anointed king? Bear thyself as befits one of thy degree in the royal presence, or by Holy Paul—

PETER. You know how we have borne ourselves in his royal presence these twelve months. We have made some of you skip. Famine and not you, has beaten us. Give me a square meal and a good sword and stake all on a fair single combat with this big bully, or his black whelp here if he is afraid of me; and we shall see which is the better dog of the two.

THE KING. Drag him to his knees. Hamstring him if he resists.

Three men-at-arms dash at Peter and drag him to his knees. They take his halter and tie his ankles and wrists with it. Then they fling him on his side, where he lies helpless.

THE KING. And so, Master Burgess—

PETER. Bow-wow-wow!

THE KING [*furious*] Gag him. Gogswoons, gag him.

They tear a piece of linen from the back of his shirt, and bind his mouth with it. He barks to the last moment. John of Gaunt laughs ecstatically at this performance, and sets off some of the soldiers.

THE KING. If a man laughs I will have him flayed alive.

Dead silence.

THE KING. And now, fellows, what have ye to say to excuse your hardy and stubborn resistance for all these months to me, your king?

EUSTACHE. Sir, we are not fellows. We are free burgesses of this great city.

THE KING. Free burgesses! Are you still singing that song? Well, I will bend the necks of your burgesses when the hangman has broken yours. Am I not your overlord? Am I not your anointed king?

EUSTACHE. That is your claim, sir; and you have made it good by force of arms. We must submit to you and to God.

THE KING. Leave God out of this! What hast thou or thy like to do with God?

EUSTACHE. Nothing, sir: we would not so far presume. But with due respect to your greatness I would humbly submit to your Majesty that God may have something to do with us, seeing that he created us all alike and redeemed us by the blood of his beloved son.

THE KING [*to the Prince*] Can you make head or tail of this, boy? Is he accusing me of impiety? If he is, by God—

EUSTACHE. Sir, is it for me to accuse you of anything? Here we kneel in the dust before you, naked and with the ropes on our necks with which you will presently send us into the presence of our maker and yours. [*His teeth chatter*].

THE KING. Ay: you may well tremble. You have cause.

EUSTACHE. Yes: I tremble; and my teeth chatter: the few I have left. But you gentlemen that see our miserable plight, I call on your generosity as noblemen, on your chivalry as good knights, to bear witness for us that it is the cold of the morning and our naked condition that shakes us. We kneel to implore your King's mercy for our wretched and starving townsfolk, not for ourselves.

THE KING. Whose fault is it that they are starving? They have themselves to thank. Why did they not open their gates to me? Why did they take arms against their anointed king? Why should I have mercy on them or on you?

[983]

EUSTACHE. Sir: one is merciful not for reasons, but for the love of God, at whose hand we must all sue for mercy at the end of our days.

THE KING. You shall not save yourself by preaching. What right have you to preach? It is for churchmen and learned divines to speak of these mysteries, not for tradesmen and usurers. I'll teach you to rebel against your betters, whom God has appointed to keep you in obedience and loyalty. You are traitors; and as traitors you shall die. Thank my mercy that you are spared the torments that traitors and rebels suffer in England. [*Rising*] Away with them to the hangman; and let our trumpeters summon the townspeople to the walls to take warning from their dangling corpses.

The three men-at-arms begin to lift Peter. The others lay hands on his five colleagues.

THE KING. No: let that hound lie. Hanging is too good for him.

The Queen hurries in with her ladies in great concern. The men-at-arms release the burgesses irresolutely. It is evident that the Queen's arrival washes out all the King's orders.

THE QUEEN. Sir, what is this they tell me?

THE KING [*hurrying across to intercept her*] Madam: this is no place for you. I pray you, retire. The business is one in which it becomes you not to meddle.

THE QUEEN [*evading him and passing on to inspect the burgesses*] But these gentlemen. They are almost naked. It is neither seemly nor sufficient. They are old: they are half frozen: they should be in their beds.

THE KING. They soon will be. Leave us, madam. This is business of State. They are suffering no more than they deserve. I beg and pray you—I command you—

THE QUEEN. Dear sir, your wishes are my law and your commands my duty. But these gentlemen are very cold.

THE KING. They will be colder presently; so you need not trouble about that. Will it please you, madam, to withdraw at once?

THE QUEEN. Instantly, my dear Lord. [*To Eustache*] Sir: when his Majesty has ended his business with you, will you and your friends partake of some cups of hot wine in my pavilion? You shall be furnished with gowns.

THE KING [*choking with wrath*] Hot w—!

EUSTACHE. Alas, madam, when the King has ended his business with us we shall need nothing but our coffins. I also beg you to withdraw and hasten our despatch to that court where we shall not be held guilty for defending our hearths and homes to the last extremity. The King will not be baulked of his revenge; and we are shriven and ready.

THE QUEEN. Oh, you mistake, sir: the King is incapable of revenge: my husband is the flower of chivalry.

EUSTACHE. You little know your husband, madam. We know better what to expect from Edward Plantagenet.

THE KING [*coming to him threateningly past his consort*] Ha! do you, Master Merchant? You know better than the Queen! You and your like know what to expect from your lords and rulers! Well, this time you shall not be disappointed. You have guessed aright. You shall hang, every man of you, in your shirts, to make mirth for my horseboys and their trulls.

THE QUEEN. Oh no—

THE KING [*thundering*] Madam: I forbid you to speak. I bade you go: you would not; and now you shall see what I would have spared you had you been obedient. By God, I will be master in my own house and king in my own camp. Take these fellows out and hang them in their white beards.

The King takes his place on his chair of state with his arms folded implacably. The Queen follows him slowly and desolately. She takes her place beside him. The dead silence is very trying.

THE QUEEN [*drooping in tears and covering her face with her hands*] Oh!

THE KING [*flinching*] No no no no NO. Take her away.

THE QUEEN. Sir: I have been always a great trouble to you. I have asked you for a thousand favors and graces and presents. I am impatient and ungrateful, ever asking, asking, asking. Have you ever refused me even once?

THE KING. Well, is that a reason why I should give and grant, grant and give, for ever? Am I never to have my own way?

THE QUEEN. Oh, dearest sir, when next I ask you for a great thing, refuse me: teach me a lesson. But this is such a little thing. [*Heartbroken*] I cannot bear your refusing me a little thing.

THE KING. A little thing! You call this a little thing!

THE QUEEN. A very very little thing, sir. You are the King: you have at your disposal thousands of lives: all our lives from the noblest to the meanest. All the lives in that city are in your hand to do as you will with in this your hour of victory: it is as if you were God himself. You said once that you would lead ten kings captive to my feet. Much as I have begged from you I have never asked for my ten kings. I ask only for six old merchants, men beneath your royal notice, as my share of the spoils of your conquest. Their ransom will hardly buy me a new girdle; and oh, dear sir, you know that my old one is becoming too strait for me. Will you keep me begging so?

THE KING. I see very well that I shall not be allowed my own way. [*He begins to cry*].

THE QUEEN [*throwing her arms round him*] Oh, dear sir, you know I would die to spare you a moment's distress. There, there, dearest! [*She pets him*].

THE KING [*blubbering*] I am never allowed to do anything I want. I might as well be a dog as a king. You treat me like a baby.

THE QUEEN. Ah no: you are the greatest of kings to me, the noblest of men, my dearest lord and my dearest dearest love. [*Throwing herself on her knees*] Listen: do as you will: I will not say another word: I ask nothing.

THE KING. No: you ask nothing because you know you will get everything. [*He rises, shouting*] Take those men out of my sight.

THE PRINCE. What shall we do with them, sir?

THE KING [*flinging himself back into his seat*] Ask the Queen. Banquet them: feast them: give them my crown, my kingdom. Give them the clothes off my back, the bread out of my mouth, only take them away. Will you go, curses on you.

The five burgesses kneel gratefully to the Queen.

EUSTACHE [*kissing her hand*] Madam: our ransom shall buy you a threefold girdle of gold and a cradle of silver.

THE KING. Aye, well, see that it does: see that it does.

The burgesses retire, bowing to the Queen, who, still on her knees, waves her hand graciously to them.

THE QUEEN. Will you not help me up, dear sir?

THE KING. Oh yes, yes [*raising her*]: you should be

more careful: who knows what harm you may have done yourself flopping on your knees like that?

THE QUEEN. I have done myself no harm, dear sir; but you have done me a world of good. I have never been better nor happier in my life. Look at me. Do I not look radiant?

THE KING. And how do I look? Like a fool.

JOHN OF GAUNT. Sir: the men-at-arms want to know what they are to do with this fellow?

THE KING. Aye, I forgot him. Fetch him here.

The three men-at-arms carry Peter to the King, and fling him down. The King is now grinning. His paroxysm of tears has completely discharged his ill temper. It dawns on him that through Peter he may get even with Philippa for his recent domestic defeat.

THE QUEEN. Oh, the poor man has not even a proper shirt to wear. It is all torn: it is hardly decent.

THE KING. Look well at this man, madam. He defied me. He spat at me. There is no insult that he did not heap on me. He looked me in the face and spoke to me as if I were a scullion. I swear to you by the Holy Rood, he called me Neddy! Donkeys are called Neddy. What have you to say now? Is he, too, to be spared and petted and fed and have a gown from you?

THE QUEEN [*going to Peter*] But he is blue with cold. I fear he is dying. Untie him. Lift him up. Take that bandage off his mouth. Fie fie! I believe it is the tail of his shirt.

THE KING. It is cleaner than his tongue.

The men-at-arms release Peter from his bonds and his gag. He is too stiff to rise. They pull him to his feet.

PETER [*as they lift him groaning and swearing*] Ah-ooh-oh-ow!

THE KING. Well? Have you learnt your lesson? Are you ready to sue for the Queen's mercy?

PETER. Yah! Henpecked! Kiss mammy!

THE KING [*chuckles*]!!

THE QUEEN [*severely*] Are you mad, Master Burgess? Do you not know that your life is in the King's hand? Do you expect me to recommend you to his mercy if you forget yourself in this unseemly fashion?

PETER. Let me tell you, madam, that I came here in no ragged shirt. I have a dozen shirts of as fine web as ever went on your back. Is it likely that I, a master mercer, would wear aught but the best of the best to go to my grave in?

THE QUEEN. Mend you manners first, sir; and then mend your linen; or you shall have no countenance from me.

PETER. I have naught to do with you, madam, though I well see who wears the breeches in this royal household. I am not skilled in dealing with fine handsome ladies. Leave me to settle my business with your henpecked husband.

THE QUEEN. You shall suffer for this insolence. [*To the King*] Will you, my lord, stand by and hear me spoken to in this tone by a haberdasher?

THE KING [*grinning*] Nay: I am in a merciful mood this morning. The poor man is to be pitied, shivering there in his shirt with his tail torn off.

PETER. Shivering! You lie in your teeth, though you were fifty kings. No man alive shall pity Peter Hardmouth, a dog of lousy Champagne.

THE KING [*going to him*] Ha! A dog of Champagne! Oh, you must pardon this man, madam; for my grandmother hailed from that lousy province; so I also am a dog of Champagne. We know one another's bark. [*Turning on him with bristling teeth*] Eh?

PETER [*growling in his face like a dog*] Grrrr!!!

THE KING [*returning the growl chin to chin*] Grrrr!!!!!!

They repeat this performance, to the great scandal of the Queen, until it develops into a startling imitation of a dog fight.

THE QUEEN [*tearing the two dogs asunder*] Oh, for shame, sir! And you fellow: I will have you muzzled and led through the streets on a chain and lodged in a kennel.

THE KING. Be merciful, lady. I have asked you for many favors, and had them granted me too, as the world, please God, will soon have proof. Will you deny me this?

THE QUEEN. Will you mock my condition before this insolent man and before the world? I will not endure it.

THE KING. Faith, no, dearest: no mockery. But you have no skill in dealing with the dogs of lousy Champagne. We must pity this poor trembling fellow.

THE QUEEN [*angrily*] He is not trembling.

PETER. No, by all the saints in heaven and devils in hell. Well said, lass.

He nudges her, to her extreme indignation.

THE KING. Hear that, dearest: he calls thee lass. Be kind to him. He is only a poor old cur who has lost half his teeth. His condition would move a heart of stone.

PETER. I may be an old cur; but if I had sworn to hang the six of us as he swore, no shrew should scold me out of it, nor any softbosomed beauty wheedle me out of it. Yah, cry baby! Give her your sword and sit in the corner with her distaff. The grey mare is the better horse here. Do your worst, dame: I like your spunk better than his snivel.

THE QUEEN [*raging*] Send him away, sir. He is too ugly; and his words are disgusting. Such objects should be kept out of my sight: would you have me bear you a monster? Take him away.

THE KING. Away with him. Hurt him not; but let him not come into the Queen's presence. Quick there. Off with him.

The men-at-arms lay hands on Peter who struggles violently.

PETER. Hands off me, spaniels. Arrr! Grrr! [*As they drag him out overpowered*] Gee-up, Neddy. [*He finishes with a spirited imitation of a donkey's bray*].

THE KING. That is how they build men in Champagne. By the Holy Rood I care not if a bit of him gets into our baby.

THE QUEEN. Oh, for shame! for shame! Have men no decency?

The King snatches her into his arms, laughing boisterously. The laugh spreads to all the soldiers and courtiers. The whole camp seems in a hilarious uproar.

THE QUEEN. No no: for shame! for shame!

The King stops her mouth with a kiss. Peter brays melodiously in the distance.

Author's Note

(From the Programme of the Open Air Theatre,
Regent's Park, London, 17 July 1934)

My first collaborator, Jean Froissart, has been dead these five hundred years. He told the story, but got it all wrong; for though he was the most voluminous of chroniclers, and the father of all tufthunters, he understood women so little that the only lady he ever loved pulled his hair and would have nothing to do with him. Auguste Rodin contributed the character of Peter Hardmouth; but his manner of creation was that of a sculptor and not that of a playwright. Nothing remained for me to do but to correct Froissart's follies and translate Rodin into words.